WAR, DIPLOMACY AND THE RISE OF SAVOY
1690–1720

This book deals with the crucial relationship between war and state formation in early modern Europe by considering the role of the Duchy of Savoy and the rise of this hitherto weak state into one of the regular members of the anti-French coalitions of the eighteenth century.

Through his participation in the Nine Years War (1688–1697) and the War of the Spanish Succession (1701–1714), Victor Amadeus II, duke of Savoy, acquired a reputation for unrivalled 'Machiavellian' double-dealing on the international stage. The book puts this diplomacy in context, both to justify the duke's diplomacy and to rehabilitate his reputation. It also charts the process of administrative change necessitated by war – considering how the duke raised men and money (at home and abroad), the administrative changes forced by war, the resulting domestic pressures, and how these were dealt with – while emphasising the continuing importance of traditional structures. In contrast to previous histories, the book explores for the first time the way in which war could provoke opposition to ducal policy and also how it could generate new bonds and an unusual version of state nationalism. There is also a re-evaluation of the role of the nobility in the Savoyard state, which argues that they were as much collaborators with as victims of ducal absolutism.

CHRISTOPHER STORRS is Lecturer in History, University of Dundee.

CAMBRIDGE STUDIES IN ITALIAN HISTORY AND CULTURE

Edited by GIGLIOLA FRAGNITO, Università degli Studi, Parma
CESARE MOZZARELLI, Università Cattolica del Sacro Cuore, Milan
ROBERT ORESKO, Institute of Historical Research, University of London
and GEOFFREY SYMCOX, University of California, Los Angeles

This series comprises monographs and a variety of collaborative volumes, including translated works, which concentrate on the period of Italian history from late medieval times up to the Risorgimento. The editors aim to stimulate scholarly debate over a range of issues which have not hitherto received, in English, the attention they deserve. As it develops, the series will emphasise the interest and vigour of current international debates on this central period of Italian history and the persistent influence of Italian culture on the rest of Europe.

For a list of titles in the series, see end of book

Relief of Victor Amadeus' coronation as King of Sicily, Palermo 1714

WAR, DIPLOMACY AND THE RISE OF SAVOY 1690–1720

CHRISTOPHER STORRS

CAMBRIDGE
UNIVERSITY PRESS

CAMBRIDGE UNIVERSITY PRESS
Cambridge, New York, Melbourne, Madrid, Cape Town, Singapore, São Paulo

Cambridge University Press
The Edinburgh Building, Cambridge CB2 8RU, UK

Published in the United States of America by Cambridge University Press, New York

www.cambridge.org
Information on this title: www.cambridge.org/9780521551465

© Cambridge University Press 1999

This publication is in copyright. Subject to statutory exception
and to the provisions of relevant collective licensing agreements,
no reproduction of any part may take place without the written
permission of Cambridge University Press.

First published 1999
This digitally printed version 2007

A catalogue record for this publication is available from the British Library

Library of Congress Cataloguing in Publication data
Storrs, Christopher.
War, diplomacy and the rise of Savoy, 1690–1720/Christopher Storrs.
p. cm. – (Cambridge studies in Italian history and culture)
Includes bibliographical references and index.
ISBN 0 521 55146 3
1. Victor Amadeus I, King of Sardinia, 1666–1732. 2. Savoy (France and Italy) – History. 3. Sardinia (Italy) – History – Aragonese and Spanish rule, 1297–1708. 4. Sardinia (Italy) – History – 1708–1861. I. Title. II. Series.
DG618.53.S76 1999
944′.48 – dc21   98-50779 CIP

ISBN 978-0-521-55146-5 hardback
ISBN 978-0-521-03829-4 paperback

For my mother and Anne-Marie

CONTENTS

List of illustrations		page x
Acknowledgements		xi
List of abbreviations		xiii
Map: The Savoyard state, 1690–1720		xv
	Introduction	1
1	The Savoyard army, 1690–1720	20
2	Savoyard finance, 1690–1720	74
3	Savoyard diplomacy, 1690–1720	122
4	Government and politics in the Savoyard state, 1690–1720	171
5	The Savoyard nobility, 1690–1720	221
6	Regions and communities in the Savoyard state, 1690–1720	265
	Conclusion	313
Select bibliography		319
Index		338

ILLUSTRATIONS

	Relief depicting Victor Amadeus' coronation as king of Sicily, Palermo, 1714	*Frontispiece*
1.1	Print depicting Victor Amadeus II with, in the background, the plans of Casale and Pinerolo (Biblioteca Reale, Turin, Iconografia Sabauda, Vittorio Amedeo II, 9/29)	28
1.2	Soldier of new provincial (or militia) battalion (or regiment) of Casale (Monferrato), 1713 (Biblioteca Reale, Turin, Manoscritti Militari, 134)	69
1.3	Soldier of new provincial (or militia) battalion (or regiment) of Mondovì, 1713 (Biblioteca Reale, Turin, Manoscritti Militari, 134)	70
3.1	Illustration depicting bust of Victor Amadeus, the arms of the House of Savoy and his territories, including the kingdoms of Cyprus and Sicily (Biblioteca Reale, Iconografia Varia 26/249)	157
4.1	Medal, 1706, celebrating victory at Turin (Biblioteca Reale, Iconografia Varia 21/2)	210
4.2	Part of firework display in Turin, September 1713, to celebrate the conclusion of the War of the Spanish Succession (Biblioteca Reale, Turin, Miscellanea di Storia Patria, 302)	211

All illustrations reproduced by permission of Il Ministero per i Beni e le Attività Culturali.

ACKNOWLEDGEMENTS

Like the achievements of the absolute princes of early modern Europe, those of many authors are in fact the results of co-operation on the part of numerous unsung collaborators. I am delighted to see the departure of this typescript to the publisher, not least because it allows me to acknowledge various obligations. I should like to thank the staff of the many archives and libraries in which I have worked on this project, and above all dottoressa Isabel Massabo Ricci of the Archivio di Stato, Turin. The foreign research needed to complete this study would have been impossible without substantial financial help. I should therefore also like to thank the Italian and Spanish governments, the Central Research Fund of the University of London, the Scouloudi Foundation, the Carnegie Trust, the Research Fund of the Faculty of Arts of the University of Dundee, and the Department of History of the University of Dundee for grants towards the cost of research abroad and the purchase of research materials. For their support in the pursuit of such grants, thanks go to Graham Gibbs and to Dr Derek McKay, who also supervised my Ph.D. thesis. Dr Hamish Scott, the external examiner of that thesis, and subsequently an inspiring collaborator on the European nobilities project, deserves thanks for commenting on an early version of one of the present chapters. I must also thank the editors of the present series, and in particular Dr Robert Oresko and Dr Geoffrey Symcox, for giving me the opportunity to publish this book, and for their encouragement and interest in my work over the years. Thanks are also due to Geoffrey for reading an early (and inevitably overlong) version of this book in typescript. I must also acknowledge the patience of Bill Davies of CUP in awaiting the arrival of this book, and of my copy-editor at CUP, Sheila Kane. Special thanks go to my friend, Dr Sandro Lombardini, of the University of Turin. Over many years he has proved invaluable in overcoming many of the difficulties encountered when researching abroad, in Turin. Our discussions of some of the issues dealt with in this book may have led him to expect something different, but I hope he is not too disappointed. On recent trips to Turin I have also enjoyed the hospitality, and otherwise benefited from the enthusiastic interest and help of two new friends, Dr Paola Bianchi and Dr Andrea Merlotti. Last, but certainly not least, I am delighted to be able to give public thanks to two women. One is my mother, who has done so much. The other is my wife, Anne-Marie, an inspiring combination of integrity, intelligence and generosity. Without the affection, patience and support she has shown over many years, this book might not have been completed. It was a lucky day, in October 1978, when I walked into the bar of the Colegio Mayor Padre Poveda in Madrid.

ABBREVIATIONS

Archival references

AST	Archivio di Stato, Turin
BRT	Biblioteca Reale, Turin
CDC	Camera dei Conti
LM	Lettere Ministri
LP	Lettere di Particolari
LPDS	Lettere di Principi, Duchi e Sovrani
MC	Materie Criminali
ME	Materie Ecclesiastiche
MG	Materie Giuridiche
MM	Materie Militari
UGS	Ufficio Generale del Soldo
PCF	Patenti Controllo Finanze
ARAH	Algemeen Rijks Archief, The Hague
EA	Eerste Afdeeling
SG	Staaten Generaal
AGS	Archivo General de Simancas
E	Estado series

PRO   Public Record Office, London
SP   State Papers
Add   British Library, Additional Manuscripts

Individuals

DLT   Comte and president de la Tour
ST   Marquis de Saint-Thomas (elder and younger)
VA   Victor Amadeus II, duke of Savoy
VDM   Albert van der Meer

Bibliographical

ASI   *Archivio Storico Italiano*
BSBS   *Bollettino Storico-Bibliografico Subalpino*
BSSV   *Bollettino della Societa di Studi Valdesi* (formerly *Bulletin de la Société d'Hisotire Vaudoise*)
CGP   C. Contessa *et al.*, eds., *Le Campagne di Guerra in Piemonte (1703–1708) e l'assedio di Torino (1706)*, 10 vols. (Turin, 1908–1933)
DBI   *Dizionario Biografico degli Italiani*, 33 vols. (Rome, 1960–87)
Duboin   F. A. and C. Duboin, *Raccolta per ordine di materia delle leggi . . . emanati negli stati sardi sino all'8 Dicembre 1798*, 23 vols. (Turin, 1818–69)
MAST   *Memorie dell'Accademia delle Scienze di Torino*
MSI   *Miscellanea di Storia Italiana*
MDSSHAC *Mémoires et Documents publiés par la Société Savoisienne d'Histoire et d'Archéologie*, Chambéry
RSI   *Rivista Storica Italiana*

The Savoyard State, 1690–1720

INTRODUCTION

I

In 1690, the Savoyard state (comprising the Duchy of Savoy, the Principality of Piedmont, the Duchy of Aosta and the County of Nice) was a minor European power, a satellite of its more powerful neighbour across the Alps, the France of Louis XIV, whose troops (garrisoned in the imposing fortresses of Pinerolo in the Val Chisone and of Casale in the Monferrato) threatened the Savoyard capital, Turin, and it was widely regarded as a satellite.[1] However, this would change with Savoyard participation in the Nine Years War (1688–97) and the War of the Spanish Succession (1701–13). In the summer of 1690, the duke – whose territories were going to be caught up in the escalating Nine Years War whether he liked it or not[2] – joined the Grand Alliance powers ranged against Louis XIV by means of treaties with Emperor Leopold and with Spain, England and the Dutch Republic, all of whom promised to help him in his struggle against the French king, and to secure for him Pinerolo. Thereafter, Victor Amadeus II's states became more familiar to informed opinion in Europe as one of the theatres of war. The duke was twice defeated by Louis XIV's forces (at the battles of Staffarda, 1690, and Marsaglia, or Orbassano, 1693) and came close to the complete loss of his

---

[1] The diplomat, Ezechiel Spanheim thought the Savoyard state less important than the Swiss cantons in 1690: see J. Mathiex, 'The Mediterranean', in J. S. Bromley, ed., *New Cambridge Modern History*, vol. VI: *The rise of Great Britain and Russia 1688–1715/25* (Cambridge, 1970), 559. In late 1689 troops from Pinerolo supplemented the ducal forces countering the Vaudois and others who had entered Piedmont in the so-called 'Glorieuse Rentrée', see G. Symcox, *Victor Amadeus II: absolutism in the Savoyard state 1765–1730* (London, 1983), 102.

[2] The Grand Alliance was preparing, in the spring of 1690, an expedition of Protestant irregulars who were to cross Victor Amadeus' territories (with or without his consent), relieve the remnant of the 'Glorieuse Rentree' and enter France, see C. Storrs, 'Thomas Coxe and the Lindau Project', in A. de Lange, ed., *Dall'Europa alle Valli Valdesi* (Turin, 1990), 199 ff.

states (particularly in the spring and summer of 1691). But his remarkable steadfastness, and occasional successes – in 1692 he led a brief invasion of Dauphiné, the only allied incursion into France during this war – ensured that he remained one of the great hopes of the anti-French coalition.[3] In 1695, anxious that the war was allowing the emperor to become too powerful in north Italy, Victor Amadeus did a secret deal with Louis XIV who surrendered Casale (which was besieged by the allies) to its immediate lord, the Duke of Mantua, rather than to the emperor.[4] In the summer of 1696, after further secret negotiations with Louis XIV's agents, Victor Amadeus (who increasingly despaired of his allies' commitment to recovering Pinerolo, his main war aim) concluded a separate peace with the French king. This, the treaty of Turin, not only secured Pinerolo but also the recognition by Louis XIV of Victor Amadeus' right to send envoys to, and receive envoys from, other courts (which Louis had effectively vetoed before 1690), a prestigious marriage between his eldest daughter, Marie Adelaide, and Louis' grandson, the Duke of Burgundy (and possible future king of France), and the 'royal treatment' at the French court.

The treaty was a clear measure of the importance attached by Louis XIV to the war in Piedmont, and his desire to end it in order to concentrate his forces elsewhere (above all, on the Rhine and in Flanders). It also held out for Victor Amadeus the prospect of the conquest of the Milanese if his allies rejected peace in Italy. In the late summer of 1696, the duke, now a subsidy-receiving ally of the French king, led a Franco-Savoyard invasion of the Spanish Milanese. This effectively forced his erstwhile allies, led by Spain and the emperor, to agree at last to the neutralisation of Italy in the treaty of Vigevano (October 1696). The emperor's envoy even held out the prospect of Victor Amadeus' mediation of the general peace. This latter prize was denied the duke but within a year the treaties of Turin and Vigevano had been incorporated in the general peace concluding the Nine Years War (the treaty of Rijswijk, 1697), which had itself been hastened by the ending of the war in Italy. The acquisition of Pinerolo, the first accession of territory by the Savoyard state in half a century, increased its security and

---

[3] In 1693 Carlos II's queen argued that Victor Amadeus' imminent capture of Pinerolo (and the French retreat from Catalonia) meant that this was no time for talk of peace: Mariana of Neuburg to the Elector Palatine, 2 Sept. 1693, in duke of Maura and Adalbert of Bavaria, eds., *Documentos ineditos referentes a las postrimerias de la Casa de Austria*, 3 vols. (Madrid, 1927–31), II, 128.

[4] For the recreation of *Reichsitalien* in north Italy in this period, see K. O. Freiherr von Aretin, 'Kaiser Joseph I zwischen Kaisertradition und Österreichischer Grossmachtpolitik', *Historische Zeitschrift*, 215, 1972, 529 ff. and C. Ingrao, *In Quest and Crisis: Emperor Joseph I and the Habsburg monarchy* (West Lafayette, 1979). Developments in the 1690s remain largely unexplored.

independence. That state had also been catapulted, as a result of its crucial role in the Nine Years War, from relative obscurity to one of European prominence. In the summer of 1696, with justifiable exaggeration, Victor Amadeus was seen by some of his own subjects as the arbiter of Europe.[5]

Within a few years, however, the Savoyard state seemed doomed again to Bourbon satellite status (and to the abandonment of all hopes of territorial expansion in north Italy), following the accession to the Spanish throne in 1701 of Louis XIV's grandson, Philip V, squeezing the Savoyard state between Bourbon France and Bourbon Milan. Victor Amadeus, who later argued that the position of the Savoyard state was worse in 1701 than when Louis XIV had held Pinerolo,[6] was obliged to make the best of a bad job. He joined the Bourbon monarchs in an alliance which provided for the marriage of his younger daughter, Marie Louise, to Philip V and which promised him subsidies and the supreme command of a Bourbon–Savoyard army in a war against the emperor (which, whether he wished it or not, would inevitably be fought in and across his territories, as had the Nine Years War). Not surprisingly, in 1701 Victor Amadeus' imperial suzerain, Leopold, ordered the duke and his ministers to appear before the imperial Aulic Court, in Vienna, to answer a charge of felony against the empire and perhaps to hear sentence stripping him of his imperial fiefs (and freeing all imperial vassals of obligations to him). This threat was underpinned by the despatch to Italy of an imperial army commanded by Victor Amadeus' cousin, Prince Eugene. Good relations with Vienna and imperial grants of one sort and another had contributed enormously hitherto to the emergence of the Savoyard state. All that had been achieved now seemed threatened.

Once again, however, Victor Amadeus transformed an unfavourable situation by means of a diplomatic *volte-face* at the expense of Louis XIV (and Philip V). In secret negotiations, only concluded after Victor Amadeus had broken with his Bourbon allies in October 1703, the emperor and the Maritime Powers promised the duke military and financial aid and territorial gains in north Italy. In subsequent years, again as in the Nine Years War, the duke obstinately held on, despite the fact that the Bourbon powers overran the greater part of his territories. In the summer of 1706 Victor Amadeus was obliged to send his immediate

---

[5] C. Contessa, 'I regni di Napoli e di Sicilia nelle aspirazioni italiane di Vittorio Amedeo II di Savoia (1700–13)', in *Studi su Vittorio Amedeo II* (Turin, 1933), 15. For attitudes elsewhere in Italy in 1696, see L. Muratori, *Annali d'Italia*, ed. G. Falco and F. Forti, 2 vols. (Turin, 1976), II, 410 ff.

[6] D. Carutti, *Storia della diplomazia della Corte di Savoia*, 4 vols. (Turin, 1875–80), III, 300.

family for refuge to Genoa and was himself hunted by the enemy across his own territories (taking refuge briefly in the Vaudois valleys). He seemed about to be expelled, possibly for good, from his states. However, Europe was again astonished as Victor Amadeus denied the Bourbons his capital, Turin, and from the autumn of 1706 turned the tide of the war in Italy.[7] As in 1696, northern Italy was largely neutralised in the spring of 1707, this time at the insistence of the emperor, who (having secured the Milanese), wished to secure Naples. However, that same year Victor Amadeus led an abortive attempt on Louis XIV's great naval base at Toulon; and in subsequent years successful campaigns in and about the Alps secured him a number of invaluable frontier fortresses (including Exilles and Fenestrelle) and the Pragelato valley. In the meantime, the emperor had invested (1707) Victor Amadeus with various territories of the Milanese (Alessandria, the Lomellina, Val Sesia) and (1708) with the Mantuan Monferrato, confiscated from its Gonzaga Duke; and had also confirmed Victor Amadeus' right to acquire limited suzerainty over the imperial feudatories of the Langhe, in accordance with their treaty of 1703. However, his failure to fulfil all the terms – above all regarding the cession of the Vigevanasco (or an equivalent) – embittered relations between Turin and Vienna henceforth. These successes, Victor Amadeus' vital contribution to the defeat of the Bourbons,[8] and the goodwill towards him of Queen Anne and her ministers, stood him in good stead at Utrecht in 1712–13. Victor Amadeus recovered his lost territories (Savoy and Nice), kept most of his conquests (although he was obliged in return to surrender the Barcelonette valley to Louis XIV). Against the wishes of the emperor, he also secured Sicily (which he had not conquered and which was at the disposal of British naval power), and with it elevation to true royal status. Victor Amadeus was promised the greater prize of Spain and its overseas empire, if Philip V died without heirs.

By 1713, then, the Savoyard state had been transformed, in a variety of ways. The state and its ruler had freed themselves from French tutelage, secured substantial territorial and other gains (including a more defensible

---

[7] For one English politician, this (along with Ramillies and negotiation of the Union with Scotland) was 'one of the great victories' of 1706, G. Holmes, *British Politics in the Age of Anne*, 2nd edn. (London, 1987), 85. For changing English perceptions of the duke from *c*. 1690, see S. J. Woolf, 'English public opinion and the Duchy of Savoy', *English Miscellany*, 12, Rome, 1961, 211 ff.

[8] According to intelligence received from Berlin in 1708, six Scots exiles at the Court of James II planned to assassinate Victor Amadeus for this reason, A. Segre, 'Negoziati diplomatici della Corte di Prussia e colla Dieta di Ratisbona', in C. Contessa *et al.*, eds. *Le campagne di guerra in Piemonte (1703–08) e l'assedio di Torino (1706)*, 10 vols. (Turin, 1907–33), VI, 316 (hereafter *CGP*).

Alpine barrier against France and, most strikingly, the distant island kingdom of Sicily). Victor Amadeus had also won an enduring European reputation for skilful (even duplicitous) manoeuvring between the greater powers to secure these.[9] By that date, too, it has been suggested, the duke of Savoy – whose ancestor Charles Emanuel I (1580–1630) had unsuccessfully attempted to exploit the French Wars of Religion to expand into southern France – had largely abandoned any lingering hopes of conquests in France. Henceforth the Savoyard state would see its future in Italy.[10] The prospects there were the more promising because that state was now also more clearly distinguished from its Italian neighbours, many of which had merely exchanged the dominion of Habsburg Spain for that of Habsburg Austria. At the end of the War of the Spanish Succession, many observers anticipated a glorious future for what just a generation earlier had been a minor power.[11]

Subsequently, however, the Spanish conquest of Sicily (1718–19) and the decision of the Quadruple Alliance (Austria, Britain, the Dutch Republic, France) that Victor Amadeus must exchange Sicily for the much inferior island kingdom of Sardinia – finalised in August 1720 when Victor Amadeus' first viceroy took possession of Sardinia, completing the transformation of the 'risen' Savoyard state into the newly independent kingdom of Sardinia, by which name it would be known until the creation of the Kingdom of Italy in 1861 – revealed that the Savoyard state was weaker than many observers realised in 1713. Nevertheless, that state had expanded substantially and enhanced its standing, and did not revert after 1713 to its earlier obscurity, while later commentators could justifiably see Victor Amadeus II as the re-founder of his state. Many of those who have taken this view have in mind both the territorial and the domestic transformation of the Savoyard state which occurred after 1713, notably the overhaul of the army, the administration and the finances –

---

[9] That Victor Amadeus soon acquired a reputation for treachery and machiavellianism is clear from the work of one of his admirers, the Genoese Paolo Mattia Doria: see F. Torcellan Ginolino, 'Il pensiero politico di Paolo Mattia Doria ed un interessante profilo storico di Vittorio Amedeo II', *BSBS*, 59, 196. A host of references could be cited to demonstrate the extent to which Victor Amadeus II remains a byword for 'Machiavellian' manoeuvring on the international stage: see G. M. Trevelyan, *England under Queen Anne, 1: Blenheim* (London, 1930), 314–15 and (in the sphere of international relations theory) M. Wight, *Power Politics* (Harmondsworth, 1979), 263.

[10] A. Lossky, 'International relations in Europe', *NCMH*, VI, 159. Victor Amadeus had hopes in 1690 of gains in France, C. Storrs, 'Machiavelli dethroned. Victor Amadeus II and the making of the Anglo-Savoyard alliance of 1690', *European History Quarterly*, 22, 3, 1992, 361.

[11] Typically, the Tuscan representative at the peace congress at Utrecht thought the Savoyard state the only one in Italy of any independent importance there: A. Bozzola, 'Giudizi e previsioni della diplomazia Medicea', in *Studi su Vittorio Amedeo II*, 145.

above all the so-called *perequazione* and the revocation of fiefs held by the nobility.[12] These were important developments, and have attracted substantial historical attention. They were also, in part at least, forced by the need to protect and maintain the enlarged and reshaped state (and the new status) won between 1690 and 1713 without the foreign support which had been so important in their acquisition. Indeed, one of the contentions of the present study is that the overhaul of 1717 was in part a response to the threat to Victor Amadeus' enhanced territory and status. However, as the present study also hopes to show, by 1713, and largely because of the need to wage war, the 'unreformed' Savoyard state had in fact experienced important domestic changes. Many of these anticipated the reforms of post-1713 and were the domestic counterpart of the Savoyard state's transformation on the international stage.[13]

The transformation of the Savoyard state after 1690 was clearly related to the larger European picture, and above all to the struggle over the Spanish Succession and the desire of many of France's neighbours to restrain and reduce Louis XIV. It is no coincidence that Victor Amadeus, descended from a daughter of Philip II, was one of the claimants to that succession and therefore due some increase in territory (and dignity) after the death of the last Spanish Habsburg, Carlos II. However, this is not the only explanation for Victor Amadeus' success. Also important was the fact that the Savoyard state straddled the Alps between Louis XIV's France and Habsburg Lombardy. In wars in part fought over the latter, Victor Amadeus might facilitate the conquest of Lombardy by the forces of Louis XIV. Alternatively, he might ensure a successful allied invasion of southern France, and perhaps trigger a Huguenot revolt. Naval operations, particularly against the recently developed French naval base at Toulon, might make use of the duke's one important harbour, Nice. For the Grand Alliance, then, Victor Amadeus' states seemed to offer the opportunity for a decisive breakthrough denied them on other fronts. Indeed, following the invasion of Dauphiné in 1692, William III even

---

[12] See G. Quazza, *Le riforme in Piemonte nella prima metà del Settecento*, 2 vols. (Modena, 1957) and Symcox, *Victor Amadeus*, passim. For G. Ricuperati, 'L'Avvenimento e la storia: le rivolte del luglio 1797 nella crisi dello stato sabaudo', *RSI*, 1992, 349 ff., a long reform era began in 1696. For V. Ferrone, 'The Accademia Reale delle Scienze: cultural sociability and men of letters in Turin of the Enlightenment under Vittorio Amedeo III', *Journal of Modern History*, 70, 1998, 528–9, the elevation from ducal to royal status was a crucial stimulus in the ensuing reconstruction of the Savoyard state.

[13] See Storrs, 'Savoyard diplomacy in the eighteenth century', in D. Frigo, ed., *Politics and Diplomacy in Early Modern Italy* (Cambridge, forthcoming). For later perceptions of Victor Amadeus, see Foscarini's *relazione* (1743), in L. Cibrario, *Relazioni dello stato di Savoia negli anni 1574, 1670, 1743, scritte dagli ambasciatori veneti Molini, Bellegno, Foscarini* (Turin, 1830), 89 ff.

thought of himself taking troops to north Italy to launch just such an attack.¹⁴ For his part, Louis XIV was obliged to divert (to a border hitherto considered safe) forces which might otherwise be used to decisive effect elsewhere – in Flanders, on the Rhine or in Catalonia – in order to deny his enemies the strategic advantages against himself which Victor Amadeus' states offered, and to exploit those they offered him for intervention in Italy.¹⁵ However, despite a recognition by historians of a new importance of Italy in international relations in the half century and more after 1680,¹⁶ the military struggle there continues to be overshadowed by that in Flanders, on the Rhine and (at least during the War of the Spanish Succession) in Spain and by the war at sea.¹⁷ This focus, admittedly, reflects contemporary military and political priorities. Both Louis XIV and the allies invariably made their greatest efforts in the Low Countries, fielding there armies of 100,000 and more during the Nine Years War. But the inevitable stalemate in Flanders (at least in the 1690s) underpinned the view that a decisive breakthrough could and should be effected elsewhere.¹⁸ It is hoped that the present study, besides contributing to a fuller understanding of the development of the Savoyard state during the Nine Years War and the War of the Spanish Succession, will also enhance knowledge and understanding of the war in Italy (and its importance) in both these conflicts.

---

¹⁴ C. Storrs, 'Diplomatic relations between William III and Victor Amadeus II 1690–96', Ph.D. thesis, University of London, 1990, 160 ff. Perhaps the best assessment of the strategic role of the Savoyard state, as a guardian of the Alpine passages, although dealing with the later war of the Austrian Succession, is S. Wilkinson, *The Defence of Piedmont 1742–1748: a prelude to the story of Napoleon* (Oxford, 1927), 3–5.

¹⁵ In 1704, Victor Amadeus justified his requests for military help from his allies as his own situation deteriorated on the grounds that the diversion of French troops to Italy had contributed to the recent Allied victory in Germany, VDM to Fagel, 12 Sept. 1704, Turin, ARAH/EA/VDM/29, 159.

¹⁶ A. Lossky, 'International relations', 159 ff.; G. Quazza, *Il problema italiano e l'equilibrio europeo 1720–1738* (Turin, 1965), passim.

¹⁷ In an otherwise excellent study, for example, David L. Smith, *A History of the Modern British Isles 1603–1707: the double crown* (Oxford, 1998), 308 notes that the peace of 1697 reflected stalemate in the Nine Years War, but makes no mention of the contribution of the war in Italy or Victor Amadeus' separate peace of 1696, and also ignores the war in Italy in the following conflict. Symptomatic of this neglect is the fact that many accounts incorrectly conflate the Casale deal of 1695 and the *volte-face* of 1696: see G. Clark, 'The Nine Years War 1688–97', *NCMH*, VI, 250.

¹⁸ See the figures in Clark, 'Nine Years War' and A. J. Veenendal, 'The War of the Spanish Succession in Europe', *NCMH*, VI. In the winter of 1695–6 William III refused Victor Amadeus additional troops (for his intended siege of Pinerolo) from Flanders because Louis XIV was believed to be planning to put into the field in the Low Countries in 1696 30,000 more men than in 1695. William believed that Louis could only do this by weakening his forces in other theatres, including Piedmont, making the diversion unnecessary, DLT to VA, 20 Dec. 1695, London, AST/LM/GB, m. 8.

Whether the duke of Savoy could exploit these advantages was another matter. Other lesser princes with a claim on the Spanish Succession – including Victor Amadeus' cousin, the Wittelsbach electoral prince of Bavaria, Max Emanuel – might have been expected to do well in these decades. Indeed, with his appointment as governor of the Spanish Low Countries from 1691, the elector seemed to be making more headway than Victor Amadeus. But Max Emanuel did disastrously in the War of the Spanish Succession. On the other hand, other lesser princes, without any claim on the Spanish Succession, did well. These included the Hohenzollern electoral prince of Prussia (elevated to King in 1701) and the duke of Hanover, promoted ninth elector in 1692 and elevated to the throne of Britain in 1714. In part the difference between success and failure between 1690 and 1713 depended upon good decisionmaking. But Victor Amadeus' success also rested upon his ability to mobilise effectively the necessary resources (essentially men and money). This, in turn, depended in part upon the extent to which an effective state structure of sorts – and political and social cohesion – existed, or could be developed, to mobilise those resources.[19]

II

The experience of the Savoyard state between 1690 and 1713 largely conforms to a larger European pattern of successful state formation – the emergence of a territorially well-defined sovereign unit, whose independence was in part underpinned by the development of institutions mobilising its resources in favour of its prince or government – by contrast with, for example, the 'failure' (and disappearance) in this period of the Gonzaga Mantuan state, hitherto one of the Savoyard state's rivals in north Italy. The question of state formation has recently come back into fashion among historians.[20] But the issue is not a simple one, not least because of the many different conceptions of the state. For some time, the early modern state in process of formation has been conceived of as approximating to the modern state: characterised by all-powerful, centralised, bureaucratic government of the sort specified by Max Weber, whose view that 'the state is that agency in society which has a monopoly of legitimate force' underpins that of many subsequent historians.[21] Not

---

[19] See G. Symcox, *War, Diplomacy, and Imperialism 1618–1763* (London, 1974), 1 ff.
[20] See E. Fasano Guarini, '"Etat moderne" et anciens états italiens. Eléments d'histoire comparée', *Revue d'Histoire Moderne et Contemporaine*, 45, 1, 1997, 15 ff.
[21] Cited in T. C. W. Blanning, *The French Revolutionary Wars 1787–1802* (London, 1996), 30. See C. H. Carter, *The Western European Powers 1500–1700* (London, 1971), 28 ff. For a simple schema of the distinguishing features of 'modern' states and societies,

all historians share this view, which is increasingly recognised as too stark for early modern Europe,[22] where the 'proprietary dynasticism' identified by Herbert Rowen seems at least as convincing an interpretation of the relationship between princes and their states.[23] In fact, these differing perceptions of the state are not necessarily wrong, because the state is in a constant process of formation, undergoing (or in need of) constant 'modernisation' (a concept which poses at least as many problems as it seems to solve).[24] Indeed, the nature of statehood and the institutions of the state have varied over the centuries, so that the typical state – if there was such a thing – of the Renaissance differed from that of the Baroque and that of the age of Enlightenment from that of the nineteenth and twentieth centuries.[25] The present study takes the view that there was a Savoyard state, one conforming to the definition of state used by John Brewer (and which more or less approximates to that given at the start of this paragraph),[26] and one contemporaries clearly recognised. It also assumes that that polity experienced a recognisable phase of state forma-

---

see T. C. W. Blanning, *Joseph II* (London, 1994), 20–1. For Blanning, Joseph II's 'Enlightened despotism' was essentially about the creation of an Austrian Habsburg state.

[22] See G. Chittolini, 'The "private", the "public", the state', in J. Kirshner, ed., *The Origins of the State in Italy 1300–1600* (Chicago, 1996), 545. (This collection was originally published as a special supplementary issue of the *Journal of Modern History* in 1995.) Modern historians are more likely to accept the criticisms of Weber's approach and definitions associated with, for example, Otto Brunner: see H. Zmora, *State and Nobility in Early Modern Germany: The knightly feud in Franconia 1440–1567* (Cambridge, 1997), 6.

[23] H. H. Rowen, *The King's State: proprietary dynasticism in early modern France* (New Brunswick, 1980).

[24] See the critical discussion of 'modernisation' concepts in H. G. Brown, *War, Revolution and the Bureaucratic State: Politics and army administration in France 1791–1799* (Oxford, 1995), 265 ff.

[25] See F. Chabod, 'Y a-t-il un état de la Renaissance?' *Actes du Colloque sur la Renaissance* (Paris, 1958), English translation in H. Lubasz, ed., *The Development of the Modern State* (New York, 1964); W. Barberis, *Le armi del principe: la tradizione militare sabauda* (Turin, 1988), which is informed by a sense of a distinct 'baroque' state; and M. Raeff, *The Well-Ordered Police State: social and institutional change through law in the Germanies and Russia 1600–1800* (New Haven, 1983). Blanning's perception of Joseph II (above) is founded in part upon an acceptance of Robert Evans' compelling argument that until at least 1700 the Habsburg monarchy was not a monolithic state characterised by powerful central institutions, but a highly successful alliance of dynasty, nobility and Church, R. J. W. Evans, *The Making of the Habsburg Monarchy 1550–1700* (Oxford, 1978), passim.

[26] 'a territorially and jurisdictionally defined political entity in which public authority is distinguished from (though not unconnected to) private power, and which is manned by officials whose primary (though not sole) allegiance is to a set of political institutions under a single, i.e. sovereign and final, authority', J. Brewer, *The Sinews of Power: war, money and the English state 1688–1783* (London, 1989), 252 n. 1.

tion, defined as a twin process of asserting itself as an independent player in the European power system, which was in turn founded (in part) upon the development of more effective means to mobilise its own resources – what Ricuperati still prefers to call 'modernisation' – between 1690 and 1713.[27]

Seen as process, state formation comprised a number of distinct developments. Firstly, there is territorial expansion. This is possibly the simplest aspect. Nevertheless, growth of this sort meant, on the one hand, a great increase in the potential resources of the state (armed manpower, tax and other revenues), and might represent a distinct and conscious alternative to state-building by administrative centralisation.[28] On the other hand, territorial expansion posed problems of integration. Secondly, there is the assertion of the state's independence on the international scene, which was increasingly the preserve of not just sovereigns but of sovereigns of a certain resource and standing.[29] As we have seen the Savoyard state effectively threw off its satellite status in and after 1690. But that achievement must be qualified in two important respects: firstly, by the extent to which Victor Amadeus depended upon his allies for the resources to combat the French and Bourbon threat; and secondly, by the extent to which the Savoyard state was juridically part of the Holy Roman Empire and subject to the (Austrian Habsburg) emperor, whose authority in those parts of north Italy which were traditionally subject to the empire, *Reichsitalien*, was reasserted in this period. This could create problems for the duke of Savoy. However, as member of the empire, he could also expect imperial protection, while as agent of the emperor he could seek grants (office, fiefs). Indeed, the rise of the House of Savoy (and most of its titles) since the middle ages – as ducal ministers were well aware when they debated how to react to the developing crisis in north Italy in 1690 – had been founded on a close association with empire and emperor.[30] Thus, the sovereignty of this small state might at the same time be underpinned and qualified by its imperial status.

---

[27] 'L'Avvenimento', 349.
[28] This notion is articulated by Paul Sonnino in an e-mail review (H-France, 2 Apr. 1998) of J. Lynn, *Giant of the Grand Siècle: the French army 1610–1715* (Cambridge 1997). On frontiers, see P. Sahlins, *Boundaries: the making of France and Spain in the Pyrenees* (Berkeley, 1989).
[29] Lucien Bély, *Espions et ambassadeurs au temps de Louis XIV* (Paris, 1990), 215, discusses the abortive efforts of the cardinal de Bouillon and the princesse des Ursins (who sought an independent princely sovereignty) to have the Utrecht congress deal with their private concerns and ambitions.
[30] See *mémoire* regarding the policy Victor Amadeus must adopt as war threatened in north Italy, Feb. 1690, AST/Negoziazioni/Austria, m. 4/24. Against the pressure from Louis XIV to declare for him it was pointed out that no duke of Savoy in recent history had fought the emperor.

The third major process in the larger one of state formation was the creation of new state structures to make more effective the authority of the central government, i.e. the prince and his ministers, and to integrate newly acquired territories. Victor Amadeus was obliged to make enormous demands on his subjects (seeking men for his armies, and money), who also had to bear all the suffering associated with war. It is inconceivable that these demands should not have affected his subjects and territories. In fact they contributed to, even necessitated, important administrative and political changes which anticipated the larger transformation which occurred after 1713 and which also add up to the achievement of a political stability which could not be assumed before 1690. Before Victor Amadeus' 'coup' of 1684, when he had effectively seized power from his mother, the regent Madama Reale (Marie-Jeanne-Baptiste de Savoie-Nemours), the latter had taken a number of initiatives which historians increasingly recognise as a 'state project' of sorts.[31] However, despite these efforts, it seems fair to say that before the cycle of wars which began in 1690, and particularly before 1684, the Savoyard state was disturbed by domestic disorder in a way which it was not after 1720. We must not exaggerate the contrast, or relate the change too exclusively to participation in the Nine Years War and the War of the Spanish Succession. Nevertheless, the resolution of some of these issues was closely related to the wars, such that the domestic and 'foreign' aspects of state (trans-)formation represented two sides of the same coin.

This aspect of state formation is related to an important historical debate, not always easily distinguished from that about the nature of the early modern state, regarding the degree to which that state was 'absolute'. Until about a generation ago, historians seemed broadly agreed that 'absolutism' was the defining characteristic of the European monarchies in the seventeenth and eighteenth centuries. According to this view, the era was characterised by the rule of more powerful monarchs, their authority backed by new resources and instruments of coercion (standing armies, centralised bureaucracies and greater revenues), so-called 'administrative monarchies' able to reduce the independence of any independent or rival forces in the state (peripheral provinces, great nobles, representative tax-voting assemblies) which had hitherto obstructed princely power. Essentially, the state, or absolute monarch, exemplified in the person and reign of Louis XIV, was seen as imposing his will on the rest of the state/society from above. Historians might disagree about just

---

[31] See C. Rosso, 'Il Seicento', in P. Merlin *et al.*, *Il Piemonte Sabaudo: stato e territori in età moderna* (Turin, 1994), 260 ff.

why absolutism happened – some urging its function as defender of the interests of the traditional landed noble elite, others preferring to emphasise the role of ideologues and others, finally, stressing the primacy of war – but that absolutism was a reality few denied.[32]

Since at least the 1960s, however, this image of the absolute state has come under sustained attack. For one thing, the contemporary understanding of absolutism has been refashioned, above all to differentiate it from despotism and tyranny. Historians have also sought to distinguish the assertions and claims of royal apologists from a reality which, it has been argued, was far from 'absolute'. William Beik, in one of the most impressive and influential reinterpretations of the phenomenon of French absolutism, accepts that Louis XIV's rule was more effective, but seeks to explain the obedient order which distinguished the reign of the Sun King from the disorder of the preceding decades by reference to the fact that – at least in Languedoc – the king was ruling with, and in the interests of the elite.[33] Sharon Kettering, another influential revisionist, has emphasised the role of local power brokers in making effective the will of the prince and his ministers in the locality, rather than the nascent bureaucracies (which, on closer investigation can often reveal themselves as clienteles of ministers and others).[34] Recently, too, Andreas Gestrich has argued that in seventeenth and eighteenth-century Germany supposedly absolute regimes were even then aware of a 'public' and the need to court (or at least inform) it, well before the acknowledged emergence of Habermas' late eighteenth-century 'public sphere',[35] while Beik has argued that the politically excluded classes were not without means of dissent, opposition and resistance.[36] Alternative, less traditi-onally absolutist models of state formation have been suggested, notably that of Robert Evans for seventeenth-century Austria, while the nobilities, hitherto regarded as among

---

[32] See M. Beloff, *The Age of Absolutism 1660–1815* (London, 1954), and F. Dumont, 'French kingship and absolute monarchy in the seventeenth century', in R. M. Hatton, ed., *Louis XIV and Absolutism* (London, 1976), 55.

[33] W. Beik, *Absolutism and Society in Seventeenth-Century France: state power and provincial aristocracy in Languedoc* (Cambridge, 1985). See Jeremy Black's definition of absolutism not as a constitutional structure but as a way of conducting politics which essentially represented a compromise between prince and elites: *A Military Revolution? Military change and European society 1550–1800* (London, 1991), 67–8.

[34] S. Kettering, *Patrons, Brokers, and Clients in Seventeenth-Century France* (Oxford and New York, 1986). For the incorporation of this approach into modern textbooks, see J. B. Collins, *State in Early Modern France* (Cambridge, 1995); and W. Reinhard, ed., *Power Elites and State Building* (Oxford, 1996).

[35] A. Gestrich, *Absolutismus und Öffentlichkeit: politische Kommunikation in Deutschland zu Beginn des 18. Jahrhunderts* (Gottingen, 1992).

[36] W. Beik, *Urban Protest in Seventeenth-Century France: the culture of retribution* (Cambridge, 1997).

absolutism's most striking victims, are increasingly seen to have shown remarkable resilience.[37]

The revisionists have not had it all their own way. What we might call traditionalists, or counter-revisionists, have reasserted the reality of what they label absolutism.[38] Nor are the revisionists confined to France.[39] Indeed, John Brewer has reasserted the importance of the effective assertion of a monopoly of tax-raising and military might (the two often, of course, closely related) in a study of a Britain which after the Revolution of 1688 looks more like the traditional 'absolute' European state.[40] The issue is of course in part a relative one, and one of perception. For the observer in Cracow, where the monarch really was weak, the authority of Louis XIV, whatever revisionists might say about it, looked formidable.[41] Not surprisingly, many historians of seventeenth and eighteenth-century Europe, while not necessarily giving it the same content as their predecessors, continue to find the label 'absolutism' useful.[42] Nevertheless, the effect of the accumulated attack on the traditional image and understanding of absolutism in early modern Europe has been to raise important questions about the effective power of the early modern state within its own borders, to question whether that state was quite so independently all-powerful *vis-à-vis* the forces in state and society over which it once seemed to dominate serenely, and to suggest that 'absolutism', in part redefined as simply a less disordered polity, was more of a compromise with (than an imposition on) the ruled.[43]

[37] See H. M. Scott and C. Storrs, 'Introduction: the consolidation of noble power in Europe *c.* 1600–1800', in H. M. Scott, ed., *The European Nobilities in the Seventeenth and Eighteenth Centuries*, 2 vols. (London, 1995), I, 1 ff.

[38] R. J. Knecht, *Richelieu* (London, 1992), 135 ff., has reaffirmed that Richelieu contributed to the development of absolutism in seventeenth-century France; while J. A. Lynn, *The Wars of Louis XIV 1667–1719* (London, 1999), 17–19, asserts the continued validity of the term 'absolutism' to describe that monarch's style of government. For W. Doyle, *Origins of the French Revolution* (Oxford, 1980), 53, 'The king of France was an absolute monarch. This meant there was no institution in the state with the right to prevent him from doing whatever he chose to do, in contrast to a state like Great Britain.'

[39] C. Rahn Phillips, *Six Galleons for the King of Spain* (Baltimore, 1986), and D. Goodman, *Spanish Naval Power 1589–1665. Reconstruction and defeat* (Cambridge, 1997), 181 ff., both to some degree question I. A. A. Thompson's thesis (see below), that the absolutism of the Spanish Habsburgs in the seventeenth century was little more than a shell. Goodman reveals that the Habsburgs sometimes found regional privilege a weak barrier against a determined executive. [40] Brewer, *Sinews of Power*, passim.

[41] See R. Bonney, *Society and Government in France under Richelieu and Mazarin 1624–61* (London, 1988), xiii.

[42] D. Parker, *The Making of French Absolutism* (London, 1983).

[43] See W. Beik, 'Celebrating Andrew Lossky: the reign of Louis XIV revisited', *French Historical Studies*, 17, 2, 1991, and (for Sweden) A. Karlsson, *Den jamlike undersaten: Karl XII's formogenhetsbeskattning 1713* (Uppsala, 1994) – as reviewed in *EHR*, 92, 447,

Explaining the process (or processes) of state formation identified above is also a matter of debate, in part simply reflecting changes in historical fashion.[44] On the one hand, there are those for whom state building was a deliberate policy, one in which would-be absolute monarchs were following a blueprint (often the model supposedly offered by Louis XIV). On the other hand, however, the rejection of 'absolutism' has been accompanied by increasing scepticism about deliberate state formation of this sort.[45] Some of those who take the latter view prefer to emphasise the influence of external pressures, and above all of war. For Charles Tilly and Theda Skocpol, state-formation was largely an unintended result of the efforts of state-builders to create and fund armies, to fight wars (and to suppress disorder).[46] However, this interpretation has recently been criticised as offering a point of departure for, rather than constituting itself, a full explanation, ignoring the fact that the same pressures can work against state formation.[47] It is hoped that the present study will provide food for thought on many of these issues. It takes the view that, without necessarily having a blueprint, Victor Amadeus

765–6 – for revisionist studies of specific areas. These revisionist approaches have recently been articulated, not altogether satisfactorily, by Nicholas Henshall, *The Myth of Absolutism: change and continuity in early modern European monarchy* (London, 1992), which focuses narrowly on England and France (and makes, p. 169, only passing reference to Victor Amadeus II). More satisfying broad surveys reflecting or surveying the last generation's work are J. Miller, 'Introduction', in Miller, ed., *Absolutism in Seventeenth-Century Europe* (London, 1990), and H. M. Scott, 'Introduction: the problem of enlightened absolutism', in Scott, *Enlightened Absolutism: Reform and reformers in later-eighteenth century Europe* (London, 1990). M. Mann, 'The autonomous power of the state', in J. S. Hall, ed., *States in History* (Oxford, 1986), offers a useful social science perspective.

[44] See, recently, S. Hanley, 'Engendering the state: family formation and state building in early modern France', *French Historical Studies*, 16, 1989.

[45] O. Raggio, *Faide e parentele: lo stato genovese visto dalla Fontanabuona* (Turin, 1990), ix ff., is very critical of the nineteenth-century model of the emerging modern state, one preoccupied with identifying and charting the development of centralised and centralising institutions.

[46] C. Tilly, ed., *The Formation of National States in Western Europe* (Princeton, 1975), passim; T. Skocpol, *States and Social Revolution: a comparative analysis of France, Russia and China* (Cambridge, 1979).

[47] Brown, *War, Revolution and the Bureaucratic State*, 3. For I. A. A. Thompson, the demands of war (often seen as the motor of absolutist state creation) could in fact undermine the reality (though not necessarily the shell) of absolutism: see Thompson, *War and Government in Habsburg Spain 1560–1620* (London, 1976), passim and '"Money, money and yet more money!" Finance, the fiscal-state and the military revolution: Spain 1500–1650', in C. J. Rogers, ed., *Military Revolution Debate: readings on the military transformation of early modern Europe* (Boulder, CO and Oxford, 1995). This view is shared by many historians of the second half of Louis XIV's reign: see G. Symcox, *The Crisis of French Sea Power 1688–1697: from the Guerre d'Escadre to the Guerre de Course* (Hague, 1974).

understandably sought greater power at home, and sometimes imitated Louis XIV (and other examples of effective government). But his main concerns were, necessarily, diplomacy and war. The latter inevitably impacted upon the domestic development of the Savoyard state.

III

Without ignoring the good work done on this subject regarding states other than France, it is immediately apparent that the great bulk of studies of both absolutism and state formation (indeed of any major theme in early modern Europe) focus on France or one of the other larger states, or Great Powers, in process of formation. There are many good reasons for this, of course, but the majority of states in early modern Europe, including the Savoyard state, were much smaller than these traditional foci, suggesting the need for alternative models.[48] One of the arguments of the present study is that there was a Savoyard special way, or *Sonderweg*, to 'absolutism' and statehood, which was founded above all upon its ability to insert itself into the states system at this crucial time of change, exploiting the rivalries of its more powerful neighbours, whom it managed to lever into channelling crucial resources (above all, armed forces and money) which were otherwise unavailable to it, although enormous efforts were also made to raise as many men and revenues from its own territories. The Savoyard state's ability to manoeuvre between the Great Powers is reasonably familiar at least to historians of international relations in this period, for whom Victor Amadeus seems often to be little more than an habitual turncoat. In fact, the duke's supposed 'treachery' was intimately related to his limited options as ruler of a small and weak state. The experience and conduct of both Victor Amadeus and his state should repay further study, not least because most studies of absolutism and state formation focus on the givers of resources, whose route to statehood was fundamentally different. This was not least because Victor Amadeus (and his subjects) might have to pay a price for those additional resources, in the form of a privileged regime within the absolute state for the Protestant Vaudois, which the latter could not have secured for themselves.

Despite its importance in this period, and its potential contribution to our understanding of crucial aspects of early modern Europe, the Savoyard state remains relatively unknown, at least by comparison with the

---

[48] It would be unfair not to acknowledge the work done on a number of lesser states. See J. A. Vann, *The Making of a State. Württemberg 1593–1793* (Ithaca, 1984), and P. H. Wilson, *War, State and Society in Württemberg, 1677–1793* (Cambridge, 1995) for one German state. For the Italian states, see E. Fasano Guarini, 'Etat moderne'.

great interest shown in some of the other Italian states.⁴⁹ But the Savoyard state in these decades is not completely terra incognita. Indeed, above all because of a Risorgimento-inspired belief that it was the only independent state in Italy between the late sixteenth and eighteenth centuries with any vigour or future, the history of the early modern Savoyard state was – as least until relatively recently, when there has been a new interest in the other states of early modern Italy (which were absorbed into the Kingdom of Italy from 1861) – somewhat privileged. The fine old nineteenth-century histories of the reign, and of specific aspects of the military and diplomatic history of the Savoyard state, produced by a group of men (above all Domenico Carutti) who successfully combined government, history and politics,⁵⁰ and the impressive published collection of Savoyard state papers and introductory essays in the splendid *Campagne di Guerra* in Piemont series, focusing on the first years of the War of the Spanish Succession, are testimony to the contrary.⁵¹

However, the older works suffer from three very different defects. Firstly, those Italian historians influenced by nineteenth-century Risorgimento attitudes towards the Savoyard state, such as Carutti, for whom Victor Amadeus was taking the first steps towards the creation of the unified Italian kingdom proclaimed in 1861, have sometimes in consequence distorted ducal policy and its concerns⁵² – not least because Victor

---

⁴⁹ See Tilly, *Formation of National States*, and M. Greengrass, ed., *Conquest and Coalescence: the shaping of the state in early modern Europe* (London, 1991). The latter (which usefully identifies three distinct means of state formation (conquest, integration, coalescence) acknowledges the need to look at Savoyard state formation but largely ignores it. There are no references to Savoy in J. Shennan, *The Origins of the Modern European State 1450–1725* (London, 1974). The Savoyard state is also largely absent from both Kirshner, *Origins of the State in Italy* and Fasano Guarini, 'Etat moderne'. Recently, however, an attempt has been made to draw on the Savoyard experience in an attempt at a broad theory of early modern state development: S. Clark, *State and Status: the rise of the state and aristocratic power in Western Europe* (Cardiff, 1995).

⁵⁰ For Carutti, see *DBI*, *sub voce*. Others included Bianchi, Cibrario, Ricotti, Sclopis, to name just a view: see M. Fubini Leuzzi, 'Gli studi storici in Piemonte dal 1766 al 1846: politica culturale e coscienza nazionale', *BSBS*, 81, 1983. See also S. J. Woolf's review of Quazza, *Le riforme*, in *BSBS*, 1958, 473 ff., commenting on the harmful impact on Piedmontese historiography of the Risorgimento and the tradition, associated with Claretta, of 'cronistoria'; and G.-P. Romagnani, 'Il "Rimpatrio" nella storiografia italiana fra Sette e Ottocento', in de Lange, *Dall'Europa alle Valli Valdesi*, 487 ff.

⁵¹ C. Contessa, et al., eds., *Le campagne di guerra in Piemonte (1703–08) e l'assedio di Torino (1706)*, 10 vols. (Turin, 1907–33).

⁵² Carutti, *Diplomazia*, III, 551–2 gives Victor Amadeus' forced exchange of Sicily for Sardinia a Risorgimento-inspired gloss, claiming that in this way a territory which had become hispanised was restored to 'Italy' and that this was the most important and enduring aspect of the exchange. This was completely at odds with Victor Amadeus' understanding of this traumatic episode. For a critical evaluation of this Risorgimento-

Amadeus was not pursuing an 'Italian' policy of the Risorgimento type (see Chapter 3). Secondly, however, non-Italian histories are too ready to dismiss Victor Amadeus as little more than a habitual turncoat, without attempting to account in any very meaningful way for his conduct. Thirdly, there is the tradition, in part related to the first strand above, which identifies Victor Amadeus' reign, and above all the era after 1713, with the creation of a rather traditionally conceived 'absolutist' state, as a result of the reforms which were the subject more than a generation ago of a seminal study by Guido Quazza.[53] This perception of the Savoyard state as an absolutist archetype is, inevitably, reflected in Geoffrey Symcox' impressive synthesis study of Victor Amadeus II's reign — the first major study of its subject in English (and the first in any language since Carutti's biographical study, published over a century ago[54]) — which more than any other work has drawn attention (particularly outside Italy) to the Savoyard state. For Symcox, 'the way in which Victor Amadeus formulated and then implemented his policies provides a definitive illustration of the methods and objectives of absolutism at work'; and — anticipating what has been said above about the need to pay attention to the experience of the smaller states of early modern Europe — 'The small size of the state he ruled makes it a purer "laboratory" specimen of absolutism than larger states like France'.[55]

Symcox' study of Victor Amadeus must be the starting point for any subsequent attempt to understand the reign. However, as Symcox himself acknowledges, his view of the duke as absolute prince *par excellence* is increasingly difficult to sustain in its entirety, in the face of further research. Sandra Cavallo's work on charitable giving in early modern Turin, for example, exposes the claim that Victor Amadeus launched an 'absolutist' transformation of the Savoyard welfare system after 1713, and instead sees what was attempted as little more than a paean to his new royal status.[56] Other historians, too — notably Giovanni Levi, Simona Cerutti, Claudio Rosso, Angelo Torre, Sandro Lombardini, Daniela Frigo and Walter Barberis — have thrown valuable new light on the early

---

inspired approach, see D. Frigo, 'L'Affermazione della sovranità. Famiglia e Corte dei Savoia tra Cinque e Settecento', in C. Mozzarelli, ed., *"Familia" del principe e famiglia aristocratica*, 2 vols. (Rome, 1988), I, 279.

[53] Quazza, *Le riforme*.
[54] D. Carutti, *Storia del regno di Vittorio Amedeo II* (Turin, 1863).
[55] Symcox, *Victor Amadeus*, passim; Symcox, 'L'Età di Vittorio Amedeo II', in Merlin *et al.*, *Il Piemonte sabaudo*, 271 ff., passim.
[56] Sandra Cavallo, *Charity and Power in Early Modern Italy: benefactors and their motives in Turin 1541–1789* (Cambridge, 1995), 195–6. Significantly, the word 'absolutism' occurs only three times in Cavallo's index.

modern Savoyard state, questioning some of the old 'absolutist' certainties.[57] On the other hand, the reign of Victor Amadeus II, once regarded as one of the two defining reigns (the other being that of Emanuel Filibert in the second half of the sixteenth century) has been 'squeezed' recently between, on the one hand, an interest in the early seventeenth century, associated above all with Enrico Stumpo and, on the other hand, a new concern, particularly on the part of Giuseppe Ricuperati, with the reforming reign of Charles Emanuel III and the creation of a 'well-ordered police state' of the sort identified by Marc Raeff (and much like the regimes of the classic 'enlightened despotism') and its breakdown in the reign of Victor Amadeus III.[58] However, it is important not to lose sight of the earlier, 1690–1720, phase of state formation on which (as will become clear) subsequent reform ultimately built, not least because there are significant gaps in our knowledge and understanding of the Savoyard state in this earlier period. This is particularly true of the Nine Years War, the second half of the War of the Spanish Succession and the war for Sicily (1718–20).

The present study, which makes no claim to be exhaustive – it does not, for example, consider the cultural and intellectual 'renewal' (embodied in the reform of the University of Turin, reopened in 1720) or Victor Amadeus' quarrel with the Papacy of which that renewal was an offshoot[59] – essentially seeks to assess the multiple and varied impact of war on the Savoyard state between 1690 and 1720. Chapter 1 considers the Savoyard army, the relative military contributions of Victor Amadeus' own states and of those who were not his subjects and the extent to which the state imposed new obligations of military service on its subjects (and developed an appropriate administrative structure) as a result of the pressures of war. Chapter 2 looks at Savoyard finances, the contribution of foreign subsidies. Chapter 3 considers Savoyard diplo-

[57] See G. Levi, *L'eredità immateriale: carriera di un esorcista nel Piemonte del Seicento* (Turin, 1985); published in English as *Inheriting Power: the story of an exorcist* (Chicago, 1988); S. Cerutti, *Mestieri e privilegi: nascita delle corporazioni a Torino secoli XVII–XVIII* (Turin, 1992); C. Rosso, *Una burocrazia di Antico Regime: i Segretari di Stato dei Duchi di Savoia, I (1559–1637)* (Turin, 1992); A. Torre, 'Politics cloaked in worship: state, church and local power in Piedmont 1550–1770', *Past and Present*, 134, 1992; S. Lombardini, 'La costruzione dell'ordine: governatori e governati a Mondovì (1682–1687)', in G. Lombardi, ed., *La Guerra del Sale (1680–1699)* (Milan, 1986); D. Frigo, *Principe, ambasciatori e 'Jus Gentium': l'amministrazione della politica estera nel Piemonte del Settecento* (Rome, 1991); W. Barberis, *Le armi del principe: la tradizione militare sabauda* (Turin, 1989).
[58] G. Ricuperati, 'Gli strumenti dell'assolutismo sabaudo: Segreterie di Stato e Consiglio delle Finanze nel XVIII secolo', *RSI*, 103, 1991. But, *ibid.* 'L'Avvenimento', p. 350, describes a long (1696–1775) phase of 'modernisation'.
[59] Symcox, *Victor Amadeus*, 217–21.

macy, both as a sphere of operation of the ducal state and for its role in mobilising the resources of Victor Amadeus' allies (thus helping to bridge the gap between a lesser and the greater powers) and in providing a sphere for the assertion of Savoyard independence and dignity. Chapter 4 considers the degree of administrative change which accompanied the process of state formation, above all the developing system of intendants, but also the persistence of older sources of state cohesion, the degree of domestic opposition to the duke's wars and the demands they made, the methods used by Victor Amadeus to counter the latter, and the way new bonds of cohesion were generated during the wars, helping to generate a new sense of Savoyard state indentity and cohesion. Chapter 5 considers the experience of the Savoyard nobility in these years and its relationship with and contribution to the emerging state, arguing that that nobility collaborated with Victor Amadeus, and found its own interest in co-operating in his 'state project' rather than merely being the victims, as in more traditional accounts of the 'absolutist' state. Chapter 6 considers the different processes of integration into the Savoyard state in these decades experienced by the province of Mondovì, a trouble spot before 1690, the Duchy of Aosta and the Protestant Vaudois communities, the reinsertion of the latter being clearly related to the duke's foreign alliances.

IV

One final point needs clarification, by way of introduction: the proper designation of the Savoyard state. This causes many problems to those unfamiliar with the state, who seek to identify it with a variety of labels which it is felt reflect power realities. Thus, it is often called Piedmont-Savoy to indicate the fact that, although Victor Amadeus was duke of Savoy, the most important part of his territories (in terms of extent, population and revenues yielded) was the principality of Piedmont. These efforts to give the Savoyard state an adequate name reflect the degree to which this typically composite early modern state fitted (and continued to fit after 1713, with the added complication of the acquisition of the Kingdom of Sicily and later of Sardinia) ill into our 'modern' notions of statehood. For the most part, it will be referred to in this book as the Savoyard state, unless otherwise appropriate[60]

---

[60] See the remarks of R. Oresko, 'The House of Savoy in search for a royal crown in the seventeenth century', in R. Oresko, G. C. Gibbs and H. M. Scott, eds., *Royal and Republican Sovereignty in Early Modern Europe: essays in memory of Ragnhild Hatton* (Cambridge, 1997), 272. For Victor Amadeus' various territories and the differing titles he enjoyed in each, see *CGP*, VII, 42.

CHAPTER I

THE SAVOYARD ARMY, 1690–1720

Armies, particularly standing ones, and their development, have figured largely in accounts of state formation, particularly for those who see this as being about the state's assertion of a monopoly of legitimate force within its own borders.[1] Some historians are now less inclined to see this as of overriding importance, rightly urging the need to beware of seeing the use of coercive force by the prince as the only (or even the decisive) element in the consolidation of the state.[2] However, it would be difficult to deny the contribution of armed might in the formation of the Savoyard state between 1690 and 1720. Firstly, it defended that state from foreign conquest, removed threats (Casale, Pinerolo) to its independence and ultimately underpinned its sovereignty.[3] Secondly, the ducal forces conquered places and territories which contributed to the enlargement and reshaping of Victor Amadeus' state. These included the conquest of the Alpine fortresses, which provided that state thenceforth with a more defensible frontier, and of the Pragelato. After securing the latter, Victor Amadeus rejected a request that he respect the Pragelato's traditional liberties, instead asserting his own right of conquest.[4] This episode reveals, thirdly, that the duke's army could assert his authority within his

---

[1] T. Blanning, *The French Revolutionary Wars 1787–1802* (London, 1996), 30. See S. E. Finer, 'State and nation building in Europe: the role of the military', in C. Tilly, ed., *The Formation of Nation States in Western Europe* (Princeton, 1975), 84 ff. and S. Clark, *State and Status: the rise of the state and aristocratic power in Western Europe* (Cardiff, 1994), 12.

[2] See J. Lynn, *Giant of the Grand Siècle: the French army 1610–1715* (Cambridge, 1997), 1 ff. and S. Lombardini, 'La costruzione dell'ordine: governatori e governati a Mondovì (1682–1687)', in G. Lombardi, ed., *La Guerra del Sale (1680–1699): rivolte e frontiere del Piemonte barocco*, 3 vols. (Milan, 1986), I, esp. 220 ff.

[3] R. D. Handen, 'The Savoy negotiations of the comte de Tessé 1693–1696' (Ph.D. thesis, University of Ohio, 1970), 129, notes Victor Amadeus' determination to avoid restrictions on the size of army which he, as a sovereign prince, could maintain in peacetime.   [4] VDM to Fagel, 2 Jan. 1709, Turin ARAH/EA/VDM/33, f. 1.

dominions. The entry of his forces was a crucial symbolic, and real, part of his assumption of territories ceded to him. His troops also supplemented the exiguous 'police' forces which the duke had at his disposal[5] and (see below, p. 38) were used to chivvy communities felt to be too slow in fulfilling their obligations to supply men, provisions, draught animals, transports and taxes. In the interval between the Nine Years War and the War of the Spanish Succession, the duke successfully concentrated his forces (many of them veterans of the Nine Years War) against Mondovì, bringing that province to heel at last in a way which had eluded his mother (see Chapter 6). Not surprisingly, the acquisition by Victor Amadeus of a permanent and powerful instrument which he could use to assert his authority at home – against, for example, rioters at Cigliano (1724) protesting against new taxation associated with Victor Amadeus' new law code, the so-called Constitutions (1723) – and to defend his independence, or sovereignty, against foreign attack, is one that most historians of the subject still feel they cannot ignore.[6]

This aspect of state formation is sometimes linked with another phenomenon which some historians have identified in the early modern period. The thesis of the 'Military Revolution', formulated by Michael Roberts forty years ago, suggested that fundamental changes in the nature of warfare between the middle of the sixteenth and the middle of the seventeenth centuries had important knock-on effects and ultimately contributed to state formation and the rise of centralised absolutism, an implication more fully worked out by some of the later contributors to the discussion. Not all agree with this formulation. Frank Tallettt, noting the enormous gulf between what armies attempted and what (held back by logistical problems) they could do, has questioned the notion of a 'revolution'. Jeremy Black, on the other hand, has argued that if there was a revolution in warfare, it occurred after 1660 and was the consequence, not cause, of an absolutist consensus. Among the examples Black cites in support of this contention is the Savoyard state.[7]

---

[5] G. Prato 'Il costo della Guerra di successione Spagnuola e le spese pubbliche in Piemonte dal 1700 al 1713', in *CGP*, X, 248 ff. puts at just 200 men the ordinary forces of law and order in the Savoyard state. In 1713, Victor Amadeus reinforced Turin's garrison on the occasion of the peace celebrations, Payne to Ayerst, 26 July 1713, Turin, SP 92/27, f. 623.

[6] See F. Venturi, 'Il Piemonte dei primi decenn: del Settecento nelle relazioni de: diplomatici inglesi', *BSBS*, S4, 1956, 237–8.

[7] M. Roberts, 'The military revolution 1560–1660', in Roberts, *Essays in Swedish History* (London, 1967); G. Parker. *The Military Revolution: military innovation and the rise of the West 1500–1800* (Cambridge, 1988); F. Tallett, *War and Society in Early Modern Europe 1495–1715* (London, 1992); J. Black, *A Military Revolution? Military change and European society 1550–1800* (London, 1988). See, also, C. J. Rogers, ed., *The Military Revolution Debate: readings on the military transformations of early modern Europe* (Boulder, CO, 1995).

In fact, we still know relatively little about the Savoyard army in the early modern era. This is not to deny the existence of some fine older general histories of that army[8] and of an exceptionally well documented account of the first years of the War of the Spanish Succession,[9] whose continuing importance as a quarry of information will be evident from the following pages. There are also some impressive more recent monographs. However, most of these focus largely on the era after 1713, while the Savoyard army hardly figures in most English-language surveys of early modern European armies (and is notable by its absence from Geoffrey Symcox' otherwise excellent survey of the reign of Victor Amadeus II).[10] Apart from the War of the Spanish Succession (and above all the years between 1703 and the end of the siege of Turin in 1706), the Savoyard army between 1690 and 1720 remains relatively unexplored. And yet, these decades were crucial in transforming the Savoyard state from one characterised by a propensity to violence which was not monopolised by, and was in fact in large part directed against the 'state' (the Parella and Mondovì revolts, 1682) to one in which after 1713 (despite such apparently provocative measures as Victor Amadeus' revocation of fiefs, 1720), armed resistance of the earlier sort failed to materialise and was in fact simply inconceivable. For most historians of the subject, the Savoyard state after 1713 was, on the other hand, highly 'militarised', a higher proportion of its population being under arms than in most other states.[11] Although the development of a nucleus of standing regular ducal forces was largely the achievement of Charles Emanuel II after 1659, for many, not surprisingly, Victor Amadeus II was the creator of the Savoyard army.[12]

However in recent years some older views of the Savoyard army, and its role in Savoyard state and society, have come under fire, above all from Walter Barberis. Whereas, for Quazza and others, the Savoyard army perfected by Victor Amadeus II was very much the instrument of the

---

[8] Comte A. de Saluces, *Histoire militaire du Piémont*, 5 vols. (Turin, 1818), still probably the best general account of the evolution of the Savoyard army between the sixteenth and eighteenth centuries (containing valuable details on administration and individual corps) and of its campaigns; N. Brancaccio, *L'Esercito del vecchio Piemonte: sunti storici dei principali corpi*, (Rome, 1922); Brancaccio, *L'Esercito del vecchio Piemonte: gli ordinamenti*, (Rome, 1923).

[9] All the *CGP* volumes include a mass of relevant materials from the Archivio di Stato, Turin.

[10] Symcox, *Victor Amadeus*; G. Quazza, *Le riforme in Piemonte nella prima metà del Settecento*, 2 vols. (Modena, 1957), I, 108 ff.; W. Barberis, *Le armi del principe: la tradizione militare sabauda* (Turin, 1988); S. Loriga, *Soldati: l'istituzione militare nel Piemonte del Settecento* (Venice, 1992). P. Bianchi, 'Esercito e riforme militari negli stati sabaudi del Settecento: un bilancio storiografico', in Società di Storia Militare, *Quaderno 1995* (Rome, 1995), 7–38 is a useful survey.   [11] Quazza, *Le riforme*, I, 105.

[12] *Ibid.*; Saluces, *Histoire militaire*, I, 310 (and passim); Prato, 'Il costo', *CGP*, X, 258 ff.

absolute state, for Barberis it was just another arena in which state (i.e. the duke) and society (i.e. his subjects) 'negotiated' service for rewards. Related to this is Barberis' attack on a Piedmontese historical tradition, which sees the Savoyard army as an alliance between a warrior dynasty and a loyal, warrior people (symbolised by the hitherto obscure 'sapper' Pietro Micca, killed in Victor Amadeus' service during the siege of Turin in 1706), a union which achieved its apotheosis in the nineteenth century with the expulsion of the 'foreigner' and the unification of Italy under the Casa Savoia.[13]

The object of the present chapter is threefold: firstly, and above all, simply to detail just how Victor Amadeus fought the two major wars which played so important a part in the longer-term process of Savoyard state formation; secondly, to show the extent to which the success of the Savoyard state between 1690 and 1713 was based upon non-Savoyard military resources; and, thirdly, to demonstrate the degree to which the needs of war (and after 1713 the problem of defending an enlarged state without outside help) obliged Victor Amadeus to impose new military obligations upon his subjects and to elaborate new military insitutions. Consideration of these issues should help to enlarge the debate about armies and warfare (and their relationship to the wider polity and society) in the early modern era, not least because most discussion of this subject focuses on a rather restricted range of armies.

ARMY EXPANSION

The years between 1690 and 1713 saw a remarkable growth in the size of the Savoyard army.[14] This was the more remarkable, in the Nine Years

[13] See Saluces, *Histoire militaire*, V, 139–40, 178, for the loyalty of the duke's subjects in the military crises of 1690, 1703 and 1706. The first eulogy of Micca was published in 1781 in Bava di San Paolo's *Piemontesi Illustri*, Barberis, *Le armi*, 237. For a criticism of some of Barberis' more general contentions, see E. Stumpo, 'Tra mito, leggenda e realtà storica: la tradizione militare sabauda da Emanuele Filiberto a Carlo Alberto', *RSI*, 103, 1991, 560 ff.

[14] All troop numbers, including official ones, must be treated with caution and some scepticism. Most figures, derived from the periodic troop reviews (below) were just a snapshot of the situation at one point in time and were invariably promptly rendered out of date by desertion, loss of life and illness on the one hand and by new levies and recruiting on the other. The original review may, anyway, have fraudulently exaggerated the numbers of men (to enable officials to draw the pay of non-existent men). In 1692 Victor Amadeus observed the difference between the Miremont regiment as reviewed and as seen by him, and suspected fraud, F. Guasco, 'Vittorio Amedeo II nelle campagne dal 1691 al 1696', *Studi su Vittorio Amedeo II* (Turin, 1933), 270. For a general discussion of the unreliability of official records, and their tendency to overestimate the number of troops at Victor Amadeus' disposal, see Prato, 'Il costo', *CGP*, X, 326. See also J. Lynn, 'Recalculating French army growth during the Grand Siècle 1610–1715', *French Historical Studies*, 18, 4, 1994.

Table 1.1. *The growth of the Savoyard army 1690–1696*

	Infantry	Cavalry and dragoons	Total
1690	7,250	1,420	8,670
1691	11,107	2,775	13,882
1692	14,467	2,775	17,242
1693	14,499	2,683	17,112
1694	15,745	2,682	18,427
1695	20,752	2,537	23,289
1696	21,508	2,515	24,023

Source: Figures taken from Prato, 'Il costo', *CGP*, X, p. 260. For 1691, cf. ARAH/SG/8643/140. For a much higher total in 1695 of 26,290 (23,800 infantry and 2,490 cavalry) cf. *mémoire* sent to Madrid in AGS/E/3421/20. For a lower estimate of Victor Amadeus' forces in 1696, of just 20,000 (but with no indication of all the units involved) cf. VDM to Fagel, 16 July 1696, Turin, ARAH/SG/8644/279.

War, given the despatch to France in 1689 of three of Victor Amadeus' regular regiments (Aosta, Marine, Nizza), in response to a request by Louis XIV for troops for the war which had begun in Flanders in 1688. (They were also a pledge of Victor Amadeus' good faith in the escalating European crisis.) This was not the first time that the ducal army had grown as a result of the Savoyard state's participation in major conflict. In 1625 when Victor Amadeus' great grandfather, Charles Emanuel I, joined with Louis XIII of France in an attack against Genoa and Spain, the Savoyard army rocketed to an astonishing 26,500, a figure not reached again before the War of the Spanish Succession. Between the late 1630s and the Peace of the Pyrenees (1659), war between Spain and France, which had inevitably extended to Italy, affected the Savoyard state, whose army again grew to nearly 18,000 in 1649. After 1659, however, the Savoyard army dwindled substantially. This was only interrupted by the expansion associated with the disastrous war against Genoa (1672) and with the fears of renewed war between France and Spain in north Italy in 1683–84. Generally speaking, however, the Savoyard forces in the generation after 1660 fluctuated between 5,000 and 6,000, reflecting in part the extent to which the dukes of Savoy were satellites of the French king, who was suspicious of any attempt on their part to maintain a larger army (and perhaps pursue a more independent foreign policy).[15] At the start of 1690, before his breach with Louis XIV, but following Victor Amadeus' efforts to increase his forces to meet the challenge of the returned Vaudois (see

---

[15] See Prato, 'Il costo', *CGP*, X, 259–60, for the general evolution in overall numbers (and costs); and C. de Rousset, *Histoire de Louvois et de son administration militaire*, 4 vols. (Paris, 1879), IV, 284 ff. for concern about the size of the Savoyard army at the French court.

Chapter 6), the Savoyard army totalled just over 8,000 men: 6,800 infantry (in six regiments: Guards, Savoy, Piedmont, Monferrato, Saluzzo, Chablais, and the recently levied Fusiliers), 490 cavalry (four companies of guards and four of gendarmes) and 800 dragoons (in two regiments: Verrua and the recently levied Chaumont or Genevois).[16] Thereafter, the Savoyard army expanded as shown in Table 1.1. In all, there was a substantial, if uneven, threefold increase in the size of Victor Amadeus' forces between 1690 and 1696. Growth was especially notable between 1690 and 1691, when the duke's forces nearly doubled,[17] between 1691 and 1692 and again between 1694 and 1695, when they grew by 25 per cent. Expansion was slowing down by the end of the war[18] but only really faltered between 1692 and 1693. This expansion, way beyond anything allowed by Louis XIV before 1690, was also notable given the losses sustained by Victor Amadeus' forces in successive campaigns.[19]

Growth of this sort has often been seen as part of a much longer-term growth in armies in early modern Europe.[20] However, although the Savoyard army expanded over the early modern era as a whole it was by no means continuous and cumulative[21]. Victor Amadeus's *volte-face* of 1696 was followed by a reversal of the recent growth. Partly to satisfy the terms of the neutralisation of Italy, partly to reverse the haemorrhage of funds associated with nearly seven years of war (see Chapter 2), between 1696 and 1698 the duke's forces were reduced to under 10,000 (8,000 infantry and 1600 cavalry and dragoons).[22] This was still sizeable, and was a measure of the extent to which Victor Amadeus had freed himself from French tutelage, obliging Louis XIV to recognise his right to have an independent army. Nevertheless, the Savoyard state remained a third (or even fourth) rank military power by contrast with both Louis XIV and the emperor, whose much larger armies caused him some anxiety.[23] Indeed, by 1700 his army was smaller than on the eve of his entry into the Nine Years War: 8,569 (7,291 infantry and 1,278 cavalry and dragoons).

---

[16] J. Humbert, 'Conquête et occupation de la Savoie sous Louis XIV (1690 à 1691)', *Mémoires de l'Académie des Sciences, Belles-Lettres et Arts de Savoie*, 6th ser., IX, 1967, 18.

[17] See the order to levy thirty new companies, Jan. 1691, Duboin, XXVI, 117.

[18] In the winter of 1695–96 Victor Amadeus increased his Chablais and Monferrato regiments by a battalion each but this was offset by a reduction of five men in every company in all his regiments, DLT to ST, 20 Jan. 1696, London, AST/LM/GB, m. 8.

[19] At the battle of Marsaglia (1693), the duke's losses were put at 1,500 (of an allied total of 5,500), about 9 per cent of his total forces: VA to DLT, 12 Oct. 1693, Turin, AST/LM/Olanda, m. 4.

[20] This issue is discussed in Lynn, 'Recalculating French army growth'.

[21] See figures for Savoyard forces 1580–1795 in Loriga, *Soldati*, 5.

[22] Prato, 'Il costo', *CGP*, X, 260; Duboin, XXVII, 78 (artillery) and XXVI, 127 (Guards) and 1851 (general); and Bazan to Carlos II, 15 Nov. 1697, Turin, AGS/E/3659/95.

[23] See Bazan to Carlos II, 17 Apr. 1698, Turin, AGS/E/3660/27.

Table 1.2. *The growth of the Savoyard army, 1701–1710*[24]

	Infantry	Cavalry and dragoons	Total
1700	7,291	1,278	8,569
1701	11,078	2,678	13,756
1702	10,915	2,678	13,593
1703	10,855	2,660	13,515
1704	23,087	3,460	26,547
1705	12,905	3,360	16,265
1706–7	13,395	3,539	16,934
1707–8	13,664	3,540	17,204
1708–9	13,978	3,500	17,478
1710	15,611	3,753	19,364

Nevertheless, this was still higher than the level which had prevailed before 1690. Expectation of war, and war itself from 1701, prompted renewed growth of the duke's forces (as in Table 1.2). Once again, expansion was erratic. The ducal army nearly doubled between 1700 and 1701 and again between 1703 and 1704. The latter achievement was the more astonishing because of the detention of about 4,500 of his regular troops by the Bourbon forces at San Benedetto in Lombardy in the autumn of 1703.[25] But expansion at this rate was impossible to sustain: the duke did not again in the War of the Spanish Succession have as many troops in his service as in 1704. Nevertheless, his army did expand,

[24] Prato, 'Il costo', X, 260. An alternative set of figures, prepared on a rather different basis and with different results by the Ufficio del Soldo in 1712, *ibid.*, 320 ff. are given below mainly because they give an idea of troop levels after 1710. For a figure for 1708 (of 12,885 infantry and 3,640 cavalry, a total of 16,525) given by Victor Amadeus himself, see VDM to Fagel, 25 Apr. 1708, Turin, ARAH/EA/VDM/32, f. 64. For the 1710 figure given below, see Loriga, *Soldati*, 5. The 22,000 given below for 1712 is also in Saluces, *Histoire militaire*, V, 263. The discrepancies emphasise the problem of harmonising different sets of figures, but the growth is unmistakable.

	Infantry	Cavalry and Dragoons	Total
1701	12,410	2,864	15,274
1702	12.304	2,864	15,168
1703	13,044	2,864	15,908
1704	26,326	3,697	30,033
1705	15,223	3,587	18,810
1706	16,575	3,760	20,335
1707	15,301	3,768	19,069
1708	16,032	3,769	19,801
1709	16,697	3,750	20,447
1710	18,739	3,753	22,492
1711	18,535	3,398	21,933
1712	18,507	3,398	21,905

[25] See figures calculated in *CGP*, I, 24 ff.

steadily rather than dramatically, in the second half of the conflict. Inevitably, peace in 1713 was accompanied by a 'reform', or reduction, of this enlarged army (see below, p. 68), but it did not again fall below 10,000 men and rose again to well over 23,000 during the struggle for Sicily (1718–20). It had risen just above this level a decade later, in 1730. Participation in the European struggle since 1690 had thus underpinned the long-term expansion of the Savoyard army.[26]

Any consideration of the enormous military undertaking of the Savoyard state in these decades must also take into account the importance of the fortresses around which most contemporary warfare revolved.[27] Apart from the defences of Savoy (notably Montmélian) and Nice, Piedmont was ringed by a number of modern bastioned fortresses, guarding the exit from and entrance to the passages through the Alps between Piedmont and Dauphiné and Provence in the west and defending the more open parts of the Savoyard state in the east. These included Cuneo, Demonte, Susa, Bard, Ivrea, Vercelli and Verrua. Turin, too, was heavily fortified.[28] These places were, and were expected by others to be, key concerns of the duke of Savoy.[29] Similarly, sieges of most of these places were among the most important actions of the wars fought by the Savoyard state in these decades, and were at least as important as the three big battles fought in 1690, 1693 and 1706. The siege of Turin in 1705–06, which was ended by Victor Amadeus' and Prince Eugene's victory there in September 1706, followed the surrender of virtually all of the duke's other major fortresses. Besides these major operations, there were numerous sieges of lesser fortified towns, suddenly placed in the front line. The extent to which the security, definition and enlargement of the Savoyard state was seen in terms of fortresses is suggested by Victor Amadeus' argument in 1709 for his gaining the French fortress of Briançon in the coming peace: that he had no major fortress between Briançon and Susa, leaving his states exposed to Louis XIV.[30]

[26] Loriga, *Soldati*, 5; Brancaccio, *Esercito. Ordinamenti*, I, 184; Symcox, *Victor Amadeus*, 168–9. In 1716, VA's forces totalled 16,423 (14,620 infantry and 1,803 cavalry), AST/MM/UGS, m. 1 *d'addizione*, no. 9. The 23,600 men (Brancaccio) for 1720 include 6,000 militia.   [27] See Parker, *Military Revolution*, esp. ch. 1, passim.

[28] For the setting and appearance of the fortresseses of the Savoyard state, see the *Theatrum Sabaudum*, of 1682, ed. L. Firpo, 2 vols. (Turin, 1984–5).

[29] In 1689 the duke's apparent unconcern about a threat from the Milanese to Vercelli (on which vast sums had been spent *c.* 1680), was one indicator at the French court of his waywardness, R. Oresko, 'The diplomatic background to the Glorioso Rimpatrio: the rupture between Vittorio Amedeo II and Louis XIV (1688–1690)', in A. de Lange, ed., *Dall'Europa alle Valli Valdesi: atti del convegno 'Il Glorioso Rimpatrio 1689–1989'*, Turin, 1990, 262.

[30] VDM to Fagel, 25 Sept. 1709, Turin, ARAH/EA/VDM/33, f. 161. The war in Sicily, 1718–20 also revolved around sieges of key positions, including Messina, Trapani and Siracusa: Carutti, *Storia della Diplomazia*, III 548, 550.

Fig. 1.1 Print depicting Victor Amadeus II with, in the background, the plans of Casale and Pinerolo (Biblioteca Reale, Turin, Iconografia Sabauda, Vittorio Amedeo II, 9/29)

Victor Amadeus necessarily took a great personal interest in the condition of the fortresses which defended his state. In the summer of 1691, for example, when his state faced arguably its most serious challenge in this era apart from that of 1705–06, and with substantial works being carried out in and about Turin itself to withstand a siege, he visited Avigliana, to ensure that it could resist any French force invading Piedmont through the Susa valley.[31] Equally important, as an indicator both of the value he placed on these fortresses (and of his distrust of some of his own subjects in this time of crisis) was the fact that, once a major fortress was threatened, the duke sometimes replaced its commander with a close confidant or somebody known to be reliable. He did this on various occasions in both the Nine Years War and the War of the Spanish Succession.[32] These decades saw extensive (and costly) improvements to many of the fortifications of the Savoyard state, both in war and peace (when the opportunity was taken to repair and rearm those places which had been seriously damaged during the fighting).[33] Despite the expulsion of the Bourbons from Piedmont towards the end of 1706, the duke could not completely ignore the French threat thereafter[34] and was also increasingly concerned – because of his growing difficulties with the emperor – with the defences of eastern Piedmont.[35] In 1713, Victor Amadeus visited some of the key fortresses of his mainland territories, to ensure their effectiveness, before he departed for Sicily.[36]

Supplying garrisons for these fortresses substantially reduced the number of men Victor Amadeus could put into the field. In 1691, he blamed his inability to go to the relief of Nice on the governor of Milan's failure to supply him with Spanish troops (freeing his own garrisons for the field). He could therefore only field 6,000–7,000 men (about half his

---

[31] VDM to Fagel, 5 May 1691, Turin, ARAH/SG/8643/133.

[32] In 1691, following the French incursion into the Val d'Aosta, the duke sent to Ivrea conte Francesco Provana di Frosasco, hero of the recent siege of Nice, VDM to Fagel, 23 June 1691, Turin, ARAH/SG/8643/152. In 1704, after the loss of Susa and Vercelli, the emperor demanded that his men share the command of some of the duke's key fortresses, Saluces, *Histoire militaire*, V, 150. (Of course, this might also prevent the duke from effecting the sort of *volte-face* he had made in 1696.) In 1706, the besieged Turin was under the command of the imperial commander, Marshal Daun.

[33] See *DBI*, 'Caraglio' (Nice) and Nicolas, *La Savoie*, I, 42 (Montmélian).

[34] Fears about French designs on Susa in 1708 prompted the rapid transfer of troops there, VDM to Fagel, 18 Feb., 28 Mar. and 25 Apr. 1708, Turin, ARAH/EA/VDM/32, fs. 32, 51 and 65.

[35] Chetwynd to Dartmouth, 24 Aug. and 2 Dec. 1712, Turin, SP 92/28.

[36] Chetwynd to Dartmouth, 14 June and 12 Aug. 1713, Turin, SP 92/28, fs. 607, 631; L. Einaudi, *La finanza sabauda all'aprirsi del secolo XVIII e durante la guerra di successione spagnuola* (Turin, 1908), 412.

army).³⁷ That same summer, the duke was informed that he needed 12,000 infantry (in effect all the available allied infantry) to defend Turin.³⁸ Victor Amadeus might raid his garrisons for a prized object: in 1692, he offered 3,000 men (from his garrisons) if the allies should besiege Pinerolo.³⁹ At other times he might take more drastic action to reduce this drain on his military manpower. In 1694, in order both to reduce the need for garrisons and to prevent the enemy from establishing themselves in Piedmont, he destroyed a number of secondary fortifications there.⁴⁰ But the normal practice was to give priority to the defence of fortresses. This widely acknowledged need could facilitate Victor Amadeus' other schemes. In 1696, with a large French force invading Piedmont, he had ample justification for strengthening his garrisons at the expense of his contribution to the allied field army,⁴¹ weakening the latter and facilitating his diplomatic and military *volte-face*. In the first years of the War of the Spanish Succession, large numbers of ducal troops were again tied up in garrisons. In July 1704 the despatch of troops to Avigliana, Ivrea and Vercelli (whose garrison totalled about 8,000 men) was said to have left Victor Amadeus with a field army of just 8,000.⁴² After 1706, with Piedmont largely free of enemy forces, the duke could put far more of his forces into the field, and reduced his garrisons for the Alpine campaigns of 1708 and 1709.⁴³ Nevertheless, the expansion of Victor Amadeus' own forces between 1690 and 1713 could not, alone, have ensured a field army large enough to successfully oppose that of his enemy.

---

³⁷ VA to DLT, 3 Apr. 1691, Turin, AST/LM/Olanda, m. 1; VDM to Fagel, 21 Apr. 1691, Turin, ARAH/SG/8644/127.
³⁸ VA to DLT, 17 June 1691, Turin, AST/LM/Olanda, m. 1.
³⁹ VA to DLT, 28 July 1692, Arches, AST/LM/Olanda, m. 3.
⁴⁰ VDM to Fagel, 23 and 30 Apr. 1694, Turin, ARAH/SG/120, 121. For a similar policy in the subsequent conflict, see VDM to Fagel, 11 Mar. 1705, Turin, ARAH/EA/VDM/30, 20. Vauban calculated that fewer fortresses would give Louis XIV thousands more troops: J. Lynn, 'The trace Italienne and the growth of armies; the French case', *Journal of Military History*, 55, 1991, 10.
⁴¹ ST to DLT, 10 Mar. 1696, London, AST/LM/Olanda, m. 4; VDM to Fagel, 27 Apr. and 18 May 1696, Turin, ARAH/SG/8644/255, 262.
⁴² VDM to Fagel, 4 July 1704, Turin, ARAH/EA/VDM/29, 114. The surrender of Vercelli meant the loss of large numbers of men, C. Faccio, 'Assedio di Vercelli. Primo periodo della campagna di Guerra per la Successione di Spagna: anno 1704', *CGP*, X, 411 ff.
⁴³ See VDM to States, 31 Mar. 1708, Turin, same to Fagel, 25 Apr. 1708, Turin, and 28 Aug. 1708, Balbote, ARAH/EA/VDM/32, fs. 53, 64–5, 164. The duke claimed to have left only two battalions in garrison: one in Turin, the other divided between Alessandria, Valenza and Casale. In 1709, Victor Amadeus put all his troops into the field, using the urban militia to defend Turin, Chetwynd to Townshend, 20 July 1709, Turin, *HMC, 11th Report, Appendix IX, part IV*, 53.

COMPOSITION OF VICTOR AMADEUS' FORCES

The expansion of Victor Amadeus' forces depended upon a substantial supply of manpower: his regiments required 3,000 recruits for example in the winter of 1708–09.[44] Just how was the Savoyard army raised to the extraordinary levels achieved in both the Nine Years War and the War of the Spanish Succession, and who were the men who made up his forces? As we shall see, like most of his contemporaries, Victor Amadeus necessarily relied on a mix of both 'nationals' and foreigners to man his armies. However, these labels are themselves deceptive. Even those regiments nominally filled by the duke's own subjects, and which we might be tempted to label 'national', were often much more diverse in composition. At the end of 1694, for example, Victor Amadeus agreed to the levy of two German and three Irish companies to complete the second battalion of his Chablais regiment; and in 1701, his recruiting captains were allowed ten foreigners per new company of fifty men.[45] Clearly, the distinction between units comprising Victor Amadeus' own subjects and those made up of 'foreigners' was not always easy to draw.

However, the duke's subjects did provide a substantial proportion of his own troops, as he acknowledged: in 1709 Victor Amadeus claimed to have recruited since 1700 (roughly speaking, since the start of the War of the Spanish Succession) a total of 70,000 men, 55,000 of his own subjects and 15,000 foreigners.[46] The company of miners in which Pietro Micca served was overwhelmingly 'native', the vast majority of Micca's fellow sappers originating from the Valle d'Andorno and Savoy.[47] The duke's own subjects were particularly likely to be used in times of crisis when it might take foreign corps some time to arrive, assuming negotiations for them had been successful (see below, p. 46). Thus in November 1689, when Victor Amadeus was increasing his forces to deal with the returned Vaudois (and the escalating European crisis), he agreed a capitulation with one of his subjects, the marquis de Chaumont, a captain of dragoons and member of the Senate of Savoy, for the levy of a dragoon regiment of 400 men (8 companies of 50 men each) in three months. The regiment, largely raised in Savoy, was complete by the spring of 1690.[48] Victor Amadeus continued to look to his own subjects as a source of military

---

[44] VDM to Fagel, 30 Jan. 1709, Turin, ARAH/EA/VDM/33, f. 12.
[45] Duboin, XXVI, 1132, 1134 (1694); *CGP*, I, lxv (1701).
[46] VDM to Fagel, 13 Mar. 1709, Turin, ARAH/EA/VDM/33, f. 36.
[47] E. Casanova, 'Contributo alla biografia di Pietro Micca e di Maria Chiaberge Bricco e alla storia del voto di Vittorio Amedeo II', *CGP*, VIII, 196 ff.
[48] L. Provana di Collegno, 'Lettere di Carlo Ciacinto Roero, conte di Guarene, capitano nel reggimento dragoni di Genevois, 1704–1707', *CGP*, VIII, 339; Saluces, *Histoire militaire*, I, 330; *CGP*, I, passim.

manpower in the War of the Spanish Succession, successfully appealing to his Protestant Vaudois subjects in the crisis of 1703–04.[49] Inevitably, however, following the loss of Savoy (and Nice) at an early stage in the Nine Years War and the War of the Spanish Succession, relying on the duke's own subjects meant in effect depending on Piedmont and (to a much lesser degree) on his other remaining territories.[50]

One source of veterans among Victor Amadeus's own subjects in 1690 were his three regiments in Louis XIV's service in Flanders, and whose retention by the French king was a serious blow to the duke's military strength. But, not least because these regiments were far from Piedmont, recovering them was not easy.[51] Victor Amadeus' envoy, de la Tour, who was contacted soon after his arrival at The Hague in 1690 by the chevalier de St George (a major in the Marine regiment), sought to co-ordinate the escape of some of these troops, initially with little sucess;[52] and in early 1691 obtained an order from the governor of the Spanish Low Countries, the marques de Gastanaga, for the reception of any deserters from those regiments in the fortresses of Spanish Flanders and sought funds from William III for the project. By late April 1691, 100 men had been collected. De la Tour despatched them to Piedmont (via Cologne, Frankfurt, the Grisons and the Milanese), with passports from the emperor. He hoped to secure more men in the summer, with the armies in the field (and desertion rather easier), although little more seems to have been achieved in 1691.[53] However, in 1693, another forty Piedmontese reached Turin from Flanders.[54] Victor Amadeus now saw this source as a means of compensating for his failure to secure German hire troops (see below, p. 46), especially as both William III and Elector Max Emanuel of Bavaria (now governor of Spanish Flanders) favoured the scheme (which

---

[49] Symcox, *Victor Amadeus*, 146–7.
[50] The governor of the tiny coastal exclave of Oneglia raised 100 men for the duke in 1695, Duboin, XXVII, 1382. Victor Amadeus might still look to Savoy. In the autumn of 1693, he gave a commission to the marquis de Sales to recruit a Savoyard regiment, Duboin, XXVI, 108; and in the later stages of the War of the Spanish Succession took the opportunity of his incursions into French-occupied Savoy to raise men. In 1711 Victor Amadeus ordered the levy of 1,100 men there, to complete his Savoy regiment, Chetwynd to Dartmouth, 15 Aug. 1711, Marches, SP 92/27.
[51] Primarily because of Victor Amadeus's insistence that they not be used against his suzerain, the emperor. This meant they could not serve on the Rhine, Oresko, 'Diplomatic background', 260–1.
[52] DLT to VA, 5 Sept. 1690 and same to ST, 13 and 20 Oct. 1690, Hague, AST/LM/Olanda, m. 1. What, above all, prevented the officers from leaving the French king's service was a lack of money.
[53] DLT to VA, 4 Mar., 3 and 27 Apr. and 17 and 25 May 1691, Hague, AST/LM/Olanda, m. 2.   [54] VDM to Fagel, 4 May 1693, Turin, ARAH/SG/8643/31.

for them had the advantage of weakening Louis XIV's forces in the Low Countries). Victor Amadeus expected to form a new regiment in this way, hoping to obtain cash help from William, arms and uniforms from the Dutch, and an assembly point and staging posts, or *étapes, en route* to Piedmont from Max Emmanuel.[55] An assembly point (at Louvain) was obtained from the latter and a contribution from William III of 4 écus plus a daily bread ration per man during their stay in those quarters and by mid-summer Victor Amadeus' envoy at Brussels, conte Tarino, had assembled sixty men.[56] This was an expensive and not plentiful source of recruits. But the duke continued to seize any opportunity to recover these troops: in 1695 he ordered Tarino to obtain as many men as possible from his regiments which were in garrison there when the fortress of Namur surrendered to his allies.[57]

Prisoners of war were another source of veterans. They were particularly important in the first phase of the War of the Spanish Succession, because of the detention by the Bourbons in 1703 of so many of the duke of Savoy's regular troops and the fact that the Bourbon armies were taking far more enemy prisoners in Italy than were the allies. There was an established procedure for the exchange of prisoners, i.e. the conclusion of formal agreements or cartels, of the sort concluded after the battles of Staffarda, 1690 and Marsaglia, 1693. However, between 1703 and 1706 the French king was apparently determined to retain the troops taken by his forces, in the belief that Victor Amadeus would be unable to replace his losses and thus could not fight on.[58] Inevitably, some of these prisoners were able to escape and to rejoin Victor Amadeus' forces.[59] He could also seek to turn to his own advantage the victories of his allies in Germany and the Low Countries, and to ensure that the cartels for prisoner exchange concluded in those theatres provided for his own recovery of

---

[55] VA to ST, 4 June 1693, Chieri, AST/LPDS, m. 68 13/271; ST to DLT, 9 June 1693, Turin, AST/LM/Olanda, m. 3. The duke hoped to obtain further *étapes* from the emperor.

[56] DLT to VA, 14 July 1693, Hague, AST/LM/Olanda, m. 3. De la Tour did not seek cash help from the Dutch, since they never gave more than a third of what William gave, in this case a trifling sum.

[57] ST to DLT, 19 Aug. 1695, Turin, AST/LM/Olanda, m. 4.

[58] Symcox, *Victor Amadeus*, 148. In 1705 Victor Amadeus allowed the governor of the besieged Verrua to capitulate if he could save its garrison, although this proved impossible, Saluces, *Histoire militaire*, V, 164.

[59] Of the more than 21,000 troops Victor Amadeus hoped to have in 1704, 1,000 were returned prisoners, *CGP*, I, 67. In reply to enemy complaints of prisoners breaching their parole in this way, the duke claimed that nothing could dispense subjects from the duties they owed their sovereign and that the French had violated their treaty obligations by seizing (1703) his troops, *CGP*, I, 66.

some of those men whom the French king refused to return – yet another example of the multifaceted 'dependence' of the Savoyard state in this era on its allies.[60] After 1706, with Victor Amadeus himself on the offensive, this problem was less serious.[61]

However, recovered prisoners of war were an uncertain source of military manpower and could never fully make good the losses incurred from one campaign to the next, or supply the foundation of a substantial increase in numbers.[62] Clearly, if Victor Amadeus was to raise substantial numbers of men from among his own subjects, he must try other means, including voluntary enlistment. Pay and conditions might attract some of Victor Amadeus' subjects into the ranks. They included 5 soldi a day, a rate of pay laid down by Charles Emanuel II in 1673, and a bread allowance of 24 ounces a day, with occasional bonuses and gratifications.[63] Officers, whose basic pay was increased by Victor Amadeus in December 1693,[64] also enjoyed extra allowances, while colonels of regiments were allowed to claim a certain number of 'dead places' (no doubt, in part, to prevent greater fraud). However, there were also remarkable differences both within and between the various ducal regiments.[65] The most generously treated were Victor Amadeus' Guards and White Cross regiments, whose officers and men enjoyed pay and conditions superior to his other national regiments. In 1692, whereas a colonel in the Guards received 7,400 lire a year, a colonel in the Savoy regiment received just 3,000 lire.[66] In 1703 Victor Amadeus again increased army officers' pay, at a time when the emoluments of other officials were being cut – no doubt as an incentive to service and loyalty – but the differentials within

---

[60] See VA to Duke of Marlborough, 13 Jan. 1706, Turin, *CGP*, V, 450; and VDM to Fagel, 10 June 1705 and 10 Feb. 1706, Turin, ARAH/EA/VDM/30, 65, 196.

[61] See cartel for exchange of prisoners between the allies and the Bourbons in north Italy, Mar. 1707, *CGP*, VIII, 356 ff.; and VDM to Fagel, 19 Sept. 1708, Turin, ARAH/EA/VDM/32, f. 179.

[62] The same was true of another source of recruits, the 'reform' of existing units and the distribution of their soldiers among the duke's other regiments. In 1710, Victor Amadeus' White Cross regiment, which had lost many men at the siege of Turin, was incorporated into his Piedmont regiment, *CGP*, VIII, 295, n. 1.

[63] See *CGP*, I, lxxiv–lxxv; Saluces, *Histoire militaire*, I, 252; Barberis, *Le armi*, 148, for terms (including 5 soldi a day pay) offered to those who would serve in the seven new regiments the duke was hoping to raise for 1704. For rewards for bravery and merit, see Prato, 'Il costo', *CGP*, X, 278.

[64] See the *mémoire* of contadore Filippone, AST/MM/UGS, m. 1/14 (no. 51).

[65] In 1691 Victor Amadeus ordered that bombardiers should receive 10 soldi a day, plus the bread allowance, Duboin, XXVII, 69.

[66] Victor Amadeus, hoping to obtain foreign hire troops for 1693, was prepared to pay what his White Cross regiment received, and (if absolutely necessary) what he paid his Guards, VA to DLT, 28 July 1692, Arches, AST/LM/Olanda, m. 3.

and between regiments persisted.⁶⁷ The benefits (bread, uniform, winter quarters – in effect a supplement to normal pay during the six winter months) enjoyed by the soldiers were not entirely free. During the Nine Years War, of each 5 soldi of pay received by the infantry, 1 (the so-called *droit de la Tésorerie*) was deducted centrally to pay for the uniform provided, and another by the company captain for those provisions for which he was responsible.⁶⁸ The soldier therefore only received 3 soldi a day. Senior officials were paid quarterly, but the troops received their pay every five to ten days, in the form of an advance from the captain on their monthly pay. (According to the duke, this prevented the men from wasting their money in the cabarets.)⁶⁹ Similar deductions were made from the pay of the cavalry.⁷⁰

Voluntary recruitment, not surprisingly, was most effective at times of dearth, including the years 1694–95 and 1708–09, when the army was at least a guarantee of bread. However, in less pressing times (and at a time of crisis, as in 1703–04, when many more recruits were required than was normal) it was much harder for captains to find enough recruits, not least because a soldier's pay was less than the average civilian wage.⁷¹ The duke was therefore obliged to resort to other means. In 1688–89 he raised men for the Aosta, Nizza and Marine regiments by offering pardons to those convicted of minor offences who would join up.⁷² This means was used again in 1703–04⁷³ and 1706.⁷⁴ Victor Amadeus might also resort to coercion of sorts. In both the Nine Years War and the War of the Spanish Succession, he banned his subjects from entering foreign service and

---

⁶⁷ Prato, 'Il costo', *CGP*, X, 266 ff.; Barberis, *Le armi*, 171–2; Saluces, *Histoire militaire*, I, 308.

⁶⁸ These deductions did not, however, always cover the outlay: see a *mémoire* on the cost of clothing 640 of Victor Amadeus' Guards regiment in 1690, AST/MM/UGS, m. 2/44.

⁶⁹ See *mémoire* re pay of recently levied Protestant battalions, 1691, ARAH/SG/8643/165; VDM to Fagel, 14 Nov. 1692, Turin, ARAH/SG/8643/287 and same to same, 12 June 1693, Turin, ARAH/SG/8644/45; and *CGP*, I, lxxiv–lxxiv. and 113 (pay arrangements for militia, Oct. 1703).

⁷⁰ See Duboin, XXVII, 1061 (for order, Jan. 1689, to deduct 3 lire a month from the pay of his Guardie del Corpo for remounts). In 1698 Victor Amadeus issued new orders, for deductions for clothes and remounts for his cavalry and dragoon regiments, Duboin, XXVIII, 1856 ff. (and *CGP*, I, lxxiv).

⁷¹ Prato, 'Il costo', *CGP*, X, 269.

⁷² Duboin, XXVI, 78 (1688) and VI, 577 (1689).

⁷³ In October 1703, the Turin diarist, Soleri, recorded the release of seventeen prisoners, who subsequently served in the marchese di Cavaglia's cavalry regiment (Piemonte Reale), *CGP*, I, 66. In Nov. 1703 peasants arrested for attacks on feudal property in Savoy were released before trial, to serve in the army, J. Nicolas, *La Savoie au 18e siècle: noblesse et bourgeoisie*, 2 vols. (Paris, 1978), I, 523.

⁷⁴ VDM to States, 1 and 4 Sept. 1706, Genoa, ARAH/EA/VDM/30, 336, 338.

ordered all those who were serving abroad to return home.[75] The duke might also exploit the local influence of his own subjects, particular the nobility (see Chapter 5). In addition, he could accept the offers of any of his subjects ready to serve in their own more or less independent 'free companies', reflecting the extent to which, again particularly in the crisis years of the War of the Spanish Succession between 1703 and 1706, Victor Amadeus could not (if he wished to survive the military challenge facing him) assert a monopoly of recruitment within his state, though it is by no means clear that he wished to do this anyway. More importantly, since these measures could not provide sufficient numbers of troops, Victor Amadeus was obliged to impose military service on his subjects in a rather new way. The imposition of new military obligations anticipated (or came to fruition in) the post-1713 establishment of provincial militia regiments (see below, p. 68) and represented a striking aspect of Savoyard state formation in these years.

As elsewhere in Europe, there was in Piedmont a general obligation on adult males to serve in time of emergency, in the general militia which had been reformed at various times since the middle of the sixteenth century,[76] and which was (briefly) called out by Victor Amadeus after his defeats in both 1690 and 1693. (The nobility had its own, distinct military obligation, the feudal levy, see Chapter 5.) However, even before the breach with Louis XIV in 1690, and reflecting the way other states provided models for reorganisation within the Savoyard state in these decades, there was extensive discussion in Turin of reform of the militia, along the lines of that in France in 1688.[77] Surveys and consultations were undertaken to ascertain the numbers of men each province could provide. Then, in March 1690, no doubt anticipating the need to mobilise men rapidly in the near future – but also wishing to reduce the impact of a massive mobilisation (which would disrupt agriculture and the economy of his states) and to avoid massive evasion – Victor Amedeus overhauled the militia. Henceforth just 6 per cent of those liable constituted the select militia, or *battaglione*, of Piedmont. The duke clarified who was liable

---

[75] Duboin, VI, 303 (1690) and 314 (1703); *CGP*, I, 66. In 1694, the inheritance of conte Carlo Amedeo Maurizio Tana, who continued to serve Louis XIV, was, briefly, confiscated: see G. Levi, *L'Eredità immateriale: carriera di un esorcista nel Piemonte del Seicento* (Turin, 1985), 155 ff.; English trans., *Inheriting Power: the story of an exorcist* (Chicago, 1988), 132 ff.

[76] See Barberis, *Le armi*, 5 ff. and P. Bianchi, 'Guerra e politica nello Stato Sabaudo (1684–1730). Le riforme militari: di Vittorio Amedeo II tra istituzioni, reclutamento e organizzazione territoriale, Ph.D thesis, University of Turin, 1997, 58 ff.

[77] See the copy of Louis XIV's order (1688) for the reform of the French militia, in AST/MM/Levate di Milizia, m. 1/10. (This *mazzo* contains projects for the levy and reform of the militia from 1689.)

(and exempt), how they were to be chosen, the privileges they were to enjoy and terms of service (including training, to ensure the militimen were effective). The system would be monitored by local magistrates and officials.[78]

The select militia was soon in action, being called out by Victor Amadeus after his first defeat, at Staffarda, in 1690, as part of his larger mobilisation of his subjects, to make good his losses and prevent Catinat conquering Piedmont.[79] More importantly, the militia was increasingly used both in place of, and as a source of recruits for the duke's regular, front-line troops. In the spring of 1691, Victor Amadeus used the militia as an interim source of garrisons, and to plug the gaps in his regular forces.[80] The following year, too, hard pressed financially, and finding it difficult to complete his infantry (to 10,000 men), the duke resorted to the militia. In February 1692 each village in Piedmont was required to supply a fixed number of men and to have replacements ready in case of loss (by death, desertion and so on). In April of that year the duke ordered the provisional incorporation of a third of the *battaglione* of Piedmont into his regular forces, promising that those involved would enjoy the same conditions.[81] In the summer of 1693, too, no doubt to maximise his forces for the siege of Pinerolo, Victor Amadeus ordered the provincial governors to call out the select militia.[82] In 1694, too, he demanded recruits from his own subjects, imposing quotas on individual communities and forbidding his captains from accepting recruits from areas outside those assigned them.[83] In the spring of 1696, Victor Amadeus again sought to complete his infantry by ordering the villages of Piedmont to levy men.[84] His use of, even dependence on, the militia was not particularly pleasing to Victor Amadeus. He could not but recognise that it imposed great burdens on his subjects, disrupting agricultural life; and that it meant the use of men who were largely unused to arms and military discipline and who were likely to desert. Use of the militia, particularly as a source of front line troops, was due, above all, to his

---

[78] Duboin, XXVI, 892 ff. See, also, the invaluable account in Saluces, *Histoire militaire*, I, 264 ff. For those exempted from service in Turin's distinct urban militia in 1690–1, see F. Rondolino, 'Vita Torinese durante l'assedio (1703–1707)', *CGP*, VII, 194.
[79] Saluces, *Histoire militaire*, V, 22 ff. Victor Amadeus was thus able to dispense with the general militia, but established a system of signals in each province, to summon it if and when necessary.
[80] Duboin, XXVI, 118, 910; Rondolino, 'Vita Torinese', *CGP*, VII, 187.
[81] Duboin, XXVI, 913 ff.; Saluces, *Histoire militaire*, I, 266–7; VDM to Fagel, 1 and 17 Mar. 1692, Turin, ARAH/SG/8643/212, 258.
[82] Duboin, XXVI, 917; AST/Levate di Milizie, m. 15; VDM to Fagel, 8 May 1693, Turin, ARAH/SG/8644/32.   [83] Duboin, XXVI, 821, 918 (1694).
[84] VDM to Fagel, 3 Feb. 1696, Turin, ARAH/SG/8644240.

desperate need for troops and his inability to secure them in any other way.

Victor Amadeus' exit from the Nine Years War in 1696 largely removed this pressure. However, in 1701, as war threatened in north Italy, the duke ordered a general levy of adult males;[85] and in the crisis following the loss of a large part of his regular forces at San Benedetto, again resorted to the militia to raise seven new regiments, totalling 4,200 men, from among his own subjects.[86] In the summer of 1705, Victor Amadeus again recruited his regular troops by forced levies from the communities of Piedmont;[87] and in 1706, he levied another seven militia battalions, which he used to supply garrisons.[88] In 1707, in what may have been a further formalisation of the system in 'liberated' Piedmont – and perhaps a return to a system which had been evolving in the Nine Years War, but which may have been undermined by the crisis and chaos of 1703–06) – each of Victor Amadeus' 'national' regiments was assigned a distinct province in Piedmont which must supply its recruits, thus preventing overlapping and competition.[89] By the later stages of the War of the Spanish Succession, it was the norm for the villages of Piedmont to supply recruits as requested for Victor Amadeus' regiments each winter for the forthcoming campaign in what seems an increasingly regularised manner.[90] This obligation was extended to Victor Amadeus' newly acquired territories in the later stages of the War of the Spanish Succession, representing an important aspect of their inte-

---

[85] Saluces, *Histoire militaire*, I, 266–7; Barberis, *Le armi*, 142 ff.
[86] *CGP*, I, 60 ff., 239 ff., 260; Barberis, *Le armi*, 146 ff.; Saluces, *Histoire militaire*, I, 267. Initially, it had been hoped to raise twelve provincial battalions (two from Turin and one each from the ten provinces of Piedmont), totalling 10,000, men in this way. Nevertheless, these new militia regiments contributed 25 per cent of the infantry Victor Amadeus hoped to have in 1704. For the Dutch envoy this was an admission that the duke had no other means of raising men, VDM to States, 24 Dec. 1704, Turin, ARAH/EA/VDM/29, 199.
[87] Duboin, XXVI, 153 ff.; Saluces, *Histoire militaire*, I, 263; VDM to Fagel, 15 July and 5 Aug. 1705, Turin, ARAH/EA/VDM/30, 27, 83, 92. Seven militia companies were sent to defend Asti, same to States, 16 Sept. 1705, ARAH/EA/VDM/30, 119. In 1705 the marchese di Pianezza wrote a *mémoire* on the militia for the duke, Rondolino, 'Vita Torinese', *CGP*, VII, 187.
[88] VDM to States, 17 Mar. and 14 Apr. 1706, Turin, ARAH/EA/VDM/30, 218, 235.
[89] VDM to States, 15 Jan. 1707, Turin ARAH/EA/VDM/31, f. 13. For the receipt by the sindics of Piobesi of circulars of 8 Dec. 1707 from the conte della Trinità and the director of the province ordering all communities to choose men for the Trinità regiment (and the specific demand of three men from Piobesi), and for how this system worked in general, see O. Scarzello, 'Corneliano, Piobesi, Monticello d'Alba e Sommariva Perno negli anni di guerra 1704–1708', *CGP*, VIII, 514.
[90] See VDM to States, 15 Feb. 1708, ARAH/EA/VDM/32, 30; and (for 1709) Duboin, XXVI, 161 and Saluces, *Histoire militaire*, I, 263.

gration into the Savoyard state, sometimes in the face of local hostility.[91]

Victor Amadeus' growing reliance on his own subjects was thus accompanied by some formalisation and regulation of their military obligation and service. However, although the duke and his officials had laid down criteria for selection, the local choice of men largely rested with the oligarchs who held local office (as syndics and so on) and dominated the communities. Inevitably, they protected their families and friends. They did so in various ways, including the purchase of substitutes, in contravention of ducal orders.[92] The burden of service, in turn, fell more heavily on poorer, less influential families. Occasionally, Victor Amadeus and his ministers were obliged to intervene to ensure the proper observance of the relevant regulations. In early 1700, Victor Amadeus sent marshal Schulemburg into Savoy following reports that the duke's order of December 1699 for recruitment of his Savoy regiment in the communities was not being properly obeyed and that many young men were fleeing the Duchy. Schulemburg dismissed 75 of the 252 men raised so far on the grounds that their recruitment breached the regulations in some way. (Many had taken money to serve, others were married and/or heads of families.) When the marshal reviewed more than 450 recruits a month or so later, these abuses seemed to have been eradicated.[93] The communities sought to find the men demanded by the duke in various ways. These included choosing by lots and the use of inducements of one sort or another.[94] However, abuse and evasion, which Victor Amadeus' own officials might sometimes abet,[95] would never be completely eradicated. In addition, the duke himself

---

[91] In 1709 the conte della Rocca, governor of Alessandria, sent 150 men to Roccavignale, in the recently acquired Monferrato, where the sindics refused to accept the obligation being imposed on Victor Amadeus' subjects to provide recruits, and had abused a recruiting segeant sent for that purpose, VDM to Fagel, 4 May 1709, Turin, ARAH/EA/VDM/33, f. 73.

[92] In 1690–1, however, many inhabitants of Turin were allowed to buy themselves out of service in the urban militia, Rondolino, 'Vita Torinese', *CGP*, VII, 194.

[93] See Schulemburg's account, 24 May 1700, Turin, AST/MM/Levate Truppe nel Paese, m. 2/14.

[94] Of the 450 or so men reviewed by Schulemburg, 108 had been chosen by lots. In Oct. 1707, the syndics of Fossano promised exemption to anybody otherwise eligible who could denounce two others who were eligible but had not presented themselves, C. Salsotto, 'Fossano e la battaglia di Torino (1706). Contributo alla storia della guerra di Spagna', *CGP*, VIII, 435.

[95] In 1702 the conte di Rivera, governor of the province of Alba, his secretary, and an official of the Ufficio del Soldo were accused of taking money to exempt many who should have been taken when the duke had recently ordered recruitment in the province for the 3rd battalion of his Guards, provoking local resentment: see AST/MC, m. 10/8.

urged recruiting men from among the ranks of the poor and unemployed.⁹⁶

The two major wars fought by the Savoyard state in the 1690s and early 1700s thus brought with them a major call to arms of the population of, above all, Piedmont and the rather novel and striking intrusion into local life of a central authority demanding a quota of the local population for military service. These obligations did not cease with the military crisis of 1703–06 but in fact became more entrenched and routine thereafter. More of the duke's subjects were thus called on to play a part in the crucial military events which saved and shaped the Savoyard state in these years. How did they respond? The simple answer, one which belies traditional Savoyard historical writing and supports the contentions of Barberis, is that they served reluctantly. As elsewhere in Europe, military service was far from popular. The duke himself acknowledged as much. At the end of 1690 he believed that if he was to have more infantry in 1691, he must hope for foreign troops since his own subjects were unwilling to serve.⁹⁷ This reluctance was also evident during the War of the Spanish Succession, the general militia levy ordered in 1701 prompting an exodus of young men abroad.⁹⁸ Similarly, the attempt to levy 8,000 men by assigning the villages of Piedmont quotas in the winter of 1704–05 was initially, at least, unsuccessful,⁹⁹ while Victor Amadeus' hopes, in the winter of 1705–06, of recruiting and expanding his forces by imposing similar quotas seemed unduly optimistic to many.¹⁰⁰ That this pessimism was not unfounded is suggested by the experience of Fossano, where in the spring of 1706 the levy of 100 men for the provincial battalion, ordered to be done within five days, took three months, due to the reluctance of those eligible to come forward and to the frequent desertion of those chosen.¹⁰¹ Things were little different after 1706: in early 1708, the Piedmontese countryside was said to be denuded of men, as many joined their regiments while others

---

⁹⁶ Ducal order for levies in communities of Monferrato, 6 Feb. 1709, AST/Levate Truppe nel Paese, m. 2/16.

⁹⁷ VDM to Fagel, 29 Nov. 1690, Turin, ARAH/SG/8643/77. Apparently, Victor Amadeus hoped to recruit his troops for 1693 from among those provided by the villages in 1692, most of whom had deserted – hardly a very promising sign, VDM to Fagel, 13 Apr. 1693, Turin, ARAH/SG/8643/23.

⁹⁸ Saluces, *Histoire militaire*, I, 265 ff.

⁹⁹ VDM to Fagel, Feb. 1705, Turin, ARAH/EA/VDM/30, 12.

¹⁰⁰ VDM to States, 6 Jan. 1706, Turin, ARAH/EA/VDM/30, 175. Many of these forced recruits arrived in Turin under armed escort, to prevent their escape, same to Fagel, 3 Feb. 1706, Turin, ARAH/EA/VDM/30, 193.

¹⁰¹ Salsotto, 'Fossano', *CGP*, VIII, 453. In 1707, too, three months were necessary for the levy of just fourteen men there, to replace deserters supplied earlier by the town, *ibid.*, 465 (1707).

fled to avoid having to fulfil their community's quota.[102] Some sought to mobilise influential connections.[103] Ultimately, in the face of this reluctance to serve, and emphasising the extent to which his army did underpin and enhance ducal authority within his state, Victor Amadeus might despatch regular troops to enforce his demands.[104]

Evasion of militia service was in part a variant on the older problem of desertion,[105] one familiar to all armies of the period and which, far more than mutiny, seems to have been the means of protesting against conditions – and forced service – in Victor Amadeus' armies at this time.[106] Within just a few days of the opening of the siege of Casale in wintery conditions in April 1695, for example, Victor Amadeus' Piedmont regiment lost considerable numbers due to desertion.[107] During the subsequent conflict, too, many men were lost through desertion, including about 2,000 in garrison in Turin during the sieges of 1705–06.[108] Deserters were not always lost for good and might subsequently be recovered from enemy forces, additionally weakening the latter.[109] Nevertheless, it represented a loss of armed manpower which Victor Amadeus could ill afford. One solution to this problem was to reduce the opportunities for desertion. In November 1703 the marchese di Pianezza was so concerned about desertion from the Asti regiment that he sought to have it sent away

---

[102] VDM to States, 15 Feb. 1708, Turin, ARAH/EA/VDM/32, f. 30.

[103] For the marchese di Susa's (unsuccessful) attempt to save a prospective tenant and his sons in the province of Fossano from the levy in 1705, see Salsotto, 'Fossano', *CGP*, VIII, 444.

[104] In 1705, Bra was threatened with twenty dragoons if it did not provide twenty-five recruits demanded of it, E. Milano, 'La partecipazione alla guerra di successione spagnuola della città di Bra illustrata negli Ordinati del Consiglio con appendice di tre documenti su Alba', *CGP*, VIII, 396.

[105] In 1705, van der Meer attributed a striking fall in the duke's forces (see Table 1.2, above) to his reliance on subjects who were too inclined to desert, VDM to Fagel, 12 Aug. 1705, Turin, ARAH/EA/VDM/30, 7. See, generally, Prato, 'Il costo', *CGP*, X, 310 ff.

[106] Swiss troops might refuse to serve if not paid, *CGP*, I, 254 (1703) but I have not discovered instances of mutiny among Piedmontese units in this period. There is nothing like those described by G. Parker, 'Mutiny and discontent in the Spanish army of Flanders 1572–1607', *Past and Present*, 58, 1973. Mutinies on this earlier scale were largely a thing of the past by the late seventeenth century, due in part to more effective organisation.

[107] VDM to States, 11 Apr. 1695, Turin, ARAH/SG/8644/186. For desertion in similar circumstances in the following conflict, see VDM to Fagel, 28 Jan. 1705, Turin, ARAH/EA/VDM/30, 94.

[108] The Cortanze regiment lost forty-five men through desertion on 6 Aug., M. Zucchi, 'Giornale inedito dell'assedio . . .', *CGP*, VIII, 279.

[109] In 1707 a Swiss colonel, formerly in the Bourbon service, returned twenty-five deserters from Victor Amadeus' forces, VDM to States, 6 Apr. 1707, ARAH/SG/VDM/31, f. 75.

from its home territory, where desertion was thought to be much easier.[110] Another solution was to enforce and tighten existing laws against desertion, and to periodically send detachments into the provinces to round up deserters,[111] while rewards were offered to those who denounced them.[112] Victor Amadeus also acted against those suspected of aiding deserters.[113]

However, the sheer repetition of such measures suggests that they were not wholly successful, and that the duke simply could not afford to maintain a tough stance. The need for experienced troops dictated the offer of frequent amnesties for those deserters who returned to their units.[114] Thus, although Victor Amadeus put pressure on the communities of Piedmont to provide men, he sometimes found it more politic to bargain with his subjects for their military service. From at least 1690, in a development which reflected the way that state formation and the creation of privilege could go hand in hand, he granted concessions and privileges to those who would serve in the militia.[115] These included promises (1703) not to incorporate the militias into his regular troops[116] – although the duke might be forced to break his word, by sheer need – and tax and other privileges.[117] Victor Amadeus also found it politic to appoint leading figures in the state (invariably nobles, see Chapter 5) to militia commands (exploiting their influence and standing to inspire confidence and encourage co-operation).[118] The duke also had to make

[110] *CGP*, I, 177 n. 1. What was worse, in this case many of the deserters joined the enemy forces.

[111] See Duboin, XXVI, passim, for legislation against desertion, the sheltering of deserters and the purchase of military equipment from them. For the rounding up of deserters in 1707, see E. Milano, 'La partecipazione', *CGP*, VIII, 409.

[112] Duboin, XXVI, 1688 (Sept. 1695).

[113] At the end of 1692, the duke, informed that deserters from his troops reached Genoese territory via Ceva, ordered that public officials (*intendenti, prevosti* and *giudici*) there be reminded of their duties (and punished if necessary), Guasco, 'Vittorio Amedeo II', 270–1.

[114] Duboin, XXVI, 1670 (Feb. 1691), 1684 and 1685 (Jan. and Mar. 1694); VA to conte di Monasterolo, 14 Oct. 1703, Turin, *CGP*, I, 97.

[115] See Victor Amadeus' decree ordering the levy of 4,000 militiamen, Oct. 1690 (above), with grant of privileges, Duboin, XXVI, 899. This was not of course very new: see Barberis, *Le armi*, passim.

[116] *CGP*, I, lxv.; Saluces, *Histoire militaire*, I, 266–7.

[117] According to the Turin diarist, Soleri, in 1703–4 Victor Amadeus gave the Turin militiamen doing garrison duty 10 soldi and a bread ration daily, *CGP*, I, 67. In 1704, with the emperor having failed to supply troops promised, and his own regular units falling into enemy hands, the duke offered the peasantry of the provinces of Ivrea and Biella exemption from all taxes for a year in return for military service, VDM to States. 29 Aug. 1704, Turin, ARAH/EA/VDM/29, 152.

[118] Saluces, *Histoire militaire*, I, 266–7.

other concessions, accommodating the rivalries of the provincial militias, which did not always see the need to sacrifice their claims against one another for some greater good, i.e. that of the state. In 1703–04, for example, the defence of the Duchy of Savoy was made more difficult by precedence disputes between the militias of the Duchy's different provinces, hindering their effective co-operation against the French.[119] As in the previous conflict, the demands of an agrarian economy also, and inevitably, constrained the duke's ability to make unfettered demands on his subjects: in the summer of 1705, the militia was allowed home to collect the harvest – without which neither his subjects nor the duke could really have waged war.[120] Clearly, Victor Amadeus might (particularly at times of crisis) have to bargain with his subjects, and to make concessions, to ensure they served in his armed forces.

FOREIGN TROOPS IN VICTOR AMADEUS' PAY, 1690–1713

Victor Amadeus' own subjects and territories, or those that remained to him, clearly supplied the bulk of his forces in these decades, and were being increasingly integrated into a network of obligation to their prince. However, as we have seen, the duke's subjects alone could not supply troops in the numbers necessary to successfully defend his states from the armies sent against him by Louis XIV from 1690, and to make the conquests which helped transform the extent and standing of Victor Amadeus and his state thereafter. The survival and success of the Savoyard state in these decades therefore depended to a remarkable degree on its ruler's ability to mobilise not only his own subjects but also substantial numbers of foreign troops, both those taken into the duke's own pay and those provided by his allies, although the distinction was not always a clear one. Ever since the restoration of the Savoyard state by Emanuel Filibert in the middle of the sixteenth century, the dukes of Savoy had depended on foreign mercenaries, particularly in wartime, and Victor Amadeus was no exception.[121] Whereas in 1689–90 there were very few foreign troops in his forces, by 1696 – according to one calculation – German, Swiss and French (i.e. the Huguenots sometimes known as 'religionaries') units contributed 9,000, more than one third of the ducal army. Similarly, whereas in September 1703 Victor Amadeus had just two foreign regiments, Schulemburg's Germans and Reding's Swiss, totalling 3,000 men, he expected to have 18,600 infantry in 1704,

[119] Marquis de Sales to VA, 12 Sept. 1703, Arbin, *CGP*, 1, 256.
[120] VDM to States, 15 July 1705, Turin, ARAH/EA/VDM/30, 83.
[121] See Barberis, *Le armi*, passim.

including 7,800 foreign troops.[122] Victor Amadeus was well aware of the limits of his own states, and the importance of foreign troops in enhancing his military strength, and sought to turn this to advantage. In 1708, he told the Dutch envoy in Turin that his states could only provide 12,000 men and that if he was to oppose any future attack by Louis XIV, the latter must be pushed beyond the Alps in the coming peace. Only in this way would he have the time in such a crisis to turn to his allies to secure the troops without which he could not fend off the French king.[123]

Foreign troops could be secured in various ways, including a steady stream of enemy deserters. Substantial numbers of these came in the Nine Years War from the garrisons at Pinerolo and Casale. Following the capitulation of Casale in 1695, Victor Amadeus allowed many of his captains to complete their units with those among the garrison (including Savoyards, Lorrainers, Burgundians and Netherlanders) willing to join them. However, these enemy deserters were not wholly reliable. Within two months, 120 of those obtained at Casale had deserted back to the enemy; and, following the desertion of the entire night watch outside Turin's citadel, in December 1695 the duke ordered that no company should have more than 5 deserters.[124] Nevertheless, in 1703–04, when Victor Amadeus again needed all the troops he could get, he used Irish and French deserters to complete the second battalions of his Guards and Monferrato regiments respectively.[125]

However, the most reliable and usual way to recruit substantial numbers of foreign troops was by capitulation, as with the Swiss, to whom Victor Amadeus inevitably looked for troops, not least because of their proximity to his states and his alliances with the Catholic cantons. In October 1693, following his defeat at Marsaglia, he concluded a capitulation with their captains for the completion of the Swiss units already in his service to 200 men per company,[126] and in the spring of 1694 agreed to

---

[122] The departure of foreign Protestant, Bavarian and Brandenburg troops in his pay in 1696 reduced Victor Amadeus' forces to 15,350, AST/MM/Riforme, m. 1/5. See van der Meer's *mémoire*, ARAH/SG/8644/298. In the winter of 1693–4 Victor Amadeus apparently hoped, in vain to increase his forces by an astonishing 6,000, using foreign troops: VDM to Fagel, 8 Jan. 1694, Turin, ARAH/SG/8644/100.

[123] VDM to Fagel, 30 May 1708, Turin, ARAH/EA/VDM/32, f. 99.

[124] VDM to Fagel, 18 Nov. and 23 Dec. 1695, Turin, ARAH/SG/8644/224, 229. Van der Meer doubted the efficacy of this order given the enormous dependence on enemy deserters.

[125] VA to Deshais, 10 Dec. 1703, Turin, *CGP*, I, 194. A group of Scots who were said to be planning Victor Amadeus' murder in 1708 apparently intended to enter his states in the guise of enemy deserters, A. Segre, 'Negoziati diplomatici della Corte di Prussia e colla Dieta di Ratisbona', *CGP*, VI, 316.

[126] Duboin, XXVII, 1378.

take another Swiss battalion.[127] In November 1695 Victor Amadeus agreed with the marchese d'Andorno for the completion of the latter's Swiss regiment.[128] In the summer of 1696, the duke was planning to raise new Swiss units, and in a series of capitulations from 1699, identical to those for the German (Schulemburg) regiments in his service, he secured Reding's Swiss, a total of three battalions.[129] Not surprisingly, the expansion of Victor Amadeus' forces from late 1703 included renewed efforts to secure substantial numbers of Swiss. In the winter of 1703–04, he was negotiating with both the Protestant and Catholic cantons for eight regiments totalling 4,800 men. These negotiations were not entirely successful, but by the spring of 1704, all the Catholic cantons except Soleure had agreed to levies for Victor Amadeus, and some of the troops were already *en route* to Piedmont,[130] while the duke also had two regiments levied in Protestant Bern.[131] The use of Swiss troops was not without its problems. For one thing, they were reluctant to serve offensively against the French, and were therefore largely used for garrisons.[132] In addition, their capitulations could be problematic. In 1706, Victor Amadeus's attempt to incorporate into a new regiment (commanded by the Swiss Colonel Ghidt) the depleted Alt regiment fell foul of the capitulation concluded with the canton of Freiburg. Nevertheless, Swiss levies continued to be a mainstay of Victor Amadeus' forces for the rest of the war: Ghidt's regiment was increased, by capitulation with its colonel in 1709, to 1,800 men, and again in 1713, at a time when the duke was reducing his 'national' regulars, to 2,200.[133]

Victor Amadeus' desire for a steady, reliable supply of Swiss troops resulted, in the early years of the War of the Spanish Succession, in an abortive attempt to permanently settle on privileged terms a Swiss 'military colony' in part of his state. In 1701, Reding, whose troops were suffering in the malarial Vercelli, suggested that they be allocated healthier quarters elsewhere in the duke's dominions, and requested that the territory assigned him and his men should be given him personally as a marquisate, with accompanying tax privileges. Reding identified a substantial property, in Biella province, whose existing population Victor Amadeus would have to resettle/compensate, and on which thriving

---

[127] Galway to Trenchard, 19 Mar. 1694, Turin, SP 92/26, f. 87.
[128] Duboin, XXVI, 1140.   [129] *CGP*, I, xl.
[130] VDM to Fagel, 22 Jan., 14 Mar. and 11 Apr. 1704, Turin, ARAH/EA/VDM/29, 11, 48, 63.
[131] Saluces, *Histoire militaire* I, 381; Brancaccio, *Esercito Ordinamenti*, I, 210–11.
[132] DLT to VA, 9 Dec. 1695, London, AST/LM/GB, m. 8.
[133] Saluces, *Histoire militaire*, I, 370. See *CGP*, I, xl, for Mellarède's agreement with the canton of Freiburg for Alt's regiment. For the obstacles to 'reform' posed by the capitulations, see VDM to States, 5 May 1706, Turin, ARAH/EA/VDM/30, 249.

new, Catholic Swiss communities would be erected. Although not all of Victor Amadeus' officials approved the project, he granted Reding's request. But the project was not a success. Almost from the start Reding complained about the quality of the land and the hostility of the local population: on one occasion about 200 women, led by a priest, invaded the colony. This pilot 'military colony' scheme was finally knocked on the head by Reding's surrender to the French of the fortress of Bard (1704) and subsequent defection, an episode reflecting a larger problem of Swiss unreliability, revealed on various occasions between 1703 and 1706.[134] Nevertheless, the episode reflects the importance of the Swiss as a source of troops to Victor Amadeus and his openness to new ideas about how to ensure a constant supply of them and at the same time to develop his own states.[135]

Germany was another important source of troops for Victor Amadeus. The individual military enterpriser was still seen as an important supplier, contracting to provide and keep up to strength a given number of men. Indeed, Victor Amadeus' need for troops in both the Nine Years War and the War of the Spanish Succession (especially between 1703 and 1706) and the difficulty of levying the required numbers in his own states, made him greatly dependent on these foreign enterprisers in these decades. In the winter of 1693–94, for example, a German officer promised to raise a regiment for Victor Amadeus, helping the duke to make good his heavy losses in the 1693 campaign. By February 1694, it was clear that the officer was unlikely to fulfil his commitment, having raised only 150 men.[136] However, for want of anything better Victor Amadeus continued to look to this means, agreeing in October 1695 with one Haxmann for another German regiment.[137] Following the end of the Nine Years War, the duke secured more German troops in this way. In 1697, conte Tarino concluded an agreement with Count Schulemburg, for a battalion of 400 Saxons.[138] In 1698 this force was raised to regimental strength by adding to it 300 Germans already in the duke's service.[139] In 1706, Baron

---

[134] In 1704, the flight of recently levied Swiss facilitated the French passage of the Small St Bernard into the Val d'Aosta, VDM to Fagel, 8 Oct. 1704, Turin, ARAH/EA/VDM/29, 170.

[135] For this episode, see Prato, 'Il costo', *CGP*, X, 279 ff. and Barberis, *Le armi*, 152 ff.

[136] VDM to Fagel, 12 Feb. 1694, Turin, ARAH/SG/8644/105. See, generally, F. Redlich, *The German Military Enterpriser and his Workforce, 13th to 17th Centuries, Vierteljahrschrift für Sozial- und Wirtschaftsgeschichte* (Wiesbaden, 1964).

[137] Duboin, XXVI, 1138.

[138] *CGP*, I, lxxxvi ff. details some of the terms (including pay) of this and some of the other capitulations mentioned below.

[139] *CGP*, I, xxvii. In 1704 the Schulemburg regiment was expected to comprise 1200 men in two battalions, *CGP*, I, 67.

Leutrum, a colonel in the service of the Prince of Ottingen, came to Piedmont with 500 men who were also incorporated into the Schulemburg regiment;[140] and in 1707 another German unit for which Victor Amadeus had been negotiating was used to form the 3rd battalion of the Schulemburg regiment.[141] In the meantime, in October 1703 a capitulation had been concluded which gave the duke another, short-lived, German (Fridt) corps on much the same terms as the Schulemburg regiment, i.e. 600 men in 6 companies of 100 men each.[142]

The difficulties encountered in the efforts to deal with individual German soldiers in the Nine Years War reflected an important shift. Increasingly, the old style military enterpriser was giving way to the German territorial princes in the so-called *Soldatenhandel*, or trade in soldiers.[143] However, securing troops from the princes could also be problematic, especially as Victor Amadeus was determined to get any troops on as good terms (and above all as cheaply) as possible.[144] Typical of just how problematic this could be were the negotiations for Saxe-Gotha troops in 1692–93. In July 1692, Victor Amadeus informed de la Tour of his desire for 2,000–3,000 foreign infantry for 1693, declaring that he could not repeat the dangerous and damaging expedient used in 1692, of obliging his own communities to provide men (see above, p. 37).[145] Thereafter de la Tour began troop negotiations with the ministers of various lesser German princes at The Hague. Unfortunately, the bishop of Münster claimed to need all his troops and refused to let them leave the empire, a lame excuse given Victor Amadeus' status as a prince of the empire and the reassertion of imperial authority in north Italy during the Nine Years War. De la Tour expected similar replies from the princes of the House of Lüneburg and the elector of Saxony. As for the bishop of Hildesheim, he would willingly have given Victor Amadeus one of his own infantry regiments, but it was in the service of the duke of Wolfenbüttel. The bishop intended to raise a new regiment in the winter of 1692–93, but this was expensive (at 25 écus per man, armed and clothed) and significant numbers would probably desert *en route* to Piedmont. De la Tour advised his master to apply to the duke of Württemberg for troops.[146]

Rather unexpectedly, de la Tour then received an offer from the

---

[140] Saluces, *Histoire militaire*, I, 362–3.
[141] VDM to States, 6 Apr. 1707, Turin, ARAH/EA/VDM/31, f. 75.
[142] *CGP*, I, xl.
[143] See P. H. Wilson, *War, State and Society in Württemberg 1677–1793* (Cambridge, 1995), passim.
[144] See VA to DLT, and ST to same, both 3 Oct. 1690, Moncalieri, AST/LM/Olanda, m. 1.   [145] VA to DLT, 28 July 1692, Arches, AST/LM/Olanda, m. 2.
[146] DLT to ST, 30 Sept. 1692, Hague, AST/LM/Olanda, m. 3.

elector of Saxony of a regiment of 1,000 infantry and was soon negotiating with the elector, and with the duke of Saxe-Gotha for a regiment the latter had in William III's service in Flanders. By October 1692, de la Tour had hopes of two infantry regiments (one each from Saxony and Saxe-Gotha), each of two battalions, for his master for 1693, totalling between 2,000 and 3,000 men. Unfortunately, these negotiations proved fruitless. The elector of Saxony refused the 1,500 men de la Tour had been hoping for, claiming that the emperor had asked him to send his troops to the Rhine in 1693. As for the negotiations with the duke of Saxe-Gotha, the latter's negotiators insisted that the infantry regiment de la Tour sought must be part of a larger package to include two cavalry regiments (which Victor Amadeus did not need). They also insisted that Victor Amadeus find winter quarters for these troops in the empire for three months, and that he pay 35 écus per man, armed and clothed (substantially more than what had been demanded earlier by the bishop of Hildesheim), besides the costs of the march and pay of 5 écus per month, all of which de la Tour thought more expensive than levying two new regiments. De la Tour had also learnt that the regiment was very weak, little more than 700 men, and that it was available only because William III, thinking it of little use, no longer wanted it.

However, Victor Amadeus was now offered two other Saxe-Gotha regiments, totalling more than 2,000 men, which had served on the Upper Rhine in 1692. Apparently, better regiments could not be found in Germany. Nor, equally importantly, were there any better placed for getting promptly from the empire to Piedmont. De la Tour was increasingly aware that it was a seller's market; Tarino had informed him from Vienna that the duke of Württemberg had snapped up the Saxe-Gotha regiment offered to de la Tour earlier, to recruit his own troops in Flanders. As the campaigning season drew nearer, he urged that, if his master wanted the 2,000 plus Saxe-Gotha troops offered he must act quickly, not least because the Imperial Circles of Swabia and Franconia, yet more buyers in the market for German troops, would probably seek to have them serve again on the Upper Rhine.[147] An agreement was concluded in Turin, early in 1693, for the two Saxe-Gotha regiments to serve in Piedmont that year. However, in the spring of 1693 Victor Amadeus learnt that the duke of Saxe-Gotha had given the regiment to the Franconian Circle in breach of their agreement. This was the more serious in that, in expectation of securing more than 2,000 Saxe-Gotha troops, Victor Amadeus had neglected to recruit his own forces in

---

[147] This story can be pieced together from DLT to VA, 2 and 31 Oct. 1692, Hague, and same to ST, 10 Oct. 1692 and 11 Nov. 1692, Hague, AST/LM/Olanda, m. 3.

Piedmont over the winter. He appealed to the emperor (hoping that Leopold would oblige the duke of Saxe-Gotha to honour their agreement) and continued to delay full recruiting as an alternative, partly because of the need to save the funds to pay the Saxe-Gotha troops if he eventually secured them. But Victor Amadeus could put little real pressure upon the duke who had so sabotaged his campaign preparations.[148]

Victor Amadeus' efforts to secure German hire troops were not entirely unsuccessful, however. In the winter of 1693–94, he accepted an offer made to Priè in Vienna of a regiment of 1,500 men, belonging to the prince of Saxe-Eisenach, at 36 Rixdollars per man[149]. During the Nine Years War, Victor Amadeus also secured troops from his cousin, the elector Max Emanuel of Bavaria and the elector of Brandenburg. In 1691, Max Emanuel of Bavaria personally led 6,000 of his troops to Piedmont to help prevent his cousin's complete military collapse. At the end of 1691, Max Emanuel departed with most of his troops, but left in Piedmont two infantry regiments (Guards, Steinau), totalling 2,000 men, who were maintained by the emperor out of the contributions demanded of the imperial vassals in north Italy. At the end of 1692 Max Emanuel agreed, under pressure from Victor Amadeus (and – more importantly – from William III, who guaranteed the provisioning of the elector's forces) to leave these regiments in Piedmont for another campaign; and in November 1693 concluded a two-year capitulation, renewed in 1695, with Victor Amadeus, who took into his own pay the Steinau regiment (but not the Guards, which left Piedmont), which totalled 1,400 men in July 1696. In the winter of 1695–96, since Max Emanuel had more infantry than he could afford, Victor Amadeus negotiated for two more Bavarian regiments. However, these negotiations were rendered abortive by the duke's inability to rid himself of two Protestant regiments which the Bavarian regiments were to replace; and he took no more Bavarian troops before abandoning the Grand Alliance in 1696.[150]

Victor Amadeus' greatest success in securing German hire troops in the Nine Years War was in obtaining those of the elector of Brandenburg. As early as 1690–91, the elector Frederick sent to Piedmont at his own cost a regiment of Huguenot refugees, led by Colonel Corneaud. However, at

---

[148] VDM to Fagel, 13 Mar. and 13 Apr. 1693, Turin, ARAH/SAG/8644/17, 23.
[149] VDM to Fagel, 12 Feb. 1694, Turin, ARAH/SG/8644/105.
[150] DLT to ST, 24 Oct. 1692, Hague, and same to VA, 31 Oct. 1692, Hague, AST/LM/Olanda, m. 3; VA to Tarino, 14 Sept. 1693, Pinerolo, AST/LM/Olanda, m. 3; ST to DLT, 10 Sept. and 3 Dec. 1695, Turin, AST/LM/Olanda, m. 4; VDM to Fagel, 23 Nov. 1693, Turin, ARAH/SG/8644/89; C. Storrs, 'Diplomatic relations between William III and Victor Amadeus II of Savoy 1690–1696' (Ph.D. thesis, University of London, 1990), 311. See L. Winkler, *Der Anteil der Bayerischen Armee an den Feldzügen in Piemont 1691 bis 1696*, 2 vols., Munich, 1886–7.

the end of 1692 the elector, from whom the duke had in fact hoped for more troops, declared his intention to recall Corneaud's regiment, which he could no longer afford to maintain.[151] In fact, Frederick was ready to leave his regiment in Piedmont if Victor Amadeus would assume the costs. Unfortunately, the duke found it extremely difficult to decide one way or the other. His irresolution, mainly the product of his financial difficulties (see Chapter 2), greatly embarrassed his envoy at The Hague, who was constantly pressed for a decision by the elector's ministers. In September 1693, after eight months of procrastination on the part of his master, de la Tour, rather unusually and bluntly, urged Victor Amadeus not to alienate a prince with great influence in the empire and told Saint-Thomas that irresolution and delay, in this as in other matters, damaged his master's standing with his allies.[152] De la Tour was greatly relieved to learn, later that month, that his master was sending a Colonel Rossignol to the elector's court to resolve the issue of Corneaud's regiment and to request more troops.[153]

The elector, irritated perhaps at Victor Amadeus' hesitation and delay, claimed that he now had no troops to spare, because of his extensive obligations to the emperor, the king of Spain, the States-General and William III.[154] However, a capitulation for the Corneaud and another two Brandenburg regiments was concluded by Rossignol in November 1693, with the elector agreeing in February 1694 to supply a fourth regiment.[155] But this was not the end of the matter, since the capitulation negotiated by Rossignol (not an experienced diplomat), and the ratification sent by Victor Amadeus' secretary of war, conte Benzo di Cavour, in the absence of his master, were regarded by the latter as yielding too much in the traditional battle for dignity between the dukes of Savoy and the electors of the empire (see Chapter 3). De la Tour was therefore ordered to Berlin, where he renegotiated the capitulation. Subsequently, too, the terms of service in Piedmont were regarded as unsatisfactory by the elector and his ministers. The bread ration of 24 ounces per man each day, which was that given to Victor Amadeus' own troops, was regarded as inadequate, especially as the Brandenburg troops in Dutch service received the cash equivalent of 32 ounces. The discrepancy was the more serious since the cost of living in Piedmont was far from cheap (as

---

[151] DLT to VA, 16 Dec. 1692, London, AST/LM/Olanda, m. 3.
[152] DLT to VA, 8 Sept. 1692 and same to ST, 8, 15 and 22 Sept. 1692, Hague, AST/LM/Olanda, m. 3. Some (according to de la Tour) suspected Victor Amadeus of dealing with the French.
[153] DLT to ST, 22 Sept. 1693, Hague, AST/LM/Olanda, m. 3.
[154] DLT to ST, 2 Oct. 1693, Hague, AST/LM/Olanda, m. 3.
[155] Duboin, XXVI, 1124 ff.

Rossignol had claimed), making the purchase of additional bread by the elector's officials rather costly. Consequently, following negotiations between the Brandenburg officers and conte Benzo, each Brandenburg captain was promised 300 Rixdollars (about 75 lire) for recruits and 32 ounces of bread a day per man (with compensation for what the captains had spent so far on this). This was approved by the elector and formed the basis on which his troops, totalling 3,000 men, served in Piedmont until the summer of 1696.[156]

These were by no means the only troops hired from German princes by Victor Amadeus in this period.[157] But the use of foreign hire troops was, as the preceding paragraphs make clear, no simple matter and fuelled a debate in Turin (as elsewhere) about the merits of different types of troops and means of recruitment. Various factors influenced this debate. These included questions of cost and the availability of funds, timing and the availability and reliability of troops. Decisions could be difficult, one option often delaying a decision on another, resulting in frustration and unsatisfactory, hasty and *ad hoc* measures in the short term. Among the advantages of troops raised in this way were that, although expensive (the main drawback), they freed Victor Amadeus of the burden of recruitment, since the contracting prince or other supplier undertook to provide in Piedmont by a fixed time an agreed number of men, armed and clothed, and to maintain them at that strength for a specific period. Troops raised in this way minimised the disruptive impact on Victor Amadeus' subjects of his levying men in his own states. Such arrangements made demobilisation, too, less of a problem, effectively shifting it outside his own states, although difficulties could still arise. In the summer of 1696, for example, Victor Amadeus' efforts to satisfy the terms of the capitulations of 1693/94 (and to remove promptly from his territories increasingly unwelcome allied troops) briefly created difficulties with the commanders of the Brandenburg troops.[158]

Besides troops sold by their princes, Victor Amadeus could also use

---

[156] See VDM to Fagel, 7 Dec. 1694, Turin, ARAH/SG/8644/156 and Duboin, XXVI, 1137 ff.

[157] In 1711, a capitulation was concluded with the duke of Württemberg for two grenadier regiments to serve in Piedmont under Marshal Rhebinder, who had come to Piedmont in 1706 at the head of the troops made available to the duke of Savoy by the elector palatine and thereafter transferred into Victor Amadeus' service: Saluces, *Histoire militaire*, I, 363; D. Carutti, 'Il Maresciallo Rhebinder. Nota biografica', *CGP*, VIII, 153 ff.

[158] F. Guasco, 'Vittorio Amedeo nelle campagne dal 1691 al 1696', 309 ff. Capitulations often underpinned privileged religious and judicial regimes which could be problematic for Victor Amadeus: Molesworth to Stanyan, 28 June 1721, Turin, SP 92/30 and Fontana to Lanfranchi, 5 Dec. 1728, Turin, AST/LP/F, m. 53

exiles and rebels. These included Irish soldiers of fortune dispersed across Europe following William III's conquest of Ireland in the early 1690s. Many entered the duke's service in the Nine Years War as deserters from that of Louis XIV[159] and in 1696 formed a distinct battalion in Victor Amadeus' Chablais regiment.[160] In the crisis of 1703–04, the duke hoped to secure valuable additional military manpower by encouraging further desertion among the Irish in Louis XIV's pay.[161] He also sought to secure whole units of Irish more directly, at source. He hoped to relieve the pressure on his own states at the end of 1704 by securing from Queen Anne's government permission to levy in Ireland itself up to 4,000 men.[162] The Irish, being largely Catholic, caused fewer problems for Victor Amadeus than did the many Protestant troops serving in Piedmont in these decades, but their loyalty could not be taken for granted. In 1704, the duke had arrested the chaplain of one of the Irish battalions in his service, an Irish Capuchin, who was telling the soldiers that in the present war only the French king was the true champion of the Roman Catholic religion.[163] However, the Irish remained a valuable potential source of military manpower and in the winter of 1707–08, Briançon successfuly negotiated in London with the earl of Kilmour for a regiment of 1,400 men to serve in Piedmont.[164]

As a source of military manpower, however, the Irish were overshadowed in the Savoyard state between 1690 and 1713 by the many French Huguenots in exile following Louis XIV's Revocation of the Edict of Nantes in 1685. The first of these Huguenot units to enter Victor Amadeus' service, the de Loches, Julien and Malet infantry battalions and the Balthasar and Rocca cavalry units, more than 2,000 men in all, had been raised in Switzerland in the spring and summer of 1690 by the envoys of the Maritime Powers to effect an invasion of southern France from Victor Amadeus' states, with or without his approval. Following the duke's accession to the Grand Alliance, these were incorporated into his own forces.[165] In 1691, efforts were made to raise another three

---

[159] For the arrival at Cuneo of fifty Irish deserters from the French forces in the Barcelonette valley, see VDM to Fagel, 3 Feb. 1696, Turin, ARAH/SG/8644/240.

[160] VDM to States, 11 May 1696, Turin, ARAH/SG/8644/257.

[161] See conte Benzo di Santena, governor of Mondovì, to Victor Amadeus, 3 Feb. 1704, *CGP*, II, 8.

[162] See correspondence between Victor Amadeus and the comte de Briançon, Sept. to Dec. 1704, *CGP*, V, passim. The duke, who seems to have underestimated how long such a levy might take, had to abandon it and rely on his own subjects: VDM to Fagel, 24 and 31 Dec. 1704, Turin, ARAH/EA/VDM/29, 198, 200.

[163] VDM to Fagel, 28 Mar. 1704, Turin, ARAH/EA/VDM/29, 55.

[164] VDM to Fagel, 4 Apr. 1708, Turin, ARAH/EA/VDM/32, f. 57; Segre, 'Negoziati ... Prussia', *CGP*, VI, 316.

[165] See C. Storrs, 'Thomas Coxe and the Lindau Project', in A. de Lange, ed., *Dall'Europa alle Valli Valdesi*, 199 ff.

Huguenot battalions, those of Colonels Montbrun, Montauban and Miremont, besides the levying of two other corps under the Swiss Oberkan, and pastor Henri Arnaud, leader of the Glorieuse Rentrée of 1689.[166] These efforts were only partially successful and for the rest of the Nine Years War the various units totalled little more than 3,000–3,500 men (significantly less than the intended 5,500).[167] Victor Amadeus also secured forces of this sort in the War of the Spanish Succession. In 1703–04, when he necessarily took whatever he could get, he agreed the levy of the Desportes and Cavalier regiments, both largely made up of Huguenot refugees, the former being increased (from 700) to 1,200 men in November 1709;[168] and levied a number of Huguenot 'free companies'.[169]

However, the use of these Protestant units was also very contentious, particularly in the 1690s, much more so than was the use of other foreign troops Victor Amadeus took into his service. De la Tour urged his master from the Protestant capitals, London and The Hague, to provide for and make more effective use of the Protestant 'religionaries'. He argued that, since his own negotiations for other (above all, German) troops were not very successful, Victor Amadeus should therefore use the Huguenot units (which were, anyway, cheaper). By doing so, the duke would also convince the Protestant Maritime Powers of his commitment to the allied cause.[170] De la Tour had to argue this way because his master was generally averse to the Protestant troops. For one thing, he distrusted them as former subjects of the French king, believing that their ultimate loyalty would always be to Louis XIV, thus constituting a 'fifth column' in his own states.[171] In addition, their Protestantism (like that of the elector of Brandenburg's troops) set the religionaries apart from the duke's other forces. It also helped make them a symbol of the more negative consequences of his war against Louis XIV and a focus of opposition to it in the 1690s (see Chapters 4 and 5).

---

[166] VA to DLT, 8 Apr. 1691, Turin, AST/LM/Olanda, m. 1.
[167] For 1696, see van der Meer's *mémoire*, ARAH/SG/8644/300. As always, numbers must be used with caution.
[168] CGP, I, xxxix–xl and 66; Saluces, *Histoire militaire*, I, 368–9.
[169] VDM to Fagel, 29 Apr. and 2 May 1704, Turin, ARAH/EA/VDM/29, 76, 78. The duke later incorporated into his regular forces two free companies (of Huguenots) which had suffered greatly in the defence of Nice, same to States, 24 Feb. 1706, Turin, ARAH/EA/VDM/30, 206.
[170] See DLT to ST, 2 Oct. 1693, Hague, AST/LM/Olanda, m. 3.
[171] See VA to marquis de Sales, 16 Oct. 1703, *CGP*, I, 244. See Storrs, 'Diplomatic relations', passim, for the articulation of similar concerns during the Nine Years War. Colonel Julien did desert to Louis XIV, in 1691, although this was due largely to jealousies among the Huguenot leaders.

Above all, however, the 'religionaries' resisted Victor Amadeus' efforts to establish his authority over, as he saw it, his army. This was in part the consequence of the inevitable distrust by Protestants of a Catholic prince. But this was not all. Initially, the Maritime Powers had paid the religionaries, but they subsequently handed over this responsibility to the duke. One of his first measures was to reduce their pay, which was higher than that enjoyed by his own troops, thus releasing funds to pay for more troops. Inevitably, this provoked resentment among the Protestant troops. In addition, those troops had been raised and were still largely financed, although indirectly, by the Maritime Powers; and they continued to be known as the troops of the king of Great Britain (who appointed their commander, the duke of Shomberg). Like any other military unit, including Victor Amadeus's own regular forces, they were determined to defend their independent identity and privileges. This caused frequent disputes between the duke's officers and the Protestant commanders, who questioned the orders of the former and insisted on their special status.[172] In 1693, after one dispute, Victor Amadeus ordered the arrest of a major in Miremont's regiment for abusing the intendant of the province of Mondovì.[173] These difficulties continued under Shomberg's successor, the earl of Galway, between 1694 and 1696,[174] but did not recur during the War of the Spanish Succession, due mainly to the fact that Victor Amadeus simply did not have as many troops of this type and that his authority over those that he had was more clearly defined.

VICTOR AMADEUS' MILITARY DEPENDENCE ON HIS ALLIES, 1690–1713

So far we have considered the role of Victor Amadeus' own subjects and of the foreign troops of one sort or another which he took into his pay. However, his success against Louis XIV in both the 1690s and 1700s also depended considerably, perhaps even primarily, on troops made available by his allies, and which remained in the pay and under the direction of the

---

[172] VA to DLT, 5 Dec. 1691, Turin, AST/LM/Olanda, m. 3. For Victor Amadeus' resentment at the refusal of the Huguenot forces to obey him as sovereign, see VDM to Fagel, 5, 22 and 26 Dec. 1692, Turin, ARAH/SG/8644/297, 307, 308.

[173] VDM to Fagel, 13 Apr. 1693, Turin, ARAH/SG/8644/23.

[174] In 1695 there was a dispute in the camp at Demont between the duke's commander, the marchese di Bagnasco, and colonel Montauban, Bagnasco having ordered the arrest of one of the latter's captains in breach of the Protestant regiments' privileged jurisdiction, VDM to States, 29 July 1695, and same to Fagel, 18 Nov. 1695, Turin, ARAH/SG/8644/198, 224.

allies. Above all, this meant the forces of the emperor and (in the Nine Years War) the king of Spain. Just as Victor Amadeus depended on substantial military support from the French king to help him suppress the Vaudois in 1686, so in 1690 the promise of Austrian and Spanish Habsburg military support against the much larger forces advancing on Turin under Marshal Catinat was a crucial factor in the duke of Savoy's decision to break with Louis XIV and in his survival following his first defeat at Staffarda. Between then and 1696, when the French king's forces in Piemont again greatly exceeded Victor Amadeus' independent military capacity,[175] the emperor and the king of Spain made available forces without which he simply could not have continued to resist Louis as he did. The Spaniards sent to Piedmont 12,000 men a year (as laid down in their treaty of June 1690 with Victor Amadeus) from the so-called army of Lombardy,[176] while the emperor also sent substantial forces.[177] The extent to which Victor Amadeus depended on foreign troops was forcibly demonstrated in 1691 when he faced the almost complete loss of his territories until the arrival of 12,000 imperial and 6,000 Bavarian troops who halted the French conquest and ensured that the duke retained Piedmont and Aosta.[178] This military dependence persisted for the rest of the war, as indicated in Table 1.3. As the war progressed the duke contributed a growing share of an allied field army in Piedmont which fluctuated around 40,000 men. Nevertheless, his projects in the winter of 1695–96 for a siege of Pinerolo in 1696 revealed that he could still barely contribute half of the allied army in Piedmont and that if he was to successfully besiege that fortress it could only be with outside help.[179] For some allied ministers, Victor Amadeus' military dependence was a guarantee of his loyalty to his allies. The events of 1696

[175] In the summer of 1696, the forces of Louis' commander in Italy, Catinat, were put at 90 battalions of infantry and 45 squadrons of cavalry, about 55,000 men, out of which he must provide garrisons for Pinerolo, Susa and Fenestrelles (and a force to defend the Pragelato) – 10,000 men in all. This left 45,000 with which to invade Piedmont, VDM to States, 11 May 1696, Turin, ARAH/SG/8644/257.

[176] See C. Storrs, 'The Army of Lombardy and the resilience of Spanish power in Italy in the reign of Carlos II (1665–1700), Part One', *War in History*, 4/4, 1997, 382.

[177] See D. McKay, *Prince Eugene of Savoy* (London, 1977), 32 ff. The imperial military effort in Italy in the 1690s still awaits its historian. Limited help was also made available by the emperor in the form of the military service of neighbouring imperial vassals: Saluces, *Histoire militaire*, V, 13.

[178] Storrs, 'Diplomatic relations', 100 ff. There were already imperial troops in Piedmont from 1690.

[179] See VA to DLT, 29 Nov. 1695, Turin, and accompanying documents, AST/LM/Olanda, m. 4.

Table 1.3. *Allied forces in Piedmont 1691–1696*

	Victor Amadeus	Spain	Emperor	Total
1691	10,000	12,000	23,000	45,000
1692	12,000	14,000	15,000	41,000
1693	12,000	14,000	15,000	41,000
1694	17–18,000	12,000	10,500	40,000
1695	17,500	11,000	12,500	41,000
1696	18–20,000	15,000	10,000	43–45,000

Source: Storrs, 'Diplomatic relations', 114, 153, 189, 240, 251, 320.

exposed the falsity of this argument and demonstrated that, particularly as a result of the expansion of his forces after 1690, the duke was able to hold the balance between the armies of Louis XIV on the one hand and those of the Austrian and Spanish Habsburgs on the other. But we should not allow this, or his switch of sides,[180] to obscure the fact that Victor Amadeus' independent military strength was overshadowed by that of his far more powerful neighbours.[181]

In the War of the Spanish Succession, Victor Amadeus remained dependent on his allies, above all the emperor. According to their treaty of 1703, the emperor was to contribute 20,000 men and the duke 14,000 to an anti-Bourbon army in north Italy. It was the emperor's initial inability to fulfil his commitments which brought Victor Amadeus near to collapse in the face of superior enemy numbers in 1704.[182] By the same token, in 1705 it was the need to deal with the advance of Prince Eugene's imperial army (and the resistance of the besieged Chivasso and Verrua) which prevented the French taking Turin that year and thus completing the ruin of the Savoyard state.[183] The imperial troops also played a key role in that *annus mirabilis* of the Savoyard state, 1706. Victor Amadeus had about 16,000 troops (10,000 of them in garrison in Turin) to face a besieging army of 40,000 and a further 40,000 French and Spanish troops in north Italy. He simply could not have contemplated resistance, let alone achieved victory outside Turin in September 1706,

---

[180] By one estimate, the duke's *volte-face* increased Louis XIV's forces in Italy to 55,000 and reduced those of the allies to 22,000, DLT to ST, 11 Sept. 1696, Hague, AST/LM/Olanda, m. 5.

[181] Most of these figures (it must be repeated), should be regarded as approximate, see Storrs, 'Diplomatic relations', 114, 153, 189, 240, 251, 320. Victor Amadeus' troops include the Protestant 'religionaries', Bavarians (from 1692) and Brandenburg troops discussed in the previous section. The total given for the emperor in 1691 includes the 12,000 imperial and 6,000 Bavarians despatched to Piedmont in that year.

[182] See VDM to Fagel, 17 June 1704, Turin, ARAH/EA/VDM/29, 102. Early in February 1704 there were only about 12,0000 imperial troops of an allied total of 30,000, *CGP*, II, 6.   [183] Symcox, *Victor Amadeus*, 149.

without the 50,000 men led to Piedmont by Prince Eugene that summer.[184] About a third of these were German troops hired by the Maritime Powers, who supplied Victor Amadeus with a remarkable 28,000 men in this way in the middle years of the war.[185] Many of these troops were subsequently deployed elsewhere, but as late as 1712 the Prussian and Saxe-Gotha troops made available by the Maritime Powers in 1706 continued to boost the allied total in Piedmont.[186] But the emperor's contingent remained the most significant. In the winter of 1707–08, allied ministers at The Hague decided that the emperor should contribute the largest single contingent – 20,000 men – and Victor Amadeus 15,000 to a total allied force in Piedmont of 46,000 men.[187] In the last years of the war, the duke was contributing the largest single contingent to the allied army in Piedmont.[188] Generally speaking, however, for most of the period under consideration the duke's own troops were a minority of the forces which underpinned his own successes. After 1713, Victor Amadeus could not realistically consider a war for the defence of Sicily without the support of at least one of the greater powers: following the arrival, in May 1719, of Austrian troops, his own forces were increasingly sidelined from the conflict in Sicily.[189]

Victor Amadeus also in some measure depended upon his more powerful allies for war matériel. Before 1690 the Turin arsenal was largely able to meet the limited requirements of the ducal army.[190] However, major warfare clearly stretched the resources of the Savoyard state, while defeat meant the loss of weaponry and munitions. A fire in the Turin arsenal in 1692 also reduced what Victor Amadeus could contribute to the

---

[184] C. Ingrao, *In Quest and Crisis: Emperor Joseph I and the Habsburg monarchy* (West Lafayette, 1979), 79 ff.; Saluces, *Histoire militaire*, V, 178, 202; Symcox, *Victor Amadeus*, 149–51.

[185] *CGP*, II, 3–4; Ingrao, *In Quest and Crisis*, 84; H. Snyder, ed., *The Marlborough–Godolphin Correspondence*, 3 vols. (Oxford, 1975), II, 862. Planning for the 1708 campaign assumed the participation of 11,000 Prussian troops and 3,000 from Saxe-Gotha, E. Pognisi, *Vittorio Amedeo II e la campagna di 1708 per la conquista del Confine Alpino* (Rome, 1930), 33 ff.

[186] Chetwynd to Dartmouth, 27 June 1711 (enclosing muster rolls for four Saxon regiments in Queen Anne's pay) and 29 June 1712, Turin, SP 92/28. See Segre, 'Negoziati . . . Prussia', *CGP*, VI, 299.

[187] Mémoire regarding the 1708 campaign. AST/MM/Imprese, m.11.14, printed in Pognisi: *Vittorio Amedeo II e la campagna di 1708*, 34–7

[188] In the spring of 1712, the allies in Piedmont expected to have fifty-six battalions in the coming campaign (more or less the same as in 1711), comprising twenty-three Piedmontese, twenty imperial, eleven Prussian and two Saxe-Gotha corps, Chetwynd to Dartmouth, 27 Apr. 1712, Turin, SP 92/28.

[189] Victor Amadeus' forces were no match for the Spanish force sent to Sicily in 1718, comprising 30,000 men, 23 warships, other vessels: W. Coxe, *Memoirs of the Kings of Spain of the House of Bourbon from the accession of Philip V to the death of Charles III 1700 to 1788*, 2nd ed. (London, 1815), II, 318–19.   [190] See, generally, *CGP*, I, lv–lvi.

allied war effort, at least for that year.[191] On the other hand, the duke's capacity in these respects was enhanced in the course of the Nine Years War, not least because of Victor Amadeus' share in what was taken from the enemy.[192] He was also able to secure munitions of various sorts from his allies, including by purchase.[193] This was indicative of the duke's dependence, evident from 1690. His treaty with Spain of that year obliged them to supplement his artillery needs, and an abortive project to raise 4,000 of Victor Amadeus' subjects to occupy the mountain passages at the end of the 1690 campaign depended upon the governor of Spanish Milan's supplying 500 muskets and bayonets, 200 barrels of powder and 200 boxes of bullets.[194] Subsequently, the governor of Milan offered heavy artillery from other parts of Spanish Italy, above all Naples, for the sieges of Pinerolo and Casale (which would, of course, have advanced Spanish interests and security in north Italy).[195] This reflected the fact that a successful siege, particularly of a major fortification, depended (as the duke himself acknowledged), on what his allies could do to supplement his own lack of the necessary weaponry and expertise, i.e. experienced military engineers.[196] Victor Amadeus did contribute artillery to the invasion of Dauphiné in 1692 and the siege of Casale in 1695,[197] but could not undertake independently the siege of the latter (or in 1696 of Pinerolo) without substantial help from his allies.[198] During the War of the Spanish Succession, too, mobilisation, expansion and the losses of 1703–06 again

---

[191] VDM to Fagel, 6 June 1692, Turin, ARAH/SG/8643/241. The fire (following the dropping of a grenade) caused damage estimated at the equivalent of 18,000 florins.

[192] See E. A. de Rochas d'Aiglun, ed., *Documents inédits relatifs à l'histoire et la topographie militaire des Alpes: la campagne de 1692 dans le Haut-Dauphiné* (Paris and Grenoble, 1874), 77 ff; English translation in G. Symcox, *War, Diplomacy, and Imperialism* (London, 1974), 149.

[193] In 1691, with the help of the Amsterdam Admiralty, de la Tour purchased powder and lead for his master, DLT to VA, 13 and 20 July, 3 Aug., 7 Sept. and 20 Oct. 1691 and same to ST, 24 July 1691, Hague, AST/LM/Olanda, m. 1.

[194] Solar de la Marguerite, *Traités publics de la maison royale de Savoie depuis la paix de Cateau Cambrésis jusqu'à nos jours*, 8 vols. (Turin, 1836–61), II, 121 ff.; Project, Oct. 1690, AST/Trattati Diversi, m. 12.

[195] VA to DLT, 28 July 1692, Arche, AST/LM/Olanda, m. 3.

[196] VA to DLT, 1 Jan. 1693, Turin, AST/LM/Olanda, m. 3.

[197] For the Dauphiné expedition, see VDM to Fagel, 6 and 13 June 1692, Turin, ARAH/SG/8644/241, 243. In 1695, the duke ordered the departure from the Turin arsenal of twenty heavy cannon and eight mortars for the siege of Casale, VDM to Fagel, 28 Mar. 1695, Turin, ARAH/SG/8644/184.

[198] In 1696, de la Tour ordered his agent at The Hague to send to the generale delle finanze (so that an account could be kept in the Ufficio del Soldo), a record of all sums disbursed to artillery and engineer officers going to Piedmont, DLT to ST, 9 Mar. 1696, London, AST/LM/GB, m. 8.

stretched the resources of the Savoyard state,[199] and until 1706 Victor Amadeus was greatly dependent upon gifts, loans and sales of essential munitions and weapons on the part of his allies.[200] As in the previous conflict, the capture of enemy munitions (particularly outside Turin in 1706 and during the Alpine campaigns thereafter) were a valuable windfall.[201] These helped ensure that, by the later stages of the conflict, the duke was able to contribute more substantially to the allied projects in the Alps and was less dependent on outside help.[202] Nevertheless, the limitations of his state in this sphere remained considerable and were amply demonstrated after 1713 during the struggle for Sicily, which exhausted Victor Amadeus' stocks of munitions. From 1720, therefore, he was anxious to recover the war matériel of Sardinia, which the island's Spanish conquerors were removing in anticipation of its transfer to him.[203]

Victor Amadeus also relied on his allies for naval help, particularly in the defence of Nice and Oneglia against Louis XIV's powerful Toulon squadron, since – apart from one or two galleys and other vessels, which were effectively in private hands, those of the Military Order of Saints Maurice and Lazarus – he had no navy to speak of before 1713.[204] This naval power was boosted by the use of privateers operating under ducal letters patent out of Nice and Oneglia,[205] but this did little to redress the naval imbalance. In the Nine Years War, the duke could rely on the Spanish galley squadrons (and the main Spanish fleet when it, occasionally,

[199] In 1703 the governor of Mondovì, following urgent requests from Victor Amadeus to his provincial governors for muskets from their arsenals, sent 2,000 of these to Turin, *CGP*, I, 100.

[200] For 1705–6, see the details in PRO/War Office 47/22, fs. 35–6; 23 f. 337; and 24 f. 206.

[201] Saluces, *Histoire militaire*, V, 211. The king of Prussia demanded some of the artillery which his troops helped capture in 1708, VDM to Fagel, 20 Feb. 1709, Turin, ARAH/EA/VDM/33, 28.

[202] In 1708, Victor Amadeus offered fifty cannon and more than sixty mortars (apart from the field artillery) for the campaign, VDM to Fagel, 25 Apr. 1708, Turin, ARAH/EA/VDM/32, f. 65.

[203] In fact, Victor Amadeus had to accept an indemnity from the king of Spain (in lieu of the artillery) of 100,000 écus (not even the 150,000 he demanded), A. Mattone, 'La cessione', 75 ff.

[204] G. B. Cavalcaselle, 'I Consigli di Guerra: genesi e sviluppi della giurisdizione militare negli stati sabaudi da Amedeo VIII a Vittorio Amedeo II', *BSBS*, 59, 1964, 113 ff.; Gerbaix de Sonnaz, *I Savoiardi ed I Nizzardi nella marina di Guerra di Casa Savoia dal 1300 al 1860: cenni storici*, Turin, 1914, 18 ff; Bianchi, 'Guerra e politica', 303–4. In 1703, Victor Amadeus rejected the emperor's proposal that he receive Sardinia on the grounds that he had no naval force with which to defend the island, A. Mattone, 'La cessione', 12.

[205] See Prato, 'Il Costo', *CGP*, X, 317–18. This was typical of that 'privatisation' of warfare, resorted to when the state could not effectively monopolise the sector, see G. Symcox, *The Crisis of French Sea Power 1688–1697* (Hague, 1974), passim.

entered the Mediterranean) and in that and the succeeding conflict on the fleets of the Maritime Powers, Britain and the Dutch Republic, who dominated the Mediterranean in 1694 and 1695.[206] His allies' fleets could help Victor Amadeus in various ways. They could contribute to the defence of his coastal territories, using their cannon (sometimes even landing them, and men) as at Nice in 1705–06. They could also transport men, money, artillery and so on to help him wage war. Above all, of course, they were crucial to the success of that combined land and sea 'descent' on Provence from Victor Amadeus' territories which was one of the key strands in allied strategic thinking,[207] and which was only partially realised in the abortive Toulon expedition of 1707.[208]

Dependence had its disadvantages for Victor Amadeus. For one thing, these forces often arrived too late to seize the initiative from the enemy, and left the field too early, to go into winter quarters.[209] More seriously, the troops and ships promised by his allies might be diverted elsewhere, ruining his own plans. Thus in 1696 the duke's plans to besiege Pinerolo were undermined by a reduction in the number of troops kept in north Italy by the emperor, who was also fighting the Turks in Hungary.[210] In addition, the contributions and winter quarters demanded of the imperial vassals in north Italy by the emperor simply did not yield sufficient funds to maintain a larger imperial contingent.[211] As for naval support, the

---

[206] See J. Ehrman, *The Navy in the War of William III* (Cambridge, 1953), J. C. de Jonge, *Geschiedenis van het nederlandsche Zeewezen*, 6 vols. (Haarlem, 1860), and C. Storrs, 'The army of Lombardy and the resilience of Spanish power in Italy in the reign of Carlos II (1665–1700) (Part II)', *War in History*, 5/1, 1998, passim, for the allied naval presence in the Mediterranean.

[207] See DLT to VA, 25 Oct. 1692, Hague, AST/LM/Olanda, m. 3.

[208] Saluces, *Histoire militaire*, V, 220–1; J. H. Owen, *The War at Sea under Queen Anne* (Cambridge, 1938), passim.

[209] In the Nine Years War, the Spanish troops generally waited until the imperial troops had crossed the Milanese before leaving for Piedmont, VA to DLT, 28 July 1692, Arche, AST/LM/Olanda, m. 3. In the later conflict, the recruits for the Hessians and Saxe-Gotha troops (and most of the Prussians) serving in Piedmont in 1707 still had not arrived by mid-summer, VDM to Fagel, 22 June 1707, Turin ARAH/EA/VDM/33, f. 126.

[210] Storrs, 'Diplomatic relations', 300 ff. After 1713, Victor Amadeus sought to justify to an irate Emperor his acceptance of the Utrecht peace by claiming (*inter alia*) that the emperor's failure to maintain his army in Piedmont at 20,000 (as laid down in their treaty of 1703) had made it difficult to continue the war there, A. Tallone, 'Vittorio Amedeo II e la Quadruplice Alleanza', *Studi su Vittorio Amedeo II* (Turin, 1933), 196.

[211] ST to DLT, 31 Dec. 1695, Turin, AST/LM/Olanda, m. 4. In 1693, the diversion of imperial troops against the duke of Modena, to enforce payment of those contributions, delayed their arrival in Piedmont and the start of the campaign, ST to DLT, 28 Apr. 1693, Turin, AST/LM/Olanda, m. 3. In the War of the Spanish Succession, the failure of the imperial commissariat to supply the German troops serving under Victor Amadeus in the pay of Queen Anne and the Dutch provoked numerous difficulties and delays: see Chetwynd to Sunderland, 18 June 1710, Turin, SP 92/28.

Anglo-Dutch vessels which had wintered at Cadiz in 1695–96, and which might have participated in a combined assault on Provence from Piedmont, or have diverted French forces while Victor Amadeus besieged Pinerolo, were recalled to the Channel in the spring of 1696 because of the threat of a French descent on England in favour of James II.[212] It is not wholly surprising then that Victor Amadeus sought to secure Pinerolo by means of a separate deal with Louis XIV. The fact that his allies had their own ambitions compounded these problems. The emperor's preoccupation with the reassertion from the 1690s of imperial authority in north and central Italy both distracted from the conflict in Piedmont and complicated Victor Amadeus' relations with some of the other Italian states.[213] Similarly, the partial armistice concluded in the spring of 1707 which effectively ended the war in north Italy (but not in Savoy, southern France and the Alps) was largely the work of the emperor, who was more concerned with securing the Spanish inheritance in southern Italy than with an invasion of France.[214] Victor Amadeus could seek to replace uncooperative imperial and Spanish commanders, and even (as in 1692) secure the supreme command for himself, asserting his authority as generalissimo to insist on acceptance of the capitulation of Casale in 1695.[215] However, his supreme command remained limited because the local commanders of the imperial and Spanish armies had little difficulty in evading ducal orders with which they disagreed, such as wintering in Dauphiné in 1692–93. Like the Protestant battalions in Victor Amadeus' service, the Spanish and imperial armies were also jealous of their independence and privileges. The presence of substantial numbers of foreign troops, even those of allies, could also represent a threat of sorts to ducal dominion, as became clear in the difficulties between Turin and Vienna in the War of the Spanish Succession over the quartering of troops in the imperial fiefs recently ceded to Victor Amadeus.[216] Last, but by no means least, the troops of his allies could cause as much devastation and suffering in Victor Amadeus' own states as those of his enemy.[217]

[212] Storrs, 'Diplomatic relations', 307.
[213] In 1692 Victor Amadeus opposed a project to divert imperial troops against the Duke of Mantua (weakening the allied effort against France and offering Louis XIV diplomatic opportunities in Italy), VA to DLT, 28 July 1692, Arche, AST/LM/Olanda, m. 3.
[214] In the spring of 1712, ten imperial battalions were absent from Piedmont at the siege of Porto Ercole in central Italy, Chetwynd to Dartmouth, 27 Apr. 1712, Turin, SP 92/28.
[215] Carutti, *Diplomazia*, III, 35.
[216] In 1710, ducal troops had to be deployed to defend Victor Amadeus' authority in the recently ceded Monferrato (and his new subjects there) from the demands of the imperial troops, Cockburn ro Chetwynd, 20 Dec. 1710, and Cockburn to Dartmouth, 27 Dec. 1710, all Turin, SP 92/27, f. 430 ff.
[217] See Levi, *Inheriting Power*, 125.

ADMINISTRATION, ORGANISATION AND SUPPLY

The expansion of Victor Amadeus' army from 1690 increased the number of those of his subjects in the pay of, and dependent upon the Savoyard state. Since army officer posts were not purchasable in that state, it also meant an increase in the amount of (military) patronage available to the duke. But the growth of the Savoyard army and the need to provide for his own forces (and at least some of the needs of the troops his allies made available) in these decades also, inevitably, created some problems.[218] Expansion certainly put great pressure on the administrative structure, developed before 1690, which had administered and provided for a much smaller military establishment, necessitating further development.[219] Among the organisational changes within the armed forces were the fixing of the number and proportion of grenadiers (what we would think of as shock-troops) and the division of regiments into battalions. The trend was towards regiments of two battalions, although this could not always be maintained in the face of financial pressures (including the cost of a high command, which each regiment had to have) and the depletion of individual regiments. Lack of uniformity therefore persisted, especially in wartime. By 1706, for example, Victor Amadeus' Guards (one of only two regiments comprising three battalions in 1703) had been reduced to two battalions, while the Savoy regiment (comprising a single battalion in 1703) received a second (1708) and a third (1709) battalion. A less hectic situation in the later stages of the War of the Spanish Succession allowed the resumption of progress towards a more uniform structure, Victor Amadeus ordering the dissolution of all third battalions as peace approached in 1712.[220] Growing standardisation also affected

---

[218] After his victory at Turin, in 1706, the indiscipline of some of the light troops necessarily resorted to by Victor Amadeus in the first years of the War of the Spanish Succession obliged him to bring them to heel: Saluces, *Histoire militaire*, I, 264–5. Generally speaking, and not surprisingly, many of the *ad hoc* measures of 1703–6 were regularised after 1706.

[219] *Ibid.*, I, 251 ff. and Bianchi, 'Guerra e politica', give the best account of organisational change.

[220] Saluces, *Histoire militaire*, I, 260, 310; *CGP*, I, xxix ff.; Prato, 'Il costo', *CGP*, X, 259. Broadly speaking, each battalion included 400 men in the 1690s and 600 in the 1700s, excluding the high command. The latter (colonel, lieutenant colonel, major, company captains and lieutenants) totalled 26 per battalion, about 1/23 of the battalion strength. The 400–600 men who made up the battalion were distributed among 7 companies (6 of 90 men each and one of grenadiers, of 53 men) in the (exceptionally privileged, see above) Guards regiment and among 12 companies of 50 men each in most of Victor Amadeus' remaining regiments. Each company comprised 44 soldiers, 4 corporals and 2 sergeants, these lower officials comprising the great bulk of officialdom within the army: in 1699, for example, there were 2,483 officials (1,755 of them lesser officials) and 8,584 soldiers. See these figures (and ratios) with those in the Dutch Republic *c*. 1600, Parker, *Military Revolution*, 20.

weaponry and dress, with the general adoption of musket and bayonet and of less varied uniforms.[221]

One further aspect of the development of the Savoyard forces, and one also related to the need to make greater provisions for the greatly increased number of old soldiers and families of the dead, and echoing developments elsewhere in Europe, was the organisation of new so-called Invalids corps The first Invalids unit had been established in 1685, and sent to Vercelli, the new corps also providing a partial solution to the need for garrisons. Others followed and in 1710 the corps was completely remodelled. In the 1700s admission to the ranks of the Invalids, which was a privilege, reflected the impact of the Nine Years War. In 1702, for example, five men were admitted (four of them non-commissioned officers) aged between 50 and 60, one of whom had been wounded at the battle of Staffarda (1690) and two at that of Marsaglia (1693). The dependents of wounded and dead soldiers might also be pensioned, especially if the latter died meritoriously: Pietro Micca's widow was assigned two daily rations of bread for herself and her son.[222]

At a more senior political and administrative level, the period saw the emergence of the secretary for war, the elaboration and further systematisation of the Uditorato di Guerra (responsible for military discipline and justice) and the further development of the office known as the Ufficio del Soldo (developments considered more fully in Chapter 4). However, it is worth considering here the function of the latter in so far as it related to the ducal forces. The Ufficio del Soldo, headed by the contadore generale, directed a network of commissaries, familiar enough in other states, who accompanied the troops and carried out on the ground the tasks which were the Ufficio's responsibility.[223] Above all, this meant the reviews. These were effected when a regiment was newly formed and at the start and end of each campaign with occasional extraordinary reviews if necessary.[224] Reviews were crucial to proper control and planning. They revealed how many men had been lost during the campaign (and thus how many must be recruited during the winter),[225] kept pay rolls and budgets up to date and were a crucial

---

[221] *CGP*, I, xxxiii ff., xlv.   [222] *CGP*, I, lxxxviii; Saluces, *Histoire militaire*, I, 372.

[223] See Victor Amadeus' general order of Oct. 1694, Duboin, XVII, 328, *CGP*, I, lxxii and Saluces, *Histoire militaire*, I, 263. For orders in July 1710, from the contadore generale to the commissary accompanying the force in and about Demonte and the valleys, see Duboin, XXVII, 351. For the Uditorato di Guerra, Bianchi, 'Guerra e politica', 200.

[224] See the reviews of the Genevois dragoons (at Vercelli, Mar. 1690), Provana di Collegno, 'Lettere di Carlo Ciacinto Roero', *CGP*, VIII, 339; of Victor Amadeus's troops in Lombardy in 1703, prior to their disarming by the Bourbon forces, *CGP*, I, 24 ff.; and of Pietro Micca's company (reviewed five times between Sept. 1705 and Feb. 1706), Casanova, 'Contributo', *CGP*, VIII, 196 ff.

[225] VA to DLT, 5 Dec. 1691, Turin, AST/LM/Olanda, m. 1.

weapon in the constant struggle against fraud on the part of both officers (who, as in other armies, sometimes claimed more 'dead men' than they were allowed) and deserters moving from one company to another to gain recruitment premiums.[226] Reflecting the extent to which participation in the Nine Years War and the War of the Spanish Succession stimulated the further elaboration of pre-war methods of control, the norms for the conduct of reviews (their frequency, and so on) were newly laid down by Victor Amadeus at the end of 1694,[227] and again in 1709. Among the measures used to keep track of individual soldiers was the giving to each man of a so-called *nom de guerre*, often simply the surname but sometimes (to avoid duplication where surnames were common) one indicating the place of origin or a distinguishing physical feature.[228] Officers were subject to monitoring of a different sort, senior officers (and the duke himself) keeping records of their junior officers with a view to their suitability for promotion.[229]

If the Savoyard state was to wage war effectively it was also crucial that it supply its forces with food, transports[230] and other needs.[231] Something has already been said about the conduct of warfare, and the importance of sieges. However, the issue of supply could also decisively influence both strategy and the outcome of a campaign. Any venture required meticulous organisation to ensure the availability of essential supplies. If not, operations could not continue. The availability of forage might determine how early an army could take the field and how early it must leave it. In 1708 and again in 1709 (i.e. at the height of the European subsistence crisis), allied offensive operations from Piedmont were cut

---

[226] *CGP*, I, lxxiv–lxxv.

[227] Duboin, XXIX, 328 ff.; *CGP*, I, lxxii–lxxiii; Saluces, *Histoire militaire*, I, 263.

[228] Pietro Micca's *nom de guerre* was the rather common one of 'Pasapertut', Casanova, 'Contributo', *CGP*, VIII, 203. Salsotto, 'Fossano', *CGP*, VIII, 415 ff., notes the problems the use of *noms de guerre* posed for local communities trying to trace their war dead.

[229] For pen portraits, 1711, of the colonels of Victor Amadeus' Guards, Piedmont and Chablais regiments, see *CGP*, I, lxxiii.

[230] It is difficult to overestimate the importance of transports and their co-ordination. In 1694, it was calculated that nearly 2,000 mules a month were needed for the carriage of munitions from Piedmont to Finale for a projected invasion of Provence, Stato delle vetture e tempo per il trasporto de materiali dal Piemonte al Finale, Add. MSS. 22921. In 1709, the allied forces in Savoy were without bread for three days because of the desertion of a number of the mule drivers and the diversion of some of the other mules to the carrying of the sick over the mountains to Aosta, disrupting the supply system, VDM to Fagel, 14 Sept. 1709, Turin, ARAH/EA/VDM/33, f. 158.

[231] See M. van Creveld, *Supplying war: logistics from Wallenstein to Patton* (Cambridge, 1977) and J. A. Lynn, *The Wars of Louis XIV 1667–1714* (London, 1999), 52–58.

short by the lack of forage in enemy territory.²³² Denying forage could be an effective, if undramatic, defensive strategy. In 1694, following Victor Amadeus's second defeat in 1693, and the failure of an allied fleet to apear for a planned joint offensive against Provence, the duke's cavalry spent the summer consuming the grass without which the enemy could not take the offensive against his states – a strategy which shielded Piedmont and its harvest (and which was also that of his allies in Flanders).²³³ In the spring of 1696, van der Meer unsuspectingly stumbled on an indication of Victor Amadeus's forthcoming *volte-face*, when reporting that he found it odd, if the duke expected a French attempt against Turin, that he ordered a retreat instead of seeking to deny them forage between Pinerolo and his capital.²³⁴ Magazines helped offset some of the uncertainties involved in depending on the climate and season, and a network of these were established in the Savoyard state for the stocking of both animal forage and the grain (or rice, where appropriate) which Victor Amadeus' subjects were obliged to supply for the maintenance of the ducal army. However, magazines occasionally benefited the enemy. Following his victory in 1693 Catinat ranged widely in Piedmont seizing the contents of the magazines stocked by the duke for that campaign.²³⁵ Nevertheless, reflecting practice elsewhere, such magazines were an important aspect of Savoyard military administrative development in the Nine Years War and the subsequent conflict.²³⁶ Troops on the march, for example those intended to go to the relief of Montmélian through the Duchy of Aosta in 1691, had to be directed to properly supplied *étapes* along their route.²³⁷ The system of *étapes*, developed before 1690, was another aspect of military organisation which underwent development in this period,

---

²³² See VDM to Fagel, 24 Aug. 1708, Balbote, ARAH/EA/VDM/32, f. 163 and same to same, 21 Sept. 1709, Turin, ARAH/EA/VDM/33, f. 159.

²³³ ST to DLT, 14 Aug. 1694, Turin, AST/LM/Olanda, m. 4; and DLT to ST, 15 June and 2 July 1694, Hague, AST/LM/Olanda, m. 4.

²³⁴ VDM to Heinsius, 21 May 1696, Turin, ARAH/SG/8644/263. In Sept. 1708, fearing that the enemy might attempt to offset their losses that campaign with an incursion into the Val d'Aosta, Victor Amadeus ordered that in this event his commanders should concentrate on the defence of the Fort of Bard, since there was no forage for the enemy elsewhere in the Duchy, VDM to Fagel, 13 Sept. 1708, Mantoules, ARAH/EA/VDM/32, f. 177.

²³⁵ Catinat, *Mémoires*, II, 253 ff. During the War of the Spanish Succession, too, especially before 1707, the ducal magazines were sometimes at the mercy of the Bourbon forces.

²³⁶ In the winter of 1708–9 the duke established forage magazines at Susa and Pinerolo for the draught animals of the artillery train for the campaign, VDM to Fagel, 27 Feb. 1709, Turin, ARAH/EA/VDM/33, f. 33. In 1712, forage stored in the magazine at Susa was used to supply the cavalry stationed nearby, Chetwynd to Warre, 3 Aug. 1712, Turin, SP 92/27, f. 489.

²³⁷ Guasco, 'Vittorio Amedeo II nelle campagne', 262.

Victor Amadeus ordering reform in September 1700 in the light of the lessons of the Nine Years War.[238]

Responsible for the commissariat, i.e. for the provision of supplies in the field, field hospitals,[239] and transports (including the artillery train) was the intendenza generale.[240] This office was directed, between 1706 and 1709, when he secured the post of contadore generale, by Gian Giacomo Fontana, one of those able officials who began a very successful career in Victor Amadeus' service in these decades of war.[241] As contadore generale, he continued to direct the Intendenza after 1709.[242] The Intendenza sometimes fulfilled its responsibilities directly. It also sometimes relied on the simple requisitioning of animals, labour and materials from Victor Amadeus' subjects.[243] However, as before 1690,[244] the Savoyard state, like many others, still depended heavily on private contractors for a wide range of services.[245] The supply of both uniforms and the troops' bread ration were contracted out, although the grain for the bread was supplied by ducal officials (from that owed by Victor Amadeus' subjects, see below, p. 77).[246] In wartime, field hospitals also largely depended on private con-

[238] Duboin, XXVII, 293.
[239] Of the 4,500 ducal troops taken prisoner by Victor Amadeus' Bourbon allies in Lombardy in 1703, about 2,000 were in hospital, CGP, I, 24 ff.
[240] See order of intendente generale, June 1691, forbidding the purchase of supplies in the camp for transport to Turin, Duboin, XXVII, 718, and of 1 Feb. 1693 for an equalisation of the burden of lodging the troops among all communities subject to the winter quarters tax, Duboin, XXI, 1100. For the Intendenza in the War of the Spanish Succession, see Prato, 'Il costo', CGP, X, 104–5.
[241] Fontana was praised by Prince Eugene for providing the transports which he thought played a key part in the allied victory at Turin in 1706, D. Carutti, Storia del regno di Vittorio Amedeo II (Turin, 1863), 338. In 1709, Fontana accompanied the imperial general count Daun's expedition into Savoy, giving the necessary orders for supply in his master's absence. For Fontana, ennobled as conte di Monastero di Vico (1722) and marchese di Cravanzana (1731), see Quazza, Le riforme, I, 49–50.
[242] In 1710, he was sent by Victor Amadeus to co-ordinate with Daun, commanding the allied troops on campaign, the supply of forage to the latter, Chetwynd to Dartmouth, 8 Oct. 1710, Turin, SP 92/28. The following year, he co-ordinated with their commissary the march of the imperial troops, same to same, 24 Oct. 1711, Turin, SP 92/28.
[243] See Duboin, XXVII, 277 ff. (orders, 1691, for forced work on military sites) and XXI, 1094 (order of 1691 regarding draught animals and wagons). See Salsotto, 'Fossano' and Scarzello, 'Corneliano . . .', CGP, VIII, passim, for demands on the communities in the following conflict.
[244] See Bianchi, 'Guerra e politica', 106–7 and Duboin, XVII, 900 (contract for barracks, 1684).
[245] In 1699, the Piedmontese contractor supplied beds (and firewood) at just over 35 lire a bed, while in Nice another contractor supplied the same for just over 22 lire, Prato, 'Il costo', CGP, X, 271.
[246] See the deal (1703) between contractors and conte Maffei for clothing the latter's new regiment, CGP, I, xxxv and Duboin, XXVII, 751, for the duke's approval (1711) of a bread contract.

tractors.[247] The Intendenza sometimes purchased or had built its own transports, including boats (for use on the Po),[248] but generally hired what it needed, either for the duration of the conflict or for each campaign.[249] Ducal officials regulated the operations of these contractors,[250] but this reliance on the latter reflected the fact that there were limits to what the ducal state, or administration, could do, to what Victor Amadeus' subjects might bear and to what his states could realistically supply. Agreements with private contractors were an obvious, tested and tried solution to many of these problems. Occasionally, foreign contractors were used. In 1709, for example, disappointed of hopes of obtaining mules from the emperor, the duke agreed with a Milanese contractor for 3,500 mules and 800 pairs of asses.[251] However, more usually he relied on a few Piedmontese, men like Basilio and Sola, who might contract to supply a variety of different services, and for whom the Nine Years War and the War of the Spanish Succession were clearly very profitable.[252]

The reliance on contractors reveals that, as has already been made clear and will become clearer (see Chapter 4), the military sphere was not characterised simply by the growth of uniformity, centralised bureaucracy and an all-embracing and impersonal state. Despite progress towards greater standardisation, there were still remarkable differences between (and within) regiments which had been raised in many different ways and were still often known by the name of their commander (invariably the nobles who had played a crucial role in their levy and often still commanded them). Similarly, regimental commanders still had a great deal of independence.[253] In many respects in fact, early modern armies – often regarded as the essence and a crucial foundation of absolutism – were influenced by particularist attitudes more often associated with its antithesis.[254] The pay of senior officers was not always according to a fixed

---

[247] *CGP*, I, lxxxvii–viii (contract of Apr. 1704); Prato, 'Il costo', *CGP*, X, 302 ff. (including contract with one Basilio for 1707).

[248] Prato, 'Il costo', *CGP*, X, 295.

[249] In March 1704, Giorgio Sola agreed to supply 162 horses for the ducal artillery train for the duration of the war, Duboin, XXXIX, 87 ff. and *CGP*, I, lvi.

[250] See Duboin, XXVII, 750 (order regarding measures to use in daily bread supply, 1710).

[251] VDM to Fagel, 20 Mar. 1709, Turin, ARAH/EA/VDM/33, f. 45. In 1713, Fontana contracted at Genoa for transports and provisions for the ducal troops going to Sicily, Chetwynd to Dartmouth, 19 July 1713, Turin, SP 92/27, f. 619.

[252] *CGP* I, lxxxvii. In 1711, Fontana used again the contractor who had supplied transports in 1710, Chetwynd to Dartmouth, 30 May 1711, Turin, SP 92/28.

[253] A nobleman levying a new regiment would enjoy various privileges (including that of appointing officers) which represented an extension of his own (rather than ducal) patronage.

[254] See F. Andujar Castillo, *Los militares en la Espana del siglo XVIII: un estudio social* (Granada, 1991), passim.

hierarchical scale, but reflected the rewards received by the individual from his master,[255] while promotion too, might be as much the result of political pressures as the good of the service (see Chapter 4). In addition, control systems were never completely effective. The growing Savoyard army was, to a degree at least, as much the instrument of the elite which ran the machinery of government and collaborated with the duke as of an impersonal state, and was used by those with influence to defend their private interests. Troops were sent, for example, to defend Buttigliera, property of the Carron de Saint-Thomas, from French raids.[256] Nor, finally, was the armed struggle always monopolised by the 'state'. On the contrary, the peasantry of Piedmont, who suffered greatly from the depredations of the French (and of Victor Amadeus' allies), sometimes fought back in a sort of guerrilla war which may have helped the duke's war effort but was not always strictly part of it.[257] In some respects, too, earlier attempts by the state to assert a monopoly of force were necessarily relaxed in wartime and had to be reasserted after 1713.[258] Given these remarks, it is not wholly surprising that Victor Amadeus continued to play a pivotal role. He dealt directly with his commanders and took a close personal interest in both his troops and army administration.[259] He also fulfilled the role of warrior prince, risking his own life in battles and sieges, and conforming wholly to an ideal of the prince as warrior which still had great force (and which could, particularly when accompanied by military success, be a useful prop of authority).[260] Above all, he supplied the most effective central co-ordination of a military (and larger administrative)

---

[255] Prato, 'Il costo', *CGP*, X. 273.

[256] In the winter of 1692–3 a detachment of dragoons were ordered to the Susa valley following reports of French plans to attack Buttigliera, VDM to Fagel, 5 Jan. 1693, ARAH/SG/8644/1.

[257] In 1693, after Marsaglia, Parella exploited peasant fury, offering a pistole for every French soldier brought in dead or alive; but in 1707, as the Bourbon position collapsed in north Italy, and as the peasants of Piedmont took their revenge for the destruction of their harvests in preceding years, Victor Amadeus was obliged to send a president of the Camera di Conti on special mission to put a stop to such incidents, VDM to States, 27 Apr. 1707, Turin, ARAH/EA/VDM/33, f. 85. In the Vaudois valleys, the war was further embittered by the issue of religion (see Chapter 6).

[258] Victor Amadeus' Constitutions (1723) restricted the carrying of arms except by soldiers and 'persons of quality', Molesworth to Newcastle, 3 June 1724, Turin, SP 92/31, f. 361. (The duke had relaxed the ban on arms in the Nine Years War and War of the Spanish Succession, *CGP*, I, 68.)

[259] See the Duke's autograph comments (1702), on the Chablais regimental roll, *CGP*, I, lxxiii.

[260] Saluces, *Histoire militaire*, V, 279–81. For war and the image of the ruler as warrior in contemporary understanding of kingship and sovereignty see J. Cornette, *Le roi de guerre: essai sur la souveraineté dans la France du Grand Siècle* (Paris, 1993), passim.

Fig. 1.2 Soldier of new provincial (or militia) battalion (or regiment) of Casale (Monferrato), 1713 (Biblioteca Reale, Turin, Manoscritti Militari, 134)

Fig. 1.3 Soldier of new provincial (or militia) battalion (or regiment) of Mondoví, 1713 (Biblioteca Reale, Turin, Manoscritti Militari, 134)

structure which before 1717, at least, was by no means completely bureaucratised or impersonal (see Chapter 4).

CONCLUSION

The approach of peace in 1712–13 allowed Victor Amadeus to think about relieving his hard pressed finances and subjects of the burden of alarge army. In the spring of 1713 he ordered the reduction of both his cavalry and infantry, although this was briefly interrupted as relations further deteriorated between Turin and Vienna.[261] But he also needed to provide for the longer-term defence needs of his enlarged and extended state after his departure for Sicily, accompanied by 6,000 troops, a substantial proportion of his regular forces.[262] This was the more serious in view of the Savoyard state's increasing isolation after 1713. The need to ensure that he could (in the absence of so many troops in Sicily) mobilise in his mainland territories perhaps as many as 10,000 militiamen quickly and cheaply in an emergency (which he had signally failed to do in 1703–04), while he sought outside help, powerfully influenced army reform from 1713. The overhaul of the militia was already under discussion long before the end of the War of the Spanish Succession, and thus pre-dates the fundamental overhaul of the Savoyard state in and after 1717. The outcome was an order, issued by Victor Amadeus from Sicily in 1714, for the creation of 10 provincial militia regiments in his mainland territories (1 in Aosta, 1 in Nice, 1 in the newly acquired Monferrato, 2 in Savoy and 5 in Piedmont), each of 600 men – a total of 6,000 (briefly increased to 10,000 in 1727) – in place of the select militia of 1690. Recruits were to be found from among all males aged between 18 and 40 and had to attend training manoeuvres (twice a year from 1716). Recruitment remained the responsibility of local agencies (including the communities) but selection criteria were strictly laid down (and some exemption privileges removed). Substitutions were only allowed from within the same family, while fathers became responsible for sons who deserted. The new units were to be led by officers drawn from the regular troops, who were to enjoy the same privileges as the regulars. Effective implementation of these guidelines would be difficult without some

[261] Chetwynd to Dartmouth, 10 May, 10 June and 12 Aug. 1713, Turin, SP 92/28, f. 586, 605, 631. Typical, however, of the non-military thinking behind armies (and of the personal style of Victor Amadeus' government) was his creation of a new Guards regiment, in 1714, to accomodate his new Sicilian subjects, as requested by the Sicilian parliament, Saluces, *Histoire militaire*, I, 305.

[262] Carutti, *Storia della Diplomazia*, III, 470. Payne to Ayerst, 2 Aug. 1713, Turin, SP 92/27, f. 625. In 1718, at the time of the Spanish invasion, there were nearly 10,000 Savoyard troops in Sicily, *ibid*, 538.

co-operation on the part of Victor Amadeus' subjects, but the new militia represented both a substantial reinforcement of his military strength and a remarkable new assertion of his authority within the state.[263]

After 1713, too, Victor Amadeus – who depended on British warships to carry him to his new island kingdom in that year – sought to establish an independent navy, to maintain communications with, and defend Sicily (and, after 1720, Sardinia).[264] With Sicily he received its galley squadron; and once on the island he set about making this more effective. He ordered the maintenance of a squadron of five galleys and three other vessels, and the creation of a new regiment of marines to serve on them; and hoped (without success) to receive, in exchange for his outstanding English subsidy arrears (see Chapter 2) a number of French vessels captured by the English navy in the War of the Spanish Succession.[265] In 1717, he issued comprehensive regulations for the fleet[266] – the first issued by a duke of Savoy since the reign of Emanuel Filibert – which were typical of the long-term administrative restructuring of that year (see Chapter 4) and support the view that that overhaul was closely associated with defending Victor Amadeus' possession of Sicily. In the short term these schemes left a lot to be desired. While they matured, Victor Amadeus necessarily relied on foreign support for his defence of Sicily (against, among others, the Turks).[267] Unfortunately for him, the Spaniards seized (1718) most of this tiny nascent Savoyard fleet (which Victor Amadeus recovered as part of the Sardinian exchange). Nevertheless, the first steps had been taken towards the development of a navy, one for which ducal officials (rather than the Order of Saints Maurice and Lazarus) were increasingly responsible.[268]

Between 1690 and 1720 the Savoyard state was almost constantly at war. Victor Amadeus had had to mobilise men to a degree not seen in the Savoyard state for more than half a century. Occasionally, notably in 1703–04, the duke had to find troops how and where he could. However, over the longer term those men were mobilised, and new obliga-

---

[263] See Chetwynd to Dartmouth, 28 Jan. 1713, Turin, SP 92/27, f. 540; Duboin, XXVI, 440; Brancaccio, *L'Esercito . . . Gl: Ordinaamenti*, I, 209–10 and Saluces, *Histoire militaire*, I, 282 ff. The latter emphasises the fact that the select militia of 1690 was now too great a burden for the Savoyard state. Foreign models were again in evidence: see project for raising provincial regiments as in Sweden, AST/MM/Levati Reggimenti Provinciali, m. 1/5.

[264] Cavalcaselle, 'I Consigli di Guerra', 114 ff.; Gerbaix de Sonnaz, *I Savoiardi ed I Nizzardi*, 28 ff.; Symcox, *Victor Amadeus*, 172. The development of a Savoyard navy after 1713 merits further study, not least as a case study of the emerging Savoyard state.

[265] VA to marquis de Trivié, 21 Oct. 1713, Palermo, AST/Negoziazioni/Inghilterrra, m. 4.   [266] Duboin, XXVII, 1213 ff.   [267] Mattone, 'La cessione', 22.

[268] During this struggle, Victor Amadeus again resorted to privateers: see his agreement with G.-B. Belgrano of Oneglia, 1719, in AST/PCF/1717–20, I, f. 88–9.

tions imposed, tying men to the state in a way which was rather new. These obligations were part of the developing state structure. They helped form the enlarged state, were extended to the new territories of the Savoyard state, and were further elaborated after 1713 in order to protect what they had helped to achieve. The duke's success in levying men, as Barberis has argued, by no means reflected a willingness to fight. (Indeed, the ducal demands offered a new arena for resistance.) But neither did it simply represent an imposition by an all-powerful prince or state. Coercion was sometimes used, but successful mobilisation of the military manpower of the Savoyard state also depended on co-operation of some sort, on the part of those who found their own interest in the expansion of the ducal army or the preservation of the Savoyard state (for example, Victor Amadeus' Vaudois subjects see Chapter 6), or who could reconcile ducal impositions with their own local influence. Clearly, the wars fought by the Savoyard state between 1690 and 1720 had given a decisive stimulus to the emergence of a more all-embracing and effective state military structure. Not all of the gains which redefined the territorial configuration of the Savoyard state in these years were the result of direct military action, or war, or solely of armed force. Victor Amadeus' success also depended upon substantial numbers of foreigners serving in his own forces (and continued to do so after 1720), and upon the forces of his allies. The Savoyard state remained weak and vulnerable when fighting alone. Nevertheless, its enhanced European standing undoubtedly owed much to its enlarged military establishment, while the growth of the armed might at its disposal – while by no means a simple tool of government[269] – strengthened the hand of the ducal (now royal) state *vis-à-vis* resistance at all levels to its growing demands. At the same time, and despite the continued use of private contractors for some essential military services, the enlarged military establishment had necessitated organisational changes which represented further progress towards a more sophisticated administrative structure.

[269] During the Nine Years War the ducal and foreign auxiliary troops engaged in a variety of illegal activities, necessitating frequent ducal orders: see those of 21 Sept. 1694, AST/Editti Originali, m. 15/79, and of 8 May 1696, AST/Editti Originali, m. 16/20 against illicit dealing in tobacco.

CHAPTER 2

SAVOYARD FINANCE, 1690–1720

Money was, necessarily, a constant concern of Victor Amadeus II in these decades because war, as contemporaries never tired of pointing out, could not be fought without it.[1] Ordinary peacetime revenues were often sharply reduced while expenditure rocketed. By the same token, however, war might be the single most important factor in the drive towards that long-term increase in government revenues, and the ability of the state to extract tax (and other) revenues which was a marked feature of early modern Europe.[2] How governments responded to the fiscal demands of warfare could have important implications for the process of state formation, whether defined as simple territorial expansion or as the assertion of greater, 'absolute' authority (or its weakening) within the existing or expanding state, or both. Historians of Habsburg Spain and of Louis XIV's France, for example, have argued that the sheer cost of war necessitated compromises to secure the required funds which undermined an earlier 'absolutist' achievement (itself often created in response to the challenge of war). By contrast, the decades after 1688 saw the development in Britain, in large part to meet the demands of war against France, of new political and fiscal institutions and practices – what John Brewer has dubbed the 'fiscal-military state' – which represented an alternative to the 'absolutist' model across the Channel but which in some respects approximated to it.[3]

---

[1] See P. G. M. Dickson and J. Sperling, 'War Finance 1689–1714', in J. S. Bromley, ed., *New Cambridge Modern History, VI: The rise of Great Britain and Russia 1688–1715/25* (Cambridge, 1970), 284. F. Tallett, *War and Society in Early Modern Europe 1495–1715* (London, 1992), 10 ff. emphasises the role of financial resources (and an 'arms race') rather than developments in tactics, weaponry and organisational capacity in explaining changes in the scale of warfare.   [2] Tallett, *War and Government*, 175–6.
[3] See I. A. A. Thompson, *War and Government in Habsburg Spain 1560–1620* (London, 1974); D. Dessert, *Argent, pouvoir et société au Grand Siècle* (Paris, 1984); G. Symcox, *The Crisis of French Sea Power 1688–1697; from the Guerre d'Escadre to the Guerre de Course* (The Hague, 1974); J. Brewer, *The Sinews of Power: war, money and the English state 1688–1783* (London, 1989), xvii.

The present chapter considers the relationship between war finance and Savoyard state formation between 1690 and 1720. Between these dates Victor Amadeus' expenditure and revenues increased by between a third and a half, underpinning his ability to maintain large forces, with which to defend his authority at home and abroad. But, on occasion, especially in wartime (for example between 1704 and 1713) his outlay and income were double, even treble, what they were in 1690 – suggesting that, as with army growth (see Chapter 1), state formation was often a process less of steady growth than of fits and starts, and occasional retreat, largely following the rhythm of war and peace itself.[4] The long-term increase in revenue was in part due to the territorial growth of the state. It also owed something to Victor Amadeus' ability to extend and increase the tax burden within his existing territories (above all Piedmont). This involved both an extension of 'state' activity in the fiscal sphere and the achievement of greater integration and uniformity at the expense of hitherto privileged areas and groups, including the clergy and nobility.[5] Success also, however, depended to a considerable degree on the duke's ability both to encourage his own subjects to advance him money and to secure foreign funds in the form of subsidies from his wealthier allies, which were made available to enable him to wage war more effectively and to swing the military balance in north Italy. These other sources had important implications for the Savoyard state. On the one hand, foreign subsidies enabled Victor Amadeus to avoid making greater (and perhaps politically risky), demands on his subjects threatening the earlier achievement of Savoyard 'absolutism'. On the other hand, the short-term sacrifice of resources and authority at home, and the near chaos associated with fiscal crisis and expediency necessitated a programme of retrenchment and reform after 1713, one which was part and parcel of the major overhaul of the institutions of the Savoyard state of 1717.

The financial history of the Savoyard state in this era is well understood, due primarily to the magnificent and still unsurpassed work of Luigi Einaudi and Giuseppe Prato on the War of the Spanish Succession.[6] Our understanding of the financial aspects of Savoyard participation in

---

[4] For a temporary decline in ducal (or royal) revenues after 1713, see G. Quazza, *Le riforme in Piemonte nella prima metà del Settecento*, 2 vols. (Modena, 1957), I, 175.

[5] G. Levi, *L'Eredità immateriale: carriera di un esorcista nel Piemonte del Seicento* (Turin, 1985), 171; English translation: *Inheriting Power: the story of an exorcist* (Chicago, 1988), 145.

[6] L. Einaudi, 'Le entrate pubbliche dello stato sabaudo nei bilanci e nei conti dei Tesorieri durante la Guerra di Successione Spagnuola' in *CGP*, IX, and *La finanza sabauda all'aprirsi del secolo XVIII e durante la guerra spagnuola* (Turin, 1908); G. Prato, 'Il costo della Guerra di Successione Spagnuola e le spese pubbliche in Piemonte dal 1700 al 1713', *CGP*, X.

the Nine Years War has also been enhanced by Enrico Stumpo's study of the relationship between Savoyard state finance and society in the seventeenth century as a whole, a work underpinned by a view that ever since the reign of Emanuel Filibert the Savoyard state and its development – fiscal and otherwise – was intimately bound up with war.[7] However, Stumpo's account of the fiscal aspects of Savoyard participation in the Nine Years War, the most expensive fought by the Savoyard state in the seventeenth century, but less abundantly documented than the subsequent conflict, is not exhaustive. In addition, although Symcox makes excellent use of the work of both Einaudi and Stumpo in his study of Victor Amadeus II, the Savoyard experience between 1690 and 1720 has not received the attention it merits in broader treatments of war and finance in this era. Dickson and Sperling's invaluable brief survey of war finance in these decades focuses on the Great Powers, Austria, Britain, the Dutch Republic and France, all of whom (except Austria) were givers rather than receivers of subsidies. Similarly, a recent collection of essays, edited by Philip T. Hoffmann and Kathryn Norberg, on fiscal crisis and political systems in early modern Europe ignores the smaller states of Italy (and Germany) and, in consequence, fails to consider a number of issues, including the crucial importance of foreign subsidies, at least for many of the smaller states, which were the norm in early modern Europe, with important implications for the editors' thesis regarding the superiority of one type of regime over another as a means of raising revenues. More recently, the volume on state finance, edited by Bonney in the European Science Foundation's Origins of the Modern State in Europe project also effectively ignores the role of foreign subsidies in state formation. It is hoped that the present chapter, on the relationship between finance, war and state formation in the Savoyard state between 1690 and 1720 will not only illuminate that subject but also extend the larger discussion of finance and state formation in early modern Europe.[8]

---

[7] E. Stumpo, *Finanza e stato moderno nel Piemonte del Seicento* (Rome, 1979), esp. 149 ff. For Stumpo the reign of Charles Emanuel II represented an abortive attempt (by means of that duke's mercantilist policies) to break out of a cycle of dependence upon development by war.

[8] P. T. Hoffmann and K. Norberg, eds., *Fiscal Crises, Liberty and Representative Government 1450–1789* (Stanford, 1994), esp. 1 ff. (but see the critical remarks of Jeremy Black, particularly of the editors' thesis regarding the greater ability of representative institutions to raise revenues, in *Parliamentary History*, 14/3, 1995, 349 ff). R. Bonney, ed., *Economic Systems and State Finance* (Oxford, 1995). For subsidies, see G. Otruba, 'Die Bedeutung englischer Subsidien und Antizipationen für die Finanzen Österreichs 1701 bis 1748', *Vierteljahrschrift für Sozial- und Wirtschaftsgeschichte*, LI, 1964. There is not an extensive literature on subsidies in English, but see P. G. M. Dickson, *Finance and Government under Maria Theresia 1740–1780* (Oxford, 1987), II, 157 ff.

SAVOYARD FINANCES c. 1689

On the eve of Victor Amadeus' entry into the Nine Years War, his ordinary revenues (i.e. those he was entitled to in peacetime) totalled 7.5 million lire net. This represented a substantial increase, of nearly 20 per cent during the previous twenty years and signalled the Savoyard state's prosperity and recovery from the consequences of the plague of 1630, the civil war of 1639–41 and foreign wars to 1659. The vast bulk, over 75 per cent, of these revenues came from Piedmont, which contributed nearly 5.9 million lire. The Duchy of Savoy supplied just under 1.7 million, the County of Nice just over 16,000 lire. Only in the Duchy of Aosta was the duke of Savoy still constrained by the need to deal with an assembly with power to vote or not vote some of his revenues (i.e. those collected directly).[9] In many respects the fiscal structure of the Savoyard state in 1689 remained very much that created by Emanuel Filibert in the later sixteenth century. In Piedmont, revenues were raised in fairly equal proportion by direct and indirect taxes. The former included the *tasso*, a land tax, to which most of the non-exempt population was subject, although individual communities, each responsible for its own quota, might prefer to raise it indirectly. The *tasso* was effectively fixed, and its yield only increased with the acquisition of new territories (for example, the provinces of Alba and Trino in 1631). Allocated between Piedmont's fourteen provinces, the largest single quota being paid by Turin, the *tasso* raised just under 1 million lire in 1689, although since substantial parts of the *tasso* had been alienated in the past, both to reward and to raise funds in the short term, the burden it represented was greater than the amount received by the duke of Savoy. Calculated largely on the same basis as the *tasso* was the *sussidio militare*, introduced in 1659 as a temporary measure to finance the army and confirmed thereafter on an annual basis. By 1689 it was effectively (but not officially) permanent, and yielded 1.2 million lire (net). The *comparto dei grani*, introduced in 1572 to feed the army and decreed each year at the time of the harvest, was also raised largely according to the criteria of the *tasso*, but payable in kind or cash. Turin again supplied the largest provincial quota, towards an ordinary annual total of 30,000 sacks of grain.

---

[9] This and the next paragraph largely follow Stumpo, *Finanza e stato moderno*, esp. ch. 1. M. Abrate, 'Elementi per la storia della finanza dello Stato Sabaudo nella seconda metà del XVII secolo', *BSBS*, LXVIII, 1969, is useful but should be read with Stumpo's remarks on its misunderstanding of Savoyard budgets (and consequent exaggeration of the growth in revenues to 1689) in mind. There is a very brief account of the tax system in C. Salsotto, 'Fossano e la battaglia di Torino (1706)', *CGP*, VIII, 428–9.

Indirect taxes meant above all the general gabelles. These included that on salt (from which the province of Mondovì remained exempt in 1689), and the customs, exploiting the transit trade across the duke's territories between France and Italy which had been deliberately encouraged by successive dukes of Savoy, in order to stimulate the economic development of their state. The salt gabelle, founded on an obligation on all over five years (and their animals) to consume, or buy, a fixed quantity of salt a year, was particularly valuable, yielding just over 1 million lire (net) in 1689. This explained the preoccupation with the maintenance (and updating) of the tax rolls, or *consegne*, and with the prevention of evasion, fraud and contraband, although these were facilitated by the many imperial and papal fiefs enclaved within Victor Amadeus' territories and by Mondovì's privileged status. As for expenditure, one third of ducal income in 1689 went on the army. Another third was taken by the ducal and other households, including that of Victor Amadeus' mother, Madama Reale, and by the appanages established by Charles Emanuel I in the 1620s for his two younger sons, Tommaso and Maurizio. Administration, diplomacy, pensions and so on absorbed another 1 million lire, as did repayment of debt (the long-term debt totalling just over 16 million lire).[10]

Tax revenues were collected in two basic ways, familiar to students of *ancien régime* Europe: directly by state officials (what was called *economia* or *économie*) and indirectly, by the contracting out or 'farming' of collection to private organisations. The *tasso* (and, in Savoy, its equivalent, the taille) and *sussidio militare* were in the former category and the gabelles in the latter, different gabelles generally being farmed to a number of different contractors. Collection seems to have been effective enough, local communities being responsible for getting their quotas to the ducal receivers/treasurers, but since the sums collected were paid to a variety of central agencies, it is often difficult to get a clear view of revenues and expenditure at any single moment. Most revenues in fact went to the treasurer general (of Piedmont) but the *sussidio militare* went to the treasurer general of the militia while the revenues from Savoy were assigned to the treasurer of the royal household. Compensating in some degree for this confusion was the obligation on ducal officials and private tax farmers to present their

---

[10] E. Casanova, 'Contributo alla biografia di Pietro Micca e di Maria Chiaberge Bricco e alla storia del voto di Vittorio Amedeo II', *CGP*, VIII, reproduces the *gabelle* roll or *consegna* of Sagliano, one of the six communities of the marchesato of Andorno, 1701, 182 ff., and that of Pianezza for 1702, 206 ff. On the concern with fraud, see the Senate of Turin's lengthy investigation from 1677 into tax exemptions granted by the *podestà* of Santena, which ultimately bogged down in the outbreak of war and death of the *podestà* (1690) and the supposed loss of many relevant papers following French raids in 1691, Levi, *Inheriting Power*, 118–19. The Carignano appanage included the proceeds of the *tabellionato* (or tax on legal contracts) in Piedmont, Einaudi, 'Entrate pubbliche', *CGP*, IX, 34.

accounts, the first via the controllore generale and the second via the generale delle finanze, to the Turin Camera dei Conti in Piedmont and in Savoy to the Chambre des Comptes at Chambéry. The co-operation of these two bodies was also necessary for any new tax measures (which they must formally register). Such co-operation, to a limited degree, compensated for the demise of representative assemblies with tax-granting powers in most of the constituent territories of the Savoyard state, but could not be taken for granted (see Chapter 4). The same was true of the Duchy of Aosta, where such a tax-granting assembly survived.[11]

Despite the persistence of traditional structures and practices, there were important developments in financial, as in some other areas of Savoyard, administration before the cycle of wars, suggesting that it would be wrong to see 1690 as the start of a wholly unprecedented reforming phase in the Savoyard state. Fiscal policy was the responsibility of the Council of Finance, established by Charles Emanuel I (1588), and reformed (1678) during Madama Reale's regency, which was attended by the duke and his leading financial officials. Victor Amadeus, however, was very much in control of financial as of other aspects of government.[12] In 1687 the duke had abolished the posts of intendente generale of the *sussidio militare* and of generale delle finanze of Savoy and created a new post, that of generale delle finanze (held by conte Marelli), to oversee the ordinary functioning of the fiscal machinery of both Savoy and Piedmont. The budget of 1689 represented a new development in integrating revenues from Savoy with those of Piedmont, and also in listing net revenues (hitherto gross revenues had been recorded, plus the alienations and resulting net revenue). There was still a long way to go: some persistent problems, particularly communal debt (largely accumulated to meet ducal tax demands in previous wars) and the unequal distribution of the tax burden both within and between communities, although acknowledged, remained largely unaddressed.[13] Nevertheless, the financial

[11] In Jan. 1690, Victor Amadeus' future envoy to London and The Hague, the comte and président de la Tour, of the Chambéry Chambre des Comptes, was negotiating with potential farmers of the Savoy tobacco gabelle, which the duke was still undecided whether to farm or to administer directly, VA to DLT, 28 Jan. 1690, Turin, AST/LM/ Olanda, m. 1; see G. Pérouse, 'Etat de la Savoie à la fin du XVIIe siècle (1679–1713). Documents inédits recueillis aux archives de Turin', *MSSHA*, LXIII, 1926, 37 ff. Accounting procedures are described by Einaudi, 'Entrate pubbliche', *CGP*, IX, 3 ff. For the assigning of specific expenditure to specific funds in 1710, see *ibid.*, 27–8.

[12] See VA to DLT and others requesting draft edicts on a number of measures to raise money, including the wine gabelle of Chambéry, Jan. or Feb. 1690, AST/LM/ Olanda, m. 1.

[13] Stumpo, *Finanza e stato moderno*, 236 ff., queries the extent of communal debt, but detailed studies confirm its seriousness. By 1690, Pancalieri had a total debt equal to more than sixteen times its average annual income (and a consolidated debt, in the form of *censi*, i.e. long-term obligations, equal to more than six times that average).

administration of the Savoyard state was already increasingly sophisticated and was making for fuller integration of the different territories into a single structure before 1690.

THE FISCAL CRISIS

Between 1690 and 1713 Victor Amadeus' expenditure grew enormously. Not all of this was military. In 1690, the duke promised what was for him a very large sum, 1 million lire, to the emperor, in return for the grant of the prestigious so-called royal treatment (see Chapter 3) and the confirmation of an earlier imperial grant, to Victor Amadeus I, of the right to purchase the mediate superiority over a number of imperial vassals in the territories enclaved within and adjacent to the Savoyard state.[14] Thereafter, and particularly during the interval of peace between the Nine Years War and the War of the Spanish Succession, the duke spent substantial sums on what we might call 'cheque-book state building', acquiring fiefs in the Langhe district: Desana, Camerano, Berneglio and part of the marquisate of Gorzegno.[15] But the driving force behind the rocketing expenditure was war. Between the summers of 1690 and 1696, a series of military budgets (which may underestimate the real total) put Victor Amadeus' extraordinary military spending during the Nine Years War as a whole at over 50 million lire (see Table 2.1). War effectively meant a doubling of pre-war expenditure.[16]

Peace from mid-1696 allowed a sharp reduction in the military budget, to a level closer to that before 1690. However, participation in the War of the Spanish Succession again pushed up spending (Table 2.2). Overall, between 1701 and 1713, extraordinary expenditure probably totalled 84

Most of that debt had been accumulated in the wars between 1620 and 1660, S. Caligaris, 'Vita e lavoro in una comunità rurale piemontese: Pancalieri nei secc. XVII–XVIII', *Bollettino della Società per gli Studi Storici Archeologici ed Artistici della Provincia di Cuneo*, 90–1, 1984, supplemento, 7 ff.

[14] D. Carutti, *Storia della diplomazia della Corte di Savoia*, 4 vols. (Turin, 1875–80), III, 175. Victor Amadeus justified to the French court this payment on the grounds that it enabled him to end the contraband traffic which exploited the proximity of these imperial territories and reduced his revenues, R. Oresko, 'The dipomatic background to the Glorioso Rimpatrio: the rupture between Vittorio Amedeo II and Louis XIV (1688–90)', in A. de Lange, ed., *Dall'Europa alle Valli Valdesi* (Turin, 1990), 272.

[15] G. Tabacco, *Lo stato sabaudo nel Sacro Impero Romano* (Turin, 1939), 143 ff.

[16] Stumpo, *Finanza e stato moderno*, 87, 93 ff. and budgets in AST/Contabilità Generali Diverse, Categoria 1, Ser. 1, Bilancio Militare Annuale, 1674–96 and 1695–6. Prato, 'Il costo', *CGP*, X, 260, gives Victor Amadeus' military costs in a rather different form. However, they broadly agree with those above: the cost of Victor Amadeus' army, which had averaged 1.8 million lire p.a. in the late 1680s, had nearly doubled to 2.8 million in 1690 and leapt to 4 million in 1691. It continued to grow, to 5.8 million in 1692, 6.2 million in 1693 and 7.5 million in 1694, at which level it remained in 1695, before rocketing to a peak of almost 9.4 million in 1696.

Table 2.1. *Savoyard military expenditure 1690–1696*

1690 (budgeted before June 1690)	3,233,990 lire	
1691 (Jan.–Oct. inclusive)	4,045,440	
	6 months winter quarters (Nov.–Apr. inclusive)	6 months of campaign (May–Oct. inclusive)
1691–2	3,306,521	2,794,422
1692–3	4,803,959	2,875,670
1693–4	5,306,104	3,744,030
1694–5	5,723,243	4,196,380
1695–6	5,980,033	4,617,041

Table 2.2. *Savoyard military expenditure 1700–1709*

Year	Lire
1700	2,750,000
1701	4,738,341
1702	5,330,000
1703	5,450,000
1704	9,877,230
1705	4,917,002
1706–7	7,896,546
1707–8	7,268,000
1708–9	8,000,000

Source: Prato, 'Il costo', *CGP*, X, 260.

million, or another 6.5 million lire a year – although, since Victor Amadeus' ordinary, peacetime revenue had risen by a third to between 10 and 11 million lire between 1688 and 1700, this represented a smaller relative increase in expenditure than during the previous conflict. It is also noteworthy that although victory outside Turin in 1706 eased the pressure on the Savoyard state, the fiscal burden of the war remained high thereafter. The conclusion of the war in 1713 again allowed Victor Amadeus to reduce his outgoings. However, the war for Sicily (1718–20), despite its limited scale – by contrast with those fought between 1690 and 1713 – was also very costly.[17]

All aspects of warfare involved substantial new expenditure.[18] Recruit-

---

[17] See Quazza, *La riforme*, I, 101 ff.
[18] Prato, 'Il costo', *CGP*, X, 260 (but note Stumpo's criticisms of these figures as underestimating the true level of war expenditure, *Finanza e stato moderno*, 13 ff). According to the calculations of the generale delle finanze's office in 1711, Victor Amadeus' military expenditure between 1703 and end 1710 totalled just under 57.5

ing in Victor Amadeus' own states was costly; levies abroad more so.[19] Horses, which could only be purchased abroad in sufficient numbers, were expensive, as were draught animals.[20] War also meant a need for more arms and munitions, which were also sometimes purchased abroad (see Chapter 1). Clothing the growing number of troops in Victor Amadeus' pay was also expensive,[21] and might necessitate expensive imports,[22] as might grain to feed those men following both the loss of territory and poor harvests (see below, p. 84). The supply of provisions and funds to Victor Amadeus' own allies, above all to the poorly financed and supplied imperial troops, who might not otherwise have been of use, further burdened ducal finances. In the War of the Spanish Succession, when the duke effectively subsidised the emperor's war effort in Italy, it contributed to the deteriorating relations between Turin and Vienna.[23] Victor Amadeus' fortifications also required substantial expenditure, which (by contrast with most of the items above) remained high between the wars.[24] The problems caused by this increase in expenditure were

million lire, an average of just over 7 million lire a year, whereas peacetime expenditure on the army averaged just under 2.9 million lire (remarkably close to the figure before 1690), P. Derege di Donato, 'Stato generale dei danni patiti dal Piemonte nella Guerra di Successione di Spagna dall'ottobre 1703 a tutto il 1710', *CGP*, IX, 422.

[19] Victor Amadeus generally allowed his captains about 30 lire per man recruited in this period, and in 1689 gave 1,148 lire for the recruiting of companies of forty men to a number of his infantry captains, AST/MM/UGS, m. 2/11. For various sums issued to recruiting captains as part of Victor Amadeus' entry into the Nine Years War, see AST/PCF reg. 1692–93, f. 1 (L3673 to major Fasanini, for recruiting the Savoy regiment), f. 2 (L8480 to marchese Pallavicino for the levy of the Aosta regiment), f. 10 (L315 to cavaliere Pensa and cavaliere Tana to make good shortfalls of men in their companies); see W. Barberis, *Le armi del principe: la tradizione militare sabauda* (Turin, 1988), 142–3, for sums spent by one officer levying men in Savoy in 1702. The previous year the duke had given nearly 74,000 lire to Colonel Reding, to bring a regiment of 600 Swiss to Piedmont, Prato, 'Il costo', *CGP*, X, 282.

[20] In 1704 the bankers Lullin and Nicolas advanced (i.e. lent) 468,000 lire for the purchase of 1,300 horses in Switzerland; while after the victory at Turin in 1706 Victor Amadeus sent agents abroad to buy the nearly 2,000 horses of which his cavalry were short, Prato, 'Il costo', *CGP*, X, 292–3. In 1703 the contractors who were to supply the artillery train demanded more than 29,000 lire, Prato, 'Il costo', *CGP*, X, 292 ff.

[21] In 1703, Gamba advanced over 320,000 lire for the clothing of various units, Prato, 'Il costo', *CGP*, X, 302.

[22] Between the winter of 1708–9 and 1713, Victor Amadeus spent substantial sums on imported English cloth for this purpose: see G. Symcox, 'Britain and Victor Amadeus II: or the use and abuse of allies', in S. B. Baxter, ed., *England's Rise to Greatness 1660–1763* (Berkeley, 1983), 175.

[23] By early 1706, the emperor owed more than 7 million lire for supplies since 1703, VA to Briançon, 3 Apr. 1706, Turin, *CGP*, V, 468 ff. After 1713, Victor Amadeus used this debt, now put at 9 million lire, to justify to the emperor his acceptance of the Utrecht peace, A. Tallone, 'Vittorio Amedeo II e la Quadruplice Alleanza', *Studi su Vittorio Amedeo II* (Turin, 1933), 196.

[24] J. Nicolas, *La Savoie au 18e siècle: noblesse et bourgeoisie*, 2 vols. (Paris, 1978), I, 47 ff.;

magnified by its often erratic character, and by severe wartime inflation.[25] The six months of winter quarters (November to April) always involved much greater expenditure (on new levies, recruits and other preparations for the campaign) than did the six months (May to October) of campaigning itself. Initial mobilisation, and defeat, also meant substantial, unbudgeted costs. The fiscal pressure was severe throughout the Nine Years War, but was especially acute following Victor Amadeus' defeats in 1690 and 1693.[26] In the War of the Spanish Succession, he was particularly hard pressed in the winter of 1703–04[27] and the summer of 1706.[28]

That Victor Amadeus managed to finance this growing expenditure was the more remarkable in view of the fact that his peacetime revenues from Savoy and Nice, both occupied by the enemy, and sometimes those from much of Piedmont too, were severely reduced. The French conquest of Savoy and Nice in the first year of the Nine Years War effectively deprived the duke of the revenues he received from those territories.[29] The situation worsened in early 1691, when the French occupied much of western Piedmont as well.[30] The French were soon cleared from Piedmont, but the duke was obliged to grant tax exemptions for war devastation and to encourage loyalty.[31] In addition, those communities

Prato, 'Il costo', *CGP*, X, 327 ff.
[25] S. J. Woolf, 'Sviluppo economico e struttura sociale in Piemonte da Emanuele Filiberto a Carlo Emanuele III', *NRS*, 46, 1962, 1, 25 ff.; F. Bonelli, 'Mercato dei cereali e sviluppo agrario nella seconda metà del Settecento: un sondaggio per il Cuneese', *RSI*, 80, 1968, 807–8.
[26] Victor Amadeus spent about 1 million pistoles to make good his losses following his defeat at Marsaglia, VDM to Fagel, 19 Oct. 1693, Turin, ARAH/SG/8644/78.
[27] See VA to the duke of Marlborough, 1 Dec. 1703, Poirino, *CGP*, V, 278, claiming that, since declaring for the allies (in October) he had spent over 600,000 écus on increasing his troops, and on his fortresses, and must spend more levying troops in Switzerland.
[28] In the spring of 1706, the duke put his expenditure on fortifications at the equivalent of 60,000 Dutch gilders a week and on transports at 8,000 gilders a day; and claimed only to have funds for the first two months of campaigning, VDM to Fagel, 1 Apr. 1706, Turin, ARAH/EA/VDM/30, 230.
[29] The loss of Nice also affected the duke's other revenues. Before 1691, much of the salt for the salt gabelles was imported through Nice whose loss disrupted supply until, in the winter of 1692–3 the Genoese allowed Victor Amadeus to import salt through their territories, VDM to Fagel, 5 Jan. 1693, Turin, ARAH/SG/8644/1. Some of this salt came from Venice and, following the fall of Casale (1695) Victor Amadeus began to ship it along the Po. Unfortunately, the king of Spain banned its passage across the Milanese, provoking the duke to threaten that he might negotiate with the French to again import salt through Nice, same to same, 5 May 1696, Turin, ARAH/SG/8644/ 256.   [30] VA to Operti, 15 July 1691, Moncalieri, copy in AST/LM/Olanda, m. 1.
[31] Cuneo, both strategically important and the capital of a province which yielded the third highest share of both the *comparto dei grani* and the *tasso*, was rewarded for its successful resistance to enemy siege in 1691 by exemption from all taxes for three years, Duboin, XXIII, 252.

within reach of Pinerolo remained vulnerable to French raids, while Victor Amadeus' second defeat, in 1693, was followed by a wider French irruption into Piedmont, weakening taxpaying capacity and impeding collection of the duke's revenues.[32] These problems continued to dog the ducal finances until the end of the Nine Years War.[33] In the War of the Spanish Succession, too, Victor Amadeus' revenues were hit by enemy occupation,[34] the devastation caused by troops on both sides,[35] and the need (particularly in 1705–06) to 'trade' revenues, in the form of tax exemptions, for loyalty and service.[36] In early 1706, it was calculated that the war had reduced ducal revenues by 5,298,963 lire (whereas expenditure since October 1703 totalled 29,067,593 lire). The worst was over by 1707, but ducal revenues did not recover immediately thereafter. When, in December 1710, with the conflict apparently drawing to an end, Victor Amadeus began to prepare an (unsuccessful) claim for a war indemnity from Louis XIV, the generale delle finanze's office put his lost revenues since 1703 at 26 million lire in total.[37]

Victor Amadeus' financial problems were compounded by the impact of some of the worst harvests of the seventeenth and eighteenth centuries. These caused high grain prices and dearth, reduced the ability of his subjects to pay rents and taxes, and obliged him to purchase grain abroad. In the Nine Years War, the worst years were 1693–94, but late snows in 1694–95 also hit the 1695 harvest, again reducing the ability of his subjects to supply the war effort. In October 1695 he attributed the arrears owed to two Huguenot regiments in his service to the fact that the communities of Piedmont on which their pay was assigned had been

---

[32] For the vulnerability of the area between Carmagnola and Turin (including Santena) between 1690 and 1693, see Levi, *Inheriting Power*, 59, 125. Much of the devastation of late 1693 was recorded in a survey by ducal officials in early 1694: see the deposition of the priest of Pianezza in E. Casanova, 'Contributo alla biografia di Pietro Micca e di Maria Chiaberge Bricco', *CGP*, VIII, 178–9.

[33] William III's envoy attributed Victor Amadeus' severe shortage of funds in part to the presence of the French in Piedmont, preventing the collection of his revenues: earl of Galway to Shrewsbury, 19 June 1696, Turin, W. Coxe, *Private and Original Correspondence of Charles Talbot, Duke of Shrewsbury* (London, 1821), 295–7.

[34] In the winter of 1707–08 it was estimated that the revenue from the gabelles (which before the war had yielded 4 million lire) had been halved by the loss of Savoy and Nice, VDM to Fagel, 4 Jan. 1708, Turin, ARAH/EA/VDM/32, 1 ff.

[35] See Derege di Donato, 'Stato generale dei danni', *CGP*, IX, passim; and Einaudi, *Finanza sabauda*, 370 ff.

[36] In 1705, the duke remitted the community of Govone's *tasso* for that year, and exempted the inhabitants of Mosso from the *tasso* for ten years, for resisting French demands, VDM to States, 20 May and 17 June 1705, Turin, ARAH/EA/VDM.30, 54, 68.

[37] P. Derege di Donato, 'Stato generale dei danni', *CGP*, IX, 422–3. It would clearly be unwise to accept this calculation at face value. Nevertheless, it is a useful indicator, particularly of the provinces and communities most affected.

badly hit by the poor weather, and later claimed that dearth throughout Piedmont meant that he could not expect his normal revenues.[38] During the War of the Spanish Succession, the poor harvests of 1708 and 1709 again caused dearth in Piedmont, reducing the ability of Victor Amadeus' subjects to pay taxes and obliging him to purchase foreign grain.[39] The Savoyard state was not alone in being vulnerable to the vagaries of the weather in an overwhelmingly agrarian European economy,[40] in which all recognised that tax yields depended on harvests.[41] Victor Amadeus could even benefit by selling grain to his own subjects at a profit, as in 1708–09.[42] But these considerations did not make his predicament any the less serious or easier to bear.

This erosion of revenues could affect Victor Amadeus' military preparations: in the winter of 1693–94, he had to reject a proposal to take a Swiss regiment of two battalions and take just one, because he simply did not have the funds for more.[43] As for the conduct of the war, he was obliged to do what he could to defend his tax base, detaching small units to fend off French raids, and arming his subjects when and where necessary.[44] He was also obliged to turn a blind eye to trade between his subjects and the enemy, working against his own strategic interests and provoking difficulties with those among his allies who wanted a complete ban on trade with France. In the winter of 1692–93, the Dutch commissary in Turin learnt that, despite the blockade of Pinerolo ordered by Victor Amadeus, his subjects were in fact supplying it, with his permission. Saint-Thomas explained that Victor Amadeus' subjects had been

[38] VA to DLT, 22 Oct. and 5 Nov. 1695, and ST to DLT, 22 Oct. 1695, all Turin, AST/LM/Olanda, m. 4. See M. Dossetti, 'Aspetti demografici del Piemonte occidentale nei secoli XVII e XVIII', *BSBS*, 75, 1977, 127 ff. and Levi, *Inheriting Power*, 125–6.

[39] VDM to Fagel, 3 Sept. 1708, Balbote, ARAH/EA/VDM/32, f. 170; same to same, 6 Feb. and 16 Mar. 1709, Turin, ARAH/EA/VDM/33, f. 15 and 43. The price of grain in Piedmont doubled between 1700 and 1709 (peaking at 5 lire a measure) but had returned to its 1700 level by 1713, Einaudi, 'Entrate pubbliche', *CGP*, IX, 345. In 1709, Victor Amadeus spent over 1,000,000 million lire in Venice alone on grain purchases, Prato, 'Il costo', *CGP*, X, 292 ff.

[40] See Dickson and Sperling, 'War finance', 305. In 1709, the commissary accompanying the imperial troops in north Italy had to pay much more than in 1708 to the bread contractors, VDM to Fagel, 9 Jan. 1709, Turin, ARAH/EA/VDM/1709, f. 6.

[41] In June 1696, Galway approved the duke's supposedly innocent negotiations with the French since it allowed his subjects time (before the negotiations were broken off) to get in the harvest, thus preventing famine and providing the revenues without which Victor Amadeus could not fight the coming campaign, Galway to Shrewsbury, 19 June 1696, Turin, Coxe, *Shrewsbury Papers*, 295 ff.

[42] Einaudi, 'Entrate pubbliche', 41. His profit was said to be 1,000,000 lire.

[43] Galway to Trenchard, 13 Feb. and 19 Mar. 1694, Zurich, SP 92/26, f. 53, 87.

[44] In the winter of 1690–1, following an order from the French intendant at Pinerolo, that the nearby Piedmontese villages pay extraordinary contributions for its garrison, further reducing his tax base, the duke armed the population to resist, VDM to Fagel, 17 Feb. 1691, Turin, ARAH/SG/8643/105.

allowed to supply the garrison there with wine (but not food) largely in response to the demands of the local population, particularly the inhabitants of Cumiana and Bricherasio, who otherwise could not pay the ducal taxes.[45] During the War of the Spanish Succession, too, the duke permitted the transit of goods to and from France and Italy, partly in response to demands from the local merchant community, partly out of a desire not to lose badly needed customs revenues.[46]

Victor Amadeus could and did reduce his non-military expenditure. From 1690 the annual ducal grant to the Turin Ospedale di Carità, of 9,000 lire and 200 sacks of corn, was stopped (and only resumed in 1700); and in the winter of 1693–94 the duke cut his usual subsidy to the Turin carnival festivities.[47] Similarly, only half of 60,000 lire promised by Victor Amadeus (May 1703) to conte Galleani and the banker Antonio Costeis for a silk manufactory was paid, in the multifaceted crisis following his *volte-face* in autumn 1703.[48] Victor Amadeus' ability to meet his financial obligations might also prevent him from achieving other major objectives. At the end of the 1690 campaign, unable to pay the emperor the 1 million lire promised earlier for the royal treatment and the right to acquire imperial fiefs, he feared that Leopold might not confirm these grants. Clearly, the cost of war might reduce the duke's ability to exert patronage and give a lead within his own territories, and threaten the achievement of other ambitions.[49] He therefore needed to find new sources of revenue.

THE CONTRIBUTION OF VICTOR AMADEUS' STATES, 1690–1713

Victor Amadeus' revenues necessarily expanded to meet his rocketing expenditure between 1690–96 and 1701–13. Between 1690 and 1696, he raised more than 70 million lire, to fund not just the cost of his war effort (50 million), but also to offset the loss (perhaps 20 million) of his ordinary revenues from Savoy, Nice and Piedmont, funding total expenditure of about 100 million lire.[50] During the War of the Spanish

---

[45] VDM to Fagel, 20 Feb. and 13 Apr. 1693, Turin, ARAH/SG/8644/14, 23; ST to DLT, 4 May 1693, Turin, AST/LM/Olanda, m. 3.

[46] VDM to States, 3 June 1705, Turin, ARAH/EA/VDM/30, 61.

[47] Cavallo, *Charity and Power in Early Modern Italy: benefactors and their motives in Turin 1541–1789* (Cambridge, 1995), 133; VDM to Fagel, 15 Feb. 1694, Turin, ARAH/SG/8644/106.   [48] Prato, 'Il costo', *CGP*, X, 354.

[49] VA to conte Tarino, 20 Oct. 1690, Turin, AST/LM/Austria, m. 22. In January 1692, however, the duke's ambassador was finally received at the Imperial court with the so-called 'royal treatment', Tarino to VA, 6 Jan. 1692, Vienna, AST/LM/Vienna, m. 25.

[50] Stumpo, *Finanza e stato moderno*, 91 ff.

Succession, the duke's revenues rose from just under 9.5 million lire in 1700 to a wartime peak of more than 18.5 million lire in 1708, falling back to below 12.5 million lire in 1713.[51] Victor Amadeus could not have waged war between 1690 and 1713 without foreign subsidies and to a much lesser degree some domestic windfalls.[52] However, his own subjects shouldered the burden of his wars. Despite the losses of territories and revenues in both conflicts, and the resort to extraordinary means, the duke's ordinary revenues (i.e. those normally received in peacetime as opposed to the extraordinary ones levied in wartime), especially those he received from Piedmont, remained the foundation of his finances in both the Nine Years War and the War of the Spanish Succession. Broadly speaking, Victor Amadeus' subjects contributed 60 million of the more than 70 million lire he raised in extraordinary revenues (and 85 million of the 100 million in total) in the Nine Years War; and 75 per cent of all his revenues in the War of the Spanish Succession.[53]

The duke's ordinary peacetime revenues, above all the gabelles, remained crucial.[54] They could (by contrast with the fixed-rate *tasso*, for example) be made to yield more by being farmed out after competitive bidding. In January 1696, Victor Amadeus farmed the salt and customs together for that year, for 2.1 million lire, on condition that no compensation would be given for any shortfall but that he should receive 75 per cent of any profit.[55] In 1698 the gabelles were again farmed together, for five years, to a French consortium, reflecting the extent to which the inability of the duke's own subjects to take the farm left him, in this sphere at least, still something of a French satellite after 1696.[56] However, on the expiry of this contract, the farm was won with a higher bid for the

---

[51] Einaudi, 'Entrate pubbliche', *CGP*, IX, table XXX and passim. As with the figures for Victor Amadeus' armed forces, extreme caution is necessary when dealing with any figures: see *ibid.*, passim.

[52] Victor Amadeus was a beneficiary from the death (1692) of Princess Maria Ludovica, widow of Prince Maurizio (who had died in 1659). Although she made bequests to other members of the ducal family and to the members of her household, the princess made Victor Amadeus her 'universal heir'. This meant the final liquidation of one of the two apanages created by Charles Emanuel I for his sons.

[53] Einaudi, *Finanza sabauda*, 342 ff.; Woolf, 'Sviluppo economico e struttura sociale', 3.

[54] The pursuit of contraband salt in the valleys near Pinerolo provided various ducal officials – notably Gropello, intendant of justice and finance from 1695 – with excellent opportunities for secret negotiations with the French there (and a plausible explanation for their being in the locality if their presence became known): see ST to DLT, 17 Apr. 1696, Turin, AST/LM/Olanda, m. 5.

[55] VDM to Fagel, 6 Jan. 1696, Turin, ARAH/SG/8644/231; Duboin, XXII, 1991. That same month the tobacco, pipes and acquavita gabelles were farmed to a merchant of Lyons, Duboin, XXII, 67.

[56] Einaudi, *Finanza sabauda*, 2 ff. According to one report, the 1,000,000 lire advanced by the farmers funded new artillery, Bazan to Carlos II, 15 Nov. 1697, Turin, AGS/E/3659, 95.

five years from 1703 to 1708 by a Piedmontese consortium, led by barone Marcello Gamba and conte Silvestro Olivero, both ducal 'officials' (auditors in the Camera dei Conti), but also important 'financiers' without whose help Victor Amadeus could not have kept going in the War of the Spanish Succession.[57] Subsequently, however, falling receipts (reflecting the impact of war) led the duke to adopt a different approach, direct administration, once the consortium's contract ended in 1708. Gabelle revenues grew thereafter, although this upward trend had begun in 1707 and owed as much to the French and Spanish retreat from Piedmont as to any change in administration.[58]

This innovation in the administration of the crucial gabelle revenues in 1708, part of a wider disillusionment with poor yields from tax-farming in Europe in these decades, was in some respects a step of sorts towards greater 'state' control,[59] and had been anticipated by Victor Amadeus' assumption (1697) of the direction and profits of the posts.[60] We should not, however, exaggerate the implications of a measure which was intended above all to maximise revenues, not least by preventing fraud on the part of the tax farmers. Indeed, with the duke less dependent on the financiers who had been so crucial earlier in the War of the Spanish Succession, Gamba and Olivero were accused of fraudulent operation of the farm of the gabelle, and were fined 250,000 lire and 100,000 lire respectively in 1712, in an episode reminiscent of Louis XIV's Chambre de Justice of the 1660s.[61] Direct administration of the gabelles was in fact disappointing and short-lived,[62] while in 1710–11 it was decided to farm the *macina* tax,[63] hitherto collected by local receivers, to improve the yield (without success). A scheme to establish a state bank, imitating developments in other states where this seemed to be a solution to war loans, also failed.[64] Victor Amadeus' approach to financial administration was (as before 1690) a pragmatic one, determined by the

---

[57] Einaudi, 'Entrate pubbliche', *CGP*, IX, 35 ff. Gamba supplied the imperial troops for Victor Amadeus, *CGP*, V, xci. He and Olivero, who held the post of intendente generale (see Chapter 1) in the Nine Years War, were also governors of the Ospedale di Carità in Turin, Cavallo, *Charity and power*, 150–1. For these and other Turin bankers, see F. Rondolino, 'Vita Torinese durante l'Assedio (1703–1707)', *CGP*, VII, passim.

[58] Einaudi, 'Entrate pubbliche', *CGP*, IX, 36.

[59] Ibid., 35; Dickson and Sperling, 'War finance', 313. See the discussion of 'administration' and 'privatisation' in I. A. A. Thompson, *War and Government*, passim.

[60] Einaudi, *Finanza sabauda*, 38; Cavallo, *Charity and power*, 151.

[61] Einaudi, *Finanza sabauda*, 89–90; Einaudi, 'Entrate pubbliche', *CGP*, IX, 87–8; *CGP*, V, xcvii and Prato, 'Il costo', *CGP*, X, 349.

[62] Einaudi, 'Entrate pubbliche', *CGP*, IX, 36.   [63] Einaudi, *Finanza sabauda*, 157–8.

[64] Quazza, *Le riforme*, I, 180; Dickson and Sperling, 'War finance', 310; and A. E. Murphy, 'John Law's proposal for a Bank of Turin (1712)', *Economies et Sociétés, série oeconomia*, 15, 1991.

greater likelihood of one method (farming or direct control) producing more revenue. However, he was also taking an interest in fiscal reform, in the later stages of the War of the Spanish Succession, in part in response to problems thrown up by the integration of newly acquired territories. As in other spheres, reform after 1713 did not emerge from a vacuum.[65]

It was generally accepted that, in wartime, Victor Amadeus could impose certain extraordinary taxes. The single most important of these was the *quartiere d'inverno*, or winter quarter tax, which was levied during the first winter following Victor Amadeus' entry into the Nine Years War. Among the great advantages of the *quartiere d'inverno* from the duke's point of view was that it was not fixed. He could therefore increase it as necessary, more than doubling the annual rate and yield between 1690–91 (12 lire per scudo of tasso, raising nearly 2.6 million lire) and 1695–96 (26 lire per scudo of tasso, yielding over 5.6 million lire). In this way, the duke raised about 26 million lire, i.e. about half of all the extraordinary revenues raised in his own states in the conflict (and nearly double what he received in foreign subsidies). The *quartiere d'inverno* was levied again during the War of the Spanish Succession, from 1704, but at a lower rate than during the previous conflict (especially after 1706) and it raised significantly less, about 18 million lire between then and 1713, than in the six years between 1690 and 1696.[66] From July 1690, Victor Amadeus was also able to double the peacetime *sussidio militare*. Unlike the *quartiere d'inverno*, the *doppio sussidio* was a fixed sum, 1.4 million lire a year, and yielded a total of 9.8 million lire during the Nine Years War.[67] The *sussidio militare* was formally declared permanent (i.e. 'ordinary') by the duke in 1700, substantially increasing his basic revenue.[68] The duke was also able to increase by five-sixths the *comparto dei grani*. This nearly double *comparto* yielded nearly 53,000 sacks of corn a year, worth during the Nine Years War as a whole just under 3.5 million lire. The *comparto* was levied at this rate again

[65] In 1709 Victor Amadeus appointed a commission to consider reform of the customs, partly to facilitate the integration of his newly acquired territories in the Monferrato, Einaudi, *Finanza sabauda*, 24 ff. In 1711, a *mémoire*, probably commissioned by the duke, considered how to improve the administration and yield of the salt gabelles, ibid., 13 ff.

[66] See Stumpo, *Finanza e stato moderno*, 94, and Einaudi, *Finanza sabauda*, 166, for the Nine Years War; and Einaudi, 'Entrate pubbliche', *CGP*, IX, 168 ff., for the War of the Spanish Succession. For what the *quartiere d'inverno* meant locally, see E. Milano, 'La partecipazione alla guerra di successione spagnuola della città di Bra . . .', *CGP*, VIII, 389 ff. and O. Scarzello, 'Corneliano, Piobesi, Monticello d'Alba e Sommariva Perno negli anni di guerra 1704–1708 . . .', *CGP*, VIII, passim.

[67] Duboin, XX, 1442 (July 1690), 1450 (Apr. 1692).

[68] Ibid., 1458. For this reason, although levied during the War of the Spanish Succession it can no longer be included in the category of extraordinary wartime taxes.

between 1704 and 1712.[69] As for the fiscally exempt feudal nobility, in wartime Victor Amadeus could (and did, on a number of occasions from 1691) demand the *cavalcata* from those nobles not serving personally in his armies;[70] and he found other means to tap their wealth.

But Victor Amadeus went further, introducing some new extraordinary revenue-raising measures in the Nine Years War. These included the levy of one-sixth and two-sixths on constituted rents, or *censi*, the *dritto della macina* (levied on corn sent for milling), both introduced in the spring of 1691,[71] a levy on alienated *tasso* (see below),[72] the soap gabelle and stamped paper tax (both in 1694)[73] and the monopoly of the manufacture and sale of candles (1695).[74] These innovations were merely the tip of an iceberg. As in most of the other states at war, the era was fertile in plans for new revenue-raising devices in the Savoyard state. There was talk in Turin of a new tax on pepper, modelled on the tobacco gabelle, in 1693 and in 1695; and of a *capitation* or poll tax (clearly modelled on that introduced in France the previous year), and a house or window tax, in 1696.[75] The sesta and doppia sesta was one of the many extraordinary wartime revenue-raising measures abolished by Victor Amadeus in December 1696 following the end of the war in Italy.[76] But some of the other recent innovations (including the stamped paper tax and the candle monopoly) survived the end of the Nine Years War, and were extended to Savoy following its recovery in 1696 (but not to Aosta, Nice or Oneglia),[77] permanently enhancing ducal revenues. The War of the Spanish Succession inevitably resulted in the reintroduction of some of those innovations of the Nine Years War which had been abolished in 1696 (including, from 1701, the *macina*), some newer measures, including the imposition of a *capitation* in the Duchy of Savoy in 1702[78] and renewed discussion (again without any practical consequences) of some of the abortive revenue-raising schemes considered in the 1690s.[79] However, the later conflict was less fertile in

---

[69] Einaudi, *Finanza sabauda*, 162, 166; Einaudi, 'Entrate pubbliche', *CGP*, IX, 195.

[70] Duboin, XXI, 886. For *cavalcata* payments by the Falletti di Barolo (1691, 1701, 1706 and 1708) see S. J. Woolf, *Studi sulla nobiltà piemontese nell'epoca dell'assolutismo* (Turin, 1963), 69–70.

[71] Duboin, XXI, 1088 ff.; ST to DLT, 8 Apr. 1691, Turin, AST/LM/Olanda, m. 1.

[72] Duboin, XX, 1451.

[73] Duboin, XXII, 422 ff. (stamped paper tax, Sept. 1694) and XXII, 329 ff. (soap monopoly, Feb. 1695). The soap gabelle was replaced in 1700 by a fixed duty, Duboin, XXII, 335.   [74] Duboin, XXII, 337 ff.; Einaudi, *Finanza sabauda*, 35.

[75] VDM to Fagel, 20 May 1695 and 9 Apr. 1696, Turin, ARAH/SG/8644/188, 252.

[76] However, the duke ordered a levy, totalling 500,000 lire to cover the cost of his troops (i.e. their winter quarters) for November and December 1696, Duboin, XX, 1453.

[77] Einaudi, *Finanza sabauda*, 40 ff., 85; Duboin, XXI, 1092, 1099.

[78] Nicolas, *La Savoie*, I, 9 ff., 273 ff. Other extraordinary measures included a levy on Turin's Jewish community, in return for confirmation of its privileges, in 1701, Duboin, II, 401 ff.

new devices than had been the Nine Years War. As in 1696, peace in 1713 saw some wartime fiscal devices (including the *quartiere d'inverno* and the *macina*) removed.[80] But by the end of the War of the Spanish Succession, Victor Amadeus' subjects (particularly those in Piedmont) paid more taxes, which in turn enhanced the duke's revenues.

War also prompted moves to tap the resources of the church, one of the wealthiest institutions in the Savoyard state but also one of the most fiscally privileged. As early as 1692, Victor Amadeus had raised the possibility of taxing the clergy in his states.[81] In 1695, his chief minister Saint-Thomas suggested that the duke approach the archbishop of Turin with a view to securing a grant from the Piedmontese clergy.[82] Subsequently, a number of the bishops of Piedmont assembled in Turin preparatory to an assembly which was to decide upon a free gift, funded by a 10 per cent levy on clerical property.[83] In fact, no specific contribution was made by the clergy before the end of the Nine Years War, but the issue of clerical taxation had been broached. During the fiscal crisis of the spring of 1696, Victor Amadeus ordered the extension of the tax burden to those who had not yet taken holy orders,[84] and in 1697 introduced measures limiting ecclesiastical tax exemptions and their abuse. That same year, the duke asserted a claim to appoint the heads of three major abbeys in his states, and (revealing the fiscal imperative behind this) to receive their revenues in the meantime, resurrecting a long-running argument with Rome over the extent of the ecclesiastical patronage of the duke of Savoy in his states (laid down in an Indult of 1451).[85] These differences exacerbated and were themselves embittered by the clash between Victor Amadeus and Rome which followed his edict of toleration for his Vaudois subjects (1694), which was the price he had to pay for the subsidies he received from England and the Dutch Republic.[86] From 1713 these issues were further complicated by the question of papal recognition of Victor Amadeus as king of Sicily, and later of Sardinia, and were not resolved until the Concordats of 1727 and 1741 which significantly enhanced royal control of the Church in the Savoyard state.

[79] Einaudi, *Finanza sabauda*, 124 ff.
[80] Quazza, *Le riforme*, I, 133; Einaudi, *Finanza sabauda*, 162.
[81] Duboin, XXIII, 204.
[82] VA to ST, 18 June 1695, Frassineto, AST/LPDS, m. 68/13/289.
[83] VDM to Fagel, 2 Dec. 1695, Turin, ARAH/SG/8644/226. According to Einaudi, *Finanza sabauda*, 58, the duke had Pope Innocent XII's permission to tax the clergy to subsidise his war effort.
[84] See decree of intendant of Ivrea and Trino, 17 May 1696, Duboin, XXIII, 217.
[85] Symcox, *Victor Amadeus*, 127 ff.
[86] See Woolf, 'Sviluppo economico e struttura sociale', 47; Symcox, *Victor Amadeus*, 130–1.

Victor Amadeus' wars also gave a decisive stimulus to the so-called *perequazione* (or equalisation, of taxation), a major reform of the fiscal burden which for many historians was the distinctive achievement of Savoyard absolutism in the eighteenth century. A reform of the tax burden (above all of the *tasso*), both to spread that burden more fairly and to increase its yield, had concerned successive dukes of Savoy since the 1560s. In part, therefore, Victor Amadeus was simply pursuing an earlier line of policy. He had initiated a survey in 1688 which was, not surprisingly, abandoned following his entry into the Nine Years War. However, in the fiscal crisis of 1696, the duke ordered that the fiscal burden be properly shared in the communities – not least because the demands of war since 1690 had further wrecked the finances of many communities, necessitating some alleviation. This was followed, once the war ended, by a major enquiry (the first in the Savoyard state), from 1697 onwards, into land values and tax burdens in the County of Nice. This was subsequently extended to the neighbouring provinces of Cuneo and Mondovì, and then to the rest of Piedmont (providing, by the way, a useful insight into the impact of the recent war). Much of southern and western Piedmont had been surveyed by late 1703, when this first phase was, again inevitably, interrupted by the military crisis. Once the crisis of the war was passed, the survey was resumed, from 1709 and had largely been completed by 1711. But whereas the survey had proceeded hitherto on the basis of declarations by local people, henceforth it was entrusted to ducal surveyors and estimators, agents of the state. Checking the reliability of the vast amount of data after 1711 delayed completion of the *perequazione*, which was finally implemented by Victor Amadeus' successor, Charles Emanuel III, from 1731. As implemented, it did away with numerous abusive tax exemptions and increased revenues; and became a byword for effective state intervention.[87]

In the financial as in the military sphere, and despite the Risorgimento historiographical tradition, of a people co-operating with its prince,[88] it is by no means clear that Victor Amadeus' subjects willingly bore the cost of his wars. His Vaudois subjects mobilised his subsidy-paying allies, or their

[87] This paragraph largely follows D. Borioli, M. Ferraris and A. Premoli, 'La perequazione dei tributi nel Piemonte sabaudo e la realizzazione della riforma fiscale nella prima metà del XVIII secolo', *BSBS*, 83, 1985, 130 ff.; and Quazza, *Le riforme*, I, 134 ff. For English language accounts of the *perequazione*, see Symcox, *Victor Amadeus*, 125–6, 202 ff. and Levi, *Inheriting Power*, esp. 86–7. Curiously, given the expansion of the Savoyard state in this era, the *perequazione* seems to have been the only major state mapping project between the 1690s and 1770s.

[88] See *CGP*, V, xcv–xcvi, contrasting the sacrifices of prince and people during the War of the Spanish Succession (with an eye to future material and 'moral' gains) with the desire for profit of the bankers/financiers (Gamba, Olivero and so on) on whom the duke depended.

representatives in Turin, to shield themselves from that burden – prompting Victor Amadeus to assert that taxation was an issue of sovereignty in which he would not be restrained (see Chapter 5). Orders had frequently to be issued for the compulsion of those refusing to pay some of the extraordinary fiscal measures.[89] The duke's revenue-raising projects might also provoke opposition of sorts among the elite and his own collaborators.[90] That the fiscal burden created difficulties for Victor Amadeus' increasingly exhausted subjects, and fanned a widespread desire for peace among them by the summer of 1696 (when the financial screw was tightening as never before) was evident.[91] Victor Amadeus did not make peace in 1696 because of the financial exhaustion of his states, but it would be wrong to completely exclude this from his calculations at that time. Not surprisingly, once the Nine Years War was over, the duke sought to ease the pressure, abolishing most of the extraordinary taxes introduced since 1690. During the War of the Spanish Succession, too, the duke's subjects might be hard pressed to meet the burdens he imposed. The town of Fossano, for example, found it difficult to meet the torrent of fiscal (and other) obligations imposed between 1703 and 1706, a largely unsympathetic Victor Amadeus frequently despatching troops to coerce the town.[92] In 1706, as in 1696, once the immediate crisis was over the duke acted quickly to ease the pressure on his hard-pressed subjects.[93]

The inability, or reluctance, of his subjects to pay obliged Victor Amadeus to find more attractive ways to encourage those among them with the necessary resources to contribute to his war effort. These included the sale of fiefs and infeudation. The first, i.e. the sale of existing fiefs or the creation and sale of new ones, with the grant of seigneurial and jurisdictional rights, was rare.[94] Since infeudation of this sort was understandably unpopular in the affected communities, the duke was also able

[89] Duboin, XXI, 1100.
[90] According to VDM to Fagel, 20 May 1695, Turin, ARAH/SG/8644/188, a pepper *gabelle*, rumoured in 1695 had been rejected in 1693 because of the opposition of the Camera dei Conti. See same to same, 9 Apr. 1696, Turin, ARAH/SG/8644/252, for anticipated resistance in the Camera dei Conti and Senato to the rumoured capitation and house/window tax.
[91] VDM to Heinsius, 21 May 1696, Turin, ARAH/SG/8644/263.
[92] Salsotto, 'Fossano . . .', CGP, VIII, passim. In Nov. 1708 the director of Mondovì requested troops to enable him to combat evasion of the *macina* tax there, Einaudi, *Finanza sabauda*, 159 ff.   [93] Salsotto, 'Fossano . . .', CGP, VIII, 457 ff.
[94] In the crisis following Victor Amadeus' defeat at Marsaglia in 1693, Janus de Bellegarde, marquis d'Entremont, purchased various properties and jurisdictions in Savoy. The inheritance of the marchesa di Pancalieri, these had been bequeathed to Madama Reale, who resigned them to the duke in 1686 (as part of the settlement of her pension and household). Patent of 16 Oct. 1693, in ADS/B1457 f. 102. See Nicolas, *La Savoie*, I, 33.

to raise funds by threatening infeudation but allowing communities to buy him off.[95] Far more widely exploited, however, was the sale of the right to infeudate hitherto allodial land subject to the *tasso*, thereby effectively alienating the revenues of the property concerned and adding to the fiscal burden for those still subject to taxation. This device, which had been used extensively in the wars up to 1659, and intermittently thereafter, was resorted to by Victor Amadeus in 1690, before he broke with Louis XIV, and much more extensively following his defeat at Staffarda.[96] It was again exploited during the crisis of spring 1691, in the early summer of 1692 (to fund preparations for the invasion of Dauphiné) and in the summer of 1693 (to finance the siege of Pinerolo).[97] In the crisis following Victor Amadeus' defeat at Marsaglia later in 1693, another round of infeudation raised 400,000 lire.[98] In all, just over 6 million lire was raised in this way during the Nine Years War. After 1696, the sheer extent of infeudation since 1690 and its damaging impact on ducal finances (reducing revenues) necessitated some sort of clawback, in the so-called 'disinfeudation' of 1698, which brought most of the properties infeudated back into the ducal tax system.[99] Infeudation was resorted to again from 1703: in May 1706, up to 6 per cent of the tax register was offered for infeudation. However, the post-1696 disinfeudation had made potential purchasers wary and infeudation during the War of the Spanish Succession yielded only about 10 per cent of that obtained in the Nine Years War.[100]

Victor Amadeus also alienated revenues, or rather their collection, in return (as with infeudation) for an invaluable short-term lump sum. Above all, this meant the *tasso*, the main direct tax in Piedmont and a mainstay of his finances. As with infeudation, this was not new, but between 1690 and 1696 annual *tasso* revenues totalling nearly 250,000

[95] Duboin, XXIV, 361 (July 1694). In 1697 the communities of the Barcelonette valley and Sospello bought out for 145,000 lire new fiefs threatened by Victor Amadeus, and in the War of the Spanish Succession Bra successfully reversed its own infeudation in favour of the marchese di Caraglio, *Finanza sabauda*, 237 ff.

[96] Duboin, XXIV, 347, 348. Purchasers after Staffarda included Carlo Lodovico Falletti di Barolo who infeudated 650 giornate of allodial land for 22,000 lire, Woolf, *Studi sulla nobiltà*, 52.

[97] Duboin, XX, 1293 ff. In 1691, the fief of Chiavazza was sold for over 19,500 lire, Quazza, *Le riforme*, I, 174.   [98] Duboin, XXIV, 358.

[99] Since he did not have the capital necessary to reimburse those who had bought infeudations in the war years, Victor Amadeus introduced the special 308,000 lire tax (this being the annual sum, 5 per cent of the capital, lost in revenue because of interest payments, Symcox, *Victor Amadeus*, 123–4. This impost was also declared permanent in 1700, Woolf, 'Sviluppo economico', 8. For the way the disinfeudation worked in practice, see Woolf, *Studi sulla nobiltà*, 53.

[100] Duboin, XXIV, 381; Einaudi, *Finanza sabauda*, 239 ff. Among the takers in 1706 was conte Olivero, who infeudated Montalto, AST/PCF/1706–7. f. 24. He forfeited it in 1712.

lire were alienated.[101] After the war, in 1699, the duke sought to redeem some of the *tasso* alienated since 1690.[102] However, in 1700, of just under 3.5 million lire due under the heading of *tasso, sussidio militare* and *imposto delle* 308,000 lire, only 2 million reached the Treasury, while in 1702 the total of alienated *tasso* was still nearly 900,000 lire.[103] Not surprisingly, the War of the Spanish Succession saw further alienations, again on a lesser scale than in the Nine Years War – in part at least due to reluctance to buy.[104] As with infeudation, sale of the *tasso* could be regarded as a retreat by the duke, trading public authority and resources for short-term advantage. The main beneficiary was the nobility, which acquired nearly 75 per cent of the *tasso* alienated in 1706.[105]

Victor Amadeus also resorted to the alienation of office in one form or another. Outright sale of the sort practised in France did not exist on the same scale in the Savoyard state before 1690. But heritability did exist, that is purchase of the right to pass an office on to an heir, or otherwise, which was granted to certain officials by successive dukes of Savoy since the 1620s, and more recently in 1681.[106] Victor Amadeus not only confirmed this right of so-called *sopravvivenza* (or survival) in July 1690, but thereafter greatly extended the scope of venality to raise funds.[107] Venality of one sort or another was regularly seen as the solution to pressing financial need,[108] and, during the fiscal crisis of the spring and early summer of 1696, a swathe of new offices was created, specifically for sale, and a

---

[101] Duboin, XX, 1289 (Mar. 1690), 1290 (Mar. 1691), 1293 (June 1692), 1310 (July and Aug. 1692), 1294 (Dec. 1692), 1297 (June 1693), 1299 (June 1694), 1300 (Mar. 1695), 1302 (Dec. 1695), 1317 (June 1696), 1318 (July 1696).

[102] Duboin, XX, 1321 (for a reduction of 5 per cent of the receipts of those enjoying alienated *tasso* and the redemption of *tasso* from those who refused the reduction).

[103] See Einaudi, *Finanza sabauda*, 66 ff., for 1700 and Borioli, Ferraris and Premioli, 'La perequazione', 195 for 1702. Some of this total of alienated *tasso* dated from before 1690.

[104] Duboin, XX, 1324 (June 1704 and Feb. 1706), 1327 (June 1706) and 1327 (Feb. 1708, hoping to raise 900,000 lire and promising return of 6 per cent). In 1710 the Saluzzo di Paesana purchased *tasso* to the value of 46,500 lire on Saluzzo, Woolf, *Studi sulla nobiltà*, 125. According to VDM to States 12 May 1706, Turin, and same to Fagel, 26 May 1706, Turin, ARAH/EA/VDM/30, 260, 266, a poor response to another proposed alienation obliged the duke to convert it into a forced loan.

[105] Quazza, *Le riforme*, I, 168, 201.

[106] See Stumpo, *Finanza e stato moderno*, 156 ff.; Nicolas, *La Savoie*, I, 240 ff.

[107] Duboin, III, 15 (Mar. 1691) and 20 (May 1693). In 1692 the marchese della Chiesa di Cinzano was appointed first president of the Senate of Piedmont, on payment of a *finanza* of 20,000 lire, 'for the pressing needs of the war', *DBI*, *sub voce*. Baldassare Saluzzo di Paesana purchased (1692) a life senatorship for 10,400 lire, Woolf, *Studi sulla nobiltà*, 126.

[108] In 1692, Victor Amadeus, needing funds for new fortifications at Cuneo, thought the best solution would be to accept offers for vacant offices there, F. Guasco, 'Vittorio Amedeo II nelle campagne dal 1691 al 1696 secondo un carteggio inedito', in *Studi su Vittorio Amedeo II* (Turin, 1933), 267.

finanza (or cash advance) demanded of the provincial intendants.[109] During the war years venality was largely confined, inevitably, to those of his states in his own hands, but he could also sell in anticipation of his recovery of lost territories.[110] In all, sale of office raised just 840,000 lire between 1690 and 1696. This was not the end of venality, Victor Amadeus creating a number of new offices for sale after 1696 and extending aspects of venality to other parts of that state, including Aosta.[111] In 1704 Victor Amadeus' offer for sale of the (now hereditary and noble) office of syndic in the communities enabled local factions and oligarchs to consolidate their grip on local government. But the general response to this attempt to extend venality was disappointing and seems to have put an end to efforts to develop this form of state funding.[112] The practice of requiring a *finanza* for some appointments continued,[113] but venality contributed far less to ducal finances during the Succession War than in the previous conflict. That the Savoyard state did not become one in which princely authority was both underpinned and restrained by an extensive system of venal office (as in France) must be attributed, at least in part, to the reluctance, or inability of Victor Amadeus' subjects to buy.[114]

Most of these measures were in effect forms of borrowing, which in

[109] Duboin, III, 20 and X, 87 (Apr. 1696) and VIII, 513 (May 1696); Quazza, *Le riforme*, I, 93; Symcox, *Victor Amadeus*, 123. In 1696, too, Victor Amadeus ordered that henceforth the office of notary could only be held by those who purchased one of the (fixed number of) hereditary and alienable posts he then created for sale. Existing notaries could continue to practise, but were denied the right to exercise a number of offices open to the new ones (thus making the latter more attractive to potential purchasers). Purchasers were also promised other benefits, including personal nobility, M. Roggero, *Il sapere e la virtú* (Turin, 1987), 63. The measure was extended to Savoy following its recovery later that year, Nicolas, *La Savoie*, I, 73. War finance, in this case venality, could thus become (limited) social engineering of sorts and help in the definition, if not creation, of what Nicolas sees as a constituent of the so-called 'bourgeoisie' of privileged notables in eighteenth-century Savoy.

[110] In March 1696, Victor Amadeus issued letters patent appointing Melchior Duchat counsellor and senator in the Senate of Savoy on the Duchy's recovery, ADS/B1457, f. 85. Victor Amadeus later banned all who had been appointed magistrates in the Duchy's sovereign courts by the French king from again holding office there, ADS/B1457, f. 75.

[111] See Duboin, VIII, 524 ff. (creation of provincial treasurers, Oct. 1699).

[112] Einaudi, *Finanza sabauda*, 248 ff. Conte Olivero purchased the right to appoint the syndic of Cavallermaggiore, AST/PCF/1704–5, f. 64.

[113] In 1708, the intendente generale, Fontana (see Chapter 1), paid a *finanza* of 70,000 lire, one of the highest, on his appointment to the post of contadore generale, Einaudi, *Finanza sabauda*, 245. Clearly, public office (especially, as in this case, where large sums were handled) would be lucrative. Fontana's *finanza* could be seen as the duke's levy on the anticipated profits, or as a form of loan.

[114] Einaudi, *Finanza sabauda*, 250 ff; Quazza, *Le riforme*, I, 73. According to one report, Victor Amadeus had expected to raise 40,000–50,000 pistoles by selling the office of syndic, VDM to Fagel, Feb. 1705, Turin, ARAH/EA/VDM/30, 12.

the Savoyard state (as elsewhere), was a crucial means of financing war in these decades. By this means Victor Amadeus raised 15.4 million lire in the Nine Years War, little short of the total he received in foreign subsidies in the same period. Between 1690 and 1702 the Savoyard debt rose from 16 million to 26 million lire, equivalent to about 2.5 times annual income. The interest on this, 1.5 million lire, absorbed one-sixth of annual revenue by the later date. As for the War of the Spanish Succession, debt/borrowing contributed a similar proportion of total expenditure, i.e. 43.2 million of a total of 211.1 million lire,[115] although in the last years of the conflict the duke began to redeem short-term debt (reducing it to just 3 million lire by 1713), and to consolidate at lower rates of interest the long-term debt.[116]

Borrowing took many forms, which were not always clearly distinguishable, and could be a mix of both the forced and the voluntary.[117] The former category included the arrears of salary and pensions, and the sums owed to other creditors. These were accumulating in the winter of 1690–91,[118] and were resorted to again in the winter of 1692–93 and in 1696.[119] Inevitably, Victor Amadeus 'borrowed' in this way during the most difficult periods of the following conflict.[120] The nobility, the wealthiest sector of Piedmontese society, some of whose members were hit by the arrears of wages and pensions, by war destruction and poor harvests, were an obvious target for ducal efforts to borrow within his own states. In 1695–96 Victor Amadeus pressed his wealthier nobles to

[115] Stumpo, *Finanza e stato moderno*, 308 ff. These proportions stood midway between the 10 per cent of the rather 'backward' Austria and the 30 per cent plus of the more advanced and prosperous Maritime Powers: see Dickson and Sperling, 'War finance', 313.

[116] For the debt accumulated between 1690 and 1696 and between 1701 and 1713, and debt repayments in the later stages of the later conflict, see Prato, 'Il costo', *CGP*, X, 365 ff. See also Symcox, *Victor Amadeus*, 201. In 1709, Victor Amadeus' former confessor, Father Sebastiano Valfrè, perhaps voicing wider concern, urged him to repay debts contracted during the war, F. Rondolino, 'Vita Torinese durante l'Assedio (1703–1707)', *CGP*, VII, 405.

[117] Gropello and his officials put great pressure on magistrates and the wealthy throughout Piedmont in 1705–06 to lend, Einaudi, *Finanza sabauda*, 212 ff.

[118] VA to DLT, 10 Feb. 1691, Turin, AST/LM/Olanda, m. 1. The English consul at Nice, who supplied Victor Amadeus' garrisons there, was still pursuing in 1695 nearly 100,000 lire owed him for provisions supplied on the outbreak of war in 1690, Boit to [?], 8 Nov. 1695, Turin, SP 92/26, f. 147. In 1711 the custodian of the Holy Shroud sought salary arrears owed since 1690, Prato, 'Il costo', *CGP*, X, 365 ff.

[119] Victims included the duke's mother, Madama Reale, who pawned her jewels (for 50,000 lire) to maintain her household, VDM to Heinsius, 21 May 1696, Turin, ARAH/SG/8644/263.

[120] In May 1706, Victor Amadeus was living on credit, Madama Reale's allowance had been unpaid for some time, and the duke's officers had not been paid for months, according to VDM to Fagel, 19 May 1706, Turin, ARAH/EA/VDM/30, 265.

'invest' in (i.e. lend to) the so-called *società dei grani*, which he set up (in September 1695) to buy grain abroad in the wake of the food and fiscal crisis then affecting his states, and which raised about 300,000 lire.[121] Nobles were inevitable recipients of ducal orders (1691, 1706) to hand over silverware for coining.[122] Other wealthy groups, notably Turin's banking and merchant elite, could expect similar approaches, which were difficult to refuse.[123]

As in many other European states, where the credit of towns was often better than that of princes and governments, Turin contributed substantially to Victor Amadeus' finances in both the Nine Years War and the War of the Spanish Succession. It did so in various ways. Among the most important was the city's administration of the so-called Monti (a bank originally established in Turin in 1653), which raised loans (by subscription) for the government using its own superior credit, the government reimbursing the city by alienating revenues to it. Loans of this sort were raised on a number of occasions between December 1689 and June 1708, particularly in 1705 and 1706.[124] The city could also simply advance money itself, again secured on the alienation of ducal revenues or on ducal permission to increase the local consumption taxes it levied. Between the winter of 1691–92 and that of 1695–96, Victor Amadeus alienated to the city various of his gabelle revenues in return for loans of one sort of another; and in November 1703 (again) conceded the gabelle to the commune for fourteen years, in return for a substantial loan.[125] Finally, Turin could guarantee other ducal loans. In 1696, for example, it stood as surety for the forced loans to the *società dei grani*.[126] Not surprisingly, in the spring and summer of 1696, Victor Amadeus was again obliged to rely on Turin, since his own credit was insufficient. He therefore asked Turin to raise a sum equivalent to 300,000 Dutch gilders

---

[121] Duboin, XI, 560 ff. Carlo Lodovico Falletti di Barolo was asked for 30,000 lire, which (partly due to the effect of the war on his own revenues) he raised by selling investments and borrowing. He had still not been repaid in 1700, Woolf, *Studi sulla nobiltà*, 53. In 1696 the duke sought to borrow additional sums through the *società*, Duboin, XXIII, 396 and XX, 1317.   [122] Einaudi, *Finanza sabauda*, 265 ff.

[123] In 1691, emergency works on Turin's defences were largely financed by a forced loan from the capital's merchant community, VDM to Fagel, 5 May 1691, Turin, ARAH/SG/8643/133.

[124] Duboin, XXIII, 372 (Dec. 1689), 376 (May 1690), 380 (Apr. 1691), 386 (Dec. 1692), 403 (Mar. and July 1705 and Feb. 1706), 410 (Aug. 1706), 422 (Dec. 1707), 430 (Apr. and June 1708); Einaudi, *Finanza sabauda*, 185 ff.; F. Rondolino, 'Vita Torinese', *CGP*, VII, 142 ff. See VDM to Fagel, 6 May and 22 July 1705, Turin, ARAH/EA/VDM/30, 42, 85.

[125] Duboin, XXV, 383 (Dec. 1691), XXIII, 390 (July 1693), 393 (June 1694), XXIV, 76–7 (Dec. 1695, Jan. 1696); Rondolino, 'Vita Torinese', *CGP*, VII, 140–1 (Nov. 1703).   [126] VDM to Fagel, 9 Sept. 1695, Turin, ARAH/SG/8644/206.

(i.e. about 1,200,000 lire). It proved difficult, but the city authorities lent the equivalent of 100,000 gilders, raised a similar sum from Turin's merchant community, and stood surety for a loan to raise the rest, which was to be paid into the Senate with the promise of repayment within two months.[127] A loan-raising Monte was successfully established in Cuneo in 1706,[128] but no other town in Piedmont could help Victor Amadeus as did Turin, which (either directly or via the Monte) was the main source of government credit in the two wars against France between 1690 and 1713.[129]

But for all the frantic efforts of the generale delle finanze to raise loans in the Savoyard state, the sheer weight of demands could soon exhaust the capacity of Victor Amadeus' diminished and relatively poor territories.[130] This, and the high interest rates sometimes prevailing in his own states, led the duke to seek loans abroad, notably in Genoa and Geneva (following the example of his predecessors). He pawned the ducal jewels at Genoa in the Nine Years War and again (in 1703 and 1706) in the War of the Spanish Succession.[131] As for Geneva, in the summer of 1696, Victor Amadeus borrowed 150,000 lire there from Lullin and another 150,000 from Berlia, against his foreign subsidies.[132] Membership of the Grand Alliance, particularly in the War of the Spanish Succession, seemed to open up cheaper, alternative sources of loans, in the shape of the Maritime Powers. The latter helped some of their allies raise cheap loans in England and the Dutch Republic, to enable them to pursue the war against France and Spain. In the winter of 1707–08 Victor Amadeus hoped to borrow more than 1.5 million lire to be repaid over ten years from his gabelle revenues, and guaranteed by the Dutch Republic, in order to obtain lower rates of interest than the 20 per cent otherwise offered him. However, this ambitious scheme failed, as had another to borrow in England in the winter of 1706–07 to finance the forthcoming Toulon expedition. The collapse of these projects, due mainly to the refusal of the Maritime Powers to give the necessary guarantees, may

---

[127] VDM to Heinsius, 21 May 1696, Turin, ARAH/SG/8644/263.
[128] Duboin, XXIII, 404 (June 1706).
[129] G. Symcox, 'From commune to capital: the transformation of Turin, sixteenth to eighteenth centuries', in R. Oresko, G. C. Gibbs and H. M. Scott, eds., *Royal and Republican Sovereignty in Early Modern Europe. Essays in honour of Ragnhild Hatton* (Cambridge, 1997), 266–7.
[130] See VDM to Fagel, 13 June 1704, Turin, ARAH/EA/VDM/29, 98.
[131] Einaudi, *Finanza sabauda*, 385–86. For Genoa's role in international finance, see G. Felloni, *Gli investimenti finanziari genovesi in Europa tra il seicento e la Restaurazione* (Genoa, 1871), passim.
[132] Buttigliera (deputising for Saint-Thomas) to DLT, 5 June 1696, Turin, AST/LM/Olanda, m. 5. Lullin offered more once his London correspondent had the Treasury's tallies for the subsidy.

have helped inspire that 'reform' of some aspects of the Savoyard finances in and after 1708–09 referred to earlier, as an alternative source of war funds.[133]

If all else failed, Victor Amadeus could resort to perhaps the most desperate (because of its disastrous consequences) measure to raise money, that standby of early modern governments in wartime: manipulation of the coinage. In the spring of 1691, facing the loss of Nice if he did not act, with his allies unable to remit their subsidies promptly and in the quantities promised, and with the revenues provided by his own territories dwindling, the duke tampered with the coinage to raise the funds needed. He ordered the revaluation of the coinage, to one third above its intrinsic value, and used silver from his own wardrobe and the churches to mint more of the new coin.[134] Thereafter, Victor Amadeus took advantage of the need to remedy the currency disorder caused by the flooding of Piedmont with German coins, brought by the thousands of troops in his own or his allies' pay, to make a further profit of this sort. These measures had disastrous inflationary consequences for the duke and his subjects. This, in turn, obliged him to take further remedial action, although his mounting difficulties perhaps inevitably led him to seek to profit again from the reform of the coinage effected in 1695–96.[135] In the War of the Spanish Succession, between 1701 and 1711, Victor Amadeus raised over 2,000,000 lire in this way.[136]

War generated its own revenues, including contributions levied in enemy territory. Victor Amadeus took a share of the contributions and booty acquired during the invasion of Dauphiné in 1692; and in the War of the Spanish Succession again profited from war contributions levied in Provence, Bugey and Dauphiné.[137] The duke also shared in the profits of

---

[133] Briançon to VA, 5 Nov. 1706, London, *CGP*, V, 585; VDM to Fagel, 4 Jan. 1708, Turin, ARAH/EA/VDM/32, f. 1; Einaudi, *Finanza sabauda*, 390 ff. For the high interest rates the duke sometimes faced, see Prato, 'Il costo', *CGP*, X, 379. See Dickson and Sperling, 'War finance', 296, for the allies allowed to borrow in the Dutch Republic 1687–1713, and 307–8 for English and Dutch loans to the emperor in both ways.

[134] Duboin, XVIII, 1230; D. Promis, *Monete dei reali di Savoia*, 2 vols. (Turin, 1841), I, 298. ST to DLT, 8 Apr. and 25 July 1691, Turin, AST/LM/Olanda, m. 1.

[135] Duboin, XIX, 711 (Victor Amadeus' letters patent, and remonstration of Camera dei Conti, Nov. 1695) and Duboin, XVIII, 1241 (order, 1696, to coin 5 soldi pieces to value of I million lire). See Promis, *Monete*, I, 300; Woolf, 'Sviluppo economico e struttura sociale', 25 ff.

[136] Einaudi, *Finanza sabauda*, 257 ff. For the melting of silver (including from the chapel of the Holy Shroud) in the War of the Spanish Succession, see Einaudi, 'Entrate pubbliche', *CGP*, IX, 10.

[137] See the agreement (1692) for the payment of contributions by the community of Guillestre in Dauphiné, in E. A. de Rochas d'Aiglun, ed., *Documents inédits relatifs à l'histoire et topographie militaire des Alpes: la campagne de 1692 dans le Haut Dauphiné* (Paris and Grenoble), 1874, and English translation in G. Symcox, ed., *War, Diplomacy and*

the privateers who flew his flag[138] and benefited from the confiscation of the property of those of his subjects serving foreign princes who refused to return home[139] and of enemy subjects in his territories.[140] But these were trivial sums and could never be the foundation of a major war effort. More important, particularly during the War of the Spanish Succession, were Victor Amadeus' revenues from the Italian territories ceded by the emperor and those he conquered from France. In 1707 the duke confirmed the traditional tax regime in the Monferrato — although from the winter of 1707–08 he extended there the *quartiere d'inverno* tax levied in Piedmont. Victor Amadeus also initially adhered to the existing tax regime in his new Lombard provinces (which Prince Eugene had already modified in early 1707, before their cession to his cousin). The duke ended the practice of farming the local gabelles there *en bloc*, but only following the conclusion of the War of the Spanish Succession would Victor Amadeus, in a self-conscious act of sovereignty, replace Eugene's main fiscal innovation, the so-called *diaria*, with an equivalent of the Piedmontese *sussidio militare*. In sharp contrast, he promptly extended to the conquered Pragelato the main Piedmontese taxes (the salt and tobacco gabelles, the stamped paper tax and the *tabellion*), while abolishing some taxes raised hitherto by Louis XIV. By 1713, the newly acquired territories were contributing nearly 2 million lire a year (more than 10 per cent of the total) of Victor Amadeus' revenues.[141]

Discussion so far has focused largely on the war years. However, fiscal innovation was not limited to the years when the Savoyard state was at war. Indeed, the interval of peace between 1696 and 1701 – when the *perequazione* was begun, some of the taxes introduced in Piedmont between 1690 and 1696 were introduced into other constituent parts of the Savoyard state, and what remained of the ducal domain in the Duchy of Savoy was sold off (leaving the duke dependent upon his tax revenues) – was in many respects at least as innovative and important as the war years. The explanation is fairly straightforward. Before 1696 Victor Amadeus was too busy fighting, but thereafter he needed money to reduce the debts accumulated in the Nine Years War. Inevitably, this meant confrontation with those communities, territories and institutions in the Savoyard state (notably the Duchy of Savoy, the Duchy of Aosta, the County of Nice and the province of Mondovì) which claimed some sort of fiscal privilege. Against the claims of the syndics of Nice, the

Imperialism 1618–1763 (London, 1970), 149 ff.; Einaudi, *Finanza sabauda*, 294 ff.; and, Tallett, *War and Society*, 56 ff.

[138] See Prato, 'Il costo', *CGP*, X, 318 and Einaudi, *Finanza sabauda*, 298.
[139] Duboin, XXIV, 269. For the way this was implemented, see Levi, *Inheriting Power*, 132–3.   [140] Duboin, XXIV, 71.
[141] This paragraph largely follows Einaudi, *Finanza sabauda*, 299 ff.

lawyer, Pierre Mellarède, was commissioned to write a tract defending Victor Amadeus' right to tax without restraint. Mellarède subsequently oversaw a massive extension of most of the taxes raised in Piedmont (including many of those introduced between 1690 and 1696), Nice largely losing its distinct fiscal identity. In the Duchy of Savoy, too, the extension there in 1696 of the Piedmontese *tabellion* (i.e. the compulsory registration of notarial deeds), and the resistance by the Chambéry Chambre des Comptes (which had to register the edict), prompted high-flown declarations on behalf of Victor Amadeus' sovereignty. In response, the Chambre des Comptes articulated its own view of fiscal privilege, as being an integral part of noble status and having originated with (and being inseparable from) the state itself.[142] The Estates of Aosta, following threats that Victor Amadeus was planning to abolish their independence, voted an unusually generous free gift in 1699. That same year saw probably the most striking assertion of ducal sovereignty within the state in this period, the defeat of the Mondovì rebels and the incorporation at last of that province into the tax regime operating in the rest of Piedmont (see Chapter 6).

Victor Amadeus clearly 'won' most of these struggles. However, we should be wary of attaching too much importance to the rhetoric used in these episodes and of seeing the privileged bodies as 'losers' in a decisive round in the progress towards eighteenth-century absolutism. For one thing, Victor Amadeus was not determined to eradicate privilege from his states, and in 1696–97 was ready enough to confirm the privileges of the towns of Savoy in return for cash to aid his hard-pressed finances.[143] Similarly, since the blackmailing of the Estates of Aosta in 1697–99 achieved its essential objective, a substantial grant, there was no need to further undermine the Duchy's privileged status. Finally, the Chambéry Chambre des Comptes retained considerable powers to delay measures it disliked, including the *tabellion* which had not been implemented by the time the French occupied the Duchy in 1703. Although Victor Amadeus was asserting 'sovereign' claims in the fiscal sphere in the Savoyard state, and making them more effective, he was not hostile to these privileged regimes *per se*, as long as they did what they could to supply his needs. This pragmatism could not but make him aware that there were limits to what his own subjects and territories could provide by way of war funds.[144]

---

[142] J. Nicolas, *La Savoie*, 2 vols. (Paris, 1978), I, 42.
[143] *Ibid.*, 49–50, 110. Montmélian was given additional fiscal privileges to help with the rebuilding of the town and its defences, *ibid.*, 51.
[144] Symcox, *Victor Amadeus*, 118 ff. By the end of 1702, with the extension to Nice and Oneglia of the tobacco monopoly, Aosta alone remained exempt from the latter, *ibid.*, 31.

FOREIGN SUBSIDIES

Looking back, in 1743, over a half century of Savoyard aggrandisement, the Venetian diplomat Marco Foscarini marvelled at how successive dukes of Savoy had had the wars which underpinned the rise of their state paid for by foreign powers, a view largely shared by later historians.[145] Indeed, perhaps the most remarkable extraordinary revenues to which Victor Amadeus had access between 1690 and 1713 were the subsidies he received at one time and another from England, the Dutch Republic, Spain (and France, in the summer of 1696 and between 1701 and 1703). In all, the duke's subsidies from his allies in the Grand Alliance peaked at 80,000 écus a month (i.e. 960,000 a year) in the later stages of the Nine Years War, a level of commitment renewed by the Maritime Powers alone from late 1703 in the War of the Spanish Succession. The relative contribution of these subsidies to Victor Amadeus' finances as a whole in the two conflicts differed greatly. In the Nine Years War, subsidies contributed just 15.7 million lire of a total raised in extraordinary revenues of about 75 million lire (see above), i.e. about 20 per cent of extraordinary (and 15 per cent of total) ducal revenues. During the War of the Spanish Succession, subsidies contributed a rather larger proportion, a half, of the 87 million lire of extraordinary revenues raised to finance the war. Between 1704 and 1713 English and Dutch subsidies alone made up 37,282,935 lire, or just over 25 per cent of all revenues actually received (rather than simply budgeted for by Victor Amadeus' ministers). In the crisis year of 1706 subsidies contributed an astonishing 41 per cent of ducal receipts. Thereafter, the significance of subsidies as a proportion of total ducal income diminished, to just 4 per cent in 1713 (which was not, or course, a year of full war). Nevertheless, as Symcox observes, it is difficult to believe that without these subsidies the Savoyard state could have sustained these wars as it did.[146]

Spain had long paid subsidies to lesser states and princes, as a means of buying troops to defend its substantial European empire. Its first commitment to Victor Amadeus during the Nine Years War was the promise of winter quarters for his troops in the Duchy of Milan, in the treaty of

[145] L. Cibrario, ed., *Relazioni dello stato di Savoia nei secoli XVI, XVII e XVIII* (Turin, 1830), 91 ff.; Stumpo, *Finanza e stato moderno*, 87.

[146] Stumpo, *Finanza e stato moderno*, 87, 97, Tables 9 and 12 (do not include all extraordinary revenues in the Nine Years War); Einaudi, 'Entrate pubbliche', *CGP*, IX, table of revenues for War of Spanish Succession; Symcox, 'Britain and Victor Amadeus II, 164 (arguing that Einaudi's calculation, based on budgets not receipts, underestimated their importance in the later conflict); and Symcox, *Victor Amadeus*, 169 (1706). For the French subsidy, of 600,000 écus a year (on both occasions), see R. Handen, 'The Savoy negotiations of the comte de Tessé 1693–96' (Ph.D. thesis, University of Ohio, 1970), 196, Einaudi, *Finanza sabauda*, 278–9; In 1718, Victor Amadeus hoped for a Spanish Subsidy in case of war: Carutti, *Diplomazia*, III, 535–6.

alliance concluded in June 1690. However, in the winter of 1690–91, with the French threatening his territories, the duke could not allow his troops to winter in the Milanese; as he was in dire financial straits, he therefore insisted on a cash equivalent. The governor of Milan was reluctant to give anything, but finally offered 5,000 écus a month for six months (i.e. the period of winter quarters) which Victor Amadeus was obliged to accept.[147] The duke was also promised, by the Spanish king, a number of one-off payments between 1690 and 1692 from various sources.[148] However, the governor of Milan regarded these as fulfilling his own obligations to Victor Amadeus, while the sums promised by Carlos II came in too slowly and simply did not keep pace with the duke's dwindling revenues. Victor Amadeus therefore pressed for a regular Spanish subsidy.[149] At last, in January 1692, Carlos II assigned the duke 30,000 écus a month on the revenues of Naples and Sicily for the duration of the war.[150] In all, between 1690 and 1696, Spain paid Victor Amadeus 5,777,148 lire, just over a third of the total received by him in subsidies in the Nine Years War and second only to the subsidy paid him by William III from England.[151]

Victor Amadeus broke with Louis XIV in June 1690 in the expectation of cash aid from the Maritime Powers, which the emperor and Spain promised to help him secure. Initially, the subsidy negotiations were conducted by his envoy in Switzerland, conte Govone, although these were switched to The Hague following the arrival there of the comte de la Tour in September 1690. Due mainly to the way the Dutch minister with whom Govone initially negotiated had reported the approach, the

---

[147] See VDM to Fagel, 29 Oct. 1690, to Heinsius, 20 Dec. 1690, and to States, 29 Dec. 1690, Turin, ARAH/SG/8643/64, 85, 88. The treaty is in C. Solar de la Marguerite, ed., *Traités publics de la Maison Royale de Savoie depuis la paix de Cateau-Cambrésis jusqu'à nos jours*, 8 vols. (Turin, 1836–61), II, 121 ff.

[148] In 1691, Carlos II granted the duke another 100,000 écus on the kingdom of Naples, although the first 100,000 écus was not yet fully paid, VA to Carlos II, 9 Mar. 1691, Turin, AGS/E/3654/35. In 1692, conte Carretta returned from Spain with 100,000 écus which had been assigned the duke from the Indies fleet recently arrived at Cadiz, VA to Operti, 27 Feb. 1692, Turin, AST/LM/Spagna, m. 36.

[149] For the duke's difficulties in securing the sums promised from Milan and Spain, see VA to DLT, 10 Feb. 1691, AST/LM/Olanda, m. 1; and same to Operti, 15 July 1691, Turin, AST/LM/Spagna.

[150] VA to Carlos II, 25 Mar. 1692, AGS/E/3655/18. Spanish ministers thought a regular subsidy would be cheaper than frequent irregular payments, see consulta of 12 Nov. 1691, AGS/E/3654/159.

[151] VA to Operti, 15 July 1691, Moncalieri, copy in AST/LM/Olanda, m. 1; Stumpo, *Finanza e stato moderno*, 97. This calculation may omit some additional payments (or promises of them): see later complaints that orders to charge Victor Amadeus a discount price for munitions from Spanish Italy had not been obeyed, consulta of Council of State of 15 July 1697, AGS/E/3659/66.

Dutch and English ministers believed mistakenly that the duke sought 30,000 écus a month in total, the cost to be shared between them. This proved acceptable to the Dutch, who agreed to pay it according to the usual proportion (i.e. two-thirds to be paid by England and one-third by the Republic). However, they only agreed to pay a subsidy for six months (to tide Victor Amadeus over the initial phase of the war), not least because William III was negotiating in Switzerland for troops which might ultimately benefit the duke. The Maritime Powers also hoped that the money could be used to maintain the troops they had levied earlier in 1690 to execute the so-called Lindau Project to invade France.[152] Victor Amadeus' defeat at Staffarda complicated the negotiations by, on the one hand, increasing the pressure on the Maritime Powers to help him but, on the other, driving up his subsidy demand, to compensate for shrinking revenues, to 50,000 écus a month. In addition, the Maritime Powers insisted that any treaty must include guarantees for Victor Amadeus' Vaudois subjects, which the duke wished to avoid (see Chapter 5). However, Victor Amadeus' financial situation, and the promise of an immediate three-month subsidy advance once the treaty was concluded, weakened his position and a treaty was concluded at last at The Hague on 20 October 1690. It promised the duke 30,000 écus for six months (i.e. 180,000), two-thirds to be paid by England. Half (i.e. 90,000 écus) was to be advanced immediately for Victor Amadeus to spend as he wished, the other half was to be spent on the Protestant battalions raised for the Lindau project. A secret article committed the duke to an edict of toleration for the Vaudois.[153]

Not surprisingly, Victor Amadeus was disappointed with the treaty. He returned only a conditional ratification of the subsidy clause and refused to accept the letters of change given him by the Dutch commissary in Turin towards the Dutch share of his advance.[154] However, his deteriorating military and financial situation in the first months of 1691 again forced his hand, obliging him to return a full ratification, although this was made easier by a promise from the Dutch and William III (whose Swiss negotiations had stalled) to pay the subsidy. Indeed, the Maritime Powers went on to increase their subsidy to the duke of Savoy. From December 1691, to enable him to maintain the three new Protestant

---

[152] See Storrs, 'Thomas Coxe and the Lindau Project', in A. de Lange, ed., *Dall'Europa alle Valli Valdesi* (Turin, 1990), 199 ff.
[153] See C. Storrs, 'Diplomatic relations between William III and Victor Amadeus II of Savoy 1690–96' (Ph.D. thesis, University of London, 1990), 34 ff.; Storrs, 'Machiavelli dethroned: Victor Amadeus II and the making of the Anglo-Savoyard Alliance of 1690', *European History Quarterly*, 22, 3, 1992, 347 ff.
[154] VDM to States, 4 Nov. 1690, Turin, ARAH/SG/8643/66.

battalions raised by the Maritime Powers earlier that year, they increased his subsidy by 6,000 écus a month, to 36,000. Following Victor Amadeus' second defeat in 1693 they increased it by another 12,000 écus a month (payable in the same proportions as before) to 48,000 making this the largest subsidy paid by England in the Nine Years War.[155] Between them the Maritime Powers gave over 10 million lire to Victor Amadeus between 1690 and 1696, England supplying 6,688,000 and the Dutch 3,341,332.

However, Stumpo's figures ignore the additional sums paid to, or on behalf of the duke. Apart from contributing to the initial levy in 1691 of the three additional Protestant battalions, in the winter of 1691–92 William promised Victor Amadeus a lump sum of 8,000 écus towards the cost of their completion (i.e. recruiting).[156] In October 1693, William and the States promised Victor Amadeus an extraordinary grant of 50,000 écus towards making good the losses sustained by those battalions at the battle of Marsaglia. William III also contributed to the costs incurred in recovering men from the duke's regiments in Louis XIV's service in Flanders (see Chapter 1) and in 1694 agreed to pay the costs incurred in remitting the subsidy to Turin (which had increased 7–8 per cent on 1693).[157] The Maritime Powers also allowed the duke to buy munitions in their states at a discount;[158] and financed indirectly Victor Amadeus' war effort by subsidising the despatch of other troops to his aid. In 1691, to prevent his military collapse, William III agreed to pay the emperor 300,000 and Max Emmanuel 100,000 écus for 18,000 men that between them they sent to Piedmont.[159]

Victor Amadeus' switch of alliances in 1703 was in part founded upon the expectation of subsidies from the Maritime Powers. In his treaty with England, negotiated in Turin and concluded in August 1704, and that with the Dutch in January 1705, the duke was promised an advance of 100,000 écus, and a monthly subsidy of 80,000 écus (equivalent to that received from England, the Dutch and Spain at the end of the Nine Years War), payable from Victor Amadeus' declaration against Louis XIV in October 1703. England again paid two-thirds (in bi-monthly instalments) and the Dutch one-third. Victor Amadeus promised to maintain an army of 15,000 (12,000 infantry and 3,000 cavalry) and to put as many

[155] See BL Add. 38,698, f. 87 (1693–4).
[156] DLT to ST, 26 Feb. 1692, London, AST/LM/GB, m. 8.
[157] DLT to ST, 27 Apr. 1694, London, AST/LM/GB, m. 8.
[158] In 1691, de la Tour bought lead and powder through the Amsterdam Admiralty, although the Dutch insisted that most of the 3,000 écus saved go to the Protestant battalions in the duke's service, or to the Vaudois, DLT to VA, 20 Oct. and 15 Nov. 1691, Hague, AST/LM/Olanda, m. 1.
[159] See Storrs, 'Diplomatic relations', passim.

of these into the field as possible. The duke again (secretly) promised toleration/restoration for the Vaudois and also agreed to open his states to the exports of the Maritime Powers.¹⁶⁰ As in the Nine Years War, the subsidy paid to Victor Amadeus was the largest given by England in the War of the Spanish Succession.¹⁶¹ Once again, too, the regular subsidy, as Symcox has pointed out, was by no means the limit of the Maritime Powers' generosity. In the spring of 1706 Queen Anne made a gift of £50,000, and the Dutch gave a supplement of 30,000 écus to the desperate Victor Amadeus. They continued to supplement the duke's subsidy after 1706. In January 1707 parliament voted him an additional £50,000 towards the costs of the Toulon expedition and in 1708 granted him a further £100,000 for leading it, a good example of the use of subsidies to direct allied strategy in British interests (against French naval power in the Mediterranean). As in the 1690s, the English and Dutch governments paid for substantial German reinforcements to go to Piedmont (see Chapter 1); and in 1706 the English government helped speed Prince Eugene's march to the relief of Turin by arranging a loan of £250,000.¹⁶² Between 1708 and 1711 Victor Amadeus' English subsidy was supplemented by a contribution for transports. Without them it was feared that little would be achieved by the allies on the French side of the Alps, in view of the poor showing of the imperial transports during the Toulon expedition (due partly to lack of funds) and the duke's inability alone to provide or pay for all the transports needed for offensive operations.¹⁶³

Subsidies, which clearly differed greatly in character from Victor Amadeus' other revenues, fuelled his war effort in many ways. For one thing, they enabled him to spend necessary sums abroad and reduce the losses incurred in remitting money to and from Turin.¹⁶⁴ During the Nine Years War, for example, of the 100,000 écus received on Victor Amadeus' behalf at Cadiz in early 1692, nearly 15,000 were spent locally.¹⁶⁵ In this way subsidies helped, for example, to offset the cost of

---

[160] Both treaties are in Solar de la Marguerite, *Traités publics*, II, 222 ff.; and *CGP*, V, 264 ff.

[161] In 1707, of a total paid in subsidies of just over £471,0000, £160,000 was due to Victor Amadeus (the equivalent of 640,000 crowns or écus), *HMC, House of Lords, 1710–11*, no. 2730, 77–9.   [162] Symcox, 'Britain and Victor Amadeus II', 163 ff.

[163] Chetwynd to Godolphin, 5 July 1710, Turin (for 1709) and same to Dartmouth, 30 May 1711, Turin, SP92/28. In 1712, the duke was reluctant, before he knew whether Queen Anne would renew this supplement (or whether the emperor would grant one) to hire more than 700 mules for the campaign, far fewer than in recent years, Chetwynd to Dartmouth, 20 Apr. 1712, Turin, SP 92/28.

[164] See DLT to ST, 21 May 1694, Hague, AST/LM/Olanda, m. 3, making just this point.   [165] *Memoria* in AST/LM/Spagna, m. 39.

Victor Amadeus' expanding diplomatic network.[166] They could be used, too, to purchase necessary munitions abroad,[167] to pay those German princes who hired out troops to Victor Amadeus,[168] and to fund a variety of lesser schemes which might ultimately enhance the duke's armed might and contribute to the success of his war effort – including the repatriation of men from the three ducal regiments in Flanders and the despatch from Flanders to Piedmont of the skilled artillery men and engineers lacking in Piedmont for the sieges of Casale and Pinerolo during the Nine Years War (see Chapter 1).

In Piedmont, those subsidies might arrive as a valuable lump sum, at a critical moment. In January 1692, for example, following the receipt of part of what had been promised from Spain, Victor Amadeus was able to give the Protestant battalions badly needed recruiting money, without which they could not participate effectively in the coming campaign;[169] and in the summer of 1693, having received some of his English subsidy, the duke was able to advance the money necessary for the purchase of two German regiments totalling more than 2,000 men.[170] Subsidies might also contribute to the success of some of the duke's other extraordinary wartime revenue-raising measures, including the purchase of silver to mint new coin and the minting of what was received in payment of those subsidies.[171] Above all, his subsidies enabled the duke to borrow, although this was sometimes made necessary by delays in paying those same subsidies (see below, pp. 113–14). In the winter of 1690–91, for example, following the receipt of a letter of change from Carlos II for 25,000 pistoles, and the assignment of another 100,000 on the Kingdom of Naples (on top of that already assigned on the Kingdom of Sicily), the duke was able not only to pay his troops their arrears but also to borrow

---

[166] De la Tour deducted his monthly salary of 300 écus, and other costs, from his master's English and Dutch subsidies, DLT to ST, 3 Mar. and 26 Aug. 1691, and same to VA, 29 June 1691, Hague, AST/LM/Olanda, m. 1. From 1692 he used the subsidies to pay the salary and expenses of the duke's envoy at Brussels, conte Tarino: see conte Marelli to DLT, 13 Apr. 1692, Turin and ST to same, 14 June 1693, AST/LM/Olanda, m. 3. In 1712–13 the duke's Dutch subsidy was used to defray costs incurred by his plenipotentiaries at Utrecht, Prato, 'Il costo', *CGP*, X, 242.

[167] De la Tour spent nearly half of the 30,000 écus of the Dutch subsidy for the quarter to 20 Apr. 1691 purchasing munitions in the Republic, DLT to ST, 27 July 1691, Hague, AST/LM/Olanda, m. 1.

[168] In 1694 de la Tour was ordered to pay the envoy of the elector of Brandenburg at The Hague 36,000 écus in settlement of Victor Amadeus' obligations to the elector's troops in Piedmont, DLT to ST, 16 Apr. 1694, London, AST/LM/GB, m. 8.

[169] VA to DLT, 24 Jan. 1692, Cuneo, AST/LM/Olanda, m. 3.

[170] ST to DLT, 30 Aug. 1693, La Perosa, AST/LM/Olanda, m. 3.

[171] DLT to VA, 7 Apr. 1692, Hague, AST/LM/Olanda, m. 2; VDM to Fagel, 25 Apr. 1695, Turin, ARAH/SG/8644/187.

(on the strength of what he was promised) to finance their winter quarters and pre-campaign recruiting.[172] Later, in the spring and early summer of 1696, a time of enormous financial difficulty for Victor Amadeus as we have seen, he borrowed at least 300,000 livres from various bankers (including 150,000 livres from Lullin and another 150,000 from Berlia) on the strength of his unpaid English subsidy.[173] In the War of the Spanish Succession, too, the duke anticipated his subsidies, borrowing in the spring of 1704 from Lullin and Nicolas against his English subsidy.[174] In 1706, he assigned monthly remittances of his English subsidy as security for future payment to the Turin financier, Gamba, who supplied the imperial troop,[175] while Olivero advanced money on the strength of Victor Amadeus' Dutch subsidy.[176]

But, despite their undoubted value, subsidies were by no means a problem-free revenue for Victor Amadeus. It was not the policy of the English and Dutch governments to assume direct responsibility for paying their subsidies in Turin. Instead, the English government, i.e. the Treasury, negotiated with individual merchants for the remittance of letters of change in satisfaction of the subsidy for a whole year (October to October), in return giving assignments on funds which were sometimes redeemable months or even years ahead. In the spring of 1694, for example, the Treasury agreed with some London merchants to remit Victor Amadeus' subsidy (384,000 écus for the year October 1693–October 1694) as follows: it should be paid at Genoa or Leghorn, at 65 sols to the écu, in six instalments, the first (in April 1694) of 128,000 pieces of eight, then four monthly instalments (July to September) of 48,000 each and a final instalment (October 1694) of 57,000 pieces of eight.[177] As for the States General, they paid cast at The Hague, but in small sums, with which de la Tour (or his agent) bought letters of change on the Amsterdam bourse for despatch to Turin. These methods, pioneered in the 1690s, were repeated during the War of the Spanish Succession.[178] The

---

[172] VDM to Fagel, 10 and 13 Jan. 1691, Turin, ARAH/SG/8643/91, 92; VA to DLT, 10 Feb. 1691, Turin, AST/LM/Olanda, m. 1.
[173] Marelli to DLT, 17 Mar. 1696, Turin, AST/LM/Olanda, m. 3; Buttigliera to DLT, 5 June 1696, Turin, AST/LM/Olanda, m. 5. De la Tour subsequently complained that he could not pay all the letters of change drawn on him by Marelli, DLT to ST, 18 Sept. 1696, Hague, AST/LM/Olanda, m. 5.
[174] Generale delle Finanze to Mafferi, 18 Mar. and 1 Aug. 1704, Turin, *CGP*, V, 287, 307.   [175] Generale delle Finanze to Tarino, 19 May 1706, Turin, *CGP*, V, 47.
[176] See Conto delle spese 31 marzo 1706, sent to the duke's envoy in London, *CGP*, V, 471–2.
[177] *Mémoire* of agreement sent by de la Tour, 1604, in AST/LM/GB, m. 8.
[178] See ST to Maffei, 21 Jan. 1704, Cocconato, *CGP*, V, 280 for the principle; and *CGP*, V, 365 (1705), 552 (1706) and 511, 620, 623 (1707) for the remittance of letters of change from London.

duke's Spanish subsidy was also generally paid in Turin in the form of letters of change. Pressing for prompt payment, urging officials to give Victor Amadeus preference in the struggle for scarce resources by assigning a 'sure' fund to the bankers responsible for remitting his subsidy, and arranging the purchase and despatch of letters of change, were among the key functions of Savoyard diplomats in those states which paid subsidies. This also explains why from 1691 he had a minister resident in Naples, which was not an independent court but was an important source of his Spanish subsidy (and of other, military and naval, help).[179] Success might also depend on the payment of gratifications to the local officials who allocated the funds from which the subsidy was paid.[180]

Remitting the subsidies to Turin, once the funds were made available in London or The Hague (or Naples) was no easy matter either. It was complicated by a number of factors: the availability of letters of change, where these were to be paid (or drawn), at what rate of exchange and at how much notice. In March 1691, de la Tour reported that, following the English Treasury's assignation of his master's subsidy on a secure fund for nine months, a banker had promised to remit the subsidy regularly until October 1691 at a fixed exchange rate (another crucial issue in subsidy remittances) of 57.5 sols to the piece of eight, payable at Genoa in cash within twenty days. However, when de la Tour received three letters of change later that month for the subsidy for the previous two months he was surprised to find that they were not payable at twenty days, nor at Genoa. The banker responsible for remitting the subsidy attributed the difficulty to the fact that there were virtually no letters of change available in England and that the exchange costs had risen considerably.[181] In fact, since the banker had agreed beforehand the rate of exchange, the loss was not borne by Victor Amadeus, in contrast with his Dutch subsidy. In June 1691, de la Tour remitted letters of change for 16,000 écus of the Dutch subsidy via Venice, which proved less advantageous than he had hoped, prompting the generale delle finanze to send him a *mémoire* of the different rates of exchange at Venice, Genoa and

---

[179] C. Morandi, 'Torino e Napoli durante la guerra della Grande Alleanza nel carteggio diplomatico di G.-B. Operti (1690–97)', in *Archivio per le provincie napoletane* (Naples, 1935).

[180] De la Tour deducted 400 écus from the first remittance of the English subsidy, to 'gratify' the secretary of the Treasury and other junior officials who might influence how promptly that subsidy was paid, DLT to VA, 15 Dec. 1690, London, AST/LM/GB, m. 8; and was later authorised to give the senior clerk in the Treasury 100 écus a year, VA to DLT, 23 May 1693, Chieri, AST/LM/Olanda, m. 3.

[181] DLT to ST, 3 Mar. 1691, and same to VA, 22 Mar. 1691, Hague, AST/LM/Olanda, m. 1.

Leghorn for future guidance.[182] Typical of the rather *ad hoc* manner in which the subsidy was often paid was the fact that in the spring of 1692, de la Tour received from the English merchant and banker, Sir Joseph Herne, nine letters of change for varying amounts drawable on different places in Italy, and payable at varying dates, ranging from one to more than three months.[183] Victor Amadeus' Spanish subsidy, assigned on Naples and Sicily, posed similar problems. In the spring of 1692, the duke received 100,000 écus (in letters of change) towards the cost of the winter quarters of the first campaign (i.e. 1690–91) but found that the rate of exchange reduced its value and that the letters would not be paid for a month.[184] The scarcity of letters of change also affected payment of Victor Amadeus' Dutch subsidy: the States General had de la Tour paid 20,000 écus in July 1692, but the envoy was not able to remit the sum to Turin immediately because of the lack of letters of change drawable on Geneva on the Amsterdam bourse.[185]

These difficulties intensified as the strain of war finance began to affect Victor Amadeus' subsidy-paying allies. In 1694, de la Tour's negotiations in London for the remittance of the subsidy during his absence at The Hague were clouded by concern over exchange costs which had risen 8 per cent since 1693, reducing the value of the increase in the subsidy granted by William III at the end of 1693.[186] Towards the end of 1694 there was another shortage of letters of change in both Amsterdam and London while some of those that were available were being 'protested' (i.e. refused), again delaying payment of the subsidy in the short term.[187] In 1695, the Bank of England assumed responsibility for the payment of Victor Amadeus' subsidy from William III. Since it could not obtain letters of change; it took advantage of the English fleet's presence in the Mediterranean to have hard cash carried from Cadiz to Genoa and Leghorn, to be paid at Victor Amadeus' order in six monthly instalments as in 1694. This raised yet another problem, the result of Victor Amadeus' own extraordinary measures to raise money at home. De la Tour received

---

[182] VA to DLT, 16 June 1691, Turin, and 4 Aug. 1691, Moncalieri, AST/LM/Olanda, m. 1. The duke had earlier sent a similar *mémoire*, prepared by the Turin bankers, Gioanetti and Beria, same to same, 4 Jan. 1691, AST/LM/Olanda, m. 1.

[183] See Herne to DLT, 22 Mar. 1692, London, AST/LM/Olanda, m. 3.

[184] VA to DLT, 23 Mar. 1692, Turin, AST/LM/Olanda, M. 3. Earlier, the 100,000 escudos granted Victor Amadeus on Sicily had been reduced in value for similar reasons, consulta of Council of State, 23 Nov. 1690, AGS/E/3654/10.

[185] DLT to VA, 29 July 1692, Hague, AST/LM/Olanda, m. 2.

[186] DLT to ST, 6 Apr. 1694, London, AST/LM/GB, m. 8.

[187] DLT to ST, 15 Oct. 1694, Hague, AST/LM/Olanda, m. 4. For the 'protesting' an earlier letter of change (for the Dutch subsidy), see VDM to Fagel, 29 Dec. 1690, Turin, ARAH/SG/8643/88.

from the bank letters of credit for 103,000 écus payable at Genoa and for 25,000 payable at Turin in local coin. Since this meant payment in the debased coinage which was the result of Victor Amadeus' successive manipulations since 1691, de la Tour initially resisted these terms but recognised the difficulty of his position and accepted the arrangement, on the promise that future payments would be in pieces of eight.[188] The situation in 1696 was even worse, following the English currency crisis. Initially, no English banker would take on the remittance of Victor Amadeus' subsidy in return for the Treasury's promises to pay (i.e. its wooden tallies). It was suggested that de la Tour take the tallies, sell them at a loss (of about 12 per cent) and carry the loss of the exchange (another 10 per cent), substantially reducing the value of the subsidy. All de la Tour could do before departing for The Hague was to leave the tallies with a London banker (to prevent the Treasury assigning them elsewhere) and await an improvement in the situation in London. In the meantime he urged his master to borrow on the security of the tallies.[189] However, in July 1696 the only bankers prepared to remit the subsidy wanted 20 per cent of Victor Amadeus' English subsidy for the year 1695–96. That subsidy remained unpaid when the duke abandoned his allies that summer.[190]

The negotiations for subsidies from the Maritime Powers in the War of the Spanish Succession sought to avoid some of the difficulties experienced in the previous conflict; Victor Amadeus' treaty (1704) with Queen Anne, for example, fixing the écu at 82 Piedmontese sols (or 4.2 lire).[191] Nevertheless, many of the earlier problems did resurface, and for largely the same reasons. In February 1704, Lullin and Nicolas, who had originally offered to remit Victor Amadeus' subsidy at 4.16 lire, declared they would only offer 4 lire, while in the spring of that year Hill, the English envoy in Turin, received two letters of change in satisfaction of the subsidy, one drawn on Genoa (which in fact had to be sent to Lullin and Nicolas) and the other on Leghorn, and not Turin. In the summer of 1704, Lullin and Nicolas defaulted, claiming they had not been paid in London, although they did subsequently remit much of the Dutch

---

[188] DLT to ST, 19 Apr. and 10 May 1695, London, AST/LM/GB, m. 8.

[189] DLT to ST, 11 and 29 May 1696, London, AST/LM/GB, m. 8. According to the earl of Ailesbury, who knew de la Tour (but who was no friend of William III's regime), on being issued with the wooden Treasury tallies, the envoy wittily replied 'What do you give me gentlemen, a faggot to warm me? God be praised my master gives me all necessaries', W. E. Buckley, ed., *Memoirs of Thomas, Earl of Ailesbury: written by himself* (1890), I, 241–2.

[190] DLT to ST, 10 July 1696, Hague, AST/LM/Olanda, m. 5. In fact, desperate for money, Victor Amadeus had decided (in his Council of Finances) that his envoy should sell the tallies, for the best price he could get, as soon as possible, ST to DLT, 26 June 1696, Turin, AST/LM/Olanda, m. 5.   [191] *CGP*, V, 264 ff.

subsidy. In 1705, G–B Gropello, (generale delle finanze since 1697) agreed that the banker, Colomba, should hence forth remit the English subsidy (he had remitted part of that for 1704). It was to be paid in eighty days. This arrangement seems to have functioned well enough.[192] It was, inevitably, disrupted as the crisis in Piedmont reached its peak in 1705–06.[193] After 1706, however, the subsidy payment mechanism worked reasonable well.

Perhaps the most serious defect of subsidies was that they were almost always in arrears, whereas the obligations they put Victor Amadeus under and the expenditure they were intended to support pressed constantly. Not until mid December 1690 was de la Tour able to remit a letter of change for William III's share of the advance promised in the treaty concluded eight weeks earlier.[194] Despite the fact that the campaign was about to open, obliging Victor Amadeus to advance money to the troops for whom the subsidy was intended, the English subsidy was in permanent arrears between then and October 1691, and (despite its clearance in the winter of 1691–92) by mid February 1692 was again in arrears, by five months (i.e. 100,000 écus).[195] Not until April 1692 could de la Tour send letters of change for a massive 144,000 écus, bringing the English subsidy up to date.[196] The arrears steadily rose again, however. De la Tour remitted to Turin, in September 1692, 72,000 écus towards the English subsidy, but this did not clear the arrears.[197] Only in March 1693, with the English subsidy eight months in arrears, was de la Tour able to send letters of change for 6 months' subsidy (i.e. the last quarter of the 1691–92 subsidy year and the first quarter of 1692–93), leaving it still in arrears.[198] By the end of the 1693 campaign William owed 100,000 écus which were only paid in December;[199] and not until April 1694 did the Treasury

[192] VA to Maffei, 3 Mar. 1704, *CGP*, V, 286; Gropello to same, 29 Apr. 1704, 13 May and 17 June 1704, Turin, *CGP*, V, 300, 301, 305; same to comte de Briançon, 29 Apr., 15 May, 18 July, 10 and 31 Aug. and 9 Sept. 1704, 7 and 14 Feb. and 1 and 21 Mar. 1705, Turin, *CGP*, V, 308, 361 and 365. For Victor Amadeus' profit and loss, according to fluctuating exchange rates, on the Dutch subsidy during the War of the Spanish Succession, see Einaudi, *Finanza sabauda*, 291.

[193] In 1705, the Turin merchant in receipt of the letters in payment of the English subsidy was obliged to find the money in Genoa. His return thence was delayed by the presence of enemy galleys (which he evaded by travelling by night and avoiding Finale), VDM to Fagel, 14 Oct. 1705, Turin, ARAH/EA/VDM/30, 135. In 1706, Colomba was unsure whether he could honour two letters of change sent to Turin for the duke's subsidy, same to same, London, 23 July 1706, *CGP*, V, 568.

[194] DLT to VA, 15 Dec. 1690, London, AST/LM/GB, m. 8.
[195] DLT to VA, 15 Feb. 1692, London, AST/LM/GB, m. 8.
[196] DLT to VA, 7 Apr. 1692, Hague, AST/LM/Olanda, m. 2.
[197] DLT to ST, 19 Sept. 1692, Hague, AST/LM/Olanda, m. 2.
[198] DLT to VA, 3 Mar. 1693, London, AST/LM/GB, m. 8.
[199] DLT to VA, 20 Oct. 1693, Hague, AST/LM/Olanda, m. 3; same to ST, 1 Dec. 1693, London, AST/LM/GB, m. 8.

conclude an agreement with the bankers, Herne and Evans, for the remittance of Victor Amadeus' subsidy for the subsidy year which had begun in October 1693. This agreement worked reasonably well. De la Tour regarded the fact that less than 10,000 écus were still unpaid in November 1694 as admirable, although he was unable to remit this sum until February 1695.[200] By the time the Bank of England agreed, in March 1695, to remit Victor Amadeus' subsidy for 1694–95, it was again six months overdue.[201] It was again in arrears by December 1695, de la Tour fearing that his master had little chance of receiving anything before April 1696.[202] In fact, none of Victor Amadeus' English subsidy for the year commencing October 1695 had been paid by the time the duke abandoned his allies in the summer of 1696 (although, as we have seen, he was able to borrow against it in Geneva in the spring and early summer of 1696). The subsidies paid by the duke's other allies were also frequently in arrears. At the end of 1694, the Dutch arrears totalled the equivalent of 120,000 florins, which de la Tour was still seeking in 1696.[203] The subsidy Victor Amadeus received from Spain was perhaps the least punctually paid and in the most substantial arrears. By July 1692, Victor Amadeus' regular Spanish subsidy was six months, or 180,000 écus, in arrears – i.e. none of it had been paid – and he was owed another 50,000 on the sums promised him in 1691.[204] This subsidy was twenty months, nearly 700,000 écus, in arrears by early 1696.[205] Victor Amadeus' subsidies were not always promptly paid during the War of the Spanish Succession. At the conclusion of the war, in 1713 he was still owed 1,000,000 lire on his Dutch subsidy (one-third of the total) and nearly 4,000,000 lire on his English subsidy.[206] Pursuit of these arrears was among the objectives of Victor Amadeus' diplomacy after 1713.[207]

Victor Amadeus was not alone in being owed substantial subsidy arrears, which were testimony to the fact that his wealthier allies had as

[200] DLT to ST, 26 Nov. 1694 and 1 Feb. 1695, London, AST/LM/GB, m. 8.
[201] DLT to ST, 1 Apr. 1695, London, AST/LM/GB, m. 8.
[202] DLT to VA, 2 Dec. 1695, London, AST/LM/GB, m. 8.
[203] Galway to ?, 15 Dec. 1693, Hague, SP 92/26, f. 57; de la Tour's *mémoires*, 26 July and 3 Nov. 1694, Hague, ARAH/SG/6919; DLT to ST, 26 June 1696, kHague, AST/LM/Olanda, m. 5.
[204] Operti to Carlos II, 6 July 1692, AGS/E/3655/32.
[205] VDM to Fagel, 5 May 1696, Turin, ARAH/SG/8644/256.
[206] Einaudi, *Finanza sabauda*, 281 ff., 288. In 1713 the English envoy noted the duke's eagerness for the conclusion of peace, which would enable him to reduce his troops (which he could not afford without his long overdue subsidies), Chetwynd to Dartmouth, 8 Feb. 1713, Turin, SP 92/28, F. 547.
[207] See the Instructions given the marquis de Trivié going to London in 1713 as Victor Amadeus' ambassador extraordinary, AST/Negoziazioni/Inghilterra; and Einaudi, *Finanza sabauda*, 292 ff.

much difficulty as he had in financing a long and costly war.²⁰⁸ One of the consequence of these problems, in England and the Dutch Republic, was an abortive attempt to substitute manufactured products for cash as a form of subsidy in the later stages of the Nine Years War. As the largest subsidy paid by the Maritime Powers in that conflict, that of Victor Amadeus became the focus from 1694 of a scheme to use the presence in the Mediterranean of the Anglo-Dutch fleet to restrict the drain of bullion (in subsidies) from their own states, and at the same to advance Anglo-Dutch commercial interests and to prevent the resurgence of Louis XIV's political influence after the war on the back of French economic success. In the winter of 1694–95, the idea of paying Victor Amadeus not in cash but in cloth for his growing army, as part of a larger package which would commit the duke to reducing tariffs on English and Dutch imports, rapidly gained ground in England and the Dutch Republic. There were serious practical obstacles to such a scheme. These included both the dependence of the Piedmontese silk industry (a major source of revenues for the duke of Savoy, and a livelihood for many of his subjects) on the French market, and the lack of necessary mercantile contacts in London and The Hague, of the Piedmontese merchants who had to pilot the scheme. Despite these difficulties, some progress was made and in the summer of 1695 a representative of the English Lustring Company arrived in Turin with cloth samples, Victor Amadeus appointing commissioners to negotiate with him. Unfortunately, those commissioners were less than enthusiastic about the scheme in the negotiations in the winter of 1695–96, for the reasons already noted. The project was not realised and seems to have been abandoned long before Victor Amadeus' *volte-face* of 1696. Despite the renewal of subsidy payments from 1703 and of a trade in cloth between Piedmont and England thereafter, it was not taken up during the War of the Spanish Succession.²⁰⁹

In some circumstances subsidy arrears could be turned to other advantage. During the War of the Spanish Succession, for example, some of Victor Amadeus' Dutch subsidy arrears were offset against military supplies purchased in the Republic.²¹⁰ This trading of arrears was most marked in dealing with Spain, which already owed substantial sums (in

---

²⁰⁸ In 1692 the elector of Brandenburg was reportedly owed 400,000 écus for the 5,000 infantry and 2,000 horses he had in Spanish service, DLT to VA, 25 Apr. 1692, Hague, AST/LM/Olanda, m. 2.

²⁰⁹ For this scheme, see C. Contessa, 'Aspirazioni commerciali intrecciate ad alleanze politiche della Casa di Savoia coll'Inghilterra nei secoli XVII e XVIII', *MAST*, ser. II, 64, 3, 1914; Storrs, 'Diplomatic relations', 284, 326 ff.; and Symcox, 'Britain and Victor Amadeus II', 172 ff.

²¹⁰ See Conto dei sussidi, Jan. 1706, *CGP*, V, 460 and VDM to Fagel, 14 May 1707, Turin, ARAH/EA/VDM/31, f. 101.

the form of the dowry of the wife of Charles Emanuel I, the Infanta Catherine, daughter of Philip II),[211] and the proximity of whose territories encouraged attempts to trade arrears for further military and other help and the cession of territory. In the spring of 1692, for example, a small portion of the duke's subsidy arrears was offset against supplies of powder and saltpetre.[212] That was not all. In 1694 and 1695, following the poor harvests in Piedmont, Victor Amadeus successfully sought to have some of his Spanish subsidy arrears paid in the form of grain exports from Spanish Naples, Sardinia and Sicily.[213] In 1695, too, the duke made even bolder, but unsuccessful, efforts to trade his subsidy arrears in Madrid. Operti was initially ordered to suggest the exchange of those arrears for nineteen fiefs in the Langhe, held by the king of Spain, as duke of Milan from the emperor, which would clearly have extended and consolidated Victor Amadeus' territorial dominion in north Italy.[214] Subsequently, in May 1695, Victor Amadeus sent conte Vernone to Madrid, in an attempt to exchange his subsidy arrears for the governorship of Milan. This would have ensured he was well placed to secure the Milanese on the Spanish king's death.[215]

Subsidies, then were an invaluable supplement to ducal finance, without which Victor Amadeus could not have achieved what he did between 1690 and 1713. They helped make good the lost revenues he normally received from his own states and helped him to meet the enormous increase in costs that warfare involved. Indeed, it was almost axiomatic among the envoys of the Maritime Powers in Turin in these decades, when the duke's loyalty to the Grand Alliance was under discussion, that Victor Amadeus profited from the subsidy, since he received more in subsidies than he lost by enemy occupation of his

---

[211] Victor Amadeus never lost sight of this other debt, see Instructions for Operti, 16 July 1693, AST/Matrimoni della Real Casa/m. 24, no. 19.

[212] *Mémoire* of subsidy arrears presented by Operti, 1692, AGS/E.3655/22. See *mémoire* of munitions supplied by the Milanese Artillery Commissioners to 1694, AST/Negoziazioni/Spagna, m. 5, no. 23.

[213] He was allowed to export 9,000 salmas of wheat, 2,000 to be debited to his subsidy account, consulta of Council of State, 8 Sept. 1694, on Operti's *mémoire* of 30 Aug. 1694, AGS/E/3656/74, 76. See also consulta of 22 Oct. 1695, on VA to Carlos II, 31 Aug. 1695, AGS/E/3657/140, 141.

[214] Indicative of the close relationship between the jurisdictional and fiscal aspects of state formation were some of the arguments used in Madrid: it was claimed that possession of the fiefs would enable Victor Amadeus to end the smuggling there which reduced his revenues, Operti to Carlos II, 16 Mar. 1695, AGS/E/3657/41.

[215] Carutti, *Diplomazia*, III, 225 ff.; Storrs, 'Diplomatic relations', 280 ff. In 1694, the Duke's envoy in Naples, seeing little hope of securing his master's subsidies thence, suggested that Victor Amadeus seek compensation in Milan or Naples, Morandi, 'Torino e Napoli', 350–1.

territories, and that it was not therefore in his interest to abandon his allies.[216] This view, which was shared by the duke's opponents,[217] had some foundation. We can contrast the less than 1.7 million lire Victor Amadeus received from Savoy and Nice in 1689 with the 2.25 million lire a year he received in subsidies between 1690 and 1696, and even more strikingly, the 26 million lire in lost revenues between 1703 and 1710 and allied subsidies in the same period totalling (according to Victor Amadeus' own officials) nearly 49 million lire (an average of nearly 3.9 million lire a year).[218] Victor Amadeus, however, saw things very differently and was anxious to dispel the notion that he lived in opulence on allied subsidies.[219] He might have argued, in both wars, that he had lost more than just the revenues of Nice and Savoy, and that if he had retained those territories he might have extracted more from them, as he did from Piedmont. More importantly, perhaps, the duke had greater need of his subsidies at some times than at others – for example, in 1696 when his own states were revealing that they were exhausted,[220] and again in 1705–06.[221]

Subsidies were clearly not an unalloyed gain. In the Nine Years War a substantial portion of those given by the Protestant Maritime Powers were initially assigned to the maintenance of the Protestant battalions they had raised, while Victor Amadeus was expected to tolerate the Vaudois in return for them. The representatives of those powers sometimes made the link explicit, threatening delays in the subsidy if a

---

[216] See Galway to Lexington, 12–22 Jan. 1695, Turin, in H. Manners Sutton, ed., *The Lexington Papers, or Some Account of the Courts of London and Vienna at the Conclusion of the Seventeenth Century, Extracted from the Official and Private Correspondence of Robert Sutton, Lord Lexington, British Minister at Vienna, 1694–1698, Selected from the Originals at Kelham* (London, 1854), 45. Van der Meer believed that the duke made a profit on the subsidy increase granted in Oct. 1691 for the three Huguenot battalions, VDM to Fagel, 22 Dec. 1692, Turin, ARAH/SG/8643/307, and same to same, 15 May 1693, Turin, ARAH/SG/8644/33. For Ingrao, *In Quest and Crisis*, 211, 219, the various supplements granted the duke in the War of the Spanish Succession were little more than (successful) bribes to prevent him switching sides as in 1696.

[217] See Vauban's memorandum on privateering, 1695, in Symcox, *War, Diplomacy, and Imperialism*, 236 ff.

[218] See Stumpo, *Finanza e stato moderno*, 39, 98 for the Nine Years War; and, for the War of the Spanish Succession, Derege di Donato, 'Stato generale dei danni', *CGP*, IX, 422.

[219] See VA to DLT, 23 Mar. 1692, Turin, AST/LM/Olanda, m. 3.

[220] See ST to DLT, 12 June 1696, Turin, AST/LM/Olanda, m. 5. Victor Amadeus' anxiety to secure his English subsidy may also have been influenced by his pending defection to Louis XIV.

[221] In the spring of 1705, Gropello told the Dutch envoy that his foreign subsidies were the only revenues the duke could count on, VDM to Fagel, 6 May 1705, Turin, ARAH/EA/VDM/30, 42.

toleration edict was not promptly issued. This was greatly resented by the duke, not least because the unpopularity of toleration of the Vaudois in Piedmont in the 1690s contributed to hostility to the new course in foreign policy from 1690 (see Chapters 4 and 5). Nor were those subsidies wholly reliable. Indeed, just when, in the spring and summer of 1696, Victor Amadeus' own exhausted subjects and territories were revealing their inability to contribute further, increasing the domestic pressure to end the war,[222] the duke's foreign subsidies also effectively collapsed. This not only reduced Victor Amadeus' ability to ignore – in what we might be tempted to call an 'absolutist' manner – that pressure, but also gave him another good reason to settle with Louis XIV. The duke's *volte-face* may have been further encouraged by the fact that the French king was himself offering substantial subsidies. However, although it would be wrong to deny a financial dimension to Victor Amadeus' abandonment of the Grand Alliance in 1696, it would be equally incorrect to see subsidies as the key to ducal policy. In 1696, the duke switched allies because the Grand Alliance had acknowledged its inability to secure Pinerolo, his main war aim, whereas Louis XIV had at last agreed to surrender it. In 1703, too, Victor Amadeus may have gained a larger subsidy by switching alliances but the key to his conduct was his fear of Bourbon domination of north Italy and its implications for his own independence and prospects of expansion. Subsidies were a valuable supplement to, even substitute for lost domestic revenues, enabling the duke to pursue a favoured policy. They might also (as in 1707, the Toulon expedition) influence strategy in the interest of the donor. But subsidies were not allowed to determine, or to distort Victor Amadeus' objectives.

CONCLUSION

Participation in the Nine Years War and the War of the Spanish Succession was a major financial challenge for the Savoyard state. (Indeed, the domestic background to the duke's *volte-face* of 1696 was a major fiscal crisis, although it would be difficult to establish a clear link between the two.) Bridging the gap between declining peacetime revenues and rocketing military expenditure was achieved by extracting more from the territories left to the duke (above all, Piedmont) and exploiting those he

---

[222] According to Buttigliera to DLT, 12 June 1696, Turin, AST/LM/Olanda, m. 5, there were no takers for more infeudation, *tasso* alienation or the sale of office, suggesting that exhaustion point had been reached. Not entirely coincidentally, opinion in Turin favoured a positive response to any French peace proposals, VDM to Heinsius, 21 May 1696, Turin, ARAH/SG/8644/263.

acquired, by borrowing and by subsidies from allies, all of which were pursued more successfully in the War of the Spanish Succession than in the Nine Years War. The first of these sources was by far the most important and contributed to a permanent increase in the duke's ordinary (peacetime) revenues. War finance contributed in other ways to state formation, including the resolution of the problem of Mondovì (1699) and the commencement of the *perequazione*, the ruin of communal finances being largely completed during the Nine Years War and the War of the Spanish Succession.[223] By 1720, with the exception of the Duchy of Aosta, the Savoyard state had made significant advances towards fiscal uniformity, modelled on the tax system of Piedmont.

That Victor Amadeus' states bore the fiscal pressure of war after 1690 without greater political difficulties was testimony to a substantial degree of cohesion before 1690 – although there were limits to what could be demanded. That the point beyond which the duke's subjects could not be pushed was not passed, was in part due to his success in attracting funds on a more or less voluntary basis from the wealthiest sectors of Savoyard society. This meant above all the nobility and clergy. Although Victor Amadeus' wars offered new opportunities for some bankers, financiers and 'moneyed men', they did not provide the springboard for new social groups. Indeed, the alienation, or 'privatisation' of public authority and resources (i.e. infeudation, and alienation of the *tasso*) apparent in these wars benefited primarily the nobility (see chapter 5). That greater, and politically dangerous (for Victor Amadeus), pressure did not have to be put on the duke's own subjects was also due, however, to the availability of foreign subsidies, especially those paid by the Maritime Powers. Subsidies could be as problematic as any other revenue. But it is difficult to understand how the small and relatively poor Savoyard state could have financed war as it did between 1690 and 1713 without these extra resources, which could be (as in 1706) the key to its survival.[224] This was a Savoyard model of the fiscal-military state, largely perfected by Victor Amadeus and successfully imitated in the 1730s and 1740s by his successor, Charles Emanuel III. They drew from foreign allies the sums which bridged the gap between what their own states could support (economically and politically) and what successful war required. This means of financing state formation was not unique to the Savoyard state, but the latter was among its most successful practitioners. The exception

---

[223] For the many burdens imposed on the communities, and the impact on their finances, see O. Scarzello, 'Corneliano, Piobesi, Monticello d'Alba e Sommarive Perno', *CGP*, VIII, passim.

[224] In 1689 Louis XIV's minister in Turin could not understand how the duke could increase his forces without foreign subsidies, Oresko, 'Diplomatic background', 263.

which proves the rule was Victor Amadeus' disastrous war for Sicily (1718–20) when foreign subsidies were not available.

After 1713 Victor Amadeus, like most of his recent allies and enemies, needed to address the awful fiscal legacy of two major wars. This was the background to an impressive and wide-ranging programme of measures between 1713 and 1720 (and indeed beyond) which to some extent echoed the initiatives taken after the end of the Nine Years War but which were more extensive and thorough. In October 1713 the duke established a system of local tax collection by salaried local receivers, backed by intendants who could use royal troops if necessary to enforce payment.[225] Before the conclusion of peace in 1713, he had struck at some at least of the financiers who had played a crucial role earlier in the war. He had also begun to reduce the burden represented by the short- and long-term debts. These policies were continued after 1713, reducing Victor Amadeus' (fiscal and, potentially, political) dependence on those who had invested in the debt.[226] The same pressures, and above all the great cost of the war for Sicily and Sardinia, in which Victor Amadeus received no outside financial help, prompted him to order the revocation, in January 1720, of fiefs alienated from the ducal demesne by his ancestors without adequate recompense and/or whose holders could not prove their titles. Of more than 800 fiefs, whose status was called into question, 172 were resumed as having been illegally alienated, largely at the expense of the old nobility. Many of these recovered fiefs were then sold to raise funds.[227] Meanwhile, in 1717, Victor Amadeus had overhauled the central financial institutions of his state, integrating the various receiving, spending (above all the Ufficio del Soldo) and accounting institutions under the overall direction of a reformed Council of Finance, which was headed by the newly appointed *generale delle finanze*, the former intendant, Carlo Francesco Vincenzo Ferrero (the future

---

[225] Quazza, *Le riforme*, I, 134, noting the admiration of Foscarini and others.
[226] For Symcox, *Victor Amadeus*, 201, the duke's success in tackling the debt averted the threat of power in the Savoyard state falling (as in Genoa) into the hands of those who controlled the state debt.
[227] Quazza, *Le riforme*, I, 169–70; Victor Amadeus justified this on the grounds that the demesne was the property of the state rather than of the prince and not therefore alienable, Woolf, *Studi sulla nobiltà*, 71. It is tempting to conclude that he had reached a new concept of the state through his wars, but we should beware of making too much of what was clearly a useful argument for a very pragmatic Victor Amadeus. That same year saw the tightening up of the administration of the gabelles, Quazza, *Le riforme*, I, 128–9, and the abolition of the *comparto dei grani*, the only remaining tax levied in kind, *ibid.*, 133. Henceforth the Savoyard tax system was wholly monetised.

marchese d'Ormea).[228] This ensured more effective control of expenditure than before 1690 (and during the recent wars, when chaos had sometimes reigned)[229] and more effective use of the relatively low tax yields of territories which were still rather poor and undeveloped.[230]

---

[228] C. Narducci, 'Il Consiglio di Finanze del Regno di Sardegna: profili istituzionali con particolare riguardo alla prima metà del xviii secolo', *BSBS*, 94, 1996, 167 ff.; Quazza, *Le Riforme*. I, 55–60. The former incumbent, G–B Gropello, had held the office of generale delle finanze for twenty years, since 1697.

[229] Einaudi, 'Entrate pubbliche', *CGP*, IX, 154 ff. makes this suggestion in the context of a discussion of the difficulty after 1713 in clearing the accounts for the War of the Spanish Succession (and the Nine Years War) of the tesoriere di milizia, Antonio Bagnolo. The matter was not resolved until 1724, Bagnolo having died in 1716. The difficulty was in large part due to the multiplicity of treasurers (especially in wartime) a situation which facilitated fraud, inefficiency and waste.

[230] See the remarks of G. Caligaris, 'Crisi bancaria a Torino: il fallimento della Casa Monier, Moris e C. (metà xviii Secolo)', *BSBS*, 86, 1988, 523 ff., on the collapse of one Turin banking house after the war of the Austrian Succession.

CHAPTER 3

SAVOYARD DIPLOMACY, 1690–1720

Hitherto, while noting the important contributions, of men and money, to Victor Amadeus' war effort between 1690 and 1713 of his own territories, mobilised by an ever more demanding and effective state structure, we have also been obliged to acknowledge the sometimes crucial additional resources which he received from his allies. This brings us to the importance of diplomacy, not least in helping to redress the inequality between the lesser powers and the so-called 'Great Powers' which increasingly dominated international relations in Europe,[1] and to the striking achievements of Savoyard diplomacy in these decades. These included Victor Amadeus' *volte-faces* of 1690, 1696 (and the separate peace of that year) and 1703 – occasions on which his diplomacy outwitted that of his more powerful allies and neighbours – and the general peace settlement of 1712–13. These diplomatic triumphs secured for the duke territorial and other gains which enlarged and transformed the Savoyard state. They also helped underpin his claims to domestic authority. Indeed, the changing shape, even the existence, of the Savoyard state in these decades was determined by and founded upon international agreements. Not surprisingly given its crucial importance, after 1713, diplomacy too was caught up in the overhaul of the key institutions of the Savoyard state, with the creation (1717) of a specialised secretariat responsible for foreign policy. This was made necessary by an enormous expansion of diplomatic business which put the pre-1690 arrangements for the management of foreign policy under some strain, although as in some other spheres, the diplomatic achievement after 1690 was also testimony to the capacity of the unreformed Savoyard state.

Savoyard diplomacy was not, however, completely successful in these

---

[1] See the observatons of Count Kaunitz, 1767, on the crucial contribution of diplomacy (as well as arms) to the security and survival of the smaller European powers, in F. Szabo, *Kaunitz and Enlightened Absolutism 1753–1780* (Cambridge, 1994), 287; and D. McKay and H. M. Scott, *The Rise of the Great Powers 1648–1815* (London, 1983), passim.

decades. In 1690 Victor Amadeus' first switch of allies, in favour of the Habsburgs, went off prematurely, contributing to the military crisis which overwhelmed his states later that year, while his efforts to secure an alliance with the Protestant Swiss cantons collapsed following his breach with Louis XIV.[2] In 1696, too, his efforts to have the Grand Alliance powers support his Italian peace, thus putting pressure on Louis XIV to grant him even better peace terms, including the fortification of the recovered Pinerolo (which was vetoed by the French king), and to secure the mediation of the general peace, also failed; the duke was only allowed to send observers, and not full plenipotentiaries, to the peace congress at Rijswijk (1697).[3] Victor Amadeus' gains at the end of the War of the Spanish Succession should not blind us, either, to the fact that he did not obtain all that he had hoped for: an indemnity for war damage from Louis XIV; Naples, Sicily and the Tuscan garrisons (an ensemble which he hoped for when the allied peace negotiations with France were resumed in 1710); and a more extensive Alpine barrier (extending further into France). He also failed to realise his ambitions on both the Milanese and the port of Finale.[4] Nor did he secure Spain and its overseas empire in exchange for his existing territories, as the British minister, the earl of Oxford, proposed.[5] At one stage, Victor Amadeus was so uncertain even of obtaining Sicily that he ordered his ministers at Utrecht, in that event, to request the inferior island kingdom of Sardinia. As it was, Philip V's ratification of the act of cession of Sicily included provisions restricting Victor Amadeus' sovereignty there.[6] In addition, the duke was obliged to surrender to Louis XIV the Barcelonette valley, to secure his Alpine barrier.[7] Finally, the peace settlement in 1712–13 in which Victor Amadeus joined with Britain in what was largely a separate peace made by the latter, exacerbated Victor Amadeus' difficulties with both the emperor and Spain, disappointing his hopes of a marriage between his own son and heir, the prince of Piedmont, and a daughter of the emperor (who had no sons), and contributed to his subsequent diplomatic isolation and the Sicilian debacle of 1718–20.

But these disappointments and failures cannot obscure the fact that the

[2] C. Storrs, 'Diplomatic relations between William III and Victor Amadeus II of Savoy 1690–96' (Ph.D. thesis, University of London), 1990, 49.
[3] D. Carutti, *Storia delle diplomazia della Corte di Savoia*, 4 vols. (Turin, 1875–80), III, 407–8.
[4] *Ibid.*, III, 404; A. Tallone, 'La vendita de Finale nel 1713 e la diplomazia piemontese', *BSBS*, 1–2, 1896–7.   [5] E. Gregg, *Queen Anne* (London, 1980), 355.
[6] G. Symcox, *Victor Amadeus: absolutism in the Savoyard State 1675–1730* (London, 1983), 172–3. The county of Modica was, in effect, a Spanish exclave.
[7] In the late 1720s, when his alliance was again in demand among the rival powers, Victor Amadeus hoped (without success) to regain Barcelonette, Symcox, *Victor Amadeus*, 184.

Savoyard state's standing and role were transformed between 1690 and 1713, with considerable implications for the process of state formation. Despite temporary breaches with the French king, Savoyard diplomatic contacts grew, culminating in an important, independent presence at the great peacemaking congress at Utrecht, the first occasion when a duke of Savoy had played such a part at a European assembly of this sort. New connections were established, many of which continued after 1713, and which gave Savoyard subjects who came to maturity in this generation a new sense of their state's position in Europe.[8] At the same time, a more substantial foreign diplomatic community developed in Turin itself. This expansion and realignment represented an assertion of independence, or sovereignty whose full exercise by the duke of Savoy had been curtailed before 1690 by Louis XIV. In turn, Savoyard diplomacy contributed vitally to the process of state formation between 1690 and 1713, securing for Victor Amadeus crucial additional resources, and ensuring that other states valued an independent, strong Savoyard polity. The sheer number of international agreements concluded by that state, many of which transformed the European strategic and diplomatic landscape, were testimony to its new international standing, as a member of the coalitions which finally restrained Louis XIV, and in striking contrast with its relative obscurity before 1690. The achievements of Savoyard diplomacy in these decades also won it an enduring reputation for diplomatic expertise,[9] and for an inclination to cynically manoeuvre on the international stage in pursuit of aggrandisement.

Savoyard diplomacy in this era also offers an excellent example of the constant interaction between war and diplomacy – between campaigning and negotiating – what John Lynn identifies as a key component in the type of 'war as process' which characterised contemporary warfare. Yet few studies exist either of Savoyard diplomacy in practice, or of the attitudes which animated it.[10] This is, largely, no doubt due to a widely

---

[8] In 1732, the marchese d'Ormea (b. 1680) told the English minister in Turin that the subjects of the king of Sardinia were very aware of the advantages gained with England's help, 'it being no more than what had occurred within their own days and the remembrance of which was fresh among them', Allen to Newcastle, 10 Apr. 1732, Turin, SP 92/33.

[9] Typical of the many contemporary appreciations of the quality of Victor Amadeus' diplomats and diplomacy was that of the Tuscan minister at Utrecht in 1712–13: A. Bozzola, 'Giudizi e previsioni della diplomazia medicea sulla Casa di Savoia durante la guerra di successione spagnuola', in *Studi su Vittorio Amedeo II* (Turin, 1933), 146. Carutti, *Diplomazia*, III, 413–14, noted (approvingly) how on one occasion during the Utrecht negotiations Maffei refused to be diverted from the key issues (including Victor Amadeus' Alpine barrier) by a French diplomat's flattery.

[10] J. A. Lynn, *The Wars of Louis XIV 1667–1714* (London, 1999), 373–74. For the Nine Years War, see Storrs, 'Diplomatic relations'. For the War of the Spanish Succession, the introductions to the documents in the relevant *CGP*, volumes are almost a

held view that Savoyard diplomacy amounted to little more than exploitation of the invaluable strategic position of the territories which made up the Savoyard state, located as they were between the main contenders in an era of major war, and that Victor Amadeus, and his son, Charles Emanuel III, were just better at the game of betrayal of allies which is generally assumed to have characterised eighteenth-century diplomacy. There is some truth in this, and even something engaging in the way this lesser prince manoeuvred in a dangerous world of greater powers. Nevertheless, more can and must be said about the nature of Savoyard diplomacy in this crucial epoch, not least because for many historians of early modern state formation, the emergence from 1500 of 'modern' diplomatic networks was yet another defining element of that state, which alone had the resources to participate in the developing international system.[11] In recent decades, however, historians have become more critical of traditional diplomatic history, focused on the formulation and execution of policy by a narrowly defined foreign office and diplomatic corps, and the understanding of the early modern state which informed it. It is increasingly clear that in the early modern era there was a less clearcut distinction between the public and the private, while the concerns, methods and objectives of diplomacy could seem very alien to modern observers.[12] What has been called a 'New Diplomatic History' has emerged, 'an intricate and sensitive blending of social and international history with the history of ideas', eager to integrate diplomacy and foreign policy with domestic politics in a way older diplomatic history did not.[13] The present chapter seeks to analyse Savoyard diplomacy in the light of some of these concerns and to identify the character and concerns of one of the key instruments in the rise of the Savoyard state from 1690.

---

monograph. For the period after 1713, see G. Quazza, *Il problema italiano e l'equilibrio europeo 1720–1738* (Turin, 1965). Relations with England are dealt with by F. Sclopis, 'Relazioni tra Savoia ed il governo Brittanico 1240–1815', *MAST*, 2nd ser., 14, 1854 and J. Black, 'The development of Anglo-Sardinian relations in the first half of the eighteenth century', *Studi Piemontesi*, 12, 1983.

[11] A. Torre, *Stato e società nell'Ancien Régime* (Turin, 1983), 24. The best accounts of the new diplomatic structures are G. Mattingly, *Renaissance Diplomacy* (London, 1955); and M. S. Anderson, *The Rise of Modern Diplomacy 1450–1919* (London, 1993).

[12] For this traditional approach, see C. H. Carter, *The Western European Powers 1500–1700* (London, 1971), 28 ff. For the newer approaches, see D. Frigo, *Principe, ambasciatori e 'Jus Gentium': l'amministrazione della politica estera nel Piemonte del Settecento* (Rome, 1991), esp. ch. 1; and L. Bély, *Espions et ambassadeurs au temps de Louis XIV* (Paris, 1990).

[13] See John C. Rule, 'Review Article: gathering intelligence in the age of Louis XIV', *International History Review*, 19, 4, 1992, 732 ff. (at 732) and J. Black, *A System of Ambition? British foreign policy 1660–1783* (London, 1991), 4 ff.

THE EXPANSION OF SAVOYARD DIPLOMATIC CONTACTS ABROAD FROM 1690

On the eve of the Nine Years War, Savoyard diplomacy was limited in scale and in its geographical, political and confessional range. The only 'permanent' missions were those to the court of Louis XIV, to Victor Amadeus' Wittelsbach cousins at Munich,[14] and to the pope at Rome.[15] Since 1686 Victor Amadeus had also had a resident, conte Solaro di Govone, at Lucerne, in the Catholic Swiss cantons, his only strict allies before 1690 (above all because of their common interest against the Protestant Vaudois),[16] and at the Imperial Diet at Ratisbon, where Carlo Caroccio had resided since 1666.[17] He also had a resident in Milan, conte Landriani, to report on the army of Lombardy, the most immediate threat to his territories apart from the French at Casale and Pinerolo,[18] and another, the chevalier de Bellegarde, in the adjacent Catholic canton of Valais. Contacts with England were very limited, apart from *ad hoc* missions associated with family occasions.[19] So, too, were contacts with the emperor and the king of Spain, Louis XIV effectively vetoing regular diplomatic links with his Habsburg opponents, despite the fact that Victor Amadeus had interests to pursue which would have benefited from a presence at both courts. In 1689, the death of Victor Amadeus' sister-in-law, Marie-Louise, wife of Carlos II of Spain, gave him an opportunity to send a minister, conte Martiniana, to Madrid, but he was obliged to defend Martiniana's continued presence there in the face of French criticism.[20] Links with the Dutch Republic were non-existent. Equally striking was the absence of continuous formal contacts between Turin and the other independent Italian states apart from Rome. This restricted

---

[14] A. Segre, 'Negoziati diplomatici della corte sabauda colla Corte di Baviera dalle origini al 1704', *CGP*, VI, passim.   [15] *DBI*, 'De Gubernatis'.
[16] See Duboin, XXIX, 347 (alliance with the canton of Soleure, Oct., 1685).
[17] A. Segre, 'Negoziati diplomatici della corte di Prussia e colla Dieta di Ratisbona', *CGP*, VI, 302; G. Tabacco, *Lo stato sabaudo nel Sacro Impero Romano* (Turin, 1939), 139, 162.
[18] See C. Morandi, 'Lo stato di Milano e la politica di Vittorio Amedeo II', *ARISI*, 4, 1938, passim.
[19] The marchese di Roero went on the occasion of the birth of the Prince of Wales in 1688: E. Ferrero, 'La rivoluzione inglese, 1688, e l'inviato di Savoia', *MAST*, ser. 2, 32, 1880.
[20] C. de Rousset, *Histoire de Louvois et de son administration*, 2 vols. (Paris, 1862–3), II, 52. Victor Amadeus' despatch of a minister to Augsburg, that same year, to participate in the election of a Habsburg king of the Romans also had to be defended to Louis XIV, as a duty incumbent on him as a vicar of the empire, R. Oresko, 'The diplomatic background to the Glorioso Rimpatrio: the rupture between Vittorio Amedeo II and Louis XIV (1688–1690)', in A. de Lange, ed., *Dall'Europa alle Valli Valdesi: atti del Convegno "Il Glorioso Rimpatrio 1689–1989"* (Turin, 1990), 270–1.

diplomatic range reflected the Savoyard state's weakness and unimportance, and its status as a French satellite. The abortive project during his minority to marry Victor Amadeus to the Portuguese infanta would have transformed the Savoyard state's wealth, power and diplomatic importance; the project's failure left the duke in his diplomatic backwater.[21]

This picture was transformed between 1690 and 1713. War against France, and membership of the Grand Alliance from the summer of 1690, meant the ending of formal contacts with France. But this was the only real example of contraction of Savoyard diplomatic relations during the Nine Years War. Victor Amadeus retained an envoy in Switzerland (where, however, Govone had increasing dealings with the Protestant as well as Catholic cantons), and kept Lanteri in Munich and Landriani in Milan. The duke also kept Caroccio at Ratisbon, where the Imperial Diet acquired a new importance in Savoyard diplomacy, as Victor Amadeus exploited his status as a member of the empire to seek the protection and military aid of that far from moribund body.[22] Much more striking, however, was the expansion of the duke's diplomatic contacts associated with missions to the courts of his new allies. In 1690, he sent Président de la Tour to reside at The Hague, which was a focal point of allied diplomacy because of the role of the Dutch Republic, the frequent presence there of William III and the existence of an informal congress of allied ministers, which sought to co-ordinate the operations of the Grand Alliance. In addition, although Victor Amadeus had originally intended to send de Gubernatis, his minister in Rome, to London,[23] de la Tour followed William III to London in the winter of 1690–91, a pattern maintained for the rest of the war.[24] From 1690, too, the duke also had a resident minister at the emperor's court in Vienna, which also assumed a new importance for the duke in these years because of his own status as an imperial vassal (particularly in view of the reviving power and authority of the emperor in north Italy after 1690), the emperor's contribution to the war in Italy, and the existence in Vienna of a gathering of allied ministers which could rival that at The Hague. For similar reasons, 1690

---

[21] For fears for the independence of the Savoyard state *vis-à-vis* France and recognition of the potential of the Portuguese connection, see C. Contessa, 'La congiura del marchese di Parella (1682)', *BSBS*, 1933, passim.

[22] Segre, 'Negoziati . . . Prussia', *CGP*, VI, largely ignores ducal diplomacy at Ratisbon in the 1690s.

[23] Alexander Stanhope to earl of Nottingham, 13 Sept. 1690, Madrid, Kent Record Office, U1590 033/3–5.

[24] In his absence, an agent at The Hague (a merchant named Normandie) collected and despatched the Dutch subsidy and de la Tour's mail. O. Schutte, *Repertorium der Buitenlandse Vertegenwoordigers residerende in Nederland 1584–1810*, Hague, 1983, 640–1, has details (for the period after 1697).

also saw the start of a permanent formal mission to Madrid, with the despatch there of Costanzo Operti.[25] From 1691, the latter's brother, Gian Battista Operti, resided on Victor Amadeus' behalf at Naples.[26] Finally, in 1692, following Max Emanuel of Bavaria's appointment at governor of the Spanish Low Countries, the duke sent conte Tarino to his cousin's court in Brussels.[27] Formal, permanent relations were resumed with the French court from 1696.

The War of the Spanish Succession again disrupted Savoyard diplomatic contacts. Initially, alliance with the Bourbons against the emperor in 1701 led to the withdrawal of the duke's minister from London. In 1701 Victor Amadeus was obliged to withdraw his minister in Vienna, Priè, after the Aulic Council declared the duke a felon of the empire for his alliance with France, a sentence not to be taken lightly (as the fate of the Gonzaga duke of Mantua who suffered the confiscation of Monferrato in 1708 as a rebellious vassal of the empire would make clear).[28] Relations with Rome had been disrupted by an escalating dispute over jurisdiction which was in part a consequence of Victor Amadeus' grant of legal toleration to his Protestant Vaudois subjects (1694). This dispute led to de Gubernatis' recall from Rome in 1700, although he was briefly replaced by conte Granieri. Victor Amadeus' switch of alliances in 1703 meant the end of formal contacts with Louis XIV, Philip V and Max Emanuel of Bavaria, who remained an ally of the French king.[29] However, membership of the Grand Alliance from 1703 also meant a full renewal of contacts with the allies. From then until 1713, Victor Amadeus was again represented by resident ministers at the courts of Queen Anne, of Emperors Leopold I, Joseph I and Charles VI, of 'Charles III' of Spain, at Barcelona, and in the Dutch Republic. In 1713 formal contacts were resumed with the Bourbon powers. Thereafter, despite the emperor's expulsion from Vienna of Victor Amadeus' minister, conte Provana, in 1714[30] – and in contrast with the situation before 1690 – it was the norm for Victor Amadeus to have diplomatic representation in the major capitals of western Europe.

[25] C. Salsotto, 'Fossano e la battaglia di Torino (1706)', *CGP*, VIII, 450; Stanhope to Warre, 30 Aug. 1690, Madrid, SP 94/73, f. 15.

[26] C. Morandi, 'Torino e Napoli durante la Guerra della Grande Alleanza nel carteggio di G.-B. Operti (1690–97)', *Archivio per le Provincie Napoletane*, 1935.

[27] A. Segre, 'Negoziati . . . Baviera', *CGP*, VI, 168 ff. Apart from the family relationship, and the advisability of maintaining good relations with a prince who had sent troops to Piedmont (see Chapter 1), it was easier for Tarino to reach Max Emanuel and William III in the camp in Flanders in the summer months than it was for de la Tour from The Hague.

[28] Segre, 'Negoziati . . . Baviera', *CGP*, VI, 172. Carroccio expected to be expelled from Ratisbon, Segre, 'Negoziati . . . Prussia', *CGP*, VI, 286–7.

[29] See Carutti, *Diplomazia*, III, 345 and Bély, *Espions*, 116 ff.

[30] Carutti, *Diplomazia*, III, 453–5.

The permanent, resident missions were increasingly the norm, and are rightly the focus of a study of the transformation of the formal structures of Savoyard diplomacy in these decades. However, they were supplemented by a host of equally important brief, *ad hoc* missions. Births, marriages and deaths among the ruling houses of Europe, including the Casa Savoia itself, were traditional occasions for such missions, as was the birth, in 1699, of a son and heir to Victor Amadeus and his duchess.[31] However, the new pressures on the Savoyard state also prompted a series of *ad hoc* missions, with more urgent military or political objectives, including that of conte Orazio Provana di Pratolongo to the court of Louis XIV in the spring of 1690 to explain to the French monarch the recent imperial diploma in the duke's favour (and in this way fend off the looming French invasion of Piedmont), and that a few months later of the conte Brandizzo to Milan, where he concluded with the governor of Spanish Milan the first of the treaties between Victor Amadeus and the members of the Grand Alliance.[32] In the subsequent war, in 1705, Victor Amadeus' minister in Vienna, the marchese di Priè, visited Berlin, to discuss the despatch to Piedmont of Prussian troop paid for by the Maritime Powers.[33] Some of these missions plugged the continuing gaps in the expanding Savoyard diplomatic network.[34]

When the system of resident diplomats first developed, in fifteenth-century Italy, there were relatively few gradations of diplomatic rank. The basic distinction had been between ambassadors (ordinary and extraordinary) and lesser ministers (residents). By the end of the seventeenth century, however, this simple hierarchy had evolved into something much more complex. For one thing, the rank of plenipotentiary (essentially ministers with powers to conclude) was increasingly disregarded (in favour of that of ambassador), while the relatively new rank of envoy extraordinary, which was increasingly distinguished from the resident (a rank rapidly declining in status) was particularly favoured at this time

---

[31] These included the despatch of the marquis d'Ussol to Lisbon, one of the few formal contacts with that court between 1681 and 1720, AST/Cerimoniale, Nascite e Battesime, m. 1/24.

[32] L. Barberis, 'Il conte Orazio Provana ambasciatore sabaudo (1630–97)', *BSBS*, 1928, 105 ff. The following year, conte Prelà was one of many ministers sent by the duke to the allied capitals to seek help to stave off his own collapse: see VA to DLT, 17 Feb. 1691 and DLT to ST, 6 Apr. 1691, Hague, AST/LM/Olanda, m. 1 and *DBI*, 'della Chiesa, marchese di Cinzano'.

[33] Briançon to VA II, 6 Feb. 1705, London, *CGP*, V, 392. In the winter of 1707–8, the marchese di Cortanze went to Vienna to co-ordinate the coming campaign, E. Pognisi, *Vittorio Amedeo II e la Campagna del 1708* (Rome, 1930), 33 ff.

[34] In January 1691, de la Tour briefly visited the court of the elector of Brandenburg, to discuss the despatch of troops to Piedmont, DLT to VA, 26 Jan. 1691, Cleves, AST/LM/Olanda, m. 1.

throughout Europe.³⁵ All sovereigns – royal and republican – were equally alert to the distinctions and their implications.³⁶ Victor Amadeus did sometimes send ambassadors but the great majority of diplomats he sent abroad after 1690 were envoys extraordinary. This was the rank at The Hague of de la Tour and del Borgo, in London of de la Tour, Maffei and Briançon, in Vienna of Tarino, in Brussels/Munich of Tarino and Briançon, at Rome of de Gubernatis, in Switzerland of Govone, at Naples of Operti, and at Barcelona of Melazzo and Trivié. At the lower end of the diplomatic hierarchy, secretaries and *chargés d'affaires*, who had credentials from their prince and thus a public 'character', did not have the access at court of other ministers but could still secure intelligence and negotiate and were especially favoured where a court or republic did not recognise Victor Amadeus.³⁷

The preference for envoys extraordinary and for the only very occasional use of ambassadors was not peculiar to the Savoyard state,³⁸ for good reason. For one thing, envoys were cheaper. Savoyard diplomatic salaries were not especially generous but ambassadors were better rewarded while embassies were much more formal, showy and expensive. This was of some importance to a regime which was anxious to control its expenditure (see Chapter 2). Envoys were also less encumbered by the ceremonial which ensured that the movements of ambassadors were both more public and more likely to come up against local court etiquette, potentially obstructing effective negotiation. Nevertheless, envoys did enjoy the status and access, above all at court, which was denied lesser figures, i.e. those without a character. The Savoyard court also felt bound by the conventions of diplomatic ceremonial.³⁹ The decision to send

---

[35] Mattingly, *Renaissance Diplomacy*, passim. In the best known diplomatic manual of the age, *De la manière de négocier avec les Souverains*, published in 1716 and drawing on wide practical experience, a French foreign office official set out the hierarchy: ambassadors, envoys extraordinary, residents, secretaries, agents: F. de Callières, *The Art of Diplomacy*, ed. H. M. A. Keens-Soper and K. W. Schweizer (Leicester, 1983), 101 ff.

[36] In 1706, the Genoese senate would not grant the English envoy the ceremonial they accorded an envoy extraordinary since his credentials did not give him this character, VDM to States, 2 Oct. 1706, Genoa, ARAH/EA/VDM/30, 364.

[37] In 1713, Victor Amadeus replaced del Borgo, his envoy at The Hague since 1703, with a secretary, Giovan Battista Despine, because of Dutch reluctance to recognise him as king of Sicily.

[38] See D. B. Horn, *British Diplomatic Service 1689–1789* (Oxford, 1961). Van der Meer went as Dutch extraordinary envoy to Turin in 1703, and to the Republic of Genoa and the grand duke of Tuscany in 1706, VDM to Fagel, 11 Sept. and 16 Dec. 1706, ARAH/EA/VDM/30, 342, 419.

[39] In 1696, the claims of the imperial plenipotentiary, Count Mansfeld, to the treatment enjoyed by ambassadors were rejected on the grounds that the Savoyard court followed what had been practised at the congress of Nijmegen (1676–8) in distinguishing

ambassadors was above all influenced by the persistence of older attitudes, dating from the early days of Renaissance diplomacy, which held that only sovereigns, or kings, could send an ambassador. This had important implications for the Savoyard preoccupation with its own claims to royal status and the so-called royal treatment, or *regio trattamento* (see below). To those courts which agreed to treat his ambassadors as those of a crowned head, Victor Amadeus invariably, even if briefly, sent an ambassador. Operti expected in 1690 to be replaced by an ambassador following the Spanish king's grant of the royal treatment;[40] Prié made his public entry into Vienna as ambassador, receiving the royal treatment, in December 1691;[41] and in 1696 the duke sent an ambassador, conte Vernone, to France following Louis XIV's recent promise to treat his ambassadors as those of a crowned head.[42] In 1705, the accession of Emperor Joseph I offered an opportunity to confirm the enjoyment of the royal treatment in Vienna: hence Prié's brief assumption again of the character of ambassador.[43] Generally speaking, too, the rank of ministers sent by the Savoyard court to foreign courts was determined by the rank of the ministers of those same courts in Turin.

So far, the emphasis has been upon the public face of Savoyard diplomacy. However, Victor Amadeus' achievement in these decades depended in large part, too, on less public contacts. Where official relations did not exist, and sometimes even where they did, Savoyard interests might be the responsibility of more or less official agents, who were often the instruments of crucial secret negotiations. Agents played an important role in maintaining links with and a flow of information from those states with whom the duke had limited or sporadic formal contacts, including Venice, Genoa and Rome;[44] and – between 1713 and 1720 – Vienna.[45] Victor Amadeus' subjects in foreign service might also supplement his formal diplomatic network, particularly in supplying

---

between ambassadors and plenipotentiaries, Bazan to Carlos II, 1 Dec. 1696, Turin, AGS/E/3659/6.
[40] Stanhope to Nottingham, 13 Sept. 1690, Madrid, Kent RO/U1590/033/3–5. Operti himself was subsequently promoted ambassador: Stanhope to [?], 31 Mar. 1694, Madrid, SP94/73 f. 277.
[41] Tarino to VA, 6 Jan. 1692, Vienna, AST/LM/Vienna, m. 25.
[42] Carutti, *Diplomazia*, III, 236; *London Gazette*, 2730.
[43] VA to Prié, 16 June 1705, Chivasso, *CGP*, IV, 365.
[44] See G. Roberti, 'Vittorio Amedeo II . . . e le potenze nemiche o neutrali (1703–07)', *CGP*, VI, for the duke's relations with Genoa, Venice and Rome. Subsequently, Philip V's ambassador to Turin before the rupture of 1703, sought to open negotiations for a separate peace with Victor Amadeus' minister in Genoa, the abate d'Angrogna, VDM to Heinsius, 12 Oct. 1709, Turin, ARAH/EA/VDM/33, f. 169.
[45] A. Tallone, 'Vittorio Amedeo II e la Quadruplice Alleanza', *Studi su Vittorio Amedeo II*, passim.

useful intelligence.⁴⁶ The duke also had various unidentified correspondents, in neutral and enemy states (including occupied Savoy for much of the 1690s and 1700s), the latter constituting a spy network of sorts.⁴⁷ The unofficial diplomatic channels and contacts of both Victor Amadeus and his ministers, of the sort identified by Lucien Bély, might be the legacy of an earlier official mission.⁴⁸ But these contacts, and secret diplomacy, were by no means the preserve of the professional diplomats. Among those involved in the duke's secret negotiations with the French king during the 1690s were the intendant of Pinerolo, Giovanni Battista Gropello, the abbé di Cumiana (Victor Amadeus' court almoner) and the Pinerolo lawyer, Peracchino.⁴⁹ During the War of the Spanish Succession, in 1709 the duke's private secretary, Lanfranchi, acted as intermediary between his master and the commander of Louis XIV's forces on the Alpine frontier, the duke of Berwick, in further secret negotiations.⁵⁰

The expansion of Savoyard diplomacy and the enormous importance of prompt and secure communications between the duke of Savoy and his ministers abroad, particularly in wartime, also inevitably affected postal arrangements. Before 1690 these were largely oriented towards France, Turin lying along the main post route between Paris and Rome. As early as the summer of 1690, measures were taken to improve postal links with Augsburg (and the allied capitals beyond), via Geneva, although following Victor Amadeus' defeat at Staffarda a postal convention was concluded with the French, which also sought to remove some of those abuses of the postal system by the French couriers which had contributed to Victor Amadeus' resentment of his French satellite status before 1690. Steps were also taken to improve links with Milan (which was another key point for connections with the duke's allies) in 1691, and Vienna in 1692. This was the system which underpinned Savoyard diplomacy for the rest of the Nine Years War, the end of that conflict being followed by the resumption (and improved regulation) of the pre-war system of posts through Turin. However, the connections established between 1690 and 1696 survived and were reactivated after 1703.

---

⁴⁶ See Carlo Giuseppe Gastaldi, secretary of the bishop of Como, to ST, 19 May 1696, AST/LP/G, m. 12, declaring his loyalty to his natural sovereign, Victor Amadeus, and reporting the passage of the Spanish minister to the Catholic cantons.

⁴⁷ See VDM to Fagel, 9 Apr. 1707, Turin, ARAH/EA/VDM/31, f. 76, for intelligence from the duke's correspondents in France; and Bély, *Espions*, 59, for a Savoyard spy at the congress of Utrecht.

⁴⁸ De Gubernatis corresponded with the abbé de Masserano, whom he had met during his embassy to Rome, and whose brother, the prince of Masserano, used this means to attempt to mediate a separate peace between Victor Amadeus and the Bourbons in the War of the Spanish Succession, VDM to Fagel, 18 May 1709, Turin, ARAH/EA/VDM/33, f. 77.

⁴⁹ Carutti, *Diplomazia*, III, 210; A. de Saluces, *Histoire militaire du Piémont*, 5 vols. (Turin, 1818), V, 64.   ⁵⁰ Sir Charles Petrie, *The Duke of Berwick* (London, 1953), 242.

The end of the War of the Spanish Succession again offered an opportunity to attempt to resolve some of the problems which had dogged the administration of the French posts passing through the Savoyard state before 1690, above all the abuse of diplomatic exemptions to carry commercial goods at the expense of Victor Amadeus' customs dues, but with limited success. As with Savoyard diplomacy as a whole, by 1713 Victor Amadeus had re-knit his relations with France, asserting his own interests, but had also established new, wider-ranging postal connections which underpinned a new European role for the Savoyard state.[51]

Despite its expansion, the Savoyard diplomatic network remained limited. Victor Amadeus had no formal diplomatic contacts with eastern Europe. Perhaps surprisingly, in view of the efforts of his father, Charles Emanuel II, to stimulate the economy of the Savoyard state, as yet a network of Savoyard consuls hardly existed, a situation which lasted until well into the eighteenth century.[52] More strikingly, no Savoyard diplomats were sent to reside at any of the German courts (apart from that of Max Emanuel of Bavaria in the 1690s), although these were now allies of Victor Amadeus.[53] The explanation for this lacuna was manifold. It is difficult to ignore the crucial importance of ceremonial issues, discussed more fully below, in inhibiting diplomatic contacts between Turin and the German (and Italian) courts before and after 1690. In addition, the job could be done more cheaply and equally effectively at Ratisbon, The Hague or Vienna where the German princes and/or their ministers could

[51] This paragraph largely follows M. Abrate, 'Posta e valigia diplomatica negli Stati sabaudi 1690–1713', *Studi Piemontesi*, IV, 1975, 255 ff. See also Storrs, 'Diplomatic relations', 32 ff. For tensions between Turin and Versailles over the posts before 1690, see C. de Rousset, *Histoire de Louvois*, II, passim. Communications between Turin and London (via The Hague) faced the additional hazards of storms and enemy ships in the North Sea: in 1695 the ship carrying Buttigliera to England had to return to port in the Dutch Republic because of the privateers, DLT to ST, 8 Mar. 1695, London, AST/LM/GB, m. 8. Of course, the most sensitive orders and reports might be carried by courier, and/or ciphered. These measures were extensively used in times of crisis. In May 1706, two of Victor Amadeus' secretaries were said to have fallen ill after days spent deciphering quantities of despatches from Maffei, VDM to Heinsius, 5 May 1706, Turin, ARAH/EA/VDM/30, 254–5. The difficulties of maintaining the vital diplomatic correspondence with a prince resident in Sicily helped put an end to any prospect of Palermo becoming the new centre of the Savoyard state (at the expense of Turin) after 1713.

[52] C. Storrs, 'Savoyard diplomacy in the eighteenth century (1684–1798)', in D. Frigo, ed., *Politics and Diplomacy in Early Modern Italy* (Cambridge, forthcoming), p. 219. But see payment to Don Sebastiano Tomasso Nosoglio, 'per console di marina' at Cadiz, AST/PCF, 1702–04, f. 16.

[53] It might also be thought surprising, given the supposed (and consciously elaborated) Saxon origins of the House of Savoy, that closer links were not developed with the Saxon princes: see 'The House of Savoy in search for a royal crown in the seventeenth centory', in R. Oresko, G. C. Gibbs and H. M. Scott, eds., *Royal and Republican Sovereignty in Early Modern Europe* (Cambridge, 1997), 322 ff.

easily be found.⁵⁴ Indeed, where direct formal links did not exist, diplomatic contacts might be maintained indirectly, through another court or courts. In both the Nine Years War and the War of the Spanish Succession, most matters at issue between Victor Amadeus and the Republic of Venice were handled by their ministers at other courts.⁵⁵ To some extent, too, Victor Amadeus' allies supplemented his diplomatic activities as they did his military, financial and naval activities in these years. During the War of the Spanish Succession the Maritime Powers sought – with limited success – to ensure that the emperor fulfilled his treaty obligations towards Victor Amadeus (regarding the cession of territory promised him in his alliance with Leopold of 1703), not least because they feared that otherwise the duke of Savoy might undermine the allied war effort in north Italy.⁵⁶ Despite these reservations, by 1713, when diplomatic contacts were renewed with both France and Spain, the Savoyard diplomatic network had expanded to cover a wider geographical and confessional range. Not until the period 1760–89 would Savoyard foreign links again extend so remarkably. In part because of this earlier (1690–1713) expansion, it is possible to discern the emergence of a more self-aware, 'professional' or expert Savoyard diplomatic corps, typical of that generation of self-conscious diplomats in Europe as a whole, which, according to Bély, came to maturity in these decades.⁵⁷ The same few men might be sent on a number of missions: de la Tour to The Hague, London, Versailles, Tarino to Vienna, Brussels and Munich, Briançon to Brussels, Munich, London, Trivié to Barcelona and London, and de Gubernatis to Madrid, Lisbon and Rome. Not surprisingly, the accumulated expertise of de Gubernatis in the affairs of Rome clearly identified him as a man to send there again. The same was no doubt true of others. In the case of del Borgo this growing specialisation resulted in his appointment as the first secretary of state specifically responsible for foreign policy from 1717.

---

[54] In 1707, following a request from the prince of Anhalt, commanding the Prussian troops in Piedmont, for a share of the contributions levied by the allies in Provence during the Toulon expedition and of the artillery found at the recently recaptured fortress of Susa, Victor Amadeus ordered Maffei to settle matters with the Prussian minister at The Hague – claiming that he found the prince offensive, VDM to Fagel, 18 Oct. 1707, Turin, ARAH/EA/VDM/31, f. 176.

[55] In the winters of 1692–3, and 1706–7, the Venetian ministers at Madrid and London respectively suggested to the duke's ministers the renewal of formal diplomatic links: Operti to ST, 26 Dec. 1692, Madrid, AST/Cerimoniale/Venezia, m. 4 and Maffei to VA, 21 Jan. 1707, London, *CGP*, V, 605.

[56] See Symcox, *Victor Amadeus*, 157 ff.

[57] Bély, *Espions*, 322 ff; Rule, 'Gathering intelligence', 745.

THE GROWTH OF A DIPLOMATIC COMMUNITY IN TURIN FROM 1690

The expanding Savoyard diplomatic presence abroad was matched by a growing foreign diplomatic presence in the Savoyard state's ducal residence and capital, Turin. In 1684, there were hardly any resident diplomats there.[58] The 1690s saw the disappearance (until 1696) of the French minister, but the appearance of representatives of Victor Amadeus' allies (notably William III, the Dutch Republic and Carlos II), although few of these remained after the duke's *volte-face* of 1696. The Nine Years War also saw the appearance in Turin of representatives of a number of the Italian princes called on as imperial vassals for contributions to the emperor's forces, some of whom hoped Victor Amadeus might act as mediator.[59] The War of the Spanish Succession saw a renewal of the pattern of the previous conflict, the French and Spanish envoys being replaced in 1703 by an influx of allied ministers.[60] As in the Nine Years War, many of these diplomats temporarily left Turin, often unwillingly, to accompany Victor Amadeus on campaign, reflecting the fact that they were accredited to the duke and (equally important) that he was the real motor of government, but foreign ministers were an ever more visible part of public and court life.[61] After 1713 the diplomatic corps returned to something more akin to the situation before 1690. Nevertheless, although it was still rather small and nothing like those at Versailles, Vienna, The Hague, Madrid or London, a diplomatic community of sorts had emerged in Turin. This growth was in part self-sustaining, because the presence of diplomats made Turin an important centre of negotiation and intelligence and so attracted more diplomats.[62]

---

[58] See A. Landi, 'Il rimpatrio dei Valdesi nei documenti dell'Archivio Segreto Vaticano (1686–91)', in A. de Lange, *Dall'Europa alle Valle Valdesi* (Turin, 1990), 173 ff.

[59] VDM to Fagel, 21 Nov. 1692, Turin, ARAH/SG/8643/291 (Duke of Modena).

[60] See VDM to States, 27 Apr. 1707, Turin, ARAH/EA/VDM/31, f. 86, for the arrival of an extraordinary envoy from 'Charles III' of Spain.

[61] In May 1709 the foreign ministers resident in Turin went to the palace of Veneria Reale to congratulate the prince of Piedmont on his tenth birthday. Later that year the imperial commander, Daun, sought their help in his abortive efforts to have Victor Amadeus reconsider his decision not to lead the allied troops on campaign, VDM to Fagel, 8 May and 3 Aug. 1709, Turin, ARAH/EA/VDM/33, f. 73, 123.

[62] Turin also attracted a growing number of private foreign visitors, some attending the prestigious Accademia Reale (which was temporarily closed during both the Nine Years War and the War of the Spanish Succession) and others drawn by Victor Amadeus' developing European reputation. The most distinguished visitors would have an audience of the duke, who would thus extend his connections among Europe's elite: see D. Carutti, 'Relazione sulla Corte d'Inghilterra del Consigliere di Stato Pietro Mellarède, plenipotenziario di Savoia al Congresso di Utrecht', *MSI*, 2nd ser., 24, 1885, 235 and *Dictionary of National Biography*, *sub voce*, for the future English secretary of state Henry St John, viscount Bolingbroke (in Turin, 1698–9).

The development of this more substantial, and visible, diplomatic corps besides representing another remarkable achievement of Victor Amadeus II, had important domestic implications. For one thing, the more numerous ceremonial occasions associated with a growing body of resident foreign ministers, notably the public entry and first public audience, stimulated and enriched the ceremonial life of Turin, focusing attention on the ducal court.[63] This more frequent ceremony also reinforced the efforts of the duke and his predecessors to embellish their capital and to establish it as part of a larger European circuit.[64] An allied diplomatic presence might also strengthen Victor Amadeus' position in times of crisis. He was understandably concerned therefore at the failure of William III's first envoy to Turin, Edmund Poley, to take his audience in 1691. The duke also pressed the taking of their public audiences by the English and Dutch ministers in Turin in the winter of 1706–07, which had been postponed because of the continuing crisis since their arrival there in 1704, and which in part represented a public recognition of the survival and success of the Savoyard state.[65] A public demonstration of confidence of this sort was one reason why Victor Amadeus expected his allies to send residents to Turin.[66] These ministers were rewarded, when they left Turin, with gifts, usually portraits of Victor Amadeus in a diamond studded frame, which allowed him to further propagate his own image abroad – although William III's envoy, the earl of Galway refused to accept a gift in 1696 from a prince who had just betrayed his own master.[67]

The emergence of a diplomatic corps was not an unalloyed gain. Among the most obvious disadvantages were the prying of the foreign

---

[63] For an account of the public entry into Turin of the Spanish envoy, Bazan, Jan. 1694, see AGS/E/3656/22; and for the public audiences of the count of Castelbarco, the emperor's envoy, and of the English envoy, Chetwynd, see VDM to States, 5 Jan. 1707, Turin, ARAH/EA/VDM/31, f. 9.

[64] On the development of Turin, see Symcox, *Victor Amadeus*, 42 ff., 77–8, 226–7 and M. D. Pollak, *Turin 1564–1680* (Chicago, 1991).

[65] VDM to Fagel, 1 Mar. 1692, Turin, ARAH/SG/8644/212; same to same, 8 and 12 Jan. 1707, Turin, ARAH/EA/VDM/31, f. 9, 11. Other sovereigns were equally concerned to publicise the fact that foreign ministers at their courts went through these (legitimating) formal ceremonies. William III, who was regarded as rather hostile to ceremony, but who was anxious after the Glorious Revolution for recognition of his English title, had published de la Tour's speech at his first public audience in London, in 1690, Storrs, 'Diplomatic relations', 82.

[66] See Maffei's Instructions as envoy to the English court, 1706, *CGP*, V, 273 ff.

[67] Galway to Shrewsbury, 15 Sept. 1696, San Mazaro, W. Coxe, ed., *Private and Original Correspondence of Charles Talbot, Duke of Shrewsbury* (London, 1821), 308. In 1713 Victor Amadeus purchased one such portrait from the marquis de Trivié, for the emperor's departing minister, Prato, 'Il costo', *CGP*, X, 220. For the significance of portraits, see K. Sharpe, *The Personal Rule of Charles I* (Yale, 1992), 180 ff.

ministers in Turin – who were sent to obtain, among other things, intelligence of Victor Amadeus' policy and conduct – and the way those envoys pressed the duke to fulfil his treaty commitments.[68] But there was more to it than that. Although not legally incorporated, and still very small in number, the members of the diplomatic community enjoyed various privileges. These were the result of the broad development of diplomatic practice throughout Europe in the preceding two centuries and were much the same as those enjoyed by diplomats elsewhere: financial (including the import and export duty free of goods declared to be for the diplomats' own use), ceremonial (rights of *entrée* at the ducal court), judicial (including the right to judge their own servants in criminal cases) and religious (Protestant ministers having the right to their own chapel in this otherwise Catholic state). Just as Victor Amadeus' own ministers in other capitals jealously guarded their privileges (and were expected to do so by the duke), so the diplomats who made up the emerging diplomatic community in Turin insisted upon – and sought to extend – their rights and privileges.[69] Few of these problems were really new, but a larger resident diplomatic community in Turin inevitably provoked more of these traditional difficulties and required more vigilant 'policing'.[70] More seriously, perhaps, the religious privileges claimed by the Protestant envoys (i.e. those of the Maritime Powers), seemed to be promoting Protestant worship in the heart of the Savoyard state, drawing to the capital Vaudois and others who attracted the attention of the ecclesiastical authorities, complicating relations between the latter and the duke (see Chapter 6).

From the start, then, the presence of foreign diplomats in some numbers, while testifying to Victor Amadeus' new international standing and enhancing his reputation and authority within his own state, could also create difficulties for the ducal and ecclesiastical authorities. It could

[68] In 1692, the marchese di Dronero, governer of Turin, reporting the suspicions of the English envoy, Poley, and of the duke of Shomberg that the Duke of Savoy had done a deal with the French king, declared that foreign ministers were honourable spies, sent to watch the movements of the sovereigns to whom they were accredited, Dronero to VA, 12 July 1692, Turin, AST/MM/Imprese Militari, m. 3/21. De Callières described diplomats similarly: Rule, 'Gathering intelligence', 743.

[69] In 1699, the envoy of Max Emanuel of Bavaria complained at his exclusion from the procession of carriages on the occasion of the departing French ambassador's formal leavetaking, declaring that in Brussels the coach of the duke's envoy always followed that of the elector. He was told that it was the practice of the Savoyard court to allow only ambassadors and princes of the blood (and not mere envoys), to take part, Segre, 'Negoziati . . . Baviera', *CGP*, VI, 178–9.

[70] In 1711, conte Tarino, Victor Amadeus' master of ceremony, had to remind the Spanish envoy that the studding on his coach exceeded what was allowed ministers of the second rank at the Savoyard court: see AST/Cerimoniale/Spagna, m. 1/33.

also expose some of the domestic limitations on ducal authority, and the extent to which the latter, in order to be effective, must sometimes (paradoxically) be flexible. In January 1696, the Dutch commissary, van der Meer, protested at an assault on two of his servants, despite their wearing of his livery, in the market in front of Turin's town hall. His insistence on the punishment of this violation of his own dignity (and, through his person, that of the Dutch Republic) coincided with Victor Amadeus' desire to prevent disorder in the capital. However, following pressure from the well connected (one of the perpetrators of the assault was connected to the household of the prince of Carignano), van der Meer agreed not to insist on severity. It was then claimed by Victor Amadeus that the transgressor had only escaped harsh punishment through the intercession of the commissary.[71] Problems of this sort were yet another reason for the persistence of more informal (even secret) contacts with foreign courts. However, the advantages of a substantial foreign diplomatic presence clearly outweighed the attendant difficulties and symbolised the new European importance of the Savoyard state, its prince and its capital.

THE ADMINISTRATION AND ORGANISATION OF SAVOYARD DIPLOMACY

The growth of the Savoyard diplomatic network from 1690 was by no means without its problems. Some of the resident envoys sent abroad by Victor Amadeus in the Nine Years War were operating in unfamiliar territory and – at least initially – the mechanisms for supplying them with the funds they needed to maintain their own (and their master's) dignity, and to pay for the running and incidental expenses of their mission, was barely adequate.[72] More important in the longer term, however, was the impact of expansion on the administration of foreign policy in Turin itself. Between 1690 and 1717 Savoyard foreign policy was just one of

---

[71] VDM to Fagel, 9 and 27 Jan. 1696, Turin, ARAH/SG/8644/234, 239. That same month, after complaints from William III's envoy, a satire against the king on sale in Turin was seized and one of the booksellers involved punished, ST to DLT, 1 Jan. 1696, Turin, AST/LM/Olanda, m. 5.

[72] For de la Tour's difficulties at The Hague, see DLT to ST, 27 Oct. 1690, 18 Apr. 1691 and 30 May 1692, Hague, AST/LM/Olanda, m. 1. From early 1691 de la Tour deducted his regular salary from the subsidy paid Victor Amadeus by William III, and any additional sums from that paid by the Dutch Republic (see Chapter 2). For the problems of Tarino at Brussels from 1692, see DLT to ST, 8 June and 23 July 1694, Hague, AST/LM/Olanda, m. 4. De la Tour observed that it was better not to send ministers abroad than to provide so poorly for them. Similar problems resurfaced during the first phase of the War of the Spanish Succession: see *CGP*, IV, 149.

the many responsibilities of the principal, or first (of three) secretaries of state and his office. There was no separate department of state responsible exclusively and solely for foreign affairs. Instead the principal secretary of state functioned as both foreign and domestic minister and on occasion himself negotiated foreign treaties, including those of Vigevano (1696) and of Turin (1701 and 1703).[73] Throughout these years the secretaryship was the preserve of the Carron de Saint-Thomas family: held until 1696 by Carlo Giuseppe Vittorio Carron, marquis de Saint-Thomas, and thereafter by his son, Giuseppe Gaetano Giacinto Vittorio, marchese di Buttigliera and (on his father's death, in 1699) marquis de Saint-Thomas. Giuseppe Gaetano had been prepared for the secretaryship (his father — who had succeeded his own father in the post — having purchased the right to have Buttigliera succeed) with a brief mission of condolence to William III in 1695 following the death of Queen Mary,[74] and by occasionally substituting for his father as secretary.[75] Indicative of the degree to which the diplomatic and other work of the first secretary's office was increasingly routinised well before 1713, is the fact that the secretary's absence, because of illness, for example, did not impair its functioning. During both the Nine Years War and the War of the Spanish Succession, one of the junior officials, Audiberti, occasionally stood in for his chief with no apparent ill consequences in the general conduct of Savoyard diplomacy.[76]

The first secretary of state's office had various diplomatic functions. It was a source of information and guidance on procedure.[77] The secretary himself acted as intermediary between the duke of Savoy and foreignministers and others in Turin.[78] But the main responsibility of the

---

[73] See Chamlay to ST, 23 Jan. 1692, Pinerolo, AST/Negoziazioni/Francia, m. 16 (two volumes of correspondence 1691–6), and passim; and Carutti, *Diplomazia*, III, 343 (for 1703).

[74] Buttigliera's mission had an additional, political, objective: a renewed commitment from William to secure Pinerolo, Storrs, 'Diplomatic relations', 261 ff.

[75] Buttigliera substituted when Saint-Thomas took the waters at San Moritz, in 1695, Buttigliera to DLT, 22 July 1695, Casale, AST/LM/Olanda, m. 4.

[76] See Audiberti to DLT, 18 Aug. 1693, Santa Brigida, AST/LM/Olanda, m. 3, explaining that Saint-Thomas had been obliged to attend Victor Amadeus following the arrival of a courier from Vienna, and had ordered Audiberti to write. In 1704, Audiberti again stood in, *CGP*, IV, 98 ff.

[77] In 1691 de la Tour wished to know how Victor Amadeus addressed the foreign ministers of other courts, following representations from the Spanish minister in London, Ronquillo, regarding a letter he had received from the duke, DLT to ST, 16 Mar. 1691, Hague, AST/LM/Olanda, m. 1.

[78] In 1690 Victor Amadeus, who was absent in the camp, sent Saint-Thomas copies of letters he had received from his father-in-law, the duke of Orleans, with orders to show these to the governor of Milan (to ensure that the Spaniards fulfilled their promises), VA to ST, 18 July 1690, Carignano, AST/LPDS, m. 68, 13. In 1708, the younger

secretary's office was the despatch and receipt of diplomatic correspondence. The effectiveness and success of Savoyard diplomacy depended in part upon information and its prompt transmission (for the proper assessment of a given situation and the issue of appropriate orders). Savoyard diplomats were therefore expected to correspond regularly with Turin.[79] De la Tour was a typically conscientious correspondent during the Nine Years War. Between his arrival at The Hague in August 1690 and his departure thence in November 1696, de la Tour wrote more than 450 letters (i.e. at least one a week and often two) from there or from London. Those to Saint-Thomas (345) greatly outnumbered those to Victor Amadeus (113), suggesting that the letter to the office was the norm. De la Tour received far fewer letters from Turin, 236 from Saint-Thomas (or, in his absence, from Buttigliera or a secretary) and just 77 from Victor Amadeus. Saint-Thomas was clearly acting as intermediary between the duke (often absent from Turin, especially in the camp, and generally overwhelmed with business) and his ministers abroad. The generale delle finanze and de la Tour corresponded about the subsidies paid by the Maritime Powers, and in the winter of 1694–95 the prince of Carignano, rather exceptionally, asked de la Tour, as the duke himself had done, to seek William III's support for the prince's claims on Neuchâtel. But few others in the Savoyard state dealt, at least officially, with Victor Amadeus' diplomats.[80] The secretary could exploit his monopoly of the official diplomatic correspondence to 'manage' the duke's information and influence policy. In 1694, Saint-Thomas, who agreed with de la Tour that their master could only succeed in the war with the support of his allies, encouraged the envoy to report the dissatisfaction of the Maritime Powers at Victor Amadeus' failure so far to issue an edict of toleration for the Vaudois. Saint-Thomas then exploited de la Tour's despatches against the edict's opponents in Turin to ensure that an edict of toleration was issued in May 1694.[81]

> Saint-Thomas, on the duke's orders, informed the English and Dutch ministers of his master's intended ratification of the agreement for Prussian troops to serve in Piedmont, VDM to Fagel, 17 Oct. 1708, Turin, ARAH/EA/VDM/32, f. 191.

[79] In November 1700, following the death of Carlos II of Spain, Victor Amadeus ordered both Vernone and de la Tour to report fully all developments, to ensure that his own decisions were as informed as possible, C. Contessa, 'I regni di Napoli e Sicilia nelle aspirazioni italiani di Vittorio Amedeo II di Savoia (1700–1713)', *Studi su Vittorio Amedeo II*, 37–8.

[80] Calculations on the basis of correspondence in AST/LM/Olanda and Gran Bretagna. Between July 1704 and Mar. 1707, Briançon wrote at least one letter a week on average to Victor Amadeus from London, with supplementary letters to Saint-Thomas, see *CGP*, V, passim for 1704–7. From 1696, the prince of Carignano corresponded with the duke's ambassador at the French court regarding his French properties, AST/Principi del sangue/Principi di Carignano, m. 1/25, 26.

[81] See ST to DLT, 20 and 27 Mar. 1694, Turin, AST/LM/Olanda, m. 4.

There were important differences between the correspondence between Savoyard diplomats and their master and that with the secretary of state's office. The letters from Victor Amadeus (drafted of course by a secretary), which often made up in sheer length what they lacked in frequency,[82] enabled the duke to update the initial instructions given to his minister in response to changing circumstances, to train and control his diplomats, and to explain ducal interests and policy, if necessary.[83] This correspondence was above all about issues of strategy and high policy. Victor Amadeus sometimes gave very specific advice on what his ministers should say and do.[84] Victor Amadeus might respond positively to suggestions from his envoys, but for most of the latter this correspondence was in some part an opportunity to demonstrate to their master their own zeal and talent, thus establishing a claim to future rewards.[85] The correspondence between the envoy and the first secretary in Turin did not ignore high policy but was much more about the humdrum aspects of diplomatic life and included complaints (about pay, for example) which were not appropriate to the correspondence with the duke. Ultimately, of course, many of these issues, including the allowing of additional salary and expenses, would be referred to Victor Amadeus but it was as well if the envoy first secured the support of the secretary of state. The correspondence between secretary and envoy was also an opportunity for the latter to retain an indirect presence in Turin, although personally absent.[86] It also allowed the envoy to advise and comment on (and even to criticise) his master's policy. In the early years of his mission de la Tour frequently complained of being left in the dark and requested regular campaign reports from Piedmont, not least to

---

[82] Victor Amadeus' despatch to de la Tour of 10 Feb. 1691, and that to Operti of 15 July 1691, both in AST/LM/Olanda, m. 1, totalled respectively forty-six and thirty-nine roughly A4 size pages.

[83] For example, in the spring of 1705, when peace negotiations became an issue: VA to Briançon and del Borgo, 29 Apr. 1705, Turin, *CGP*, V, 367 ff.

[84] In 1691, following precedence disputes between the imperial and Spanish forces in Piedmont, Victor Amadeus ordered his minister in Madrid to try to secure orders for the Army of Lombardy to co-operate with the other allied forces there, and detailed specific arguments he might use, VA to Operti, 15 July 1691, Moncalieri, AST/LM/Olanda, m. 1. See marchesa Vitelleschi, *The Romance of Savoy*, 2 vols. (London, 1905), II, 476–7, for another example of this sort of advice in 1717.

[85] In 1710 the duke approved del Borgo's proposal for the exchange of his master's existing territories for Naples, Sicily, and the Tuscan ports, Contessa, 'I regni', 68 ff. In 1713 Mellarède boasted of having trounced in legal argument (regarding a formal declaration of Victor Amadeus' rights on the Spanish crown) the foremost Dutch jurist, M. Gasco, 'La politica sabauda a Utrecht nella "relazione Mellarède"', *RSI*, 1935, 318–19.

[86] The envoy might also secure the goodwill of the secretary by doing him small favours: see ST to DLT, 8 June 1694, Turin, AST/LM/Olanda, m. 4.

satisfy the allied ministers at The Hague.[87] Later, during the Utrecht negotiations, Maffei complained to Saint-Thomas of the difficult position in which the Savoyard plenipotentiaries found themselves following their master's contradictory orders, on the one hand, not to abandon the demand for an alpine 'barrier' against France, which included Mont Genevre and villages along the Rhone, and, on the other hand, to do nothing which might prejudice his chances of securing Sicily and recognition of his claims to the Spanish succession.[88]

While acknowledging a degree of routinisation of the work of the secretary's office, we must not exaggerate 'bureaucratic' development in the administration of Savoyard foreign policy before 1717. We should not allow what was said earlier about the emergence of a core of career diplomats to obscure the fact that the 'official' diplomatic 'service' remained extremely small and would be necessarily supplemented by non-professionals. Among those whom it would be difficult to describe as professionals but who could play an important role was the marchese di Parella, whose family contacts in Vienna made him useful in negotiations there.[89] As for those 'professionals' identified earlier, such as the comte de Briançon, it would be equally correct to see their careers as reflecting the continued influence on appointments of kinship and clientage (see Chapter 4). The Savoyard diplomatic network was not in 1690, nor did it become by 1720, the sort of narrowly recruited professional, 'modern' corps that the term 'diplomatic service' might imply. As for the secretary's office, it was still, like most others in the state, very small, comprising (apart from the secretary himself) just five subordinate secretaries in 1699.[90] For another, the secretary had many other responsibilities. Reflecting the fact that his office originated as one serving the prince, the secretary was also still the ducal notary, responsible for the private contracts of the duke and his family. In addition, the man (and the degree to which he retained the confidence of the prince) was still in many

---

[87] In June 1691, de la Tour claimed that five posts had passed without his receiving any despatches from Turin. This was particularly worrying given rumours at The Hague of Piedmont's desperate situation, the country being near revolt, and the court 'confused' – all of which he was hard put to counter, DLT to ST, 8 June 1691, AST/LM/Olanda, m. 1. In 1696, with a general peace apparently about to be concluded, de la Tour (who was ignorant of his master's secret negotiations with Louis XIV) thought that Victor Amadeus must not risk a third military defeat against the French forces then entering Piedmont, DLT to ST, 11 May 1696, Hague, AST/LM/Olanda, m. 5.

[88] Gasco, 'La politica sabauda', 346.

[89] It was intended to send Parella to Vienna in 1687, although he did not go: Vitelleschi, *Romance of Savoy*, I, 267 ff. Parella did go in 1689; see the draft instructions, for Parella to negotiate Victor Amadeus' investiture with his imperial fiefs, the acquisition of the Langhe fiefs and the royal treatment, 1689, AST/Materie d'Impero/Investiture, m. 3/7. [90] Prato, 'Il costo', *CGP*, X, 243.

respects, as elsewhere in Europe, more important than his office, which largely depended upon him, while the distinction between public and private spheres remained vague.[91] Victor Amadeus, who may not have had as much confidence in the younger Saint-Thomas as he had had in the latter's father, might circumvent his 'foreign office'. In May 1701, he instructed Maffei to send any proposals he received for the exchange of his master's territories for a share of the Spanish Succession through the secretary's office but not to refer to the present letter, which was presumably sent without Saint-Thomas' knowledge.[92]

Indeed, although he might be influenced by the older Saint-Thomas' greater experience, Victor Amadeus was very much his own foreign minister. In 1695, his insistence on seeing all important documents delayed the return to The Hague of his ratification of the renewal of the Grand Alliance, which Saint-Thomas thought required little more than a signature. The duke might even reject the elder Saint-Thomas' advice. On the occasion, again, of the renewal of the Grand Alliance, Victor Amadeus, who rightly feared that some of his more powerful allies were negotiating a separate peace behind his own back, had sent to de la Tour a *mémoire* outlining his own sacrifices on behalf of the allied war effort, which he insisted (against the advice of Saint-Thomas) must be given in writing.[93] Partly, no doubt, as a security measure, Victor Amadeus sometimes also kept his envoys ignorant of important developments, de la Tour and Tarino both being surprised by his switch of alliances in 1696, although reports of secret deals between Victor Amadeus and Louis XIV had been circulating since 1690. The duke might even avoid the use of an intermediary, dealing personally with Louis XIV's negotiator, Tessé in 1693–94 and 1696, and again in the alliance negotiations of 1701.[94] The duke might also obtain useful information, even negotiate, by means of his correspondence with members of his family abroad, above all his two daughters, married into the French and Spanish courts, again circumventing what we might call the 'official structures'.[95] Foreign subjects,

---

[91] On the death of Giuseppe Gaetano (1749) a quantity of official documents were recovered from the private papers of the Saint-Thomas family: see AST/RAC/Scritture Regi Archivi/Inventari, m. 3 (4).

[92] Contessa, 'I regni', 55. Priè was promoted minister of state on his return from Vienna (1701), and effectively rivalled Saint-Thomas as the duke's chief minister, Carutti, *Diplomazia*, III, 327.

[93] ST to DLT, 22 Sept. 1695, Turin, AST/LM/Olanda, m. 4. Saint-Thomas preferred to allow de la Tour to decide between this and a less damaging oral representation.

[94] Carutti, *Diplomazia*, III, 218–19; P. Canestrier, 'Comment M. de Tessé prepara en 1696 le traité de paix entre Louis XIV et Victor-Amédée de Savoie', *Revue d'Histoire Diplomatique*, 48, 1934, passim.

[95] Victor Amadeus' correspondence with his daughter, Marie-Louise, Philip V's first queen, was used by his Bourbon opponents to make him peace proposals during the War of the Spanish Succession: see Carutti, *Diplomazia*, III, 382, for a letter of Jan.

too, might be a useful alternative to Victor Amadeus' own officials. Particularly striking in this respect is the duke's use of the venetian abbé, Vincenzo Grimani, as an intermediary in his 'unofficial' negotiations with both the Republic of Venice and the emperor before (and after)1690.[96] In part, Grimani was preferred because of his contacts in Vienna and because using a resident minister in this sort of work could undermine the latter's longer-term position at the court where he resided. But, as in other spheres of government, another crucial factor was the personal relationship between the individual and Victor Amadeus.

This did not mean that Victor Amadeus could ignore advice, or that foreign policy was not the subject of debate and disagreement, even among his closest collaborators. In the summer of 1696, Priè, an advocate of the Austrian Habsburg alliance, from Vienna urged the unwisdom of Victor Amadeus' *volte-face*;[97] and during the Utrecht negotiations the duke occasionally followed the advice of his plenipotentiaries who were not only very experienced but had a better sense, being on the spot, of what was possible.[98] In addition, no ducal attempt to monopolise control of, and to stifle, debate about foreign policy among his subjects could completely succeed, given the great importance of these issues between 1690 and 1720. The Vaudois (and Huguenot) exiles who swarmed to the duke's states in the 1690s continued to appeal to the Protestant powers, and their envoys in Turin, against the measures of Victor Amadeus and his minister (see Chapter 6). Some of Victor Amadeus' other, especially his noble, subjects had their own contacts with foreign courts, which, as in the case of Parella, the duke might exploit for his own purposes. Some of these nobles were determined to pursue their own claims: the marquis d'Aix protested, as a claimant to the principality of Orange, against the relevant provisions of the peace of Utrecht.[99] Finally, although we should beware of exaggerating the existence (and influence) of what we might call 'public opinion' in Turin, or in the wider Savoyard state, something of the sort did exist.

1708, and VDM to Heinsius, 19 Oct. 1709, Turin, ARAH/EA/VDM/33, f. 176, for the duke's communication of a similar letter.

[96] V. Dainotti, 'Vittorio Amedeo II a Venezia nel 1687 e la Lega di Augusta', *BSBS*, 35, 1933, 465 ff. Victor Amadeus used Grimani, to put pressure on his allies in the winter of 1693–4, see G. P. O. de Cléron, comte d'Haussonville, *La duchesse de Bourgogne et l'Alliance Savoyarde sous Louis XIV*, 3 vols., 4th edn (Paris, 1906), I, 57 ff.

[97] Rimostrazione . . . dal marchese di Priè, 17 June 1696, Vienna, AST/Negoziazioni/Austria, m. 5 (17).

[98] Those plenipotentiaries urged the duke to surrender the Barcelonette valley, to secure his alpine barrier and not to take exception to Philip V's limited ratification of the cession of Sicily, which otherwise he might lose: Gasco, 'La politica sabauda', 355 and passim.

[99] Comte Marc de Seyssel-Cressiau, *La Maison de Seyssel: ses origines, sa généalogie, son histoire*, 2 vols. (Grenoble, 1900), 20.

Victor Amadeus could not wholly ignore his subjects' desire for peace (see Chapter 4) and during the critical early phase of the War of the Spanish Succession sought to prevent enemy peace proposals becoming widely known in his states, since he might then come under pressure to respond to, or even accept them. This was another argument – the domestic political one – for secret diplomacy.[100]

Despite these reservations, however, diplomacy and foreign policy were spheres in which ducal authority was more firmly asserted, and a more 'modern' state structure achieved, in these decades. The remarkable expansion of Savoyard diplomacy from 1690 inevitably generated a great deal of paperwork. This vastly increased documentation, reflected in the enormous growth in the volumes of diplomatic materials in the Archivio di Stato, inevitably put growing pressure on the traditional administrative framework within which Savoyard diplomacy operated. This was certainly one of the reasons for the reform of the spring of 1717 which split the first secretary's office and created (echoing the practice in Louis XIV's France) a distinct foreign ministry, now able to concentrate on the task of co-ordinating an enlarged Savoyard diplomacy.[101] But that reform (and the more wideranging overhaul of the central institutions of the state of which it was part) was also necessitated – something which most accounts largely ignore – by the intense diplomatic activity of the Savoyard state after 1713, as Victor Amadeus sought to defend his new states and status in an unfavourable international climate.[102] This reform of the direction of Savoyard diplomacy finally ended the century-long domination of the Carron de Saint-Thomas,[103] confirming Victor Amadeus' control of the key institutions of the state through his own creatures, the marchese del Borgo becoming the first foreign secretary. The change undoubtedly meant a step towards specialisation, freeing the first secretary for foreign

---

[100] In 1695, 'the public' in Turin was said to be eager to know how William III would provide for the government of his realms in his absence on campaign following the death of Queen Mary, ST to DLT, 13 and 16 May 1695, Frassineto, AST/LM/Olanda, m. 4. In 1709, apparently, opinion in Turin (following the publication in Milan of the emperor's edict denying Victor Amadeus' sovereignty in the Monferrato) variously feared and wanted war against the emperor, VDM to Fagel, 19 Oct. 1709, Turin, ARAH/EA/VDM/33, f. 175 ff.

[101] There are accounts of this major reform in Frigo, *Principe, ambasciatori*, 17 ff.; Symcox, *Victor Amadeus*, 195, Quazza, *Le riforme*, I, 55 ff. and Storrs, 'Savoyard diplomacy in the eighteenth century', 220 ff.

[102] See Tallone, 'Vittorio Amedeo II e la Quadruplice Alleanza', 194.

[103] In fact, Saint-Thomas still played some part in the direction of affairs in 1717–18: see Tallone, 'Vittorio Amedeo II e la Quadruplice Alleanza', 219–20, 228, 238, 241, and *DBI, sub voce*, for his disastrous mission to Vienna in 1718. The ministers of George I suspected him of plotting with the Swedes (against Britain), VA to Cortanze, 10 Jan. 1720, Turin, AST/LM/GB, m. 24. If for no other reason, it was politic for Victor Amadeus to dispense with Saint-Thomas at this critical juncture.

affairs from (most of) his distracting domestic responsibilities. But del Borgo was little more than the instrument of his master, whose determination to control foreign policy was now underpinned by long experience. Indicative of the continued primacy of Victor Amadeus was the fact that between December 1719 and December 1720, at the height of the Sicily–Sardinia exchange crisis, the marchese di Cortanze, Victor Amadeus' minister in London, sent 90 letters to Turin, barely 10 of them to del Borgo. Of the 120 letters received by Cortanze, half came from the king and half from del Borgo. As before 1717, the former were by far the most important.[104]

THE FUNCTIONS AND OBJECTIVES OF SAVOYARD DIPLOMACY

Savoyard diplomats had three basic functions: the discovery and transmission of intelligence, negotiation and the representation of their master and his state. Military (and naval) intelligence included details of enemy plans and preparations affecting Victor Amadeus' states[105] and local campaign reports.[106] Political intelligence was equally diverse, ranging from reports on the health of Carlos II[107] to information about what Victor Amadeus' allies were up to. In June 1695, de la Tour informed his master of reports from Paris which suggested that William III's confidant, Dijkveld, was negotiating secretly with the French, the magistrates of Amsterdam and the emperor's ministers at The Hague, to the exclusion of both de la Tour himself and the Spanish ambassador there. It was reports such as these which enabled Victor Amadeus to decide which way the wind was blowing and to make his own separate peace in 1696.[108] Reflecting the relative isolation of Savoy before 1690, information on a host of other subjects, including court ceremonial, was also welcome in

---

[104] Storrs, 'Savoyard diplomacy in the eighteenth century', p. 233.
[105] In 1705, the English ministry supplied intelligence of French contacts inside Nice, Briançon to VA, 3 Apr. 1705, London, *CGP*, V, 398 ff.
[106] In 1695 de la Tour reported the progress of the allies' successful siege of Namur in Flanders. During the following war, Victor Amadeus' minister at the court of 'Charles III', the cavaliere Melazzo, was a valuable source of information on the war in Spain, VDM to Fagel 3 and 15 June 1707, Turin, ARAH/EA/VDM/31, f. 113, 118.
[107] Contessa, 'I regni', passim.
[108] DLT to ST, 14 and 28 June 1695, Hague, AST/LM/Olanda, m. 4; Storrs, 'Diplomatic relations', 263 ff. Indicating the importance of intelligence in Savoyard diplomacy, de la Tour observed that, although nothing positive could be proved, the matter was so important that even the simplest suspicions should not be ignored. In the subsequent war, del Borgo's reports from The Hague of proposals made by the Portuguese envoy for a peace settlement (including the settlement of Philip V in Italy) enabled Victor Amadeus to instruct his diplomats to ensure that they were prepared for negotiations on this basis, VA to Briançon, 27 May 1705, Turin, *CGP*, V, 374.

Turin.[109] Foreign intelligence could have important implications for the process of state formation: Victor Amadeus' diplomats at Vienna kept him informed about the activities there of those imperial feudatories transferred to the duke's sovereignty following his treaty with the emperor of 1703, but who resented their incorporation into the Savoyard state and were manoeuvring to avoid it.[110] In addition, diplomats could supply information about institutions and practices elsewhere which might provide an organisational model for the developing Savoyard state.[111] Negotiations revolved around the conclusion of those treaties which ensured Victor Amadeus the additional resources of men and money crucial to successful warfare and the peace treaties which enshrined his territorial and other successes, but could involve much more.[112] As for representation, the diplomat was always in a sense representing his master, but on occasion did so when specific grants and honours were bestowed (and oaths given).[113] Representation also meant, more broadly, projecting abroad the image of Victor Amadeus and his state.[114] Savoyard diplomats also carried out many lesser tasks, including private purchases for their master, further reflecting the degree to which the diplomatic 'service' was still the personal instrument of the prince (rather than of an impersonal state).

But what were Victor Amadeus' larger diplomatic objectives? Essen-

---

[109] In October 1691, de la Tour pointed out that if he returned to London he must have letters for Queen Mary, who ruled jointly with William III. It had been taken ill that he had none the previous winter, DLT to ST, 26 Oct. 1691, Hague, AST/LM/ Olanda, m. 1.

[110] VDM to Fagel, 4 May 1709, Turin, ARAH/EA/VDM/33, f. 73.

[111] In 1711 conte Provana sent from Vienna a *mémoire* detailing the system of Austrian military tribunals, discipline among his expanded forces being a matter which greatly interested Victor Amadeus, P. Bianchi, 'Guerra e politica nello stato sabaudo (1684–1730). Le riforme militari di Vittorio Amedeo II fra istituzioni, reclutamento e organizzazione territoriale' (Ph.D. thesis, University of Turin, 1997), 213 ff.

[112] In 1691, the duke hoped to take advantage of the arrival of German troops to relieve Montmélian and to take winter quarters in the Duchy of Savoy. He ordered Govone to concert with William III's envoy in Switzerland the secret provision (with or without Bern's connivance) of 30,000 sacks of corn in the Pays de Vaud, VA to DLT, 17 June 1691, Turin, AST/LM/Olanda, m. 1. Ricuperati, 'Gli Strumenti', 805 notes the influence of foreign (especially French and Spanish Bourbon) models, reported by Victor Amadeus' diplomats, on his administrative reorganisation of 1717.

[113] In March 1692, Victor Amadeus' ambassador in Vienna took, on his master's behalf, the oath of fidelity to the emperor as commander-in-chief of the imperial forces in Italy, *London Gazette*, 2749.

[114] In 1692 de la Tour relayed requests, received from the Blaeu brothers of Amsterdam, for payment of the so-called *Atlas de Savoye*, which their father had printed for Charles Emanuel II (as part of his attempts to enhance the image of his states). He urged that the brothers be paid what was owed them since they were influential officials of Amsterdam, DLT to ST, 3 June 1692, Hague, AST/LM/Olanda, m. 2. See L. Firpo, ed., *Theatrum Sabaudiae: teatro degli stati del Duca di Savoia*, 2 vols. (Turin, 1984–5).

tially, Savoyard diplomacy sought security and aggrandisement, primarily territorial (but also 'moral' i.e. the so-called royal treatment). This clearly lay behind the preoccupation with Pinerolo in the Nine Years War, Victor Amadeus' desire for Milan and the Monferrato, and his determination to secure the alpine barrier in 1712–13. It may also have influenced de la Tour's initial hopes of exploiting the anticipated success of the Grand Alliance against France in the 1690s to secure for Victor Amadeus part of southern France. These hopes, although they were ultimately disappointed, reflected the degree to which Savoyard diplomats (and their master) saw great new opportunities of expansion opening up in these decades, but also the extent to which Savoyard diplomacy sought to recover territories lost in the past, including both Geneva and Pinerolo, and to make the most of an extensive inheritance of claims of all sorts which could either be realised or bartered for some other advantage.[115]

Hopes of territorial expansion were focused primarily on securing the Spanish monarchy, or a part of it – particularly the Milanese – as compensation for surrendering Victor Amadeus' claims on the whole. In this respect it must be stressed that, contradicting the later 'Risorgimento'-inspired views of historians like Carutti and Contessa, for whom the acquisition of Pinerolo in 1696 and of Sicily in 1713 were steps towards a Savoyard unification of Italy, Victor Amadeus was not pursuing any policy of Italian integration. Victor Amadeus was certainly ready to use the language of a 'free Italy' with his allies, to gain their support against Louis XIV. In the winter of 1694–95, for example, he urged the emperor that securing Pinerolo for the duke of Savoy would ensure the freedom of Italy and the security of Milan, and would be of enormous value to the emperor should the Austrian Habsburgs succeed Carlos II.[116] But this was little more than self-interested rhetoric, intended to ensure that his allies helped him secure Pinerolo. Victor Amadeus' attitude did not change markedly thereafter. The duke was quite prepared to swop his territories in north Italy for Naples and/or Sicily and even to abandon them completely to secure the larger prize of the Spanish monarchy;[117] and in 1712 he told his plenipotentiaries at Utrecht that he was concerned less with the common interest of Italy

---

[115] C. Storrs, 'Machiavelli dethroned: Victor Amadeus II and the making of the Anglo-Savoyard Alliance of 1690', *European History Quarterly*, 22/3, 1992, 362. See the *relazione* detailing Savoyard claims on the Auvergne, Clermont and the Duchy of Brittany, 1697, in AST/Negoziazioni/Francia, m. 17/18.

[116] VA to DLT, 5 Dec. 1694, Turin, AST/LM/Olanda, m. 4. The duke also suggested to one imperial minister that possession of Pinerolo was one of the means whereby Louis XIV deprived Italy of imperial protection, VA to Count Kinsky, 1 Jan. 1695, Turin, AST/LM/Olanda, m. 4 (copy).   [117] Contessa, 'I regni', passim.

than with his own.[118] Victor Amadeus' diplomacy fully conforms to that 'proprietary dynasticism' identified by Herbert Rowen. It was emphatically not that of a putative 'Italian'.[119]

On the other hand, providing for the various members of the different branches of the House of Savoy, or Casa Savoia, one of the oldest dynasties in Europe, was a key concern of Victor Amadeus' foreign, or rather dynastic policy, one unduly neglected in some traditional and more recent surveys of the subject. That Savoyard diplomacy operated on behalf of the 'house', rather than of an impersonal, modern Savoyard 'state', was asserted repeatedly by Victor Amadeus himself,[120] and was taken for granted by his ministers.[121] Savoyard diplomacy worked in favour of the ruling house in a number of ways, including efforts to make good the territorial and other claims of the various branches of the dynasty, claims which (if realised) might extend the dominion and enhance the prestige of both the duke and the Casa Savoia. In the winter of 1694–95, for example, Victor Amadeus ordered de la Tour to seek William III's support for the duke's uncle, the prince of Carignano, one of many claimants to the county and sovereignty of Neuchâtel, then in the possession of the duchess of Nemours, who was not expected to live long. The duke believed that William's support might help overcome any opposition to the prince on the part of neighbouring Protestant Bern.[122] In 1704, when ratifying the treaty for the despatch to Piedmont of 8,000 troops of another claimant, the king of Prussia (see Chapter 1), the duke specifically reserved his uncle's claim on Neuchâtel. However, when the duchess of Nemours at last died in 1707, the king of Prussia (who had the backing of the Grand Alliance and of the Neuchâtel estates) triumphed. Since Victor Amadeus needed the king's support in the

---

[118] Gasco, 'La politica sabauda', 335. This followed Venetian approaches at Utrecht, seeking to interest the duke in the defence of Italian interests against an all-powerful emperor, which Victor Amadeus (probably correctly) saw as little more than a cover for more narrowly Venetian concerns.

[119] H. H. Rowen, *The King's State: proprietary dynasticism in early modern France* (New Brunswick, 1980).

[120] Victor Amadeus observed in 1700, that the Spanish Succession was a momentous issue both for himself and his house, Contessa, 'I regni', 18; and in 1713 explained his agreement to cede the Barcelonette valley in return for the alpine barrier by referring to the need to contain a power which had in the past been so threatening to 'our house', Gasco, 'Politica sabauda', 355.

[121] In 1691, informed that the Grand Priorate of Castile, a major Spanish dignity, was vacant, and assuming that Victor Amadeus would want it for his cousin Prince Eugene (but without the duke's order), Saint-Thomas ordered Operti to press the latter's candidacy in Madrid, ST to VA, 26 Sept. 1691, Turin, AST/LP/C, m. 36.

[122] VA to DLT, 5 Feb. 1695, Turin, AST/LM/Olanda, m. 4. William, who also claimed Neuchâtel, declined his aid: DLT to ST, and to Prince of Carignano, 10 May 1695, London, AST/LM/GB, m. 8.

empire in his increasingly difficult dealings with the emperor, he preferred at this stage to sacrifice the claims of the prince of Carignano – who had his own 'diplomats' representing and pursuing his interests in Neuchâtel – in order to pursue his own.[123] Victor Amadeus was also prepared to use his diplomatic network to secure prestigious marriages for the females of the house. In 1704, for example, he pressed (unsuccessfully) the candidacy of Princess Maria of Carignano as a bride for 'Charles III' of Spain.[124]

Occasionally, Savoyard diplomats were also ordered to secure foreign niches (above all in the service of the emperor, Louis XIV or Carlos II of Spain) for junior members of the Casa Savoia who might otherwise represent a liability and embarrassment. Victor Amadeus' efforts on behalf of Prince Eugene are well known[125] but were by no means the limit of the duke's efforts on behalf of his relations. In 1695, Prince Eugene's elder brother, Prince Thomas, comte de Soissons, abandoned the service of Louis XIV, and headed for Milan, hoping to enter that of Carlos II of Spain. Victor Amadeus, partly out of a concern to allay any suspicions among his allies that the prince was mediating a separate peace between himself and the French king, received his cousin coolly and encouraged his departure for the Low Countries, where he sought the support of William III in a bid for employment in Madrid. Prince Thomas followed William to London, where he was arrested for non-payment of a debt contracted during an earlier visit. De la Tour paid 2,000 écus to save the prince from this indignity, in the knowledge that Victor Amadeus would not want a member of the Casa Savoia to become an object of public contempt. Subsequently, Operti in Madrid was ordered to press there Prince Thomas' case for suitable, i.e. prestigious and remunerative, employment within the Spanish monarchy, employment which might in turn advance Victor Amadeus' own interests in Madrid.[126] In the meantime, Prince Thomas' amity with William

---

[123] Segre, 'Negoziati . . . Prussia', *CGP*, VI, 314 ff.
[124] See VA to Priè, 24 Feb. and 2 Mar. 1706, Turin, *CGP*, 5, 23 ff.
[125] See D. McKay, *Prince Eugene of Savoy* (London, 1977), 12, 25.
[126] DLT to ST, 22 Apr. 1695, London, AST/LM/GB, m. 8; ST to DLT, 16 May 1695, Frassineto, AST/LM/Olanda, m. 4. In the winter of 1697–8, Victor Amadeus hoped, with the aid of Carlos II of Spain, to secure for a sister of Prince Eugene (whose scandalous conduct in Paris was embarrassing the Casa Savoia) the co-adjutorship of the abbey of Nivelle in Spanish Flanders, where she could soon expect to succeed the ailing abbess, Bazan to Carlos II, 1 Nov. 1697, Turin, AGS/E/3659. The attempt failed, the duke being informed that the appointment was not among Carlos' regalian rights, Carlos II to VA, 31 Jan. 1698, Escorial, AGS/E/3660/74. On the princess, see R. Devos, 'Couvents et dames galantes en Savoie, Marie-Jeanne-Baptiste de Savoie-Soissons (1665–1705), soeur du prince Eugène, à la Visitation à Annécy', *MMSSHAA*, XCVI, Mélanges offerts à Bernard Grosperion, 225 ff.

usefully supplemented de la Tour's efforts in London on Victor Amadeus' behalf. Unfortunately, the prince's efforts to find a new niche in Spain, paralleling (and to some extent a consequence of) the switch of alliances since 1690 of the head of the Casa Savoia, was a victim of Victor Amadeus' own *volte-face* of 1696.[127]

Having relations in high office in other states was no guarantee that they would use their position to Victor Amadeus' benefit. Eugene's relations with the duke were increasingly strained following the latter's *volte-face* of 1696, a process completed by the recriminations following the abortive Toulon expedition and Eugene's loyalty to the emperor.[128] During the crisis associated with the loss of Sicily, Victor Amadeus' efforts to reach an agreement with the emperor with the help of Eugene were thwarted by, in part, Eugene's refusal to help.[129] Nevertheless, the Casa Savoia clearly constituted an important dimension of Savoyard diplomacy in these decades. For the duke himself, it might mean the need for wider consultation within the House, particularly where a given policy drastically affected its ancestral territories. Thus, in 1710, during the preliminary allied peace negotiations with the French at Geertruydenberg, Victor Amadeus ordered Mellarède to discover Eugene's view on an exchange of his existing states for the kingdoms of Naples and Sicily, which represented a major transplanting of 'our House'.[130]

Victor Amadeus' claim to the Spanish Succession, derived from the marriage of Philip II's daughter, the Infanta Catherine, with Charles Emanuel I, was just one of many which might be exploited. In 1696, with his allies apparently hoping for a general peace on the basis of the Westphalia settlement of 1648 (which had confirmed the cession of Pinerolo in 1631), de la Tour suggested that his master might instead demand Pinerolo as heir of the House of Valois.[131] These claims were constantly being reinforced and added to by marriage. Victor Amadeus' own marriage (1684) to Anne-Marie of Orleans, niece of Louis XIV, Charles II and James, and granddaughter of Charles I, brought with it a claim to the English (and from 1707 British) throne, in an era when the English succession was another issue in international relations. The duke made little, at least publicly, of his claim to William III's crown in the early 1690s, but was aware of it, and the need to retain at least the

---

[127] DLT to VA, 2 Dec. 1695, London, AST/LM/GB, m. 8; VA to DLT, 31 Dec. 1695, Turin, AST/LM/Olanda, m. 4.   [128] McKay, *Prince Eugene*, 106–7.

[129] A. Tallone, 'Vittorio Amedeo II e la Quadruplice Alleanza', 195 and passim.

[130] Contessa, 'I regni', 73. The previous year Eugene had claimed that Briançon, the French town sought by the duke as part of an extensive Alpine barrier, contributed nothing to the latter, VDM to Heinsius, 5 June 1709, Turin, ARAH/EA/VDM/33, f. 87.

[131] DLT to ST, 3 and 10 Apr. 1696 and attached *mémoire*, AST/LM/Olanda, m. 5.

goodwill of the exiled James II, who sent agents to Turin to press James' interests and to remind Victor Amadeus of the family connection. Like many contemporaries, Victor Amadeus may also have had doubts about the long-term viability of the revolutionary regime in England. These different considerations may all have influenced his conduct in 1696 when he formally acknowledged James II as part of his switch of alliances.[132] However, following the peace of Rijswijk the duke (like Louis XIV) again recognised William III as king of England.[133] The birth of Victor Amadeus' sons, the prince of Piedmont, in 1699, and the future Charles Emanuel III in 1701, and the death of the future Queen Anne's son, the duke of Gloucester, gave the duchess of Savoy's claim new importance. In 1701, therefore, Victor Amadeus' minister in London, Maffei, formally protested to the English parliament against the Act of Succession, which set aside the rights of the duke's wife and her son in favour of the Protestant elector of Hanover, a move which reflected both anti-Catholic feeling and lingering hostility in England towards Victor Amadeus following his treachery in 1696.[134] Despite this setback, the duke continued to conduct his relations with the English court – or courts – with an eye to exploiting his dynasty's claims on the English succession.[135] Queen Anne was well aware of this family connection. Indeed, her sense of the need to compensate Victor Amadeus' duchess and her heirs for the injustice done in 1701 influenced her generosity towards the duke in the peacemaking of 1712–13.[136] Unfortunately,

[132] In early 1696, Victor Amadeus rejected a request from William III's envoy in Turin that he publicly celebrate the failed attempt to assassinate the king, claiming that this might further antagonise Louis XIV, ST to DLT, 27 Mar. 1696, Turin, AST/LM/Olanda, m. 5. Govone's formal speech to James II, at his audience in 1696, as reported in J. Barnardiston, *Transactions in Savoy* (London, 1697), referred to promises made by the duke to agents sent by James to Turin and looked forward to the exiled Stuart monarch's restoration at the general peace. [133] Carutti, *Diplomazia*, III, 250.

[134] *Ibid.*, 293 ff. and appendices. G. M. Trevelyan, *England Under Queen Anne: Blenheim* (London, 1930), 127, claims that disgust in London deprived Victor Amadeus of the chance to instal a Savoyard prince on the throne of England following the duke of Gloucester's death. This may refer to Charles Emanuel, but the issue (which has not been properly explored) is a complex one and would repay further study. The formal protest may have been, in part, prompted by a *mémoire* given by James II to the duke's minister at the French court: see 'memoria del Re Giacomo . . .', AST/Scritture Relativi alle Corti Stranieri, Inghilterra, m. 1/18.

[135] In 1713, Victor Amadeus' ambassador to the French court was instructed to maintain good relations with James II's widow. This was because her son, 'James III' (who had not been recognised as king by Victor Amadeus in 1701), if elevated to the British throne, might be useful to the duke's sons (and not, incidentally, the Savoyard 'state'): Vitelleschi, *Romance of Savoy*, II, 421–2.

[136] Anne and Anne-Marie had briefly grown up together, and in her last years the queen referred fondly to the latter as the only remaining member of her immediate family, Gregg, *Queen Anne*, 8.

from 1714 the new Hanoverian (and whig) regime in London was less sympathetic to its Savoyard rival, the dynastic issue contributing to the collapse of the close relationship and a projected defensive alliance between the two courts.[137]

Victor Amadeus II, like his predecessors (and other European princes and republics) was also greatly preoccupied with questions of ceremonial, dignity, precedence and rank. This was not least because of the contemporary distinction between (the select group of) crowned heads and the great number of uncrowned rulers and the growing differentiation between them in later seventeenth and eighteenth-century Europe. Diplomatic ceremonial, and above all, the so-called 'royal treatment', or *trattamento regio* (i.e. the rather more splendid treatment of a diplomat regarded as the representative of a crowned head) was one of the spheres in which this status could be most clearly given expression. Not surprisingly, the great majority of uncrowned heads sought royal status, by acquiring territories carrying crowns[138] or by grant of the 'royal treatment' (i.e. the treatment of their ministers at foreign courts as the representatives of crowned heads). At the same time they had to exercise vigilance to ensure that their own claims and rights were not ignored by rivals and that the latter did not steal a march in the competition for status. The dukes of Savoy had claimed crowned head status from 1632 when Victor Amadeus I assumed the title of king of Cyprus and the style of Royal Highness (*Altezza Reale*), a title and style which Victor Amadeus II used throughout this period.[139] Nineteenth-century historians had little sympathy with this issue, but the pattern and conduct of Savoyard diplomacy was as much influenced by the desire for recognition of the Casa Savoia's royal status as by the search for territory.[140] There were some successes before 1690, Charles II of England granting the royal treatment in 1682. However, securing wider recognition of this

---

[137] D. McKay, 'Bolingbroke, Oxford and the defence of the Utrecht settlement in Southern Europe', *EHR*, 86, 1971, 284. Victor Amadeus' relations with the Jacobite court in exile, especially after 1713, have hardly been dealt with in the secondary literature.

[138] See generally, Anderson, *Rise of Modern Diplomacy*, 17 ff. The Spanish Succession was very important in this respect, since it made so many crowns available.

[139] The claim to the crown of Cyprus derived from the marriage of Charlotte of Lusignan, queen of Cyprus (d. 1487) and a son of the duke of Savoy. This issue of crowned head status has recently been thoroughly treated by R. Oresko, 'The House of Savoy', 272 ff.

[140] The negotiations (1681) for a Portuguese bride for Victor Amadeus included a Savoyard demand for the royal title, D. Frigo, 'L'Affermazione della sovranità: famiglia e Corte di Savoia tra Cinque e Settecento', in C. Mozzarelli, ed., *'Familia' del principe e famiglia aristocratica*, 2 vols. (Rome 1988), I, 282. See the remarks of Oresko, 'House of Savoy', 338.

royal status, which was also a crucial aspect of Savoyard claims to sovereignty, was a major concern of Victor Amadeus' diplomacy in this era.[141]

Indicative of the degree to which the issue could influence ducal policy was the fact that the emperor's decision (1690) to grant Victor Amadeus royal treatment was one of the lures which led the duke to abandon his French connection. As for William III, he respected Charles II's earlier grant of royal treatment when de la Tour – who had initially appeared in London incognito because of uncertainty about just how the king would treat him – had his public audience of the king in November 1690.[142] Not all of the duke's new allies were so accomodating. On the occasion of the conclusion of Victor Amadeus' accession to the Grand Alliance, at The Hague in 1690, the Dutch representatives asserted their own claims to precedence. De la Tour was unwilling to press the issue, for fear of losing (or at the least delaying) the treaty, suggesting that Savoyard diplomats, like their master, recognised that they must sometimes yield in this matter, in order to achieve other goals.[143] Louis XIV's concession of the royal treatment was another factor in the duke's decision to abandon his allies and join the French king in 1696.[144]

Victor Amadeus' main competitors in the struggle for status were the lesser princes and states. In Italy the duke's main rivals were the Republic of Venice[145] and the grand duke of Tuscany.[146] In Germany, competition

[141] This preoccupation was not confined to a narrowly conceived diplomatic sphere. In 1706, at the height of the crisis of the Savoyard state, Victor Amadeus' duchess made difficulties about giving the title Excellency to the Genoese admiral welcoming her as she and her sons took refuge in the Genoese republic, and about allowing him to 'cover' himself in her presence. She claimed to be unaware that any sovereign granted him that title and that only ambassadors were permitted to 'cover' themselves before sovereigns, VDM to Fagel, 30 June 1706, Oneglia, ARAH/EA/VDM/30, 296.

[142] DLT to VA, 15 Sept. 1690 and 17 Nov. 1690, Hague, AST/LM/Olanda, m. 1.

[143] This episode is more fully treated in Storrs, 'Machiavelli Dethroned . . .', 372–3.

[144] R. D. Handen, 'The Savoy negotiations of the comte de Tessé 1693–1696' (Ph.D. thesis, University of Ohio, 1970), 140. In 1708, however, the Bourbons failed to detach him from the Grand Alliance with the offer of the Milanese with the royal title, Contessa, 'I regni', 54. The duke's response might be surprising. But just how the Bourbons would realise their offer was not obvious.

[145] Dainotti, 'Vittorio Amedeo II a Venezia', 464; In 1696, William III's reception in London of the embassy of recognition from the Republic of Venice provoked concern in Turin – above all as to whether there had been innovations in the established ceremonial to the advantage of the Venetians and to the detriment of Victor Amadeus. ST to DLT, 22 May 1696, Turin, AST/LM/Olanda, m. 5; DLT to ST, 4 May 1696, London, AST/LM/GB, m. 8; same to same, 19 June 1696, Hague, AST/LM/Olanda, m. 5.

[146] In Feb. 1691, following a grant to the grand duke of Tuscany by the emperor, Victor Amadeus secured an imperial decree that the grant did not prejudice his own claim, AST/Ceremoniale/Toscana, m. 1.

was keenest with the electors.[147] The remarkable expansion of Savoyard diplomacy in the 1690s and 1700s, while offering more opportunities to assert Savoyard claims, also ensured more conflicts. In December 1693, the prospect of the duke's envoy, Operti, being promoted to ambassador in Madrid to take advantage of Carlos II's grant of the royal treatment, prompted a flurry of activity there among the representatives of the German and Italian princes, who were all anxious about the implications for their own claims and standing.[148] Inevitably, new adjustments and arrangements were necessary and possible.[149] But evasion, too, was sometimes necessary.[150] Victor Amadeus might also have to acknowledge the gains of others to achieve other goals. In 1707, for example, he found it expedient (if he was to have the empire fall in with his own wishes in north Italy) to recognise at last the ninth electorate granted to the House of Hanover in 1692, another of the successes of this period in terms of status.[151] But Victor Amadeus himself scored one of the greatest successes, with his acquisition of Sicily (1713), which was at least as important for the royal dignity the island kingdom brought with it as for the additional territory and resources it represented. These remarks apply with even greater force to the much smaller and poorer island realm of Sardinia, which was of value to the House of Savoy only

---

[147] In 1690, when sending de la Tour powers to participate in the congress of allied ministers at The Hague, the duke pointed out that it would be greatly prejudicial if de la Tour yielded precedence to the minister of an elector, VA to DLT, 3 Oct. 1690, Turin, AST/LM/Olanda, m. 1. In fact, to avoid disputes of this sort (which would have made the congress inoperable), it had been agreed that the congress would ignore ranks, DLT to ST, 17 Oct. 1690, Hague, AST/LM/Olanda, m. 1.

[148] Wiser to elector palatine, 24 Dec. 1693, Madrid, in Adalbert of Bavaria and G. Maura Gamazo, eds., *Documentos ineditos referentes a las postrimerias de la Casa de Austria*, 3 vols. (Madrid, 1927–31), II, 154.

[149] In 1691, de la Tour was informed that the duke of Celle's envoy at Vienna would be ordered to treat Victor Amadeus' ambassador there as the duke of Celle (or his envoys) treated the emperor's ambassador, if Victor Amadeus reciprocated. De la Tour promised that his master's ministers would do so where the envoys of the House of Luneburg enjoyed crowned head treatment. DLT to VA, 22 Mar. 1691, Hague AST/LM/Olanda, m. 1. In 1709, the elector of Mainz agreed to address Victor Amadeus as 'Most Serene Royal Highness', Segre, 'Negoziati . . . Prussia', *CGP*, VI, 317.

[150] In 1702, Victor Amadeus met his son-in-law, Philip V of Spain, at Acqui. Despite acknowledging the duke's crowned head status, Spanish court etiquette emphasised the inferiority of Victor Amadeus who evaded further indignity by feigning illness, Vitelleschi, *Romance of Savoy*, II, 398–9.

[151] VDM to Griffier, 2 Mar. and 6 Apr. 1707, Turin, ARAH/EA/VDM/31, fs. 48, 75. Victor Amadeus seems to have made no difficulties in recognising the new status of the elector of Brandenburg as king (1701) in Prussia, Segre, 'Nagoziati . . . Prussia', *CGP*, VI, 287 ff.

because it carried a royal title[152], at least before Bogino's attempts to develop the island after 1750. It was this dramatic elevation of Victor Amadeus from duke to king, and the resulting dilemma for other states about whether to recognise his new status, which help make the period after 1713 such a distinct one. Victor Amadeus had succeeded in creating a new, royal, Savoyard state, one which benefited from the privileged standing of crowned heads, which some other candidates for royal status (including his cousin the elector of Bavaria), had failed to achieve.

THE ATTITUDES, CHARACTERISTICS AND METHODS OF SAVOYARD DIPLOMACY

How did Victor Amadeus and his collaborators see the world around them? The traditional view of the duke as successful manipulator might suggest a prince confidently surveying the international scene. Nothing could be further from the truth. Victor Amadeus was acutely aware of his own weakness in a Europe dominated by greater powers. This awareness made him very uncertain about how to act in a crisis. In 1690, for example, he just did not know whether to remain in the French camp or to join that of the emperor as the escalating European conflict threatened his own states at last and forced him to opt for one side of the other.[153] The debate surrounding the death of Carlos II and the outbreak of the War of the Spanish Succession about whether to ally with the Bourbons (urged by de la Tour) or the emperor (urged by Priè), echoed the uncertainty and division of 1690. Anxiety also contributed to a certain procrastination, as Victor Amadeus postponed crucial decisions for war and peace, which could frustrate his own ministers and, after 1713, to a frantic search for security.[154]

So-called 'maxims of state' regarding the interests or policy of other states might be one guide in this situation, although it was recognised that not all states acted according to (or even recognised) their own true interests. It was axiomatic among Savoyard policy makers in the 1690s, for example, that it was a Spanish maxim of state to run not risks, despite

---

[152] In 1713 Victor Amadeus' style changed from 'His Royal Highness' to 'His Majesty': I. Lameire, *Les occupations militaires en Italie pendant les guerres de Louis XIV* (Paris, 1903), 346. In 1718 Victor Amadeus sought, without success, to secure Tuscany with the title 'King of Liguria' instead of Sardinia: Carutti, *Storia della Diplomazia* III, 547–8.

[153] See 'memoria de capi da esaminarsi in consiglio circa li negozi correnti di SAR . . .', 1 Feb. 1690, AST/Negoziazioni/Austria, m. 4/24.

[154] In 1693, in reply to one of de la Tour's many outbursts on this score, Saint-Thomas declared (in confidence) his sympathy and explained that the problem was getting Victor Amadeus to decide for one of the various options, ST to DLT, 30 Aug. 1693, La Perouse, AST/LM/Olanda, m. 3; McKay, 'Bolingbroke, Oxford', 273 (for 1714).

Fig. 3.1 Illustration depicting bust of Victor Amadeus, the arms of the House of Savoy and his dominions, including the kingdoms of Cyprus and Sicily (Biblioteca Reale, Iconografia Varia 26/249)

the fact that this cautious policy had resulted in substantial Spanish territorial losses, and that Spanish ministers were resolved not give the governorship of Milan to the duke of Savoy.[155] Some other states –

[155] See VA to Operti, 15 July 1691, Turin, copy, and DLT to VA, 25 May 1691, Hague, both in AST/LM/Olanda, m. 1. In 1710, del Borgo claimed the same of Vienna, Contessa, 'I regni', 70.

notably England – were thought to be so unstable that no firm policy could be founded on them. In these circumstances, again reflecting his real weakness, Victor Amadeus must either, in the case of Spain, seek to change what were seen as the established maxims of state, or, in the case of England, accommodate himself to the political ebb and flow. In fact, a readiness to adapt to changing circumstance was – necessarily given its weakness – probably the most important maxim of Savoyard policy in these decades. It was articulated in the instructions given de la Tour following the second Partition Treaty agreed between William III and Louis XIV in March 1700, which had largely neglected the duke's own claims.[156] Despite this setback, he was not especially pessimistic, above all because execution of the project had to await the death of Carlos II. In fact, thought Victor Amadeus, both Louis XIV and William III, the former more than sixty and the latter nearly fifty, were more likely to die before Carlos because 'age is the most dangerous illness'. Therefore, he believed it was worth waiting on time and the workings of Providence, which often upset the best plans. Victor Amadeus turned to history for confirmation of this, claiming that there were no examples of such ambitious projects having succeeded, because men and conjunctures changed. This was no fatalistic philosophy, but provided the duke with invaluable guides for the conduct both of himself and of his diplomats.

Victor Amadeus also thought that the prince must remain free (of treaty commitments) as far as possible. It might be thought that this attitude underpinned his apparent readiness to ignore treaty obligations and abandon his allies. However, it would be quite wrong to emphasise his *volte-faces* at the expense of the duke's real concern (which was again essentially the product of his weakness) that all – above all his allies – fulfil their treaty obligations. In the winter of 1690–91, he was extremely anxious that his allies should not think he was wavering, fearing that in that case they might abandon him.[157] This did not mean that he might not negotiate secretly with the enemy, as he (and each of his allies) did throughout both the Nine Years War and the War of the Spanish Succession. It was difficult to maintain the secrecy for long. Indeed, Victor Amadeus might inform his allies of these negotiations. In 1692, when the question of whether to conclude a separate peace was debated by Victor Amadeus and his ministers,[158] he hoped to exploit the French offers to bind his allies (who were conducting their own separate secret negoti-

---

[156] These instructions are cited extensively in Contessa, 'I regni', 17 ff.
[157] See VA to Tarino, 20 Dec. 1690, Turin, AST/LM/Austria, m. 23.
[158] President Provana's consideration of the state of the war and whether Victor Amadeus should fight on or make peace with France, no date [but 1692?], AST/Negoziazioni/Francia, m. 15/17.

ations with the French king), more firmly to him and to secure a renewed commitment from them to his own full restoration (i.e. the recovery of Nice and Savoy) in any peace settlement.[159] To a degree, this policy worked. In 1693, William III's secretary at war, William Blathwayt, urged the departure of the long-delayed Mediterranean fleet, which might ensure the success of Victor Amadeus' plans of a joint land and sea assault on Provence, declaring that 'the Tempter is at hand and that more than the strongest assurances are requisite to keep that duke steady to the alliance'.[160] It was only in 1695–96, when his more powerful allies – who effectively regarded him as of secondary importance – seemed to be about to renege on their own treaty obligations, evading his efforts to secure from them renewed commitments to secure Pinerolo, that Victor Amadeus believed he had little option but to make his own deal with Louis XIV.[161] In addition, the failure of conte Vernone's mission to Madrid, 1695, to secure the governorship of Milan, meant that the conquest of the latter with the aid of Louis XIV seemed the only means for Victor Amadeus to secure this Savoyard objective (and forestall the emperor).[162] During the War of the Spanish Succession, this reputation for switching sides might be useful in ensuring Victor Amadeus' allies made greater efforts on his behalf, to prevent another betrayal, and it was deliberately exploited by the duke.[163]

However, such a reputation had its disadvantages. It made Victor Amadeus' own allies wary – at least initially – of wasting resources in case he should defect, provided his enemies with useful propaganda[164] and

---

[159] In the winter of 1691–2, Victor Amadeus informed his envoy in Switzerland, following French peace proposals to the Swiss (which he believed were aimed at himself), that the better terms the French offered him the better his allies would treat him, VA to Govone, 24 Jan. 1692, Turin, AST/LM/Svizzera, m. 27.

[160] Blathwayt to Nottingham, Dighem, 25 May 1693, Add. MSS 37992, f. 7.

[161] Storrs, 'Diplomatic relations', passim. Victor Amadeus may also have feared the disintegration of the Grand Alliance, as relations between the Maritime Powers and Spain effectively broke down following the expulsion (1695) of the agent of the former, Schonenberg, from Madrid, *ibid.*, 297 ff.

[162] A. Legrelle, *La diplomatie française et la succession d'Espagne*, 4 vols., 2nd edn, (Paris, 1888–92). I, 450.

[163] In 1704, as his enemies occupied his states, the duke informed his allies that if not helped he must take his own measures, reporting approaches by Louis XIV, VDM to Fagel, 26 Sept. and 3 Dec. 1704, Turin, ARAH/EA/VDM/29, 165, 191. In 1711, Victor Amadeus' resentment of his treatment by the emperor vented itself in declarations that he knew how to take care of his own interests to the British envoy, who feared a 'scurvy trick', Chetwynd to Dartmouth, 1 July 1711, Turin, SP 92/27, f. 458.

[164] Louis XIV's declaration of war (1703) referred to Victor Amadeus' notorious duplicity, J. Klaits, *Printed Propaganda under Louis XIV: absolute monarchy and public opinion* (Princeton, 1976), 198.

tarnished the duke's reputation or *gloire*.¹⁶⁵ In fact, he was remarkably loyal to his allies during the War of the Spanish Succession, despite French efforts to exploit his growing resentment of the emperor's conduct and of the latter's expanding power in Italy to achieve a repeat of the *volte-face* of 1696, and spreading rumours that it was imminent.¹⁶⁶ Allied success from 1706, and Britain's lead in concluding what was largely a separate peace from 1711, made this difficult. Victor Amadeus was not therefore obliged by the disparity between himself and his more powerful allies, as he had been in 1696, to adopt a line of conduct which won him renown but also widespread condemnation. Instead he made a virtue of necessity and stressed the obligations of his more powerful allies, not least as a reward for his loyalty.¹⁶⁷ As in the previous war, the duke and his diplomats found it advantageous to articulate the rhetoric of the 'common cause' of the allies against Louis XIV.¹⁶⁸ After 1713, Victor Amadeus was particularly concerned to see treaties respected since his hold on Sicily rested upon those concluded at Utrecht.

This emphasis on treaty obligations reflected a larger emphasis on the legal and historical claims of the duke of Savoy. For this reason, for example, the three-man team sent to negotiate at Utrecht in 1712 included the lawyer Mellarède, who had been involved in the very legalistic negotiations in Milan and Vienna regarding the cession of imperial fiefs in north Italy.¹⁶⁹ This emphasis was not peculiar to Savoyard diplomacy, since all princes and states needed a legal cover of some sort for their claims. Nor was legal expertise the only, or even the most important, quality sought in a diplomat. Mellarède, was only one, and by no means the most important, of the Utrecht negotiating team. But legal right might

---

¹⁶⁵ This was one of the arguments against the duke's *volte-face* put to de la Tour in 1696 by William III and Max Emanuel of Bavaria, the latter claiming to feel it all the more strongly because he was 'family', DLT to VA, 24 July 1696, Brussels, AST/LM/Olanda, m. 5. One English diplomat, disgusted by the duke's betrayal in 1696, referred to Victor Amadeus thereafter by various double-edged epithets, including that of 'the juggler', George Stepney to Richard Hill, 31 Oct. 1703, Vienna, in W. Blackley, ed., *The Diplomatic Correspondence of the Right Hon. Richard Hill, envoy extraordinary from the court of St James to the duke of Savoy*, 2 vols. (London, 1845), I, 52.   ¹⁶⁶ Carutti, *Diplomazia*, III, 382 ff. (1709).
¹⁶⁷ See VDM to Fagel, 22 Apr. 1705, Turin, ARAH/EA/VDM/30, 35.
¹⁶⁸ Following his second defeat, in 1693, the duke restated both the value to the allies of a diversion in Piedmont (which he claimed cost Louis XIV three times more than the same allied effort elsewhere) and his own sacrifices for the 'common cause', VA to DLT, 22 Oct. 1693, Turin, AST/LM/Olanda, m. 3. References of this sort fill most contemporary diplomatic correspondence.
¹⁶⁹ Carutti, 'Relazione sulla Corte d'Inghilterra', 221 ff.; Carutti, *Diplomazia*, III, 389–90. Del Borgo was also an able lawyer, *DBI*, *sub voce*. Other lawyers sent on 'diplomatic' missions included President Graneri, appointed to settle (with Prince Eugene) the duke's differences with the emperor, VDM to Griffier, 3 Mar. 1708, Turin, ARAH/EA/VDM/32, f. 39.

also, particularly for a smaller state, to some extent counter real weakness. Arguments drawn from history, too, might underpin schemes of aggrandisement and help Victor Amadeus and his ministers fend off otherwise unwelcome schemes (without the offence of outright rejection). In 1696, among the arguments which Priè was ordered to deploy in Vienna to justify the duke's *volte-face* was the uncertainty of Victor Amadeus' restoration, if he did not accept Louis XIV's offers. He was told to support this claim by reference to his master's sixteenth-century ancestor, the unfortunate duke Charles the Good (1504–53).[170] For these reasons, Savoyard diplomats often collected local legal and historical materials.[171]

In the instructions given de la Tour in 1700, Victor Amadeus also declared that the wise prince should protect his own interests without betraying anxiety, although this was probably the dominant emotion underlying Savoyard diplomacy in these decades, and that he who knew how to 'possess his soul' was the master of affairs. This brings us to another of those key characteristics of Savoyard diplomacy, related to the duke's supposed inclination towards double-dealing, which has dominated perceptions of Savoyard diplomacy ever since: its penchant for dissimulation or duplicity. In the winter of 1691–92, for example, Victor Amadeus sought to replace the imperial commander in Italy, Count Caraffa, hoping that this might ensure a more vigorous (and successful) campaign in Piedmont in 1692. However, he ordered his minister in Vienna, Priè, to go about it in a very roundabout way, avoiding open confrontation. Only the advice of the Spanish ambassador, marques de Borgomanero, and the imperial minister, Count Stratmann (both of whom the duke said Priè must be guided by) that he should speak openly led Priè (with his master's approval) to adopt this bolder, more forthright approach.[172] Of course, dissimulation was by no means confined to diplomacy, and was widely regarded as one of the distinguishing traits of the courtier. Nor was it peculiar to Savoyard diplomacy. But there is no doubt that dissimulation characterised Savoyard diplomacy more obviously than it did that of the Great Powers. It is almost impossible to conceive of Savoyard diplomats adopting the bullying tone used by the imperial minister at Utrecht, Count Sinzendorf, in conversation with del Borgo about Sicily in December 1713. Del Borgo evaded a tricky situation by declaring that Sicily was in the gift of Queen Anne, and not something on which Victor Amadeus could have his own ideas – which was typical of the way Savoyard diplomacy exploited its own

---

[170] VA to Priè, 4 July 1696, Turin, AST/LM/Olanda, m. 5. During the Utrecht negotiations unwelcome proposals regarding Sicily were met with arguments drawn from the island's history, Gasco, 'Politica sabauda', passim.

[171] See AST/Scritture Relativi alle Corti Stranieri/Spagna, m. 2/13 (Operti) and *DBI*, 'De Gubernatis'.   [172] VA to DLT, 9 Jan. 1692, Turin, AST/LM/Olanda, m. 3.

perceived and real weakness.[173] During those same negotiations Maffei won the confidence of the English Tory ministry, in part by not betraying Victor Amadeus' real hostility to the peace policy and proposals of the new ministry, and by refusing to join the other allied ministers in London in a formal representation to the queen in favour of the recently ousted Whigs (who favoured an energetic war). Maffei's dissimulation convinced the Tories that he alone of the allied ministers in London understood and dispassionately pursued his own master's true interests. They therefore took him into their confidence, enabling Maffei to discover from them what other foreign ministers had to wait to read in the London *Gazettes*.[174] Dissimulation was not an innovation in Savoyard diplomacy associated with this war. In 1695, following the discovery of the secret negotiations with the French of William III's confident, Dijkveld, from which Victor Amadeus, the German princes and Carlos II had been excluded, de la Tour urged that his master should at least 'insinuate' his resentment, even if he did not think fit to complain openly.[175] Weakness ensured that dissimulation would remain a key instrument of Savoyard diplomacy.

Despite Victor Amadeus' awareness of the possibilities offered to him by faction and party struggles, Savoyard diplomats did not interfere to any considerable extent in the domestic politics of the states where they resided. De la Tour seems to have been able to rely in the 1690s on the support of a number of MPs and peers favourable to his master.[176] Whether these contacts were with any distinct political group within parliament is not clear, but de la Tour was subsequently thought by Victor Amadeus to have been too pro-Whig. The duke advised Maffei to be less partial, thus ensuring that Savoyard interests remained invulnerable to a change of government,[177] but it could still be difficult to chart a steady course in the choppy waters of English politics. In 1713, Bolingbroke's praise of Maffei was qualified by the latter's intimacy with the disgraced Whig leader, the duke of Marlborough.[178] However, Maffei at least did not try to influence the queen's choice of ministers, as did the imperial minister in London. After 1713, with the Whigs back in power under George I, Victor Amadeus lost favour in London as a major beneficiary of the 'Tory' peace of Utrecht. In other courts, too, while

---

[173] Del Borgo to VA, 12 Dec. 1712, Contessa, 'I regni', 112 ff.
[174] Carutti, 'Relazione sulla Corte d'Inghilterra', 235.
[175] DLT to ST, 28 June 1695, Hague, AST/LM/Olanda, m. 5. In 1700, de la Tour pressed his master not to dissimulate over the Spanish Succession, Contessa, 'I regni', 34, 39 ff.
[176] See London newsletter of 8 Dec. 1693, in *HMC 7th Report*, Appendix, 216; and Storrs, 'Diplomatic relations', 213 for Victor Amadeus' escaping criticism of subsidies to allies.   [177] See Carutti, *Diplomazia*, III, 398.
[178] Carutti, 'Relazione sulla Corte d'Inghilterra', 235.

ready to work with those sympathetic to their master,[179] closer involvement in faction fighting seems to have been largely avoided. The wisdom of this approach was confirmed on the only occasion when Victor Amadeus did seriously attempt to intervene in the domestic politics of a foreign court, funding the opponents of his cousin Eugene (who opposed the marriage of the emperor's daughter with the future Charles Emanuel III), in Vienna in 1719. The effort proved counter-productive and Victor Amadeus was obliged to replace his minister at the imperial court, the marquis de Saint-Thomas.[180]

On the other hand, and despite his financial difficulties, the duke could not afford not to give, or at least promise, gratifications[181] or even bribes,[182] not least because some ministers seemed to expect (and even to tout for) them.[183] There was a clear expectation that these gifts would benefit Savoyard diplomacy: in 1694, for example, Victor Amadeus hoped that the Prussian chief minister, Danckelman, would co-operate with de la Tour's efforts in Berlin to resolve a recent difference over ceremonial, which was hindering the despatch of the elector's troops to Piedmont (see Chapter 1), not least because he paid Eberhard von Danckelman an annual pension.[184] However, gratifications did not guarantee success.[185] They, and pensions, were (like subsidies paid to

---

[179] See VA to conte Tarino, 8 Dec. 1703, Turin, CGP, IV, 39–40, urging him to co-operate with all the factions at the imperial court, but especially with Prince Eugene.   [180] DBI, sub voce; D. McKay, Prince Eugene, 169 ff.

[181] In 1692 the elector of Mainz and his chief minister were each rewarded with a diamond for their support in Vienna, Priè to ST, 11 June 1692, Vienna, AST/LM/Austria, m. 25. Subsequently, de la Tour's proposals to give presents to Lord Ranelagh, the minister largely responsible for the payment of the duke's English subsidy, and other English lords, were approved, ST to DLT, 6 Oct. 1694, Aosta, AST/LM/Olanda, m. 4; same to same, 5 Feb. and 29 Mar. 1695, Turin, AST/LM/Olanda, m. 5. See, in general, R. M. Hatton, 'Gratifications and foreign policy: Anglo-French rivalry in Sweden during the Nine Years War', in R. M. Hatton and J. S. Bromley, eds., *William III and Louis XIV 1680–1720: essays for M. A. Thomson* (Liverpool, 1968). There was a great difference between such gifts and the corruption of a secretary of the French ambassador in Turin, Phélypeaux, giving access to the latter's correspondence, Carutti, *Diplomazia*, III, 321–2.

[182] In 1709, Victor Amadeus briefly considered paying the duke of Marlborough more than 100,000 doppie for his help in securing the Milanese in the peace negotiations, Contessa, 'I regni', 66.

[183] DLT to ST, 1 July 1695, Hague, AST/LM/Olanda, m. 4.

[184] VA to DLT, 29 June 1694, Turin, AST/LM/Olanda, m. 4. Danckelman in fact refused cash but accepted a gift of Piedmontese silk to his wife, DLT to ST, 1 Oct. 1694, AST/LM/Olanda, m. 4.

[185] In 1693, Colonel Rossignol went to Saxony, to collect two regiments for which a capitulation had been concluded, taking 1,000 pistoles as presents for various ministers and officers, ST to DLT, 14 Mar. 1693, Turin, AST/LM/Olanda, m. 3, but did not secure the promised troops.

allies) an uncertain tool, in part because they were often a victim of the crisis affecting ducal finances in the war years. In 1703, a document drawn up in connection with Mellarède's mission to the Swiss cantons, to have the Duchy of Savoy taken into Swiss protection and to secure troops, showed that the Swiss pensions which the duke was obliged to pay according to his father's and his own treaties, had remained unpaid from 1690. An attempt was then made to pay 5,000 écus, or three years arrears, but the contribution of these moneys to the limited success of Mellarède's mission must remain uncertain.[186]

In the instructions of 1700 cited earlier, Victor Amadeus also declared that the prince should not foment jealousy among his neighbours and rivals by precipitate negotiations. Instead, he should be ready to exploit any opportunity. One consequence of this was to make Savoyard diplomacy opportunist and largely reactive. The duke and his ministers had to be alert to and exploit opportunities opened up by others. Typical of this approach was the Geneva renunciation scheme which surfaced briefly during the Nine Years War. Despite formal renunciations of their claims on Geneva and the Pays de Vaud, which had been lost in the middle decades of the sixteenth century when the Savoyard state had nearly disappeared altogether, the dukes of Savoy had not completely resigned themselves to their loss. Indeed in 1688–89 Victor Amadeus put a number of projects to the French king for operations against Bern (following reports that the latter was aiding Vaudois exiles from his states), suggesting that if Louis had responded, Victor Amadeus might have joined him against the Grand Alliance in the Nine Years War and continued the process of state formation as a French satellite.[187] These ambitions continued to worry the duke's Swiss neighbours. In 1692, in the course of discussions in Vienna about an invasion of France from Piedmont that year, the Dutch minister, Heemskerk, suggested that Victor Amadeus again formally renounce his claims to Geneva in order to gain that city for the Grand Alliance, facilitating the intended invasion. Victor Amadeus' minster, Priè, recognised the strategic advantages of the scheme but sought to turn it to advantage. He proposed that the duke of Savoy receive compensation for his renunciation, about which Heemskerk had said nothing, in the form of satisfaction of ducal claims on the Monferrato, i.e. in terms of long-established Savoyard ambitions. Priè even suggested that Victor Amadeus surrender to William III the port of Villefranche (which the duke could not defend) in return for support in Vienna for the grant at last of the Monferrato in exchange for renouncing

---

[186] P. Valente, 'Relazioni diplomatiche di Vittorio Amedeo II, duca di Savoia, coi Cantoni Svizzeri e colla Repubblica del Vallese durante il secondo periodo della guerra in Italia per la successione di Spagna (1703–1707)', *CGP*, VI, 391 and passim.

[187] Carutti, *Diplomazia*, III, 167.

Savoyard claims on Geneva. In fact, the scheme foundered on Geneva's understandable reluctance to defy Louis XIV, and the House of Savoy did not finally renounce its Genevan claims until the middle of the eighteenth century. Nevertheless, the episode reveals the way in which Savoyard diplomats were alert to new possibilities being opened to their master to exploit traditional Savoyard claims[188] and the extent to which they saw his new allies as a source of additional diplomatic leverage, notably in Vienna and Madrid, to achieve objectives which Victor Amadeus alone could not secure.[189] The essentially reactive approach revealed in this episode was equally in evidence during the Utrecht peace negotiations, when Victor Amadeus' plenipotentiaries were ordered not to raise the issue he was really concerned about, the acquisition of some or all of the Milanese, but to wait until some other power raised it.[190]

REACTIONS AND RESPONSES TO WIDER CONTACTS ABROAD

What effect, if any, did increased foreign, diplomatic contacts have on individual diplomats, and on the Savoyard state? Did they supply new political models, or suggest ones to avoid? One way of attempting to assess this interaction is to consider the attitudes expressed in the final *relazioni* increasingly required of Savoyard diplomats at the end of their mission. Unfortunately, this requirement was by no means uniformly expected or enforced, one further indication of the continued lack of uniformity in Savoyard diplomacy in this era. In addition, *relazioni* themselves varied remarkably in nature. In general, the *relazione* was expected to be an account of a mission or negotiations, with some broader description and assessment of the court, government, personalities and military, fiscal and other resources of the state concerned. Both Operti (Naples, 1691–96) and Trivié (Spain/Barcelona, 1707–11) produced lengthy *relazioni* of this

---

[188] The renunciation scheme is pieced together in Storrs, 'Diplomatic relations', 144 ff. In 1697 the duke was concerned to exclude Geneva from the general peace, since its inclusion would represent a blow to his claims: see the *mémoire* in AST/Negoziazioni, Francia, m. 17/15. Another renunciation was briefly considered by the duke in his abortive efforts to secure the Swiss guarantee from 1703, Carutti, *Diplomazia*, III, 349 ff. Suspicions of Savoyard ambitions in Switzerland were a gift to French propaganda there in the War of the Spanish Succession: Klaits, *Printed Propaganda*, 198.

[189] In 1691 de la Tour urged on William III the more effective contribution to the allied war effort in north Italy that the Milanese could play if the governorship were given to the dynamic and vigorous Victor Amadeus, DLT to VA, 25 May 1691, AST/LM/Olanda, m. 1. But if William did press this traditional Savoyard aspiration in Madrid, he clearly could not overcome Spanish objections.

[190] Symcox, *Victor Amadeus*, 163. This approach is amply demonstrated for the War of the Spanish Succession by both Contessa, 'I regni', and Gasco, 'Politica sabauda', passim (and 321 for a statement that this was their policy by Victor Amadeus' plenipotentiaries, Mar. 1712).

type, but they were in fact rather rare. Nothing of the sort was produced by de la Tour, for example, at the end of his mission to The Hague and London. Another type of *relazione* was the account of a mission, which was effectively a collection of relevant papers (instructions, correspondence and so on), or *précis* of them, preceded by an introduction. Typical were Mellarède's (four-volume) and del Borgo's (one-volume) accounts of the Utrecht peace negotiations, the former including an account of a brief mission to (and assessment of) the English court. However, if there are fewer Savoyard *relazioni* from this period than we might expect or wish for, valuable insights into attitudes and reactions are provided by the abundant correspondence which is the single most important legacy of Savoyard diplomatic activity.[191]

In fact diplomats, not surprisingly, were much less likely to seize the apparent opportunities to see a wider world than the independent traveller, because of the need to remain close to the centres of decision making and communications. None of the Savoyard diplomats sent to the Dutch Republic and England between 1690 and 1713 got much beyond London (apart from journeys to and from the coast) and The Hague. Briançon got no further than Winchester while no Savoyard envoy visited Wales, Scotland or Ireland (and rarely discussed these countries unless they thrust themselves to the political fore – as in the case of Scotland in 1707 and 1708). De la Tour made very occasional forays to the camp in Flanders and into the Dutch Republic in search of William III at his palace-cum-hunting lodge at Het Loo in the province of Utrecht; and journeyed twice (1691, 1694) into Germany, but this was a rather limited geographical range.[192] Trivié, Victor Amadeus' envoy to the court of 'Charles III' of Spain, saw little more of Spain than Barcelona, apart from Charles' brief sojourn in Madrid in 1710.[193] Nevertheless, this restricted geographical range did not necessarily mean a limited ability to observe or appreciate foreign states and societies.

The reactions of Savoyard diplomats to the Dutch Republic and to England could be positive. In September 1690, following the French victory at Fleurus in Flanders, de la Tour compared the Dutch to the

---

[191] C. Morandi, ed., *Relazioni di ambasciatori sabaudi, genovesi e veneti durante il periodo della grande alleanza e della successione di Spagna (1693–1713)* (Bologna, 1935). Trivié's *relazione* of 1711 is printed in full in Quazza, *Il problema italiano*, 359 ff.; Gasco, 'Politica sabauda', 317 ff.; C. Baudi di Vesme, 'Le "relazioni" diplomatiche Sarde', *BSBS*, 1970, 656 ff., focuses on the eighteenth century.

[192] DLT to VA, 10 Apr. 1692, Amersfoort, AST/LM/Olanda, m. 2; same to ST, 6 Oct. 1693, Loo, AST/LM/Olanda, m. 3; same to same, 22 Sept. 1695, Utrecht, AST/LM/Olanda, m. 5; same to VA and ST, 3 Sept. 1696, Dieren, AST/LM/Olanda, m. 6; Briançon to VA, 17 Sept. 1705, Winchester, *CGP*, V, 427.

[193] Quazza, *Il problema ialiano*, 359.

ancient Romans in their determination in defeat. Generally, however, taking what we might call an 'absolutist' view, he was critical. Reflecting a belief in the need for any polity to be directed by a single firm hand, from the start de la Tour thought this was lacking in the Republic, which was thus an easy target for French efforts to exploit discontent with the war. In October 1690 de la Tour reported a riot in Rotterdam during which a mob destroyed the house of a magistrate. The envoy feared revolution (revealing more perhaps about the differences between the Savoyard and Dutch states than about the real likelihood of upheaval in the latter) and looked forward to the arrival of William III and a strong hand. He was critical of the formalities (i.e. the need of the deputies of the States General with whom he negotiated to refer back to their provincial sovereigns) which he thought inevitable in a 'government of the many' but which delayed his negotiations. In fact, de la Tour soon recognised that, despite the presence of malcontents and French sympathisers in the Dutch towns, William III and the regents who dominated those towns and the Republic kept the latter steady. Nevertheless, things were allowed there which would not be permitted in Turin. In December 1692, reporting a notice in one of the Dutch *Gazettes* that Saint-Thomas had withdrawn from Victor Amadeus' court (which might have been French propaganda, intended to undermine confidence at The Hague in the war in Piedmont), de la Tour observed that thousands of stories of this sort were published daily with impunity. He found this general freedom, and what he saw as an inclination to disorder, particularly disconcerting following his master's *volte-face* in 1696. In September he sought permission to return to Turin since he feared for his own safety among a 'free and discontented people' in the event of a complete rupture between the duke and his former allies; and in November, following much invective in the Dutch *Gazettes* and rumours of a plot to attack his house (and despite Pensionary Heinsius' despatch of an armed guard to protect him), de la Tour fled to the greater safety of Brussels.[194]

De la Tour's contact with England prompted equally negative reactions, although Roero's hasty withdrawal thence in the wake of the Revolution of 1688 would have already confirmed an established image of England as disorderly. According to de la Tour, the English people were touchy and violent, extremely sensitive about their rights and violations of them. In 1695, reporting a riot sparked off by the impressment of men for

[194] DLT to VA, 1 and 29 Sept. and 13 Oct. 1690, Hague, same to ST, 21 Sept. 1696, Hague, AST/LM/Olanda, m. 5. In 1712 del Borgo's windows at Utrecht were smashed by a Dutch mob angry at Savoyard perfidy in collaborating with England in a separate peace, Bély, *Espions*, 405.

service in the navy, he observed that public opinion backed the rioters since forced recruitment of this sort was against the law, of which the English were as jealous as of their defence (i.e. against foreign enemies). As for political life, from the first de la Tour drew attention to the factions which disrupted and delayed business, and therefore explained his own failure to achieve more for his own master. Parliament, an institution by now effectively dormant in the Savoyard state (apart from the Duchy of Aosta), was constantly described by de la Tour as the venue for this destructive factionalism. In a critical appreciation of William III, written (in cipher) in 1693, he attributed what he saw as the king's damaging irresolution in part to the political divisions which also made it difficult for William to end the corruption. This, in turn, thought the envoy, absorbed much of the money granted by parliament, which, in de la Tour's view, could have been put to much better use helping his own master.[195] This view of England as a factious, violent polity had not altered by the time Mellarède wrote his *relazione*.[196]

It may be that the criticisms directed at these relatively freer polities and societies with which an expanding Savoyard diplomacy was coming into contact were little more than commonplaces, or even flattery, of the prince who would read them and himself expressed similar views: Victor Amadeus observed to Govone in July 1690 (regarding Bern's hesitation about how to react to the developing crisis in north Italy) that popular states, where private interests prevailed over those of the state, could not be depended upon.[197] Victor Amadeus does not seem to have articulated views like these on England or the Dutch Republic in these decades, but it is clear that the new exposure to alternative political models did not stimulate new ideas about how to run their state among those collaborators of Victor Amadeus II, Savoyard diplomats. Rather, it seems (admittedly only on the basis of 'official' correspondence) that diplomatic experience confirmed a preference for princely absolutism on the part of both diplomats and their prince.[198] The experience of Savoyard diplomats elsewhere largely conforms to the same pattern. Trivié's *relazione* at the end of his mission to Spain attributed that state's 'decline' to the fact that, after the primacy of Cardinal Ximenez in the early sixteenth century, that monarchy had lacked ministers ready to put the public interest before personal advantage or (where they were so public minded) princes ready

---

[195] DLT to ST, 22 Apr. and 24 Nov. 1695, London, and same to VA, 10 Feb. 1693, London, AST/LM/GB, m. 8.
[196] Carutti, 'Relazione sulla Corte d'Inghilterra', 236 ff.
[197] VA to Govone, 13 July 1690, Carignano, AST/LM/Svizzera, m. 27.
[198] In 1691, de la Tour commented on recent political changes in Madrid, where seven new councillors of state had been appointed, that too many ministers ruined states, DLT to ST, 13 July 1691, Hague, AST/LM/Olanda, m. 1.

to support them. This, he argued, had prevented the removal of abuses and their replacement by those solid foundations which were the basis of the happiness of a state. The implication, of course, one often explicitly made by Savoyard diplomats in this period, was that Victor Amadeus was just such a firm, public-minded prince, who could galvanise and make effective any state (in this case, Spain and its empire), identifying and mobilising resources (above all for war) in a way his weaker fellow-princes could not emulate.[199]

CONCLUSION

In 1709, the opening of peace negotiations saw Victor Amadeus articulating a desire to rearrange not just the borders between the Savoyard and French states to his own advantage but also, thereby, the entire structure of international relations in western Europe, to prevent a resurgence of that French hegemony whose victim he had been in the 1680s. He not only proposed the continuation beyond the conclusion of peace of the war-time alliance, in order to defend the independence of his state but also urged that the allies must exploit Louis XIV's need for peace to erect a new international 'system' in place of that which had underpinned Louis XIV's earlier domination. This meant stripping France of whole provinces, to the benefit of, among others, Victor Amadeus himself.[200] Unfortunately for the latter, these hopes of transforming the international system, and securing an extensive barrier, to include not just the alpine watershed but also Briançon, Monaco and even Bugey (which had been exchanged by Charles Emanuel I in 1601 for Saluzzo) failed. But they are worth remarking. It was clearly possible in 1709 to envisage, if only briefly, the partition of Louis XIV's France to the great advantage of the duke of Savoy (among others), because of his enhanced European role. Associated with this new role was, as we have seen, an expansion of the Savoyard diplomatic presence abroad – one which put some pressure on the established arrangements for administering Savoyard diplomacy (which was very much the duke's instrument, although his ministers had some scope for manoeuvre) and thus helped prepare the way for the creation of a distinct 'Foreign Office' in 1717 – and some major successes in terms of territory and dignity or status. Success abroad also underpinned ducal authority and sovereignty at home. After 1713, discontented subjects were far less likely to look abroad for support (or to find it) to make effective their sense of grievance than they were before 1690. Victor Amadeus' success owed a great deal both to the instability in

---

[199] Quazza, *Il problema italiano*, 360–1.
[200] VDM to Fagel, 29 Mar., 12, 20 Apr. 1709, Turin, ARAH/EA/VDM/33, f. 49 ff.

Europe between 1690 and 1713, associated above all with the Spanish Succession, and to the devising of new approaches to achieving peace and stability in Europe on the part of statesmen and policy-makers. These included the emergence of a network of alliances designed to restrain Louis XIV's France, which became known as the 'Old System',[201] of which an independent Savoyard state was an integral part, and the growing hold of the notion of 'natural frontiers', which helped Victor Amadeus secure the alpine watershed frontier in 1713 – but no more.[202] Clearly, despite the enormous successes of the Savoyard state on the international scene between 1690 and 1713, there were limits to what was possible. The Savoyard state remained a small operator in a world dominated by a few Great Powers. Victor Amadeus (like his predecessors and successors) might exploit his strategic position in the quarrels between those more powerful states to his own advantage, as in 1696. Thereafter he might exploit his reputation for duplicity to blackmail his allies. But this was a weapon of weakness. The duke and his diplomats exploited that weakness, convincing the Maritime Powers – who had earlier seen Victor Amadeus as helping to maintain the European balance against Louis XIV – of the need, during the War of the Spanish Succession, to strengthen the Savoyard state in Italy as a counter to the growing power of the Austrian Habsburgs there.[203] However, after 1713, the true weakness of the Savoyard state was exposed when Victor Amadeus was effectively abandoned by England. Isolated, he was obliged to exchange Sicily for Sardinia, to facilitate a revision of the Utrecht settlement to accommodate Spain, a far more important power, in order to achieve a more stable European balance. At the same time and reflecting the close relationship between the 'foreign' and 'domestic' spheres in Savoyard state formation, Victor Amadeus' authority – or sovereignty – in Sardinia was limited by the terms of its cession (as had been the case with Sicily).[204]

[201] See H. M. Scott, '"The true principles of the revolution": The duke of Necastle and the idea of the old system', in J. Black, ed., *Knights Errant and True Englishmen: British foreign policy 1600–1800* (Edinburgh, 1989), 55 ff.
[202] See P. Sahlins, 'Natural frontiers revisited: France's boundaries since the seventeenth century', *American Historical Review*, 95, 1990, 1423 ff.; and Rule, 'Gathering intelligence', 749.
[203] In this, Victor Amadeus was successfully exploiting the contemporary inclination towards balance of power principles: see Bély, *Espions*, 577 ff.; and Rule, 'Gathering intelligence', 749.
[204] Following Charles Emanuel III's issuing (1770) of new Constitutions, the Sardinian feudal barons claimed these breached the terms of the island realm's cession in 1720, and appealed to the King of Spain, Charles III, who according to the act of cession would inherit Sardinia in the event of the extinction of the House of Savoy, as guarantor of the island's 'constitution': A. Mattone, 'La Cessione' p. 47ff.

CHAPTER 4

GOVERNMENT AND POLITICS IN THE SAVOYARD STATE, 1690–1720

Historians of state formation in early modern Europe have tended, applying the insights of the sociologist Max Weber, to emphasise the development of centralised, formal, impersonal, specialised and 'bureaucratic' structures within the polity, not least as instruments for the mobilisation of the resources (notably men and money) necessary for war. Federico Chabod, for example, saw the development of bureaucratic structures and mentalities in sixteenth-century Milan as the most significant contribution of the Renaissance to the emerging modern state, while, for Matthew Anderson, disunity and the failure to develop an effective central administration cast serious doubts on whether in 1713 the Austrian monarchy could be called a state at all.[1] Since the 1960s, however, the concept of what has sometimes been called the 'administrative monarchy', i.e. a centralised personal royal absolutism based on a network of local agents, such as the French intendants, has come under attack from a number of directions.[2]

Just how far both the older and the more recent approaches go to understanding the newly effective power of princes and the state – explanations which have largely been developed in relation to early modern France – is one of the concerns of the present chapter. It seeks, firstly, to understand just how far the process of Savoyard territorial state

---

[1] F. Chabod, 'Y a-t-il un état de la Renaissance ?', *Actes du Colloque sur la Renaissance* (Paris, 1958), English translation in H. Lubasz, ed., *The Development of the Modern State* (New York, 1964); M. S. Anderson, *Eighteenth-Century Europe 1713–1789* (Oxford, 1966), 11 ff. Most books on the early modern state make reference to Weber: see J. M. Smith, *The Culture of Merit: nobility, royal service and the making of absolute monarchy in France 1600–1789* (Ann Arbor, 1996), 163 (and passim for its attempt to synthesise older and more recent, 'cultural', concepts of early modern state formation).

[2] See W. Beik, 'Celebrating Andrew Lossky: the reign of Louis XIV revisited', *French Historical Studies*, 17, 1991, 526 ff.

formation in these decades was accompanied by, even necessitated, the development of more bureaucratic, centralising and 'rational' administrative structures – what John Brewer has called the 'hidden sinews' of power – to mobilise more effectively the resources of the 'fiscal-military state'.[3] It aims, secondly, to consider the nature of politics in the Savoyard state in these decades, and above all to assess both the channels and extent of opposition to two wars which made enormous demands on Victor Amadeus' subjects, and how it was dealt with; and, thirdly, to identify new sources of state cohesion, what we might call a Savoyard national identity generated by war.

Traditionally, historians of the Savoyard state have identified the major leap forward of the type identified above as occurring in the reign of Victor Amadeus II in 1717, when three major Secretariats of State, for internal affairs, foreign policy and war – in part a conscious imitation of French practice – a reformed Council of Finances (headed by the generale delle finanze), and a network of provincial intendants were established as part of a tightly knit structure intended to more effectively mobilise the limited resources of a small, relatively poor state.[4] In fact, we know relatively little about Savoyard government (and politics) between 1690 and 1713, a period which largely falls between the studies of Stumpo and Rosso on the early seventeenth century and that of Quazza on the eighteenth. Yet the Nine Years War and the War of the Spanish Succession were characterised, not surprisingly, by a remarkable interest on the part of Victor Amadeus II in alternative (including foreign) administrative, fiscal and military models, and by important new developments which the reforms of 1717 – in part at least a specific response to an immediate problem (the threat to Victor Amadeus' possession of Sicily) – built on.[5] The overhaul of 1717 was by no means therefore a complete innovation. It is also increasingly clear that interest in administrative reform in the Savoyard state pre-dated 1690, but that it had few practical successes.[6] War from 1690 proved a powerful force for change.

[3] J. Brewer, *The Sinews of Power: war, money and the English state 1688–1783* (London, 1989), xv–xvi and passim.

[4] G. Quazza, *Le riforme in Piemonte nella prima metà del Settecento*, 2 vols. (Modena, 1957), passim; G. Symcox, *Victor Amadeus II: absolutism in the Savoyard State 1675–1730* (London, 1983), 190 ff.; Symcox, 'L'Età di Vittorio Amedeo II' in P. Merlin et al., *Il Piemonte sabaudo: stato e territori in età moderna* (Turin, 1994), 373 ff.; C. Rosso, *Una burocrazia di Antico Regime: i segretari di stato dei Duchi di Savoia*, I (1559–1637) (Turin, 1994), 14–15.

[5] See *mémoires* on the composition of the councils and secretariats of the emperor and the king of France, sent by Victor Amadeus' ministers to Vienna and Paris, conte Provana and conte Vernone, AST/MG/Ministri e Segreterie di Guerra, m. 1/12.

[6] See Rosso, *Una burocrazia*, 59, for the abortive attempt of Victor Amadeus' mother to introduce French style secretariats of state in 1677, and the marquis de Saint-Thomas'

BUREAUCRACY, INTENDANCY AND THEIR LIMITS

For Symcox the chief administrative achievements of Victor Amadeus were the reordering of the finances, the *perequazione* and the intendants.[7] The first two have been dealt with in Chapter 2, and the intendants will be discussed below. However, there were also important administrative developments at the centre. Among the most significant of these was the creation of the specialised secretaryship of war, the history of which – despite recent interest in the Savoyard army and Savoyard administration in the early modern era – remains obscure. On the eve of Victor Amadeus' entry into the Nine Years War, the various officials and departments (*veedor*, *contador*, inspectors and vice-auditors) responsible for the Savoyard military operated largely independently of each other, and answered only to the duke himself, who thus provided the crucial co-ordinating role, along with Saint-Thomas, his first secretary and effective chief minister.[8] However, the sheer scale of military activity from the summer of 1690 meant that this arrangement soon proved inadequate. From at least the spring of 1691 conte Giuseppe Antonio Benzo di Cavour, president in the Camera dei Conti, councillor of state and military auditor general, was *de facto* secretary for war, a situation which was regularised by the issue of ducal letters patent in June 1692.[9]

The secretary for war had a wide range of functions. According to a breakdown of the responsibilities of Victor Amadeus' chief officials in 1691, the job of the secretary (aided by four clerks) included arranging the *étapes* for the duke's troops and ensuring that the barracks contractors fulfilled their obligations. In effect, the secretary's office despatched all

---

mémoire (*c.* 1685) on the French and Spanish secretariats of state. Rosso seeks to dispel the traditional view of a Savoyard state which was overhauled under Emanuel Filibert in the later sixteenth century and by Victor Amadeus in the early eighteenth century, with little of relevance occurring between the two reigns, *ibid.*, 9 ff. On the reform of 1677, see also D. Frigo, *Principe, ambasciatori e 'Jus Gentium': l'amministrazione della politica estera nel Piemonte del Settecento* (Rome, 1991), 27–8. [7] Symcox, *Victor Amadeus*, 62.

[8] A. de Saluces, *Histoire militaire du Piémont*, 5 vols. (Turin, 1818), I, 292. According to P. Bianchi, 'Guerra e politica nello stato sabaudo (1684–1730). Le riforme militari di Vittorio Amedeo II fra istituzioni, reclutamento e organizzazione territoriale' (Ph.D. thesis, University of Turin, 1997), 175–6, Madama Reale had appointed a secretary for war in 1676, but the difference between this figure and the secretary of state after that date was a superficial one.

[9] Duboin, XIV, 887. Saluces, *Histoire militaire*, I, 292, says Victor Amadeus created the office in 1692, and is followed by Quazza and others, but Benzo was frequently referred to as secretary for war before then: see VDM to Fagel, 2 and 26 May 1691, Turin, ARAH/SG/8643/132, 146. The English secretaryship at war emerged in similar circumstances in the 1690s: see M. A. Thomson, *The Secretaries of State 1681–1782* (London, 1968), 65 ff.

orders relating to the army received from the duke.[10] The secretary for war sometimes played a personal role in the arranging of winter quarters in provincial Piedmont, particularly when their allocation (and payment) were a sensitive issue, and he received representations and appeals from affected localities against their obligations.[11] He also become involved in disputes between Victor Amadeus' subjects, particularly where they focused on military obligations.[12] In essence, the secretary for war was the intermediary between Victor Amadeus and his developing military establishment and between the latter and the rest of the Savoyard state[13] and was effectively acknowledged as such, even by those colleagues and others resentful of his authority. Inevitably, the secretary for war rapidly emerged as an important political figure during the Nine Years War: Benzo was one of that small group of ministers left in charge in Turin by Victor Amadeus during his recuperative absence at Chieri in the spring of 1693. Peace in 1696, the subsequent reduction in the military establishment and Benzo's disgrace (1698) for fraudulent irregularities were followed by a reduction in the size of the office establishment (to just three secretaries in 1699), but did not result in the new secretariat's demise.[14] More importantly, participation in a major conflict again from 1701, and the need to maintain a sizeable defence establishment after 1713, underpinned the need for a specialised war office. As far as the Secretariat of War was concerned, the reform of 1717 simply confirmed the existence of an office

[10] Distribuzione dell'aziende che concerne le Finanze . . . 1691, AST/MM/UGS, m. 1/17. Accordingly, in 1691, Victor Amadeus wrote to conte Benzo as the man responsible for co-ordinating measures for the defence of the Duchy of Aosta, F. Guasco, 'Vittorio Amedeo II nelle campagne 1691–1696 secondo un carteggio inedito', *Studi su Vittorio Amedeo II* (Turin, 1933), passim. Thirty years later, the secretary for war supplied a route plan (and arranged halting-places or *étapes*, or 'tappe') for various units moving to and from Turin, VA to Rhebinder, 22 Apr. 1721, Turin, AST/MM/Impieghi, m. 1 d'addizione.

[11] See conte Felice Dionisio Carron to ST, 6 Nov. 1693, AST/LP/C, m. 37, for the departure of deputies sent by the town of Trino to Benzo, to make representations about the lodging of troops in the town.

[12] In the winter of 1693–4 Benzo played a mediatory role between the Vaudois and the inhabitants of Barge, following the former's seizure of contributions sent by the latter to Pinerolo, VDM to Fagel, 8, 15, 22 and 25 Jan. 1694, Turin, ARAH/SG/8644/100–03.

[13] This included the foreign troops made available and/or funded by his allies. For the secretary as mediator between the commanders of the Protestant battalions, through their own intermediary, van der Meer, see VDM to Fagel, 13 Apr. 1693, Turin, ARAH/SG/8644/23. Benzo also dealt with foreign dignitaries, visiting Milan in 1692 to co-ordinate with the governor of the Milanese the defence of Piedmont and the Milanese (against attack from Casale) during the allied invasion of Dauphiné.

[14] Victor Amadeus' order regarding remounts for his cavalry, of April 1698, AST/MM/UGS, m. 1/21, was countersigned by Buttigliera and others, suggesting a brief loss of autonomy.

which, because of war since 1690, had become an established feature of the Savoyard administrative and political structure.¹⁵

Another institution of central administration which survived the overhaul of 1717 (no doubt because it was reformed between 1690 and 1713) when it became one of the four *aziende*, or departments, responsible to the Council of Finances, was the Ufficio del Soldo, or Army Pay Office. It had been established by Emanuel Filibert in 1560 and was headed by a succession of *veedori generali* until 1688 (when the post was suppressed) and thereafter by its contadore generale, a post created in 1674.¹⁶ The Ufficio's main task was to keep a record of the duke's troops and their pay (and other costs), to conduct the reviews of the troops, to expedite orders to pay contractors for services and to prepare an annual military budget.¹⁷ The Ufficio also serviced other parts of the developing military structure.¹⁸ Inevitably, the pressures of war brought changes, and a first attempt to regularise and consolidate the Ufficio del Soldo in the summer of 1695. Not surprisingly, the number of officials seems to have expanded with the growth in workload, to include a headquarters staff of the contadore generale plus eight others (four officials and four secretaries), whose salaries reflected the office hierarchy,¹⁹ and a network of war commissaries and/or military intendants in the field.²⁰ Subsequently, in 1698 Victor Amadeus suppressed the traditional privilege, enjoyed by the

---

¹⁵ For subsequent holders of the office, see P. Bianchi, 'Guerra e politica', 196 ff. Typically, in 1713 the then secretary for war, Lanfranchi, countersigned the duke's orders for remounts for the cavalry, AST/MM/UGS m. 1/21.

¹⁶ Bianchi, 'Guerrae politica', 173 ff.

¹⁷ See the distribution of tasks among the duke's officials in 1691, AST/MM/UGS, m. 1/17. All new levies and new officers appointed were recorded by the Ufficio since they involved additional expenditure. In Feb. 1690 the Ufficio received Victor Amadeus' letters patent of November 1689 commissioning the marquis de Chaumont colonel of the Genevois dragoons regiment which he was to levy, L. Provana di Collegno, 'Lettere di Carlo Giacinto Roero, conte di Guarene, capitano nel reggimento dragoni di Genevois 1704–07', *CGP*, VIII, 339.

¹⁸ In 1695 Victor Amadeus ordered the contadore to prepare an annual military budget, copies of which were to be given to the generale delle finanze and to the secretary for war, Regolamento economico delle Truppe, Frassinetto, 29 June 1695, AST/MM/UGS, m. 1/20.

¹⁹ The first official (auditor Balestrero) was to have 1,500 lire p.a., and the others lesser sums (Giovanni Sala, 1200 lire p.a.; Stefano Boyero and the conte di San Michele 600 lire p.a. each). The secretaries (Stefano Brianza, Garretto, Picono and Giovanni Paolo) were each to have 400 lire p.a. See Victor Amadeus' order to the Ufficio Generale del Soldo, 29 June 1695, Frassinetto, AST/MM/UGS, m. 1/13.

²⁰ Regolamento Economico . . ., 1695, AST/MM/UGS, m. 1/20. By the summer of 1696 the Ufficio comprised the contadore generale, three officials, four secretaries, two intendants and eight commissaries, see budget in AST/MM/UGS, m. 2/28. A very good idea of the range of activities of a military intendant in the Nine Years War is given by the correspondence of G.-B. Gropello in AST/LP/G, m. 53.

Ufficio del Soldo and the Tesoreria Generale di Milizia, to a very small percentage of the pay of the troops which passed through their hands. Henceforth, the heads of these bodies were to enjoy an annual salary, of 15,000 lire a year, regardless of the number of troops in Victor Amadeus' pay. In effect, they were being turned into salaried officials.[21] The appointment as contadore generale in 1709 of Gian Giacomo Fontana, hitherto intendente generale of the army (see Chapter 1), provided an opportunity, following substantial discussion about the shape of the Ufficio del Soldo (henceforth generally known as the Ufficio Generale del Soldo),[22] to consolidate many of these developments and to define more clearly the functions and responsibilities both of the Ufficio and its own staff.[23] This reform of the Ufficio, which was increasingly staffed by long-serving 'career' officials, progressing up a more clearly structured hierarchy, in part at least as a reward for their service,[24] was followed in 1710 by reform of the Tesoreria Generale di Milizia.[25]

The reforms of 1717 also integrated within the new structure of government another example of administrative reorganisation associated with the preceding war years, the Council for Artillery, Building and Fortifications. War, inevitably, meant a much higher profile for both artillery and fortifications (see Chapter 1). This was reflected in the creation, in 1696, of a separate battalion of bombardiers and the amalgamation, in 1697, of the artillery and engineers, both independent units hitherto, into a distinct service arm.[26] Finally, in 1711 the new council was created, amalgamating the existing Intendancy General of Artillery with the other two bodies.[27] The reorganisation meant little change in terms of the individuals who staffed the new body, most of

[21] Minute of Victor Amadeus' order of 1 Apr. 1698 in AST/MM/UGS.
[22] See Progetto comandato da SAR per l'Ufficio Generale del Soldo, AST/MM/UGS, m. 1/37.
[23] See Duboin, XXVII, 344 ff. The regulations defined the responsibilities of the central office staff, the commissaries, who were graded in terms of function and salary, their auxiliary clerks and the Ufficio's officials stationed in the major garrisons. They also provided for a secretary, nodaro (sic) Chiavarino, for the contadore generale. Besides their cash salaries, all officials (except the war commissaries) received a daily bread ration.
[24] See patents appointing Bartolomeo Boyer, for his long service in the Segreteria di Guerra and Ufficio del Soldo, war commissary in the latter, AST/PCF, reg. 1709–11 f. 7 and Progetto, AST/MM/UGS, m. 1/37, in which Sala (still enjoying the 1,200 lire p.a. laid down in 1695) is said to have served in the Ufficio for thirty-three years. The family relationship (if any) between Bartolomeo and Stefano Boyer is unclear. See the emergence of the '1st official' in the Finance Office: L. Einaudi, 'Le entrate pubbliche dello stato sabaudo nei bilanci e nei conti dei tesorieri durante la guerra di successione spagnuola', *CGP*, IX, 1 ff.   [25] AST/MM/Ordini e Regolamenti, m. 4/27.
[26] Symcox, *Victor Amadeus*, 145. Bianchi, 'Guerra e politica', 160 ff, provides the best modern account.   [27] Duboin, VIII, 550; *CGP*, IX, 12–13.

them simply being reappointed from the former institutions.[28] From 1717 this Council was one of the four *aziende*, responsible (as a major spending department) to the reformed Council of Finances. Clearly, some at least of the elements which made up the reformed, post-1717 Savoyard state, characterised by a structure of offices with more clearly differentiated functions, staffed by a relatively small hierarchy of bureaucrats, their different ranks reflected in their salaries, were in place well before that date and had emerged as a practical response to the challenges of war since 1690.[29]

What has been outlined above was by no means the limit to the contribution made between 1690 and 1713 in the way of central institutions to the shape of the reformed post-1717 Savoyard state. In 1707, once the great crisis of the Savoyard state had passed, Victor Amadeus set about reordering the archives, which had been the object of frantic concern during the crises of 1691 and 1705–06.[30] In that year, the archives – which could play a crucial role in the process of state formation (underpinning ducal claims and reforms)[31] – were transferred to the royal palace, where the archivist began cataloguing them.[32] Thereafter, the duke was anxious to secure the archives of newly acquired territories.[33] In this way, Victor Amadeus initiated that reordering of the Savoyard archives which was to be another of the successes of the Savoyard

[28] See the appointment of Giovanni Giacomo Vaniera, as controller, with a salary of 2,400 lire p.a. (out of which he had to pay a secretary), that of Vittorio Amedeo Riccaldini (hitherto intendant general of artillery) as intendant general of the new body, with a salary of 3,300 lire, that of Giacinto Filippa as first secretary in the office of the intendant general at 1,100 lire, and that of Giovanni Battista (hitherto secretary of the Artillery) as secretary of the new Council, with a salary of 400 lire, AST/PCF, reg. 1709–11, f. 165 ff.

[29] See the appointment of a first secretary in the Ufficio delle Finanze, Einaudi, 'Entrate pubbliche', *CGP*, IX, 1 ff.

[30] See letters from Cesare Felice Rocca, archivist, to ST, summer 1691, AST/RAC/Inventari, m. 1 and E. Casanova, 'Gli Archivi Camerali durante l'assedio di Torino (1705–06)', *CGP*, VIII, 219 ff.

[31] In 1690, Victor Amadeus personally scrutinised the copies in the royal archives of the treaties signed by his predecessors with the kings of France (and the imperial diploma granted earlier that year), AST/RAC/Scritture Regi Archivi, Registri delle Scritture date ai Ministri, m. 1/1, 16 May and 15 July 1690. In 1716, the royal archivist supplied information on the organisation of the inquisition in the other Italian states, again demonstrating the importance of foreign models as Victor Amadeus sought to restructure his state: L. Braida, 'L'Affermazione della censura di stato in Piemonte dall' ed: 40 del 1648 alle Costituzioni del 1772', *RSI*, 102, 1990, 723.

[32] See AST/Archivi di Corte, Categoria 2o, m. 1/16, printed notice, Jan. 1707.

[33] See AST/RAC, 20, m. 1/12, for an inventory of papers carried from Casale, 1709–10. In 1720, Victor Amadeus was anxious that the Spaniards should not remove documents from the Sardinian archives, A. Mattone, 'La cessione del Regno di Sardegna dal Trattato di Utrecht alla presa di possesso sabauda (1713–20)', *RSI*, 104, 1992, 82.

administration in the eighteenth century.[34] However, without ignoring the importance of developments at the centre, it is the creation of a network of provincial intendants which has hitherto seemed to be the distinct contribution of this generation of war to administrative centralisation and princely absolutism in the Savoyard state;[35] in this conforming to a supposedly European-wide pattern pioneered by Richelieu and Louis XIV and imitated by many of France's neighbours — including Victor Amadeus' son-in-law, the first Bourbon king of Spain, Philip V.

The intendants in the Savoyard state did not emerge in Victor Amadeus' reign from a complete vacuum in local government.[36] The foundation of all local government were the communities, run by their sindics and magistrates (or *podestà*). These did much of the work of government in the localities, and continued to do so after 1690 (and after 1713).[37] Their working was overseen by various ducal officials operating at provincial level. The number of Piedmontese provinces had increased from seven under Emanuel Filibert to twelve (1622), and (from 1653) eighteen. From 1565, these provinces were directed, by prefects, or *prefetti* (who in Piedmont replaced the so-called *juges mages* who continued to function in the Duchy of Savoy), whose role was primarily judicial.[38] This system was formalised and defined (1622) by Charles Emanuel I, who also (1624) codified the functions of another provincial official dating from at least the sixteenth century, the referendary or *referendario*, who had both administrative and judicial functions. However, the referendary now acquired much more wide-ranging duties, with a particular emphasis on the protection of ducal revenues, and was to reside in the provincial capital (in this anticipating the intendant). Finally,

---

[34] See I. Massabo Ricci *et. al.*, 'Archivio di Stato di Torino', in *Guida Generale degli Archivi di Stato Italiani*, IV (Rome, 1994), 376.

[35] See Quazza, *Le riforme*, I, 65 ff.; Symcox, *Victor Amadeus*, esp. 120 ('The intendant system became the most critical administrative structure holding the state together') and A. Torre, 'Politics cloaked in worship: state, church and local power in Piedmont 1570–1770', *Past and Present*, 134, 1992, 89.

[36] Henri Costamagna, 'Pour une histoire de l'Intendenza dans les états de terre ferme de la Maison de Savoy à l'époque moderne', *BSBS*, 83, 1985, has thrown new light on the subject. Unless otherwise indicated, this and the succeeding paragraphs depend largely on Costamagna's account of the intendancy's origins, 373 ff. Costamagna's article focuses largely on developments after 1713.

[37] See Levi, *Inheriting Power: the story of all exorcist* (Chicago, 1988), for how local government worked in one Piedmontese community (Santena) before (and after) 1690, and E. Casanova, 'Contributo', *CGP*, VIII, 182, 206 (execution by the syndics and magistrate of the communities of the marquisate of Andorno, and by the *podestà* and sindics of the community of Pianezza, of Victor Amadeus orders, 1700, to draw up a new *consegna* for the salt gabelle.

[38] See order of Senate of Piedmont to prefects and judges, Dec. 1702, to send monthly accounts of criminal cases in which decisions required higher confirmation, Duboin, III, 1386.

there were the provincial directors, or *direttori*. These were the creation of the Delegation set up in 1661 by Charles Emanuel II to oversee and reorganise the economic life of the provinces, following the mid-century wars which had so devastated much of Piedmont and ruined the finances of numerous communities. The Delegation devised regulations to this end and in 1668 designated directors to execute them in each province of Piedmont. The duke of Savoy was not therefore short of administrative, fiscal and judicial agents in the provinces on the eve of the Nine Years War. They could also rely on the provincial governors, who were responsible for the military and political direction of the province.[39]

The history of the intendancy in the Savoyard state is traditionally dated from Victor Amadeus' edict of May 1696 for the appointment of an intendant in every province in Piedmont. In fact, five successive intendants of justice, or *intendenti di giustizia*, served in the province of Pinerolo before 1690, the first having been appointed in 1658. The intendancy (general) of the Duchy of Savoy dated from 1686, and that for the County of Nice from January 1689 when the cavaliere Morozzo (who had served as intendant in the Vaudois valleys in 1687–88) was appointed intendant general.[40] The functions of these first intendants were primarily but not only financial, Morozzo playing a key role in the resettlement of the Vaudois valleys after the expulsion of the Protestants.[41] Not surprisingly, therefore, the intendants were already prominent figures: on the outbreak of war in 1690 the intendants of Savoy and of the province of Pinerolo were enemy targets, both becoming prisoners of war.[42] As yet,

---

[39] For general accounts of the various officials in the localities before 1690 (and 1717) and their different responsibilities, see P. Merlin, 'Il Cinquecento', in Merlin, *Piemonte sabaudo*, 105, 254 ff., Costamagna, 'Pour une histoire . . .', 373, 388 ff.; and C. Salsotto, 'Fossano e la battaglia di Torino (1706)'. Contributo alla storia della guerra di successione di Spagna, *CGP*, VIII, 424–5. The official who is least well treated, particularly in view of his importance, in the historical literature is the provincial governor, but see B. A. Raviola, 'Carriere, poteri; ed onori di un elite: i governatori nei Domini sabaudi da Emanuele Filiberto a Carlo Emanuele I (1559–1630)', tesi di laurea, University of Turin, 1995–6, and S. Lombardini, 'La costruzione del ordine: governatori e governati a Mondovì (1682–1687)', in G. Lombardi, ed., *La Guerra del Sale (1680–1699): rivolte e frontiere del Piemonte barocco* (Milan, 1986), 179 ff.

[40] Costamagna, 'Pour une histoire . . .', 391; P. Petrilli, 'Alle Origini dell'Intendenza in Piemonte: il Caso della Provincia di Pinerolo 1658–1717' tesi di laurea, University of Turin, 1989–90; Symcox, 'Two forms of popular resistance in the Savoyard state of the 1680s: the rebels of Mondovì and the Vaudois', in Lombardi, *Guerra del Sale*, 276.

[41] In November 1689 the intendant of Savoy, conte Tarino, agreed with one Lorenzo Datal for the supply of two vessels to serve on Lake Geneva (no doubt to prevent a repeat of the so-called Glorieuse Rentrée), AST/MM/Imprese Militari, m. 1/40. Morozzo's instructions are in Duboin, IX, 8.

[42] In 1690, conte Tarino was captured by the French forces invading the Duchy, J. Humbert, 'Conquête et occupation de la Savoie sous Louis XIV (1690 à 1691)', *Mémoires de l'Académie des Sciences, Belles-Lettres et Arts de Savoie*, IX, 1967, 21, while an

however, intendants only operated in a very few, peripheral areas. They were hardly in evidence in Piedmont, and certainly did not constitute a structure covering the entire Savoyard state.

It was war from 1690 which prompted the extension throughout the Piedmontese provinces of a network of intendants. This seems to have been largely in place by 1693, when Victor Amadeus issued instructions to a number of intendants of justice and finance, or *intendenti di giustizia e azienda* (a significant change in both name and function) in various provinces. The responsibilities of the intendants now extended into the judicial and military spheres, but they remained above all fiscal agents[43] and should not be confused with the military intendants, or *intendenti di guerra*, who were responsible to the Ufficio Generale del Soldo, and with whom the intendants of justice and finance often liaised.[44] In view of their extensive responsibilities, the intendants were given permission to employ subordinates. The functions and responsibilities of the intendants continued to expand with the demands of the war effort, the threat in 1694–95 of famine (see Chapter 2)[45] and the evolving fiscal and political situation. In 1695, as relations with the church deteriorated (and in view of Victor Amadeus' pressing fiscal needs), the intendants were ordered to ensure that the communities of their provinces declared all those properties claiming fiscal immunity because of their ecclesiastical status (and proved their claim to exemption).[46] Not all of these early intendants proved up to the job, the intendant of the province of Pinerolo, Balustre, being replaced, as ineffective, by the rising Giovanni Battista Gropello in 1695.[47] But for the latter, and men like him, the developing intendancy offered the prospects of advancement and power, not least because as ducal agents they enjoyed some local patronage.[48]

---

aggrieved local noble seized the intendant of the province of Pinerolo, Giovanni Antonio Frichignono, and handed him over to the French, Petrilli, 'Alle origini', 168 ff.

[43] Petrilli, 'Alle origini', 18 ff. See standard instruction, May 1693, Duboin, IX, 15.

[44] Victor Amadeus' regulations for the arrangement and financing of *étapes*, June 1695, ordered that the intendants of war should send, each month, to the intendants of justice of each province a certificate of sums paid by the communities by way of *étapes*, so that the intendant of finance could set these against their tax obligations, AST/MM/UGS, m. 1/20, para. 7.

[45] In 1695 Victor Amadeus ordered the governor of Turin, the marchese di Dronero, not to allow grain to leave the province of Turin without a passport from the provincial intendant, Gropello, Guasco, 'Vittorio Amedeo nelle campagne', 286.

[46] See instructions to Gropello, as intendant of the provinces of Torino and Susa, 27 Apr. 1695, AST/ME/Category 11: Immunità Reale del Piemonte, m. 1/14.

[47] VDM to Fagel, 9 Sept. 1695, Turin, ARAH/SG/8644/206.

[48] See Carlo Giacinto Ferrero to ST, 15 Mar. 1695, requesting for his brother the post of judge of Rivarolo, soon to be vacated by its incumbent, whose successor was to be appointed in Victor Amadeus' name by the intendant, Gropello, AST/LP/F, m. 36.

These developments culminated in Victor Amadeus' edict of May 1696. Hitherto, whereas individual intendants had often been responsible for more than one province, some provinces had no intendant.[49] Victor Amadeus now ordered the establishment of an intendant of justice and finance in every province of Piedmont, laid down their principal duties and salary and offered the new posts for sale.[50] The extension and consolidation of the intendancy in Piedmont in the spring of 1696 was, at least in part therefore, a fundraising measure at a time of fiscal crisis (see Chapter 2). The same no doubt applies to Victor Amadeus' reform of the provincial structure in January 1697, reducing the number to twelve.[51] More importantly, however, by 1700, when conte Giuseppe Ignazio di Rezzano, intendant of Saluzzo and Fossano (1698) and director of Mondovì (1699) was appointed intendant-general of the Duchy of Savoy on the promotion from that post of conte Nicolis di Robilant,[52] the network of intendants developed in the Nine Years War, one in each of the Piedmontese provinces, had been extended to most of the Savoyard state, except for Aosta.[53] Indicative of the new importance of the inten-

[49] A Riparto degli'intendenti di guerra e azienda (c. 1694–96), AST/MM/UGS, m. 1/24, shows most intendants as responsible for two provinces. Gropello was intendant of both the Val Luserna and Saluzzo province (as was his predecessor), VDM to Fagel, 9 Sept. 1695, Turin, ARAH/SG/8644/206.

[50] Duboin, III, 1230. See the (draft) Istruzione agl'Intendenti delle provincie di Piemonte, e per quello di Saluzzo, 31 Mar. 1697, Duboin, IX, 20 ff. in which (inter alia) the intendant is also to enjoy the status (and authority) of vice-auditeur de guerre in his province. For a sort of auction for the intendancy of Alba in June 1696, conte Della Chiesa di Benevello offering 20,000 lire and intendente Coppa offering 27,000 on behalf of his son (and on condition that Coppa himself could exercise the office during his son's minority, the latter being aged just 14), see mémoire from Marelli and Gropello, 4 June 1696, AST/PA/Finanze, Intendenze e loro Segretarie, m. 1/3. For sums raised in this way in the summer of 1696, see AST/MM/UGS, m. 2/89. Clearly, the view of the otherwise excellent Petrilli, 'Alle origini', that there is no firm evidence of sales needs qualification.

[51] Duboin, IX, 23 (n.1); Costamagna, 'Pour une histoire', 379. Carmagnola, Ceva, Cherasco, Chieri, Savigliano and Trino were incorporated into neighbouring provinces. This reorganisation must also be related to the recent recovery of Pinerolo.

[52] J. Nicolas, La Savoie au 18e siècle: noblesse et bourgeoisie, 2 vols. (Paris, 1978), I, 192. See Petrilli, 'Alle origini', 287, for the career of Rezzano, conte di Rodoretto.

[53] In September 1696 the cavaliere Solaro di Moretta was appointed intendant of the province of Pinerolo (which now included Pinerolo itself), Petrilli, 'Alle origini', 204–5. In 1696–7, the lawyer and magistrate Marco Antonio Pusterla (who had already carried out a number of missions for Victor Amadeus) acted as interim intendant of Chieri and Carmagnola, L. Marini, 'La Valle d'Aosta fra Savoia e Piemonte 1601–1730', Relazioni e Communicazioni presentate al XXXI Congresso Storico Subalpino, 1956, 2 vols. (Turin, 1959), II, 637. In 1697 Baldasare Saluzzo di Paesana was appointed intendant of Asti, S. J. Woolf, Studi sulla nobiltà Piemontese nell'epoca dell'assolutismo (Turin, 1963), 126. See list of provincial intendants [1696–7], AST/MG/Senato di Piemonte, m. 1, 43, 44–5; and AST/PCF, reg. 1697–99 f. 86, for letters patent appointing senator and conte Avenato intendant of Turin and Ivrea.

dants and of their essentially fiscal role was the leading role of the intendant of Nice, Pierre Mellarède, in efforts to maximise ducal revenues there,[54] and that of the intendant of Mondovì in the reordering of that province during and after the last phase (1698–1700) of the so-called Salt War.[55]

During the War of the Spanish Succession, the opportunity was taken to appoint intendants in Victor Amadeus' newly acquired territories.[56] But we must not exaggerate either the primacy of the intendants before 1713 or the smooth progression from 1690 towards their later supremacy. Before 1717 the structure was in fact much less clearcut or systematic than the foregoing might imply. In 1697 the intendant of Pinerolo, Giovanni Antonio Zoja, lamented his lack of general instructions, inspiring some doubt about whether the intendants were part of some clearly perceived blueprint of ducal absolutism.[57] Some provinces still lacked an intendant in the War of the Spanish Succession.[58] Particularly in the early days of the intendancy, the authority of the intendants was often resented, and obstructed, by the existing representatives of the ducal government, including the provincial governors and their cronies,[59] while the duke could not always ensure respect for, or even the physical safety of his intendants.[60] More importantly, before 1713, when the system of intendants was not yet firmly entrenched, the older layer of local officials

---

[54] Symcox, *Victor Amadeus*, 126–7.

[55] See Victor Amadeus' orders of 19 July 1698, in G. Lombardi, 'La Guerra del Sale: caleidoscopio di una historia', in Lombardi, ed., *La Guerra del Sale (1680–1699): rivolte e frontiere del Piemonte barocco*, 3 vols. (Madrid, 1986), 150 ff. In 1699, following the rebels' defeats, the intendant, conte Lamberti, informed the syndics of Mondovì of the duke's order that the property of those exiled to the Vercellese be sold, G. Lombardi, 'La Guerra del Sale trecento anni dopo', in *ibid.*, 19.

[56] From the winter of 1708–9, an intendant largely assumed responsibility for the administration of the Pragelato, I. Lameire, *Les occupations militaires en Italie pendant les guerres de Louis XIV* (Paris, 1903), 319 ff. See AST/PA/Finanze, Intendenze e loro Segretarie, m. 1/43, draft instructions for intendant general di giustizia e azienda dei paesi di nuovo acquisto, 1709. The conte di Rezzano, who was clearly making a career in the intendancy, was appointed intendant-general of some of the new territories in 1712, Petrilli, 'Alle orgini', 287. [57] Petrilli, 'Alle origini', 207.

[58] There is no reference to any intendant in Levi's investigation of the commune of Santena, *Inheriting Power*.

[59] The clashes (1696) between conte Felice Dionisio Carron, governor of Trino province, and the intendant of Vercelli, are chronicled in the former's letters in AST/LP/C, m. 37. For Zoja's complaints (1697) of threats against him by the governor of Pinerolo, see Petrilli, 'Alle origini', 219.

[60] This point is well made by Petrilli, 'Alle origini', 168 ff., citing an incident (1689) in which an officer in the Monferrato regiment, a member of the Bava family, wounded the brother of the intendant of the province of Pinerolo after clashes between the intendant and the provincial governor.

continued to have an important role.⁶¹ Indeed, the apparent triumph of the intendants by the end of the Nine Years War was followed by a reversal of fortune and their temporary eclipse by the provincial directors. Typically, whereas five successive intendants had been appointed between 1693 and 1698, between 1699 and 1717 five successive directors were appointed for Pinerolo province.⁶² Significantly, too, both contemporaries and historians seem to have confused the intendants and directors in this period, suggesting that the triumph of the former was by no means clearcut and that there was little real difference between them.⁶³ The provincial directors – who were already prominent in the allocation of fiscal burdens before the renewal of war in 1701⁶⁴ – played a key role in this and other spheres during that conflict.⁶⁵

We need to beware of attaching too much importance to labels, whose meaning contemporaries were clearly not always careful (or able) to distinguish. Indeed, the directors were just one of a great number of ducal agents and officials who were pressing the communities to supply animals,

---

⁶¹ In the winter of 1696–7, Spitalier, the prefect of the valley community of Barcelonette, played a key part in abortive efforts to have the valley agree to its separation from the county of Nice, as the first step towards the introduction of a harsher ducal tax régime, Spitalier to ST, 13 Jan. 1697, Barcelonne, AST/LP/S, m. 87. In 1697, a local referendary, conte Ferraris, was appointed by Victor Amadeus to resolve (with a representative of the governor of Milan) clashes between Piedmontese and Milanese border communities, consulta of 6 June 1699, AGS/E/3427/38.

⁶² Petrilli, 'Alle origini', passim. See O. Scarzello, 'Corneliano, Piobesi, Monticello d'Alba e Sommariva Perno negli anni di guerra 1704–1708 (dagli "Ordinamenti Originali" dei suddetti comuni)', *CGP*, VIII, 497 ff. The same men often served as directors before and intendants after 1699: Petrilli, 'Alle Origini', 48

⁶³ L. Bulferetti, 'L'Elemento mercantilistico nella formazione dell'assolutismo sabaudo', *BSBS*, 54, 1956, 280, sees the directors as the ancestors of the intendants: see Symcox, *Victor Amadeus*, 245. See a reference to the director of Alba province as intendant in the communal records of Sommariva Perno, Feb. 1704, Scarzello, 'Corneliano', *CGP*, VIII, 521 and in Apr. 1704 to Gallino as 'direttore and intendente', *ibid.*, 522. However, the community's records most frequently refer to Gallino simply as direttore. According to G. Bracco, 'Guerra del Sale o guerra del tasso? Le riforme fiscali di Vittorio Amedeo II nel Monregalese', in Lombardi, *Guerra del Sale*, 354, in 1709 it was the intendant or director of Mondovì who approved a new distribution of the province's tax burden.

⁶⁴ In 1699 it was the director of Biella who gave orders regarding the repartition of that province's tax burden, Duboin, XXIII, 75.

⁶⁵ See *CGP*, I, 113 (and passim) for the role of the provincial directors (rather than intendants) in mobilising the Savoyard state's resources for war in the autumn of 1703. In the summer of 1706, Gropello ordered the directors of the provinces of Asti, Cuneo, Mondovì, Pinerolo and Saluzzo to identify who in their provinces should be asked to make a loan, and to co-ordinate their efforts with Fontana, L. Einaudi, *La finanza sabauda all'aprirsi del secolo XVIII e durante la guerra di successione spagnuola* (Turin, 1908), 213–14. In 1712, as the war drew to a close, the duke sought reports on the economic situation of his territories. Those received for the twelve provinces of Piedmont carried seven signatures, only three of which (Alba, Fossano, Mondovì) simply declared themselves intendants, Costamagna, 'Pour une histoire', 392.

men, money, wagons and so on in the War of the Spanish Succession.[66] Not entirely surprisingly, these decades of crisis were characterised as much by the use of *ad hoc* commissions as by developing permanent structures.[67] Nevertheless, despite the apparent chaos, the resurgence of the directors is noteworthy. It may have owed something to the duke's having put the office of intendant up for sale in 1696, perhaps reducing the effectiveness of the intendants as ducal instruments. On the other hand, where there were no takers, a province may have been left without an intendant. But it may also have been due to factors which in the longer term favoured the intendants. The directors, because of their earlier remit, and the need to nurture the tax-paying capacity of their provinces, too easily became the defenders of provincial interests against outsiders, including the ducal 'state'.[68] This attitude was no doubt underpinned by the fact that many provincial directors were drawn from the local elite.[69] In wartime Victor Amadeus may have had to co-operate with that elite. However, the divided loyalties of the directors gave good reason for preferring the intendants, most of whom (including Gropello and the future marchese d'Ormea) were relatively obscure and/or pliant.[70]

Not surprisingly, therefore, the later stages of the War of the Spanish Succession saw the intendants re-emerge as key ducal agents in the localities. Gropello's instructions, as generale delle finanze, to the communities regarding the use of local taxation, in 1711 and 1712, for

[66] This clearly emerges from Scarzello, 'Corneliano', *CGP*, VIII, 497 ff.
[67] Conte Giorgio Giuseppe Compans di Brichanteau, a member of the Turin Senate since 1682, was sent to Borgofranco in 1702 to remodel the local council, following revelations of faction and skulduggery there; and in 1703 to Ivrea to help improve its defences, Einaudi, *Finanza sabauda*, 248 and *CGP*, I, 78. In 1705 special commissioners were sent around Piedmont, to discover hidden grain and arrange its storage in magazines at Cuneo, Ivrea, Turin and Vercelli, Einaudi, *Finanza sabauda*, 169 ff.
[68] In Jan. 1705, Chiaverotti Chiampo, director of Ivrea province, following the arrival there of a special commissioner sent to arrange the removal of excess grain, urged the need to allow the province to retain some of that supposed excess. The director of Mondovì province seems to have responded similarly. In 1710 the director of the province of Mondovì complained about the rapacious attitude of the farmer of the meat gabelles (who for his part complained about the director) to Gropello, Einaudi, *Finanza sabauda*, 26, 171.
[69] One director of Mondovì, a local noble, Ippolito Maria Beccaria, had supported the rebels in the Salt War of 1680, Lombardi, 'La Guerra del Sale', 21. For family links between the referendary of Alba province and the local elite (1689), see A. Torre, 'Rivolta contadina e conflittualità: l'esempio di Monforte d'Alba tra Sei e Settecento', in Lombardi, *Guerra del Sale*, 322.
[70] Individual intendants, however, could also press the interests of their provinces: in June 1697 Saluzzo di Paesana urged that the province of Asti be granted some respite from its fiscal obligations, AST/Prima Archiviazione/Somministranze, Alloggi Militari e Caserme, m. 1/3 (284). This particular intendant may have been unusual in his outspoken independence, but the issue needs further study.

example, were sent through the intendants.[71] In 1713, Giovanni Francesco Palma, was appointed intendant-general of the Duchy of Savoy (following the latter's recovery from the French), having already successfully served as director of the town and province of Susa and intendant of the Pragelato. He was permitted to appoint a number of subordinate officials[72]. This developing structure no doubt contributed to the decision to amalgamate the offices of prefect and referendary, in a number of provinces in 1713.[73] In 1714 Victor Amadeus turned to the intendants for information on the extent in their provinces of tax-exempt and tax-paying ecclesiastical property,[74] and in 1716 to check the results of the first phase of the *perequazione*. Their new position was confirmed in Victor Amadeus' administrative overhaul of 1717, above all as agents of the generale delle finance. A network of provincial intendants spread across the Savoyard state, acquiring ever greater powers (over the communities) and responsibilities as local agents of ducal (or royal) authority – above all in the catchall fiscal sphere.[75]

But the search for institutional aspects of state formation should not obscure the fact that many spheres in the Savoyard state remained largely untouched in these years. This was true, for example, of the Vicariato (i.e. the institution or official responsible for the policing of Turin), which had undergone reform before 1690, and would do so again after 1713, but which was hardly affected between those dates.[76] Substantial areas of Savoyard life remained outside the direct range of the state and its agents. Poor relief, which was the resort of many more in these years of war and famine than before 1690, was the responsibility of an array of private institutions, including the Ospedale della Carità (founded in 1649 on private, not ducal, initiative). These coped reasonably well, and did not – contrary to what was once thought – need reinvigorating by an interventionist ducal absolutism after 1713.[77] Independent jurisdictions also

---

[71] Duboin, IX, 28 (Mar. 1712) and 29, Instruction to the intendant of justice and finance in city and province of Cuneo, June 1711.
[72] Letters Patent, Venaria Reale, 19 May 1713, ADS/B 1462, f. 1.
[73] In 1713 the intendant of Pinerolo province ordered the establishment of schoolmasters approved by local priests in the communities of the Pragelato and their maintenance by those communities, Duboin, XIV, 1261, 1395. This was a marked contrast with the all-powerful local role in 1708 of the vibailli of that valley, Duboin, XXVIII, 860.
[74] Duboin, XX, 181.
[75] Quazza, *Le riforme*, I, 65 ff. Costamagna, 'Pour une histoire', 393 ff.; Symcox, *Victor Amadeus*, 198. An intendant-general was appointed for Sicily after 1713, *ibid.*, 182.
[76] D. Balani, *Il vicario tra città e stato: l'ordine pubblico e l'annona nella Torino del Settecento* (Turin, 1987), 39 ff.
[77] S. Cavallo, *Charity and Power in Early Modern Italy. Benefactors and their motives in Turin 1541–1789* (Cambridge, 1994), significantly modifies the account in Symcox, *Victor Amadeus*, 199 ff, of the reform of poor relief in the state from 1716.

survived. Although Victor Amadeus reduced the power and independence of the church in his states in the quarrel which began in 1694 (and continued for most of the rest of his reign) — affecting the University of Turin, the censorship and so on — the clergy was not yet (if ever) simply a tool of the state. For that matter, Victor Amadeus continued to delegate substantial powers to private agencies, including the tax farmers, while the judges with special responsibility for disputes involving the tax farmers (who were partly paid for by them) could only loosely be called agents of the state.[78]

Even if we think that Savoyard administrative structures necessarily became larger, more specialised and more sophisticated in these decades, the product should not be confused with a modern bureaucracy. As we have seen in the case of the conduct of diplomacy and foreign policy, specialisation of function still lay (at least in 1713) largely in the future, the first secretary of state's relatively understaffed office having a wide range of responsibilities (see Chapter 3). The expansion of office-holding was a complex issue. The creation of new offices was in part a response to new administrative needs. But it was also a means of creating new resources of ducal patronage, of attaching to Victor Amadeus men who had looked elsewhere in the Savoyard state — and even outside it — for patronage. In part, too, as we have seen, it was a revenue-raising measure. Clearly, the relationship between the growth in the number of offices and the advance of state power was no simple one. Indeed, Victor Amadeus' sale of local office, notably that of syndic (see Chapter 2), to finance his wars may have sharpened the need for a new, or more intrusive, central agent (i.e. the non-venal intendancy) in the localities.[79] The Savoyard state was not a 'bureaucracy', governed and held together by its central administration, before or by 1713 (or 1720) — although it was more clearly set on that road. For one thing, the number of officials remained small.[80] For another, men were still often more important than the offices they held. This meant that, on the one hand, somebody like Gropello could extend the scope of his office as generale delle finanze, effectively intruding into the sphere of, say, the secretary for war.[81] It also meant, on the other

---

[78] Braida, 'L'Affermazione della censura', p. 717 ff. Einaudi, *Finanza sabauda*, 4 ff. See the complaint of the Turin Senate (1691) about the existence of many rival jurisdictions, AST/MG/Senato di Piemonte, m. 1/41.

[79] See Ricuperati, 'Il Settecento', in Merlin et. al., *Piemonte sabaudo*, 452. Just when the venality associated with the intendancies in 1696 was ended is not clear but those posts were no longer venal after 1717, Costamagna, 'Pour une histoire', passim.

[80] In 1696–7, there were only six people in the first secretary's office (including Saint-Thomas) and just five in that of the secretary for war (including Benzo), see AST/MG/Senato di Piemonte, m. 1/43.

[81] This impression is conveyed by, for example, the correspondence in *CGP*, I, passim.

hand, that other men were sometimes given office (or responsibility) because of their existing power, and in the hope that this could be tapped by the state. This was true of the marchese di Parella, whose reputation in Mondovì enabled him to mediate differences between the province and Turin, as he had done before 1690, in ways that 'official' government agents might not (see Chapter 6).[82]

Recently, recognising that there could be a crucial difference between 'the effective structure of state power' and 'the description of a state's institutions',[83] some historians have placed greater emphasis on more informal means of enabling early modern governments to enforce their authority, notably networks of patronage and clientage and a reliance on local power brokers.[84] 'Structures' of this sort in Piedmont before 1690 have been identified by Giovanni Levi and others[85] but perhaps the best example of such a network is that of the Carron, headed successively by the two marquis de Saint-Thomas who held the office of first secretary of state throughout our period.[86] The importance of clientage and connection, often cutting across the official structures described above, is evident in the correspondence between one member of the Carron clan, conte Dionisio Felice Carron, governor of Trino (1692–96) and Susa (1696–1704) and his Saint-Thomas cousins in the Nine Years War. Conte Dionisio articulated the view that individuals acted at least as much in accordance with their personal obligations to other individuals as out of a sense of official duty.[87] He also believed that others who sought his support in their search for place and profit did so in the expectation that, as somebody who 'belonged' to Saint-Thomas, conte Dionisio could mobilise the latter on the applicant's behalf.[88] In addition, the governor frequently wrote to his kinsman on issues which were the formal responsibility of the secretary for war, conte Benzo, with whom conte

---

[82] Similarly, marchese Pallavicino, as a leading local figure, could exert important influence on the conduct of Fossano and its administration, see Salsotto, 'Fossano', *CGP*, VIII, 434 ff.

[83] I. A. A. Thompson, *War and Government in Habsburg Spain 1560–1620* (London, 1976), 286.

[84] See S. Kettering, *Patrons, Brokers and Clients in Seventeenth-Century France* (Oxford, 1986) and C. Rosso, 'Stato e clientela nella Francia della prima età moderna', *Studi Storici*, 28, 1987.   [85] See G. Levi, *L'Eredità immateriale*.

[86] Carlo Giuseppe Carron de Saint-Thomas (d. 1699) is not the subject of an entry in the *DBI*, although his son Giuseppe Gaetano (in many respects a less important figure) is.

[87] Conte Dionisio Felice Carron [DFC] to ST, 16 Aug. and 7 Oct. 1692, Trino, AST/LP/C, m. 37 [all subsequent references are to this *mazzo*], praising the marchese di Pianezza for his help at the start of Carron's governorship.

[88] Conte DFC to ST, 28 May 1695, Trino, seeking the appointment as judge of Cuneo for avvocato Bottia; and same to same, 6 Dec. 1695, Trino, requesting the post of judge at Centallo for his protégé (who had not been appointed to Cuneo).

Dionisio's relations were poor. In 1693, he claimed that in view of Benzo's failure to reply to his letters, he needed Saint-Thomas' 'protection'.[89] The governor also relied on his cousin's influence to press his own claims, to secure favourable treatment from the other parts of the ducal administration and to protect conte Felice from the many complaints reaching Turin about his prickly and sometimes unco-operative attitude.[90] Other men on the make also looked to Saint-Thomas to promote their careers. These included some of Victor Amadeus' leading collaborators and officials in these decades: Gropello, who in 1696 was widely regarded as a creature of Saint Thomas, and Fontana, who sought the latter's protection.[91] For his part, the secretary for war, who was himself reputed to be a client of the marchese di Pianezza,[92] seemed to be trying to establish his own local clienteles, which in Trino meant effectively ignoring his own immediate official agent, the provincial governor, and using other local ducal officials.[93] A figure as quarrelsome as conte Dionisio could only last for so long; in 1704, Victor Amadeus removed him from his governorship of Susa, which was threatened with siege.[94] It is tempting to see this as a step towards the break-up of the Saint-Thomas network, a process completed with the reforms of 1717. But, clientage

[89] Conte DFC to ST, 6 and 16 Feb. 1693 and 28 June 1694, Trino. In 1693, the governor suggested to Saint-Thomas (but not to Benzo, whose responsibility it was) a solution to the vexed issue of winter quarters at Trino, justifying this course of proceeding by claiming that security in the secretary of war's office was poor, same to same, 6 Nov. 1693, Trino. In 1695, informed – not, apparently, by conte Benzo – that the garrison departing from Casale would be assigned their first *étape* at Trino, the governor hoped his cousin could have the order changed, same to same, 25 Oct. 1695, Trino.

[90] In 1693, anticipating the successful siege of Susa, conte Felice reminded Saint-Thomas of his own aspiration to that governorship, same to ST, 26 July 1693, Trino. In 1695, he sought Saint-Thomas's intervention with Gropello regarding financial payments, same to same, 2 July 1695, Trino. In 1693 the governor informed his cousin of a recent contretemps with the marchese di San Giorgio, same to same, 1 Nov. 1693, Trino.

[91] VDM to Fagel, 16 Apr. 1696, Turin, ARAH/SG/8644/253; Costamagna, 'Pour une histoire', 436. In 1695, Gropello, then a successful intendant of justice and finance, complained to Saint-Thomas that Benzo had blocked his efforts to make a career as an intendant of war, Petrilli, 'Alle origini', 247–8.

[92] VDM to Fagel, 29 Dec. 1692, Turin, ARAH/SG/8643/310. For a broad discussion of the development of noble clientage/power *pari passu* with the centralising absolute state, see S. Marchisio, 'Ideologia e problemi dell'economia familiare nelle lettere della nobiltà piemontese (XVII–XVIII secoli)', *BSBS*, 83, 1985, 116 ff. (and Chapter 5).

[93] See conte Dionisio Felice Carron to ST, 22 Aug. and 16 Oct. 1695, Trino, complaining of Benzo's cultivation of, and delegation of authority to, the local patrimonial, Salabue.

[94] See ST to conte Dionisio Felice Carron, governor of Susa, 27 May 1704, saying that he had warned him in previous letters of complaints that he was impossible to work with, which Victor Amadeus could not allow in the present crisis, *CPG*, II, 145.

relationships clearly both underpinned and undermined more formal structures in the Savoyard state as in other early modern states.[95] Indeed, in some respects many of those holding office in this era were Victor Amadeus' own creatures, constituting a ducal clientage network. Relations of this sort continued to operate alongside, and to complicate the official administrative framework of the Savoyard state after 1717.[96]

THE ROLE OF VICTOR AMADEUS AND THE DYNASTY

A concern to identify the achievement of more 'modern' 'structures' on the part of those concerned with early modern state formation in the Savoyard state also risks losing sight of other crucial elements in that process. Probably the most important single contribution to the effectiveness, coherence and integration of the Savoyard state in these decades was that of Victor Amadeus himself. The duke of Savoy did not rule entirely alone, without counsel or council. In October 1703, on learning of the detention of his forces in Lombardy, Victor Amadeus consulted together with various ministers (the marchesi Ferrero, Pallavicino, Parella, and Priè, the grand chancellor, Saint-Thomas and the president of the Senate, de Gubernatis) before ordering the arrest of the French and Spanish ambassadors.[97] The duke was expected to take advice in this way and was sometimes, as we shall see, anxious to show that contentious decisions (above all, for war) were not taken lightly. Nevertheless, the existence of a functioning formal Council of State (before the creation of the body of that name in 1717) is difficult to prove,[98] and it is questionable whether it was anything other than a source of honour and dignity to those designated councillors, or ministers of state.[99] Victor Amadeus was, as we have

---

[95] The clienteles identified above are not the only ones in the Savoyard state between 1690 and 1713. Pierre Mellarède may have been part of a Savoyard network, which included the marquis de Coudrée and the marquis d'Aix, Costamagna, 'Pour une histoire', 422–3. The clients of another of Victor Amadeus' close collaborators, the marchese di Cortanze, included a syndic of Calosso (Asti province) in 1705, *CGP*, IX, 429.

[96] For clientage after 1720, see C. Storrs, 'Savoyard diplomacy in the eighteenth century', in D. Frigo, ed., *Politics and Diplomacy in Early Modern Italy* (Cambridge, forthcoming).

[97] F. Rondolino, 'Vita Torinese', *CGP*, VII, 50 n.1.

[98] G. Galli della Loggia, *Cariche del Piemonte e Paesi uniti colla serie cronologica delle persone che le hanno occupate*, 3 vols. (Turin, 1798), II, 146–7, cites Victor Amadeus' edict of May 1680 restoring 'nostro consiglio secreto di stato', which included the archbishop of Turin, Saint-Thomas (as first secretary) and the grand chancellor; and sees, Appendix, 48–9, the reforms of 1717 as involving a functioning body deriving from that order. AST/MM/UGS, m. 2/22 gives details of the cost of this body in 1696, but there are no institutional records.

[99] Conte Orazio Provana di Pratolongo was promoted councillor of state and first

seen, in very large part his own foreign and finance minister, and often sent orders direct to his provincial governors.[100] The duke's determination to see and decide all, complicated matters to some degree, above all in wartime when he was so often absent from his capital. This was the more remarkable because monarchs, especially where administrative structures were being elaborated, were becoming more sedentary, fixed (like Louis XIV) in their capitals or palaces. Victor Amadeus, however, was more typical of those princes who still, primarily because of the pressures of war, travelled around their realms.[101] He was frequently away from Turin during the Nine Years War,[102] but his absences were especially striking during the first years of the War of the Spanish Succession. In March 1705, on Victor Amadeus' return from the camp, the Dutch envoy noted that the duke had been absent with the army for nearly eleven months without once visiting Turin.[103] Victor Amadeus' travels served various purposes. They enabled him to see what was going on for himself, underpinning his role in government; and to show himself to a much wider audience than that which saw him either at court or in Turin. They thus provided one of those personal links whose importance as a bond between monarchs and subjects in early modern Europe should not be obscured by a preoccupation with the development of more formal structures.[104]

But Victor Amadeus' travels also complicated matters because decisions were necessarily delayed until his return,[105] not least because he

president in the Senate of Savoy on his return (1687) from his embassy to Rome, Barberis, 'Il conte Orazio Provana', 105. In 1713, Pierre Mellarède was designated minister of state (and first president of the Camera dei Conti) for his role in the Utrecht settlement, D. Carutti, ed., 'Relazione sulla Corte d'Inghilterra del Consigliere di Stato Pietro Mellardède' plenipotenziario di Savoia all Congresso di Utrecht, *MSI*, 2nd ser., 24, 1885, 221.   [100] See Guasco, 'Vittorio Amedeo nelle Campagne', passim.

[101] An obvious contrast with Victor Amadeus II was Carlos II of Spain – although the latter's successor, Philip V was, necessarily, much more active, as was William III.

[102] In October 1691, Victor Amadeus (who had spent most of the preceding summer in the camp) was en route for Susa, VA to DLT, 11 Oct. 1691, Lombriasco, AST/LM/Olanda, m.1. The following December, the duke passed through eastern Piedmont on one of many journeys to Milan, ST to DLT, 3 Dec. 1691, Turin, AST/LM/Olanda, m. 1. The duke then passed through south-western Piedmont, en route to Genoa: VA to DLT, 24 Jan. 1692, Cuneo, and same and ST to DLT, 6 Feb. 1692, Genoa, AST/LM/Olanda, m. 3.

[103] VDM to Fagel, 18 March 1705, Turin, ARAH/EA/VDM/30, 23.

[104] In this way, too, the duke discovered potential servants. At Carmagnola, in the summer of 1706, he met and was impressed by the local magistrate who would soon be appointed intendant of Susa and rise to be first minister and marchese di Ormea, Ricuperati, 'Il Settecento', 458 ff.

[105] When, in 1694, the Brandenburg troops demanded additional winter quarters, Benzo di Cavour put them off until his master's return, VDM to Fagel, 15 Oct. 1694, Turin, ARAH/SG/8644/151.

would rarely delegate decision-making. His duchess, Anne Marie of Orleans, was allowed some role during her husband's absences but it was a limited one.[106] When Victor Amadeus went to Chieri to recuperate, following his smallpox attack in the autumn and winter of 1692–93, he did not relinquish control. He expected weekly reports of their activities from each of his four leading ministers (Saint-Thomas, Benzo, Marelli and Provana), and accounts of their joint sessions, and used these to keep control despite being absent.[107] Victor Amadeus clearly saw the nascent bureaucracy as his personal tool, ordering in 1695 that two officials of the Ufficio del Soldo must always remain in Turin, but that the contadore generale and many of the other officials should attend him in the camp.[108] Ducal control of this sort was undoubtedly facilitated by the relatively small size of the Savoyard state, at least by comparison with France (and the fact that for many of the war years of the 1690s and 1700s territorial losses reduced it even further). But it was also a consequence of Victor Amadeus' determination to rule.

One very practical expression of the role of the duke was Victor Amadeus' court. The last generation, inspired by the work of Norbert Elias, has seen a great deal of interest in and work on courts and their role in early modern Europe. The Savoyard court has attracted some attention, but this has largely focused on other reigns than that of Victor Amadeus II.[109] Although not as grand as the courts of Madrid, Vienna or

[106] See Victor Amadeus' patents of 1690, 1701 and 1704, authorising the duchess to issue and sign various patents in his absence, AST/Tutele e Reggenze, m. 7/3, 4 and 5. In 1705, the duchess issued an order for the levy of the militia and sent commissaries into the provinces of Piedmont to help organise it, VDM to Fagel, 17 June 1705, Turin, ARAH/EA/VDM/30, 68.

[107] VA to Benzo, Marelli, Provana and Saint-Thomas, 26 May 1693, Chieri, AST/LPDS, Vittorio Amedeo II, m. 68/30; same to ST, 23 May and 4 and 5 June 1693, Chieri, AST/LPDS, m. 68/13/269, 271, 272.

[108] Memoria del Contadore Generale (in fact a letter from Victor Amadeus, 29 June 1695), AST/MM/UGS, m. 1/13.

[109] N. Elias, *The Court Society* (Oxford, 1987); A. Barbero, 'Principe e nobiltà negli stati sabaudi: gli Challant in Valle d'Aosta tra XIV e XVI Secolo', and D. Frigo, 'L'Affermazione della sovranità: famiglia e corte dei Savoia tra Cinque e Settecento', both in C. Mozzarelli, ed., *'Familia' del principe e famiglia aristocratica* (Rome, 1988); C. Stango, 'La Corte di Emanuele Filiberto: organizzazione e gruppi sociali', *BSBS*, 85, 1987, 445 ff.; I. Massabo Ricci and C. Rosso, 'La corte quale rappresentazione del potere sovrano', in G. Romano, ed., *Figure del Barocco in Piemonte: la Corte, la città, i cantieri, le provincie* (Turin, 1988); P. Merlin, *Tra guerre e tornei. La corte sabauda nell'età di Carlo Emanuele* (Turin, 1991). See the historiographical discussion in R.O. Bucholz, *The Augustan Court. Queen Anne and the Decline of Court Culture* (Stanford, 1993), 1 ff., and the critical remarks of Trevor Dean, 'The Courts', in J. Kirshner, *The Origins of the State in Italy 1300–1600* (Chicago, 1996), 136 ff. For Victor Amadeus' court, see R. Di Gilio, 'La corte di Vittorio Amadeo II negli anni 1680–1713', tesi di laurea University of Turin, 1990–9.

Versailles, Victor Amadeus maintained a court whose numbers and formality had been growing in step with the domestic and international standing of the dukes of Savoy. The ducal court, which in the later sixteenth and early seventeenth centuries had been influenced by Spanish practice, but which was now increasingly influenced by the court of Louis XIV, served many functions and purposes. Apart from being the household of the duke and his family, it was also a means of representing Victor Amadeus' sovereign power, of asserting his princely status (not least *vis-à-vis* foreign dignitaries) and of focusing the loyalty of his subjects. Above all, and far more than the developing institutional superstructure outlined earlier, it provided the environment in which for most of this period Victor Amadeus daily moved and acted. The years between 1690 and 1713 were not an age of especial development for the Savoyard court, whose organisation into three distinct parts – the *casa* (household), the *camera* (chamber) and the *scuderia* (stables), run by the grand chamberlain, the grand master of the *casa* and the grand *scudiere* respectively, – had only recently (1680) been laid down in regulations which would endure throughout the eighteenth century.[110] Indeed, the years between 1690 and 1713 may have represented a retreat of sorts, as non-military expenditure was reined in, with inevitable consequences for the size and splendour of the court, although this pressure eased after 1706 when Victor Amadeus' sons were given their own households.[111] The list of those holding court office, or with *entrée* there in 1705, reads like a roll call of the great nobility of the Savoyard state. Some noble families enjoyed a traditional presence at court. These included the family of the marquis de Sales, in many respects the leader/representative of the nobility of the Duchy of Savoy, and the holder of important offices in the

---

[110] Frigo 'L'Affermazione', 304 ff., discusses the regulation of 1680 and its significance, within the context of a longer-term shift, from domestic institution to court and a related tripling in size of the Savoyard court, between the later sixteenth and the eighteenth centuries (i.e. *c.* 1720).

[111] See the figures for the years 1683–1712 given in Di Gilio, 'La corte', 66, and see the list of court officials and their holders (1705) in F. Rondolino, 'Vita Torinese durante l'assedio', *CGP*, VII, 49–58, although the list is not exhaustive and should be supplemented by that in the appendix to Frigo, 'L'Affermazione'. Symcox' observation, 'From commune to capital . . .', in R. Oresko, G. C. Gibbs and H. M. Scott, eds., *Royal and Republican Sovereignty in Early Modern Europe: essays in Honour of Ragnhild Hatton* (Cambridge, 1997), 257, that Madama Reale's court was unusually reduced in 1705 (no doubt because of the impact on her finances of her son's straitened circumstances, see Chapter 2) and subsequently grew markedly, is probably correct: the English envoy, Richard Hill, was certainly struck by the size of Madama Reale's household in 1699, *CGP*, X, 234. For the size, structure and cost of the ducal court in a 'normal' year (1699), see G. Prato, 'Il costo della guerra di successione spagnuola e le spese pubbliche in Piemonte dal 1700 al 1713', *CGP*, X, 199 ff.

state, including that of *primo scudiere* in the royal household.¹¹² For some other leading subjects, for example the Piedmontese marchese di Druent (grand master of the wardrobe from 1690), a post at court was the only office held. It would be wrong, therefore, to see the court purely as an instrument of state formation – not least because so few in the state actually had contact with it. Nevertheless, that it was seen as a key element in projecting duke and dynasty, and in binding the duke and his subjects was evident in 1713 when Victor Amadeus sought to recreate in Palermo a splendid court for his new Sicilian subjects (as they greatly desired).¹¹³

A very few of the duke's male courtiers would be further bound to him as members of the chivalric Order of the Annunziata, or Annunciation. This had been founded (1362) by Duke Amadeus VI of Savoy as the Order of the Collar, refounded as the Order of the Virgin Annunziata by Duke Charles III in 1518, revived by Emmanuel Filibert as part of his 'restoration' of the Savoyard state after 1560, and 'reformed' by Madama Reale during her regency. The Military Orders, most of them founded in the later middle ages and many surviving throughout the early modern era, and of which the Spanish or Habsburg Order of the Golden Fleece is probably the best known, have not been given their due weight in analyses of *ancien régime* societies, although they exemplify the degree to which a state's subjects could have a variety of different (and not necessarily mutually exclusive) relations with their sovereign. The orders served two basic purposes. Firstly, and particularly at the international level, they represented an assertion of sovereignty by the awarding prince. But they were also, secondly, an important source of linkage between sovereigns and some of their noble subjects, for whom they were a source of enormous prestige and additional privilege. Among the distinctions of the Order was the close contact it brought with the duke of Savoy – who headed it and was invariably depicted wearing the Order's distinct collar (which including the lettering of its motto *fert*, or 'ready', and a brooch depicting the Annunciation) – and the various ceremonial and other privileges enjoyed by its members.¹¹⁴ The members also played a leading

---

¹¹² For Sales, see *CGP*, I, 238 ff. See the promotion (1707) of the marchese di Cortanze (colonel in the Asti militia and later in a regular regiment) in the royal household at the same time as he was sent to take possession of Alessandria on Victor Amadeus' behalf, *CGP*, V, 622.

¹¹³ In 1713 the duke made extensive appointments in his household, filling some posts long vacant, before leaving for Sicily, Chetwynd to Dartmouth, 9 Aug. 1713, Turin, SP 92/28, f. 629. See Symcox, *Victor Amadeus*, 171 ff.

¹¹⁴ Generally, see L. Cibrario, *Statuts et ordonnances du très noble Ordre de l'Annonciade* (Turin, 1840); Duboin, I, 129 ff. and Vitelleschi, *Romance of Savoy*, I, 54 ff. Most portraits of the dukes of Savoy in the early modern era depict them wearing the

part in all major 'state' occasions, helping to define them as such, including the funeral of Charles Emanuel II in 1675 and the publication of the peace with France and Spain in August 1713.¹¹⁵ Without wishing to exaggerate the importance of an institution which involved few in the state, the Order of the Anunciation (like the ducal court) nevertheless clearly helped knit together the elite of the different territories of the Savoyard state. Victor Amadeus clearly subscribed to the Order's ethos;¹¹⁶ and in two extraordinary general promotions at the end of each of his two wars (1696, 1713) used it to reward some of his chief collaborators in all spheres (administration, army, the court): the marquises of Saint-Thomas, Parella, San Giorgio, Lucinges, Bagnasco, Tana and Caraglio, the counts of la Pierre and Tournon and General Rhebinder.¹¹⁷ To a much lesser degree, a similar function was played by the other Savoyard chivalric Order, that of Saints Maurice and Lazarus, which had been founded by Emanuel Philibert in the later sixteenth century and which, in the early seventeenth century, had spearheaded a ducal attack on the city of Turin's charity system.¹¹⁸ These more traditional institutions continued after 1713 to function alongside the newer ones in the Savoyard state identified earlier, and were equally an object of Victor Amadeus' reforming activities.¹¹⁹

Victor Amadeus was clearly aware of the value of traditional forms of linkage between a prince and his subjects. These included oaths. In the winter of 1708–09, the duke's commander in the conquered Dauphiné valleys imposed an oath on each of the communities of those valleys (and

> Order's collar: see those in Symcox, *Victor Amadeus*, and that of the marchese del Borgo, reproduced on the cover of D. Frigo, *Principe, ambasciatori*. Saluces, *Histoire militaire*, V, 48, tells the (apocryphal) story of Victor Amadeus, touched (1691) by the suffering of his subjects, giving them his own Collar. There is nothing on the Annunziata in Quazza, *Le riforme*, or Symcox, *Victor Amadeus*. I hope to discuss elsewhere the continued importance of the chivalric orders in early modern Europe, but see I. de Madariaga, *Russia in the Age of Catherine the Great* (Yale, 1981), 79, for the foundation of the first Russian order of chivalry by the 'modernising' Peter the Great.

[115] See AST, *I rami incisi dell'Archivio di Corte: sovrani, battaglie, architetture, topografia* (Turin, 1988), 238; and Payne to Ayerst, 2 Aug. 1713, Turin, SP 92/28, f. 623.

[116] He did not respond to a proposal made in 1711 (admittedly a time when his need for cash was less pressing) to sell 100 titles of 'cavaliere della Santissima Annunciata', Einaudi, *Finanza sabauda*, 138.

[117] AST/Camera dei Conti, art. 852 (Nobiltà, Cronologie de L'Ordre du Collier de Savoie). The colonels of six of the intended twelve new regiments in 1703–04 were at one time or another knights of the Annunziata. Reflecting the intimate link between Order and dynasty, the Prince of Carignano's son also received the collar in 1713.

[118] Cavallo, *Charity and power*, 86 ff.

[119] Victor Amadeus' Royal Constitutions, 1723, declared the Annunziata incompatible with the holding of any other Order (except that of Malta), Vitelleschi, *Romance of Savoy*, I, 154 ff. For the role of the Order in the Savoyard state after 1713, see G. Ricuperati, 'Gli strumenti dell'assolutismo sabaudo: Segreterie di Stato e Consiglio delle Finanze nel XVIII secolo', *RSI*, 103, 1991, 855.

upon the community of the valley as a whole), which he clearly thought of some importance in binding these new subjects. Following the cession of the Dauphiné valleys by Louis XIV in 1713, Victor Amadeus, demanded new oaths swearing *hommage lige* and *fidélité lige*. He clearly felt that the fuller oath more firmly entrenched his sovereignty in his recently acquired dominions[120] – emphasising again the need to recognise the persistence of older types of political bond alongside the more 'modern' ones emerging in these decades.[121]

Emphasising Victor Amadeus' role in government also, however, means recognising on what a slender, dynastic thread the Savoyard state hung. In many respects those processes of state formation highlighted by these historians preoccupied with processes of supposed modernisation including administrative centralisation and so on, were less important in holding together the Savoyard state – and many others – than were dynastic certainty and the avoidance of minorities.[122] Arguably, the political instability which dogged the Savoyard state in the early 1680s was a reflection less of the weakness of the state than of uncertainty about where power lay during Victor Amadeus' minority (he had succeeded his father in 1675 aged just six), and the fact that his mother, the regent, continued to govern despite formally handing over power in 1680. Her attempt to pack her son off to Portugal, and suspicions that she might be trying to poison him (and the opposition that these provoked), reveal the degree to which the identity of the state hinged on the person and quality of its prince.[123]

---

[120] Lameire, *Occupations militaires*, 305 ff., prints the oath taken in 1708–9 and describes the accompanying public ceremony (an important part of the process of oath-taking). He contrasts the elaborate oaths demanded by Victor Amadeus with the looser ones required by Louis XIV. In 1714, as King of Sicily, Victor Amadeus received the usual oath, and the so called 'Maltese falcon', from the knights of Malta in acknowledgement of his suzerainty of that island. In 1720, an essential part of the act of taking possession of Sardinia by Victor Amadeus' viceroy was the taking of oaths from the members of the island kingdom's estates, Mattone, 'La cessione', 85.

[121] See P. Sahlins, *Boundaries. The making of France and Spain in the Pyrenees* (1989), 54–5 for Louis XIV's taking oaths from his new subjects in formerly Spanish Cerdanya in the 1660s (and the importance of oath-taking as an aspect of what Sahlins defines as 'jurisdictional sovereignty' in *ancien régime* Europe); and Kamen, *War of Succession*, 96, for oath-taking by Philip V of Spain.

[122] See the table differentiating between 'traditional' and 'modern' societies and politics in T. C. W. Blanning, *Joseph II* (London, 1990), 20–1. By contrast with the survival of the House of Savoy and with it an independent Savoyard state, the death without direct male heirs of the duke of Parma (1731) and the grand duke of Tuscany (1737) meant the effective disappearance of their dynastic states. H. G. Koenigsberger, G. L. Mosse and G. Q. Bowler, *Europe in the Sixteenth Century*, 2nd edn (London, 1989), 303–4, 329 note that minorities could delay or interrupt the establishment of absolute régimes.

[123] See C. Contessa, 'La congiura del marchese di Parella (1682)', *BSBS*, 38 (1936), 100 ff.

Victor Amadeus' personal rule from 1684 only partially resolved these problems. Until the birth of the prince of Piedmont in 1699, disaster was looming for the House of Savoy and the Savoyard state because, although Victor Amadeus' duchess was frequently pregnant, she was unable to produce a son and had only two daughters, Marie-Adelaide (b. 1685) and Marie-Louise (b. 1688).[124] This difficulty was made worse by the war, duchess Anne Marie miscarrying (a boy) in the crisis provoked by the French invasion of 1691 and her enforced flight from Turin.[125] The duke's lack of direct male heirs was problematic because females were excluded from inheriting imperial fiefs, which made up an important element of the Savoyard state.[126] If Victor Amadeus died without legitimate male heirs of his own body, the succession would pass to the senior of the collateral lines of the house of Savoy, that of Carignano, in the person of his elderly uncle, the deaf and dumb Prince Emmanuel Filibert (b. 1628), and his sons, Victor Amadeus (b. 1690) and Thomas Joseph (b. 1696). Should the Carignano line fail, the succession passed to the junior collateral line, that of Soissons, headed by Prince Louis Thomas and his sons, who included Prince Eugene. Similar circumstances earlier in the seventeenth century had plunged the Savoyard state into a damaging civil war (1637–42).[127] In view of these considerations, it is not surprising that allied diplomats were often alarmed at the way Victor Amadeus frequently risked his life on campaign.[128]

The prospect of another civil war, even a 'War of the Savoyard Succession', which would surely have set back any progress towards administrative centralisation came very close during the duke's smallpox attack in the autumn and winter of 1692–93, prompting his allies and his enemies to manoeuvre to exploit the situation for their own ends. The problem for Victor Amadeus' allies was that although Prince Filibert of

---

[124] The duke had an illegitimate daughter, Vittoria Francesca (b. 1690) and later an illegitimate son (Vittorio Francesco, b. 1694) by his mistress the contessa di Verrua, see G. de Léris, *La comtesse de Verrue et la cour de Victor Amédée II de Savoie* (Paris, 1881), 98 and Duboin, VIII, 243.   [125] Vitelleschi, *Romance of Savoy*, I, 330.

[126] See L. Bulferetti, 'Il principio della "superiorità territoriale" nella memorialistica piemontese del secolo XVIII', in *Studi in memoria di Gioele Solari* (Turin, 1954), 158, 168.

[127] There is an account of the collateral lines of the House of Savoy in C. A. M. Costa de Beauregard, *Mémoires historiques sur la Maison Royale de Savoie*, vol. 4 (Turin, 1816) and *CGP*, VII, 42 ff. For the elderly prince of Carignano, see VDM to Fagel, 20 Oct. 1692, Turin, ARAH/SG/8643/282 and Braubach, *Prinz Eugen*, I, 193 ff. In 1831, Victor Amadeus' descendant in the direct line, Carlo Felice, died without heirs and the crown passed to Carlo Alberto of the Carginano line.

[128] See VDM to Fagel, 9 May 1704, Turin, ARAH/EA/VDM/29, 80. Victor Amadeus personally led a cavalry charge at the battle of Turin (1706), Symcox, *Victor Amadeus*, 151.

Carginano was inclined towards Spain and hostile to Louis XIV (who had attempted to block the prince's marriage in 1684 to the Modenese princess, Caterina d'Este), Filibert's physical handicaps might prevent him making his claim and authority effective and vigorously pursuing the war against France, particularly in the face of domestic opposition to that war. Although it was widely believed in the same circles that most of Victor Amadeus' subjects abhorred the count of Soissons (who was then in Louis XIV's service, although he abandoned it in 1695) (see Chapter 3), it was feared nevertheless that they might support him as the means to achieve peace with France. One solution was to make use of the emperor's imperial authority in Piedmont, to appoint Prince Eugene as some sort of regent for or co-ruler with the prince of Carignano. In this case the latter's authority (and Savoy's continued membership of the Grand Alliance) would be underpinned by Habsburg troops. The emperor's appointment of Eugene as field marshal in Piedmont for 1693 thus had as much to do with the political and dynastic crisis in Turin as with purely military factors. As for Louis XIV, he was urged by his foreign minister, Colbert de Croissy, to plan for the eventuality of Victor Amadeus' death, in order both to 'manage' Carignano and his son, to exploit the goodwill towards France of many of the duke's subjects, and in this way to end the war in Piedmont. Instructions were in fact drawn up, in February 1693, for the abbé de Rivarol, brother of an officer in one of the Savoyard regiments in Louis' service, to go on a secret mission to Turin to sound out Carignano about ending the war should he succeed Victor Amadeus. In fact, Victor Amadeus' recovery rendered the mission abortive. Nevertheless, in March 1693, following reports that the emperor planned to seize Carignano and his son (and Victor Amadeus' family), the French king ordered Catinat to be ready to go to the prince of Carignano's aid.[129] For the rest of the 1690s, the threat to the Savoyard state of dynastic uncertainty, particularly in wartime, was clear.

Victor Amadeus' lack of a direct male heir also posed another threat to the territorial integrity of the Savoyard state: that the husbands of his daughters (once they had married) might in the future lay claims on the territories of that state. The duke's concern to prevent such a threat was evident during the negotiations for the separate peace with Louis XIV (whose claims to the Spanish crown were based on similar foundations) in the summer of 1696, and above all in the agreement for the marriage between Victor Amadeus' daughter, Marie Adelaide, and Louis XIV's grandson, the duke of Burgundy. Although the law of succession

---

[129] This episode is discussed in Storrs, 'Diplomatic relations', 179 ff. and R.D. Handen, 'The Savoy negotiations of the Comte de Tessé, 1693–1696' (Ph.D. thesis, Ohio State, 1970), 31 ff.

excluded her from inheriting, Victor Amadeus was very concerned to have a formal renunciation of her rights by Marie Adelaide included in the treaty between himself and the French king. Louis managed to evade this, but the marriage contract (which was not settled satisfactorily until September 1696) did include a formal renunciation by Victor Amadeus' daughter (who, since she was not yet twelve, the legal age for oath-taking, was given special dispensation).[130]

If Victor Amadeus was aware of the degree to which the very existence of the Savoyard state was linked to the dynasty, and of its consequent fragility, so too were many of his subjects, whose joy at the peace in 1697 was enhanced by the announcement of Anne-Marie's pregnancy. The importance of this development is evident from the way it disrupted Victor Amadeus' plans that summer. He postponed both a planned tour of the recently recovered Duchy of Savoy and repairs to the fortifications of Turin, the latter because of the likely effect on the air of Turin (and on the duchess' health). Not surprisingly, the death of the baby, a boy, soon after its birth, in November 1697, greatly distressed the duke.[131] Not until May 1699, after frequent visits by both Victor Amadeus' mother, Madama Reale and his duchess to the leading shrines of Turin, to make vows in return for the birth of a prince,[132] and a resort to astrologers and clairvoyants by an increasingly desperate Victor Amadeus,[133] was this fundamental threat to the Savoyard state finally removed, with the birth of a son, Victor Amadeus Joseph Philip, followed by the birth of a second son, the future Charles Emanuel III, in 1701.[134] The importance of the birth of his first son in 1699 was evident from the great joy expressed by many of Victor Amadeus' subjects.[135] The birth of the two princes held out the prospect of further territorial and other gains as a result of

---

[130] P. Canestrier, 'Comment M. de Tessé prepara en 1696 le traité de paix entre Louis XIV et Victor Amédée II', *Revue d'Histoire Diplomatique*, 48 (1934), 389; and Handen, 'Savoy negotiations', 154 ff. (and Appendix E, a copy of the marriage contract). Victor Amadeus secured a promise that the renunciation would be registered by the Paris Parlement, VDM to Fagel, 10 Aug. 1696, Turin, ARAH/SG/8644/287. See also Oresko, *The House of Savoy*, 329.
[131] Bazan to Carlos II, 3 and 31 May and 15 Nov. 1697, Turin, AGSE/3659/55, 65 and 97. The keen interest of foreign diplomats in this crucial development in the Savoyard state is itself noteworthy.
[132] L. Cibrario, *Storia di Torino*, 2 vols. (Turin, 1846), II, 95–6; and Vitelleschi, *Romance of Savoy*, II, 378 ff.
[133] V. Dainotti, 'Veggenti e astrologi intorno a Vittorio Amedeo II', *BSBS*, 34, 1932, 268.   [134] See Bazan to Carlos II, 8 May 1699, Turin, AGSE/3660/95.
[135] Soleri, Diario, BRT/Storia Patria, 230, f. 19. Two hundred members of the confraternity of the Name of Jesus, led by their rector, the marchese Pallavicino, went on pilgrimage to Vercelli where they deposited a silver *ex voto* image of a baby, Cibrario, *Storia di Torino*, II, 671–2.

marriages (above all, with a daughter of the emperor). They could also strengthen the personal ties between the dynasty and the expanding territorial state. Victor Amadeus bestowed on his sons the customary territorial titles – that of prince of Piedmont on his eldest son and heir, and that of duke of Aosta on his second son – while in 1712, Maffei, on learning of Sicilian hostility at the prospect of rule from distant Turin, suggested that the prince of Piedmont (or Victor Amadeus himself) might reside in Palermo.[136]

Above all, however, the births secured a hitherto uncertain succession, and the state itself, and the prince of Piedmont rapidly became a new focus of loyalty.[137] However, in an age of high infant mortality[138] the young princes required constant vigilance. In September 1705, the duke was said to be more concerned about the prince of Piedmont's diarrhoea and fever than about the enemy threat.[139] In 1706 the princes, their mother and grandmother were evacuated by Victor Amadeus to Genoa to prevent his heir from falling into French hands at this moment of crisis for his state. The duke ordered the Ceva militia to protect the passages between Piedmontese and Genoese territory (through Spanish territory) leaving Ceva itself exposed.[140] Victor Amadeus continued to be exercised by the health and safety of his sons thereafter. In 1708, the year in which the two princes were removed from female tutelage, he was enormously relieved when a riding accident in which they were involved proved not to have serious consequences.[141] His anxiety was justified: the death of

[136] In fact, Victor Amadeus himself went to Sicily in 1713, leaving the prince of Piedmont to govern his mainland territories, but was obliged, by the deteriorating international situation and the growing threat of war, to return to Turin in 1714, Thereafter, Sicily (and from 1720 Sardinia) was governed by a viceroy, a new institution in the Savoyard state.

[137] C. Contessa, 'I regni di Napoli e di Sicilia nelle aspirazioni italiane di Vittorio Amedeo II di Savoia (1700–1713)', *Studi su Vittorio Amedeo II* (Turin, 1933), 88. Savoyard commanders sent captured enemy standards to the young prince of Piedmont during the War of the Spanish Succession. The birth of his sons may have influenced the duke's decision to legitimise (1701), his two illegitimate children by the comtesse de Verrua. He later married the daughter to the prince of Carignano.

[138] In the winter of 1705–6, a son recently born to the duchess died, Tarino to VA, 16 Jan. 1706, Vienna, *CGP*, V, 104, while in 1709 the duchess again miscarried, VDM to Fagel, 25 Sept. 1709, Turin, ARAH/EA/VDM/33, f. 162.

[139] VDM to States, 16 Sept. 1705, Turin, ARAH/EA/VDM/30, 119.

[140] VDM to States, 30 June 1706, Oneglia, ARAH/EA/VDM/30, 291. The prince and princess of Carignano had also been evacuated, but were briefly captured by the French, who may still have seen them as a useful counter, same to Fagel, 2 June 1706, Turin, ARAH/EA/VDM/30, 276.

[141] VDM to States, 18 Apr. 1708, Turin, ARAH/EA/VDM/32, f. 63. One of those involved in this incident was subsequently rewarded with the fief of Montalto forfeited by the banker, Olivero, in 1712: AST/PCF/1711–12, ff. 171–2. In late 1711, the prince of Piedmont again fell ill, contributing to Victor Amadeus' decision

the prince of Piedmont in 1715 meant that the Savoyard succession now depended upon the survival of the future Charles Emanuel III.[142]

OPPOSITION AND COHESION

Forty years ago, in a study of diplomacy in and after 1815, Henry Kissinger argued that the real test of an effective, successful foreign policy was not only its relevance to the foreign situation, but also, indeed more importantly, its ability to command general domestic support.[143] The Savoyard state between 1690 and 1720 was clearly a very different polity from those Kissinger had in mind. However, his insight remains appropriate. The Risorgimento school of historians saw the wars of the 1690s and 1700s as a common enterprise binding Victor Amadeus II and his subjects, all this despite the enormous pressures generated by those conflicts. There is clearly something to this view because, apart from one or two instances (see below) there were no major revolts or acts of betrayal in these dramatic war years to contradict it. However, this does not mean that we should ignore, as do most studies of Victor Amadeus II's reign, and of these decades in particular, the degree of dissent from, even opposition to ducal policy within the Savoyard state. The demands (in terms of money, men, animals, crops and so on) of long and intensive warfare, the single most important test of early modern (and of modern) states and societies, and the consequent suffering at all levels of Savoyard society could not but create difficulties and tensions within the Savoyard state, and provoke some questioning of ducal policy. The absence of representative assemblies where political issues, such as whether to continue or to end the war, could be formally and openly debated by a wider 'public' did not mean the end completely of serious discussion or of opposition which, instead, necessarily found other channels. Of course we must be careful not to interpret all discussion, or criticism, as an expression of hostility to ducal policy. Nevertheless, the fact that debate and dissent were not always as visible in the Savoyard state between 1690 and 1713 as in England or the Dutch Republic did not mean that they did

---

to postpone an inspection of the fortifications on his alpine frontier, Chetwynd to Dartmouth, 9 Nov. 1711, Turin, SP 92/28. In a curious episode, reflecting a wider concern for the life of both Victor Amadeus and his eldest son, in 1712 a priest was accused of making effigies of the two, with an intent to effect their deaths, S. Loriga, 'Un segreto per far morire la persona del Re Magia e protezione nel Piemonte del '700', *Quaderni Storici*, 53, 1983; published as 'A secret to kill the king: magic and protection in eighteenth-century Piedmont', in E. Muir and G. Ruggiero, eds., *History from Crime: selections from Quaderni Storici* (Baltimore, 1994), 90.

[142] See Vitelleschi, *Romance of Savoy*, II, 457, 482.
[143] H. Kissinger, *A World Restored: Europe after Napoleon* (New York, 1957), 326.

not exist, merely that they took different forms. The rest of this chapter seeks to identify these, and to show how Victor Amadeus responded to them.[144]

Formal venues for political debate, i.e. representative estates with real powers, were increasingly a thing of the past in the Savoyard state, although Victor Amadeus' wars meant the acquisition of territories (including both those detached from the Milanese, Sicily, briefly, and Sardinia) in which representative assemblies of a sort in which opposition to ducal demands could be publicly voiced continued to exist.[145] Among the most visible fora of debate, even of opposition in these years, were the sovereign courts: the Senate and the Camera dei Conti of Turin, the Senate and Chambre des Comptes of Chambéry, and to a much lesser extent both the Senate of Nice and (from 1697) the Conseil Supérieur of Pinerolo.[146] These institutions, whose members were drawn from, and formed part of the governing elite of the Savoyard state,[147] had a dual, even an ambiguous role. On the one hand, they were an integral part of the ducal administration and of the public face of the Savoyard state.[148] More importantly, the Camera dei Conti and Chambre des Comptes were important accounting institutions, approving the accounts of

---

[144] The notion of a deep traditional loyalty of the people of Victor Amadeus' states, and particularly the Piedmontese, to the House of Savoy, which was asserted at this time by Victor Amadeus' diplomats (for example, Vernone at the French court in 1700), Contessa, 'I regni', 35, was as much a ploy to ensure that Victor Amadeus yielded as little of his existing territories as possible, in return for the largest possible slice of the Spanish Succession. On the need to distinguish between criticism and opposition, see Sharpe, *Personal Rule of Charles I*, 100.

[145] Victor Amadeus' abortive plan to have the Duchy of Savoy taken under the protective wing of the Swiss from 1703 seemed to necessitate the calling of the Duchy's defunct estates to approve the move, P. Valente, 'Relazioni diplomatiche di Vittorio Amedeo II, Duca di Savoia, coi Cantoni Svizzeri e colla Repubblica del Vallese durante il secondo periodo della guerra in Italia per la successione di Spagna (1703–07)', *CGP*, VI. The terms of the cession of Sicily and Sardinia to Victor Amadeus under-pinned the continued existence of the representative, tax-granting estates of those realms, Mattone, 'La Cessione' 25 ff. In Sardinia, however, after 1720 the full assembly was effectively dispensed with, the Savoyard regime preferring to deal with the permanent committee of the estates (which had to periodically renew the taxes granted earlier), Symcox, *Victor Amadeus*, 182–3.

[146] There is no good modern study of the sovereign courts in this era, although details can be found in most studies of the Savoyard state, including Merlin *et al.*, *Piemonte sabaudo*, and Rosso, *Una burocrazia*. E. Genta, *Senato e senatori di Piemonte nel secolo XVIII* (Turin, 1983), is a prosopographical study of that institution after its reform in 1723.

[147] See the list of magistrates in 1705–6 in Rondolino, 'Vita Torinese', *CGP*, VII, 67 ff.

[148] In 1691 Max Emanuel of Bavaria was received by the Senate, Camera and council of the city of Turin, on his public entry into Turin, Soleri, Diario, BRT/Storia Patria, 230, f. 15.

receivers of taxes, investigating tax fraud and granting tax relief where appropriate (see Chapter 2). As for the Senates, they registered ducal decrees (and pardons), monitored the subordinate magistrates in the communities (those appointed by the duke and by the lords possessing independent jurisdictions) and acted as a court of appeal from inferior jurisdictions.[149] Indicative of the importance of the sovereign courts to the normal functioning of Piedmont was Victor Amadeus' decision in the summer of 1706 to split both Senate and Camera into two, one half remaining in Turin, the other accompanying him to Cherasco, which was to be the location of his administration for as long as Turin remained either cut off from the rest of his states or in enemy hands or both. The full Senate did not sit again in Turin until September, the full Camera only in November of that year.[150] The sovereign courts had supplied successive dukes of Savoy with collaborators;[151] and Victor Amadeus continued to rely upon them in wartime.[152] In fact, many of his key collaborators in this era, including both the comte de la Tour, president of the Chambéry Chambre des Comptes and envoy to the Dutch Republic and William III and conte Pralormo, a member of the Senate, who took possession (1707) in Victor Amadeus' name of Val Sesia and remained there as the duke's *podestà*, were drawn from the sovereign courts.[153] One reason for this collaboration on the part of the magistrates was that the sovereign courts were beneficiaries of the process of state expansion and formation,[154] which often meant the extension of their own jurisdiction at the expense of those of their rivals – notably the church and the emperor. Throughout his long-running dispute with the

---

[149] G. Lombardi, 'Note sul controllo degli atti del sovrano negli stati sabaudi ad opera delle supreme magistrature nel periodo dell'assolutismo', *Annali dell'Università di Roma*, 2, 1962, 1–40, passim (esp. 4, for the different competences and responsibilities of Senate and Camera). Unfortunately, Lombardi (whose approach is largely juridical and whose focus is above all the Senate) says virtually nothing about the period between 1682 and 1723.   [150] Rondolino, 'Vita Torinese', *CGP*, VII, 67, 72.

[151] Magistrates of the sovereign courts were members of the Delegation set up in 1661 to reform local finances, C. Rosso, 'Il Seicento', in Merlin *et al. Il Piemonte sabaudo* (Turin, 1994) 254. In 1685 Victor Amadeus ordered that two members each from the Senate and Camera should serve on the body framing the rules of operation of the Ospedale di Carità, Duboin, XII, 271. See Cavallo, *Charity and Power*, 151.

[152] In 1705, auditors of the Camera (four of whom held the post of referendary) played a key role in the census of Turin's population ordered by Victor Amadeus on the eve of the siege, E. Casanova, 'Censimento di Torino alla vigilia dell'assedio (29 agosto–6 settembre 1705)', *CGP*, VIII, 3 ff.   [153] *CGP*, V, 12, 92.

[154] The sovereign court of Pinerolo, originally created (1643) by the French king, was not only confirmed by Victor Amadeus when he recovered Pinerolo in 1696. In addition, he extended its jurisdication in 1697, and again (to some of his conquests of French territory) in and after the War of the Spanish Succession – although it was finally abolished, in favour of the Senate of Turin, in 1729: see M. Viora, 'Il Senato di Pinerolo', *BSBS*, 29, 1927, 174, 209, 215, 231, 247.

Pope from 1694, the duke enjoyed the backing of the sovereign courts,[155] while in 1708, the Camera dei Conti made no difficulty over Victor Amadeus' edict ordering the holders of those imperial fiefs in the Langhe (immediate superiority over which had recently been transferred to him by the emperor) to register with the Camera (thus formally acknowledging the duke's suzerainty).[156]

But the interests of sovereign courts and duke were not always or inevitably identical. The former were also expected to scrutinise ducal edicts, and to modify and even oppose them if they thought those edicts against the public interest. This right of 'remonstrance' rarely if ever seems to have been exercised in a manner reminiscent of that of the French Parlements[157], but was certainly exercised on occasion before 1690.[158] Nevertheless, this more critical function – and a certain independence of mind underpinned by the fact that members of the sovereign courts had often purchased their posts in one way or another – could put these courts on a collision course with Victor Amadeus in the three decades after 1690, because of his desperate efforts to maximise revenues. Between 1696 and 1703, for example, the Chambre des Comptes at Chambéry played a leading role in opposing – with some sucess – the duke's efforts to reform (largely at the expense of the hitherto fiscally privileged) the tax system in Savoy.[159]

Victor Amadeus' differences with the Piedmontese sovereign courts, however, remain largely unexplored. Of the many examples during the Nine Years War of difference of opinion, even opposition, at least as measured by modification of ducal edicts,[160] among the most remarkable was the Turin Senate's alteration of the edict (1694) in favour of the Vaudois (see Chapter 6). That same year the Camera dei Conti opposed Victor Amadeus' order to establish a glass manufactory, which was very

[155] In 1700, the Senate of Turin ordered the archbishop of Turin to reverse recent measures intended to counter the duke's efforts to increase the fiscal contribution of the clergy, Einaudi, *Finanza sabauda*, 56 ff. For the Chambéry Chambre des Comptes, see Symcox, *Victor Amadeus*, 130.

[156] Copies of the edict and act of registration accompanied VDM to Fagel, 22 Dec. 1708, Turin, ARAH/EA/VDM/32, f. 229.

[157] Einaudi, *Finanza sabauda*, 72. Cavallo, *Charity and Power*, 116, describes the right of remonstrance as theoretical.

[158] For earlier refusals to register ducal edicts see W. Barberis, *Le armi del principe. La tradizione militare sabauda* (Turin, 1988), 82 ff. (1611–12); Lombardi, 'Note sul controllo', 20 ff. (1681) and Duboin, XIV, 884 (1684).

[159] In 1701–2 the Chambre des Comptes refused to register, then modified to the point of making ineffective an edict obliging nobles to compensate those communities where they had bought land and wrongly withdrawn it from contributing to the communal tax quota, Einaudi, *Finanza sabauda*, 90 ff. Generally on the Chambre des Comptes in this period, see Symcox, *Victor Amadeus*, 121–2.

[160] See Barberis, *Le armi*, 134, for the Turin Senate's modification of a ducal edict of 1691 threatening those of his subjects residing abroad who did not promptly return home.

unpopular with the inhabitants of Turin, on the grounds that it would make excessive use of wood (driving up the price of the latter) and damage the forests;[161] and made representations against the stamped paper tax, claiming that it had pernicious consequences for the provision of justice – the proper administration of which was among the key duties of both prince and the sovereign courts.[162] Peace from 1696 did not mean the end of these difficulties,[163] while renewed war from 1701 provided more opportunities for confrontation. In 1702 conte Salmatoris, president of the Senate of Nice, opposed the extension there of the tobacco gabelle;[164] and in 1703, the Camera – effectively acting in defence of 'consumers' – complained at the poor quality and high price of candles consequent on Victor Amadeus' establishment (1695) of a candle monopoly.[165] In 1704, the duke's order to the Camera to register at last an edict for the storing of surplus grain in ducal magazines, about which the Camera had great reservations, was complied with. However, the Camera modified the edict. This, together with the general reluctance to comply and the lack of an effective system of local control made the scheme difficult to operate.[166] Clashes of this sort, not surprisingly, were less common after the fiscal crises of the first years of the war. However, ducal manipulation of the coinage – a persistent source of tension with the sovereign courts after 1690 could still provoke the Camera in 1709.[167]

It would be wrong, however, to think of the sovereign courts as constantly at odds with Victor Amadeus in these decades. Co-operation remained the norm and most ducal measures were registered with little or no opposition or modification. When the survival of the Savoyard state was at stake, Camera and Senate would modify, even stifle, their right to veto and oppose. Thus, in the summer of 1706, the Camera, which had initially objected to Gropello's alienating more *tasso* than cash received (in loans), gave way following receipt of a ducal letter and subsequently abandoned its plan to modify the edict once Gropello had represented that this would undermine his loan negotiations.[168] But the Savoyard sovereign courts were clearly not simply the tools of the duke. On occasion, their attempt to modify a ducal edict – for example that establishing the Reding 'military colony' in the Biellese (see Chapter 1) –

[161] Duboin, XVII, 330. See Einaudi, *Finanza sabauda*, 37.
[162] Einaudi, *Finanza sabauda*, 42.
[163] The Camera dei Conti unsuccessfully opposed (1698) Victor Amadeus' edict banning the use of private couriers, Einaudi, *Finanza sabauda*, 42–3.
[164] Einaudi, *Finanza sabauda*, 98 ff.
[165] *Ibid.*, 35. These criticisms, although not immediately effective, undoubtedly contributed to Victor Amadeus' decision to abolish (1712) the monopoly.
[166] *Ibid.*, 134, 169 ff. [167] *Ibid.* 238–9 (the sale of Santhia, 1706) and 260 ff. (coinage).
[168] *Ibid.*, 250 ff.

could reflect a wider unease, even opposition. Scrutiny by the sovereign courts thus supplied, if only to a very limited degree, the want of control of ducal government in the wake of the disappearance of powerful representative assemblies, and might at least make Victor Amadeus and his officials reconsider. These differences between the duke and his ministers on the one hand, and the sovereign courts on the other, did not fully replace the sort of bargaining (and implicit limitation on power) evident in states where representative assemblies still thrived. But they underpinned a constitutionalism of sorts, even if it is one a later generation might find it hard immediately to recognise as such.

Victor Amadeus could turn these clashes to advantage.[169] However, the sovereign courts clearly needed managing on occasion. Ministers were sometimes obliged to attend the Camera in person in order to get edicts registered.[170] The duke could also appoint his own men to the most senior posts, conte Orazio Provana serving as first president in the Senate of Savoy between 1687 and his death in 1697.[171] This may explain why an abortive project (1704) to raise money by selling the right to inherit the leading offices of state excluded those of the first president of both the Camera and the Senate, without whose support it would be more difficult to steer business through the sovereign courts.[172] Ultimately, Victor Amadeus could seek to sideline a troublesome institution, many of the functions of the Chambre des Comptes being transferred to the intendancy from the late 1690s, before being abolished in 1720. Nevertheless, this latter was an extreme step. The other sovereign courts (including the Chambéry Senate) survived, and continued to play a key role in the Savoyard polity.[173]

Rather more difficult to pin down, because less formal, were the court factions which could also be a vehicle of opposition to ducal policy. To some extent these were merely the continuation of the factions which had competed for power in Turin throughout the 1680s and which were linked with the foreign courts vying for the Savoyard alliance. They

[169] In 1705, following representations on behalf of a French Protestant refugee and his son, Victor Amadeus replied that due process (i.e. the Senate) must take its course, effectively sheltering behind the Senate – although this was an important concern and a source of potential domestic division and opposition, ST to VDM, 8 Aug. 1705, Turin, ARAH/EA/VDM/30, 98.

[170] In 1701, Gropello attended the Camera dei Conti to ensure pasage of the edict reintroducing the *macina* tax, Einaudi, *Finanza sabauda*, 152–3.

[171] L. Barberis, 'Il conte Orazio Provana', 105.   [172] Einaudi, *Finanza sabauda*, 245 ff.

[173] In 1720, the president of the Camera dei Conti was asked by Victor Amadeus to report on Sardinia as the king prepared to take over the island. The president's report represented a 'constitutional' position of sorts, urging his master to respect traditional institutions (in contrast, implicitly, with the policy he had pursued in Sicily and which had alienated the Sicilians), Mattone, 'La cessione', 9–10.

included a pro-imperial and Spanish faction led by the prince of Carignano and, to a lesser degree by the marchese di Parella (brother-in-law of one of the emperor's ministers, Count Königsegg), who had sought Austrian and Spanish Habsburg support in 1682 against the regent.[174] Parella's known links with the imperial court probably explains both his ignorance of the negotiations preceding Victor Amadeus' *volte-face* of 1696 and his despatch to Vienna later that summer, no doubt in the hope that he might be better able to convince the emperor of the advantages of a separate peace in Italy. Parella and his family continued thereafter to be closely identified with the Austrian Habsburgs: the departure without Victor Amadeus' permission for Hungary of Parella's son and heir, the marchese d'Andorno, to serve in the imperial armies, in 1698, prompted the family's temporary banishment from Turin.[175]

More important, however, in the present context is the pro-French faction and the extent of pro-French sentiment in Turin, also dating from before 1690.[176] Contemporaries were convinced of, and the envoys of Victor Amadeus' Protestant allies obsessed by, the existence of French sympathisers at the duke's court. In 1694, for example, van der Meer supported a request for more frequent intelligence from The Hague by reference to the need to counter the activities of the French faction in Turin.[177] Such vague suspicions and accusations must be treated with some caution. Nevertheless, contemporaries clearly recognised the existence of a pro-French faction in Turin headed by Victor Amadeus' mother, the former regent, Madama Reale.[178] The latter remained an important political figure after being ousted from power in 1684, maintaining (see above) a substantial court of her own in Turin, and refashion-

[174] The best, brief, recent introduction to the still largely obscure issue of Turin court factions in the 1680s is R. Oresko, 'The diplomatic background to the Glorioso Rimpatrio: the rupture between Vittorio Amedeo II and Louis XIV (1686–1690)', in A. de Lange, ed., *Dall'Europa alle Valli Valdesi* (Turin, 1990). See, also, Contessa, 'La congiura', passim.

[175] A. Ferrero della Marmora, *Notizie sulla vita e sulle geste militari di Carlo Emilio San Martino di Parella, ossia cronica militare aneddottica delle guerre in Piemonte dal 1672 al 1706* (Turin, 1863), 358 ff.; Bazan to Carlos II, 18 Sept. 1698, Turin, AGS/E/3660/60.

[176] In 1689, Louvois claimed to have seen letters about Victor Amadeus' hostile conduct from (unidentified) French sympathisers in Piedmont, C. de Rousset, *Histoire de Louvois et son administration militaire*, 4 vols. (Paris, 1862–3), 2/2, 287.

[177] VDM to Fagel, 1 Mar. 1694, Turin, ARAH/SG/8644/104. In 1706, van der Meer backed the duke's complaint against slanderous criticisms in a Dutch publication of the marchese di Caraglio, hero of the siege of Nice and one of the duke's leading subjects, claiming that such reports could be misused by French 'creatures' in Turin, same to same, 21 Apr. 1706, Turin, ARAH/EA/VDM/30, 239.

[178] In 1689, Louis XIV's minister in Turin reassured his master that a mission Victor Amadeus was sending to Munich could be of no political significance, since he was sending the abbé Pallavicino, whose house the duke thought too close to Madama Reale, Oresko, 'Diplomatic Background', 266.

ing, positively, the image of her regency.[179] More importantly, despite the role of the French court in her ejection from power in 1684, together with Louis XIV's minister in Turin, she was the champion of the French cause there, supplying Versailles with intelligence and pressing its cause on her son. In May 1690, as Catinat advanced across Piedmont, she urged Victor Amadeus not to antagonise the French king.[180] In the summer of 1691, with his allies failing to prevent a major French onslaught, Victor Amadeus was again pressed by his mother to make peace.[181] Madama Reale, whose household remained a focus for French sympathisers – and even of French spies[182] – continued thereafter to maintain links with, and to supply intelligence to the French court.[183]

There were suspicions, too, that some of Victor Amadeus' own ministers opposed his wars. According to William III's envoy in Switzerland, not only Madama Reale (and Victor Amadeus' duchess) but also most of his ministers – their estates already in French hands or threatened with it – were pressing the duke to make peace with Louis XIV following Victor Amadeus' disastrous first campaign of the Nine Years War.[184] Although sometimes no doubt exaggerated, these reports were by no means completely unfounded. In 1692, President Provana, one of Victor Amadeus' leading collaborators in the Nine Years War, in a *mémoire* debating the issue of war or peace, came down on the side of peace. He argued, *inter alia*, that when the glory of the prince (in this case loyalty to allies who were not fulfuiling their oblgations) threatened the destruction of his own interests and reason of state, then it was no longer true glory but mere vanity – a scarcely veiled criticism of Victor Amadeus' determina-

---

[179] For the attempt to rewrite the history of the Regency, see Contessa, 'La congiura', 105–6.

[180] *Mémoire* from Madama Reale, 13 May 1690, Rousset, *Histoire de Louvois*, 2/2, 310. When Victor Amadeus broke with the French court (after initially seeming to take her advice), the former Regent criticised the French Court for not handling her son as she had advised, Catinat to Louvois, 30 May 1690, Rousset, *Histoire de Louvois*, 2/2, 338.

[181] Madama Reale to VA, 21 May 1691, Turin, AST/Negoziazioni/Francia/m. 15 (no. 14).

[182] In 1693 a man in Madama Reale's household, French by birth, was arrested for corresponding with the enemy, VDM to Fagel, 26 June 1693, Turin, ARAH/SG/ 8644/49.

[183] A. Segre, 'Negoziati diplomatici della Corte Sabauda colla Corte di Baviera dalle origini al 1704', *CGP*, VI, 198–9. Madama Reale, who resented being deprived of the regency in her son's absence in Sicily, continued to confide in the French court after 1713, Vitelleschi, *Romance of Savoy*, II, 428ff.

[184] Coxe to Nottingham, 14 Oct. 1690, Berne, SP 96/7. Marshal Catinat, who clearly had good sources of intelligence in and about the Savoyard court, reported that after the loss of Susa in the winter of 1690–91, some of Victor Amadeus' ministers again urged him to settle, prompting the duke to reply, 'I can't, I won't and I must not', Catinat to Louvois, 10 Feb. 1691, Rousset, *Histoire de Louvois*, 2/2, 452. For the political crisis after Staffarda, see Saluces, *Histoire militaire*, V, 22 ff.

tion to fight on.¹⁸⁵ Dissent from ducal policy within what we might call official circles was by no means confined to the Nine Years War and could find expression in the leaking of sensitive documents.¹⁸⁶ It could also take a more public form. In 1703, de la Tour, an advocate of the French alliance, resigned his office of secretary for war (see Chapter 3) following his master's latest reversal of alliances.

Without necessarily being part of a pro-French faction, many of those outside the court and government might also eagerly desire the end of war and the difficulties associated with it. Nobles figured prominently among those identified as opposing the war, not least because of their greater access to Victor Amadeus and the fact that they had so much to lose through the devastation war brought. In early 1694, following reports of major French preparations (to deliver the knock out blow after the 1693 campaign), some of Victor Amadeus' leading nobles (unfortunately not identified) were said to have urged him, unsuccessfully, to avoid ruin by ending the war.¹⁸⁷ In the summer of 1704, too, with his allies having failed to help him as promised and with his states pressed on all sides, and his main fortresses falling into enemy hands, some at least among the nobility hoped and expected that Victor Amadeus would settle separately with the French king (as in 1696).¹⁸⁸ It is tempting to see the 'prophecies' of peace before 1696 of the so-called beata, Maria degli Angioli, of an elite family, as reflecting a more widespread desire among the Turinese elite (and the population at large) for the end of the war.¹⁸⁹ Deliberate rumour-mongering, particularly of a coming peace, during the War of the Spanish Succession exploited the widespread knowledge of Victor Amadeus' conduct in 1696.¹⁹⁰ Popular opposition, especially to

---

¹⁸⁵ AST/Negoziazioni, Francia, m. 15/17. See L. Barberis, 'Il conte Orazio Provana ambasciatore sabaudo (1630–1697)', *BSBS*, 1928, 110–11. Galway suspected that Provana (whom he called an anti-Vaudois bigot) spread false rumours of secret peace negotiations by the duke's other allies to bounce Victor Amadeus into listening to French peace proposals, Galway to William III, 18 May 1694, Turin, SP 8/15, 10.

¹⁸⁶ Louis XIV was well informed about the instructions given de la Tour for his mission to the Hague (via the French Court) in 1700, Contessa, 'I regni', 23

¹⁸⁷ VDM to Fagel, 23 Apr. 1694, Turin, ARAH/SG/8644/119.

¹⁸⁸ VDM to Fagel, 15 Aug. 1704, Turin, ARAH/EA/VDM/29, 145–6.

¹⁸⁹ F. Rondolino, 'Vita Torinese', *CGP*, VII, 396 ff. On the political resonance of prophecy in early modern Europe, see R. Kagan, *Lucrecia's Dreams: politics and prophecy in sixteenth-century Spain* (Baltimore, 1990).

¹⁹⁰ In the spring of 1705, the English envoy in Turin noted a widespread inclination there to believe the reports, put out by the French, that Victor Amadeus was secretly negotiating a separate peace, Hill to Hedges, 28 Apr. 1705, Turin, in W. Blackley, ed., *The Diplomatic Correspondence of Richard Hill*, 2 vols. (London, 1845), II, 531–3. Then, and in 1706, van der Meer attributed such rumours to French 'creatures': VDM to Fagel, 7 Oct. 1705 and 27 Jan. and 12 May 1706, Turin, ARAH/EA/VDM/30, 128, 189, 255.

the new demands the war brought with it, might express itself in a variety of ways, including armed struggles with the foreign troops (of Victor Amadeus' allies) quartered on them.[191] Even without being able to point to specific individuals or episodes, it is clear that the war, particularly at times of crisis, stimulated a desire for peace which found expression in a variety of often covert forms. The duke and his ministers could not ignore this reality.[192]

How did Victor Amadeus deal with these pressures? His own troops, and those of his allies, undoubtedly strengthened his ability to deal firmly with domestic dissent (see Chapter 1). Some certainly suffered for their dissidence, particularly when it turned to dealings with the ememy.[193] However, at least during the most difficult war years, the duke often had to turn a blind eye or effectively buy off the malcontents, particularly among the elite. In 1693, a servant of Presidente Vacca, of the Turin Senate, denounced supposedly treasonous meetings between Vacca and two leading figures, the marchesi di Pianezza and Druent. Apparently, they had voiced their opposition to the war, expressing the fear that Piedmont would become another Palatinate, laid waste by French troops. The three men were also said to have celebrated French successes and criticised the marchese di Parella. Victor Amadeus showed a keen interest in the affair, but none of the three accused (who had not, anyway, taken their grumbling further) suffered.[194] As for buying off malcontents, in 1694 Victor Amadeus promoted a number of new lieutenants general, only one of whom was expected to take the field, at a time (as we have seen) when he was under pressure from the elite. Those promotions were widely seen in Turin as an attempt to head off this opposition.[195]

Perhaps the most interesting example of Victor Amadeus' having to retreat before opposition (although not necessarily opposition to the war *per se*) was provided by the Bernardi affair in the opening stages of the War of the Spanish Succession. Just as in the Nine Years War, the duke

---

[191] The resentment of Victor Amadeus' subjects at the damage done by foraging troops (allied and enemy) was sufficiently well known in the summer of 1705 to inspire fear that those subjects might seek to exact their revenge, VDM to States, 29 July 1705, Turin, ARAH/EA/VDM/30, 89.

[192] In January 1706, no doubt on Victor Amadeus' orders, Saint-Thomas told the Dutch envoy that his subjects, great and small, complained at the demands made on them for money, grain, forage, wagons and men, VDM to Fagel, 20 Jan. 1706, Turin, ARAH/EA/VDM/30, 184. For pressure from the clergy for an end to the war in 1706, see Carutti, *Vittorio Amedeo II*, p. 316.

[193] In the War of the Spanish Succession, the councillor and referendary of state, conte Pallavicino di Perlo was tried, and condemned (to loss of office and property, and exile) for secret negotiations with the French, AST/MC, m. 9/12

[194] Contessa, 'La congiura', 139 ff.

[195] VDM to Fagel, 3 May 1694, Turin, ARAH/SG/8644/119b.

210 WAR, DIPLOMACY AND THE RISE OF SAVOY

Fig. 4.1   Medal, 1706, celebrating victory at Turin (Biblioteca Reale, Iconografia Varia 21/2)

Fig 4.2 Part of firework display in Turin, September 1713, to celebrate the conclusion of the War of the Spanish Succession (Biblioteca Reale, Turin, Miscellanea di Storia Patria, 302)

was (sometimes rightly) inclined to suspect treachery among those entrusted with the defence of strategically important fortresses when they surrendered those places, and to punish them.[196] In the summer of 1704, following the surrender of Susa, he ordered the trial of its erstwhile governor, Giuseppe Tomaso Bernardi, and was determined to have Bernardi condemned and severely punished, for treason, no doubt to serve as an example for the future. Unfortunately, the affair backfired, dividing the duke's own collaborators and the Savoyard elite as a whole. Following Bernardi's trial, at which he was defended by the cavaliere Vernone, many of Turin's female elite visited and comforted Bernardi's wife. The cavaliere Vernone was not only the younger brother of the conte di Vernone but had also himself served Victor Amadeus in Switzerland, and concluded a number of capitulations there for Swiss troops. More seriously, the cavaliere Vernone, apparently outraged by the injustice of Bernardi's condemnation (and the rigging of his trial) seems to have orchestrated a campaign designed to force the duke to pardon Bernardi. It succeeded, Victor Amadeus granting a reprieve when Bernardi was on the scaffold. But that was not the end of the matter; a week or so later on 11 September 1704, some of Victor Amadeus' other ministers met to discuss making an example of those propagating the view that Bernardi had been condemned unjustly in the first place, and that Victor Amadeus' pardon was an acknowledgement of this. According to one of those present, conte Ferraris, his wife had heard President Delescheraine condemn the role of the grand chancellor and President Peyrani in the business. Unforunately for Gropello, who was co-ordinating the business for Victor Amadeus, and perhaps reflecting the wider unease over the matter within the elite, Ferraris was unwilling to make a formal declaration against Delescheraine, who was widely regarded as playing the leading part in spreading these subversive opinions. But he was not alone. Gropello explained to the others present that he had suspended distribution of copies of the sentences against Bernardi (and the other officers at Susa who were condemned) for fear that somebody might, on the basis of these publish something critical of them, in effect appealing to public opinion. This was because a number of people, especially President Caselette and President Delecheraine had been asking the printers for copies of the sentences. At this same meeting President Peyrani reported remarks critical of Bernardi's condemnation by both the cavaliere Vernone and the conte di Lagnasco, son of the governor of Savig-

---

[196] In 1691, Victor Amadeus had arrested the governor and officers of Villefranche (Nice), following its fall to the French, VDM to Fagel, 4 Apr. 1691, Turin, ARAH/SG/8643/123. In 1718, the cavaliere Marelli, governor of Castellamare, was thought to have surrendered to the besieging Spaniards rather too promptly, and was condemned to death by a military court, Saluces, *Histoire militaire*, V, 271.

liano. The fact that none of those identified as offenders on this occasion seem to have been punished suggests that in this instance Victor Amadeus, whose pardon for Bernardi was clearly a defeat, had to accommodate dissent of a sort within his state.[197]

Victor Amadeus might seek to head off resentment and opposition in other ways. These might, ultimately, include bringing his wars to a prompt halt, as in 1696, thus ending the associated burdens as most of his subjects certainly wished – although this is not to suggest that domestic pressure of this sort was the key consideration behind the duke's *volte-face* in 1696. On the contrary, Victor Amadeus sought to ensure that his subjects recognised and accepted their obligations to help him fight his enemies by – as Luigi Einaudi observed – courting what we might call public opinion. Of course, that public opinion in the Savoyard state *c.* 1700 was hardly as developed as either its late twentieth-century descendant or even that emerging 'public sphere' which – influenced by the work of Habermas – has so influenced the last generation of work on eighteenth-century France. Nevertheless, historians are increasingly aware of the importance of public opinion in the supposedly absolute state,[198] and something of the sort did (as we have seen) exist in Turin. Inevitably, public opinion in the Savoyard capital in this period was very sensitive to foreign and military developments, as Victor Amadeus and his ministers were well aware.[199]

Clearly, there was a need to explain the enormous sacrifices that were being asked of the duke's subjects There were various ways in which this justificatory message could be communicated. One might be the consultation of certain groups in informal public assemblies, the duke explaining his breach with Louis XIV to a gathering of several hundred nobles in Turin in June 1690.[200] Another was a public manifesto which should explain the conflict the duke and his subjects found themselves caught up in.[201] Similar explanations, as Einaudi pointed out, were often inserted in the preambles of the edicts imposing new fiscal and military obligations on Victor Amadeus' subjects. Thus, in July 1690, his order to the communi-

---

[197] The Bernardi affair can be followed in *CGP*, II, 165–94, passim (which prints many relevant documents). For the session of September 1704, see AST/MC, m. 10/9.
[198] See A. Gestrich, *Absolutismus und Offentlichkeit: politische Kommunikation in Deutschland zu Beginn des 18. Jahrhunderts* (Göttingen, 1992), passim.
[199] See ST to conte Tarino, Oct. 1703, Turin, *CGP*, IV, 34, on the excellent disposition of both nobility and populace. In the winter of 1705–6, Victor Amadeus informed the English envoy that the departure of his predecessor, Hill, from the beleaguered Savoyard state had had a bad effect on the duke's subjects, VDM to States, 27 Jan. 1706, Turin, ARAH/EA/VDM/30, 190.
[200] D. Carutti, *Storia della diplomazia della Corte di Savoia*, 4 vols. (Turin, 1875–80), III, 184–5.
[201] Klaits, *Printed Propaganda*, 198; VDM to Fagel, 19 Feb. 1704, Turin, ARAH/EA/VDM/29, 38.

ties to provide fixed numbers of armed men declared that the duke was doing all he could to allow his 'most faithful subjects' to enjoy their accustomed peace and that, despite the obligation on all to follow him in taking the field, he was (implying a substantial concession on his part) only asking for some men to be supplied armed. Similarly, when Victor Amadeus joined the War of the Spanish Succession, the edict reintroducing the unpopular *macina* tax (1701) mentioned the obligation on the duke to do all in his power to ensure the peace and tranquillity of his *ben amati popoli*, who needed protection in the present circumstances, thus obliging him to increase his forces. There was also a reference to his having taken the advice of his most experienced ministers (i.e. the decision was not taken alone or lightly), and a claim that the *macina* seemed the most just means of meeting the extraordinary need (one of the key expectations of government being that it should rule justly). It was promised that the tax would only be imposed for as long as the emergency lasted. Other ducal edicts contained equally propagandistic preambles aimed at justifying Victor Amadeus' policy to his subjects.[202] In the autumn of 1703 the duke specifically instructed his provincial governors to inform the 'public' of the outrage done him at San Benedetto, and wrote to a number of towns and communities in the provinces of Biella, Ivrea and Vercelli to the same end, hoping in this way to stimulate loyalty at this time of crisis.[203] In 1719, too, Victor Amadeus sought to explain his need for funds, for the war against Spain in Sicily, to his subjects, in the preamble to an edict creating a new Monte or loan subscription.[204]

As elsewhere, public (and particularly religious) ceremonial and celebration could play an important political role.[205] Religion, and above all the Roman Catholic faith (particularly as redefined and reinvigorated by the Counter-Reformation), was another source of cohesion in the Savoyard state, although by no means peculiar to it. The return of the exiled Vaudois, and the influx in the 1690s of Huguenot refugees

---

[202] Einaudi, *Finanza sabauda*, 119–20, 152, 163 ff.; *CGP*, 1, 60 (extract from Victor Amadeus' order of 3 Oct. 1703 summoning militia) and 62 (extract from ducal order of 19 Dec. 1703 for levy of 7 militia regiments of 600 men each); AST/Editti, m. 14/38.

[203] VA to provincial governors, *CGP*, I, 71–2. Subsequently, various provincial governors reported that they had publicised the news, to good effect: *ibid.*, 74 (Susa), 78 (Ivrea), 84 (Nice). A similar letter written by Victor Amadeus to the bishop of Saluzzo in early October 1703 is published by F. Gabotto, 'Il manifesto di guerra di Vittorio Amedeo II contro I Francesi nel 1703', *BSBS*, 9, 1904, 10. See also VA to inhabitants of Val di Luserna, 3 Oct. 1703, *CGP*, I, 73 (and note).

[204] Edicts of May and June 1719, in AST/PCF/1717–20, f. 105, 111. Victor Amadeus clearly hoped to be able to borrow what he needed from his subjects.

[205] On the importance of ceremonies and celebrations in early modern Europe, see R. J. Lopez, *Ceremonia y poder a finales del Antiguo Regimen. Galicia 1700–1833* (Santiago de Compostela, 1995).

complicated this uniformity, to say the least (see Chapter 6).[206] However, this should not obscure the continued importance of religion as a political cement in the Savoyard state. One of the great advantages of the Casa Savoia and Victor Amadeus in this respect was their possession since the fourteenth century of the Santo Sindone (the so-called Holy Shroud) which had been removed by Emanuel Filibert to Turin (from Chambéry) in the 1570s. The Sindone was closely (and deliberately) identified with the House of Savoy, and was exhibited on important occasions, including, most recently, in 1686, to celebrate Victor Amadeus' triumph over the Vaudois (and the achievement at last of a Catholic Savoyard state) and again in 1692. The decades preceding 1690 saw the construction of a splendid new chapel (designed by Guarini) to house the Sindone, which was an integral part of Charles Emanuel II's attempts to link dynasty, shroud and embellished capital.[207] The Sindone was removed to the newly completed chapel in 1694 at the height of the Nine Years War. Victor Amadeus, his great nobles and various foreign princes who were then visiting Turin played a key role on this great state occasion.[208] The Sindone continued to play a part in the projection of both the royal house and the Savoyard state thereafter. In 1696 the betrothal of the duke's eldest daughter to the duke of Burgundy took place in the new chapel;[209] and in May 1697 the exhibition of the Shroud was a focal point of the peace celebrations in Turin, and may have attracted as many as 20,000 people from Victor Amadeus' own and neighbouring states.[210] Equally indicative of its importance was the fact that the Shroud was taken with her by Victor Amadeus' duchess when she and her sons fled from Turin in 1706 to avoid capture by the enemy.[211] The Shroud remained an important source of identity and prestige for the Savoyard dynasty after 1713.[212]

---

[206] There was a tiny Jewish minority, notably the Turin ghetto (from 1679), Symcox, *Victor Amadeus*, 127.

[207] *DBI*, 'Antonio Bertola', 'Carlo Emanuele II di Savoia'. For the display of the shroud in May 1692, see BRT, Storia Patria, 726: registers of masters of ceremonies, conte di Verone, G. 694.

[208] Cibrario, *Storia di Torino*, I, 394 ff. This event may have been the origin of the legend that Father Valfrè, called by Victor Amadeus, helped re-sew the fabric of the Shroud, *I rami incisi*, 282.

[209] Soleri, Diario, BRT/Storia Patria 230, f. 16. The betrothal of Victor Amadeus' younger daughter to Philip V also took place in this chapel in 1701, *ibid*. f. 22.

[210] According to the Spanish envoy this delayed the departure from Turin (to their provincial garrisons) of many of the duke's troops, Bazan to Carlos II, 3 May 1697, Turin, AGSE/3659/54.   [211] Casanova, 'Censimento di Torino', 13.

[212] After 1713, the Sindone was exhibited on the occasion of royal weddings. In 1737 the English minister claimed to have missed the post because he could not get through the crowds packing Turin's streets to see the Sindone, which was being shown on the occasion of the marriage of Charles Emanuel III to the princess of Lorraine, Villettes to Newcastle, 4 May 1737, Turin, SP 92/41.

Particularly important as an instrument of propaganda were the Te Deum masses which celebrated the victories of Victor Amadeus and of his allies in other theatres, and which helped to convince his subjects of the likelihood of support from outside in the Savoyard state's darkest moments and of ultimate allied victory.[213] Such masses, with the archbishop of Turin officiating in the cathedral church of San Giovanni (adjacent to the Royal Palace) and the ducal family and great dignitaries of state attending what were great public occasions, were frequent enough in Turin before 1690.[214] However, between 1690 and 1713 Victor Amadeus' wars prompted many more of them. There were few successes to celebrate during the Nine Years War — although in 1691 Victor Amadeus had a medal struck to commemorate the successful defence of Cuneo.[215] In 1695, however, Te Deum masses followed the surrender of Casale, and that of Namur in Spanish Flanders to Victor Amadeus' allies.[216] There was rather more to celebrate during the succeeding conflict. In July 1704, a Te Deum mass was sung in Turin to celebrate the allied victory over Max Emanuel of Bavaria, at Donauwörth.[217] Later that year a Te Deum celebration of another allied victory in Germany, at Höchstädt (Blenheim), seemed to give heart to the inhabitants of Turin (who anticipated the imminent fall of Vercelli), demonstrating the propaganda value of these occasions.[218] Not surprisingly, in 1705, Eugene's apparent success in forcing the passage of the river Adda at Cassano, as he headed to the relief of Turin prompted yet another Te Deum there (prematurely as it turned out) as did the allies' conquest of Catalonia that year.[219] The failure of the enemy siege of Barcelona in early 1706 provided an opportunity for another morale-boosting Te Deum mass in Victor Amadeus' beleaguered capital.[220]

---

[213] The Te Deum mass as propaganda was ably exploited (not least during the Nine Years War and the War of the Spanish Succession) by Louis XIV: see M. Fogel, *Les cérémonies de l'information dans la France du XVIe au milieu du XVIIIe siècle* (Paris, 1989), passim; and R. Chartier, *The Cultural Origins of the French Revolution* (Duke, NC, 1994), 127 ff.

[214] In May 1682, a Te Deum mass in Turin celebrated Madama Reale's grant of an amnesty to the Mondovì rebels, Contessa, 'La congiura', 97.

[215] Saluces, *Histoire militaire*, V, 45.

[216] VDM to States General, 10 July 1695, and to Fagel, 9 Sept. 1695, Turin, ARAH/SG/8644/196, 206

[217] See *CGP*, II, 262 with a brief description of the Te Deum mass held in Turin; VDM to States, 25 July 1704, ARAH/EA/VDM/29, f. 125; and Hill to Hedges, 22 July 1704, Turin, Blackley, *Diplomatic Correspondence*, II, 389.

[218] VDM to States, 2 Sept. and 17 Dec. 1704, Turin, ARAH/EA/VDM/29, 152–3, 197. Hill to Hedges, 2 Sept. 1704, Turin, *Diplomatic Correspondence*, II, 416.

[219] VDM to States, 26 Aug., 2 Sept. and 16 Dec. 1705, ARAH/EA/VDM/30, 105, 111, 166.   [220] VDM to States, 2 June 1706, Turin, ARAH/EA/VDM/30, 273.

Celebrations of his own successes (and of other major events connected with the House of Savoy) in these years not only focused attention on the duke and his family but identified them with these defining moments in the history of the Savoyard state. On entering the relieved Turin, in September 1706, the duke had yet another Te Deum mass sung, in the chapel of the Holy Shroud; and the deliverance of the Savoyard state was communicated to his other subjects by, among other things, Te Deum masses which he ordered the bishops of Piedmont to have sung.[221] Subsequent celebratory masses charted the success of ducal arms for the rest of the conflict and the achievement of a good peace in 1713; and in July 1718 a Te Deum celebrated the recent British naval victory over the Spaniards off Sicily – a victory which was wrongly believed to ensure that Victor Amadeus retained that island realm.[222]

More importantly, not least because of its novelty, after 1706 the victory outside Turin in that year, coinciding with the feast of the Virgin's Nativity (i.e. 8 September), was the focus of an annual celebration, which Victor Amadeus first ordered in June 1707. His edict, registered by the Senate without dissent, claimed that divine favour had saved his capital – giving that event (and, by implication the survival of the Savoyard state and its ruling dynasty) a providential interpretation.[223] The new festival was distinct from those previously celebrated in the Savoyard state in that it focused attention on an event (i.e. the lifting of the siege of Turin) which was crucial in the formation of that state, and in particular focused attention on the capital, the heart of the state, which had been rapidly renewed and extended by the dukes in the last century and which also attracted great numbers of Victor Amadeus' subjects. Indicative of the role of both the Order of the Annunziata and of the growing royal family in defining a great state occasion was their role in these celebrations. On 8 September 1712, for example, the Sindone having been exhibited the previous day, Victor Amadeus and the knights of the Annunziata, accompanied by the two

---

[221] Symcox, *Victor Amadeus*, 151; Rondolino, 'Vita Torinese', *CGP*, VII, 338 ff. For the celebration of Te Deum masses, to celebrate the relief of Turin, at Pinerolo in Sept. 1706, see C. Patrucco, 'Il 1706 a Pinerolo in relazione colla guerra e colla battaglia di Torino', *BSBS*, 10, 1905, 178.

[222] Symcox, *Victor Amadeus*, 167. Victor Amadeus' arrival in his new kingdom, Sicily, in 1713 was also the occasion for a Te Deum mass, Vitelleschi, *Romance of Savoy*, II, 432. For 1718, see BRT, Storia Patria, 726: registers of masters of ceremonies, marchese d'Angrogna, f. 590.

[223] The edict of 29 June 1707, and the Senate's registration of it, are in Casanova, 'Censimento di Torino', *CGP*, VIII, 218. On the role of the Church of the Consolata in the celebratory ceremony, see F. Venturi, *Saggi sull'Europa illuminista: Alberto Radicati di Passerano* (Turin, 1954), 43.

duchesses and the court, attended chapel in the cathedral and then solemnly processed through the 'best' part of Turin, while the town itself was illuminated in the evening. The new festival, which was to be celebrated by provincial governors and officials throughout the Savoyard state, seems to have been a success: it was, not surprisingly, regularly celebrated in Turin itself from 1707, and increasingly (although this subject needs further investigation) in the rest of Piedmont.[224] It may also have been a far more significant reminder of the events of 1706 to the duke's subjects (the great majority of whom still did not visit Turin) than was the splendid baroque basilica, monastery and – emphasising the difficulty in distinguishing between dynasty and state – dynastic mausoleum, built from 1717 to the designs of the new king's Sicilian subject, Filippo Juvarra, at Superga, outside his capital, in fulfilment of Victor Amadeus' vow on the eve of the battle of Turin.[225]

The festival celebrating the deliverance of Turin suggests that the wars between 1690 and 1713 may have generated new sources of state identity, focused on the prince and dynasty, cemented by the sense of a shared historical experience, particularly of war, which was reflected in frequent pictorial and other artistic references (again particularly to the siege and relief of Turin in 1706).[226] Indeed, one could go further and argue that such events and festivals helped create what we might call a Savoyard 'nation', united by a common culture, experience (or history) and identity; a nation which had been forged above all in the War of the Spanish Succession. This claim clearly applies to the experience of Piedmont

---

[224] See order of community of Sommariva Perno (4 Sept. 1707) for future solemnization of the two feasts of the Virgin (the Nativity, 8 Sept., and the Immaculate Conception, 8 Dec.), as in the edict of June 1707, Scarzello, 'Corneliano', *CGP*, VIII, 531; and that at Fossano: Salsotto, 'Fossano', *CGP*, VIII, 410. The celebrations in Turin were frequently reported by English diplomats in subsequent years: see Cockburn to Walpole, 7 Sept. 1709, Turin, *Historic Manuscripts Commission: 11th Report, Townshend*, 56; and Allen to Newcastle, 8 Sept. 1731, Turin, SP 92/33, f. 619.

[225] Symcox, *Victor Amadeus*, 226–7. How far Victor Amadeus' brief residence in Sicily (1713–14) threatened Turin's role as capital of the Savoyard state needs further study, in Oct. 1714 his return to Turin from Palermo was celebrated by a firework display paid for by the city authorities: BRT, Storia Patria 726, registers of masters of ceremonies, marchese d'Angrogna, f. 212. For the wider role of the Superga in Victor Amadeus' 'state' project, M. T. Silvestrini, *La Politica della Religione. il Governo Ecclesiastico nello Stato Sabaudo del XVIII Secolo* (Florence, 1997), 293.

[226] See the work of Pietro Maurizio Bolckman, referred to in A. Cifani and F. Monetti, *I piaceri e le grazie. Collezionismo, pittura di genere e di paesaggio fra Sei e Settecento in Piemonte*, 2 vols. (Turin, 1993), I, 20 and passim. Significant, too, in this context was the evidence supplied for the beatification of Victor Amadeus' erstwhile confessor, Valfrè. Much of it (but not all) focused on his conduct during the siege of Turin: see Rondolino, 'Vita Torinese', *CGP*, VII, 399 ff.

more than it does to that of the Duchy of Savoy in these decades. Indeed, these contrasting experiences may have contributed to the growing gulf between these two key components of the Savoyard state after 1713. But this qualification cannot negate the fact that through war was forged a Savoyard nation, which defined itself in part by a widespread refusal to tolerate the bullying of Louis XIV. The point merits especial emphasis because the existence of such a national identity was effectively obscured by the backward projection into this period in the nineteenth century of an 'Italian' national sentiment – which certainly did not exist in these decades – aimed at making Piedmont the cradle of Italian nationhood.

CONCLUSION

By 1713, and even more by 1720 (following the reforms of 1717), the Savoyard state was in many respects more bureaucratic, centralised, integrated and 'absolute'. Victor Amadeus employed more officials, in more central offices, which as a whole constituted a more complicated administrative structure comprising a number of more specialised bureaux, exercising delegated authority and power. He had in the meantime freed that structure from the hold of the Carron de Saint-Thomas and instead promoted a number of other men (notably Gropello and Mellarède) whose authority was essentially derived from their role as officials in the developing administrative state, and whose ability to make the ducal will effective in the localities was founded upon the emerging intendancy. These would remain integral aspects of the Savoyard state throughout the eighteenth century. Some features and institutions of this more elaborate state structure were (as this chapter has, hopefully, shown) in some degree anticipated between 1690 and 1713. Nevertheless, we should not exaggerate. In many respects the Savoyard state remained a typical state of its day, with government relatively small scale, even personal, in nature. Presiding over and directing the developing institutional structure was Victor Amadeus, whose personal authority was greatly enhanced by two successful wars. Both he and the dynasty continued to be the lynchpin of a Savoyard state which had still by 1713, or even 1720, not assumed responsibility for all the spheres of activity we associate with 'modern' government. The duke was still more or less content to co-operate with other (not necessarily antagonistic) administrative systems and jurisdictions which to a degree fragmented the unity of that state but which he could not easily do without. Nor could he entirely prevent discussion and debate. As in other states, the disappearance of representative assemblies did not mean the end of politics.[227] The domestic politics of the Savoyard state in these decades reflected both its geographical position, between two Great Powers, and the pressures imposed by two major wars. It is remarkable that (apart from the final phase of the Mondovì 'Salt War' and the episode of the San Martino Vaudois 'republic') (see Chapter 6) there was not more serious, open resistance to ducal authority or policy. Nevertheless, opposition of one sort or another — although it might express itself indirectly (for example, in opposition to the Vaudois edict of 1694) — certainly existed. Whether loyalty, the duke, the dynasty and an independent Savoyard state would have survived prolonged defeat in the 1690s and 1700s must be doubtful. However, success in the 1690s no doubt strengthened Victor Amadeus' hand in the subsequent conflict, as did the removal of the most serious pressure in 1706. Thereafter, he deliberately exploited the common experience of war to create (or perhaps confirm?) a Savoyard national identity.

[227] One further means of influencing discussion, and opinion, was the Turin *Gazette*. In 1695, following the death of William III's queen, Mary, the earl of Galway, concerned at the widely held opinion (one not confined to Turin or Victor Amadeus' states) that William ruled as Mary's consort and that her death would mean a revolution in England which would undermine the Grand Alliance, had a corrective report inserted in the Turin *Gazette*: Galway to Stanhope, 8 Feb. 1695, Turin, Kent RO, U1590, O15/1.

CHAPTER 5

THE SAVOYARD NOBILITY, 1690–1720

Effective mobilisation of the resources needed for success in war might necesitate some social restructuring as well as administrative overhaul and development.¹ Not surprisingly, many of those who have seen state formation, particularly when defined as the development of state structures and princely 'absolutism' within the state, in the making in the early modern era have regarded the nobility as among its main, even its chief victim(s). Indeed for many historians early modern Europe witnessed a multifaceted crisis of the aristocracy.² This was not least because nobles everywhere were, *inter alia*, apparently losing their traditional (military) role to the state which, together with the economic difficulties experienced by many nobles in the seventeenth century, meant a serious loss of confidence and of real authority, power and influence. More recently, however, historians have begun to reassess the situation of the European nobility in the seventeenth and eighteenth centuries and to recognise that this earlier view is too bleak. William Beik has redefined absolutism in seventeenth-century Languedoc as co-operation between monarch and local elite; and in words which reflect a growing consensus among historians, Jeremy Black declares, 'absolutism can be defined as a politico-social arrangement, rather than a constitutional system, by which the social elite was persuaded to govern in accordance with the views of the ruler, while these views were defined in accordance with the assumptions of the elite'. Increasingly, historians are acknowledging that nobles everywhere continued to play a crucial role in

---

¹ G. Symcox, ed., *War, Diplomacy, and Imperialism, 1618–1763* (London, 1974), 1.
² H. Kamen, *The Iron Century (1560–1660)* (London, 1971). For the thesis of an early modern 'crisis of the aristocracy' or nobility, see L. Stone, *The Crisis of the Aristocracy 1558–1641* (Oxford, 1965); D. Bitton, *The French Nobility in Crisis 1560–1640* (Stanford, 1969); and C. Jago, 'The "crisis of the aristocracy" in seventeenth-century Castille', *Past and Present*, 84, 1979. For the loss of power by Spain's grandees, see H. Kamen, *The War of Succession in Spain 1700–1715* (London, 1967), 83 ff.

polity and society, and to play an active rather than passive role in state formation.³

Work on the nobility of the Savoyard state, and the interpretative framework into which it is fitted, largely conforms to the general evolution of work on the early modern European nobility. Thus, Guido Quazza, whose major study of reform in the Savoyard state after 1713 is also an important contribution to our understanding of Savoyard society, saw the nobility as the main loser in a reform process largely carried out, by and benefiting, the non-noble 'bourgeoisie'.⁴ However, this view has over the last decade or so come under attack. On the one hand, Enrico Stumpo has sought both to antedate Quazza's hypothesis of a relationship between state formation and social change and to contrast the two different models of nobility provided by the Piedmontese nobility and the Tuscan patriciate, while on the other hand Giuseppe Ricuperati has queried the Quazza thesis on the relationship between reform and society in the Savoyard state in the generation after 1713 emphasising the emergence and consolidation of a service nobility rather than the empowerment of a rising bourgeoisie.⁵ This debate about the experience and role of the nobility in these crucial decades of Savoyard state formation prompts the observation that, as Geoffrey Symcox has recently noted, there are still important gaps in our knowledge of the Savoyard nobility in this period, and by contrast with Luigi Bulferetti's extensive work on the nobility in reign of Charles Emanuel II. This neglect in turn reflects a much greater interest among historians of the nobility, or nobilities of early modern Italy with the patricians of the republics and the feudal nobles in the rest of the Peninsula.⁶

---

³ W. Beik, *Absolutism and Society in Seventeenth-Century France: state power and provincial aristocracy in Languedoc* (Cambridge, 1985), passim; J. Black, *A Military Revolution? Military change and European society 1550–1800*, London, 1991, 67–8. For a recent introduction to this subject on a European scale see H. M. Scott and C. Storrs, 'Introduction: the consolidation of noble power in Europe c. 1600–1800', in H. M. Scott, ed., *The European Nobilities in the Seventeenth and Eighteenth Centuries*, 2 vols. (London, 1995), I, 1ff.

⁴ G. Quazza, *Le riforme in Piemonte nella prima metà del 1700*, 2 vols. (Modena, 1957), I, 91 ff.

⁵ G. Ricuperati, 'Gli strumenti dell'assolutismo sabaudo: segreterie di stato e consiglio delle finanze nel XVIII secolo', *RSI*, 103, 1991, and Ricuperati, 'L'Avvenimento e la storia: le rivolte del luglio 1797 nella crisi dello stato sabaudo', *RSI*, 104, 1992, 349 ff.; E. Stumpo, *Finanza e stato moderna nel Piemonte del Seicento* (Rome, 1979); Stumpo, 'I ceti dirigenti in Italia nell'età moderna. Due modelli diversi: nobiltà piemontese e patriziato toscano', in A. Tagliaferri, ed., *I ceti dirigenti in Italia in età moderna e contemporanea* (Udine, 1984).

⁶ Symcox, review in *Journal of Modern Italian Studies*, 1, 1997, 456; A. Cardoza, *Aristocrats in bourgeois Italy: the Piedmontese nobility, 1861–1930* (Cambridge, 1997). In an article which draws extensively on noble archives, Angelo Torre claims that 'The Piedmon-

In fact the picture is not as bleak as the foregoing might suggest, since there do exist studies of the Savoyard nobility which reflect the diverse approaches to the history of the nobility everywhere in Europe. These include the general, quasi-prosopograhical approach of Antonio Manno's family histories (or detailed genealogies) of the turn of the century. This approach reached its apogee in Stuart Woolf's 1963 study of three Piedmontese noble families, the Falletti di Barolo, the Saluzzo di Paesana and the Valperga di Rivara, which remains (as will become abundantly clear in this chapter) the most important single study of the Piedmontese nobility in this period, an amazingly rich quarry of both data and insights.[7] A rather different approach has been the biography of the individual noble, notably those by Alberto Ferrero della Marmora of the marchesi di Parella and Pianezza, Franco Venturi's study of conte Alberto Radicati di Passerano and, more recently, R. Gaja's biography of the marchese d'Ormea, an approach which inevitably largely excludes the mass of the lesser nobility (which remains largely unexplored).[8] At the other end of the spectrum, Luigi Bulferetti sought to grasp the nobility of the whole state (or at least Piedmont), Jean Nicolas has sought to convey the experience of the entire nobility of the Duchy of Savoy in the later seventeenth and eighteenth centuries, while Alessandro Barbero has

---

tese aristocracy has not yet found its historian', Torre, 'Politics cloaked in worship: state, church and local power in Piedmont 1550–1770', *Past and Present*, 134, 1992, 62. See also the comments of Stumpo, 'Ceti', 167–8. On the nobility – or nobilities – of early modern Italy generally, see C. Donati, *L'Idea di nobiltà in Italia (secoli XIV–XVIII)* (Bari, 1988); Donati, 'The Italian nobilities in the seventeenth and eighteenth centuries', in H. M. Scott, ed., *The European Nobilities*, I, 237 ff.; C. Mozzarelli and P. Schiera, eds., *Patriziati e aristocrazie nobiliari: ceti dominanti e organizzazione del potere nell'Italia centro-settentrionale dal XVI al XVIII secolo* (Trent, 1978); T. Astarita, *The Continuity of Feudal Power: the Caracciolo di Brienza in Spanish Naples* (Cambridge, 1994); and, more briefly, D. Sella, *Italy in the Seventeenth Century* (London, 1997), 50 ff.

[7] A. Manno, *Il patriziato subalpino. Notizie di fatto storiche, genealogiche, feudali e araldiche*, 2 vols. (Florence, 1895) (additional, unpulished typescript volumes are available in the Archivio di Stato, and in the Biblioteca Reale, Turin); S. J. Woolf, *Studi sulla nobiltà Piemontese nell'epoca dell'assolutismo*, *MAST* (Turin, 1963).

[8] A. Ferrero della Marmora, *Le vicende di Carlo di Simiane, marchese di Livorno poi di Pianezza tra il 1672 ed il 1706* (Turin, 1862); Ferrero della Marmora, *Notize sulla vita e sulle geste militari di Carlo Emilio San Martino di Parella* (Turin, 1863); F. Venturi, *Saggi sull'Europa illuminista, 1: Alberto Radicati di Passerano* (Turin, 1954); R. Gaja, *Marchese d'Ormea* (Milan, 1988). See also M. H. Siffre, 'La mode de vie d'un noble niçois à l'age classique: Honoré Grimaldi', *Revue d'Histoire Economique et Sociale*, 1973, 449 ff. This genre has been continued in attenuated form in the invaluable potted biographies in the *DBI*. For a study of one of the few non-titled nobles in the Savoyard state about whom we have more than minimum details see G. Pignet, 'Eugenio Gaspar De Tillier uomo d'arme e di legge (1630–1699)', in *La Valle d'Aosta: relazioni e comunicazioni presentate al XXXI Congresso Storico Subalpino di Aosta Settembre 1956*, 2 vols. (Turin, 1959), II, 695 ff.

essayed a briefer and narrower analysis of the nobility of the Duchy of Aosta.⁹ Other historians have focused on specific aspects of the experience of the Savoyard (or rather Piedmontese) nobility. Woolf has drawn on his family studies to explore the economic fortunes of the latter in the seventeenth century.¹⁰ Silvia Marchisio, exploiting the noble family papers in the Archivio di Stato, Turin, has analysed the attitudes and values, or ideology, they reveal.¹¹ Walter Barberis and Sabina Loriga have explored the relationship between the nobility and the army in the Savoyard state.¹² Revealing the extent to which many studies of *ancien régime* Europe must engage with the nobility, Claudio Rosso's study of the emerging state bureaucracy in sixteenth and seventeenth-century Piedmont inevitably has much to say about nobles and nobility,¹³ while Sandra Cavallo's recent study of the motives for charitable giving in early modern Turin also says much about noblewomen in particular.¹⁴ Finally, Giovanni Levi's 'microhistorical' study of the exorcist priest of Santena in the 1690s fits the latter's career into noble economic and political strategies and rivalries and an interpretation of the process of state formation which emphasises the importance of local conditions and the role of local notables as mediators between the state and the periphery.¹⁵

Drawing both on these fine modern studies — many of which reflect the new emphasis on the persistence of noble wealth, influence and power — and on some of the rich archival materials in Turin, the present chapter seeks to explore the experience of the Savoyard nobil-

---

[9] L. Bulferetti, 'La feudalità e il patriziato nel Piemonte di Carlo Emanuele II', *Annali della Facoltà di Lettere, Filosofia e Magistero dell'Università di Cagliari*, 2, 1953, an invaluable fund of information of all sorts on the Piedmontese nobility in the seventeenth century; J. Nicolas, *La Savoie au 18e siècle: noblesse et bourgeoisie*, 2 vols. (Paris, 1978); A. Barbero, 'Una nobiltà provinciale sotto l'Antico Regime: il *Nobiliaire du Duché d'Aoste* di J.-B. De Tillier', *RSI*, 109, 1997, 5 ff.

[10] S. J. Woolf, 'Economic problems of the nobility in the early modern period: the example of Piedmont', *Economic History Review*, 17, 1970.

[11] S. Marchisio, 'Ideologia e problemi dell'economia familiare nelle lettere della nobiltà piemontese (XVII–XVIII sec.)', *BSBS*, 83, 1985, 67 ff.

[12] W. Barberis, *Le armi del principe: la tradizione militare sabauda* (Turin, 1988); S. Loriga, *Soldati. L'istituzione militare nel Piemonte del Settecento* (Venice, 1992). See also the critical review of Barberis' book by E. Stumpo, 'Tra mito, leggenda e realtà storica: la tradizione militare sabauda da Emanuele Filiberto a Carlo Alberto', *RSI*, 103, 1991, 560 ff.

[13] C. Rosso, *Una burocrazia di Antico Regime: i Segretari di Stato dei Duchi di Savoia, 1 (1559–1637)* (Turin, 1992).

[14] S. Cavallo, *Charity and Power in Early Modern Italy: benefactors and their motives in Turin 1541–1789* (Cambridge, 1995).

[15] G. Levi, *L'Eredità immateriale: carriera di un esorcista nel Piemonte del Seicento* (Turin, 1985), 10 (and passim); English trans., *Inheriting Power: the story of an exorcist* (Chicago, 1988), 175–6.

ity in these crucial decades, above all from the perspective of state formation. This, as will become clear, is by no means the only valid approach to that nobility and its experience. But it is an important aspect, and one in which the nobility both played an important role, as Woolf has noted and – as Ricuperati argues – was to a degree reshaped.[16] Thus, just as important in the process of state formation as the 'disciplining' of Mondovì in 1699 (see Chapter 5) was the fact that there was no repeat of the Parella 'revolt' of 1682,[17] not even after Victor Amadeus' revocation (1720) of nearly 200 fiefs alienated to many noble families between 1637 and 1680 (and their sale often to non-nobles, creating the so-called 'nobility of 1722') or in the wake of the *perequazione* which hit the income of many, though not all, noble families (see Chapter 2). The years between 1690 and 1720, it might be argued, therefore also represented something of a watershed in relations between nobles and the Savoyard state. In the following pages, the numbers, character, values and general strategies of the Savoyard nobility on the eve of the Nine Years War are analysed, and then an attempt is made to assess just how that nobility fitted into the multiple processes of Savoyard state formation between 1690 and 1720 – although much of what is said in the first part will apply equally to the second. Victor Amadeus did deliberately exclude some 'old' nobles and some 'new' men.[18] He also integrated more fully into the developing state structure his nobility, contributing to the emergence, or consolidation, of a service nobility which fused 'old' and 'new' and which would come into its own in the so-called 'Bogino era' after 1750. Although some nobles lost as a result of some of Victor Amadeus' policies, the nobility was not simply his victim. The developing state, while obliging nobles to adapt, also offered new opportunities to pursue traditional objectives. To a degree, too, the state also depended upon the still considerable moral and material resources of its nobles. For his part, Victor Amadeus revealed his continuing commitment to the idea of nobility by, *inter alia*, ennobling his non-noble collaborators. In sum, the nobility played a key role in the Savoyard state project; and, if the rise of Savoy between 1690 and 1720 was associated with social change it was with the emergence of a variant of nobility not with the empowerment of a non-noble bourgeoisie.

---

[16] Woolf, *Studi sulla nobiltà*, 164. Ricuperati, 'L'Avvenimento', 349.
[17] C. Contessa, 'La congiura del marchese di Parella (1682)', *BSBS*, 38, 1936.
[18] A. Manno, 'Un mémoire autographe de Victor Amédée II', *Revue internationale*, I, 1884. 95; Ricuperati, 'Gli Strumenti, 815.

THE NOBILITY OF THE SAVOYARD STATE ON THE EVE OF THE NINE YEARS WAR

How numerous was the nobility (and what proportion of the population of the Savoyard state as a whole) on the eve of Victor Amadeus's wars? Unfortunately, contemporary evidence for this is scarce and we are obliged to rely on surveys related to those wars to obtain some (though still vague) idea. A survey in connection with the capitation tax imposed by Victor Amadeus on all his subjects, noble and non-noble, in the Duchy of Savoy in 1702, to finance his intervention in the War of the Spanish Succession, constitutes the most complete survey of the nobility of that part of the Savoyard state in these decades. It revealed 795 noble households (besides a further 34 households headed by secular religious who were also noble) in the Duchy. Calculating the average noble household size as 4.1 persons, Nicolas estimates the Savoyard nobility to total about 3,400 individuals in 1702, or 1.6 per cent of the Duchy's total population of 320,00. This is lower (though not dramatically so) than the 1.5–1.9 per cent calculated by Woolf for Piedmont but larger than the 0.5 per cent calculated by Barbero for Aosta in 1720.[19] More significantly, the nobility of the Savoyard state was nothing like as numerous as either the relatively large nobilities of Spain (10 per cent) and Poland (perhaps 7.5 per cent) or even that of Brittany (2 per cent).[20] But these global figures can be misleading, not least because the nobility was geographically unevenly distributed. In the Duchy of Savoy, in the mountainous areas and in those provinces (notably Tarentaise and Maurienne) where the establishment of a powerful feudal nobility had been blocked by powerful prince bishops and resistant peasant communities, the nobility was barely in evidence. Nobles preferred the plains, and above all the towns. In other parts of the Savoyard state, too, the nobility were attracted to the towns, Turin (and the lesser urban centres of Piedmont), Aosta and Nice all drawing large numbers of nobles from the surrounding rural areas.[21]

Place of residence was not the only thing which distinguished nobles from one another. The nobility of some families, including the San Martino, Valperga and Castellamonte (who traced their descent from Arduino, twelfth-century king of Italy) was much older and thus more

---

[19] Barbero, 'Una nobiltà', 10.
[20] Nicolas, *La Savoie*, I, 9ff.; Woolf, *Studi sulla nobiltà*, 11–12, 44 ff.; I. A. A. Thompson, 'The nobility in Spain 1600–1800', and R. I. Frost, 'The nobility of Poland-Lithuania 1569–1795', in Scott, *European Nobilities*, I, 174 ff., II, 191 ff.
[21] Just over a half of all nobles of the Duchy of Savoy lived in 1702 in the province of Savoy and half of these (i.e. 25 per cent of the Duchy's nobles) in the town of Chambéry, Nicolas, *La Savoie*, I, 12 ff. In Aosta the nobility was increasingly absent from the Duchy altogether, Barbero, 'Una nobiltà', 10.

distinguished than that of most other nobles and they were proud of the distinction.²² The number of nobles in the Savoyard state had substantially increased in the first half of the seventeenth century, both during the wars of Charles Emanuel I and in the conflicts of mid-century.²³ According to a list of ennoblements by ducal patent between 1560 and 1701 in the Duchy of Savoy, drawn up by ducal officials in 1701, of 627 noble families, the nobility of just over 30 per cent, i.e. nearly one-third, dated from after 1563.²⁴ There were a number of means of ennoblement, some of them overlapping: office, ducal grant (sometimes in effect a sale of nobility), 'aggregation' (a non-noble being allowed by an existing noble family to take its name and status),²⁵ foreign grant (including by the Holy Roman emperor)²⁶ and fraudulent assumption, especially at times of government weakness, as in the 'civil war' of the 1630s and 1640s.²⁷ Beneficiaries of this earlier wave of social mobility included the grandfather of Victor Amadeus' envoy to the Hague and London during the Nine Years War, the count and president de la Tour, who had been ennobled by ducal letters patent in 1634.²⁸ Between 1660 and 1690 ennoblements were rarer, not least because of the Savoyard state's reduced role in European affairs (lessening the need to raise funds by selling

---

[22] Woolf, *Studi sulla nobiltà*, 92–3, notes the prevalence of the name Arduino in some old families. The nobility of the family of Victor Amadeus' close collaborator conte Orazio Provana di Pratolungo has been traced to the eleventh century, L. Barberis, 'Il Conte Orazio Provana, ambasciatore sabaudo (1630–1697)', *BSBS*, 30, 1928, 66. The Isnardi di Caraglio responded to the enquiry of 1687 into titles of nobility, describing themselves as 'nobilissima e antichissima', *DBI*, 'Caraglio'. Generally, see the invaluable L. Cibrario, 'Iacopo Valperga di Masino. Triste episodio del secolo XV: con due appendici sulla genealogia d'alcune famiglie nobili del Piemonte e della Savoia', *MAST*, 2nd ser., 19, 1861, 213–89.

[23] See Stumpo, *Finanza e stato moderno*, 236 ff. Individual ennoblements can be traced in *DBI*, for example, 'Cacherano'. Barbero, 'Una nobiltà', 28, stresses the social mobility in Aosta of the earlier sixteenth century.

[24] See Nicolas, *La Savoie*, I, 21 ff., 28–9 for a breakdown of letters of ennoblement 1561–1700. Caution is necessary in interpreting the figures: the status of a substantial 21 per cent was not known.

[25] See the aggregation of the Perrone into the San Martino family, in P. Dagna, 'Un diplomatico ed economista del Settecento: Carlo Baldassare Perrone di San Martino (1718–1802)', in Dagna *et al.*, eds., *Figure e gruppi della classe dirigente piemontese nel Risorgimento* (Turin, 1968), 9 ff.; and that of Onorato Claretti (1631), Rosso, *Una burocrazia*, 309 ff. and *DBI, sub voce*.

[26] The Malabaila di Canale, who (despite claiming to originate in medieval Germany) can be traced to medieval Asti, were ennobled by Emperor Ferdinand III in 1640, A. Ruata, *Luigi Malabaila di Canale: riflessi della cultura illuministica in un diplomatico piemontese* (Turin, 1968), 12.

[27] For grants of nobility in the civil wars, see Barbero, 'Una nobiltà', 7.

[28] E.-A. de Foras, *Armorial et nobiliaire de l'ancien duché de Savoie*, 6 vols. (Grenoble, 1863–1950), V, 385 ff. Ricuperati, 'Gli Strumenti', 846 ff.

patents of nobility), partly because of the opposition of the institutions (notably the sovereign courts, the Senate and Chambre des Comptes in the Duchy of Savoy, the Senate and Camera in Piedmont) which, not least because of their role in protecting ducal revenues against fiscal fraud (including false claims of fiscal exemption) were in a sense the protectors of the true against false nobles.[29] Indeed, in 1679 Madama Reale ordered an enquiry into titles (and the rejection of those nobles found to be bogus), which was followed by Victor Amadeus' enquiry into titles of 1687.[30] However, upward social mobility into the nobility did not cease completely, as the fiscal pressures associated with the Portuguese marriage project and the Mondovì Salt War prompted a new wave of ennoblements.[31]

The nobility of the Savoyard state was also differentiated internally in terms of rank. The noble hierarchy was headed by the so-called princes of the blood, primarily (but not only) the junior branches of the House of Savoy (Carignano, Soissons, Nemours), and enjoying additional privileges.[32] As elsewhere in Europe, and to the confusion of historians and others who mistakenly see all untitled nobles as non-noble or 'gentry', the vast majority of nobles did not enjoy the titles (baron, count, marquis) which multiplied among the nobility of the Savoyard state in the seventeenth century but which were also restricted to an elite within the noble elite. In the Duchy of Savoy proper these included the marquisate of Bourg-Saint-Maurice, created (1635) for the Chabod family, the marquisate of Coudrée, created (1655) in favour of the Allinges, the

---

[29] For an early seventeenth-century example of opposition of this sort, see Barberis, *Le armi*, 80 ff.

[30] See *DBI*, 'Caraglio' and AST/Camera dei Conti/Nobiltà, art. 852 for examples of the consignment of arms in 1687. This was not the first enquiry of this sort. In 1645 Madama Cristina had ordered an investigation of titles in the Duchy of Aosta, aimed primarily at those nobles created by her rivals in the recent civil war, Barbero, 'Una nobiltà', 7. Just how far these enquiries represented the state establishing itself as the new arbiter of noble status, as has been claimed for Louis XIV's France, R. Bonney, *L'Absolutisme* (Paris, 1989), 116 (and how far developments in the Savoyard state were a conscious imitation of the French king) cannot be determined before more work has been done on the subject. Rosso, *Una Burocrazia*, 207 ff., is critical of Donati's claim, *Idea di nobiltà*, 177, that the Savoyard nobility was one closely regulated by the state.

[31] In 1685 the marchese di Priè purchased the fief of Pancalieri with its marchional title, S. Caligaris, 'Vita e lavoro in una comunità piemontese: Pancalieri nei sec. XVII–XVIII', *Bollettino della Società per gli studi storici, archeologici e artistici della provincia di Cuneo*, 90–1, 1984, 7–8.

[32] See F. Rondolino, 'Vita Torinese durante l'assedio (1703–07)', *CGP*, VII, 43 ff. for the families. In 1692, the marchese di Pianezza refused to go as the duke's ambassador to Rome, claiming that the right to refuse was one of the privileges of the princes of the blood, Ferrero della Marmora, *Pianezza*, 441–2. The privileges of the princes of the blood at the Turin court became a bench mark for the claims of foreign ambassadors there: Essex to Newcastle, 9 Sept. 1732, Turin, SP 92/34, f. 81 ff.

marquisate of Thorens, erected (1665) in favour of the Sales, and the marquisates of Faverge (1644), Challes (1669) and Arvilliars (1678), all in favour of branches of the Milliet family. In 1680 Madama Reale elevated the Carron fief of Aigueblanche to a marquisate.[33] Piedmont, too, saw a proliferation of titles. In 1662, Giambattista Buschetti was enfieffed as marchese with that part of the marquisate of Ceva he had acquired from Princess Lodovica, widow of Prince Maurice of Savoy, and the title of count of Mombello was granted to the Cacherano family; and in 1665–66, the fief of Robilant was erected into a 'county' in favour of Lodovico Nicolis di Robilant.[34] As with ennoblement generally, the grant of titles was less prolific after the 1660s, not least because of the opposition of many older families resentful of the social mobility of the preceding decades.[35]

The political and social changes consequent on Emanuel Philibert's restoration of the Savoyard state, and the policies of his son Charles Emanuel I had contributed to divisions within the Savoyard nobility, into what Stumpo has defined as the court, the feudal and the office-holding nobility.[36] The cleavage between these elements within the nobility took various forms. An earlier attempt by the 'rising' Onorato Claretti to secure aggregation into the Provana family had failed due to the refusal of certain branches of that house to accommodate his pretensions. Some other newly ennobled sought to disguise their true origins, by claiming a false ancestry.[37] The more recently ennobled ducal officials were also denied access to the most prestigious distinctions of the state, including the Order of the Annunziata (see Chapter 4), which remained the monopoly of the oldest and most distinguished families.[38] The gulf between old and new nobles was not unbridgeable. The recently ennobled office-holding nobility were sometimes admitted to court,[39] while intermarriage was not unknown. Such links could ultimately benefit the older noble families.[40] Nevertheless, liaisons of this sort were

---

[33] Nicolas, *La Savoie*, I, 37; *DBI*, 'Arvilliars', *DBI*, IV, 368–9. G. Galli della Loggia, *Cariche del Piemonte e Paesi uniti colla serie cronologica delle persone che le hanno occupate dal secolo IX al dicembre 1798*, 3 vols. (Turin, 1798), III, 52.

[34] *DBI*, 'Buschetti', 'Castagnole' and 'Cacherano'; AST/PCF/1665–66, f. 185.

[35] In 1688, the recently acquired fief of the controller general of finance, Francesco Giacinto Gallinati, Parpaglia, was raised to comital status, Galli della Loggia, *Cariche*, III, 95. [36] Stumpo, 'I ceti', 151 ff.

[37] Taking advantage of the destruction of the family archive by the French and Turks in 1543, Onorato Claretti (d. 1663) secured a declaration from the Senate of Nice which ratified a false (and more prestigious) ancestry, Rosso, *Una burocrazia*, 315.

[38] *Ibid.*, 218.

[39] The rise of the Gabaleone di Salmour from non-noble merchants, financiers and officials c. 1600 to Court nobility c. 1660 is charted by Barberis, *Le Armi*, 91 ff..

[40] In 1664, a daughter of the distinguished but financially hard-pressed Valperga di Rivara family married the rich, ennobled banker, conte Turinetti di Pertengo, who did much

by no means the norm, the old families marrying as far as possible with similar families. The tensions within the Savoyard nobility could quickly surface during a political crisis such as that provoked by the Genoese war fiasco in 1672, when the old nobility launched a savage assault on the newer men, including that scion of the lesser nobility, and collaborator of Charles Emanuel II, Gianbatista Truchi.[41] The closing of the Savoyard elite after 1660 may have contributed, as Sandra Cavallo has argued, to a search on the part of those who now found upward mobility blocked to find new sources of status and distinction in the Savoyard state, which found expression in Turin in distinct patterns of charitable giving in these decades.[42]

Generally speaking, the nobility as a whole was the wealthiest social group within the Savoyard state, although, reflecting the general poverty of the parts of that state, the nobility as a whole was rather poor by comparison with some of its European counterparts. The titled elite within the nobility were also generally wealthier than their fellow nobles. In Piedmont, typically, marchese Giacinto Antonio Ottavio Provana di Druent, whose ancestors had been enfieffed with Druent in the fourteenth century, enjoyed one of the largest private incomes in the state, the result largely of the accumulation by marriage and inheritance of the patrimonies of other noble families, many of them now extinct.[43] Other wealthy Piedmontese noble families included the Tana d'Entraque, the San Martino di San Germano and the Biandrate Aldobrandino di San Giorgio.[44] In the Duchy of Savoy, the marquis de Sales headed the sixty-one leading noble landowners included in the cadastral survey of 1730, with estates totalling more than 1,000 hectares and yielding an annual revenue of 9,526 lire. An enormous gulf separated these from what Nicolas calls a 'peasant nobility', nobles with very little land and income, who made up the vast bulk of the nobility. These poorer nobles were particularly dependent upon the fiscal privileges which accompanied noble status but were also the most vulnerable to ejection from the ranks of the nobility by the Chambéry Chambre des Comptes, in its dual role as defender of the ducal fisc against false claims to noble status and exemptions and defender of noble privilege in the Duchy. This was

to resolve the family's difficulties, Woolf, *Studi sulla nobiltà*, 104. The Piedmontese Pallavicino secured, by marriage, the fiefs of a recently promoted lesser noble family from Aosta, Rosso, *Una burocrazia*, 73.

[41] See C. Rosso, 'Il Seicento', in P. Merlin et al., *Il Piemonte sabaudo: stato e territori in età moderna* (Turin, 1994), 257.   [42] Cavallo, *Charity and Power*, 98 ff.

[43] *DBI*, 'Druent'; Woolf, *Studi sulla nobiltà*, 77 ff.

[44] The wealthy Tana effectively acquired the fief and title of Entraque in the later seventeenth century by purchase from the 'declining' Valperga di Rivara, Woolf, *Studi sulla nobiltà*, 95, 103.

because they were less well placed to maintain their dignity, to 'live nobly' Their difficulties were also exploited by other nobles to acquire more property. The situation elsewhere in the Savoyard state mirrored that in the Duchy.[45]

In their general attitudes and conduct, however, nobles in the Savoyard state, whatever their origin, broadly adhered to an increasingly familiar European pattern. Above all, they were concerned less with the interests of the nobility as a whole than with those of their own family,[46] or house, or clan, many older families, including the Roero, San Martino, Radicati and Solaro having over the centuries spawned new branches.[47] Noble families were particularly concerned to defend the name, renown and status of their own lineage, not least because the achievements of their ancestors were generally the origin of their own nobility, prestige and wealth.[48] The chief concern was to avoid the threat of extinction, which was probably the single most serious danger facing noble families throughout Europe in all ages. No study exists of rates of extinction among the nobility of the Savoyard state comparable with those of the nobilities of other European states, but it is clear enough that the Savoyard nobility was as vulnerable to this threat as nobles elsewhere.[49] One obvious solution to this problem was to have large families, to ensure the existence of an heir or heirs. Carlo Girolamo del Carretto, marchese di Bagnasco, hero of the siege of Montmélian (1690–91), had eleven children by his two wives, while Victor Amadeus' envoy to the Swiss

---

[45] See Nicolas, *La Savoie*, I, 121 ff. for calculations of the distribution of wealth within the nobility of the Duchy of Savoy based upon the (later) *perequazione*; and 274 ff. for calculations from a self-assessed donative (1697–8) and the capitation roles drawn up (1702) by the intendant and controller general of finances. In 1687 the president de Lescheraine wrote on behalf of a noble of Thonon who was so poor that he was obliged to join Victor Amadeus' army as a simple soldier, *ibid.*, I, 313.

[46] See Levi, *Inheriting Power*, for the struggle in the community of Santena between the Benzo and Tana families in the seventeenth and eighteenth centuries.

[47] A scion of the Solaro purchased (1646–7) the fief of La Margarita from the Del Carretto, thereby founding this branch of an old and distinguished family, Rondolino, 'Vita Torinese', *CGP*, VII, 41. See Venturi, *Saggi*, 28–9, for the offshoots of the Radicati family.

[48] The Tana archive contained notarised eyewitness accounts of past acts of military heroism, which were kept with the family's proofs of its nobility, Marchisio, 'Ideologia', 71.

[49] See the figures Nicolas gives, *La Savoie*, I, 21 ff., for the survival of families whose nobility dated from before 1560. For Piedmont, see Manno, *Il patriziato subalpino*, passim. The lines of both Carlo Luigi Caissotti and Pierre Mellarède, among Victor Amadeus' 'new' nobility, were extinguished in the second generation on the death of their sons without heirs, *DBI*, 'Caissotti' and D. Carutti, ed., 'Relazione sulla Corte d'Inghilterra del Consigliere di Stato Pietro Mellarède, plenipotenziario di Savoia al Congresso di Utrecht', *MSI*, 2nd ser., XXIV, Turin, 1885, 222.

Catholic cantons in the Nine Years War, the conte di Govone, and his wife, Maria Provana di Druent had ten children.[50]

It was not simply the family which needed to be protected. So, too, did its wealth. This really meant its landed patrimony because, despite the efforts of Charles Emanuel II to encourage his nobles to engage in commercial activity,[51] and some investment in loans (both within and outside – notably in Genoa – the Savoyard state) the nobility of the Savoyard state and its wealth were primarily rooted in the land.[52] In line with practice elsewhere in Europe was the growing use of both primogeniture (i.e. inheritance by the first born son) and entail (i.e. the limitation of the heir's freedom to dispose of the property, so that successive heirs were little more than temporary trustees, unable to alienate those parts of the patrimony included within the entail). Primogeniture and entail had been adopted by many Savoyard noble families before 1600.[53] However, the rate of adoption accelerated thereafter, particularly following the ducal edict of 1648 authorising the establishment of long-term primogeniture.[54] Not all families adopted entail or

---

[50] *DBI*, 'Bagnasco' and 'Breglio'. The old marquis de Saint-Thomas (d. 1699) was one of eleven children and himself had nine: Manno, *Il patriziato subalpino*, *sub voce*. See the family trees of the Falletti di Barolo, Valperga di Rivara and Saluzzo di Paesana families in Woolf, *Studi sulla nobiltà*, and that of the Solaro di Monasterolo in Galli, *Cariche*, III, Appendix, 30. Not all families were so large: Luigi Malabaila, conte di Canale (b. 1704), was an only child, Ruata, *Canale*, 13.   [51] Quazza, *Le riforme*, II, 283.

[52] Typically, the Costa, new nobles who had made their way by financial activity, gradually increased the proportion of land in their patrimony between the 1660s and 1680s, Nicolas, *La Savoie*, I, 280–1. For noble investments within the Savoyard state, above all in communal debt, see Woolf, *Studi sulla nobiltà*, passim. Some landowners, including the Perrone di San Martino, exploited the rich mineral deposits on those estates: see Dagna, 'Un diplomatico', 11.

[53] In 1579 the last San Martino conte di Vische established a primogenitural entail on the marriage of his niece to a Birago, in favour of their sons, on condition that they adopted his family name, thus 'creating' the Birago di Vische, P. Costamagna, 'L'Evoluzione patrimoniale dei Birago di Vische dal' 1586 alla fine del secolo XVIII' (tesi di laurea, University of Turin, 1968–9), 1 ff. The Scarampi di Camino adopted primogeniture in 1568 and founded an entail in 1646, Woolf, *Studi sulla nobiltà*, 152.

[54] In 1667, conte Filippo San Martino d'Agliè, superintendent of the duke of Savoy's finances, established inheritance by primogeniture in his will, AST/Provincia di Ivrea, m. 3/3; and in 1679, conte Carlo Osasco was given permission to establish primogeniture, AST/PCF/1679, f. 166. On the spread of entails and primogeniture in the Savoyard state see Nicolas, *La Savoie*, I, 295–6, Woolf, *Studi sulla nobiltà*, 148 ff. (and passim), and Bulferetti, 'Feudalità e patriziato', passim (some of the latter's figures are summarised in Cavallo, *Charity and Power*, 173–4. For the use of primogeniture and entail by the European nobility as a whole, see J. P. Cooper, 'Patterns of inheritance and settlement by great landowners from the fifteenth to the eighteenth centuries', in J. Goody, J. Thirsk and E. P. Thompson, eds., *Family and Inheritance in Rural Society in Western Europe 1200–1800*, (Cambridge, 1976). Dr H. M. Scott and I are preparing a study of noble entails in Europe between 1600 and 1800.

primogeniture. Nor could these instruments protect a noble patrimony against all threats. Despite, and sometimes even because of, their use many noble families bore a substantial burden of debt, particularly to ecclesiastical institutions in those parts of the Savoyard state too poor to generate other sources of credit.[55] Nevertheless, more and more of a family's inheritance and patrimony, tangible and otherwise, was being protected by these means and it seems reasonable to conclude that without them the nobility of the Savoyard state would have been poorer and weaker than in fact it was.[56] Adoption of primogeniture and entail was by no means incompatible with the tradition whereby a family group, or consortile, effectively enjoyed the revenues of an estate as a group.[57]

A clutch of children, particularly sons, helped to ensure family survival in the face of the ever-present threat of early mortality. However, providing for those children, especially the younger sons and the daughters who would not inherit the title and patrimony, to ensure that they did not pursue disreputable careers and lifestyles harmful to the family's reputation, might seriously strain the family's resources. Such activity might include commerce, although the restricted opportunitites available in the Savoyard state may have been more practical a restraint in this respect than any formal rules on derogeance.[58] The strategies whereby Savoyard noble families, like those elsewhere in Europe, provided for younger sons and daughters without compromising wealth or reputation, necessitated an obedience to parents (and above all fathers) which constituted an important aspect of the education of the young noble.[59] Those strategies were articulated by the Savoyard nobleman, René Favre, lord of la Valbonne, in his, *Le Bien Public pour le Fait de la Justice*, which was

---

[55] For defects in entails (and their impact on noble fortunes in the eighteenth century), see Woolf, *Studi sulla nobiltà*, 153. For indebtedness to ecclesiastical institutions see Nicolas, *La Savoie*, I, 289.

[56] For the inclusion of its artillery in one family entail, see M. Grosso and Mellano, 'Su una vicenda di Carlo Francesco Valperga conte di Masino', in Grosso and Mellano, *Spunti e profili nella Storia del Piemonte nei secc. XVII e XVIII* (Turin, 1961), 73 ff.

[57] See Woolf, *Studi sulla nobiltà*, 85 ff. for the consortile of the Valperga di Rivara family; and Venturi, *Saggi*, 29, for that of the Radicati. The consortile did not have to be a single family group: that at Santena comprised a number of families, including the Benzo and Tana, each with a share in the fief, Levi, *Inheriting Power*, 103.

[58] A Coardi, ambassador in Madrid, took the opportunity to invest in Spain's overseas empire c. 1670, Marchisio, 'Ideologia', 103–4.

[59] We still do not know enough about this educative process, but the attitudes (obedience and so on) it inculcated (or was intended to) are clear enough in the correspondence between the conte di Guarene and his father, L. Provana di Collengo, 'Lettere di Carlo Giacinto Roero, conte di Guarene, capitano nel reggimento dragoni di Genevois 1704–07', *CGP*, VIII, passim.

published at Annécy in 1646, and revolved essentially around four careers: the church, the law, the court and the army.[60]

Relations between nobles and the church were by no means easy. In the past many noble families had appropriated tithes and patronage (notably rights of presentation), which often meant conflict with the local clergy.[61] In addition, local churches and chapels were often a focus of conflict between lords and communities.[62] These conflicts were testimony to the sheer extent to which the church fitted into overall noble family strategies, not least as an arena for a family's display of power and status.[63] In addition, false grants of land to the church could extend the fiscal exemption enjoyed by parts of a noble family's patrimony. Above all, the church was a reservoir of decorous, influential and lucrative niches (episcopal sees, canonries and so on) for needy relations. Once ensconced in the church, these men (and women, as abbesses) were expected to – and generally did – use their patronage to benefit their relations, securing appointments and making land and credit available.[64] If an heir died, the return to the secular state of a younger son in the church could be arranged without great difficulty.[65] Not surprisingly, therefore, few Savoyard noble families with more than one son did not boast at least an abate.[66]

The court has long been regarded as a preserve of the nobility, and the Savoyard court is no exception.[67] However, the court was the preserve of the old nobility, largely to the exclusion of the more recently ennobled.

---

[60] Nicolas, *La Savoie*, I, 225.
[61] See Woolf, *Studi sulla nobiltà*, 101 for the recovery by the archbishop of Turin (1659) of tithes paid to the Valperga di Rivara consortile; and Nicolas, *La Savoie*, I, 201 for the ecclesiastical patronage of nobles in Savoy.
[62] See Bergadani, 'Un villaggio dell'Astigiano nelle vicende politiche e militari dei secoli XVII e XVIII', *BSBS*, 30, 1928, 390, and Venturi, *Saggi*, 29 ff., for long-running conflicts between noble families and communities which focused on the local church.
[63] In his will, conte Francesco Amedeo Costa di Polonghera declared (1674) his wish to be buried in the family chapel in the Augustinian church at Chieri, AST/Costa di Polonghera, m. 5.
[64] In 1686 there were three members of the de Sales family in the chapter of Saint Pierre, Annécy, while in 1699 a Milliet, archbishop of Tarantaise, appointed a nephew dean of the cathedral of Moutiers, Nicolas, *La Savoie*, I, 251. See, also Rondolino, 'Vita Torinese', *CGP*, VII, 371–2 for the canons of Turin cathedral; and M. Grosso and Mellano, 'Impressioni e commenti tratti dalle lettere di Giovanni Battista Isnardi vescovo di Mondovì (1697–1731)', in Grosso and Mellano, *Spunti e profili*, for the strong family sense of one Piedmontese noble prelate.
[65] Following the death (1604) without heirs of the eldest son of the first conte of the Perrone di San Martino family, his younger brother abandoned holy orders to prevent the family's extinction, Dagna, 'Un Diplomatico . . .', 9–10.
[66] See *DBI*, 'Breglio' for the sons of Ottavio Francesco Solaro, conte di Govone (fl. 1680).
[67] For the court appointments of successive generations of (males and females of) the Scaglia di Verrua (among the elite in the Savoyard nobility) see G. de Léris, *La comtesse de Verrue et la cour de Victor Amédée II de Savoie* (Paris, 1881), passim.

The former included conte Giacinto Antonio Ottavio Provana di Druent, and Carlo Emanuele Birago di Vische. The latter was appointed gentleman of the bedchamber to Charles Emanuel II (1660), Cavaliere Gran Croce of the Order of Saints Maurice and Lazarus (1661), conte – later marchese – di Candia and knight of the Order of the Annunziata (1668). Also to be found within this elite was Guido Francesco Maria Biandrate Aldobrandino, marchese di San Giorgio and Rivarolo, grand master of Savoy, knight of the Annunziata, whose wife, Cristina di Wicardel de Fleury had been maid of honour of Madama Reale.[68] It was from among this select group, too, that the duke chose his military chiefs and provincial governors.[69] Many other nobles went into the law, including the magistracy (i.e. the sovereign courts) and administration, including that of Turin and other towns, where influential local noble families were frequently elected syndics.[70] For some, most notably the relatively recently ennobled Carron de Saint Thomas, state office-holding was a family tradition, although some other noble careers – the most prestigious, the preserve of the court nobility – were largely closed to them.

As for military careers, as has already been noted, historians have long seen the nobility as the victim of the long-term transformation of warfare in the early modern era, the process sometimes referred to as the 'Military Revolution'. According to this view, nobles inevitably lost out with the replacement of the old feudal knight by artillery and infantry and (with the growth of large and expensive armies) by state funded, organised and controlled armies which were no longer raised by nobles and which in fact helped keep the nobility in check. The nobility was increasingly demilitarised, a process reflected in a number of developments, including the transformation of old noble fortresses into more comfortable country houses. There are certainly signs of this process, both in Europe and in the Savoyard state in particular. Not all nobles were soldiers, and some fortified houses were being demilitarised. However, as in the rest of Europe, it would be a gross misrepresentation of the experience and nature of the Savoyard nobility in the 1680s to see it as having abandoned its military ethos. On the contrary, the military ethic remained a vital element in notions of nobility, and many Savoyard nobles had experience of active military service, in the armies of their prince, in the war against Genoa (1672) and in the Salt War (1682). Some, for want of military

---

[68] *DBI*, 'Provana di Druent'; Costamagna, 'L'Evoluzione . . . Birago di Vische'; *CGP*, VIII, 347 ff.

[69] Carlo Francesco Renato della Chiesa, marchese di Cinzano of an old and distinguished family held successive provincial governorships between the 1660s and 1680s, *DBI*, *sub voce*.

[70] See C. Salsotto, 'Fossano e la battaglia di Torino (1706)', *CGP*, VII, 415 ff., for the election of members of the Bava and Operti families as syndics of Fossano.

employment at home (in the limited Savoyard army and the pacific foreign policy before 1690) served foreign princes and states, including Louis XIV, the emperor, Venice and even Lucca.[71] For some others, holy orders were combined with a military career in the Order of Malta, which attracted noble cadets throughout Europe.[72]

Many of these careers required some sort of education, and sometimes, as in the case of the church and the law, a formal qualification.[73] For this reason, many noble families in the Savoyard state, again as elsewhere in Europe, did what they could to educate their sons.[74] For most (given the expense) this still meant very little, particularly outside the home, but for others it meant study which qualified them for employment.[75] For a privileged few, education involved attendance at one of the exclusive, specialised educational institutions which had sprung up throughout Europe for the education of nobles in the seventeenth century. For most of the seventeenth century, this meant an education outside the Savoyard state (at one of the French academies, or one of those closer to home in Italy). However, Savoyard nobles also had access to the College of Nobles run by the Jesuits in Turin since 1681 and to one of Europe's premier noble education institutions, the Turin Accademia Reale, which – reflecting the general concern with the proper education of the nobility

---

[71] M. Grosso and M. F. Mellano, 'Le guerre contro i Turchi negli anni 1688–89 nel carteggio di due gentiluomini piemontesi', in Grosso and Mellano, *Spunti e profili*, 31 ff., is a veritable gazeteer of those Savoyard nobles fighting in the Balkans in these years; Pignet, 'Eugenio Gaspar De Tillier', 695 ff. See, more generally, C. Storrs and H. M. Scott, 'The military revolution and the European nobility c. 1600–1800', *War in History*, 3/1, 1996, 1 ff.

[72] See Nicolas, *La Savoie*, I, 234, for the number of nobles from the Duchy of Savoy received into the Order of Malta 1516–1700. Piedmontese nobles who entered the Order included cavaliere Pietro Francesco Federico Roero (younger brother of conte Carlo Giacinto Roero di Guarene), cavaliere Tana, and cavaliere Antonio Domenico Balbiano, Provana di Collegno, 'Lettere . . .', *CGP*, VIII, 295, 297, 302; and commendatory (i.e. holder of a commend of the Order) Costanzo Operti, second son of the marchese di Cervasca, Victor Amadeus' minister to Madrid from 1690, Rondolino, 'Vita Torinese', *CGP*, VII, 282–3.

[73] In 1688 Victor Amadeus promised to give Giovanni Battista Nicomede Doria proofs of his affection for him and his house, but emphasised that public office required appropriate capacity, Marchisio, 'Ideologia', 123 n. 274.

[74] See, generally, G. P. Brizzi, *La Formazione della classe dirigente nel Sei–Settecento. I 'seminaria nobilium' nell'Italia centro-settentrionale* (Bolgna, 1976), and M. Motley, *Becoming a French Aristocrat: the education of the court nobility 1580–1715* (Princeton, 1990).

[75] The future marchese d'Ormea studied at home, then at the University of Mondovì (graduating in 1697), and became magistrate of Carmagnola, G. Ricuperati, 'Il Settecento', in Merlin, *Il Piemonte sabaudo*, 459. Conte Giuseppe Cacherano di Cavallerleone, of an old noble family, and vicario of Turin from 1701, also (like various ancestors who served in the magistracy) had a law degree, as did conte Francesco Nomis di Castelletto e Valfenera, vicario from 1687 (and again from 1700), D. Balani, *Il vicario tra città e stato: l'ordine pubblico e l'annona nella Torino del Settecento* (Turin, 1987), 130.

of governments throughout Europe – had been established by Victor Amadeus' mother in 1677. The Academy was effectively a part of the court, being the responsibilty of the gran scudiere (see Chapter 4). Rather than technical skills and qualifications, the Academy imparted the skills necessary for court life. It was also a means to transmit and instil (reflecting the fahionable neostoicism which swept seventeenth-century Europe) what we might call an absolutist ideology. Above all, it offered a privileged introduction and access to the court.[76] This no doubt justified the great cost of attending the Academy, which inevitably excluded virtually all but the wealthiest of the duke's noble subjects.[77] Wealthier nobles would also tour Europe's capitals, the so-called Kavaliertour, to acquire additional polish, foreign languages and to make valuable contacts.[78]

So far, little has been said about noblewomen. Such neglect, however, is completely unjustified. There is a tradition which, probably rightly, sees the status of noblewomen (like that of non-noblewomen) broadly decline in the early modern period.[79] In addition, noblewomen (like younger sons) were often sacrificed for the good of the noble family's standing and wealth. Particularly when resources were scarce, daughters might be sent into the church as a means of reducing their demands on the patrimony (by way of a dowry), since spiritual dowries were generally lower.[80] However, the position of noblewomen did not completely decline and daughters were also an asset, even in the church (especially as

[76] See the extract from a textbook in use at the Accademia, G. Ponza, *La science de l'homme de qualité* (Turin, 1684), in I. Massabo Ricci and C. Rosso, 'La corte qual rappresentazione del potere sovrano', in G. Romano, ed., *Figure del Barocco in Piemonte: La corte, la città, i cantieri, le province* (Turin, 1988), 15. The Accademia, and the education it imparted, is discussed by W. Barberis, *Le Armi*, 177 ff. See, generally, G. Oestreich, *Neostocism and the Early Modern State* (Cambridge, 1982), passim.

[77] The costly education of Gerolamo (b. 1669), eldest son (and heir) of the Falletti di Barolo included attendance at the Accademia, Woolf, *Studi sulla nobiltà*, 54. The conte di Guarene was there from November 1697 to January 1699, Provana di Collegno, 'Lettere . . .', *CGP*, VIII, 289.

[78] Marchisio, 'Ideologia', 85, 106. See *DBI*, 'Breglio', for tour of Giuseppe Roberto Solaro di Govone (b. 1680).

[79] See S. Hanley, 'Engendering the state: family formation and state building in early modern France', *French Historical Studies*, 16, 1989, 4 ff. and references. Dr H. M. Scott and I are currently preparing a study of noblewomen in early modern Europe *c*. 1600–1800.

[80] In one of his wills, Carlo Lodovico Falletti di Barolo (d. 1705) justified a restricted provision for one of his daughters, should she take religious vows, on the grounds of the need to use the family's resources to ensure its continuance and standing by channelling them to the eldest son, Woolf, *Studi sulla nobiltà*, 59. Five of the six sisters of Giuseppe Roberto Solaro di Govone (b. 1680) entered convents, *DBI*, 'Breglio'. In the Nine Years War, after Victor Amadeus' defeat at Marsgalia, marauding French troops stormed an exclusively noble nunnery near Revello, VDM to Fagel, 20 Nov. 1693, Turin, ARAH/SG/8644/86.

heads of religious houses). More importantly, a family would prefer to have daughters marry, for a number of reasons. For the 'newer' office-holding nobility, a daughter's marriage might establish a connection with an older noble family.[81] For older families, it might be the means to a valuable alliance with a wealthy and influential new family.[82] A daughter's marriage might, in the absence of a son, be the only means to prevent family extinction.[83] The prospects of marriage for a noblewomen were no doubt improved by a period at court, where women played a peculiarly important role.[84] Just how successful a marriage might be (and how happy for the noblewoman) depended upon many factors, including how promptly the dowry was paid. In addition, with substantial numbers of nobles in state (or foreign) service, and with high mortality rates, a married noblewoman might be responsible for running a household and estate and even determining crucial aspects of family strategy. For the same reasons, widowhood was often a relatively enjoyable time for some noblewomen.[85] In order to prepare her for society and marriage, noblewomen too required an appropriate education, but one very different from that of their male relations.[86] Clearly, although generally less important than men in noble family strategy, noblewomen were by no means unimportant. Individual noblemen, many of whom benefited personally, as heirs of noblewomen, were invariably well aware of their female as well as of their male relatives and connections.[87]

The vast majority of those Savoyard nobles who married did so locally. However, some marriage alliances, particularly those of the oldest, wealthiest and most prestigious families, contributed to the emergence of a Savoyard nobility, i.e. one comprising the nobilities of its component

---

[81] The daughter of the first Carron de Saint-Thomas to be ennobled married a Challant, *DBI*, *sub voce*.

[82] Giuseppe Gaetano Giacinto Carron de Saint-Thomas married (*c.* 1669) Paola Beatrice Roero di Guarene, *DBI*, *sub voce*.

[83] See *DBI*, 'Buschetti', for the preservation of the name, title and patrimony (in Ceva) on the death without sons of Giambattista Buschetti (d. 1685) by their transmission to the son of his sister (who had married Filippo Carlo Ripa di Meana, conte di Giaglione) on condition of the nephew's adding the Buschetti name to his own.

[84] See Rondolino, 'Vita Torinese', *CGP*, VII, 53 ff. for the great number of women at court. On the marriage of one of the maids of honour, she received an additional dowry from the prince: Woolf, *Studi sulla nobiltà*, 94 (and Nicolas, *La Savoie*, I, 240, for that received by the daughter of the marquis de Sales in 1701).

[85] See Woolf, *Studi sulla nobiltà*, 122, for the direction of the Saluzzo di Paesana patrimony from 1659 by a widow, Caterina Marzia Gandolfi di Ricaldone, during a minority; and Nicolas, *La Savoie*, I, 280 (and passim) for a Costa widow in the 1680s.

[86] Nicolas, *La Savoie*, 1, 396 ff.

[87] Typically, Giacomo Ignazio Malabaila, 4th conte di Canale was also conte di Monale as heir of his mother, Anna Gerolama Bunea, Ruata, *Canale*, 13.

parts (Aosta, Nice, Piedmont and Savoy), and also helped to integrate older, court and newer nobilities. Typical, before 1690, were the marriages between (c. 1657) Francesca de Chabod de St Maurice (of the Duchy of Savoy) and Carlo Francesco Antonio Pallavicino della Frabosa; that (1679) between the marchese di Bagnasco and Irene Felice Isnardi di Castello di Caraglio; that (1679) between Baldassare Saluzzo di Paesana (eldest son of a family whose marriages hitherto had been largely 'local') and Costanza Camilla Arborio di Gattinara, widow of Conte Balbis (and a lady of honour at court). This process was producing a nobility increasingly interconnected by marriage: both the cavaliere d'Entraque and the old marquis de Saint-Thomas (d. 1699) were maternal uncles of the conte di Guarene.[88]

Relations between the Savoyard nobility and the Savoyard state on the eve of the Nine Years War were by no means simple. That nobility was not a ruling class, since effective power was in the hands of the duke, and only in part the governing class, following the earlier rise of non-noble office holders.[89] Following the suppression of representative assemblies, there were hardly any institutions which brought the nobility (or its representatives) together to play a formal role and/or give them a self-consciously distinct public identity outside the Duchy of Aosta.[90] Yet nobles could present a problem to ducal authority in the developing state, because of their local jurisdictions[91] and patronage, their stranglehold on the communities indebted to them, their contribution to local disorder (via their feuds and their protection of local brigands) and – as the recent regency had shown – their readiness to look outside the Savoyard state for allies in the domestic political struggle. However, it is arguable that it was the political vacuum created by Victor Amadeus' minority and their own importance in the state which forced nobles to act in this way. In fact, there was little essential or inherent antagonism or conflict between nobles and the developing ducal state. Although the latter's creation of new nobles might be resented by some older families, it also reflected a commitment to the very concept of nobility. Similarly, while ducal investigations into (and rejection of false) claims to noble status might be

[88] Provana di Collegno, 'Lettere . . .', *CGP*, VIII, 293 ff.; *DBI*, 'Bagnasco'; Woolf, *Studi sulla nobiltà*, 125 (Saluzzo di Paesana). [89] Stumpo, 'I ceti', 151 ff.
[90] In Savoy, the cornette blanche (an office held by one of the noble elite, including successive members of the Seyssel family to 1694, and the marquis de Coudrée – the last to hold the post – until his death in 1736) acted as intermediary between the duke and the duchy's nobility, Nicolas, *La Savoie*, I, 44.
[91] However, the expansion of titles in the Savoyard state in the seventeenth century was not accompanied by an expansion of jurisdictions, thus making it difficult to equate ennoblement and 'refeudalisation' in that era, see Stumpo, 'I ceti', 169–70.

seen as the intrusion of the state, imposing its own concepts of nobility and underpinning a monopoly of the right to make and break nobles, these enquiries (which were in fact often inspired by a concern to end false claims to noble tax exemptions, which harmed the ducal finances) ultimately strengthened nobles and their privileges.[92] The duke was also ready, at the request of noble parents, to use his 'absolute' authority to protect the interests of individual noble families, detaining wayward younger nobles whose conduct threatened a family's reputation, influence and patrimony.[93] More importantly, the state provided many of the material and other resources which ensured an honourable income and lifestyle for nobles and their families. Some relatively poor families, including, for example, the Valperga di Rivara, had built up a tradition of ducal or state service, precisely because the state provided or channelled invaluable additional means. For some other noble families, including the Carron de Saint-Thomas, state office-holding had been the means of entry into the nobility itself.[94]

For his part, the duke greatly depended upon his nobles. Those with feudal jurisdictions, were responsible, under the supervision of the Senate, for the local administration of justice in many parts of the Savoyard state, while others often enjoyed a privileged role in local government, as syndics in the communities.[95] As seigneurs, landowners and employers, nobles enjoyed extensive patronage on their own account.[96] Their wealth made individual nobles, and the nobility as a whole, crucial to some ducal schemes, for example those of Charles Emanuel II and Madama Reale, for the commercial development of Piedmont, all of which necessitated substantial initial capital.[97] For this and other reasons, the dukes of Savoy relied upon their noble subjects to play an important role in the development of their capital, Turin, and not least by building expensive and imposing palaces there.[98] Nobles, in effect, had the ability, authority,

---

[92] See Beik, *Absolutism and Society*, 319–20, on the way investigations of false nobility in France in the 1660s represented the regulation (by the absolute monarch) of hierarchy but also its strengthening.

[93] In 1700–1, at the request of his own family, the comte de La Forest was briefly incarcerated by ducal order in the fortress of Miolans, Nicolas, *La Savoie*, I, 412.

[94] See also, Woolf, *Studi sulla nobiltà*, 90 ff. (the Valperga di Rivara) and Rosso, *Una burocrazia*, passim.

[95] The feudal consortile appointed the *podestà* of Santena, Levi, *Inheriting Power*, 102 and passim.

[96] In 1700, forty-six under-farmers collected the revenues of the marquis de Saint-Thomas in Tarantaise province alone, Nicolas, *La Savoie*, I, 201, 223, 306. Nobles were inevitably frequent recipients of letters seeking appointments for friends and relatives: see Marchisio, 'Ideologia', 118, n. 255.

[97] Bulferetti, 'Assolutismo e mercantilismo nel Piemonte di Carlo Emanuele II', *MAST*, 3rd ser., 2, 1953, passim.   [98] See Cavallo, *Charity and Power*, 105 ff. and references.

standing and resources which the as yet imperfectly formed state still sometimes lacked and which it occasionally needed to tap for its own purposes. In return for their co-operation, nobles were rewarded by the state. Victor Amadeus backed nobles (as feudal lords) in their conflicts with their own vassals, conflicts which seem to have sharpened, at least in Savoy itself, from c. 1680 as a result of what Nicolas calls a 'feudal reaction'.[99] Superficially threatening 'state' institutions could be neutralised or even mobilised in favour of nobles, not least by means of marriage alliances with those (nobles) running them.[100] Essentially, the duke and his nobles found co-operation mutually advantageous. Victor Amadeus disliked individual nobles, including conte Carlo Francesco Valperga di Masino, his mother's erstwhile favourite, resenting the way they had selfishly exploited his minority. The duke also briefly punished some others (notably the marchese di Pianezza and his nephew, Provana di Druent) following his seizure of power in 1684. But there was no essential hostility between Victor Amadeus and the nobility as a whole. On the contrary, the latter played a key role in the Savoyard state and found its own interest in doing so.[101]

Nevertheless, Savoyard state and nobility were not as closely meshed in 1690 as they would become thereafter. For one thing, some nobles were vassals of other lords and princes and had only relatively recently 'transferred' to the Savoyard state.[102] Many still owed allegiance to a number of other sovereign princes, including the Gonzaga dukes of Mantua,[103] the

---

[99] Nicolas, *La Savoie*, II, 507 ff.; Woolf, *Studi sulla nobiltà*, 102, 119.

[100] In 1655 the community of Rivara, having appealed to the Camera dei Conti in a tax dispute with the Valperga di Rivara, objected to the Camera's appointment of its first president, conte Francesco Giovanni Cauda di Caselette (an in-law of the Valperga) to chair a commission to hear the case. The community prevailed, but still lost the case, Woolf, *Studi sulla nobiltà*, 98–9.

[101] In 1674, the marchese di Parella was invested with the marquisate of Andorno as a reward for his financial and other help in Charles Emanuel's recent (disastrous) war against Genoa: Bulferetti, 'La feudalita e il patriziato', Appendix IX, 258–61. One curious expression of this loyalty was the way many nobles were given the names of the dukes of Savoy. These included Vittorio Amedeo (born c. 1685), son of conte Giuseppe Maria Solaro della Margherita, *CGP*, VII, 41 and Vittorio Amedeo della Costa (b. 1695), *DBI*, *sub voce*.

[102] The lords of Santena were vassals of the archbishop of Turin, Levi, *Inheriting Power*, 166.

[103] Most of the fiefs in the Monferrato held by the Falletti di Barolo were held from/via the House of Savoy from 1631, although the head of the family had already sought Piedmontese 'naturalisation' before that date. Nevertheless, to which jurisdiction (Turin or Milan) some of the family's other fiefs were immediately subject was debatable, and allowed the family room for manoeuvre, Woolf, *Studi sulla nobiltà*, 19, 45–6 (and 93, 99 for the position of the Valperga di Rivara).

pope[104] and the emperor, and were able to manipulate to their own advantage their uncertain juridical status *vis-à-vis* the duke of Savoy.[105] In addition, the ambitions of many Savoyard noble families were by no means confined to the Savoyard state. The marriage strategies of some looked beyond its confines, in part reflecting the Savoyard state's satellite status and in turn contributing to the emergence of a European noble elite.[106] Finally, although some nobles found state service in their interest, many others (the vast majority) did not. So far, at least, many noble families had managed to get by with very little contact with the (Savoyard) state, which simply could not accommodate them all anyway. Their own families and affairs preoccupied most nobles at least as much as did the state and its concerns. This reality is exemplified by the experience of the Falletti di Barolo who, by 1690, had risen from relative provincial obscurity by means of profitable marriages and good management of their patrimony, but without being drawn into the institutional (administration, army, court) ambit of the Savoyard state.[107]

1690–1720

How did intensive warfare after 1690 affect Victor Amadeus' noble subjects? On the one hand, it is possible to point to further evidence of the supposed 'demilitarisation' noted earlier. Destruction, by both friend and foe, of nobles' castles, for example, although by no means new, removed one of the traditional foundations of the independent military

---

[104] For the princes of Masserano, see G. Casalis, *Dizionario geografico-storico-statistico-commerciale degli stati del re di Sardegna*, 28 vols. (Turin, 1833–56), *sub voce*.

[105] In 1655, in the case brought in the Camera by the community of Rivara (above), the Valperga produced a number of imperial investitures and a grant of fiscal exemption issued by the Holy Roman Emperor Sigismund in 1430, Woolf, *Studi sulla nobiltà*, 98.

[106] One of Parella's sisters, Eleonora Margarita, married (1) a Langhe noble, the conte di Desana and (2) Count Königsegg, a leading minister at the emperor's court: see the agreement between her and her main rival, the marchese di Crescentino, for the inheritance of her first husband, July 1689, AST/Provincia di Vercelli, m. 20 (Desana)/1. See also *DBI*, 'Caraglio', for the marriage (*c.* 1670) of the marchese di Caraglio with Christine Charlotte Havart di Senantes (Lorraine). For the marriage (1683) of conte Scaglia di Verrua with Jeanne-Baptiste d'Albert de Luynes, daughter of the duc de Luynes (and Victor Amadeus II's future mistress), and the role of Scaglia's mother (a former dame d'honneur of Madama Reale) in the marriage, see Léris, *Comtesse de Verrue*, 22.

[107] The family's ambitions were as much focused on Gonzagan Mantua as on the Savoyard state, and its insertion into the latter was largely by means of marriages into the Piedmontese nobility (with a Birago di Vische, in 1666, for example) – suggesting that independent noble family strategies might contribute in the long term to Savoyard state formation, see Woolf, *Studi sulla nobiltà*, 47 ff.

power of the nobility.¹⁰⁸ The loss of artillery from those castles, requisitioned by Victor Amadeus in 1690, in the crisis of that year, might have the same effect — even if some of this was subsequently returned.¹⁰⁹ That some of his nobles had lost the will to fight, and the ability to do so successfully, is also suggested by the failure of some to respond positively to an 'enquiry' of 1702 as to who would serve Victor Amadeus, and a very disappointing performance of the nobility of the Duchy of Savoy in the face of the French invasions of 1690 and 1703; although the nobility of Savoy were also more pro-French in inclination than were the nobles of Piedmont. In December 1703, on learning of the withdrawal of one of his regiments, commanded by the baron d'Aiguebelle, from the Duchy, Victor Amadeus lamented the apparent loss by Savoy's nobility of the military daring of their ancestors.¹¹⁰

However, Victor Amadeus' disappointment reflected an expectation that his noble subjects should both be able to fight, and that they should fight for him. During the War of the Spanish Succession, in fact, he had improved the defences of the castles and country houses of some of his nobles as a means of resisting the enemy.¹¹¹ More importantly, although difficult to quantify precisely, the evidence suggests that — far from abandoning (or evading) its military role — the Savoyard nobility played a crucial role in Victor Amadeus' armies between 1690 and 1720. For many nobles, these wars were the start of a distinguished military career,¹¹² while individual families supplied a number of officers and commanders.¹¹³ Noble families which had hitherto remained largely outside

---

[108] See VDM to Fagel, 3 Oct. 1693, Turin, ARAH/SG/8644/72, for the destruction by the French after Marsaglia of Saint-Thomas' castle of Buttigliera (although the latter had hardly underpinned Carron military power); *CGP*, I, 251, for the demolition, on Victor Amadeus's order, 1703, of the fort of Allinges (Savoy); and Woolf, *Studi sulla ' nobiltà*, 67, for enemy destruction in the War of the Spanish Succession of the castle of Pocapaglia, which its noble owner could not afford to rebuild.

[109] See Grosso and Mellano, 'Su una vicenda', *passim*, for conte Carlo Francesco Valperga di Masino's efforts to recover artillery requisitioned in 1690. It is possible that Victor Amadeus was also on this occasion disarming a man of whose conduct in the crisis associated with the duke's breach with Louis XIV he could not be certain.

[110] For the survey of 1702, see Pérouse, Etat de la Savoie . . ., 26; *CGP*, I, 282.

[111] In 1705, the marchese di Osasco had managed to fend off French troops besieging the latter. Later that year, Victor Amadeus had a number of noble castles and country houses in the Asti area garrisoned by his own and imperial troops, VDM to States, 18 Mar. and 14 Oct. 1705, ARAH/EA/VDM/30, 24, 134. For the Radicati castle at Passerano, see Venturi, *Saggi*, 31.

[112] This was true of Louis de Blonay, youngest son of the baron d'Oncieu (Savoy), who in 1690 became a cornet in the new Genevois dragoon regiment, *DBI*, 'Blonay'.

[113] In the War of the Spanish Succession, three of the four sons of the conte di Cumiana served as officers (two in the Monferrato, one in the Saluzzo regiment), Provana di Collegno, 'Lettere . . .', *CGP*, VIII, 111.

the state structure also provided it with soldiers, five Falletti di Barolo brothers serving in Victor Amadeus' forces in these years.[114] Significantly, too, although members of the magistracy did sometimes plead their office to avoid military service in 1702, some families which hitherto had been distinguished largely in what we might call civilian administration, now assumed military office.[115] Not surprisingly, nobles dominated the officer corps of Victor Amadeus' army in these decades. The list of colonels, lieutenant colonels, captains and lieutenants of the regiments campaigning in Lombardy in September 1703 reads like a roll call of the Savoyard nobility,[116] while the new regiments, raised in 1703–04, were also dominated by nobles.[117] One reason why nobles continued to dominate the Savoyard military establishment was that they still largely saw themselves as natural military leaders. In 1703, the marquis de Sales, organising the defence of Savoy, identified the local nobility as best suited to levy and command the new units to be levied for the Duchy's defence, and their social inferiors, the bourgeois, as lieutenants.[118] Equally importantly, non-nobles generally seem to have shared these views.[119]

This military role was – as Stumpo has emphasised – by no means risk free.[120] On the contrary, many nobles were killed in the service of their prince in these decades. Casualties during the Nine Years War included the eighteen-year-old Pietro Ottavio Falletti di Barolo (Staffarda, 1690), conte Michele Gabaleone di Salmour (Cuneo, 1691), the conte di Lagnasco (Embrun, 1692) and Carlo Giacinto Maurizio Solaro della Moretta, marchese di Chiusa (Marsaglia, 1693).[121] Among the noble casualties in the War of the Spanish Succession were conte Radicati di Brosolo and cavaliere Carlo Andrea Roero di Mombarone (the siege of

---

[114] Woolf, *Studi sulla nobiltà*, 64.
[115] Baron Nicola Coardi di Carpenetto, of a family ennobled in the seventeenth century, for example, served as a colonel in the Turin militia, in 1705–6, Rondolino, 'Vita Torinese', *CGP*, VII, 39.   [116] See *CGP*, I, 25 ff.
[117] See the list of colonels of projected twelve new regiments, all but one of them titled, *CGP*, I, 61. It is noteworthy that these new regiments were invariably known by the name of the colonel who had raised them (della Trinità, for example), whereas the older, ducal regiments were invariably designated by their 'regional' names: Aosta, Monferrato, Piedmont, Savoy, etc.
[118] Marquis de Sales to VA, 7 Oct. 1703, Chambéry, *CGP*, I, 241. Victor Amadeus subsequently sent Sales brevets as brigadier for two local nobles, as requested, *ibid.*, 251.
[119] In 1703, Fossano appointed conte Lelio Bava di Valle colonel of its newly raised regiment of cavalry, Salsotto, 'Fossano', *CGP*, VII, 422.
[120] E. Stumpo, 'Tra mito, leggenda e realtà storica: la tradizione militare sabauda da Emanuele Filiberto a Carlo Alberto', *RSI*, 103, 1991, 560 ff.
[121] Woolf, *Studi sulla nobiltà*, 64; *DBI*, 'Balbiano' (Gabaleone di Salmour's widow); A. de Saluces, *Histoire Militaire du Piémont*, 5 vols. (Turin, 1818), V, 60; Provana di Collegno, 'Lettera . . .', *CGP*, VIII, 348.

Turin, 1706) and the marquis de Sales (siege of Toulon, 1707).[122] These deaths no doubt meant higher rates of mortality, and even of family extinction, among the Savoyard nobility than was the case before 1690, although extinction was no doubt also hastened in some cases by the family's straitened financial circumstances.[123] Many other nobles were wounded in action, including the marchese di Voghera (Embrun, 1692) and the marquis d'Aix (Vercelli, 1704).[124] Yet others narrowly escaped death, including Parella's son and heir, the marchese d'Andorno, who had a horse killed beneath him while fighting in the valleys bordering Dauphiné in 1704[125] only to die (1719) in the defence of Sicily against the Spaniards.[126] Even if not physically harmed, nobles risked capture. Many nobles were taken prisoner at Staffarda and Marsaglia in the Nine Years War. Among those captured in the War of the Spanish Succession were conte Piossasco di None (detained at San Benedetto in 1703 and, probably because he was one of the duke's best officers, not released until after the battle of Turin in 1706), marchese Giuseppe Giacinto San Martino di San Germano, the conte della Trinità, the marquis de Trivié, the conte Benzo di Santena and Carlo Alberto Biandrate Aldobrandino, conte d'Ales (eldest son of the marchese di San Giorgio).[127]

For some nobles, service in the Savoyard army meant abandoning that of a foreign prince.[128] There is no doubt that this transfer was in part the result of pressure from Victor Amadeus, who in June 1690 and again at the start of the War of the Spanish Succession banned his subjects from entering the service of foreign princes and ordered those already serving

---

[122] *CGP*, II, 218. See Provana di Collegno, 'Lettere . . .', *CGP*, VIII, 289, 295 for the deaths of the conte di Santo Stefano, colonel of Victor Amadeus' dragoons (drowned crossing the Dora, 1706) and of cavaliere di Sciolze, of the Roero di San Severino, captain of the Genevois dragoons (killed, 1706) and the 'necrologies' of the parishes of Turin, Rondolino, 'Vita Torinese', *CGP*, VII, 346 ff., for soldier nobles killed during the siege(s) of Turin.

[123] In 1691 the last of the (Aostan) du Châtelard, whose nobility was supposedly traceable to the Crusades, was killed in action against the French, Barbero, 'Una nobiltà', 20. The unusually high incidence of noble mortality in war improved the prospects of many younger brothers and sons and no doubt strengthened the traditional noble preference for large families so that there was always a son in reserve.

[124] Saluces, *Histoire militaire*, V, 60; C. Faccio, 'Assedio di Vercelli', *CGP*, X, 439. Comte de la Roche d'Alléry was wounded at the siege of Verrua, 1705.

[125] [?] to VA, Luserna, 5 Oct. 1704, ARAH/EA/VDM/29, 172–3.

[126] Ferrero della Marmora, *Parella*, 456.

[127] See Saluces, *Histoire militaire*, V, 79, for nobles taken prisoner at Marsaglia, 1693; and list of prisoners exchanged in Mar. 1707, Provana di Collegno, 'Lettera . . .', *CPG*, VIII, 356 ff.

[128] These included conte Radicati di Cocconato and conte di Solaro, who both entered Victor Amadeus's service in the autumn of 1703, *CGP*, I, 85, 272.

abroad to return home on pain of confiscation of their property.[129] Victor Amadeus clearly sought to mobilise his noble subjects, ordering a general survey in 1691 to discover who had obeyed (or not) his earlier order to return home and further surveys in 1701 and 1702 to discover those nobles who might serve in his forces (and to discover the excuses of those who could or would not, see above).[130] It is possible to view these measures as an assertion of ducal authority *vis-à-vis* his noble subjects, one underpinned by the needs of war. More importantly, however, the expansion of the Savoyard army in these years, and Victor Amadeus' need for great numbers of additional officers, clearly allowed many of his noble subjects to pursue military careers at home, and not (as before 1690) having to go abroad, in this way transforming their relationship with their own prince (and state).[131] Not all Savoyard nobles took advantage of this opportunity. Conte Scaglia di Verrua, who had gone to reside in France following his wife's affair with Victor Amadeus, was killed in Louis XIV's service at the battle of Höchstädt in 1704, while baron Carlo Emanuele Pallavicino entered the French king's service after being taken prisoner and died on the French side at the battle of Malplaquet (1709)[132]. Nor was Victor Amadeus wholly hostile to his nobles serving in the armies of his allies or of his suzerain the emperor.[133] Individual Savoyard nobles continued to serve foreign princes and states after 1713. However, thereafter most Savoyard nobles in arms served in the ranks of the much larger army of their own sovereign, whether in the regular, standing forces or the reformed militia. The wars of 1690–1720 were in this respect a turning point in relations between the Savoyard state and its nobles.

Army service could be very expensive.[134] The cost might strain the family patrimony and necessitate loans and even sales of property.[135] This

---

[129] Duboin, VI, 303 and Levi, *Inheriting Power*, 132. Nobles formerly in French service could be a source of military intelligence, VDM to Fagel, 5 Feb. 1704, Turin, ARAH/EA/VDM/29, 21.

[130] Levi, *Inheriting Power*, 132–3, Nicolas, *La Savoie*, I, 9 ff.

[131] In 1703 Victor Amadeus was informed that a number of officers from Nice in the French service would willingly enter his own if he needed officers, Caraglio to VA, 6 Oct. 1703, *CGP*, I, 85.

[132] *CGP*, IV, 76. Pallavicino's desertion (which shocked the leading families at the ducal court) surprised Victor Amadeus the more both because of his own great affection for the baron and because the latter's parents and grandparents had held leading court offices, VDM to Fagel, 25 Mar. 1704, Turin, ARAH/EA/VDM/29, 54.

[133] In 1703 he recommended to Prince Eugene the young conte Piosasco, who was on his way to Vienna to enter the emperor's service, VA to Eugene, 20 Dec. 1703, *CGP*, IV, 10,.

[134] See the cost of conte Roero di Guarene's equipage as cornet in Victor Amadeus' Guards, 1701, Provana di Collegno, 'Lettere . . .', *CGP*, VIII, 293.

[135] In 1691 Giovenale Maria Valperga di Rivera sold his family's palace at Fossano to pay for his son's equipage. Cristina Valperga di Rivara, of another branch of the same

was typical of the degree to which, between 1690 and 1720, Victor Amadeus's wars also meant new fiscal pressure on the nobility. Many noble patrimonies and revenues suffered from war damage and the levy of contributions. Among those whose properties and revenues were affected in the Nine Years War were the conte di Scalenghe, the marquis de Fleury, the Falletti di Barolo and the Saluzzo di Paesana.[136] Nobles whose properties in the area around Turin were devastated at the height of the War of the Spanish Succession included the marquis of Saint-Thomas, Provana di Druent, Tana d'Entraque, Benzo di Cavour, de Lescheraine, Filippo di Martiniana, and San Martino di Parella.[137] Others were threatened with the same fate.[138] These pressures were intensified by the squeeze on landed revenues caused by the terrible weather and poor harvests of 1693–95 and 1708–09 (see Chapter 2), but the fiscal burdens imposed by Victor Amadeus also added to what for some (particularly the poorer) nobles was little less than a crisis.[139] These burdens included the *cavalcata* (the only tax paid by feudal land, in lieu of military service),[140] voluntary and forced loans (the latter including

---

family, had to sell *tasso* and various *censi* to equip her sons for army service in the Nine Years War and in the subsequent conflict borrowed to fund such expenditure, Woolf, *Studi sulla nobiltà*, 105. In 1708 a widowed noblewoman borrowed 840 florins from the Barnabites of Annécy for her son's equipage, Nicolas, *La Savoie*, I, 230.

[136] See the French demands on the conte di Scalenghe on his property at None and Scalenghe, 1691, AST/Provincia di Pinerolo, m. 12/3 and the representations of the inhabitants of Mortigliengo to the marquis de Fleury, June 1694, regarding their difficulties in paying dues and taxes, Opera Pia Barolo, Wicardel, Suppliche, m. 136/6. For Falletti di Barolo property in the Monferrato and that of the Saluzzo di Paesana near Saluzzo, see Woolf, *Studi sulla nobiltà*, 52, 123.

[137] Rondolino, 'Vita Torinese', *CGP*, VII, 298 ff. See Barbero, 'Una nobiltà', 48, for destruction wrought by the French in the Val d'Aosta, 1705, and its effects on one noble family, although this may just have been the final straw for a family already in straitened circumstances.

[138] In 1706 conte Girolamo Maria Costa della Trinità, who had been taken prisoner at the siege of Ivrea, and subsequently released on parole, and who had been entrusted by Victor Amadeus with escorting his duchess and family to Genoa (in breach of his parole) was threatened by the commander of the French forces in Piedmont with the devastation of his estates at la Trinità unless he returned to them. However, the threat was not carried out, apparently because of the duke of Marlborough's kind treatment of French prisoners after his victory at Ramillies, VDM to Fagel, 7 July 1706, Oneglia, ARAH/EA/VDM/30, 299.

[139] The cost of his son's equipage, war taxation, a French sack of his residence, poor harvests and a daughter's dowry together led the conte di Pocapaglia to sell (with Victor Amadeus' permission, because it breached an entail established in 1662) his share of the fief of Serralunga to the Falletti di Barolo, Woolf, *Studi sulla nobiltà*, 67.

[140] The Falletti di Barolo were called on to pay *cavalcate* on their property in 1691, 1701, 1706, 1707 and in 1708 (on the latter occasion being asked for arrears from the 1630s owed for their recently acquired fief of Pocapaglia), Woolf, *Studi sulla nobiltà*, 70.

contributions to Victor Amadeus' *società dei grani*, 1695)[141] and various *ad hoc* impositions (including the *capitation* of 1702).[142] The state was also tightening the fiscal screw for nobles in other ways. These included new demands for the registration of feudal property,[143] an edict (1699) ordering all who had acquired property within the last twenty years to compensate the communities for the damage done to their tax base,[144] and the first steps in the late 1690s towards the so-called *perequazione* (see Chapter 2).[145] Even more remarkably, perhaps, in the aftermath of his first defeat in 1690, Victor Amadeus may have considered abolishing noble fiscal exemptions, partly in order to make palatable to the rest of his unprivileged subjects the new demands he was then obliged to impose.[146]

Nobles may also have resented the increase in this period in the number of ennoblements by ducal letters patent. This was most pronounced between 1696 and 1701 when Victor Amadeus was obliged to offer noble titles to attract buyers of ducal domain (which he was selling off to reduce the debt accumulated in the Nine Years War).[147] The newly ennobled included the financiers Pierre Anselme de Montjoye, who from being a tax farmer in the Duchy of Savoy, bought an (ennobling) office in the Chambéry Chambre des Comptes in 1696 and in 1699 part

[141] Woolf, *Studi sulla nobiltà*, 53. In 1706 Victor Amadeus resorted to a forced loan from his nobles (and others) following the disappointing results of his attempt to raise funds by further alienation of the *tasso*, VDM to Fagel, 26 May 1706, Turin, ARAH/EA/VDM/30, 266. See the discussion of state creditors (and their social background) in L. Einaudi, *La finanza sabauda all'aprirsi del secolo XVII e durante la guerra di successione spagnuola* (Turin, 1908), 270 ff. Other nobles went unpaid: see marchese Tommaso Felice Ferrero della Marmora to VA, 19 July 1694, AST/LP/F, m. 36, reciting his past services in the hope that the duke would order the full payment of his stipend.

[142] Pérouse, 'Etat de la Savoie', 25. This account ignores the sum demanded of the nobility of Savoy, to finance repair of the fortifications of Montmélian, 1696, Nicolas, *La Savoie*, I, 274.

[143] Woolf, *Studi sulla nobiltà*, 89 (Rivara, consegnamento of 1691) and 120 ff. (Saluzzo family, 1691). [144] Nicolas, *La Savoie*, I, 311.

[145] Faced with the latter, during the War of the Spanish Succession, some noble families settled with the communities with whom they were in dispute, making the best of a bad job. In 1711, the Valperga di Rivara and the community of Rivara concluded a dispute dating from 1687 (and in which the Valperga had sought to have the case heard before the Senate of Casale rather than that of Turin in a typical example of the way rival jurisdictions offered scope for strategic manoeuvring), Woolf, *Studi sulla nobiltà*, 100. In Santena, too, the *perequazione* obliged the noble consortile to compromise, Levi, *Inheriting Power*, 169–70.

[146] Saluces, *Histoire militaire*, V, 24–5. Unfortunately, there is little other evidence for this.

[147] Nicolas, *La Savoie*, I, 29, 37. While not reaching the levels of the central decades of the seventeenth century, the number in the 1690s (21) was more than the total in the decades 1660–90. See Cavallo, *Charity and Power*, 107–8, and references. Some of Victor Amadeus' other fiscal expedients, including the sale of the office of syndic (1704) also required the additional incentive of ennoblement – or at least the grant of noble privilege, Quazza, *Le riforme*, I, 73.

of the alienated ducal domain in Savoy, Montjoye, which was subsequently elevated to comital status,[148] and Giovanni Berta, conte di Mongardino (1704).[149] They also included ducal officials like Giovanni Battista Gropello, promoted conte di Borgone in 1699.[150] Reflecting, too, the remilitarisation of the nobility as a whole, was Victor Amadeus' grant of patents of nobility to those who distinguished themselves in action.[151] This process continued after 1713, Mellarède being elevated to conte di Bettonet in 1717, and culminated in the elevation of some of Victor Amadeus' other non-noble collaborators (including Palma and Fontana) among the 'nobility of 1722'. Clearly, although this was by no means new, the state's greater fiscal and other needs – above all in wartime – between 1690 and 1720 offered, as they had in the past, greater opportunities for social promotion.

Equally striking was the way in which the Savoyard nobility was 'renewed' by an influx of foreign nobles, drawn into the ducal service as soldiers. This was hardly new – or peculiar to the Savoyard state. The French soldier, des Hayes (d. 1721) entered the service of Victor Amadeus' father in 1660, rising to the governorships of Mondovì (playing a leading role in the military defeat of the rebels there in 1699) and Vercelli. He was rewarded with inter alia, the fief and comital title of Dorzino (1719).[152] However, although difficult to quantify, there was a discernible foreign influx in these years. This ranged from relatively obscure Irish exiles, dispersed throughout Europe following the defeat of James II's forces in Ireland by those of William III in the early 1690s,[153] to (at the highest levels) the German Schulemburg and the Lithuanian baron Bernard Ottone Rhebinder. The latter came to Turin during the War of the Spanish Succession, as commander of the German troops sent by the elector palatine. He greatly impressed Victor Amadeus, who drew him into his own service. After a distinguished role in the Toulon campaign, Rhebinder was promoted (1707) governor of Biella; and, after further distinguished military service, knight of the Annunziata and governor of Pinerolo (1713). Rhebinder and his ilk were reliable agents of ducal and

---

[148] Nicolas, *La Savoie*, I, 34, 281–2. Anselme played a key part in the abortive cadastral reform in Savoy of 1699, *ibid.*, 123.

[149] Rondolino, 'Vita Torinese', *CGP*, VII, 117. One Ferrod, who had profited from mining investments and military contracting purchased (1708) a baronial title, Barbero, 'Una nobiltà', 47.   [150] See Quazza, *Le riforme*, I, 25.

[151] See AST/Camera dei Conti/Nobiltà, art. 852, patent of nobility in favour of Ambrogio Calzamiglia of Oneglia, 23 Apr. 1695, for his role in the defence of Nice, 1691; and Barbero, 'Una nobiltà', 20, for the ennoblement of Jean Charles de Perloz (Aosta) for serving against the French in 1706.

[152] See *CGP*, I, 48, II, 197ff. and 270 ff., and viii, 294.

[153] See Nicolas, *La Savoie*, I, 19, for an Irish nobleman, Jean Oregan, residing at Chambéry, 1702.

royal authority and policy in the Savoyard state, not least because –at least initially – they lacked an independent local position and connections.[154]

On the other hand, individual nobles from the old elite sometimes fell foul of Victor Amadeus in these years. One of the most striking of these – apart from those who suffered confiscation for not returning from abroad – was a woman, Caterina Balbiano di Colcavagno. Born (1670) into the court nobility, in 1687 she married conte Michele Gabaleone di Salmour who died at the siege of Cuneo in 1691. Her situation was typical of that of the many noblewomen in this generation who as wives, widows or mothers of noblemen absent on or killed in state service were given an enhanced role.[155] However, Caterina was readier than most to seize her opportunities. In 1694 she married again. Her second husband was Prince Charles of Brandenburg, brother of the reigning electoral prince of Brandenburg, and commander of the regiments sent by the elector to Piedmont (see Chapter 1). The elector's concern at this mésalliance on the part of his brother was a serious blow to relations between Victor Amadeus and the elector, who blamed the duke for the business. Fearing the loss of the elector's troops, Victor Amadeus immediately had Caterina incarcerated in the monastery of Santa Croce in Turin. Following Charles's death (at the siege of Casale, July 1695), Caterina sought to press her rights as Charles' widow, further complicating the situation. She was not released until January 1696 and promptly went into exile, seeking papal confirmation of her marriage and exploiting the antagonism between Turin and Rome. Clearly, Victor Amadeus was not going to allow the ambitions of one of his noble subjects to thwart his own ambitions,[156]

---

[154] For Rehbinder, see Carutti, 'Il Maresciallo Rehbinder: nota biografica', *CGP*, VIII, 153 ff., and P. Bianchi, 'Guerra e politica nello stato sabaudo (1684–1730): le riforme militari di vittorio Amedeo II fra istituzioni, reclutamento e organizzazione territoriale' (Ph.D. thesis, University of Turin, 1997), 329 ff. Quazza, *Le riforme*, I, 50, identifies Rhebinder as one of Victor Amadeus' collaborators after 1713 but says little about him. Rhebinder's receipt of the prestigious Annunziata was one of the few exceptions (the others were the two marquises of Saint-Thomas) to its monopoly by the old court nobility, see Rosso, *Una burocrazia*, 218–19.

[155] Noblewomen, as mothers and wives, had always had a role of this sort but it was more pronounced in wartime, when even more noblemen were absent: see the Turin census of 1705, Rondolino, 'Vita Torinese', *CGP*, VII, 103 ff. During Parella's absence from Turin on campaign, his wife informed him of what was being said there, about him and advised her husband on how to conduct himself, Ferrero della Marmora, *Parella*, 453. See the absentee conte di Guarene's correspondence with his mother between 1704 and 1707, Provana di Collegno, 'Lettere . . .', *CGP*, VIII, 293. From 1710, Enrichetta del Pozzo, recently married to the marquis d'Aix, effectively managed that family patrimony in her husband's absence as soldier and diplomat, Seyssel-Cressieu, *La Maison de Seyssel: ses origines, sa généalogie, son histoire*, 2 vols. (Grenoble, 1900), I, 100.

[156] See *DBI*, 'Balbiano di Colcavagno, Caterina' and A. Segre, 'Negoziati diplomatici della Corte di Prussia', *CGP*, VI, 285–6. Without going so far, many Savoyard

and in the War of the Spanish Succession asserted that should any of his own subjects fail in their duty they would be punished regardless of their quality (i.e. noble or not),[157] – a threat which he was ready to carry out on the surrender of key fortresses (see Chapter 4).

Not surprisingly, this ducal heavy-handedness made some nobles elsewhere anxious about the prospect of incorporation into the Savoyard state, particularly in neighbouring territories which were expected to pass to Victor Amadeus and whose nobles were used to a lighter touch on the part of government.[158] It also provoked some friction with his own nobles, and even prompted a rather striking assertion of what we might call a Savoyard version of 'aristocratic constitutionalism'. In 1702, the Chambéry Chambre des Comptes, which had pointed out the poverty of most Savoyard nobles by way of reply to the duke's order (1699) for the compensation of communities for the erosion of their tax base, declared that fiscal privilege (i.e. the taille exemption of the nobility, which was also then under pressure from Victor Amadeus) was a right 'born with the State itself'.[159] This view of the state, as an alliance of power and privilege, was not always adhered to by the duke in specific instances, not least because the military crisis facing Victor Amadeus meant that he sometimes recruited, rather than punished, those guilty of anti-seigneurial violence, to the disgust of many lords.[160] However, and perhaps because of the war-driven pressures of these decades, this perception of an essentially co-operative, but also contractual relationship between prince, or state, and privileged corps was restated in Jacques de Blonay's *Alphabet d'érudition*, published at Chambéry in 1708.[161]

However, while acknowledging some degree of social mobility, and of ducal coercion of some of Victor Amadeus' nobles, it would be completely wrong to see a social transformation, deliberately engineered by the Duke or otherwise, at the expense of the established noble elite of the Savoyard state in favour of newer blood between 1690 and 1713. Throughout Victor Amadeus' wars, the old court nobility retained its hold on the key positions in the state (in the administration, the army, at

---

noblewomen were determined to press their claims to precedence, including at the ducal court: see Di Gilio, *La Corte di Vittorio Amedeo II*, 231–2 for the marquise de Bellegarde (1695).
[157] VDM to Fagel, 21 Apr. 1706, Turin, ARAH/EA/VDM/30, 239. This followed critical comments in the Dutch press of the marchese di Caraglio's defence of Nice.
[158] See VA to Prince Eugene, Turin, 9 Feb. 1707, *CGP*, V, 8 ff., on such fears in the Milanese (where the nobility enjoyed a privileged role in government). Similar anxieties had been voiced during the Nine Years War.
[159] Nicolas, *La Savoie*, I, 40 ff. [160] *Ibid.*, II, 523, for an example of this in late 1703.
[161] *Ibid.*, II, 530. 1708 also saw the publication, at Turin, of another text on the nobility: Sapellani, 'La difesa necessaria della nobiltà ideale di Platone ...', Marchisio, 'Ideologia', 95 n. 133.

court and in diplomacy) and was still entrenched in these spheres at the conclusion of the War of the Spanish Succession.[162] There is no indication, for example, that the military crisis of 1703–04 saw non-nobles replace nobles in the officer corps. Nor, despite the fact that some (very few) nobles did suffer sequestration for failing to return home from foreign service, did they suffer for long. During the War of the Spanish Succession, the loyalty of the marchese di San Damiano (who levied one of the new regiments raised in the winter of 1703–04) removed the stain of disloyalty incurred by his father in the previous conflict and resulted in the reversal of the sequestration which had then been imposed.[163] Confiscation was not always effective anyway, because of the mass of claims on a noble patrimony of a wife (or widow) and children, whose interests (protected by the family systems of the nobility) Victor Amadeus could and would not harm.[164] More importantly, most of his nobles were loyal.[165] Family traditions of service, which helped distinguish nobles, were also a highly marketable commodity in a tense military and political situation. Some 'new' men of relatively humble origin, such as Gropello, could rise by application, talent and what we might call blind loyalty to Victor Amadeus' interests; they had little else to offer. Financiers and military contractors also took advantage of the needs of a state at war to gain influence, wealth and status in these decades. On the other hand, some nobles were casualties of the various pressures at work between 1690 and 1720. Nevertheless, although there was clearly some unusual social mobility in the Savoyard state, a mobility clearly related to the war and the associated growth of state bureaucracy, Victor Amadeus' needs probably worked as much to the advantage as to the detriment of the

[162] See Balani, *Il Vicario*, 130, on those appointed vicario of Turin between 1687 and 1723; and Di Gilio, 'La corte di Vittorio Amedeo II', appendix, for court officeholders.

[163] For San Damiano, see Saluces, *Histoire militaire*, V, 67; *CGP*, I, 63 and Victor Amadeus to Camera dei Conti, 22 Apr. 1704, in AST/CdC, art. 495 (Rappresaglie), m. 1. See the experience of the Tana family during the Nine Years War, in Levi, *Inheriting Power*, 132 ff.

[164] See the case of conte Gerolamo Radicati di Cocconato, who failed to obey a ducal order to appear before the grand chancellor in Turin, and instead fled to the Republic of Genoa. Following an order to confiscate his property, his wife, contessa Flavia Teresa di San Nazaro, protested on behalf of herself (claiming her dowry and other endowments) and her stepchildren, documents (1713) in AST/Provincia di Asti, m. 14/15. For the background to this episode, see Venturi, *Saggi*, 18.

[165] Some took the opportunity to make ringing declarations of this. In 1703, marchese Francesco Maria Adalberto Pallavicino delle Frabose, governor of Asti province, holder of court office and putative colonel of a new Asti regiment, prefaced an account of his own conduct with the hope that his loyal service would match that of his ancestors (to the House of Savoy), marchese Pallavicino to VA, 7 Oct. 1703, Asti, *CGP*, I, 86. See, also, Parella to ST, 18 July 1704, Luserna, *CGP*, II, 501.

existing elite, whose position may in fact have been strengthened in these decades.[166] The expanding Savoyard diplomatic network (see Chapter 3) provided new opportunities for nobles,[167] who were also entrenching themselves in the state's developing administrative cadres.[168] Some did so by purchasing offices at a time when their sale was one means for the duke to finance war but this was by no means their sole route to office.[169] For those communities and individuals feeling the pressure of Savoyard state formation, nobles (even though they were acting as officers or officials rather than in a private capacity) were often the instruments of that heavier handed and more intrusive regime.[170]

The explanation for the Savoyard nobility's continued pre-eminence was in part that the state simply could not do without the nobility. This dependence of the emerging state on the nobility is particularly striking in the case of the army. Nobles' continued military pre-eminence was founded in part upon their possession of an appropriate education and

[166] See Nicolas, *La Savoie*, 1, 292–3, for the purchase by the marquis de Sales, in 1698, from the heavily indebted marquise de Cruseilles, of the comté de Duingt and Chateauvieux, purchased by her father in 1681, and *ibid.*, 281, for the acquisition of land in Savoy by the Costa between 1685 and 1722. In Piedmont, see the Falletti di Barolo purchase of Pocapaglia (above).

[167] From 1706 the abate Carlo Alessandro Doria del Maro was Victor Amadeus' representative at Genoa, subsequently being sent to Rome and Madrid, finally crowning his official career with appointment as viceroy of Sardinia. His successor at Genoa between 1709 and 1713 was another scion of the Piedmontese nobility, the abate d'Angrogna: Tallone, 'La vendita di Finale', 270–1. Conte (and senatore) Lascaris di Castellar, of a junior branch of an old family, and conte (and referendary) Ruschis (of the Turin patriciate) were appointed Victor Amadeus's plenipotentiaries to negotiate the details of the new border with France, in 1713, following the conclusion of the War of the Spanish Succession: see instructions, 2 Oct. 1713, AST/Provincia di Pinerolo, m. 26/21.

[168] Conte Sclarandi, for example, served as war commissary in the War of the Spanish Succession, see VA to Sclarandi re the lodging of troops in various territories in the Astigiano, Nov. 1694, AST/Provincia di Asti, m. 29/3. But this was not entirely new: Levi, *Inheriting Power*, 187 n. 15.

[169] Baldassare Saluzzo di Paesana, for example, purchased a life senatorship for 10,400 lire, in 1692 and in 1697 the intendancy of the province of Asti, Woolf, *Studi sulla nobiltà*, 126.

[170] The minutes of the council of Bra during the War of the Spanish Succession show that nobles (marchese Pallavicino, conte della Rocca, marchese di Pianezza, conte di Montalenghe, marchese di Cortanze, marchese di Castagnole, conte Robilant) rather than Victor Amadeus himself were the source of orders and demands for men, money and so on, those nobles being invariably referred to by their noble titles rather than by (in fact without any indication of) their offices – by contrast with men like Gropello, the provincial director, Gallino, and the intendant, Angiono, whose names are preceded by their office – E. Milano, 'La partecipazione alla guerra di successione spagnuola della citta di Bra illustrata negli Ordinati del Consiglio', *CGP*, VIII, passim. In 1692, the cavaliere Tana d'Entraque, colonel of the White Cross regiment, arrested the marchese di Monforte, VDM to Fagel, 22 Dec. 1692, ARAH/SG/8643/305.

experience often absent in other sectors of Savoyard society.[171] But above all, Victor Amadeus depended upon the co-operation of his nobles and the deployment of their local influence (and material resources) to mobilise men for his war effort.[172] The single most compelling example, particularly in the 1690s, of the crucial role of the nobility in this respect was the marchese di Parella. His influence throughout Piedmont made him a key figure in both conflicts when it was a question of using the militia[173] and his resources were tapped in the levy (1694), of a Swiss unit for his son and heir, the marchese di Andorno.[174] Similarly, the levy of the new regiments formed in 1703–04 was largely left to the nobles (many of them from among the court nobility), who had connections and leverage in the provinces where those forces were to be raised. These included Govone in Alba, Bagnasco in Cuneo and marchese Guido Biandrate di San Giorgio in Fossano.[175] In the Duchy of Savoy, too, the resources and influence of other leading individuals and families might be exploited, necessarily, by a state with an independent infrastructure still in process of formation. In 1703 the supreme command in the Duchy was (almost inevitably) conferred on the marquis de Sales, scion of one of the Duchy's greatest families (and of the court nobility). For the same reasons, Victor Amadeus' nobles could also play an important political role: in 1704, for example, Parella was used by the duke in an abortive attempt to prevent by negotiation the defection to the French of the Val San Martino.[176]

Nobles' continued dominance of the commanding heights of the Savoyard state (army, court, diplomacy) reflected other attributes and resources which the developing state needed in this and other spheres of operation and which it found in most plentiful supply among its nobles. As we have seen, in the Savoyard state as elsewhere in Europe nobles

---

[171] In 1703, the marchese di Pianezza, given the military command of Turin and its province by Victor Amadeus in his own absence, supported a proposal to flood part of Piedmont (as a defensive measure) with reference to what he had seen in the Low Countries and to a leading text on fortification, Pianezza to VA, 25 Oct. 1703, *CGP*, I, 103 ff. The following spring, the duke sent to the commendatore Deshais, commanding at Vercelli, which was under siege, the conte de Guarene, who had attended the exclusive and expensive Accademia Reale and understood the art of fortification, VA to Deshais, 23 May 1704, *CGP*, II, 132.

[172] See *CGP*, I, 114, for commendatore Solaro as commander of local militia and *ibid.*, 87, for conte Guglielmo Antonio Radicati di Robella as captain of Asti militia.

[173] VA to Parella, 23 Sept. 1704, *CGP*, 2, 584; and Ferrero della Marmora, *Parella*, 461 ff. See VDM to States, 1 and 29 July 1705, Turin, ARAH/EA/VDM/30, 76 and 89 for Parella's role as leader of militia and of his son Andorno as leader of the Vaudois irregulars.

[174] Duboin, XXVI, 1123; Bianchi, 'Guerra e politica', 7 ff. Parella agreed to raise, clothe and arm (except for rifles) the men, who would only then become the responsibility of Victor Amadeus.   [175] *CGP*, I, 61.

[176] ST to Priè, Crescentino, 30 June 1704, *CGP*, IV, 90–1.

often did what they could to ensure the sort of education that would qualify their sons for office. However, and more importantly, a technical training was by no means crucial to success in these spheres. The extent to which men, such as Ludovico Eusebio Solaro di Moretta, marchese di Dogliani (1635–97) could easily switch from one post to another, moving from the court to diplomacy, to civil and military employments, is further evidence of the fact that government and its operations were still not yet narrowly professionalised or specialised (see Chapters 3 and 4).[177] Most importantly, nobles were likely to have that experience and understanding of, and ease in the world of courts where so much of their work would be done, which their status and education as nobles gave them. At the same time, Victor Amadeus needed to have his court attended by the distinguished, polished, old nobility to maintain its own brilliance and pretensions.[178] Only nobles would do for this sort of office.[179] Given their influence and importance, the duke also needed to associate his nobles with his most important political projects. It is worth noting, in connection with the reports circulating in the Dutch Republic critical of the marchese di Caraglio's defence of Nice, that Victor Amadeus was also anxious to ensure that a proper picture of Caraglio's conduct was disseminated abroad, reflecting the importance of the loyalty of his great nobles as a means of reassuring his allies.[180] Their high profile also gave

[177] The marchese di Dogliani, having participated in the war against Genoa (1672) and in the suppression of the Vaudois (1686), was sent as Victor Amadeus' envoy to Louis XIV's court (1686). On his return to Piedmont in 1690, he fought at the battles of both Staffarda and Marsaglia and received the Order of the Annunziata, Barberis, 'Il conte Orazio Provana', 105. According to Di Gilio, 'La Corte di Vittorio Amedeo II', 88–9, only one-third of 134 court nobles (1680–1713) held only court office.

[178] See Marchisio, 'Ideologia', 93, n. 125, for the commendatore Solaro's letter of December 1694 to the marchesa di Rosignano on Victor Amadeus' great desire to have as many women (of quality) as possible at his court; and Venturi, Saggi, 20, for that young noble (aged nine) entering the household of Victor Amadeus' nephew, Prince Thomas, in 1707.

[179] This view was not confined to Victor Amadeus, or to princes: in 1706, when the duke's family fled to the Genoese Republic, the latter deputed nobles to formally receive his duchess, VDM to Fagel, 30 June 1706, ARAH/EA/VDM/30, 292.

[180] In 1704, as his enemies occupied much of Victor Amadeus' state, the Dutch envoy noted the growing consternation of the Savoyard nobility (and its hope that the duke would avoid the worst by settling with the French king – presumably as in 1696), VDM to Fagel, 25 July and 15 Aug. 1704, Turin, ARAH/EA/VDM/29, 128, 145. In 1704, too, Parella was recalled from the valleys after having received French peace proposals, but was replaced by his son, Andorno, who could exercise his father's influence there, VDM to Fagel, 19 Aug. 1704, Turin, ARAH/EA/VDM/29, 146–7; same to States, 2 Sept. 1704, Turin, ARAH/EA/VDM/29, 154. (Parella's conduct may have embarrassed the Duke vis-à-vis his allies, his recall thus being politic.) The following year, as the French moved to besiege Turin, van der Meer reported the measures taken by the capital's principal inhabitants (nobles) to leave, VDM to Fagel, 10 June 1705, ARAH/EA/VDM/30, 65.

nobles opportunities (by contrast with non-nobles), which many were ready to exploit, in the safeguarding of their patrimonies in these difficult years.[181] Last, but by no means least, nobles were also more likely than any others to possess the material resources to bear the costs of state service at a time of extreme financial difficulty.[182]

For their part, nobles were sometimes the duke's foremost critics (see Chapter 4). However, most found it rewarding to respond positively to Victor Amadeus' needs, and to co-operate with him. As before 1690, for numerous cadets state employment meant sufficient income to maintain their status.[183] Even if not paid well or, particularly in these decades, promptly, army and diplomatic salaries were among the best in the Savoyard state. In effect, the state was channelling substantial parts of the sums it raised in taxation and received in subsidies, in the way of the nobility, thus enhancing its take of total wealth.[184] Success in one sphere might bring other appointments, honours and opportunities.[185] Nobles' own influence and patronage – and in this period particularly their military patronage – expanded as servants of the state.[186] Equally importantly, the fiscal crisis of the Savoyard state was not merely a threat:[187] it

[181] See Guarene to the Imperial commander re contributions on his property, 1706, Provana, 'Lettere . . .', *CGP*, VIII, 300; and Guarene's hopes of exploiting contacts with the Spanish commander, Colmenero, to save the family estate, in the event of an enemy advance, *ibid.*, 317.

[182] In 1690, Victor Amadeus was said to be looking for somebody to send to London who would effectively fund himself, Fuensalida to Carlos II, 7 Sept. 1690, Milan, AGS/3413/21. Similarly, only distinguished nobles could entertain and at the same time watch over the detained ambassadors in Turin in 1703 of Louis XIV and Philip V, L. Bély, *Espions et ambassadeurs au temps de Louis XIV* (Paris, 1990), 358 and VDM to Fagel, 11 Mar. 1704, Turin, ARAH/EA/29, 46.

[183] Woolf, *Studi sulla nobiltà*, 62.

[184] In addition, diplomats invariably received parting gifts from the sovereigns to whom they had been sent. Like Victor Amadeus, some gave their own portrait in a diamond frame to departing diplomats, de la Tour receiving a diamond framed portrait of the elector of Brandenburg on leaving Berlin in 1694, DLT to ST, 1 Oct. 1694, The Hague, AST/LM/Olanda, m. 4. Some princes, however, gave cash. In 1713 the British government gave his secretary Perrino £300 for conte Maffei, PRO/LC5/3, f. 15.

[185] In 1692, on his return from his extraordinary mission to Vienna and Munich, the marchese di Cinzano was appointed first president of the Senate of Piedmont (although he was required to advance a substantial cash sum, or *finanza*), *DBI*, 'della Chiesa'.

[186] The capitulations for the levy of new regiments agreed with the marquis de Chaumont (1689) and with the conte di Massetti (1690) allowed them to appoint most of the first tranche of officers, Saluces, *Histoire militaire*, I, 330.

[187] That threat could anyway be moderated: see the decision of the Camera dei Conti, 1699, reducing the *cavalcata* demand on conte Cacherano d'Osasco, given the damage inflicted on his states during the Nine Years War, AST/Prima Archivazione/Cavalcata, m. 1/1.

also offered opportunities, at least for the wealthier nobles. Carlo Lodovico Falletti di Barolo was just one of many of Victor Amadeus' noble subjects to infeudate substantial property, purchase alienated *tasso* and transform loan credits into the same.[188] Some nobles expanded their own patrimonies at the expense of the towns and communities of Piedmont, many of which suffered 'dismemberment' (i.e. the loss of subject territories and communities).[189] Nobles also exploited the enormous financial pressure created by the wars for the communities to lend to, and increase their hold on, the latter. In 1690, for example, the community of Pancalieri secured loans from, *inter alia*, the marchese di Priè, to meet the sudden and overwhelming fiscal burden associated with the start of the war.[190] Clearly, some noble families found Victor Amadeus' wars provided an excellent opportunity to enhance their own dignity and to extend their patrimonies and influence.[191] State (or ducal) service also brought more indirect rewards.[192] Sometimes these rewards were the result of corruption and the abuse of an official position.[193] Nobles were able not only to entrench themselves in the developing state but also, and because of this, to mediate beween it and others within it. They were appealed to (admittedly, not always successfully) in the hope of modifying the demands of that state. In the spring of 1706, the syndics of Fossano sent one of their number, conte Negro di Caselletto,

---

[188] Woolf, *Studi sulla nobiltà*, 52.

[189] See the infeudation of conte Carlo Giovanni Giacomo Pastoris with Lamporo (detached from the jurisdiction of Crescentino), the acquisition by conte Giacomo Nomis of the fief and *tasso* of Cossilla, and the infeudation of conte Nicola Ocello with Nichilino and its *tasso*, AST/PCF/1693–94, f. 161, 165, 238. Subsequently, Nichilino was detached from the jurisdiction of Moncalieri in favour of conte Ocello, AST/PCF/1694–95, f. 151. The marquis of Saint-Thomas had Rosta detached from Rivoli, to his own advantage: memorie di un borghese di Rivoli, BRT, Storia Patria, 4076, f. 84.

[190] Caligaris, 'Vita e lavoro', 57 ff. According to P. Bullio Dranzon, 'L'Evoluzione patrimoniale degli Scarampi di Camino dalla seconda metà del secolo XVI alla prima metà del secolo XVIII' (tesi di laurea, University of Torino, 1965–6), most of this family's *censi* were acquired in the war years (especially the 1690s). See Woolf, *Studi sulla nobiltà*, 168, for the nobles among the creditors of Bra in 1720.

[191] Conte Solaro della Margherita purchased (1698) the fief of Panfey for his son and heir, Rondolino, 'Vita Torinese', *CGP*, VII, 41; conte Lelio Bava (of the Costigliole) was invested count of Valle di Baratonia in 1699, *ibid.*, 422.

[192] In 1706, for example, Victor Amadeus ordered his minister at the emperor's court to press the interests there of the widow of the conte di Sanfrè, on behalf of the marchese di Caraglio, one of the duke's leading collaborators in the War of the Spanish Succession, VA to conte Tarino, 28 Apr. 1706, *CGP*, V, 44.

[193] See the case against the conte di Rivara, governor of Alba, in 1702, accusing him of receiving bribes to exempt those not legally excused from a recent levy of troops in his province, AST/MC, m. 10/8; and Marchisio, 'Ideologia', 121, for illegal conduct (again 1702) to benefit friends and relations.

to Turin, to seek the withdrawal of two regiments billeted in the town.[194] In May of that year, the sindics of Alba bestowed on the marchese di Cortanze the title Protector of the City, and granted him and his heirs the privileges of a native of the city, in gratitude for his efforts in defence of the town — and perhaps hoping for their future continuance.[195]

Princes, in the Savoyard state as elsewhere, needed nobles to articulate effectively the structures of their developing state. This was, no doubt, one reason why Victor Amadeus could not simply suppress criticism and dissent emanating from within that elite (see Chapter 4). Nobles served their own interests by responding positively to that need.[196] These men, their resources and influence therefore contributed crucially to the mobilisation of Savoyard resources for war and thus to the whole process of state formation, between 1690 and 1713/20, in ways that lesser men could not. Indeed, in many respects the representative figures of this phase of Savoyard state formation are not so much the non-noble Gropello and Mellarède[197] but nobles such as Ignazio Solaro di Moretta, marchese del Borgo and Ercole Tommaso Roero, marchese di Cortanze. The former was the son of parents who were both from the old court elite, his father founding the del Borgo branch of the Dogliani family. The young marchese received his first court appointment during the regency of Madame Reale, in 1680. He demonstrated, in a *mémoire* of 1700, his command of the complex legal and historical issues related to Victor Amadeus' claims to various French inheritances, thus revealing his grasp of some of the key concerns of ducal diplomacy. Between 1703 and 1713 he served as Victor Amadeus' envoy at that crucial diplomatic centre, The Hague, and led the Savoyard delegation, at the Utrecht peace congress. On his return to Turin in 1713 he was appointed instructor of the future Charles Emanuel III, member of the Council of Finance in Victor Amadeus' absence in Sicily, governor of Monferrato and (from 1717) the first of the secretaries of state for foreign affairs in the wake of Victor Amadeus' reforms of that year, a post he held until 1732.

---

[194] For a similar occurrence at Bra in 1704, see E. Milano, 'La partecipazione alla Guerra della Città di Bra', *CGP*, VII, 391. Such resort to nobles to mediate (and reduce) the demands of a more intrusive state did not end with the war: see Marchisio, 'Ideologia', 119, n. 256. [195] Eusebio, 'Alba...', *CGP*, IX, 472–3.

[196] In 1714, the Prince of Piedmont ordered the Senate of Turin not to proceed in a dispute between the marquis d'Aix and his brothers and sisters, declaring that the marquis' zeal (in the service of his prince) prevented his attendance, Seyssel-Cressieu, *Maison de Seyssel*, 120.

[197] These two are identified as among the key collaborators with Victor Amadeus in his transformation of the Savoyard state after 1713 by Quazza, *Le riforme*, I, 23 ff.

In the meantime, in 1709 he had succeeded to the substantial patrimony of his cousin, Giambattista Solaro, marchese di Dogliani (who had died without heirs). This inheritance helped ensure that del Borgo was among the wealthiest nobles in Piedmont in the 1730s.[198] As for Cortanze, he was a scion of one of the great Piedmontese families, Roero. A vassal of the Pope, he was ordered by him (1702) not to recognise Victor Amadeus as sovereign, but this does not seem to have affected his loyalty to the duke. In 1703 he was colonel of a battalion of the Asti militia, which subsequently became the Cortanze regiment. In 1707 (a year in which he was promoted within the ducal household) he took possession of Alessandria in Victor Amadeus' name and in 1708 was sent on a pre-campaign mission to Vienna. After 1713 the appointments of this able, loyal and multifaceted nobleman included the governorships of Biella, Alessandria and Turin (the citadel) and envoy to London.[199] Other versatile, noble collaborators of Victor Amadeus in this era included the Savoyard marquis d'Aix, baron Filippo Guglielmo di Saint-Rémy, the first Savoyard viceroy of Sardinia, and, last but by no means least, the marchese di Caraglio (d. 1723).[200]

Options outside the Savoyard state were narrowing for most Savoyard nobles, who were becoming more enmeshed with in the emerging state structure, a development typified by the experience of the Falletti di Barolo family. After 1713 the family's participation in the Savoyard state, at its highest levels, would be even more striking.[201] However, this could be a slow process, and was not necessarily complete by 1713. A number of Savoyard nobles retained links with foreign princes, including Parella

[198] *DBI*, 'Carlo Gerolamo Solaro Moretta, marchese del Borgo' and 'Ignazio Solaro di Moretta, marchese del Borgo'; L. Einaudi, 'Le entrate pubbliche dello stato sabaudo nei bilanci e nei conti dei tesorieri durante la guerra di successione spagnuola', *CGP*, IX, 5. See the (admittedly rather later) portrait of the latter (wearing the Order of the Annunziata) in the Palazzo Reale, Turin, reproduced on the cover of D. Frigo, *Principe, ambasciatori e 'jus gentium': l'amministrazione della politica estera nel Piemonte del Settecento* (Rome, 1991). Without wishing to claim that del Borgo's securing of the Dogliani patrimony was any other than in accordance with the proper rules of inheritance, it is highly likely that this went without hitch because of the marchese's close relation with the duke. One foreign agent at Utrecht thought del Borgo expected or hoped to secure the viceroyalty of Sicily for himself or a relation, Bély, *Espions et ambassadeurs*, 530.

[199] Biographical and career details in Rondolino, 'Vita Torinese', *CGP*, VII, 108 n. 2. For household in Turin, 1705, see E. Casanova, 'Censimento di Torino alla vigilia dell'assedio (29 agosto–6 settembre 1705)', *CGP*, VIII, 111. There is a copy of the papal monitory, Aug. 1702, in AST/Provincia di Asti, m. 30/4.

[200] See *DBI, sub voce*; Marc de Seyssel-Cressieu, *La Maison de Seyssel*; CGP, VIII, 326; and *DBI*, 'Caraglio'.

[201] Woolf, *Studi sulla nobiltà*, 61 ff.

with the emperor and the marchese Pallavicino with Carlos II of Spain.²⁰² Of course, serving their own sovereign and a foreign prince were by no means mutually exclusive for Savoyard nobles, the expulsion of the French from Casale being advantageous to both Victor Amadeus and Carlos II. In addition, the duke's lack of a male heir before 1699, the continuing vulnerability of the Savoyard state and their own interests may have suggested the wisdom of maintaining such foreign connections. Some of Victor Amadeus' nobles still sought and obtained foreign nobility and titles,²⁰³ while Ercole Turinetti, marchese di Priè took the opportunity to transfer to the emperor's service (i.e. that of an ally of his master, but one who could also offer more by way of rewards than could Victor Amadeus) during the War of the Spanish Succession.²⁰⁴ Similarly, although the general trend was towards marriage within the confines of the Savoyard state, some of Victor Amadeus' more distinguished and wealthier noble subjects still looked beyond the narrow confines of the Savoyard state when they married. These incuded the Falletti di Barolo and the Isnardi di Caraglio.²⁰⁵ Many nobles, particularly in the Duchy of Savoy, still sent their sons (and daughters) to be educated in France.²⁰⁶ Some nobles sought to defend themselves against the more intrusive, threatening symptoms of the developing state, for example the nascent *perequazione* (see Chapter 2), by denying the competence of the Senate of Turin, and appealing to other jurisdictions.²⁰⁷ Most nobles, in fact continued to see the state as something distant. Despite the tightening links between nobles and state in this period, many Savoyard nobles (and especially the head of a family) might still do little beyond managing the patrimony (a considerable responsibility for many), and have little to do with the state. The conte di Guarene, for example, retired from the army

---

[202] See marchese Pallavicino to Bazan, 18 July 1695, Casale, AGS/Estado/3659/19, and Bazan to Carlos II, 29 July 1695 and 25 Jan. 1697, Turin, AGS/E/3659/15, 16, urging payment of the arrears of a pension granted the family of the marchese Pallavicino by Philip IV, citing the marchese's service in contributing to the expulsion of the French from Casale in 1695, the influence he (and his wife) enjoyed as a member of the duke's court (and as a recently appointed knight of the Annunziata) and pointing out that an earlier order, of 1695, to pay the marchese's pension arrears had had little effect.

[203] See conte Tarino's imperial diploma. Oct. 1691, in AST/Provincia di Asti, m. 15 (Cossambrato)/7.

[204] See Provana di Collegno, 'Lettere . . .', *CGP*, VIII, 327 n. 2.

[205] Woolf, *Studi sulla nobiltà*, 54; *DBI*, 'Caraglio' for the inheritance (1703) of a substantial patrimony in Lorraine (on the death of a mother).

[206] See Nicolas, *La Savoie*, I, 293, 395, for the education of Charles-Joseph Castagnery de Châteauneuf, son of a member of the Chambéry Senate in Paris between 1695 and 1708.

[207] See Woolf, *Studi sulla nobiltà*, 99, for an appeal to the Senate of Casale by the Valperga di Rivara (*c.* 1699).

in 1707 (i.e. once the great crisis of the Savoyard state had passed in 1706) on grounds of ill health and devoted himself thereafter to his estate and growing family.[208] The concerns of most nobles (including those who were engaging more with the state) remained very traditional. They included the protection (and enlargement) of the family and its patrimony, the foundation of noble influence and power.[209] The pursuit of these objectives ensured that nobles continued to behave much as they had before 1690.[210]

CONCLUSION

For Quazza and Woolf, Victor Amadeus II's reign was one in which the nobility of the Savoyard state, having exploited ducal weakness before 1684 was, generally speaking, the duke's victim.[211] This seems especially striking after 1713. Nobles were increasingly expected to play a part in the new military structure created in the aftermath of the War of the Spanish Succession, while the emerging intendancy (see Chapters 1 and 4) would be used, *inter alia*, to discipline the lesser nobles of, for example, the Duchy of Savoy.[212] But the most striking aspects of this anti-noble policy were the fiscal ones. These included the confiscation, or revocation, from 1719 of nearly 200 fiefs which were supposedly held illegally by the Piedmonte nobility, and their sale, to the new so-called 'nobility of 1722'; and the completion of the *perequazione*, as a result of which the nobility lost nearly one-third of its fiscal exemptions.[213] However, it is by no means clear that these measures were part of a deliber-

---

[208] Provana di Collegno, 'Lettere . . .', *CGP*, VIII, 287 ff. The fifth conte di Canale's diplomatic career from the 1730s was his family's first real contact of this sort with the Savoyard state, Ruata, *Canale*, 11 ff.

[209] For the (unsuccessful) efforts of the old and distinguished Provana di Druent to avoid extinction by marrying (1695) a daughter, Elena Matilde, to a Falletti di Barolo, see Woolf, *Studi sulla nobiltà*, 55. The wedding was a major occasion for noble society in Turin. In 1713 Carlo Maria Saluzzo di Paesana urged one of his sons who had taken holy orders to abandon them and marry (to continue the family), since the only one of Carlo Maria's sons to marry had only one son, *ibid.*, 125.

[210] See Woolf, *Studi sulla nobiltà*, 105, for a primogeniture established in 1698; and Nicolas, *La Savoie*, I, 401, for a violent attack, in 1700, on the château of Belmont by the servants of one noblewoman following an unfavourable decision by the Senate of Chambéry.   [211] Quazza, *Le riforme*, 1, 164 ff.; Woolf, *Studi sulla nobiltà*, 9–10, 42.

[212] In 1718, one Savoyard noble who fell foul of Victor Amadeus denounced the latter as a tyrant, G. Symcox, *Victor Amadeus II: absolutism in the Savoyard state 1675–1730* (London, 1983), 191 and Nicolas, *La Savoie*, I, 629 ff.

[213] Woolf, *Studi sulla nobiltà*, 109, 133–4. According to *ibid.*, 71, revocation was under consideration from at least Dec. 1713. The *perequazione*, although prepared by Victor Amadeus was not in fact put into effect until after his abdication in 1730, Symcox, *Victor Amadeus*, 202 ff.

ately anti-noble policy, rather than simply expedients to reduce the massive debt accumulated during the Nine Years War and the War of the Spanish Succession, and to finance the costs of the defence of Sicily against Spanish attack (and, potentially, a European war) at a time when Victor Amadeus was isolated in Europe and thus unable to mobilise the foreign subsidies which had been so important between 1690 and 1713 (see Chapter 2). The great majority of Piedmontese fiefs and fiefholders were not affected. Nor is it as obvious as used to be thought that the supposedly new nobility of 1722 was so much of a triumph of new social forces. Among the noble titles given out in 1722 was the marquisate of Borgo San Dalmazzo received by Victor Amadeus' collaborator from the old nobility, Ignazio Solaro di Moretta, who thus became marchese del Borgo. If, and it is by no means certain, Victor Amadeus was pursuing an anti-noble policy, this may well have been because the preceding war years had strengthened, not weakened, the position of his nobility (and that of the elite within that noble elite).[214]

Indeed, the years between 1690 and 1713 had in many respects prepared the way for post-1713 developments. On the one hand, the wars necessitated the elaboration of new state structures (notably the intendancy) and the mobilisation of resources which created opportunities for 'new men' like Gropello. However, we should not allow this to obscure the enormous contribution to Victor Amadeus' success of his nobles. The nobility above all others were, not least because of the traditional bonds of vassalage, expected to serve their prince[215] and most nobles – many more than before – undoubtedly did so after 1690, often at great cost. Some families which had hitherto been largely on the periphery of the state structure were drawn into it as it expanded; and were entrenching themselves within it (and above all in the army). Loyalty was closely bound up with self-interest. As before 1690, state service met some basic noble needs which were intimately related to family strategies, not least the need for decorous niches for younger sons. Victor Amadeus' resolution of both the domestic and foreign political problems which beset the Savoyard state before 1684 largely removed the necessity for his nobles, greater or lesser, to seek (as had Parella and some of the Mondovì elite in the crisis of 1680–82) patrons and even

---

[214] According to Quazza, Le *Riforme*, I, 173, only 39% of the fiefs sold in 1722 went to the old nobility. But Quazza also notes that less than 8% of the fiefs legitimately held were not in the possession of this group. The four richest Piedmontese families at the end of the wars were from the old nobility, Woolf, *Studi sulla nobiltà*, 125–6, 147.

[215] Victor Amadeus laid great stress on these bonds at the time of his abdication and attempt to recover his throne from 1730 onwards, see D. Carutti, *Storia della diplomazia della Corte di Savoia*, 4 vols. (Turin, 1875–80), IV, 13.

refuge and to some extent deliberately restricted foreign contracts and opportunities. After 1713, Victor Amadeus institutionalised the growing military role at home of his own nobles, evident since 1690, and bound them more closely to himself and the emerging state structures.[216] Since he had also needed their wealth to help finance his wars, nobles (or rather those nobles with the resources to exploit their opportunity) turned this, too, to advantage.

Victor Amadeus was not fundamentally anti-noble,[217] and could not afford this luxury. Nobles were the most likely to have the skills he needed in arms and diplomacy. Their local influence also often made good the weaknesses of what was still an incomplete state structure (see Chapter 4). For many important offices, Victor Amadeus (like other princes) continued to see illustrious ancestry as a strong recommendation, even a necessity. In September 1713, the patents appointing conte Giorgio Michele Piosasco di None captain of the second company of Victor Amadeus' prestigious bodyguards specifically mentioned the 'splendour of his nobility' as a reason for his promotion.[218] From 1714, illustrious birth was one of the qualities required in those appointed viceroy of Sicily, and later Sardinia. Not surprisingly, therefore, certain individual and family names from the old court nobility recur in the crucial spheres of Savoyard state formation; notably the army – includ-

---

[216] This was in part, too, a solution to the European-wide problem (and increasingly perceived as such) of the existence of large numbers of idle, poor and unproductive nobles, see G. Pérouse, 'Etat de la Savoie à la fin du XVlle siècle: documents inédits . . . aux Archives d'Etat de Turin', *Mémoires et documents de la Société Savoisienne d'Histoire et d'Archeologie*, 63, 1926, 24 ff. The successful assertion of a royal right of nomination to senior ecclesiastical posts in the Savoyard state (in the Concordats of 1727 and 1741) confirmed the value of co-operation with the state in this sphere too: see M. T. Silvestrini, *La Politica della Religione. Il Governo Ecclesiastico nello Stato Sabaudo del XVIII Secolo* (Florence, 1997), 293 ff.

[217] Indeed, he used the instruments of the developing state to protect the interests of the nobility. In 1713, not long after taking possession of Sicily, Victor Amadeus granted a lieutenancy in one of his regiments to a scion of the Sicilian nobility, to get the man out of Sicily and free his family from the problems he caused them. Victor Amadeus ordered that the man be watched, but that due regard should also be paid to his distinguished birth, VA to Rhebinder, 29 Dec. 1713, Palermo, AST/MM/Impieghi, m. 1 d'addizione.

[218] Galli della Loggia, *Cariche*, 2, 512. That same year, the ducal patents mentioned Pràla's distinguished blood as one reason (besides his zeal and merit) for his appointment as governor and lieutenant general of the city and county of Nice, *CGP*, II, 272. The education of the duke's children was, almost inevitably, entrusted to members of the old court nobility: in 1708 the marquis de Coudrée was appointed governor of the prince of Piedmont and the future Charles Emanuel III, Ricuperati, 'Il Settecento', 489.

ing the pivotal provincial governorships[219] – and diplomacy. Without getting involved in day-to-day administration (which they would have felt was beneath them), such men – who were the duke's daily companions at court – were a crucial link between centre and localities. They helped mobilise the latter, and thus contributed to the process of state formation. In addition, and *pace* Quazza, many of Victor Amadeus' other collaborators, including the future marchese d'Ormea, far from being non-noble bourgeois were noble (although greatly inferior to nobles like Parella) and expected promotion within the nobility as their reward for serving the duke. For the non-noble, nobility itself was often the reward they sought and achieved. Individual nobles may have incurred ducal displeasure, and some families certainly suffered after 1713, but nobles generally were participators in – rather than being excluded from – the process of Savoyard state formation between 1690 and 1720. Typically the nobility (and particularly the lesser nobility) of Piedmont, Savoy, Aosta, Nice and many (but not all) of the new territories sought to batten onto the Savoyard state not combat it.[220]

[219] For the stranglehold of the nobility, and above all the old nobility, on this crucial, multifaceted post, see the list of governors in the autumn of 1703 in *CGP*, I, 61. A preliminary survey of the names and titles of those appointed provincial governors *c.* 1690–1720, using the Patenti Controllo Finanze, in the AST confirms this broad conclusion.

[220] Whereas many of the discontented Sicilian nobles defected to the invading Spanish forces in 1718–19 (despite Victor Amadeus' deliberate efforts to attract and even buy their loyalty from 1713), few – if any – of his mainland subjects seem to have responded to the emperor's attempt to exploit resentment at the recent investigation of fief holders and revocation, by summoning many of those fief holders to acknowledge his suzerainty, which was regarded by Victor Amadeus as an infringement of his own sovereignty: Molesworth to [?], 12 Feb. 1721, Turin. SP 92/30.

CHAPTER 6

REGIONS AND COMMUNITIES IN THE SAVOYARD STATE, 1690–1720

State formation in early modern Europe was, as we have seen, an internal as much as an external process. This involved not merely the development of new administrative structures for the more effective control of subjects and mobilisation of resources but also the greater integration into those structures of traditionally independent provinces or communities, what Giorgio Chittolini has called the progressive 'aggregation of particularisms' and what Carlo Belfanti and Marzio Romani have called the domestic *politica della frontiera*, i.e. the removal of internal frontiers, matching the rationalising of external borders with other states.[1] The Savoyard state, like so many early modern European states, comprised a number of different regions and communities, each with its own distinct sense of itself and of its relationship with its prince, and, therefore, one in which this process of integration was, in some respects, appropriate. And in fact, each region of the Savoyard state had its own distinct experience of state formation, not least in this decisive phase of the process between 1690 and 1713. Hitherto, what has most attracted attention has been the model of integration offered by the province of Mondovì, namely, the military conquest and definitive subjugation of a hitherto rebellious, and to a degree unintegrated, region of the state.

However, as Beik has demonstrated in the case of Languedoc, forced subjection was by no means the only means of integration. The same is true of the Savoyard state. Rather strikingly, at the start of both the Nine Years War and of the War of the Spanish Succession, Victor Amadeus sought to save the Duchy of Savoy from French conquest by having it

---

[1] Chittolini, cited in A. Barbero, 'Principe e nobiltà negli stati sabaudi: gli Challant in Valle d'Aosta tra XIV e XVI secolo', in C. Mozzarelli, ed., *"Familia" del principe e familia aristocratica*, 2 vols. (Rome, 1988), I, 245 ff.; Carlo Marco Belfanti and Marzio Achille Romani, 'Il Monferrato: una frontiera scomoda fra Mantova e Torino (1536–1707)', in C. Ossola, C. Raffestin and M. Ricciardi, eds., *La frontiera da stato a nazione: il Caso Piemonte* (Rome, 1987), 114.

incorporated into the Swiss Confederation. Both attempts failed, but would, if successful, have transformed the relationship between the Duchy and both its duke and the rest of the Savoyard state.[2] In fact, throughout both wars, the Duchy of Savoy was effectively detached from the Savoyard state by enemy conquest and occupation. Victor Amadeus' recovery of the Duchy in 1696 was followed by its reintegration into the Savoyard state. This included the extension to the Duchy of some of the taxes introduced in Piedmont since 1690, the confirmation of traditional privileges in return for cash grants, the sale of what remained of the ducal domain in the Duchy (constituting a further shift in its relationship with its duke) and a struggle between Victor Amadeus and the Chambéry Chambre des Comptes over reform of the *taille*, a process which was interrupted from 1703 but resumed from 1713.[3] Similarly, the recovery, after more than sixty years, of Pinerolo and the adjacent Val Perosa in 1696 was followed by their reintegration into the Savoyard state, a process briefly interrupted by French occupation during the Succession War, but resumed thereafter.[4] As for the newly acquired territories (those detached from the Milanese) in the War of the Spanish Succession, their traditional privileges were largely confirmed by Victor Amadeus before the end of the war. Only thereafter were they integrated into the Savoyard state in a more complete way.[5] The island of Sicily had to be somehow integrated between 1713 and 1718 (and Sardinia from 1720). By focusing on three different regions or communities within the Savoyard state, the province of Mondovì, in southern Piedmont, the Duchy (or Valley) of Aosta between Piedmont and Switzerland and the Protestant Vaudois inhabiting the valleys, between Piedmont and Provence, the present chapter seeks to demonstrate the variety of experiences in these crucial decades.[6]

[2] P. Valente, 'Relazioni diplomatiche di Vittorio Amedeo II, duca di Savoia, coi Cantoni Svizzeri e colla Repubblica del Vallese durante il secondo periodo della guerra in Italia per la successione di Spagna (1703–7)', *CGP*, VI, 387 ff.; and D. Carutti, 'Della neutralità della Savoia nel 1703', *MAST*, 2nd ser., 20, 1863 – both of which give details of the 1690 negotiations as well.

[3] For the reintegration of Savoy, and the accompanying problems, from 1696, see Duboin, III, 1076, XXV, 174, 179 and XXVII, 736; and J. Nicolas, *La Savoie au 18e siècle: noblesse et bourgeoisie*, 2 vols. (Paris, 1978), I, 32, 122 ff.

[4] See C. Storrs, 'Le politiche statali 1684–1748' [provisional title] in *Il Settecento Religioso nel pinerolese* (forthcoming).

[5] In August 1708 Victor Amadeus confirmed the Senate of Casale and ordered it to conform itself to the established laws of the Monferrato, Duboin, III, 1795. A ducal intendant was making his presence felt from 1708, Duboin, XI, 584, but only in 1713 did Victor Amadeus suppress the *maestrato* of Casale, Duboin, III, 597.

[6] Additional perspectives on relations between Turin and the periphery, including some provinces and regions not considered in the present chapter, are offered in M. Di. Macco and G. Romano, eds., *Diana trionfatrice: arte di corte nel Piemonte del Seicento* (exhibition catalogue) (Turin, 1989). The fullest account of the short-lived Savoyard

THE PROVINCE OF MONDOVÌ

The province of Mondovì (acquired by the dukes of Savoy in 1396, by an act of voluntary 'dedition' which underpinned its claims to a privileged tax regime) is perhaps an archetype of the traditionally independent province reduced to obedience by the powerful, centralising princely state in the age of so-called 'absolutism'. Symcox, for example, sees the province's defeat by the duke's regular troops in 1699 as 'a critical moment in the affirmation of state power by Victor Amadeus II'.[7] This was above all because in the early 1680s, on the eve of Victor Amadeus' assumption of power, the most serious attempt so far to assert ducal authority in the province at the expense of Mondovì's distinct status had been decisively rebuffed in the 'Salt War' of 1680–82. The latter had been provoked by the regent, Madama Reale's demand for the traditional free gift, or donative, on Victor Amadeus' impending marriage with the Portuguese infanta and the resulting dispute over its apportionment in the surrounding contado by the syndics of Mondovì. The failure of negotiations led Madama Reale to seek a military solution, despatching 2,500 troops to Mondovì in the spring of 1681. This was initially successful, encouraging the regent to exploit her advantage to at last end Mondovì's fiscal privilege and to introduce the salt gabelle. However, the resistance of the mountain communities, notably Montaldo, rekindled revolt while the regent foolishly reduced the military presence. In the summer of 1681, following the harvest, the rebels attacked Mondovì. Louis XIV then offered to help the regent suppress the revolt. This threat of French military intervention was one pressing reason why Madama Reale now sought a negotiated settlement of the Mondovì problem. In the spring of 1682, with the Portuguese match about to be concluded, and fearing that the rebels might seize Victor Amadeus as he travelled to Nice to embark, the regent gave in, granting a pardon and abandoning her efforts to introduce the salt gabelle.[8]

This was by no means the end of trouble in Mondovì or the neighbouring province of Ceva. In the summer of 1684 Victor Amadeus was obliged to lead 3,000 troops to Ceva, where a Mondovì-style situation

---

regime in Sicily remains V. E. Stellardi, ed., *Il regno di Vittorio Amadeo II di Savoia in Sicilia dall'anno 1713 al 1719*, 3 vols. (Turin, 1862).

[7] G. Symcox, *Victor Amadeus II: absolutism in the Savoyard state 1675–1730* (London, 1983), 133.

[8] Inevitably the best introduction to this subject in English is Symcox, *Victor Amadeus*, 79 ff. But see also the contributions to G. Lombardi, ed., *La Guerra del Sale (1680–1699): rivolte e frontiere del Piemonte barocco*, 3 vols. (Milan, 1986) and S. Lombardini, 'Le premesse ecologiche di una rivolta contadina: agricoltura e demografia nel Monregalese all'epoca delle Guerre del Sale', *Bollettino della Società per gli Studi Storici, archeologici ed artistici della Provincia di Cuneo*, 89, 1983, 107 ff.

was developing, to prevent the situation escalating into full-scale rebellion. In Mondovì itself there were further troubles in 1686, 1689 and 1690, the first and last of these arising at a time when a number of the duke's troops were required elsewhere. In 1686, engaged in war against the Vaudois, Victor Amadeus sent the marchese di Parella to pacify the province, which was rebelling against the meat gabelle, with a mixture of negotiation and threat, and was able to use the Mondovì militias against the Vaudois. In January 1687, those Monregalese who had taken up arms against their sovereign were pardoned.[9] The disturbances in Mondovì in 1689 may, as some contemporaries thought, have encouraged the Vaudois Glorieuse Rentrée (see below, p. 295).[10] The troubles in the spring of 1690 occurred just when the French king was demanding that Victor Amadeus hand over a substantial chunk of his limited military establishment as a demonstration of his good faith.[11] The duke was obliged to send the greater part of the garrisons of Asti, Vercelli and Turin itself to end the disorder in Mondovì, where the rebels badly mauled his Savoy infantry regiment. Despite Victor Amadeus' declared intention to forcibly reduce his subjects to obedience, he was obliged to negotiate and, with an eye on his deteriorating relations with Louis XIV, to grant a pardon in April 1690. The following month he visited the province as part of the pacification package.[12]

In 1690, therefore, on the eve of the cycle of wars which transformed the Savoyard state, and despite his declared wish to impose his authority in Mondovì, Victor Amadeus had not really improved on the situation there left him by his mother. Mondovì's exemption from the

[9] Symcox, *Victor Amadeus*, 92–3; S. Lombardini, '"Quand . . . l'Mondui u sia sensa bandi, 'l mond u i a da fini". Appunti per un'ecologia politica dell'area monregalese nell'età moderna', including (Appendix 4) senator Guglielmo Leone's account of Parella's negotiations; Duboin, VI, 573, 574. Parella apparently enjoyed influence in the province, partly because of contacts established there (and his conduct there) during the war against Genoa in 1672, contacts and influence which were reinforced by his role in pacifying the various crises in relations between Mondovì and Turin in the 1680s: see C. Contessa, 'La congiura del marchese di Parella (1682)', *BSBS*, 38, 1936, 81 ff.

[10] See Rott, *Histoire de la représentation diplomatique de la France auprès des Cantons suisses, de leurs Alliés de leurs Confédérés* (Bern, 1926), 206.

[11] See consulta of Spanish Council of State, 20 May 1690, AGS/E/3411/112,113; R. Oresko, 'The diplomatic background to the Glorioso Rimpatrio: the rupture between Vittorio Amedeo II and Louis XIV (1686–1690)', in A. de Lange, ed., *Dall'Europa alle Valli Valdesi: Atti del Convegno 'Il Glorioso Rimpatrio 1689–1989'* (Turin, 1990), 275.

[12] Symcox, *Victor Amadeus*, 104; Duboin, VI, 583; *mémoire* of Madama Reale, 13 May 1690, in C. de Rousset, *Histoire de Louvois et de son administration militaire*, 4 vols. (Paris, 1862–3), IV, 310. See AST/MM/Levata di Milizia, m. 1/24 for Victor Amadeus' order to Bene, Cherasco, Cuneo, Fossano, Saluzzo and Savigliano to raise men following sedition in Mondovì, Apr. 1690.

salt gabelle continued to create problems for the authorities in Turin, above all because it underpinned a profitable trade in contraband salt with those areas which were subject to the gabelle, harming ducal revenues. Indeed, the smuggling of salt (and other goods), far more than agriculture or industry, was the key to the province's wealth. There were other serious problems, too, notably the fragmentation and privatisation of power, in the hands of local family and client groups, local nobles protecting their clients among the bandits (often involved in smuggling) against the ducal authorities, and the related problems of feud and vendetta. The difficulties encountered by the authorities in Turin were in part the consequence of the fact that this was also a frontier zone, bandits and others able to escape to other jurisdictions (notably that of the Republic of Genoa and those of the many imperial feudatories, particularly those of the Langhe, whose fiefs were enclaved within or bordered Piedmont and who were extremely jealous of attempts by Turin to extend its authority and power).[13] Finally, the preceding decade had shown that Mondovì was often at its most troublesome when the Savoyard state was most seriously embroiled in foreign policy issues and war.

The Nine Years War inevitably affected Mondovì. In 1691 substantial numbers of local peasants in the form of the militia, went to the aid of Turin, Carmagnola and Cuneo;[14] and in 1693, following Victor Amadeus' defeat at Marsaglia, the Mondovì militias were again called out, to prevent the enemy seizing Cuneo.[15] Clearly, despite the preoccupation with privilege and the widespread lawlessness, the province was not fundamentally disloyal. However, it is also noteworthy that Victor Amadeus felt it advisable to use Parella to mediate between himself and Mondovì at this time. The war also meant the presence in the province of a new element: Savoyard and foreign troops. In the winter of 1692–93 the duke's own Mondovì and Savoy regiments and the Huguenot Montbrun regiment were assigned winter quarters there following a visit to Mondovì by Victor Amadeus' secretary of war, conte Benzo di Cavour.[16]

---

[13] Lombardini, 'Quand ... l Mondovì ...', is an excellent general introduction to Mondovì and the issues, and refers to the earlier local interventions of Emanuel Filibert and Charles Emanuel I. See also Symcox, *Victor Amadeus*, 85.

[14] VDM to Fagel, 23 and 26 May, 16 June 1691, Turin, ARAH/SG/8644/144, 146, 150 (noting that the Mondovì militias were disarmed by the French on the surrender of Carmagnola); Lombardini, 'Quand ... l Mondovì ...' includes an illustration of the standard of the Madonna of Vico carried by the militia to Cuneo.

[15] VDM to Fagel, 16 Oct. 1693, Turin, ARAH/SG/8644/77.

[16] VDM to Fagel, 28 Nov. and 5 Dec. 1692, Turin, ARAH/SG/8643/294, referring to the seditious attitude of the inhabitants of Mondovì, and the fact that they had not paid as much as Victor Amadeus' other subjects, 297.

In addition, and despite its fiscal privileges, the province was expected to contribute its share of the costs of war. In 1692, following a visit by Victor Amadeus himself, to negotiate this contribution, the province had granted just 75,000 lire. However, Benzo di Cavour's visit at the end of 1692 was also the occasion for negotiating a larger grant for 1693, of 500,000 lire, most of which seems to have been promptly paid. Although shielded by both its status and reputation the province was being integrated into the Savoyard war effort.[17]

Victor Amadeus' journey to Mondovì in the winter of 1691–92 was not just a fundraising exercise, but reflected real fears about the town and province.[18] These were justified given Louis XIV's hopes of exciting another rebellion there in an attempt to undermine the duke's war effort. In September 1690 marshal Catinat was authorised to levy contributions in Mondovì, but to grant exemptions, and to allow the destruction of the citadel (both symbol and instrument of ducal authority in Mondovì itself since its construction in the later sixteenth century) if he thought it in Louis XIV's interests.[19] More seriously, in the winter of 1691–92, Louis' agent at Pinerolo, Chamlay, initiated secret negotiations (which soon, however, came to light) with malcontents in both Mondovì and Ceva. These were intended to foment revolt, urging the inhabitants not to pay taxes and promising French support for their rebellion.[20] Clearly, while pursuing secret negotiations with Victor Amadeus himself (see Chapter 3), the French king was also seeking to increase the pressure on the duke to settle by exploiting the traditional rebelliousness of some of his subjects. The allied invasion of Dauphiné in 1692 made Louis XIV even more eager to foment revolt in Mondovì, while the growing demands on Mondovì of Victor Amadeus made some in the province readier to conspire. The plotting came to a head in the winter of 1692–93, when a number of those involved were arrested and brought to Turin. The plotters included members of the local nobility (Gian Giacomo Truchi di Savigliano, Carlo Francesco Ferrero di Roasio), Many were condemned and executed, although some were then pardoned and/or allowed to return from exile. This measured response, together with the failure of

---

[17] VDM to Fagel, 2 Feb., 28 Nov. and 12 Dec. 1692, Turin, ARAH/SG/8643/208, 294, 302; ST to DLT, 6 Feb. 1692, Genoa, AST/LM/Olanda, m. 3, noting that the duke's presence in Mondovì – and Ceva – would speed payment of the winter quarters due in those provinces.

[18] Poley to Nottingham, 19 Jan. 1692, SP 92/26 f. 19; *London Gazette* 2741, Turin, 2 Feb. 1692.

[19] Louvois to d'Herleville (governor of Pinerolo), 6 Sept. 1690, Rousset, *Histoire de Louvois*, III, 140.

[20] VDM to Fagel, 15 Mar. 1692, Turin, ARAH/SG/8643/216; VA to DLT, 24 Feb. 1692, Turin, AST/LM/Olanda, m. 3.

the French king to fulfil his earlier promises of military support for potential rebels, undoubtedly helped prevent further trouble. The failure of this rebellion suggests that the disloyalty of some among the provincial elite did not detract from that basic loyalty of the province as a whole noted earlier – although if Louis XIV had been able to back it more effectively the episode might have proved more testing for ducal authority.[21]

The abortive revolt of 1692–93 was in some degree linked with an equally serious, if also rather different, problem associated with the process of state formation in these years, that of the quasi-independent imperial feudatories, above all those in the Langhe, many of whom had effectively become mediate imperial vassals, depending immediately on the duke of Savoy, following the Münster settlement of 1648. Some were resentful of their new status, seizing every opportunity to throw it off. The imperial declaration of war against France in 1689 was used to justify resistance to Savoyard recruiting in these territories, although such an attitude was made more difficult by the diploma Victor Amadeus secured from the emperor in February 1690 and the duke's switch of sides in June 1690. Many of the feudatories, however, continued to resent Savoyard authority. Typical of these was marchese Carlo Francesco Del Carretto di Monforte and Novello. Some of his relatives had accepted Savoyard dominion in return for various rewards. But Carlo Francesco made great difficulties about accepting the authority of the Turin Senate, and about supplying Victor Amadeus with both money and men, and was briefly arrested and taken to Turin in May 1692 for plotting resistance with his subjects. Finally, in December 1692, Victor Amadeus had had enough and sent his White Cross regiment, in winter quarters at nearby Alba, to the castle of Monforte, which was taken and looted. The marchese was then taken prisoner to Turin. This was by no means the end of this matter, however. Victor Amadeus had to send more troops to the Langhe, before finally granting a pardon to the inhabitants of Monforte, Novello and the other villages. Nor was this the end of the difficulties the imperial feudatories posed to the expanding Savoyard state, the episode revealing the crucial importance of the emperor, and above all of the authority he could grant or delegate, in the process of Savoyard state formation. It demonstrated, too, that resistance to ducal authority could be decisively overcome using armed force but that Victor Amadeus

---

[21] VDM to Fagel, 15, 19 and 22 Dec. 1692, Turin, ARAH/SG/8643/303, 304, 305; and same to same, 5 jan. 1693, Turin, ARAH/SG/8644/1. See also Lombardi, *Guerra del Sale*, 112 ff.; and, for Truchi's incarceraton in the citadel of Turin, L. Cibrario, *Storia di Torino*, 2 vols. (Turin, 1846), I, 110 ff.

might prefer, wisely, to be magnanimous after the initial assertion of his authority and power.[22]

As for Mondovì, Louis XIV still seems to have had hopes of inciting trouble there, particularly after Victor Amadeus' second defeat, at Marsaglia, in 1693. This was one reason why Louis hoped Catinat could seize Cuneo in the aftermath of his victory, thereby encouraging potential rebels in both Mondovì and Ceva, which Louis still thought ready to revolt. A revolt there would also cut communications between Lombardy, Piedmont and Finale, thus cutting off the Milanese and the Savoyard state from the rest of the Spanish monarchy.[23] Allied leaders in Turin certainly feared that Catinat might now cut the links between Turin and both Mondovì and Cuneo.[24] However, as with French expectations of Jacobite revolt in Britain after 1688, and allied hopes of a Huguenot revolt in Dauphiné in the wake of the allied incursion in 1692, these hopes were not realised, and for the rest of the Nine Years War both Mondovì and Ceva were relatively quiet – not least because of the quartering there of, mainly foreign, troops.[25] This may explain why Victor Amadeus felt able to (plan to) destroy the fortresses of Mondovì and Ceva as part of his policy of rasing a number of fortresses in some parts of his state (see Chapter 1) – a policy which some thought mistaken because of their value in restraining the inhabitants of those two provinces.[26]

Of course, it is the years after 1696 which are generally regarded as crucial in transforming relations between Turin and Mondovì. For Symcox, conflict was inevitable in view of the new pressure for fiscal reform (leading to conflict with other fiscally privileged bodies, including the

---

[22] VDM to Fagel, 10 May and 22 Dec. 1692, and 8 and 20 Feb. 1693, Turin, ARAH/SG/8643/227, 305 and 8644/13, 14. See A. Torre, 'Rivolte contadine e conflittualità. L'esempio di Monforte d'Alba tra Sei e Settecento', in Lombardi, *Guerra del Sale*, 317 ff. and Torre, 'Faide, fazioni e partiti, ovvero la redefinizione della politica nei feudi imperiali delle Langhe tra Sei e Settecento', *Quaderni Storici*, 63, 1986, translated as 'Feuding, factions and parties: the redefinition of politics in the imperial fiefs of Langhe in the seventeenth and eighteenth centuries', in E. Muir and G. Ruggiero, eds., *History from Crime: selections from Quaderni Storici* (Baltimore, 1994); and L. Bulferetti, 'Il principio della 'superiorità territoriale' nella memorialistica piemontese del secolo XVIII: Carlo Ignazio Montagnini di Mirabello', in *Studi in memoria di Gioele Solari* (Turin, 1954), 153 ff.

[23] Louis XIV to Catinat, 10 Oct. 1693, Fontainebleau, B. Le Bouyer de St-Gervais, *Mémoires et correspondence du maréchal de Catinat*, 3 vols. (Paris, 1819), II, 253 ff. For Finale's crucial role as link between the Milanese and the Spanish monarchy, see C. Storrs, 'The Army of Lombardy and the resilience of Spanish power in Italy in the reign of Carlos II (1665–1700)', *War in History*, 4/4, 1997 and 5/1, 1998, passim.

[24] VDM to Fagel, 27 Nov. 1693, Turin, ARAH/SG/8644/89.

[25] See VDM to Fagel, 21 Oct. 1695, Turin, ARAH/SG/8644/216, for the presence in Mondovì of Huguenot troops (in winter quarters).

[26] Catinat to Vendôme, 19 Apr. 1694, Oulx, Catinat, *Mémoires*, III, 4.

church), the disloyalty in the province during the war years and, perhaps most importantly, the fact that Victor Amadeus now had at his disposal larger numbers of more experienced, regular troops. In June 1697 the duke ordered the levy of the salt gabelle in the district of Mondovì. The city and lowland areas complied reasonably peacefully, but there was serious resistance in the mountain communities, obliging Victor Amadeus to again personally lead troops to Mondovì, in July 1698. There he supervised the division of the registers of all the communities; i.e. the separation of those of the town of Mondovì from the surrounding communities effectively subject to it – part of the larger contemporary cadastral survey of the duke's territories (see Chapter 2) – a purge of Mondovì's town government, the introduction of new measures against banditry and the enforcement of existing ones on the carrying of firearms. Victor Amadeus then departed, leaving the marquis des Hayes in command. The following year, however, the disorders were renewed, encouraged by a poor harvest. In November 1698 the rebels sacked Vico, attacking and killing officials of the new gabelle. The duke therefore sent reinforcements to des Hayes, who by early 1699 had at his disposal 10,000 regular troops (8,000 infantry and 2,000 cavalry). These included Victor Amadeus' Guards, the Aosta, Chablais, Fusiliers, Monferrato, Piedmont, Savoy and White Cross infantry regiments, the Genevois dragoon regiment and the recently arrived German Schulemburg regiment, plus the militias of Cuneo, Fossano, Pinerolo and Saluzzo. As might be expected, a rebel attack on Mondovì failed in January 1699 and des Hayes, having negotiated secretly with a number of their leaders, was able to destroy the rebels at Vico in May 1699. He then occupied their last stronghold at Montaldo. Defeat was followed by severe punishments, including the expulsion of 564 families to Vercelli, the appointment of an intendant, and a determined effort to destroy the culture which had underpinned the province's resistance since the 1680s. This included further progress towards the disarming of the province, and the destruction of the chestnut trees which were an important part of the food supply. Thereafter, the cadastral reform continued and Mondovì lost it's domination of the neighbouring communities, which became autonomous bodies within the larger state structure. Mondovì had at last been subdued, and a medieval system of local authority and administrative and political relations replaced by a more 'modern' one.[27]

---

[27] This paragraph draws largely on Symcox, *Victor Amadeus*, 132–3, which provides an excellent synthesis of the substantial Piedmontese bibliography on this subject; the still very useful A. de Saluces, *Histoire militaire du Piémont*, 5 vols. (Turin, 1818), V, 97 ff.; and G. Amoretti, 'La guerriglia e le operazioni militari nel periodo della guerra del sale nella provincia di Mondovì (Ultimi decenni del XVII secolo)', in Lombardi, *Guerra del*

The renewal of war from 1701, and particularly of war against France from 1703, put renewed pressure on the province, because of military operations and the need to supply Victor Amadeus' forces;[28] although, if the duke's later efforts to recover war damages from Louis XIV are any guide, Mondovì was one of the provinces of Piedmont least affected by the War of the Spanish Succession, operations only really being conducted there in the summer of 1706.[29] The war also interrupted the cadastral survey, which was renewed, rather spasmodically, in 1709 and 1711.[30] The real interest of the Succession War lies in what it reveals about Mondovì's integration into the Savoyard state. Victor Amadeus was clearly unsure about the loyalty of the province, consulting its governor, conte Benzo di Santena, on whether the population could be trusted with arms if he withdrew the second battalion of the Schulemburg regiment, in September 1703. In fact, his need of the latter left him little choice but to order local levies to defend the province and its capital, and to allow the bearing of arms again, in part because of the persisting problem of banditry. Benzo di Santena, however, was horrified. Perhaps reflecting a widespread view among the Savoyard elite of the province's population as inherently inclined to revolt, he thought that they could not be trusted with arms and effectively refused to carry out the duke's order. Indeed, he thought it absolutely necessary that Victor Amadeus leave at least some regular troops in Mondovì to prevent revolt. The duke took the governor's advice and abandoned plans to levy men in Mondovì, instead ordering the levy of 400 men in Ceva, as Benzo di Santena had suggested, to be used to garrison Mondovì. Concern about Mondovì, and reluctance to use the local population, was also evident when, following the despatch to Mondovì of units of Victor Amadeus' Monferrato regiment, the governor disarmed those from Montaldo on guard duty there. The duke even saw enemy deserters as a way to have troops at Mondovì without arming the local population. In the worsening crisis, however, and in view of the poor condition of the defences of the province (notably the poor state of the castles of Ormea and Ceva), the governor offered in October 1703 to raise 500–600 men in Mondovì and subsequently, with Victor Amadeus' approval, levied a number of free companies in Mondovì for operations in the neighbouring imperial fiefs occupied by the French. Clearly, neither the duke nor his collaborators were convinced that Mondovì was as yet fully integrated into the Sa-

---

Sale, 401. For the substantial costs of the exile to Vercelli, borne by the duke, see Prato, 'Il costo', *CGP*, X, 250–1. For the cadastral survey, see D. Borioli, M. Ferraris and A. Premoli, 'La perequazione dei tributi nel Piemonte sabaudo e la realizzazione della riforma fiscale nella prima metà del XVIII secolo', *BSBS*, 1986.

[28] Santena to VA, 21 Nov. 1703, Priè, *CGP*, I, 161.   [29] See *CGP*, IX, 412–14, 420.

[30] Borioli *et al.*, 'La perequazione dei tributi', 165.

voyard state, but given the crisis facing the latter it was impossible to avoid arming elements of its population. Not surprisingly, the governor was also anxious about the presence of French residents in the province and its capital.[31]

These anxieties may have been exaggerated. Indeed, in October 1703 Santena himself informed Victor Amadeus that news of the detention of his troops at San Benedetto had been received in Mondovì with all the resentment that such an act against its sovereign might be expected to provoke.[32] However, the crisis of 1706 revealed that, particularly when ducal authority was weakened, the province's place in the Savoyard state might still be in question. In March 1706 Victor Amadeus had arrested three Mondovì bandits said to be in contact with the French commander, the Duc de la Feuillade.[33] That same summer Victor Amadeus' family, fleeing to Genoa, and later the duke himself, visited the town, the duke exhorting his subjects, though less than wholly confidently, to a loyal defence. He seems to have also hoped to encourage loyalty and active resistance by offering tax exemptions, as occurred elsewhere in his state during this crisis (see Chapter 2). However, the province promptly surrendered to Louis XIV's forces in early July, after which the town was garrisoned by about 3,000 French troops for three weeks. This episode remains shadowy, not least because nineteenth-century historians, committed to the notion of a Savoyard (or Piedmontese) nation loyally rallying to its prince in the wars of these decades, has tended to skirt it.[34] Soon after the departure of the French, the Monregalese sent a deputation to Victor Amadeus seeking, and ultimately securing a ducal pardon for having welcomed the French. Initially, however, Victor Amadeus, believing that his suspicions of the real loyalty of the province and its inhabitants had been confirmed, refused to receive Mondovì's deputies. It has even been suggested that this episode explains his abandonment of plans to turn the neighbouring sanctuary at Vicoforte into the pantheon of the House of Savoy, sometime before the Superga, outside Turin, was designated for this role and honour.[35]

[31] VA to Santena, 28 and 29 Sept. and 2 and 6 Oct. 1703, and 10 Jan. 1704, *CGP*, I, 47, 51, 58, 81, 216; Santena to VA, 1, 4 and 8 Oct. and 10 Nov. 1703, *CGP*, I, 57, 77, 91, 147; VA to marchese Pallavicino, commanding in Asti province, 6 Oct. 1703, Turin, *CGP*, I, 81; Santena to ST, 11 Oct. 1703, Mondovì, *CGP*, I, 96.

[32] Santena to VA, 6 Oct. 1703, Mondovì, *CGP*, I, 84.

[33] VDM to States, 17 Mar. 1706, ARAH/EA/VDM/30, 218.

[34] Van der Meer attributed the surrender of the province to its disarming between 1698 and 1700, VDM to States, 7 July 1706, Oneglia, ARAH/EA/VD/30, 298, 300.

[35] There is a good discussion of this subject in G. Lombardi, 'La Guerra del Sale trecento anni dopo: cronaca di un convegno: fatti e interpretazioni', in Lombardi, *Guerra del Sale*, 117 ff. Saluces, *Histoire militaire*, V, 185 depicts the Monregalese as erring but repentant.

For the rest of the War of the Spanish Succession, not surprisingly, there was little or no trouble in Mondovì. Indeed, in January 1707 Victor Amadeus allowed those exiled to Vercelli in 1699 to return home, a mixture of princely grace in victory and prudence.[36] By 1713, Mondovì was clearly much more integrated into the Savoyard state, and less turbulent than before 1690, although we should not ignore the extent to which traditional lawlessness persisted well into the eighteenth century.[37] In large part, integration was the result of the massive military operation of 1698–1700, which in turn reflected (and confirmed) the new resources of authority acquired by Victor Amadeus since 1690. But we should beware of focusing on armed might to the exclusion of other elements, particularly as terror alone was neither practicable nor advisable in the longer term.[38] Symcox notes how the local cohesion which had underpinned a general provincial resistance in the early 1680s subsequently weakened, undermining resistance. This fragmentation was in part due to the fact that the local elite, less inclined to look to the French court (now effectively excluded from intervention in the Savoyard state), was more integrated into both the Savoyard state and the Savoyard elite, seeing office and its rewards as an important means to maintain its position in more difficult economic circumstances. Perhaps the most striking example of this process was Carlo Francesco Vincenzo Ferrero di Roasio. Born (1680) into the lesser nobility of Mondovì, and grandson of one of the 'rebels' of 1682 he served as magistrate, was 'discovered' by Victor Amadeus in 1706 and thereafter worked his way up the developing state structure, via the intendancy, to become generale delle finanze in 1717 and (1722) marquis of Ormea. In the reign of Charles Emanuel III, he became chief minister, using his power to reward relatives and friends from Mondovì, and in this way, using the bonds of family and clientage, completed the province's integration into the Savoyard state.[39]

---

[36] E. Genta, 'Condanne, grazie e porto d'armi: proiezioni della Guerra del Sale sul riordinamento del Senato', in Lombardi, *Guerra del Sale*, 389. According to Lombardi, 'Guerra del Sale', 114, many of those allowed to return had previously fought for the duke in some of the free companies.

[37] M. Broers, 'Policing Piedmont: the 'well-ordered' Italian police state in the age of revolution 1789–1821', *Criminal Justice History*, 1994, notes the persistence of smuggling and disorder well beyond 1713.

[38] For Victor Amadeus' tempering repression with some clemency (respecting dowry and other family obligations) in the confiscations ordered in 1699–1700, see Lombardi, 'Guerra del Sale', passim.

[39] There is a need for a good modern study of Ormea, but see G. Ricuperati, 'Il Settecento', in P. Merlin et al., *Il Piemonte sabaudo: stato e territori in età moderna* (Turin, 1994), 458 ff. and R. Gaja, *Il marchese d'Ormea* (Milan, 1988). For the family's role in the Salt War, see Lombardi, 'Guerra del Sale', 155 (and 157 ff. for a late eighteenth-century historian, Gioacchino Grassi, another descendant of Salt War rebels, denouncing the latter in terms similar to those of the rebels' opponents in Turin in the 1680s and

THE DUCHY OF AOSTA

The Duchy of Aosta, roughly equivalent to the present day Val d'Aosta, lay between Piedmont and Switzerland and was the only one of the duke of Savoy's territories which could still in 1690 be called a *pays d'états*.[40] It has been largely neglected in English-language histories of the Savoyard state, no doubt because it was smaller and in all respects more peripheral than most other parts of that state, but also, and perhaps more importantly, because it does not conform to patterns of interpretation which emphasise the development of absolutism under Victor Amadeus II. Aosta had already, in the fifteenth century, forced Duke Amadeus VIII to retreat from his attempt, embodied in the Statutes of 1430, to create an integrated state which would have effectively ended the Duchy's privileged, quasi-independent status; and not until the 'enlightened absolutism' of the 1760s, in the reign of Charles Emanuel III, was the Duchy fully integrated into the Savoy state (integration being measured by the effective loss of a distinct set of institutions, together with the extension there of a more effective and intrusive centralised control). Between 1690 and 1713, the Duchy of Aosta certainly figured more largely than hitherto in the Savoyard state, and those years saw a greater integration of the Duchy into the larger state. Perhaps the most striking manifestation of this was an apparently major threat to Aosta's privileged status in 1699–1700. However, the integration achieved between 1690 and 1713 was neither complete nor a decisive step towards 'absolutist' control from Turin. As for the events of 1699–1700, the threat to the Duchy's liberties on that occasion may have been less serious than has sometimes been thought and was not inspired by a farsighted blueprint for the subversion of Aosta's distinct status. On the contrary, these decades saw the Duchy (like the Vaudois, below) achieve a significant reaffirmation of their distinct identity and place within the Savoyard state. This could be at least as effective a means of state building as the traditional 'absolutist' model.[41]

The Duchy of Aosta had long ago lost full independence, but remained jealous of its liberty, and sensitive to breaches of its privileged juridical status. In the later sixteenth century, Emanuel Filibert had left the

---

1690s). Another local man who achieved status and power in and through Victor Amadeus' developing state in these decades was Gian Giacomo Fontana, intendente generale, contadore generale, conte di Monastero di Vasco (1722) and marchese di Cravanzana: Ricuperati, 'Il Settecento', 455–56

[40] See I. Lameire, *Les occupations militaires en Italie pendant les guerres de Louis XIV* (Paris, 1903), 201.

[41] For Amedeo VIII, see Barbero, 'Principe e nobilità', 251. For later developments, see F. Negro, 'L'Inizio della perequazione nel Ducato d'Aosta (1767–73)', *Bibliothèque de l'Archivium Augustanum: sources et documents d'histoire valdôtaine*, II (Aosta, 1982).

Duchy's institutions largely intact, allowing its assembly of the Three Estates to continue to meet and the latter's interim committee, the Conseil des Commis, to continue to function; and in 1580, he formally recognised the Duchy's distinct status. The Duchy's privileges, including the right to take appeals against the decisions of the local Cour des Connaissances to the Senates of either Savoy or Piedmont, were formally laid down in the so-called Coutumier, drawn up between 1573 and 1582, which was referred to whenever the Duchy's privileges were in question. In 1610, for example, Charles Emanuel I was asked to suppress the *tabellionato* and to prohibit appeals above a certain value outside the Duchy – on the grounds that both breached the Coutumier. The Duchy enjoyed other privileges, including exemption from the Inquisition and the dogana (customs levy). Successive dukes of Savoy, including Charles Emanuel II in 1662 and Victor Amadeus II himself in 1682, were obliged to swear to respect the Duchy's privileged status, while in 1687 the latter also confirmed the privileges of the Conseil des Commis. More practically, the Duchy could play off the two Senates, of Piedmont and Savoy, each jealous of its own authority and the ambitions of the other, against each other to ensure the survival of Aosta's privileged position.[42]

The Duchy's resistance to the ambitions of the Senate of Turin frequently provoked the latter to accuse the Conseil des Commis of disobedience towards its duke. However, the Duchy remained unique in the Savoyard state in that its prince had to negotiate with its political elite through a formal representative assembly, whose members enjoyed fiscal and other privileges, if he wished to raise additional revenues there. The salt gabelle had been introduced into the Duchy in the 1570s with the agreement of the Conseil des Commis. Negotiation of this sort thereafter revolved above all around the so-called free gift, or donative. This was granted roughly every six years, and in return the duke was expected to confirm the Duchy's privileges and to make grants to the members of the Estates. The determination of the Duchy's ruling elite to defend its privileges expressed itself in a strong legal-historical tradition, exemplified by Jean-Baptiste de Tillier, whose family provided the last four secretaries of the Conseil des Commis – he succeeded his own uncle in the post in 1699 – and whose personal archive still constitutes a major source for the Duchy's history.[43]

---

[42] This and the succeeding introductory paragraphs closely follow L. Marini, 'La Valle d'Aosta fra Savoia e Piemonte 1601–1730', in *Relazioni e communicazioni presentate al XXXI Congresso Storico Subalpino 1956*, 2 vols. (Turin, 1959), I. See also M. A. Benedetto, *Ricerche sul 'Conseil des Commis' del Ducato d'Aosta*, 2 vols. (Turin, 1956, 1965), passim.

[43] For de Tillier, see Symcox, *Victor Amadeus*, 37 ff., L. Colliard, 'Les manuscrits de J.-B. de Tillier (1678–1744)', *Biblothèque de l'Archivium Augustanum: sources et documents d'histoire valdôtaine*, II (Aosta, 1982); J.-B. De Tillier, *Le Franchigie delle comunità del*

The dukes of Savoy only very occasionally visited the Duchy, instead relying on a number of officials to make their authority there effective. These included the governor (or bailli of the bailliage of Aosta), an office held since 1677 by Tommaso Felice Ferrero, marchese della Marmora, and in his permanent absence by the military commandant, an office held since 1688 by Francois-Jérôme de Challant, baron of Châtillon, and the *vibailli* (or deputy bailli). In the later sixteenth century, Emanuel Filibert had generally appointed natives of the Duchy to these posts, but the seventeenth century saw the growing appointment of non-natives, mainly men from Savoy and Piedmont, including (from 1656) a Carron, brother of the marquis de Saint-Thomas. During the tenure of men like the Piedmontese lawyer, Biagio Beltramo, *vibailli* in the 1680s, these offices could be the foundation of significant reforming initiatives. However, both governor and *vibailli* generally recognised the need to co-operate with the Duchy's privileged institutions and its elite, many of whose members remained influential (for example, the baron of Châtillon, member of an old and distinguished Aostan family). In 1677 we find Beltramo informing Madama Reale that she should send her orders via the Conseil des Commis. Turin could also generally rely on the bishop of Aosta, an ex-officio and influential member of the Conseil des Commis, which generally had a say, as did the duke of Savoy in his appointment. On the death of the bishop, Bally, in 1690, Beltrami was quick to inform Turin and to suggest the appointment of a Piedmontese successor, who would usually be drawn from the elite of the Savoyard state. The duke also enjoyed patronage rights in the Duchy, appointing for example the provost of the hospice of the Great St Bernard. Such patronage enabled the duke to attract and reward some, but not all, of the Duchy's many poor nobles. Typical of these was Eugène Gaspard de Tillier, who had served Charles Emanuel II at Vienna and Ratisbon in the 1660s. He was then obliged, for want of opportunity at home, to enter the military service of the Republics of Venice and Lucca until enabled, with the help of the bishop of Aosta, mobilised by de Tillier's own cleric brother and of the regent, Madama Reale, to return to Aosta in 1680 on his appointment as secretary to the Conseil des Commis.[44] Ducal patronage was also limited by the exiguous military establishment

Ducato di Aosta, ed. Ma. Clotilde di Charvensod and M. A. Benedetto, *MSI*, 4th ser., 71, 1965; and A. Barbero, 'Una nobiltà provinciale sotto l'Antico Regime. Il *Nobiliaire du Duché d'Aoste* di J.-B. De Tillier', *RSI*, 1997, 5 ff.

[44] Pignet, 'Eugenio Gaspare De Tillier, uomo d'arme e di legge (1630–1699)', in *La Valle d'Aosta: relazioni e comunicazioni presentate al XXX Congresso Storico Subalpino di Aosta, 1956* (Turin, 1959), 695 ff. Offering what we might call a 'bottom-up' perspective on contemporary understanding of sovereignty, de Tillier referred to the duke of Savoy as 'mon souverain naturel', in what was clearly intended to lay an obligation on the latter to offer him employment of some sort, *ibid.*, 705 ff.

of the Duchy, which reflected the latter's reluctance to tolerate or fund anything more. Finally, the duke could send occasional, *ad hoc* agents to the Duchy, including, for example, the magistrate and future intendant, Marco Antonio Pusterla, who was sent by Victor Amadeus II in the later 1680s to enquire into complaints against Beltramo's conduct as *vibailli*.

The Duchy of Aosta's peculiar political and jurisdictional position within the Savoyard state was underpinned by a geographical isolation and inaccessibility which also helped make it one of the poorest regions of the Savoyard state, particularly by contrast with Piedmont. It depended essentially on the export of its own dairy products, grain and manpower and upon the transit of Piedmontese exports *en route* to Switzerland via the Great Saint Bernard. The passage of goods between the Duchy and Piedmont via Ivrea, where duties were levied by the duke was a frequent source of concern and complaint on the part of the Estates. One reason for this was that the older Little Saint Bernard route had largely been displaced by the Simplon route. The Duchy's capital, and only significant town, Aosta, was a centre for the exchange of produce from Savoy and elsewhere and an administrative and episcopal centre. Charles Emanuel II's efforts to stimulate the economy of Aosta (as of the other parts of his state) in the 1660s had hardly affected this basic pattern, relative backwardness and poverty.[45]

The emphasis so far has been on the degree to which the Duchy saw itself as distinct from Turin and the rest of the Savoyard state, but it was not a monolithic community. There were important local divisions, not least within the ruling elite, between, for example, old and more recent nobles, and resulting in factional conflict within the Conseil des Commis. In 1688 the ducal delegate, Pusterla, noted differences between, on the one hand, the towns of the Duchy and, on the other, its capital, Aosta, the nobility and the Conseil des Commis regarding taxation. At the same time, the Assembly and the Conseil des Commis were both drawn from a narrow elite within the Valley. In addition, although distinct, the Duchy (or its elite) was increasingly integrated into the larger Savoyard elite, not least as a result of marriages between local families and those of other parts of the Savoyard state. In consequence, many Piedmontese noble families were fiefholders in the Duchy.[46] Typical at a more distinguished level was Carlo Filippo Perrone, of the

---

[45] Symcox, *Victor Amadeus*, 39. In 1669 the *vibailli* feared dearth in the Duchy following the marquis de Caselle's excessive grain exports; and in 1688–9 de Tillier's attempt to register those obliged to serve in the militia was greatly hindered by the seasonal absence of many young men.

[46] See P. Plassier, 'Les sindics de Valsavarenche pour les Paquiers et franchises accordées a la Paroisse: recognoissance (20 juillet 1698)', in *La Valle d'Aosta*, 729 ff., for an example of intermarriage of this sort and its consequences.

comital San Martino family, baron of Quart, and elected to the Estates in 1682, who was also a gentlemen of Victor Amadeus' chamber. Some Piedmontese nobles were even elected to the Conseil des Commis, as happened in 1686 with Francesco Maria Adalberto Pallavicino, marchese delle Frabose.

It was the Vaudois who, from 1688–89, first really presented the Duchy of Aosta with a military threat in this period, necessitating new levies there, following the so-called Glorieuse Rentrée (see below).[47] However, it was war against France from 1690, and above all the loss of Savoy and Nice, which thrust on Aosta a new strategic importance in the Savoyard state. The Valley was now in the front line and a crucial route through which Louis XIV's forces could invade Piedmont and the Milanese from Savoy. In early 1691, reports of French plans to invade Piedmont via the Duchy, the reputed unreliability of the latter's militia and pressure from the Conseil des Commis led Victor Amadeus to send Parella there with two regiments. In addition, he replaced the absentee marchese Ferrero della Marmora as governor, and his stand-in, the baron of Châtillon, who may have been suspect because of his role in the neutrality negotiations between the Duchy's representatives and the French (see below, p. 284–5). He appointed instead Joseph de Mesmes, marquis de Marolles.[48] Subsequently, in June about 7,000 French troops briefly advanced into the Duchy, their main purpose being to destroy roads and bridges, thus preventing Victor Amadeus marching through the Valley to the relief of Montmélian, and to levy contributions. Victor Amadeus' fear that they would try to take Ivrea, thus securing control of the Duchy and isolating it from Piedmont, and also attempt to invade Piedmont from Aosta were unfounded.[49] However, despite the declarations of loyalty to Victor Amadeus by the Conseil des Commis, the population of the Duchy showed itself all too ready to lay down their arms and welcome the French. This was nothing more than a local recognition of the superiority of French arms but could not be welcome

---

[47] Marini, 'La Valle . . .', 642 ff.; Pignet, 'E.G. de Tillier', 713 ff.
[48] The new governor nevertheless urged Victor Amadeus not to remove Châtillon completely from the Duchy because, although not highly regarded, the latter was the only man who could get things done there, and both the Conseil des Commis and the Duchy's nobility would be sorry to see him go. Indeed, the latter threatened to return to their châteaux, in effect to strike, if the bailli were given greater authority, de Mesmes to ST, 28 Mar. 1691, Aosta, AST/LP/M, m. 47. See Pignet, 'E.G. De Tillier', 717 ff.; Marini, 'La Valle', 644 ff.
[49] VA to DLT, 2 July 1691, Moncalieri, AST/LM/Olanda, m. 1. See AST/MM/Imprese, m. 2 for an account of the invasion sent to the duke by the Conseil des Commis; VDM to States, 2 June 1691, Turin, ARAH/SG/8643/147; Pignet, 'E.G. De Tillier', 720. Saluces, *Histoire militaire*, V, 40–1, emphasises the vandalism which destroyed much of the Duchy's rich architectural patrimony.

in Turin.⁵⁰ The French soon withdrew from the Duchy, taking hostages from each of the three Estates, as surety for the payment of the contributions demanded, but this did not remove the military threat. There were renewed fears for Aosta in the winter of 1692, when it was thought that the French might send a force through the Duchy to relieve Casale, and again in 1693 and 1694.⁵¹

The Duchy also became a vital strategic route in the opposite direction, from Piedmont into Savoy and even France, and a lifeline between Piedmont and Switzerland. It was no doubt for this reason, that, following the French conquest of Savoy in 1690, Victor Amadeus was said to be planning a visit to Aosta in the winter of 1690–91.⁵² Following the French retreat in 1691, the Valley was the chosen route for the abortive expedition to relieve Montmélian, Victor Amadeus' last outpost in Savoy. When that project was abandoned in favour of clearing the French from Piedmont, sending troops into the Valley was seen by Victor Amadeus as a means of at least diverting the French from the siege of Montmélian until a relieving force could be sent.⁵³ Following Montmélian's surrender in December 1691, Aosta became even more important as a means of keeping open for the allies the route into and through Savoy, particularly as the French were closing the other mountain passes. In the winter of 1691–92, when Victor Amadeus was assessing the prospects of an allied invasion of France in 1692, he thought an attempt through the Duchy had the best prospects of the three options (i.e. Aosta, Susa or the Barcelonette valley) because although it was the longest route it was also the easiest. This probably explains his visit to Ivrea in December 1691.⁵⁴ In the spring of 1692 the duke again visited Ivrea to inspect the mountain passes, accompanied by the governor of Spanish Lombardy.⁵⁵ In fact, the allies invaded Dauphiné in 1692 via the Barcelonette valley, but in the summer of 1693, Victor Amadeus again saw the Duchy as a route into Savoy and France. To this end he ordered the establishment of magazines at Ivrea and Aosta and the widening of the Duchy's

---

⁵⁰ Marini, 'La Valle', cites the governor's report, at the height of the French incursion, of pro-French sentiment in the Valley and his own impotence in face of such insubordination (as Marolles saw it). See also Pignet, 'E.G. De Tillier', 720.

⁵¹ VDM to Fagel, 29 Dec. 1692, Turin, ARAH/SG/8643/310; Pignet, 'E.G. De Tillier', 722.

⁵² VDM to States, 23 Dec. 1690, Turin, ARAH/SG/8643/87.

⁵³ See F. Guasco, 'Vittorio Amedeo nelle campagne 1691–1696', in *Studi su Vittorio Amedeo II* (Turin, 1933), 261 ff. for the duke's ordering the organisation of supplies along the route of the Spanish troops who were to march via Ivrea, Donnaz, Châtillon and Aosta (but never did so).

⁵⁴ VA to DLT, 5 Dec. 1691, and 9 Jan. 1692, Turin, AST/LM/Olanda, m. 1; ST to same, 9 Dec. 1691, Turin, AST/LM/Olanda, m. 1.

⁵⁵ VDM to Fagel, 5 Apr. 1692, Turin, ARAH/SG/8643/222.

roads – although nothing was attempted there.[56] Finally, at the conclusion of the 1694 campaign, Victor Amadeus made his first full visit to the Duchy of Aosta, partly to inspect its defences but also concerning himself with the government of what was now a front-line territory with a much more important role in the Savoyard state than before 1690.[57]

The Duchy's enhanced military role brought with it new pressures, similar to those experienced elsewhere in the Savoyard state. In June 1690 the Duchy's militia was called out (with great difficulty, given the widespread reluctance) to serve in Piedmont.[58] More importantly, there was a substantial, and rather novel, military presence. Huguenot and Vaudois units were frequently (1691–92, 1695–96) assigned winter quarters there, no doubt because of the proximity to their Swiss and German recruiting grounds.[59] Protestant troops were also occasionally, for example in 1692, stationed there during the campaigning season. Indicative of the importance of Aosta, and of the need to provide for its defence while other operations were mounted, was Victor Amadeus' order, in the summer of 1693, that all his forces should join his field army for what became the abortive siege of Pinerolo, with the exception of his Piedmont and Chablais regiments which remained at the Great St Bernard, and the Aosta regiment itself which stayed in the Duchy.[60] In 1695, while the bulk of Victor Amadeus' forces took part in the siege of Casale, large numbers of troops were stationed in the Duchy, including the Swiss/Protestant Sacconay regiment, partly to prevent the despatch through Aosta into the Po valley of a French relief or diversionary force.[61]

This military presence, of both friend and foe, could be very destructive. In 1691, for example, although the French were forced to withdraw, as we have seen this was not before they had inflicted serious material loss. Victor Amadeus ordered the repair and rebuilding of many of the roads and bridges destroyed on this occasion, as a necessary preliminary to sending troops through Aosta to the relief of Montmélian,[62] but his own and his allies' troops could be equally destructive. The presence of French and other foreign troops also flooded Aosta (as other parts of the Savoyard

---

[56] VDM to Fagel, 19 June and 3 July 1693, Turin, ARAH/SG/8644/43, 52.
[57] ST to DLT, 6 and 13 Oct. 1694, Aosta, AST/LM/Olanda, m. 4.
[58] Pignet, 'E.G. De Tillier', 715 ff.
[59] VDM to Fagel, 1 Mar. 1692, Turin, ARAH/SG/8643/212; same to same, 21 Oct. 1695 and 27 Apr. 1696, both Turin, ARAH/SG/8644/216. In the winter of 1693–4 the Protestant regiments, recruiting in Switzerland, requested and were given assembly points in the Duchy, VDM to Fagel, 27 Nov. and 11 Dec. 1693, and 15 Jan. 1694, all Turin, ARAH/SG/8644, 89, 92, 101.
[60] VDM to Fagel, 10 July 1693, Turin, ARAH/SG/8644/54.
[61] VDM to States, 15 July 1695, Turin, ARAH/SG/8644/194; Pignet, 'E.G. De Tillier', 723.   [62] VA to DLT, 26 Sept. 1691, Turin, AST/LM/Olanda, m. 1.

state) with foreign coins, creating serious short-term problems. Since the ducal authorities failed to resolve these, the Conseil des Commis took action to prevent further loss. Equally serious was the almost constant demand on the Duchy's population to supply the war in one way or another. In 1692 mules were seized to meet the enormous need of draught animals for the Dauphiné invasion and again, in 1693, for the siege of Pinerolo.[63]

This seizure of animals was effectively a form of taxation. War also imposed substantial new financial burdens, both direct and indirect, in the Duchy. In 1691 the Duchy had promised to pay the French invaders substantial contributions of 200,000 lire (although 300,000 had originally been demanded), and as late as August 1693 the Conseil des Commis was obliged to ask the Duchy's nobility to help pay off the outstanding 69,000 lire.[64] In addition, early in 1694 the Duchy agreed to pay 6,000 pistoles towards the maintenance of a force of 2,000 men which Victor Amadeus agreed to levy for the Duchy's defence. In the spring of 1694 the Assembly of the Three Estates, called by the governor, Marolles, on Victor Amadeus' order, heard a 'harangue' from the governor concerning the duke's obligations to defend his sovereignty and glory, and a request for a donative of 350,000 lire. They agreed a lesser donative, of 250,000 lire, to be paid over six years.[65] In addition, in 1695 the Duchy's treasurer, Millet, was obliged to raise short-term loans totalling 100,000 lire. Such measures were in part the result of other war-related financial obligations. These included the organisation, from 1691 (although they were not entirely new in the Duchy) of *étapes*, staging posts where soldiers could be rested and supplied *en route*, to ensure that the troops marching through the Valley were properly supplied, and therefore disciplined: at Verres-Donnas (for 300 men), at St Vincent-Châtillon (300), and at Aosta (1,000). However, these *étapes* were increasingly exhausted by the demands being made on them, including the provision of (fire)wood to the troops – yet another form of hidden taxation.[66]

Not surprisingly, perhaps, given these new pressures, from at least November 1690, the Conseil des Commis were negotiating with the French military commanders for a separate neutrality. This was, in effect, a repeat of the Duchy's conduct in the wars which had torn apart the

[63] Pignet, 'E.G. De Tillier', 721–2.
[64] In 1694, the States of Aosta heard a request for repayment of sums advanced in 1691 to help pay those contributions, F. E. Bollati di Saint Pierre, ed., *Atti e documenti delle Antiche Assemblee Rappresentative nella Monarchia di Savoia*, Monumenta Histroria Patriae series, 2 vols. (Turin, 1879, 1884), II, col. 1451–52. See Pignet, 'E.G. De Tillier', 722.
[65] Bollati di Saint Pierre, *Atti d documenti*, II, cols. 1441 ff.
[66] Pignet, 'E.G. De Tillier', 717 ff. (including a complaint by the Conseil des Commis to Victor Amadeus, Mar. 1692, that the Duchy was denuded of provisions and money by the need to supply the troops quartered there).

Savoyard state 150 years earlier, and demonstrates the degree to which Estates could still on occasion claim an independent political role extending into the international arena.[67] Victor Amadeus' attitude to these negotiations was ambiguous. On the one hand, it is possible that he saw them as a means, particularly given his inability to properly defend the Duchy, to avert the complete loss of Aosta and its use as a French military corridor into Piedmont. At the same time, he was happy for the Conseil des Commis to conduct the negotiations, perhaps because – should the negotiations become known – it might compromise less his relations with his new allies. In this light, the Duchy's exercise of its supposed privilege might dovetail with ducal policy. On the other hand, although the baron de Châtillon, who claimed to have consented to the negotiations at the instance of the Conseil des Commis, reassured Victor Amadeus that the hoped-for neutrality would not affect his sovereignty, at least if those negotiated in the past were anything to go by, the duke no doubt had some anxieties about the loyalty of the Duchy in the spring and summer of 1691.[68] The failure of the negotiations, and the fact that the French were kept out of the Duchy after 1691, meant that Aosta remained an integral part of Victor Amadeus' state.

Nevertheless, Aosta remained preoccupied with its own defence and extremely sensitive to threats to its liberty from within the Savoyard state. In the summer of 1693 the Conseil des Commis sent a deputation, which included local notables such as Challant, to Turin to protest at infringements of the Duchy's privileges, particularly regarding the role of the Cour des Connaissances, and to argue against the appointment of an intendant for the Duchy on the grounds that the Conseil des Commis traditionally filled the functions of any likely intendant.[69] The episode allows an interesting insight into the tussles between Aosta and Turin, and into the complexity of what we might call 'absolutist' attitudes. On the one hand, the Senate of Turin maintained a position which advanced, and was largely a cover for, its own authority and power throughout the Savoyard state (including the Duchy of Aosta). On the other hand, the Duchy's deputies advanced the view that Aosta depended solely on its duke – an 'absolutist' view (the assertion of princely authority) which was nevertheless intended to preserve the Duchy from a greater threat, that of subordination to Turin (and above all its Senate). Equally noteworthy is

---

[67] See the very pertinent observations on the roles of Estates and states on the European stage in R. Asch, *The Thirty Years War: the Holy Roman Empire and Europe 1618–48* (London, 1997), 4–5.

[68] Challant de Châtillon to ST, 23 Dec. 1690 and 7 Mar. 1691, Aosta, AST/LP/C, m. 62. In general, see Marini, 'La Valle', 644; Pignet, 'E.G. De Tillier', 718.

[69] Benedetto, *Ricerche*, 41 ff. shows the Conseil des Commis legislating on a number of issues arising from the war (including desertion).

the fact that the Duchy's deputies found some support for their position in Turin, from (among others) the generale delle finanze, conte Marelli, who was a fiefholder in the Duchy of Aosta.[70]

The grant of a donative was an opportunity to vent grievances and seek redress. This opportunity was seized by the States following Victor Amadeus' request for money in early 1694. In the fourth session of the Assembly of the States of Aosta, held on 28 April 1694, the inhabitants of Donnas sought exemption from the agreed donative because of their obligation to supply the *étape* located there. By way of reply the governor claimed that barracks to lodge the troops would be built at Bard, the vitally important fortress between Aosta and Ivrea, thereby reducing the pressure on Donnas. More significantly, the Assembly prepared a *mémoire* for Victor Amadeus, comprising nineteen points, on which they sought redress or ducal favour of some sort. The Estates wished to be allowed to pay the donative over ten years, rather than the usual six, because half of the previous donative remained unpaid and the Duchy had to pay Victor Amadeus 6,000 pistoles towards the cost of the 2,000 men he had agreed to station in the Duchy for its defence. On the other hand, they also wanted Victor Amadeus to order the levy of these men and ensure that they were properly controlled by their officers. Other demands were: that stationed soldiers should not be foreigners (and especially not Protestants); that no further donatives be requested; that compensation be paid (as had been promised) for the mules seized on Victor Amadeus' orders in previous years, for firewood supplied to the troops and for lodging of the troops passing through the Duchy; and that the soldiers be paid, and provided with bread in light of the exhaustion of the *étapes*. Since the Duchy's agriculture did not enable it to satisfy Victor Amadeus' fiscal demands, he was asked to introduce measures to promote their trade, specifically to allow them to export their produce to Piedmont, and exempt their animals and waggons from forced work, since they did not have enough animals to properly cultivate the land. At the same time they accepted their own obligation to make their animals available when necessary. They also sought confirmation of the privilege of the Duchy's own courts to hear certain cases and – reflecting the fact that the Duchy was by no means a monolithic community – asked Victor Amadeus to end abuses of tolls by the feudal lords. Finally, the twenty-five members of the Conseil des Commis sought the usual privileged grant to themselves of salt (now increased to 100 measures) and an increase in their salaries.[71]

---

[70] Marini, 'La Valle', 647 ff.; Pignet, 'E.G. De Tillier', 718 (for accusation in 1690).
[71] Bollati di Saint Pierre, *Atti e documenti*, cols. 1441 ff. See Pignet, 'E.G. De Tillier', 722–3, for many of the issues arising prior to 1694.

Victor Amadeus sought to accommodate the Duchy as far as possible on these demands, which revealed the strains generated by the Nine Years War and its impact on the Savoyard state. He agreed to confirm the Duchy's privileges, to extend the time in which the new donative could be paid (while pointing out that the last one should have been fully paid by July 1693), to levy no more donatives and to ensure that the 2,000 troops were properly controlled. On some of the other demands he was more circumspect, referring to the Turin Camera dei Conti both the request to be allowed to export goods to Piedmont and that for compensation for animals seized in 1692. As for the levying of contributions, this was referred to Chancellor Bellegarde and others. He also gave rather vague promises of future compensation for firewood provided and for billeted troops. Similarly, on a request to be relieved of the burden of supposedly useless fortifications in the Valley, Victor Amadeus promised satisfaction at a more favourable juncture. Victor Amadeus agreed to limit the demands made of the villages (in default of assigned barracks) but restated the obligations of the Duchy's inhabitants to supply the troops with provisions and to transport them. On the seizing of animals, Victor Amadeus ordered that they not be demanded (unnecessarily) but expressed his expectation that in an emergency the Duchy would give what was required. The duke ordered what was requested on tolls, while reserving his own rights. Finally, while agreeing to the request for salt for the members of the Conseil, Victor Amadeus ruled out the requested salary increase, declaring that his financial situation made this impossible.

What we see then in the Duchy of Aosta in 1694 is the traditional pattern of negotiation typical of an early modern *pays d'états*. On the one hand, Victor Amadeus called on his subjects to fulfil their extraordinary wartime obligations, but recognised the need to satisfy some of the grievances identified or articulated by the Estates in order to secure his grant. On the other hand, the privileged Estates acknowledged an obligation but were able to bargain and to exploit the prince's wish, or need, for money, to secure the redress of a range of grievances, the great majority of which, but by no means all, were largely the product of war. Neither side achieved all that it was seeking: the duke his larger donative and the Estates satisfaction on all points. However, each had secured enough to show that the established system of negotiation worked. Victor Amadeus was not therefore tempted into a divisive and perhaps disastrous attempt to impose stronger central authority (absolutism) while for the Duchy's inhabitants their traditional institutions clearly provided some protection against more exorbitant demands. This was also shown in the final years of the Nine Years War when proposals to extend to the Duchy the tax on stamped paper introduced in Piedmont in 1694 and the *tabellion* (the compulsory recording of deeds by state-approved notaries), whose extension to Aosta had been suspended by Charles Emanuel I in 1610 following appeals to the Coutumier, and to establish a 'college' of notaries there (reducing the existing number of notaries practising in the Duchy) were successfully blocked. These fiscal innovations still had not been introduced in the Duchy by the end of the war in 1696.[72] The Nine Years War, therefore, confirmed the traditional, contractual foundation of Aosta's place within the Savoyard state.

It was the post-war period which, as in Mondovì, saw the most serious threat, or the most serious articulation of one, to the distinct position of the Duchy of Aosta in the Savoyard state. In May 1697, on Victor Amadeus' order, the *vibailli* (since 1693, conte Buschetti, senator of Nice and Piedmont and a relation by marriage of the Balbis di Vernone) gave the Conseil des Commis a memorial on the introduction of the *tabellion* and the college of notaries. The Conseil was determined to resist, ordering de Tillier to prepare a statement of its own position which was entrusted to another deputation sent to Turin in the early summer of 1697 (who took with them dairy produce from the Duchy to 'reward' those in the capital who supported its cause). The Conseil also sought to mobilise again those Piedmontese nobles, including the marquis de Saint-Thomas, who were fiefholders in the Duchy. Soon after arriving in Turin, however, the deputation was informed by Gropello, now generale delle finanze, and by conte Casellette, first president of the Camera dei Conti, that Victor Amadeus wished to make the Duchy more like his other states, in terms of finance, and that it was not longer simply a matter of the *tabellion* and the stamped paper tax but of all other taxes levied in his other territories. The Duchy was therefore asked to produce the documents on which its claim to privileged exemption was founded, and the ducal patrimoniale generale, David, cited it before the Camera. At one point in the negotiations, the Piedmontese officials asserted that the issue was not one simply of finance but also of sovereignty, that concept which had been so frequently articulated by Victor Amadeus and his ministers during the Nine Years War and which was also frequently expressed in dealings with both Mondovì and Rome in the years after 1696. But it is difficult to know what weight to give this assertion. On the one hand, it may well have represented a new sense of ducal authority in his own territories, sharpened by the experiences of the years since 1690. On the other hand, it was simply a powerful negotiating ploy. It may be that Victor Amadeus himself was less preoc-

---

[72] This paragraph, and the following account of developments to 1700, is drawn from Marini, 'La Valle', 650 ff.

cupied with the issue of sovereignty than were his legally trained officials. In the summer of 1698 the duke, in a memorial to the Conseil des Commis, does not seem to have elevated it in the same way, but rather to have seen it as a bargaining issue. Whatever the truth of this matter, a proposal from ducal officials, echoing the duke's memorial, offering confirmation of the Duchy's privileges in return for a donative of 100,000 lire (subsequently reduced to 60,000), and acceptance of both the *tabellion* and the stamped paper tax, was followed by an order by Victor Amadeus for the matter to be settled by the Camera dei Conti (whose competence in this matter had been denied by the Duchy and its deputies).

In February 1699, Victor Amadeus' appointment of the president of the Turin Senate, Guglielmo Leone, to head a committee of the Camera to discuss the case was successfully opposed by the Duchy's deputies on the grounds that Leone was related to the former *vibailli*, Beltramo, and therefore prejudiced. Nevertheless, the affair was progressing and in August 1699 the duke ordered the recently (1697) appointed governor of the Duchy, Giovanni Battista Doria, marchese di Ciriè, to investigate the conduct of both the Conseil des Commis and the Cour des Connaissances, and abuses of the Coutumier. This might seem to be merely a further step on Victor Amadeus' part towards the eradication of the Duchy's privileged position. However, such an enquiry was by no means unjustified, and Ciriè's instructions made clear that the discovery of abuses would not prevent Victor Amadeus from confirming the Duchy's privileges. Indeed, it is difficult to interpret this as other than another bargaining ploy intended above all to force the Duchy to compromise, rather than to destroy its distinct status. Indeed, the birth of the Prince of Piedmont in May 1699 had offered a marvellous opportunity for all to solve the crisis peaceably, since the duke could now justifiably request a donative of the Duchy. Soon after the above instructions were sent to Ciriè, he and Gropello (who was also in Aosta) offered confirmation of the Duchy's privileges in return for a substantial donative. The Estates responded, offering 500,000 lire over six years. Although Victor Amadeus had hoped for 750,000 lire, the donative offered, the largest ever granted by the Duchy, was accepted. Victor Amadeus terminated David's case and confirmed the Duchy's privileges early in 1700.[73]

---

[73] Lameire, *Occupations militaires*, 203, notes that the Duchy was exempt in 1704 from the stamped paper tax levied throughout the rest of the Savoyard state. Indicative of the extent to which Victor Amadeus still felt the need for the co-operation of the local elite on important occasions was his invitation to the Conseil des Commis to lead the Te Deum mass to celebrate the birth of the Prince of Piedmont in Aosta cathedral, in 1699: Pignet, 'E.G. De Tillier', 725.

Thus ended what some among the Aostan elite had regarded as the most serious crisis facing the Duchy. And yet, as in 1694, the result had been not the destruction of the province's autonomy, the option chosen in Mondovì at largely the same time, but a confirmation of it. It is possible that there was a close link between the defeat of Mondovì's distinct status and the survival of that of Aosta between 1698 and 1700, since it would have been foolish, perhaps even disastrous, for Victor Amadeus to seriously confront Aosta at the same time as he was committed in Mondovì. The likelihood of a link between the two different outcomes in the two provinces is strengthened by the fact that intelligence reached Turin of a rebellion being planned in the Duchy of Aosta in the event of Victor Amadeus' failure to confirm its traditional privileges.[74] The threatening discourse of the ducal officials may, anyway, have been mere negotiating bluster. Whatever the truth of the matter, Victor Amadeus was not dogmatically set on the creation of a centralised, uniform absolute state; and once he had secured his object (above all the funds to help solve the financial crisis which was the legacy of participation in the Nine Years War) he was ready enough, if not necessarily happy, to confirm the traditional relationship, which had, as in 1694, largely worked.[75]

The outbreak of the War of the Spanish Succession in 1701, and particularly Victor Amadeus' *volte-face* of 1703, meant the renewal for the Duchy of Aosta of many of the strains of the 1690s. Just as in 1690, in October 1703 the Conseil des Commis received a letter from the duke justifying the breach with Louis XIV, on the grounds of the latter's provocation, as part of Victor Amadeus' propaganda campaign to sell the new war to his own subjects.[76] Initially, once again, the Duchy was a crucial lifeline to the outside world, along which so many men and so much matériel must travel if the duke was to survive the Bourbon onslaught. In December 1703 Victor Amadeus expressed his fears that a French conquest of the Valley, whither he had been able to send only very few troops, would cut communications between Piedmont and Switzerland and Germany, rendering useless his efforts to levy troops in those parts.[77] In fact, and by contrast with the brief French incursion in 1691, the Duchy was occupied for two years, following the treacherous surrender of the fortress of Bard to the besieging French by the colonel of

---

[74] See Notice from avvocato Brolliet of planned rebellion in this event, 1698, AST/MC, m. 9/9. This episode needs further exploration.

[75] Nor should we ignore the extent to which, in the background of this 'constitutional crisis', the Duchy's secular elite was largely in agreement with Victor Amadeus on a range of other issues, including that of taxation of church-owned property, a major issue between 1696 and 1703, Marini, 'La Valle', 659.

[76] VA to Conseil des Commis, 3 Oct. 1703, Turin, *CGP*, I, 73.

[77] VA to Count Starhemberg, 31 Dec. 1703, Turin, *CGP*, I, 207.

the Swiss troops in garrison there.[78] The occupying forces were careful not to alienate the Duchy by infringing its liberties, the Estates having secured promises to this effect from the start of the occupation and subsequently making clear their resentment of supposed infringements. But this change of masters meant few changes of substance in the relationship between periphery and centre.[79] The allied victory at Turin in 1706 was followed by the French abandonment of Aosta, and its recovery by Victor Amadeus who, nevertheless continued to worry about French incursions.[80] Towards the end of 1708 the duke sent additional forces into the Duchy to expel French troops who had crossed the Little St Bernard in an attempt to divert him from the siege of Fenestrelles.[81] Despite these alarms, after 1706, Aosta was more important as a possible route into the Duchy of Savoy and even France. For all these reasons, it was again closer to the front line than most of Victor Amadeus' other territories.[82]

As in the 1690s, war meant new demands of men and money. As elsewhere in the Savoyard state military service was not popular. In December 1701, the *vibailli*, Joly d'Alléry informed Victor Amadeus that following rumours of recruiting in Piedmont, the peasantry of Aosta were seeking passports to leave to look for work abroad.[83] In October 1708, in order to recruit his Savoy regiment for 1709, Victor Amadeus forbade those inhabitants of the Duchy capable of bearing arms to leave and ordered those abroad to return; and in the summer of 1709 he ordered further levies in the Duchy.[84] War also meant another tightening of the fiscal screw. This included payments to the occupying French between 1704 and 1706[85] but meant, above all, facing the demands of Victor Amadeus. Whereas in 1700 the Duchy contributed just 62,500 of

[78] For a detailed account of the French invasion and conquest of 1704, with supporting documentary evidence, see *CGP*, II, 594 ff. There is a very brief account of the French conquest in Saluces, *Histoire militaire*, V, 153.

[79] The Conseil des Commis continued, for example, to take action against those appealing to sovereign courts outside the Duchy, see Lameire, *Occupations militaires*, 204 ff.

[80] See *CGP*, V, 95 n. 1, for Victor Amadeus' fears on this score in 1707.

[81] Saluces, *Histoire militaire*, V, 230 ff. See also VDM to Fagel, 19 May and 7 and 11 July, Turin; and same to States, 31 Aug. and 3 Sept. 1708, Balbote, ARAH/EA/VDM/32, 91, 132, 137, 168, 170. In 1712, 3 of the 23 battalions available to Victor Amadeus for the campaign were assigned to the Duchy; and following reports of enemy plans to send troops into the Duchy over the Little St Bernard to levy contributions Victor Amadeus sent 1,000 foot and 600 (imperial) cavalry to reinforce the troops already stationed in the Duchy, Chetwynd to Dartmouth, 27 Apr. 1712, and to Warre, 28 Sept. 1712, both Turin, SP 92/28.

[82] In 1708 (and again in 1711) Schulemburg used the Valley and the Little St Bernard as a means of getting into and out of the Duchy of Savoy, Saluces, *Histoire militaire*, V, 247, 256.   [83] Marini, 'La Valle', 656.   [84] Duboin, XXVI, 156, 168.

[85] Lameire, *Occupations militaires*, 208, 210.

a total of 7,900,000 lire (i.e. less than 1 per cent), this promptly rose by one third in 1701, to 83,333, at which level it remained until 1704 and (after its recovery from the French) until 1711. It then fell by one third in 1712 to 60,000, and again in 1713, to just 48,333 lire.[86] But although the Duchy was shouldering a marginally heavier fiscal burden between 1701 and 1712, Victor Amadeus and his ministers clearly believed it could and should pay more. At the end of 1706 (following the Duchy's reconquest) the ducal representative rejected the donative offered by the Estates (320,000 lire over the usual six years) on the grounds of its insufficiency. Victor Amadeus subsequently sent Gropello to attend the Estates' sessions. Gropello pointed out that the last four payments towards the previous donative remained unpaid. The matter was resolved by the Estates offering an additional sum (90,000 lire) by way of 'thanksgiving' for their return to Victor Amadeus' dominion. Gropello also attended the next session of the States, convened in 1712, to consider another donative, and informed the Assembly of Victor Amadeus' difficult financial situation. However, the Estates offered just 290,000 lire, over six years, far less than had been hoped for. The implication that the Duchy had some obligation to give more, articulated by the *vibailli*, Joly de Fleury (presiding over the Assembly in the absence of the governor), displeased the Conseil des Commis who reminded Victor Amadeus of their supposed natural liberty. Victor Amadeus, very dissatisfied, nevertheless accepted, in view of the Duchy's recent suffering. Six years later, in the summer of 1718, on the expiry of the donative of 1712, Victor Amadeus sought an open-ended committment from the Aosta Estates for extraordinary funds for the duration of the Sicilian war. He was disappointed: the Estates granted just 280,000 lire over six years.[87]

Historians of the Savoyard state under Victor Amadeus have traditionally focused on the duke as determined creator of an absolute, centralised state structure, above all by reference to his destruction of the pretentions of Mondovì. However, by shifting our focus to the Duchy of Aosta, we see a Victor Amadeus who could live with much looser forms of integration, ones which do not conform to the traditional 'absolutist' pattern. The years between 1690 and 1713 certainly saw the Duchy of Aosta play a more important and visible role in the Savoyard state (not least because, with Piedmont, it was sometimes all that remained of that state). From 1714, Aosta supplied one of the new militia regiments (see Chapter 1).

[86] L. Einaudi, 'Le entrate pubbliche dello stato sabaudo nei bilanci e nei conti dei tesorieri durante la guerra di successione spagnuola', *CGP*, IX, 42 ff. (For substantially different sums actually received from the treasurer of the Duchy, Millet, see *ibid.*, 90 ff.)

[87] Bollati di St Pierre, *Atti e documenti*, II, cols. 1490 ff., 1517 ff. and 1540; see also G. De Botazzi 'Donativo del Ducato d'Aosta a Vittorio Amedeo II', *BSBS*, 11, 1907, 405–7.

Yet Aosta was not integrated more forcibly into the developing state structure. The traditional system of bargaining, underpinned by the loyalty of the elite (now serving in various ways, not least in the expanding ducal armies) was reasonably successful in tapping, when necessary, the limited resources of a rather poor region. Victor Amadeus would clearly have liked to extract more revenues from Aosta. But, it was not obvious that ducal revenues would, or could, be substantially increased by a more intrusive, 'absolutist' alternative. Tighter central control might be difficult to establish and even counter-productive. The pragmatic Victor Amadeus recognised and accepted these restraints. In this region, at least, little changed between 1690 and 1720.[88]

THE VAUDOIS

A distinct community, rather than region, in the Savoyard state was the Protestant Vaudois, who traditionally inhabited the valleys between Piedmont and France, to the north and west of Turin, above all the two main valleys radiating out from Pinerolo, the Val Pellice and the Val Chisone. The alteration of their position within the Savoyard state, in these decades, as part of the larger transformation of that state, was at least equal to the change of that of Mondovì, if very different in nature. The transformation of the position of the Vaudois has many aspects: their return from short-lived exile, the rebuilding of their communities and institutions (including the revival of assemblies of a sort which might be said to represent a partial reverse of the trend towards ducal absolutism), and a new legal guarantee of their position, which operated throughout the eighteenth century, secured largely through the intervention of the Protestant Maritime Powers. In addition, and especially as the territorial enlargement of the Savoyard state involved the addition of chunks of Protestant France, the valleys of Perosa in 1696 and of the Pragelato in the War of the Spanish Succession, this also meant a significant shift in the confessional balance and identity of the Savoyard state. Not surprisingly, this transformation, and the re-emergence of an apparently eradicated Protestantism, generated some of the fiercest opposition to Victor Amadeus' new foreign policy, especially in the 1690s, both inside and outside his state. It also resulted in a serious clash over his authority (or sovereignty) within it with the pope. Some of these issues have already been dealt with, particularly by historians of the Vaudois. However, despite the great volume of work on Vaudois history, there are still

---

[88] In Sept. 1713, Victor Amadeus declared, in reply to the Conseil des Commis, that he did not wish to undermine its privileged jurisdiction in health matters, Duboin, III, 1327.

significant gaps in our knowledge and understanding of the latter in this period. Vaudois history still revolves very largely around the so-called Glorieuse Rentrée of 1689. The present chapter is therefore intended as a contribution to the history of the Vaudois between 1690 and 1720, and to emphasise the extent to which their experience, which differed from those of both Aosta and Mondovì, revealed yet another distinct type of integration in the developing Savoyard state.[89]

In 1690 the Savoyard state was fully part of the Counter-Reformation Catholic world. It always had been, but that Catholic identity had long been qualified by the presence in the valleys between Turin and the frontier with France of a hard core of Protestants. Spasmodic efforts to eradicate this alien religious element, by persuasive missionary work and by more violent means, had not solved the problem before 1684. However, in just a couple of years, between 1685 and 1687, the Catholic identity of the Savoyard state had been confirmed with the extraordinary military suppression of the Vaudois communities of the Piedmontese valleys. This had been done initially at Louis XIV's insistence, but there is no reason to question Victor Amadeus' commitment to the eradication of Protestantism from his states. While many Vaudois converted, others preferred to resist. Vaudois resistance tested ducal might, but (with French help) Victor Amadeus was able to finally crush the Vaudois in what was a minor triumph for the militant Counter-Reformation. The defeat of the Vaudois, hitherto an integral part of the Savoyard state, transformed the latter, in a confessional sense, in a remarkable way, and was in many respects a major achievement for Victor Amadeus. It was followed by the departure into internal and foreign exile of thousands of Vaudois, whose children were often distributed among Catholic institutions and households to be brought up in the 'true' faith – and by Catholic colonisation of the valleys,[90] which in a sense represented a

---

[89] Among the most promising signs of new developments in Vaudois historiography are P. Sereno, 'Popolazione, territorio, risorse: sul contesto geografico delle Valli valdesi dopo la "Glorieuse Rentrée"', and D. Tron, 'Il Reinsediamento in val Germanasca dopo la Rentrée', both in A. de Lange, ed., *Dall'Europa alle Valli Valdesi: Atti del Convegno 'Il Glorioso Rimpatrio 1689–1989'* (Turin, 1990). Sereno, 293, notes the relative lack of source materials on the Vaudois after the Rentrée.

[90] In 1686, the village of Rorà was sold to a consortium of thirty-two Savoyards for just over 20,000 lire, Sereno, 'Popolazione, territorio', 293–4. On the forced baptism, removal (and marriage) of Vaudois children, see Tron, 'Il reinsediamento', 326. The best introduction to this subject in English is inevitably Symcox, *Victor Amadeus*, 93 ff. (and Symcox, 'The Waldensians in the absolutist state of Victor Amadeus II', in de Lange, *Dall'Europa alle Valli Valdesi*, 237 ff. For the way the Vaudois presence had helped shape Savoyard institutions hitherto, see S. Cavallo, *Charity and Power in Early Modern Italy: benefactors and their motives in Turin 1541–1789* (Cambridge, 1995), 10, 110, for charities targeting Vaudois converts to Catholicism. For previous persecutions

deliberate attempt at confessional state formation.[91]

However, those exiles had not abandoned hope of returning to their valleys and substantial numbers lingered in Switzerland. Their chance came with the outbreak of the Nine Years War in the autumn of 1688. Taking advantage of the diversion of French attention to the Rhine and Flanders, a group of Vaudois and French Protestants, led by Pastor Henri Arnaud, crossed Lake Geneva into Savoy and fought their way back into the valleys in the summer of 1689, in the so-called Glorieuse Rentrée. Despite their success, in part due to their having taken both Louis XIV and Victor Amadeus II by surprise, the situation of Arnaud's men in the winter of 1689–90 was not promising: they must expect a serious Franco-Savoyard onslaught in the spring of 1690, since Victor Amadeus and the French king were mobilising their forces. However, the Protestant irregulars had established a foothold in Victor Amadeus' states which the leaders of the anti-French coalition now hoped to exploit, to create a more serious diversion of Louis XIV's forces. In early 1690 the Hague congress agreed to back a second expedition which should march from Switzerland via Spanish Lombardy into Piedmont, Victor Amadeus still at this stage being regarded as an ally of the French king. The expedition should then fight its way through the duke of Savoy's states, relieve the remnant of the Glorieuse Rentrée, enter southern France and link up with their co-religionaries, the Huguenots, sparking off a major revolt which would ultimately force Louis XIV to a reasonable peace. This so-called Lindau Project proved difficult to execute, for various reasons. Eventually, however, it was implemented, if not in all respects as initially planned, in the late spring of 1690. More importantly, the preparation and execution of this threat to his own states obliged Victor Amadeus to make the best of a difficult situation, rather than being master of the situation, free to intervene if and when he wished, and to break with Louis XIV in June 1690.[92] The duke's switch of alliances transformed his relationship with his erstwhile Vaudois subjects. It was accompanied by

---

(1633, 1655) and the threat posed some of their neighbours in the Savoyard state by Vaudois violence (and the way hostility to them united the dukes of Savoy and some of their noble subjects), see S. J. Woolf, *Studi sulla nobiltà piemontese nell'epoca dell'assolutismo* (Turin, 1963), 112, 117.

[91] See R. J. W. Evans, *The Making of the Habsburg Monarchy 1550–1700* (Oxford, 1978), passim; and Asch, *Thirty Years War*, 15–17.

[92] There is a good brief account of the Rentrée in Symcox, *Victor Amadeus*, 102. Arnaud's (supposed) account, *Histoire de la Glorieuse Rentrée des Vaudois dans leurs vallées*, 1710, has recently been republished (Turin, 1989). For the real author, see E. Campi, 'Vincenzo Minutoli e l'histoire du retour', in de Lange, *Dall'Europa alle Valle Valdesi*, 363 ff. For Lindau, see C. Storrs, 'Thomas Coxe and the Lindau Project 1689–90', in de Lange, ed., *Dall'Europa alle Valli Valdesi*, 199 ff.

the release of those Vaudois still held in ducal prisons, and by orders to allow the Vaudois and French Huguenots free passage and to supply them. There were good reasons for this. For one thing, the Vaudois were traditionally good fighting men and the duke needed as many of these as he could get. More specifically, the Vaudois could swell the ranks of the Lindau expeditionary force against France and contribute to the defence of the Vaudois valleys, which the French were now occupying. Equally important, a more conciliatory policy towards the Vaudois might convince Victor Amadeus' new allies, the Protestant Maritime Powers, of his commitment to the 'common cause'; enough certainly to justify their granting him the substantial cash help without which he could not fight the war.[93]

Such an approach was politic, because from an early stage in the negotiations for an alliance between Victor Amadeus and the Maritime Powers, the latter made it clear that they would insist on some formal ducal enactment on behalf of the Vaudois.[94] This was, in fact, one of the main obstacles to the conclusion of a treaty. The instructions prepared for de la Tour ordered him to claim (and only if those negotiating with him raised the subject of Victor Amadeus' earlier persecution of the Vaudois) that his master had had little choice in the matter and had not continued it longer than was necessary. If the Dutch insisted on the restoration of the Vaudois, or the people of the Val di Luserna, to their former status in the Savoyard state, de la Tour must claim that it had already been done. If he saw no chance of a treaty without yielding to their demand, he must do so only in general terms. Supplementary instructions were sent to de la Tour in October 1690, following the arrival in Turin of the Dutch commissary, van der Meer, who made it clear that the Dutch would insist on the restoration of the Vaudois of the Val Luserna as the price of a treaty. Victor Amadeus repeated that de la Tour must insist that this restoration

[93] For the release, arming and despatch of Vaudois prisoners, and Victor Amadeus' orders to aid their passage, see VA to Govone, 4 and 18 June 1690, Turin, AST/LM/Svizzera, m. 27 and C. Storrs, 'Diplomatic relations between William II and Victor Amadeus II 1690–96' (Ph.D. thesis, University of London, 1990), 34. See VDM to Fagel, 24 July 1690, Geneva, ARAH/SG/8643/23 for reports of about 3,000 French troops in the Val San Martino. Victor Amadeus continued to arm returning Vaudois thereafter, VDM to Fagel, 23 May 1691, Turin, ARAH/SG/8643/144. The duke (and his successors) particularly valued Vaudois soldiers for campaigning in rocky country: in 1691, Saint-Thomas informed van der Meer that Victor Amadeus intended to take Vaudois troops to the relief of Nice because of the mountainous terrain there, VDM to Fagel, 16 Mar. 1691, ARAH/SG/8643/117.

[94] This paragraph draws upon Storrs, 'Diplomatic relations', 59 ff., Storrs, 'Machiavelli dethroned: Victor Amadeus II and the making of the Anglo-Savoyard Alliance of 1690', *European History Quarterly*, 22, 3, 1992, 347 ff. and M. Viora, *Storia delle leggi sui Valdesi di Vittorio Amedeo II* (Bologna, 1930), 171 ff.

had already been effected and that it should be recognised as an act of grace on the part of the Vaudois' sovereign – the first of many references to this key concept in the Vaudois edict negotiations. Nevertheless, if de la Tour found it impossible to avoid a formal obligation, he could agree to it. In fact, de la Tour found it impossible to escape the Dutch insistence on a treaty provision for the Vaudois. It was thus with the, extremely grudging, approval of his master that de la Tour concluded, in October 1690, a subsidy treaty which bound Victor Amadeus, in a separate, secret article (the only concession on this subject won by de la Tour) to issue a formal public edict, to be properly registered by the Senate and Camera dei Conti of Turin, revoking the anti-Vaudois edict of 1686, and restoring to his Vaudois subjects the property, privileges and children lost in 1686. Equally important, if not strictly part of the restoration of Victor Amadeus' Protestant subjects, the duke must allow foreign Protestant exiles to settle in the Vaudois valleys. These were serious commitments. They not only transformed the position of the Vaudois, but they also held out the prospect of large numbers of French Protestants, who otherwise had no real link with or commitment to Victor Amadeus or the Savoyard state, flocking to Piedmont, which was both a haven and a route back into France. Enforcement of these obligations would dog Victor Amadeus' relations with the Maritime Powers for the rest of the Nine Years War.

Not surprisingly, from the start Victor Amadeus was slow to fulfil these obligations. He initially only returned a partial ratification of the treaty concluded by de la Tour, rejecting that part of the secret article allowing French Protestants to settle in the Piedmontese valleys since he feared that they would remain loyal to the French king. He pointed out that William III and the States-General had intended to 'restore' both Vaudois and French Huguenots and that whereas the treaty provision for the Vaudois followed from this, that for the French Protestants did not. Only the Vaudois could claim a right to settle in the valleys. He declared himself ready to allow foreign Protestants into those valleys, but only with specific permission. He would not grant a blanket right. Unfortunately, Victor Amadeus' appalling military and financial circumstances in the spring of 1691 made this position difficult to maintain, against Dutch and English insistence. In April 1691 he was obliged to send a full ratification of the treaty concluded in October 1690, accepting the obligation towards Vaudois and French Protestants. Nevertheless, his dislike of it had been made clear and thereafter expressed itself in endless delays in issuing the promised edict. Not until February 1692 did William III's envoy, Poley, and van der Meer at last receive the first of many draft edicts prepared by Victor Amadeus' ministers which they found unacceptable.⁹⁵ Only in the spring of 1694 would an edict be issued at last.

Why did it take so long? Some of the issues have already been identified, but they were many and complicated with wider and more serious implications. Firstly, there was the question of the preamble. The representatives of the Maritime Powers insisted on some reference to the pressure of, on the one hand, the French king, for the reduction of the Vaudois in 1686 and, on the other, that of the Dutch and William III for an edict of toleration. Victor Amadeus did not wish to offend Louis XIV unnecessarily and was also sensitive about his own authority or sovereignty within his own territories and therefore wished only to refer to foreign powers in general. Secondly, and more importantly, there was the issue of the recovery of children and property lost and seized in and after 1686.⁹⁶ Thirdly and finally, there was Victor Amadeus' reluctance to allow free and unrestricted access to the Vaudois valleys for French Huguenot refugees. The duke made some efforts to accommodate the Maritime Powers – allowing 500–600 French refugees named by Poley and van der Meer to settle in the valleys – but objected to a larger settlement of French Huguenots, above all because he feared that Louis XIV hoped to secure the valleys for himself by this infiltration of French subjects. Van der Meer subsequently argued that the presence of non-Piedmontese Protestants, by swelling the population of the valleys, would in fact strengthen the latter as a future bulwark against Louis XIV, but the duke remained unconvinced.⁹⁷ Victor Amadeus and his ministers could not ignore either the fact that any edict on behalf of the Vaudois would inevitably complicate relations between the courts of Turin and Rome. They therefore needed to limit concessions as far as possible and to

---

⁹⁵ It safeguarded, for example, the position of the Catholics who had lived in the Val San Martino, at Prali, before 1686, VDM to Fagel, 1 Mar. 1692, Turin, ARAH/SG/8643/212; VDM to Fagel, 8 Mar. 1692, Turin, ARAH/SG/8643/213. The Italian draft of the edict is at ARAH/SG/8643/211: and a French translation, with the envoys' proposed alerations, at ARAH/SG/8643/213, 214.

⁹⁶ Victor Amadeus also wanted to limit the right of settlement to those of his own subjects born in the Protestant faith, fearing that otherwise many of them might also be attracted to the valleys, undermining (he did not specify how) his own authority, Storrs, 'Diplomatic relations', 230–1. Van der Meer was concerned about the implication of the third point for the children of Vaudois who had converted to Catholicism.

⁹⁷ VDM to Fagel, 13 and 28 June 1692, Turin, ARAH/SG/8643/242, 244 and same to same, 13 April 1693, Turin, ARAH/SG/8644/23. Perhaps surprisingly, Victor Amadeus' position on this point was strengthened by the fact that his own Vaudois subjects, often resentful of the French refugees (see below) were ready to sacrifice the interests of the foreign Protestants to secure their own, VDM to Fagel, 26 Mar. 1694, Turin, ARAH/SG/8644/113. Some refugees had already returned to the French valleys, following threats of confiscation of their property if they did not, VDM to Fagel, 22 Mar. 1694, Turin, ARAH/SG/8644/112.

prepare the ground in Rome. Last, but by no means least, we cannot ignore Victor Amadeus' real religious scruples on this point, which led him to consult various theologians – including his former confessor, Father Valfre.[98]

The slow progress of the edict was also due to the fact that it was perhaps the most divisive issue, apart from the war itself, with which Victor Amadeus' ministers had to deal between 1690 and 1696. In December 1692 Saint-Thomas, in a rare insight into the debates within Victor Amadeus' ruling circle in these years, told van der Meer of a bitter dispute with an unidentified opponent of the edict. The Dutch commissary was well aware of the hostility to the Vaudois, to the Protestant troops in Victor Amadeus' service and to the Vaudois edict of individual ministers, including both the secretary of war, conte Benzo di Cavour (a creature of that champion of Counter-Reformation Catholicism in the Savoyard state, the marchese di Pianezza) and the generale delle finanze, conte Marelli. According to van der Meer, Marelli believed that blocking the edict would lead the Maritime Powers to stop paying Victor Amadeus' subsidy, depriving him of the means to wage the present war and so lead to a peace.[99] Indeed, although both edict and war may equally have attracted the hostility of a grouping of Catholic *dévots* in Turin, it is also possible that opposition to the edict was a 'legitimate' means of arguing against a war which it was difficult to criticise head on. According to Saint-Thomas, who declared his own enthusiasm for the edict, the edict's opponents sought to make the issue one of conscience (as opposed to his own determination to regard it as one of state) and to undermine his own standing with Victor Amadeus.[100] That Saint-Thomas was not simply trying to mislead the Protestant envoys is suggested by his correspondence with de la Tour, in London in the spring of 1693. Saint-Thomas attributed the delay in issuing the edict to the efforts of unnamed casuists, or theologians, and the pope. For his part, Saint-Thomas claimed to have consulted other casuists. These had resolved his own difficulties of conscience in the affair, but were reluctant to openly defend the edict, confirming the extent to which the issue of the edict embittered political life in Turin. Recognising that the long-term objective of the edict's

---

[98] See Viora, *Storia delle leggi*, 206 ff., for the views of the theologians, consulted by Provana. In 1693, Victor Amadeus himself informed van der Meer that Valfrè, had concerns which must be addressed, VDM to Fagel, 27 Mar., Turin, ARAH/SG/8644/20.

[99] VDM to Fagel, 26 and 29 Dec. 1692, Turin, ARAH/SG/8643/308, 310.

[100] In the spring of 1693, Saint-Thomas confided to van der Meer that Valfrè, who was highly esteemed by the duke, had declared the drafter of the edict a heretic, obliging Saint-Thomas to defend himself, VDM to Fagel, 27 Mar. 1693, Turin, ARAH/SG/8644/20.

opponents might be to alienate the Maritime Powers from Victor Amadeus, and so hasten the end of the war, Saint-Thomas used his official correspondence with his master's envoy to ask the latter to collude with him to ensure the edict was issued, by preparing a *mémoire* for the duke outlining the pressing reasons for its publication – which de la Tour did in fact supply. But this was by no means the end of the divisions between Victor Amadeus' ministers on this matter.[101]

For their part, the Maritime Powers, or their envoys in Turin, were under pressure from the Vaudois, who sent frequent deputations to them from their valleys, as individual cases made clear that without an edict what had been promised the Vaudois in the treaty was difficult to enforce.[102] This pressure grew in the winter of 1693–94, in the wake of the developing European subsistence crisis; this made it much more difficult for those Protestant refugees in Switzerland to obtain charity. Many therefore headed for Piedmont, provoking a spate of clashes with the ecclesiastical and secular authorities on a wide range of issues: the recovery of children and property and access to accommodation and employment – the inquisitor forbidding Catholics to employ or lodge the Protestant immigrants –[103] into which the envoys of the Maritime Powers were inevitably drawn.[104] Another source of pressure to grant the edict was the

---

[101] See Viora, *Storia delle leggi*, 206 ff., for a disastrous earlier attempt by Saint-Thomas to secure a favourable theological opinion from the Jesuit, Raiberti, a papal brief of Nov. 1692 congratulating Victor Amadeus' religious zeal (since the edict now seemed to have been lost) and for the collusion between Saint-Thomas and de la Tour, which had little immediate effect. In late 1693, Saint-Thomas, clearly hoping to moderate van der Meer's demands for the overdue edict, informed him of the intrigues of the pro-French faction in Turin and of his own disputes over the edict with some of Victor Amadeus' other ministers, VDM to Fagel, 30 Nov. 1693, Turin, ARAH/SG/8644/90.

[102] VDM to Fagel, 12 May 1692, Turin, ARAH/SG/8643/229. In the winter of 1692–3 two Vaudois, seeking to recover the niece of one of them, were arrested by the authorities at Turin, VDM to Fagel, 16 Jan. 1693, Turin, ARAH/SG/8644/4. Pressure for the edict also arose as a result of the difficulties encountered by French Protestants from Dauphiné who returned with the allies after the abortive incursion of 1692 and wished to settle in the Val Luserna, VDM to Fagel, 21 Oct. 1692, Turin, ARAH/SG/8643/283.

[103] VDM to Fagel, 8 Nov. 1693, Turin, ARAH/SG/8644/83; and same to marquis de Marolles, governor of Duchy of Aosta, 9 Nov. 1693, Turin, ARAH/SG/8644/84. For the inquisitor's efforts from the winter of 1690–1 to help the Catholics in the valleys resist the various pressures consequent on the return of Protestant Vaudois, see A. Landi, 'Il Rimpatrio dei Valdesi nei Documenti dell'Archivio Segreto Vaticano (1686–1691)', in de Lange, *Dall'Europa alle Valle Valdesi*, 188–9. The increasingly difficult situation for the refugees in Switzerland is dealt with by M.-J. Ducommun and D. Quadroni, *Le refuge Protestant dans le Pays de Vaud* (Geneva, 1991) and M. Küng, *Die Bernische Asyl- und Flüchtlingspolitik am Ende des 17. Jahrhunderts* (Geneva, 1993).

[104] See VDM to Fagel, 15, 25 and 29 Jan. 1694, Turin, ARAH/SG/8644/101, 103 and 104, for the Dutch commissary's intervention on behalf of a young woman who had

revelation in the winter of 1692–93, and again in that of 1693–94, that Louis XIV's agents were negotiating secretly with the Vaudois in an attempt to end the fierce guerrilla war in the valleys, and prevent Victor Amadeus and his allies using the Vaudois valleys to repeat the incursion into Dauphiné of 1692. Besides offering substantial annual pensions to the hard pressed Vaudois communities if they would agree to a truce, Louis XIV (or his agents) were pointing out to the Vaudois that William III had so far failed to secure the promised edict of toleration.[105]

These pressures underpinned a determination on the part of the subsidy-paying Maritime Powers by the spring of 1694 that Victor Amadeus must finally issue the long-promised and much-delayed Vaudois edict. In tense audiences with the duke, van der Meer claimed that the excuses put forward so far were the work of Victor Amadeus' enemies. But, in conversation with Saint-Thomas, he tried a different tack, relating the edict to Victor Amadeus' hopes of support on the international scene in the long term. He argued that the only guarantee of peace and security after the present war was continued co-operation between the members of the Grand Alliance and that, if Victor Amadeus did not issue the edict, none would ally with him (because he could not be trusted to fulfil his obligations). The duke would again become a 'slave' of France.[106] From March 1694, van der Meer's efforts, which had been reinforced by occasional deputations to Victor Amadeus from the Vaudois themselves, received more sustained and forceful support from William III's new envoy, the Huguenot earl of Galway.[107] Patience was clearly running out in London and The Hague, where de la Tour was suspected of not representing to his master the true depth of feeling regarding the edict. Even William, usually so reserved, spoke sharply to de la Tour on the subject.[108] Saint-Thomas, who had championed the edict as a means to pursue the war effectively, and who had, as we have seen, borne the brunt

---

returned from Switzerland hoping to recover her father's property and who, having converted to Catholicism (hoping this would facilitate her efforts) and then reverted to her Protestant faith, had been arrested by the Inquisition as a relapsed heretic; and same to same, 5 Mar. 1694, Turin, ARAH/SG/8644/110, for his efforts on behalf of a 15-year-old Vaudois girl whose parents were trying to recover her from the Catholic family with whom she lived.

[105] See copies of a letter from a minister in Geneva to the Vaudois, end 1692, and of another written to the same from Pinerolo, 21 Jan. 1693, Turin, ARAH/SG/8644/14. It is surely no coincidence that the winter of 1692–3 saw subversive negotiations on the part of the French in both Mondovì and the Vaudois valleys. For French offers after the defeat at Marsaglia, see VDM to Fagel, 23 Nov. 1693, Turin, ARAH/SG/8644/88.

[106] VDM to Fagel, 5 Mar. 1694, Turin, ARAH/SG/8644/110.

[107] Galway's arrival prompted the despatch to Turin of a Vaudois deputation of welcome, bringing further complaints, VDM to Fagel, 22 Mar. 1694, Turin, ARAH/SG/8644/112.   [108] Viora, *Storia delle leggi*, 214 ff.

of personal attacks on his Catholic orthodoxy in consequence, used William's words and the crucial contribution to Victor Amadeus' war effort of both William and the Dutch in his campaign against the edict's opponents to good effect.[109] At last, on 5 May 1694, Victor Amadeus informed his council that he would issue the edict, although publication was delayed both to allow him personally to inform the papal nuncio and to allow his ambassador in Rome, de Gubernatis, to inform the pope. It was hoped in this way to forestall a breach with the papacy over the toleration established by the edict. The duke issued the edict at last on 23 May 1694. This was certainly not the end of the affair, since Saint-Thomas' claim that the edict did not have to be registered by the Turin Senate or Camera dei Conti, on the grounds that previous edicts had not been registered, was rejected by van der Meer, who cited the formal registration of previous Vaudois edicts issued by Victor Amadeus' predecessors and pointed out that the 1690 treaty required this formality. Registration took place on 25 May. This should have been a matter of course. However, both Senate and Camera — whether in secret collusion with the duke or in opposition to him is unclear — restricted the concessions granted the Vaudois in the edict. Van der Meer regarded these amendments as a breach of Victor Amadeus' treaty obligation, but saw little chance of redress in face of the determined opposition of clergy and pro-French elements. On 25 June he and Galway formally thanked the duke. Galway then took a copy of the edict to the valleys, where a synod of the consistories was to be held, and a Vaudois deputation subsequently visited Turin to thank both the envoys and Victor Amadeus.[110]

The struggle for the edict was, as we have seen, closely linked with the rebuilding in the valleys of the Vaudois communities and culture suppressed in the later 1680s. Perhaps the most important aspect of this process was the repopulation of the valleys as exiles returned from Switzerland and Germany. This repeopling was not easy against the multiple threat of French arms,[111] the antagonism of neighbouring Piedmontese Catholic communities,[112] internal divisions[113] and famine. But

[109] ST to DLT, 20 Mar. 1694, Turin, AST/LM/Olanda, m. 4.
[110] VDM to Fagel, 28 May, 25 June and 16 July 1694, Turin, ARAH/SG/8644/126, 131 and 135. Viora, *Storia delle leggi*, 217–19, prints the text of the edict. See also I. Soffietti, 'La legislazione sabauda sui Valdesi dal 1685 al 1730', in de Lange, *Dall'Europa alle Valli Valdesi*, 283–4.
[111] In the spring of 1692, reports reached Turin of French plans to invade the valleys and even to settle there Irish (another displaced population) — evidence of both the crucial importance of the valleys and the strategic value of colonisation schemes, VDM to Fagel, 12 Apr. 1692, Turin, ARAH/SG/8643/223.
[112] For conflicts, sometimes violent, between the Vaudois and the neighbouring communities of Barge and Bricherasio, see van der Meer's correspondence, Jan. and Feb. 1694, Dec. 1694, Jan. 1695, ARAH/SG/8644.
[113] In Oct. 1695, after receiving a deputation complaining at pastor Henri Arnaud's

with help from the Maritime Powers and Victor Amadeus[114] the Protestant population of the valleys did recover – although surveys effected by ducal officials in the valleys in 1697–98 (the first stage of *perequazione*, see Chapter 2) revealed that the total population of the valleys was less than two-thirds of what it had been in 1686.[115] The next step was the rebuilding of the Vaudois' distinct ecclesiastical, political and social institutions and structures. This, too, depended greatly upon support – mainly financial – from their co-religionaries outside the Savoyard state: William III's Queen Mary II supported a number of pastors and schoolmasters in the valleys,[116] while the Dutch States General funded both the rebuilding of ruined pastors' houses and churches, the building of new churches[117] and contributed towards the costs of a new catechism for the instruction of the young.[118] The first synod to be held since the expulsion of the 1680s, was held with ducal permission in November 1692 and was attended by a ducal representative. This set a pattern for the rest of the period under consideration. Although not political institutions, the revival of the synod (and consistories) meant a small but significant revival of autonomous institutions of a sort in the Savoyard state in these years.[119] This resurrection of the Vaudois communities and the way of life which had existed before 1687 had some less positive consequences for those involved, including not least the efforts of Victor Amadeus and his ministers to increase the revenues yielded by the valleys. In the winter of 1694–95, with the support of the envoys of the Maritime Powers, the Vaudois managed to beat off an attempt to extend to the valleys the

---

cashiering those Vaudois unable to bear arms, depriving them of a share in the contributions raised (a vital source of provisions and funds), the commissary (who was frequently called on to mediate in these quarrels) observed that their disunity was the cause of all the Vaudois' misfortunes, VDM to Fagel, 10 Oct. 1695, Turin, ARAH/SG/8644/214.

[114] In 1691, van der Meer used funds provided by the States General to purchase some of the seedcorn needed by the Vaudois, arguing that this was the best way to relieve the States of the burden of the Vaudois in the longer term, VDM to Fagel, 28 Sept. 1691, Turin, and States' Resolution approving his action, ARAH/SG/8643/180, 196.

[115] See Tron, 'Il reinsediamento', and Sereno, 'Popolazione, territorio', passim.

[116] Request to States General from Vaudois pastors, 31 Dec. 1692, Bobbio, ARAH/SG/8644/3.

[117] VDM to Fagel, 19 Feb. and 17 Dec. 1694, Turin, ARAH/SG/8644/107, 156.

[118] Resolution of States, 20 Jan. 1696, on letter from van der Meer, ARAH/SG/8644/232. Presumably, many of the children recovered by returning relatives would need proper instruction.

[119] See T. J. Pons, ed., *Actes des synodes des Eglises Vaudoises 1692–1854* (Torre Pellice, 1948). Van der Meer's account is in VDM to Fagel, 17 Sept. 1693, St Jean in the Val di Luserna, ARAH/SG/8644/67, enclosing a detailed extract of the proceedings of the synod of 1693 held at St Jean, ARAH/SG/8644/66, supplements Pons' account. See Soffietti, 'La legislazione', 287–8, for divorce rulings by successive synods (1695, 1708, 1711, 1718 and 1720).

imposts on tobacco and brandy (from which they had always been exempt) and the new duty on stamped paper. This fiscal pressure was particularly fierce in the winter and spring of 1695–96 when the duke was especially hard pressed (see Chapter 2). Gropello, now intendant of Saluzzo and the valleys, summoned various Vaudois for tax owed since 1686. More seriously, Gropello and his master were determined to introduce the salt gabelle, from which the valleys (like Mondovì) were exempt. The English and Dutch ministers secured a promise from Gropello that the Vaudois would not be unfairly or excessively taxed, but by the end of the war the decision had been taken to integrate the valleys into an increasingly uniform tax regime.[120] Clearly, the rebuilding of the Vaudois communities and way of life in the valleys was not easy, and could not have been achieved without support from their co-religionaries abroad. Nevertheless, it was one of the most striking developments within the Savoyard state after 1690.

Having finally secured the crucial edict of toleration in 1694, however, the envoys of the Maritime Powers found it nearly as difficult to have it fully implemented, for various reasons. There were deliberate, co-ordinated efforts by Catholic institutions in Piedmont to thwart the provisions of the edict regarding property, the recovery of children[121] and the restoration of institutions and practices which had flourished before 1686.[122] Some cases, which were not really covered by the edict,

[120] VDM to States, 17 Dec. 1694, Turin, ARAH/SG/8644/159 and same to Fagel, 20 Dec. 1694, 9 Sept. and 10 Oct. 1695, 10 and 13 Feb., 23 Apr. and 11 and 14 May 1696, Turin, ARAH/SG/8644/160, 206, 214, 241, 242, 245, 254, 257.

[121] In 1695, van der Meer, primed by the Vaudois, reported the efforts of the cavaliere Vercelli, the duke's own governor in the Val Luserna, to buy the property of those Catholics wishing to leave the valleys in order to prevent its return to its pre-1686 Vaudois owners and that the Compagnia di San Paolo, of Turin, and the Propaganda Fide, had created a fund to buy, through Vercelli, property in the valleys, in a deliberate attempt to thwart the permission granted Vaudois in the edict to buy Catholic owned property (once in the possession of the church, that property could never be released). Van der Meer also reported serious difficulties facing parents seeking (in accordance with the terms of the edict) to recover their children, VDM to Fagel, 1 Apr. 1695, Turin, ARAH/SG/8644/185; see Tron, 'Il reinsediamento', 334. In many respects the renewed Vaudois presence (and later the edict) reinvigorated the Catholic mission in the valleys: see VDM to Fagel, 9 Apr. 1694, ARAH/SG/8644/117, for the despatch to Villar of a Catholic priest, for the first time since 1690.

[122] Typical was the affair of the appointment of a notary of the Reformed religion in the Luserne valley, in accordance with the traditional privileges of the Vaudois. Only in Jan. 1696, after nearly a year of negotiation, and with a loan from van der Meer to pay the necessary fees, the Protestant notary was finally admitted by the grand chancellor (and with no innovations in his patents limiting his sphere of activity, as had been originally attempted), VDM to Fagel, 28 Nov. and 26 Dec. 1695 and 6 and 9 Jan. 1696, Turin, ARAH/SG/8644/228–232. Inevitably, van der Meer saw the opponents of the Vaudois at work in these various difficulties: same to same, 4, 7, 14, 25 and 28 Feb. 1695, ARAH/SG/8644/168 ff.

required clarification of it.[123] Pope Innocent XII's condemnation of the edict in August of that year, by giving rise to a long-running conflict between church and Savoyard state may have helped the Vaudois. Victor Amadeus' resentment at what he regarded as an interference with his sovereignty expressed itself in a formal ban on publication of the prohibition in his states which the Senate (resentful of any clerical jurisdictional claims) registered in September 1694. The inquisitor, however, repeated his earlier ban on Catholics (on pain of excommunication) lodging and dealing with Protestants, while he and the papal nuncio instigated the putting of questions on this matter by parish priests in the confessional. This helped inflame the dispute between Turin and Rome, which was further fuelled by Victor Amadeus' efforts to have the papal fiefs enclaved within his territories contribute men and money to his war effort. The Vaudois issue was thus part of another important aspect of Savoyard state formation in these years, i.e. the conflict with the church, which was not resolved till well after 1713. However, while ready to restrict ecclesiastical interference in lay matters in his states, the duke was by no means willing to be seen as a protector of Protestant heretics in his states.[124]

Inevitably, many of the difficulties thrown up by the edict remained unresolved when Victor Amadeus abandoned the Grand Alliance in 1696. It was, however, the duke's *volte-face* in 1696 which was perhaps the most serious threat facing the Vaudois in the short term. No longer dependent on the subsidies of the Maritime Powers, and allied again with Louis XIV, there was a strong possibility that he would end the toleration granted to his Vaudois subjects. They certainly feared this, while some refugees from neighbouring French Pragelato who had settled in the Val di Luserna during the war fled to Switzerland. In fact, few if any, of these fears were realised. In the summer of 1696, partly in order to convince William III and the Dutch of his good faith, and thus secure their support until the conclusion of the general peace in 1697, and partly as an assertion of his new independence of both Louis XIV and the pope, Victor Amadeus made clear his determination to respect the edict of

[123] In 1696 van der Meer and Galway raised the case of women who had converted to Catholicism before the expulsion of 1686, on the promise of dowries, and of parents and their children who had similarly been 'bought' for the Catholic faith before 1686. Since the issue of the edict of May 1694 many of these had reverted to the reformed faith, but were threatened by the Catholic clergy as lapsed Catholics. The envoys sought orders from Victor Amadeus, since the edict did not adequately cover such cases, VDM to Fagel, 27 Apr. and 14 May 1696, Turin, ARAH/SG/8644/255, 261.

[124] VDM to Fagel, 3 and 27 Sept. and 1 Oct. 1694, Turin, ARAH/SG/8644/141, 147, 148. For general accounts of the longrunning breach with Rome, see Symcox, *Victor Amadeus*, 129 ff., Viora, *Storia delle leggi*, 220 ff. and F. Venturi, *Saggi sull'Europa illuminista, 1: Alberto Radicati di Passerano* (Turin, 1954), passim.

1694, and sought to reassure the Vaudois that his change of policy would not affect them.[125] But this did not mean he was any more enamoured of the edict. The Huguenot inhabitants of the valley of Perosa, ceded by Louis XIV in 1696 with Pinerolo, were excluded from its benefits, by the terms of cession in the treaty of Turin of 1696, which Victor Amadeus' Protestant allies later hoped to rectify during the War of the Spanish Succession.[126] In July 1698, in accordance with his treaties with Louis XIV, and reflecting his own determination not to have his valleys occupied by a French fifth column, Victor Amadeus expelled all French Protestants, about 3,000 people in all, from the Vaudois valleys.[127] The post-war years also, in some part continuing a process begun before 1696, saw the full reintegration into the Savoyard state of the Vaudois communities, including the first stage of the so-called *perequazione* and the introduction at last of the gabelle (as in Mondovì). These developments should not, however, obscure the more important point, that the edict of 1694 formalising the position of the Vaudois Protestants in the Savoyard state survived the collapse of Victor Amadeus' alliance with its sponsors the Maritime Powers.[128]

The English and Dutch envoys, on their arrival in Turin in the winter of 1703–04 were assured by a Vaudois deputation that the duke respected the edict.[129] There were certainly some incidents during the War of the Spanish Succession reminiscent of those which had surfaced during the Nine Years War,[130] but it was in Victor Amadeus' interest to satisfy as far

---

[125] VDM to Fagel, 20 and 27 July and 3 Aug. 1696, Turin, ARAH/SG/8644/282, 283, 285. Van der Meer was told of Victor Amadeus' rejection of Louis XIV's demand for the expulsion from the valleys of foreigners, same to same, 27 July 1696, Turin, ARAH/SG/8644/283. A Vaudois deputation thanked Victor Amadeus for these assurances, same to same, 6 Aug. 1696, Turin, ARAH/SG/8644/286.

[126] Chetwynd to bishop of Bristol, 12 Mar. 1712, Turin, SP 92/27 f. 476; same to Dartmouth, 23 Aug. 1710, Turin, SP 92/28; VDM to Fagel, 22 July 1704, Turin, ARAH/EA/VDM/29, 124. For one contemporary report, see Bazan to Carlos II, 6 Aug. 1698, Turin, AGS/E/3660/55.

[127] VDM to Fagel, 8 June 1709, ARAH/SG/EA/VDM/33 f. 88; Tron, 'Il reinsediamento', 321; Viora, *Storia delle leggi*, 248 ff. (and text of edict, 252–3); and Symcox, 'The Waldensians in the absolutist state', 246. Most of those expelled went into exile in Germany.

[128] Tron, 'Il reinsediamento', and Sereno, 'Popolazione, territorio', passim.

[129] VDM to Fagel, 1 Feb. 1704, Turin, ARAH/EA/VDM/29, 21–2.

[130] The value of the edict was thrown into relief by cases like that (1705) of the French Huguenot director of one of the workshops in the General Hospital in Turin, Jean Saliens whose exclusion from the protection granted the Vaudois by the edict of 1694 was made clear when his son was effectively detained on the grounds that he wished to change his religion: see the lengthy account of the affair in VDM to Fagel, 20 May and 5 Aug. 1705, Turin, ARAH/EA/VDM/30, 48, 92; and more briefly, in the published correspondence between Turin and its minister in London in *CGP*, V, passim.

as possible the Protestant Maritime Powers who helped keep him going, while the real breakthrough as far as the Vaudois and their protectors were concerned had been achieved in 1694. Once again, the Vaudois were in the front line of Victor Amadeus' struggle against the French. In 1705, in view of the French reoccupation of Pinerolo and advance into the valleys, the duke ordered that some of the Vaudois families be evacuated from their now exposed positions and supplied with bread.[131] As in the Nine Years War, the French king sought to detach the Vaudois from their prince. Indeed, between 1703 and 1708, when the marchese d'Andorno reconquered it, the San Martino Valley effectively threw off its allegiance to Victor Amadeus, to form an independent republic under Louis XIV's protection. Not surprisingly, perhaps, in 1704 the duke asked van der Meer to visit the valleys to encourage the Vaudois to remain loyal to their prince, a remarkable indication of the mediatory role between prince and Protestant subjects acquired by the Maritime Powers.[132] At the height of the crisis threatening the very existence of the Savoyard state, in 1706 Victor Amadeus briefly fled to the valleys, where he appealed to the loyalty and self-interest of the Vaudois. His appeal seems to have worked, Vaudois resistance on this occasion preventing the French seizing the heights between the San Martino and Luserna Valleys, and attacking Victor Amadeus in his last refuge. Subsequently, 1,500 Vaudois joined the duke outside Turin before the decisive engagement there.[133] After 1706, with the war being largely fought in the Alps, the Vaudois valleys remained close to the front line.[134] Thereafter, too, the Vaudois continued to play their part in supplying Victor Amadeus' war effort,[135] although – supported by the envoys of the Maritime Powers, as

[131] VDM to States, 15 Apr. 1705, Turin, ARAH/EA/VDM/30, 33.
[132] VDM to Fagel, 4 July 1704, Turin, and Pianezza to VDM, 2 July 1704, Turin, ARAH/EA/VDM/29, 112. The leaders of the rebellion were subsequently executed, while Victor Amadeus demanded oaths of loyalty from his recovered subjects, most of whom, however, benefited from an amnesty, VDM to Fagel, 1708, ARAH/SG/EA/VDM/32, fs. 174, 187 and 196. For a general account of this episode, see Armand-Hugon, 'La Repubblica di San Martino', *BSSV*, 84, 1945.
[133] VDM to States, 17, 21 and 24 July and 4 Sept. 1706, Genoa, ARAH/EA/VDM/30, 302, 305, 311, 318. In early 1704, the Vaudois were expected to contribute the same number to Victor Amadeus' total (infantry) force that year of 16,500 men (i.e. almost a tenth of the whole), Hill to Nottingham, 15 Feb. 1704, Turin, in W. Blackley, *The Diplomatic Correspondence of the Rt. Hon. Richard Hill, Extraordinary Envoy from the Court of St James to the Duke of Savoy in the Reign of Queen Anne from July 1703 to May 1706* (London, 1845).
[134] See VDM to Fagel, 14 Sept. 1709, Turin, ARAH/SG/EA/VDM/33, f. 157, for fears of a French attack on Val Luserna.
[135] Victor Amadeus formed a regular corps of 500 Vaudois for his 1708 campaign, VDM to Fagel, 2 June 1708, Turin, and 3 Aug. 1708, Bardonecchia, ARAH/EA/VDM/32, fs. 105, 148.

in the 1690s – they were able to fend off some of the duke's fiscal demands.[136] Away from the fighting the process of rebuilding the Vaudois communities continued. Churches were again rebuilt with the aid of grants from the Maritime Powers, who continued to fund pastors and schoolmasters.[137] Synods continued to be held in the valleys, with Victor Amadeus' permission and in the presence of a ducal representative, and could be critical of the policy of their prince and his agents.[138] As in the 1690s, there were difficulties over property claims, which in the case of Protestants returning to Val Perosa, were complicated by the sale between the wars of confiscated property in order to raise funds in the short term.[139]

The Vaudois were much less of a concern during the War of the Spanish Succession than were the Protestants of the Pragelato, conquered by Victor Amadeus' forces in 1708. This was because in their treaties with the duke of 1704 and 1705 the Maritime Powers had held out the prospect of securing for him the Pragelato, Dauphiné and Provence, in return for which he promised to allow the return of Protestant exiles and full religious freedom for those Protestants forced to convert to Catholicism by Louis XIV.[140] In fact, however, Victor Amadeus was as reluctant to extend to the Vaudois of Pragelato the benefits of the edict of 1694 as he had been to issue the edict and manoeuvred to avoid making any formal grant. In December 1708, in response to a request from van der Meer for this, the duke replied that he only held the Pragelato by right of conquest and that, to satisfy the terms of the treaty (above), he must

[136] See VDM to Fagel, 12 Oct. 1709, Turin, ARAH/EA/VDM/33, f. 171, for Victor Amadeus' exempting the inhabitants of Val Luserna from taxes for 1709.
[137] From the winter of 1704–5 Queen Anne paid pensions to seven preachers in the valleys: VDM to Fagel, 18 Feb. 1705, Turin, ARAH/EA/VDM/30, 16. See same to same, 15 June 1709, Turin, ARAH/EA/VDM/33, f. 92, for grants to various communities for the rebuilding of their churches by the English envoy, and enclosing a petition from the community of Pomaret requesting funds towards the rebuilding of its church, pointing out that this was the nearest community for many of those Protestants of the Pragelato (see below) who wished to attend reformed services.
[138] In early 1708 Victor Amadeus gave permission for a synod, which had to resolve (among other things), difficulties following the appointment of two pastors who had returned from England where they had been studying, VDM to Fagel, 11 Feb. 1708, Turin, ARAH/EA/VDM/32, f. 28. In late 1708 the synod complained to Victor Amadeus at the denial to Vaudois pastors of access to one of the leaders of the San Martino 'rebellion' (who had converted to Catholicism before his execution), VDM to Fagel, 27 Oct. 1708, Turin, ARAH/EA/VDM/32, f. 196.
[139] VDM to Fagel, 8 June 1709, Turin, ARAH/EA/VDM/33, f. 88.
[140] VDM to Fagel, 31 Oct. 1708, Turin, ARAH/EA/VDM/32, f. 198. See A. Forneron, 'L'articolo segreto sul Pragelato nel trattato di alleanza colle Potenze Maritime', BSSV, 70, 1938.

await the peace and the formal cession of the Pragelato – although he would happily grant *de facto* toleration in the interim.[141] The duke evaded a similar request from Queen Anne in 1709, on the grounds that it was not advisable, while he was negotiating a settlement of his differences with the pope (in part inflamed by this very issue) to provoke the latter with a public extension of Protestant toleration in his states; and he asked the envoys of the Maritime Powers to do what they could to restrain the Vaudois from provoking the Catholics of the Pragelato.[142] However, the unofficial toleration proved an unsatisfactory second best, as was shown in 1710 following the detention of one young Vaudois woman from Fenestrelles, Catherine Borel, niece of a substantial Geneva merchant, and heiress to a large property in the Pragelato. Victor Amadeus and his ministers proved rather unhelpful, arguing that, born and baptised a Catholic, she was not protected by the duke's treaty obligations. This case understandably caused much anxiety among the reformed community in the Savoyard state. It also prompted the British envoy in Turin, Chetwynd, to press his own government to exploit Victor Amadeus' desire for an advantageous peace to include in the latter some specific obligation to the Protestants of the Pragelato. What he had in mind was something comparable to the edict of toleration of 1694, which was clearly now a benchmark for all sides.[143] However, this attempt to use diplomacy to extend religious privilege and toleration within the Savoyard state failed. Victor Amadeus, who was determined to avoid anything of the sort, was able to end the war without a formal obligation to grant a liberty of worship to his newly acquired Protestant subjects, above all by arguing that Pragelato was ceded to him by Louis XIV not at the dictate of the Maritime Powers but in exchange for his own cession of Barcelonette. The importance of this success became apparent after 1713 when the court of Turin turned against its Protestant subjects; Protestantism in the

---

[141] VDM to Fagel, 19 Dec. 1708, Turin, ARAH/SG/EA/VDM/32, f. 225.

[142] In a recent case a pastor from the Val Luserna had gone to preach at Usseau in the Pragelato, provoking the Catholics there. This in turn had obliged Victor Amadeus to repeat his order to his intendant not to interfere with freedom of worship: see VDM to Fagel, 16 and 27 Feb., 13 Mar., 1 and 4 May 1709, Turin, SP 92/27, fs. 27, 32, 36, 70, 72.

[143] Chetwynd to Sunderland, 18 June 1710, Turin, SP 92/28. There are further details on the Borel case in same to same, 28 June and 12 July 1710, Turin, SP 92/28; same to Dartmouth, 23 Aug. 1710, Turin, SP 92/28 (and enclosing copy of the same to Sunderland, 8 June 1709, Turin, on behalf of the Protestants of Val Luserna, the Pragelato and Val Perosa in the forthcoming peace negotiations); same to same, 23 May 1711, Turin, SP 92/28; same to Bishop of Bristol, 12 Mar. 1712, Turin, SP 92/27, f. 476.

Pragelato was effectively destroyed in 1730 but that of the other Vaudois valleys, while coming under pressure nevertheless survived.[144]

The position won by the Vaudois is among the most striking examples of the way war and diplomacy, and the dependence of the Savoyard state on its Protestant allies if it was to wage war successfully, transformed that state internally between 1690 and 1720. Their privileged position and the edict of 1694 could not thereafter be taken for granted in the face of attempts to whittle away its provisions. However, it survived; and in 1727, Pierre Mellarède, who had enough experience to know what he was talking about, objected to the use by the Neapolitian historian and philosopher, Bernardo Andrea Lama (one of the leading lights of the reformed University of Turin in the 1720s) of the term 'brigands' to describe the Vaudois rebels of 1655 on the grounds that it would be regarded as improper by the Protestant powers who protected the Vaudois.[145] Whatever the precise reason, and although the long-term pressure on behalf of the Catholic faith did erode the strength of Protestantism in the valleys,[146] the Savoyard state had effectively acknowledged, between 1690 and 1713, that it was no longer a single confessional state, by means of an edict mediated by foreign powers. Throughout the eighteenth century, the edict of 1694 would serve as both a reference point for those concerned to defend the religious rights and privileges of the Vaudois and a yardstick for those (notably the inhabitants of the Pragelato during the War of the Spanish Succession) seeking similar

[144] See Symcox, *Victor Amadeus*, 155–6; and L. H. Boles Jr, *The Huguenots, the Protestant Interest and the War of the Spanish Succession 1702–1714* (New York, 1997), 69 ff. The omission of the edict of 1694 from the wide ranging Constitutions (or law code) issued by Victor Amadeus for his states in 1723 sparked English protests in Turin; and although in 1730 Victor Amadeus moved against relapsed Vaudois heretics, this was far less serious than the blanket outlawing of Protestant worship in the Pragelato, which prompted a mass exodus of Protestants: Symcox, *Victor Amadeus*, 185–7 and Quazza, *Le Riforme*, 11, 370–3.

[145] In the summer of 1718, as the Sicilian war broke out, a ducal order infringing the edict of 1694 provoked another Vandois appeal to their foreign protectors, and another – successful – intervention in Turin on behalf of the Vandois: Symcox, *Victor Amadeus*, 185. For Mellarède and Lama see G. P. Romagnani, 'Il "rimpatrio" nella storiografia italiana fra Sette e Ottocento', in de Lange, *Dall'Europa alle Valli Valdesi*, 489. We should not ignore the efforts on behalf of their co-religionaries of other Protestant states and princes. In 1714, following a recent order by the intendant, Pavia, forbidding the appointment of (Protestant) schoolmasters without the approval of the local Catholic clergy, the king of Prussia, Frederick William, sought to mobilise the English and Dutch governments and the German princes against the measure: A. Pittavino, 'La Cronaca di Pragelato dal 1658 al 1724 di R. Merlin e G. Bonne', *BSBS*, 9 1904, 323–3.

[146] Tron, 'Il reinsediamento', 335, contrasts the proportions of 73.1 per cent Protestants and 26.9 per cent Catholics in 1686 with Vaudois 58.1 per cent and Catholics 41.9 per cent in 1777.

privileges. The edict had recreated a privileged community in the state, more akin to the experience of the Duchy of Aosta than that of the province of Mondovì, and might thus be thought to represent an obstacle to the absolute state. But it had also reknit and strengthened, not least because of the possibility of calling on outside support, i.e. the Maritime Powers, the ties between the Vaudois and that state, anchoring the former more firmly in the latter and thus largely (if not completely) solving the problem of the Vaudois in the Savoyard state.

CONCLUSION

By 1720, the regions and communities which traditionally made up the composite Savoyard state were probably more integrated into that state than was the case in 1690,[147] although this was (not surprisingly) less true of the more recently acquired territories.[148] Traditionally, the process of integration has been regarded as one in which an authoritarian prince, Victor Amadeus, his hand strengthened by the development of a more powerful army, was able to impose integration by force, the most obvious example of this being the province of Mondovì. However, the process in Mondovì was more nuanced than this bald outline implies, while there were in fact different patterns of integration. For the Duchy of Aosta, which had done what it could and emerged in 1713 with its distinct institutions and role in the Savoyard state confirmed (despite the strong language of the late 1690s), very little had changed by the end of the War of the Succession. Greater integration in this case did not mean that there were no more limitations on ducal absolutism; the duke still had to rely on and co-operate with the Estates of Aosta and the Conseil des Commis. Rather more striking, not least because it was inextricably bound up with the two wars fought between 1690 and 1713, was the way the recently expelled Protestant Vaudois were not only enabled to return but also secured, largely at the insistence of the duke's Protestant allies, the Maritime Powers, a newly privileged position in the Savoyard state. The

[147] This included the independent marquisate of Saluzzo, acquired by Charles Emanuel I, which in 1701 finally lost its distinct marchional identity, S. J. Woolf, 'Sviluppo economico e struttura sociale in Piedmonte da Emanuele Filiberto a Carlo Emanuele III', *Nuova Rivista Storica*, 46, 1962, 4.

[148] Victor Amadeus' new Sicilian subjects seem never, in the five years he ruled the island, to have been really won over to his rule. Given more time, his efforts to integrate the island more closely (and countering its relatively more relaxed style of government under the Spanish Habsburgs in the preceding centuries) might have proved successful. However, it certainly did not succeed in binding Sicily more than superficially into the Savoyard polity and no doubt contributed to the success of the Spanish invasion of 1718, Symcox, *Victor Amadeus*, 171 ff.

duke was clearly reluctant to avoid extending the same privileged regime to his newly acquired Protestant subjects in the Pragelato. Far, however, from weakening that state, the edict of 1694 and the mediation of England and the Dutch Republic, whose concern was above all to ensure the duke could function effectively to help restrain Louis XIV's France, bound his Vaudois subjects more closely to Victor Amadeus and the Savoyard state. Indeed, it is questionable whether Victor Amadeus really wanted to create a uniform state. For one thing, diversity itself might offer the duke useful means if one region or community should go as far as armed rebellion; in the 1680s and after Victor Amadeus was able to use Vaudois against Mondovì and vice versa. If the years between 1690 and 1713 saw an apparently more determined drive to extend central control and impositions at the expense of local liberty and exemptions it was the result less of a ducal blueprint for 'absolutism' than of a desperate search for money and men to wage wars, above all the Nine Years War, whose sheer impact and cost had simply not been foreseen.[149]

[149] Symcox, 'Two forms of popular resistance in the Savoyard state of the 1680s: the rebels of Mondovì and the Vaudois', in Lombardi, *La Guerra del Sale (1680–1699)*, I, 285.

CONCLUSION

The years between 1690 and 1720 were ones of remarkable achievement for the Savoyard state and its prince, Victor Amadeus II. Their success can be charted in a number of spheres which, taken together, represent a substantial stage in the process of state formation: territorial enlargement and the achievement of a new, more defensible alpine frontier with France; the creation of a larger army, able to enforce the will of Victor Amadeus and his ministers; the expansion of government revenues, raised both from an enlarged territorial base and from existing territories which were increasingly expected to pay more; the development of tighter administrative structures linking centre and periphery; and the greater integration of individual provinces and communities, and of powerful social groups. The experience of these decades may also have helped create a new Savoyard 'national' identity, though one which was perhaps strongest in Piedmont, and which contributed to a growing divide between Piedmont and Savoy. Last, but by no means least, Victor Amadeus secured royal status, founded upon possession of the island realm of Sicily, and later Sardinia. Indeed, the culmination of the rise of the Savoyard state from 1690 through the crucible of war and diplomacy was its emergence in the new guise, in 1720, of the Kingdom of Sardinia after the Sicilian war (1718–20). Many of these achievements were intimately associated with a successful assertion by the Savoyard state and its prince of their independence on the international stage, particularly *vis-à-vis* Louis XIV's France. Victor Amadeus' diplomacy between 1690 and 1713 also ensured that for the rest of the eighteenth century the Savoyard state would be regarded as a natural member of that 'Old System' which brought together France's neighbours in order to contain French ambition and aggression; and in consequence gained for his state the foreign backing crucial to its escape from earlier French tutelage. Deservedly, Victor Amadeus (and his state) won a new stand ing among the Italian states and princes,[1] and admiration at home and abroad, then and later, for an achievement which could, and should, not be taken for granted and which involved considerable risk.[2]

'War made the state and the state made war.'[3] The development of the Savoyard state summarised above could, it must be stressed, have been achieved, at least in part, by peaceful means. Mention has already been made of the efforts of Victor Amadeus' predecessors to effect administrative reform and that revision of the tax registers which we know as the *perequazione*. But the transformation of the Savoyard state between 1690 and 1720 was above all associated with the two major wars that accompanied the struggle for the Spanish Succession. Victor Amadeus and the Savoyard state were by no means the only princes and states to benefit; or who expected to benefit from this.[4] However, the duke of Savoy was almost unique, at least in Italy (i.e. among the independent Italian states), in doing so well out of the great territorial rearrangement effected between 1690 and 1713, and particularly that of 1712–13. This owed much to Victor Amadeus' own claim on the Spanish Succession, but rather more to the crucial strategic importance of the Savoyard state. The knock-out blow was never delivered (as had been hoped) from his states, but the war in Italy played a larger part in the outcome of both the Nine Years War and the War of the Spanish Succession than has been acknowledged. Previous historians have exaggerated the extent to which Victor Amadeus was in control of, and felt himself to be in control of the diplomatic negotiations going on around him. On the contrary, he tended to be anxious and uncertain. (The point has also been made that what seemed signs of strength, notably the switches of alliance in 1696 and 1703, were the complete opposite, symptoms of the duke's vulnerability.) Nevertheless, his success also owed a great deal to the duke's ability to exploit his strategic situation, not least to secure vital additional help from the Great Powers whose resources so far exceeded those of his own states. This was important because, although his own subjects and

---

[1] In 1692–3 the duke of Modena and other princes and states saw the duke of Savoy as a possible mediator between themselves and an emperor demanding their contributions: VDM to Fagel, 21 Nov. 1692, ARAH/SG/8643/291.
[2] S. J. Woolf, 'Sviluppo economico e struttura sociale in Piemonte da Emanuele Filiberto a Carlo Emanuele II', *Nuova Rivista Storica*, 461, 1962, p. 1, compares the situation of the Savoyard state with that of Navarre, partitioned by France and Spain in the early sixteenth century.
[3] C. Tilly, ed., *The Formation of National States in Western Europe* (Princeton, 1975), 42.
[4] In 1705–6, with Philip V of Spain in difficulties, a number of Victor Amadeus' Italian neighbours hoped to advance their own territorial ambitions in return for support of one sort or another: VDM to Fagel, 16 Dec. 1705, Turin, ARAH/EA/VDM/30, 165.

states were pushed hard to provide men and money, and shouldered a massive burden, Victor Amadeus could not have achieved what he did without outside help.[5]

If we must beware of the legendary image of Victor Amadeus II as the manipulator of the international scene, we must also be careful not to exaggerate the contrast between the Savoyard state before and after this watershed and of exaggerating the degree of integration and the reinforcement of the authority of the state which was achieved between 1690 and 1720. For one thing, the struggle with the church, in part the product, or by-product of war, had by no means been satisfactorily resolved by 1713, when it was exacerbated by new problems arising from Victor Amadeus' acquisition of Sicily, and would not be so until the conclusion of the Concordats of 1727 and 1741. It is also worth remarking the extent to which the achievement of 1690–1720 was the work of the unreformed Savoyard state and the degree to which the Savoyard state remained untransformed. Indeed, the acquisition of Sicily (and subsequently Sardinia) made the Savoyard state even more of a 'composite state' in 1720, whose different territories had little in common apart from a duke and dynasty which provided the vital glue, than it had been in 1690. The birth of an heir in 1699, and of the future Charles Emanuel III in 1701, was at least as important an element in holding the state together as was the development of those more formal, impersonal institutions and structures which have impressed historians ever since. That state, often labelled 'absolute' could be, and often was, the guarantor (as much as the enemy) of privilege, these decades affirming the distinct position of both the Vaudois and the Duchy of Aosta in the Savoyard state – but in this way, too, firmly anchoring them in that state. Nor can we ignore (*pace* the Risorgimento tradition) the importance and value to the Savoyard state of its place in the Holy Roman Empire and the extent to which (at least until the 1730s) imperial and papal vassals and enclaves continued to confuse the issues of jurisdiction and sovereignty in that state.[6] Victor Amadeus refused, in 1697, to receive Pinerolo as a fief of

---

[5] It is worth stressing here that hardly any of the great territorial gains of these years were conquered by Victor Amadeus' own forces. Typically, in 1698, Victor Amadeus sought with French help (but without success) to ensure that in the ongoing negotiations between the emperor and the Ottoman Turks following Prince Eugene's recent successes in the Balkans (notably at Zenta, 1697), his own claim to the kingdom of Cyprus should at last be realised: N. Luttrell, *A Brief Historical Relation of State Affairs from September 1678 to April 1714*, 6 vols. (Oxford, 1857), IV, p. 367.

[6] Only from 1736, with the emperor's cession of the Langhe fiefs in the wake of Savoyard intervention in the War of the Polish Succession, was Charles Emanuel III able to exact

either the king of France or the emperor, but he was ready to exploit his status as an Imperial vassal and to accommodate the empire and emperor which had played a crucial role in the rise so far of the Savoyard dynasty and state.[7] Sovereign independence was the ideal, but subject status had its advantages, especially for a weak state. At the same time, the attitudes of Victor Amadeus, the lynchpin of the Savoyard state, were very traditional, revolving around his own status and dignity and those of his house.[8]

The persistence of more traditional political bonds, and privilege, was underpinned in part by the way Victor Amadeus financed and fought his wars. His subjects supplied most of the men and money without which the latter could not have been carried to a successful conclusion. However, given the relative poverty and weakness of the Savoyard state, at least by comparison with the Great Powers who dominated the international scene, its success depended greatly on the additional resources made available by Victor Amadeus' allies. Indeed, it is difficult to believe that he could have achieved what he did without the troops, military expertise, artillery, munitions, ships and above all money provided by those allies, and which were simply not available within the Savoyard state itself. By obtaining additional resources from outside his own state, Victor Amadeus also reduced the pressure on his own subjects, thus reducing in turn the likelihood of resistance to the growing burden of war-inspired impositions. This could not put a complete end to debate about, even opposition and resistance to the duke's policies – his wars did make enormous demands and brought considerable suffering – but could help to keep it within reasonable limits. As well as helping to contain the fiscal pressure on his own subjects, the aid provided by Victor Amadeus' allies also contributed to the avoidance of the creation of a French-style

---

full vassalage and homage from the Falletti di Barolo: S. J. Woolf, 'Studi sulla nobiltà piemontese nell'epoca dell'assolutismo', *MAST*, 1963, 20.

[7] See AST/Provincia di Pinerolo, m. 4/11b. In 1697, in order to secure the agreement of the imperial ministers to the incorporation of Victor Amadeus' separate space of 1696 into the general peace settlement being concluded at Rijswijk, de la Tour gave a verbal promise that Pinerolo would be returned to the empire, D. Carutti, *Storia della diplomazia della Corte di Savoia*, 4 vols., (Turin, 1875–80), III, 244–5.

[8] In 1731, when attempting to recover the throne he had recently abdicated in favour of Charles Emanuel III, Victor Amadeus declared 'I exposed my life hundreds of times to maintain the splendour of my House, I must not allow it to be obscured now', Carutti, *Storia della Diplomazia*, IV, p. 12. The abdication episode merits further study, not least for the many indications that Victor Amadeus' perception of government, the state, the relationship between prince and subjects remained very traditional, founded on personal relations (including clientage), traditional juridical forms and so on.

state (characterised by extensive venality) which would severely limit the monarchy's field for manoeuvre (i.e. absolutism). But their subsidies gave those allies political leverage within the Savoyard state; and the Protestant Maritime Powers were able to help reinsert their Vaudois co-religionaries into the emerging Savoyard polity. Here then was a distinct, Savoyard Sonderweg towards more integrated statehood in the era of the Spanish Succession, one very different from that of the Great Powers.

Despite these qualifications, a more coherent, organised Savoyard state structure of sorts had also emerged between 1690 and 1713, something akin to traditional images of the 'absolute' state, in order above all to maximise the effective mobilisation of the resources of the state for war. Having said this, it must also be acknowledged that the Savoyard state was, in some respects, weaker (partly because more 'composite') in 1713 than it had been in 1690, becoming more fragmented with the acquisition of the distant island realm of Sicily. At the same time it lost the support of the allies who had crucially contributed to the defence and expansion of Victor Amadeus' state. There was therefore a pressing new need to overhaul the institutions of the state to combat this relative 'disintegration' brought about by success in war and maximise further the state's resources. The result was the overhaul of virtually all aspects of government from 1713, although most attention has been focused on what was attempted in and after 1717. It could be argued, therefore, that the real administrative, as opposed to territorial, transformation of the Savoyard state necessarily occurred after 1713, in consequence of developments since 1690. Major reforms were essential to defend what had been acquired with additional foreign resources before 1713, not least because (for all the supposed superiority of a small state in mobilising its resources)[9] those resources were still far inferior to those of the Great Powers and because what had been achieved was very soon after 1713 threatened. Reform thereafter, which was essentially a pragmatic response to serious external threat (rather than an 'absolutist' blueprint imposed in a sort of vacuum), produced by 1720 a more tightly knit and controlled Savoyard state - although it could not achieve its immediate purpose, the retention of Sicily.

Some of the reforms effected after 1713, notably the creation of a navy, really were new, and were a direct response to the way the Savoyard state, and its strategic and defensive problems and needs, had been reshaped by 1713. However, many other of the apparent innovations after 1713 built

---

[9] This was among the arguments of the German cameralist, Bielfeld's, analysis of state power in his *Institutions Politiques* (1760): see D. Showalter, *The Wars of Frederick the Great* (London, 1996), 264.

substantially upon developments since 1690. This was obviously true in the case of the army, and particularly the new militia. Here Victor Amadeus was in effect establishing the militia which he had wanted to raise in more urgent circumstances (and with only partial success) in 1703–4. The same was true of the system of intendants, which was simply extended throughout the Savoyard state from 1717. The continuation and implementation of the *perequazione*, too, was largely a continuation of a reform long considered but which had finally begun to take shape between 1690 and 1713. Even the division of the responsibilities of the first secretary, and the creation of distinct secretariats responsible for internal and foreign policy, which was on the face of it a radical departure in 1717, could be said to conform to a pattern of bureaucratic specialisation which had begun with Benzo's designation as secretary for war in 1691–2. Clearly, the older view, that the Savoyard state was suddenly transformed in and after 1717 needs qualification.[10]

War since 1690, and its resulting pressures, had therefore given a substantial impulse to the longer-term process of reforming, and overhauling the Savoyard state (including the development of an effective diplomatic structure to ensure that the Savoyard state could 'punch above its weight'). The wisdom of this, and the essential social and political stability of the Savoyard state were both confirmed by the debacle in Sicily, and the forced exchange of the latter for Sardinia, in 1718–20 and the search for resources at home. Ultimately, however, the Savoyard state, like all other states then and now, was constantly in process of formation, as new challenges and problems necessitated new solutions. By the later eighteenth century, monarch and ministers in Turin would be seeking new answers to rather different issues.[11]

[10] In many respects, S. Cavallo, *Charity and Power in Early Modern Italy: benefactors and their motives in Turin 1541–1689* (Cambridge, 1994), 183 ff. complements the present argument.

[11] In the last quarter of the eighteenth century a group of administrators within the Savoyard state structure recognised the need for various improvements, reforms, at the heart of that state to meet new problems, including that of public order: see M. Broers, 'Policing Piedmont: the 'well-ordered' Italian police state in the age of revolution, 1789–1821', *Criminal Justice History*, 1994, 55 n. 16.

SELECT BIBLIOGRAPHY

PRIMARY SOURCES

Turin

Archivio di Stato

Archivi di Corte: Categoria 1: m. 1, 1b; Categoria 2: m. 1; Categoria 3: m. 1
Camera dei Conti: Rappresaglie (art. 495); Nobiltà (art. 852)
Cerimoniale: Roma: m. 2; Spagna: m. 1; Vienna: m. 1
Costa di Polonghera: m. 1–3, 5
Editti Originali m. 14–16
Gioie e Mobili: m. 3, 6 d'addizione
Langhe: m. 2, 3
Lettere di Ministri: Austria, m. 23, 25; Gran Bretagna, m. 8, 9, 24; Olanda, m. 1–6; Spagna, m. 36; Svizzera: m. 27; Vienna, m. 25
Lettere di Particolari: B, m. 44 (conte Benzo di Santena); C, m. 37 (conte Felice Dionisio Carron de Saint-Thomas), 62 (Challant de Châtillon); F, m. 36 (Ferrero, various), 53–6 (Fontana); G, m. 12 (Carlo Gastaldi), 53 (G.-B. Gropello); M, m. 37 (Pierre Mellarède), 47 (de Mesmes); P, m. 47 (conte Piosasco di None); R, m. 23 (Rehbinder); S, m. 83 (conte Solaro di Moretta), 87 (Spitalier)
Lettere di Principi, Duchi e Sovrani: m. 68
Materie Criminali: m. 9, 10, 12
Materie Ecclesiastiche: Negoziazioni colla Corte di Roma: m. 1, 3, 4; Materie Benefiziarie: m. 3; Riduzioni e Vacanti: m. 1; Inquisizione, m. 2; Immunità Reale del Piemonte: m. 1; Immunità locale: m. 1; Decime, sussidi e contribuzioni degli ecclesiastici di qua da monti: m. 1; Eretici: m. 1
Materie Giuridiche: Ministri e Segreterie di Stato: m. 1; Senato di Piemonte: m. 1
Materie Militari: Levate di Milizia: m. 1; Levate Reggimenti Provinciali: m. 1; Levate Truppe nel Paese: m. 2; Levate Truppe Straniere: m. 1; Ordini e Regolamenti: m. 1–4; Riforme: m. 1; Ufficio Generale del Soldo: m. 1–9
Matrimoni della Real Casa: m. 37
Nascite e Battesime: m. 1

Negoziazioni: Francia: m. 15–17; Inghilterra: m. 1, 2, 4; Olanda: m. 1, 2
Ordini Militari: Annunziata: m. 5
Patenti Controllo Finanze: 1690–1713
Prima Archivazione/Cavalcata, m. 1; Confraternite e Congregazione di Carità: m. 1; Ducato di Aosta: m. 1; Ebrei e Religionari: m. 1; Emolumenti e Insinuazioni: m. 1; Esenzione e Privileggi: m. 1; Finanze, Intendenze e loro Segreterie: m. 1; Operato nei tempi di guerra: m. 1; Pene Pecuniarie: m. 1; Provincia di Nizza e Oneglia: m. 1; Somministrazione, Alloggi Militari e Caserme: m. 1
Principi del Sangue: Principi del Sangue diversi: m. 10; Principi di Carignano: m. 1, 2; Principi di Soissons: m. 1
Provincia di Alba: m. 5, 10
Provincia di Asti, m. 8, 10, 14, 15, 16, 17, 21, 22, 30, 44
Provincia di Cuneo: m. 1
Provincia di Ivrea: m. 3, 10
Provincia di Pinerolo: m. 4, 12, 20, 21, 25, 26
Provincia di Vercelli, m. 5, 8, 14, 20, 21, 22, 26
Testamenti di Sovrani e Principi della Real Casa Savoia: m. 5
Trattati Diversi: m. 12
Tutele e Reggenze: m. 7

Biblioteca Reale

Storia Patria 220: Diary of Francesco Lodovico Solari (1682–1721)
Storia Patria: 227, 555, 834–36: Lodovico Soleri di Moretta, Trattati e gesta di Vittorio Amedeo II
Storia Patria 407b: Memorie di un borghese di Rivoli
Storia Patria 726: Registers of Victor Amadeus' Masters of Ceremonies 1690–1722

Opera Pia Barolo

Wicardel: Suppliche: m. 136; Miscellanea: m. 154; Lettere famigliari: m. 1; Lettere private: m. 137

London

British Library

Additional Manuscripts: 9737–40; 9743; 9746; 214862; 34504; 37992; 38013–14; 46528B; 46530A; 46539

Public Record Office

State Papers: SP 79 (Genoa)/ 3; SP/92 (Italian states): 25, 26SP 80 (Empire)/ 17; SP 96 (Switzerland)/ 7, 8

SELECT BIBLIOGRAPHY 321

Archivo General de Simancas, Spain

Estado (State Papers): 3412–3419; 3659–3660

Algemeen Rijks Archief, Hague

Staten Generaal: Eerste Afdeeling: 8643–8644 (verbal of commissary Van der Meer, 1690–97)
Staten Generaal: Eerste Afdeeling: Van der Meer: 29–33: letters from Turin 1704–9

PUBLISHED PRIMARY

Printed sources

Accame, P., 'La Repubblica di Genova e la guerrra per la successione di Spagna', *CGP*, VIII
Beaucaire, de, H., ed., *Recueil des instructions données aux ambassadeurs et ministres de France depuis les traités de Westphalie jusqu'à la Révolution Française. XIV: Savoie-Sardaigne to 1748*, 2 vols. (Paris, 1898)
Blackley, W., *The Diplomatic Correspondence of the Rt. Hon. Richard Hill, Extraordinary Envoy from the Court of St. James to the Duke of Savoy in the Reign of Queen Anne from July 1703 to May 1706*, 2 vols. (London, 1845)
Bollea, L. C., ed., *Cartario di Bricherasio (1159–1859) con Appendice di Statuti e Bandi Campestri*, Biblioteca della Societa Storica Subalpina, XCIX (Turin, 1928)
Bollati di Saint Pierre, F. E., *Atti e documenti delle Antiche Assemblee Rappresentative nella Monarchia di Savoia*, Monumenta Historia Patriae, 2 vols. (Turin, 1879 and 1884)
Carutti, D., ed., 'Relazioni sulla Corte di Spagna dell'abate Doria del Maro e del conte Lascaris di Castellar, ministri di Savoia', *MAST*, ser. 2, 19, 1861
  'Relazione sulla Corte d'Inghilterra del Consigliere di Stato Pietro Mellarède, plenipotenziario di Savoia al Congresso di Utrecht', *MSI*, 2nd ser., 24, 1885
Carutti, D., 'Lettere di Vittorio Amedeo II al conte Morozzo della Rocca, ambasciatore a Madrid dal 1714 al 1717', *MSI*, X, 1870
Casanova, E., 'Contributo alla biografia di Pietro Micca e di Maria Chiaberge Bricco e alla storia del voto di Vittorio Amedeo II', *CGP*, VII
  Censimento di Torino alla vigilia dell'assedio (29 agosto–6 settembre 1705)', *CGP*, VII
'Gli Archivi Camerali durante l'assedio di Torino (1705–06)', *CGP*, VII
Cibrario, L. ed., *Relazioni dello Stato di Savoia negli anni 1574, 1670, 1743 scritte dagli ambasciatori veneti* (Turin, 1830)
Coxe, W., ed., *Private and Original Correspondence of Charles Talbot, Duke of Shrewsbury* (London, 1821)
Denina, C., *Istoria della Italia Occidentale*, 6 vols. (Turin, 1809)

Derege di Donato, P., 'Ordine di battitura di monete ossidionali di Torino (1706)', *CGP*, VIII

Dubion, F. A., *Raccolta per ordine di materia delle leggi emanati negli stati sardi sino all'otto dicembre 1798*, 23 vols. (Turin, 1818–69)

Eusebio, F., 'Alba e suo territorio nella Guerra del 1703–09. Cronaca composta con estratti dagli 'Ordinati originali' del Comune', *CGP*, IX

Faccio, C., 'Assedio di Vercelli: primo periodo della Campagna di Guerra per la successione di Spagna anno 1704', *CGP*, X

Ferrero, E., 'Campagne in Piemonte durante la Guerra per la successione di Spagna (1703–07)', ed. C. Pio de Magistris, *CGP*, I

Guasco, F., 'Vittorio Amedeo nelle campagne 1691–1996 secondo un carteggio intedito', in *Studi su Vittorio Amedeo II* (Turin 1933)

Heller, F., ed., *Militärische Korrespondenz des Prinzen Eugen von Savoyen* (Vienna, 1843)

Le Bouyer de St.-Gervais, *Mémoires et correspondance du maréchal de Catinat*, 3 vols. (Paris, 1819)

Manners Sutton, H., *The Lexington Papers, or Some Account of the Courts of London and Vienna at the Conclusion of the Seventeenth Century Extracted from the Official and Private Correspondence of Robert Sutton, Lord Lexington, British Minister at Vienna 1694–98, selected from the originals at Kelham* (London, 1854)

Manno, A., 'Un mémoire autographe de Victor Amedée II', *Revue Internationale*, I, 1894

Manno, A., ed., Relazione del Piemonte del segretario francese Sainte Croix, *MSI*, 16, 1877

Manno, A., P. Vayra and E. Ferrero, eds., *Relazioni diplomatiche della monarchia di Savoia dalla prima alla seconda restaurazione (1559–1814). Francia. Periodo III 1713–1719*, 3 vols. (Turin, 1886–91)

Milano, E., 'La partecipazione alla guerra di successione spagnuola della città di Brà illustrata negli Ordinati del Consiglio con appendice di tre documenti su Alba', *CGP*, VII

Morandi, C., ed., *Relazioni di ambasciatori sabaudi, genovesi e veneti durante il periodo della grande alleanza e della successione di Spagna (1693–1713)* (Bologna, 1935)

Morozzo della Rocca, E., 'Lettere di Vittorio Amedeo II a Gaspare Maria conte di Morozzo suo ambasciatore a Madrid dal settembre 1713 al principio del 1717', *MSI*, XXVI, 1886

Moscati, R., *Direttive della politica estera sabauda da Vittorio Amedeo II a Carlo Emanuele III* (Rome, 1941)

Pérouse, G., 'Etat de la Savoie à la fin du XVIIe siècle: documents inédits . . . aux Archives d'Etat de Turin', *Mémoires et documents de la Société Savoisienne d'Histoire et d'Archéologie*, 63, 1926

Pittavino, A., 'La Cronaca di Pragelato dal 1658 al 1724 di R. Merlin e G. Bonne', *BSBS* 9, 1904

Plassier, P., 'Les sindics de Valsavarenche pour les Paquiers et franchises accordées a la Paroisse. Recognoissance (20 juillet 1698)', in *La Valle d'Aosta:*

relazioni e comunicazioni presentate al XXXI Congresso Storico Subalpino di Aosta Settembre 1956, 2 vols. (Turin, 1959)

Pognisi, E., ed., *Vittorio Amedeo II e la campagna del 1708 per la conquista del confine alpino* (Rome, 1935)

Pons, T. J., ed., *Actes des Synodes des Eglises Vaudoises 1692–1854* (Torre Pellice, 1948)

Ponza, G., *La science de l'homme de qualité* (Turin, 1684)

Prato, G., 'L'Espansione commerciale inglese nel primo settecento in una relazione di un inviato sabaudo', in *Miscellanea in onore di Antonio Manno*, I (Turin, 1912)

Provana di Collegno, L., 'Lettere di Carlo Giacinto Roero Conte di Guarene, Capitano nel reggimento dragoni di Genevois 1704–07', *CGP*, VIII

Ricaldone, di, A., ed., 'Giornale, 1682–99, di Conte Pietro Francesco Cotti di Scurzolengo', *Il Platone*, III, 1978

Rochas d'Aiglun, M. A., *Documents inédits relatifs à l'histoire et la topographie militaire des Alpes. La Campagne de 1692 dans le Haut Dauphiné* (Paris and Grenoble, 1876)

Rousset, C. de, *Histoire de Louvois et de son administration militaire*, 4 vols. (Paris, 1862–3)

Scarzello, O., 'Corneliano, Piobesi, Monticello d'Alba e Sommariva Perno negli anni di guerra 1704–1708 (dagli "Ordinamenti Originali" dei suddetti comuni)', *CGP*, VIII

Solar de la Marguerite, C., comte de, ed., *Traités publics de la Maison Royale de Savoie depuis la paix de Cateau-Cambrésis jusqu'à nos jours*, 8 vols. (Turin, 1836–61)

Staffetti, L., 'Lettera di Vittorio Amedeo II per la guerra contro i Francesi nel 1704', *BSBS*, II, 1906

Tillier, de, J.-B., *Le Franchigie delle comunità del Ducato di Aosta*, ed. M. C. di Charvensod and M. A. Benedetto, *MSI*, 7, 1965

Viora, M., 'Documenti sulle assistenze prestate dall'Olanda ai Valdesi durante il regno di Vittorio Amedeo II', *BSBS*, 30, 1928

'Notizie e documenti sugli interventi diplomatici dell'Inghilterra in favore dei Valdesi durante il regno di Vittorio Amedeo II', *Studi Urbinati*, 1, 1928

Zucchi, M., 'Giornale inedito dell'Assedio di Torino (11 Maggio–7 Settembre 1706)', *CGP*, VIII

SECONDARY SOURCES

Guides

Archivio di Stato di Torino, 'Guida Generale', in *Guida Generale degli Archivi di Stato Italiani*, IV (Rome, 1994)

Armando, V. and A. Manno, A 'Bibliografia dell'Assedio di Torino dell'anno 1706', *CGP*, X

Bianchi, N., *Le materie politiche relative all'estero degli Archivi di Stato piemontesi* (Turin, 1876)

Loddo Canepa, F. (ed.), *Inventario della R. Segretaria di Stato e di Guerra del Regno di Sardegna* (Rome, 1934)
Manno, A. and V. Primis, *Bibliografia storica degli stati della monarchia di Savoia*, 10 vols. (Turin, 1884–1934)
Ricuperati, G., La storiografia italiana sul Settecento nell'ultimo ventennio', *Studi Storici*, 4, 1986; and in AA.VV., *La storiografia italiana degli ultimi venti anni*, 3 vols., vol. 11, *L'Età moderna* (Bari, 1989)

Monographs and articles

Abrate, M., 'Elementi per la storia della finanza dello stato sabaudo nella seconda meta del XVII secolo, *BSBS*, 67, 1969
    'Poste e valigia diplomatica negli stati sabaudi 1690–1713', *Studi Piemontesi*, 4, 1975
Allegra, L., 'L'Ospizio dei catecumeni di Torino', *BSBS*, 88, 1990
    'L'Anitisemitismo come risorsa politica: battesimi forzati e ghetti nel Piemonte del Settecento', *Quaderni Storici*, 84, 38, 1993
    Identità in bilico: il ghetto ebraico di Torino nel Settecento (Turin, 1996)
Amoretti, G., 'La guerriglia e le operazioni militari nel periodo della guerra del sale nella provincia di Mondovi (Ultimi decenni del XVII secolo)', in G. Lombardi, *La Guerra del Sale (1680–1699): rivolte e frontiere del Piemonte barocco* (Milan, 1986)
Archivio di Stato di Torino, *I rami incisi dell'Archivio di Corte, sovrani, battaglie, architettura, topografia* (exhibition catalogue) (Turin, 1982)
    Bâtir une ville au siècle des lumières: Carouge, modèles et réalités (exhibition catalogue) (Turin and Geneva, 1986)
    Il Tesoro del Principe: titoli carte memorie per il governo dello Stato (Exhibition catalogue) (Turin, 1990)
Armand-Hugon, A., 'La Repubblica di San Martino', *BSSV*, 84, 1945
Astuti, G., *La formazione dello stato moderno in Italia*, 2 vols. (Turin, 1957)
Balani, D., 'Studi giuridici e professioni nel Piemonte del Settecento', *BSBS*, 76, 1978
    Ricerche per una storia della burocrazia piemontese nel Settecento', in *L'Educazione Giuridica*, IV, 1 (Perugia, 1981)
    Il Vicario tra città e stato: l'ordine pubblico e l'annona nella Torino del Settecento (Turin, 1987)
Barale, V., *Il principato di Masserano e il marchesato di Crevacuore* (Biella, 1966)
Baraudon, A., *La Maison de Savoie et la Triple Alliance (1713–22)* (Paris, 1896)
Barberis, W., 'Continuità aritocratica e tradizione militare nel Piemonte sabaudo', *Società e Storia*, 4, 1981
    Le armi del principe. La tradizione militare sabauda (Turin, 1989)
    'Tradizione e modernità: il problema dello stato nella storia d'Italia', *RSI*, 103, 1991

Barbero, A., 'Una nobiltà provinciale sotto l'Antico Regime: il *Nobiliaire du Duché d'Aoste* di J.-B. De Tillier', *RSI*, 109, 1997
Baudi di Vesme, C., 'Le "relazioni" diplomatiche sarde', *BSBS*, 68, 1970
Baudrillart, A., *Philippe V et la Cour d'Espagne*, 5 vols. (Paris, 1890–1901)
Belfanti, C. M. and M. A. Romani, 'Il Monferrato: una frontiera scomoda fra Mantova e Torino (1536–1707), in C. Ossola, C. Raffestini and M. Ricciardi, eds., *La frontiera da stato a nazione. Il Caso Piemonte* (Rome, 1987)
Bély, L., *Espions et ambassadeurs au temps de Louis XIV* (Paris, 1990)
Benedetto, M. A., *Ricerche sul Conseil des Commis del Ducato d'Aosta*, 2 vols. (Turin, 1956 and 1965)
Berberis, L., 'Il Conte Orazio Provana, ambasciatore sabaudo (1630–1697)', *BSBS*, 30, 1928
Bergadani, R., 'Un villaggio dell'Astigiano nelle vicende politiche e militari dei secc. XVII e XVIII', *BSBS*, 30, 1928
Bianchi, P., 'Esercito e riforme militari negli stati sabaudi del Settecento: un bilancio storiografico', Società di Storia Militare, *Quaderno 1995* (Rome, 1995)
  'Guerra e politica nello stato sabaudo (1684–1730). Le riforme militari di Vittorio Amedeo II fra istituzioni, reclutamento e organizzazione territoriale', Ph.D. thesis, University of Turin, 1997
Black, J., 'The development of Anglo-Sardinian relations in the first half of the eighteenth century', *Studi Piemontesi*, 12, 1938
Bodo, P., *Le Consuetudini, la legislazione, le istituzioni del vecchio Piemonte* (Turin, 1950)
Bonelli, F., 'Mercato dei cereali e sviluppo agrario nella seconda metà del Settecento: un sondaggio per il Cuneese', *RSI*, 890, 1968
Bonjour, E., *Die Schweiz und Savoyen im spanischen Erbfolgkrieg* (Bern, 1927)
Borioli, D., M. Ferraris and A. Premoli, 'La perequazione dei tributi nel Piemonte sabaudo e la realizzazione della riforma fiscale nella prima metà del XVIII secolo', *BSBS*, 83, 1985
Bornate, C., *Gli Assedi di Nizza, in Nizza nella Storia* (Nice, 1943)
Bouquet, M.-T., 'Musique et musiciens à Turin de 1648 à 1775', *MAST*, 17, 1968
Bozzola, A., 'Venezia e Savoia al congresso di Utrecht (1712–13)', *BSBS*, 35, 1933
  'Giudizi e previsioni della diplomazia medicea sulla Casa di Savoia durante la guerra di successione spagnuola', in *Studi su Vittorio Amedeo II* (Turin, 1933)
Bracco, G., *Terra e fiscalità nel Piemonte sabaudo* (Turin, 1981)
  'Guerra del Sale o guerra del tasso? Le riforme fiscali di Vittorio Amedeo II nel Monregalese', in G. Lombardi, ed., *La Guerra del Sale (1680–1699).* (Milan, 1986)
Braida, L. 'L'Affermazione della censura di stato in Piemonte dall'editto del 1648 alle Costituzioni del 1772', *RSI*, 102, 1990
Brancaccio, N., *L'Esercito del vecchio Piemonte. I sunti storici* (Rome, 1922)

L'Esercito del vecchio Piemonte. Gli ordinamenti (Rome, 1923)
Braubach, M., *Prinz Eugen von Savoyen*, 5 vols. (Vienna, 1963–66)
Boggio, P. C., *La chiesa e lo stato in Piemonte: sposizione storico-critica dei rapporti fra la S. Sede e la Corte di Sardegna dal 1000 al 1854*, 2 vols. (Turin, 1854)
Bulferetti, L., 'La feudalità e il patriziato nel Piemonte di Carlo Emanuele II', *Annali della Facoltà di Lettere, Filosofia e Magistero dell'Università di Cagliari*, 2, 1953
  'Assolutismo e mercantilismo nel Piemonte di Carlo Emanuele II', *MAST*, 2nd ser. 2, 1953
  'Il principio della "superiorità territoriale" nella memorialistica piemontese del secolo XVIII', in *Studi in memoria di Gioele Solari* (Turin, 1954)
  'La fine del Parlamento di Saluzzo nel secolo del capitalismo feudale', in *Studies Presented to the International Commission for the History of Representative and Parliamentary Institutions*, XVIII (Louvain, 1955)
  'L'Elemento mercantilistico nella formazione dell'assolutismo sabaudo', *BSBS*, 54, 1956
  'I Piemontesi piu ricchi negli ultimi cento anni dell'assolutismo sabaudo', in *Studi storici in onore di Gioacchino Volpe*, I (Florence, 1953)
  'Nobiltà subalpina e patriziato genovese nel secolo XVII', 12 *Conference Internationale des Sciences Historiques* (Vienna, 1965)
Bullio, P., 'Problemi e geografia della risicoltura in Piemonte nei secoli XVII e XVIII', *Annali della Fondazione Luigi Einaudi*, III, 1969
P. Bullio Dranzon, 'L'Evoluzione patrimoniale degli Scarampi di Camino dalla seconda metà del secolo XVIII' (tesi di laurea, University of Turin, 1965–6)
Caligaris, S., 'Vita e lavoro in una comunita piemontese: Pancalieri nei sec. XVII–XVIII', *Bollettino della Societa per gli studi storici, archeologici e artistici della provincia di Cuneo*, 90–1, 1984
  'Crisis bancaria a Torino: il fallimento della Casa Monier, Moris e C (metà XVIII secolo), *BSBS*, 86, 1988
Canestrier, P., 'Comment M. de Tessé prépara en 1696 le traité de paix entre Louis XIV et Victor Amédée II', *Revue d'Histoire Diplomatique*, 48, 1934
Cappelletto, A., 'La costruzione e l'amministrazione di Venaria Reale (secoli XVII–XVIII)', *BSBS*, 89, 1991
Carutti, D., *Storia del regno di Vittorio Amedeo II* 3rd. edn. (Turin, 1897)
  Storia del regno di Carlo Emanuele III (Turin, 1859)
  'Della neutralità della Savoia nel 1703', *MAST*, 2nd ser., 20, 1863
  Storia della diplomazia della Corte di Savoia, 4 vols. (Turin, 1875–80)
  'Il Maresciallo Rehbinder. Nota Biografica', *CGP*, VIII
Casalis, G. *Dizionario geografico- storico- statistico-commerciale degli stati del re di Sardegna*, 28 vols. (Turin, 1833–56)
Castronovo, V., 'Storia del primo giornale degli stati sabaudi', *BSBS*, 58, 1960
Cavalcaselle, G. B., 'I Consigli di Guerra: Genesi e sviluppi della giurisdizione militare negli stati sabaudi da Amedeo VIII a Vittorio Amedeo II', *BSBS*, 62, 1964
Cavallo, S., *Charity and Power in Early Modern Italy: benefactors and their motives in*

Turin 1541–1789 (Cambridge, 1994)

Cerutti, S., 'Cittadini di Torino e sudditi di Sua Altezza', in G. Romano, *Figure del Barocco in Piemonte* (Turin, 1988)

Mestieri e privilegi: nascita delle corporazioni a Torino secoli XVII–XVIII (Turin, 1992)

Chabod, F., 'Y a-t-il un état de la Renaissance?', *Actes du Colloque sur la Renaissance* (Paris, 1958); English trans. in H. Lubasz, *The Development of the Modern State* (New York, 1964)

Cibrario, L., *Statuts et ordonnances du très noble Ordre de l'Annonciade* (Turin, 1840)

Storia di Torino, 2 vols. (Turin, 1846)

'Iacopo Valperga di Masino. Triste episodio del secolo XV: con due appendici sulla genealogia d'alcune famiglie nobili del Piemonte e della Savoia', *MAST*, 2nd ser., 19, 1861

Cifani, A. and F. Monetti, *I piaceri e le grazie. Collezionismo, pittura di genere e di paesaggio fra Sei e Settecento in Piemonte*, 2 vols. (with Introduction by R. Oresko and appendix by G. Ferraris) (Turin, 1993)

Claretta, G., *Sui principali storici piemontesi e particolarmente sugli storiografi della Real Casa di Savoia* (Turin, 1878)

Clark, S., *State and Status: the rise of the state and aristocratic power in Western Europe* (Cardiff, 1995)

Contessa, C., 'Decadenza della diplomazia italiana . . . relazioni veneto-sabaude nel secoli XVII', *Miscellanea di Storia Patria*, 42, 1906

'Aspirazioni commerciali intrecciate ad alleanze politiche della Casa di Savoia coll'Inghilterra nei secoli XVII e XVIII', *MAST*, 64, 1914

'Progetti economici della seconda Madama Reale fondati sopra un contratto nuziale (1678–1682)', *MSI*, 48, 1915

'I regni di Napoli e di Sicilia nelle aspirazioni italiane di Vittorio Amedeo II di Savoia (1700–13)', in *Studi su Vittorio Amedeo II* (Turin, 1933)

'La congiura del marchese di Parella (1682)', *BSBS*, 38, 1936

Contessa, C., et al., eds., *Le campagne di guerra in Piemonte (1703–1708) e l'assedio di Torino (1706)*, 10 vols. (Turin, 1908–33)

Cordero di Montezemolo, M., 'Cenni sul comune di Mondovì nel periodo in cui si costituisce il Regno di Sardegna', *Bollettino della Società per gli Studi Archivistici ed Artistici nella Provincia di Cuneo*, 28, 1950

Costa de Beauregard, C. A. M., *Mémoires historiques sur la Maison Royale de Savoie*, 4 vols. (Turin, 1816)

Costamagna, H., 'Pour une histoire de l'Intendenza dans les états de terre ferme de la Maison de Savoye a l'époque moderne', *BSBS*, 83, 1985

Cuaz, M., 'La Valle d'Aosta fra Cinque e Settecento nella storiografia degli ultimi vent'anni', *BSBS*, 76, 1978

Dagna, P., 'Un diplomatico ed economista del Settecento: Carlo Baldassare Perrone di San Martino (1718–1802), in Dagna et al., *Figure e gruppi della classe dirigente piemontese nel Risorgimento* (Turin, 1968)

Dainotti, V., 'Veggenti e astrologi intorno a Vittorio Amedeo II', *BSBS*, 34, 1932

'Vittorio Amedeo II a Venezia nel 1687 e la Lega di Augusta', *BSBS*, 35, 1933

Davico, R., 'The Devil and the "Viva Maria": psychoses and revolts in the Savoyard state (1680–1700)', in A. de Lange, ed., *Dall'Europa alle Valli Valdesi* (Turin, 1990)

Della Porta, G., *La politica ecclesiastica di Vittorio Amedeo II* (Casale, 1914)

De Rege Di Donato, P., 'Stato Generale dei danni patiti dal Piemonte nella Guerra di successione di Spagna dall'ottobre 1703 a tutto il 1710', *CGP*, IX

Devos, R., 'Couvents et dames galantes en Savoie: Marie-Jeanne-Baptiste de Savoie-Soissons, soeur du Prince Eugène à la Visitation d'Annécy (1665–1705)', *MDSSHA* 96: *Mélanges offerts à Bernard Grosperrin*

Devos, R. and B. Grosperrin, *La Savoie de la réforme à la révolution française* (Rennes, 1985)

Di Gilio, R., 'La Corte di Vittorio Amedeo II 1680–1713' (tesi di laurea, University of Turin, 1990–1)

Di Macco, M. and G. Romano, eds., *Diana trionfatrice: arte di corte nel Piemonte del Seicento* (exhibition catalogue) (Turin, 1989)

Dossetti, M., 'Aspetti demografici del Piemonte occidentale nei secoli XVII e XVIII', *BSBS*, 75, 1971

'La demografia delle valli valdesi dal 1686 al 1800', *BSBS*, 79, 1981

'Fronti parentali in una comunità alpina del Settecento', *BSBS*, 90, 1992

Einaudi, L., *La finanza sabauda all'aprirsi del secolo XVIII e durante la guerra di successione spagnuola* (Turin, 1908)

'Le entrate pubbliche dello stato sabaudo nei bilanci e nei conti dei tesorieri durante la guerra di successione spagnuola', *CGP*, IX

Fazy, H., *Les Suisses et la neutralité de la Savoie 1703–1704* (Geneva, 1895)

Fellone, G., *Il mercato monetario in Piemonte nel sec. XVIII* (Milan, 1968)

Ferrero, E., 'La rivoluzione inglese, 1688, e l'inviato di Savoia', *MAST*, 32, 1880

'L'Esercito Piemontese al principio del secolo XVIII', *CGP*, I

Ferrero della Marmora, A., *Le vicende di Carlo di Simiane, marchese di Livorno poi di Pianezza tra il 1672 ed il 1706* (Turin, 1862)

Notizie sulla vita e sulle geste militari di Carlo Emilio San Martino di Parella, ossia cronica militare aneddottica delle guerre in Piemonte dal 1672 al 1706 (Turin, 1863)

Foa, S., *La politica economica della Casa Savoia verso gli Ebrei dal sec. XVI fino alla rivoluzione francese* (Rome, 1962)

Forneron, A., 'L'Articolo segreto sul Pragelato nel trattato di alleanza colle Potenze Marittime', *BSSV*, 70, 1938

Frigo, D., 'L'Affermazione della sovranità. Famiglia e Corte dei Savoia tra Cinque e Settecento', in C. Mozzarelli, ed., *"Familia" del principe e famiglia aristocratica* (Rome, 1988)

Principe, ambasciatori e "Jus Gentium": l'amministrazione della politica esterna nel Piemonte del Settecento (Rome, 1991)

Fubini Leuzzi, M., 'Gli studi storici in Piemonte dal 1766 al 1846: politica culturale e coscienza nazionale', *BSBS*, 81, 1983

Gabotto, F., *Storia di Cuneo* (Cuneo, 1898)

Gaibotti, E., 'La segreteria di stato per gli affari esteri dello stato sabaudo: storia dell'istituzione e documenti d'archivio', *Studi Piemontesi*, 15, 1986

Gaja, R., *Il marchese d'Ormea* (Milan, 1988)

Galli della Loggia, G., *Cariche del Piemonte e Paesi uniti colla serie cronologica delle persone che le hanno occupate dal secolo IX al dicembre 1798*, 3 vols. (Turin, 1798)

Garufi, C. A., ed., *Rapporti diplomatici fra Filippo V e Vittorio Amedeo II di Savoia nella cessione del regno di Sicilia 1713–1720* (Palermo, 1914)

Gasco, M., 'La politica sabauda a Utrecht nella "Relazione Mellarède" ', *RSI*, 6, 1935

Gaudio, G., 'Ricerca sull'intendenza dei paesi di nouvo acquisto: le provincie di Alessandria e Lomellina nel Piemonte del '700: figura e mansioni dell'intendente sul territorio' (tesi di laurea, University of Turin, 1979–80)

Gaziello, F., 'Les registres d'Ordinati di Conseglio de Saorge et la guerre de succession d'Espagne', *Recherches Regionales (Côte d'Azur et Contrées Limitrophes)*. Centre de Documentation des Archives des Alpes Maritimes, Nice, 8e année, 3, 1968

Genta, E., *Senato e senatori di Piemonte nel secolo XVIII* (Turin, 1983)

'Condanne, grazie e porto d'armi: proiezioni della Guerra del Sale sul riordinamento del Senato', in G. Lombardi, *La Guerra del Sale (1680–1699)* (Milan, 1986)

Gerbaix de Sonnaz, de, A., 'Quelques diplomates savoyards et nicards au service de la maison de Savoye, de France, de l'empire et du Saint Siège', in *Miscellanea di studi storici in onore di A. Manno* (Turin, 1912)

Girgenti, A., 'Vittorio Amedeo II e la cessione della Sardegna: trattative diplomatiche e scelte politiche', *Quaderni di Storia*, 40, 1990

Gros, A. *Histoire du Diocèse de Maurienne*, 2 vols. (Chambéry, 1948)

Grosso, M. and M. F. Mellano, *Spunti e profili nella Storia del Piemonte nei secoli XVII e XVIII* (Turin, 1961)

Guerci, L., *Le monarchie assolute, II: Il Settecento* (Turin, 1986)

Handen, R., 'The Savoy negotiations of the comte de Tessé 1693–1969', Ph.D. thesis, University of Ohio, 1970

'End of an era: Victor Amadeus II and Louis XIV 1690–96', in R. M. Hatton, ed., *Louis XIV and Europe* (London, 1976)

Haussonville, G. P. O. comte d', *La duchesse de Bourgogne et l'alliance Savoyarde*, 4 vols. (Paris, 1898–1908)

Istituto della Enciclopedia Italiana, *Dizionario biografico degli Italiani*, 33 vols. (Rome, 1960–87)

la Lumia, I., 'La Sicilia sotto Vittorio Amedeo II di Savoia', *ASI*, 3rd, XIX, XX, XXI, 1874–5

la Rocca, L., 'Una proposta di lega italiana al re di Sicilia nel 1719', *Archivio Storico Siciliano*, XXXII, 1907

Lameire, I., *Les occupations militaires en Italie pendant les guerres de Louis XIV* (Paris, 1903)

Landi, A., 'Il rimpatrio dei Valdesi nei documenti dell'Archivio Segreto

Vaticano (1686–1691)', in A. de Lange, ed., *Dall'Europa alle Valle Valdesi* (Turin, 1990)
Lange, A. de, ed., *Dall'Europa alle Valli Valdesi: atti del Convegno 'Il Glorioso Rimpatrio 1689–1989'* (Turin, 1990)
Léris, de, G., *La comtesse de Verrue et la cour de Victor Amédée II de Savoie* (Paris, 1881)
Levi, G., 'La seta e l'economia piemontese del Settecento, *RSI*, 79, 1967
— 'Mobilità della popolazione ed immigrazione a Torino nella prima metà del Settecento', *Quaderni Storici*, 17, 1971; reprinted as 'Como Torino soffocó il Piemonte', in G. Levi, *Centro e periferia di un stato absoluto: tre saggi su Piemonte e Liguria in età moderna* (Turin, 1985)
— 'Distruzioni belliche e innovazione agricola: il mais in Piemonte nel 1600', in AAVV, *Agricoltura e trasformazione dell'ambiente, secoli XIII–XVIII* (Prato, 1979)
— *L'Eredità immateriale: carriera di un esorcista nel Piemonte del Seicento* (Turin, 1985); English edn. (trans. L. Cochrane): *Inheriting Power: the story of an exorcist* (Chicago, 1988)
Lombardi, G., 'Note sul controllo degli atti del sovrano negli stati sabaudi ad opera delle supreme magistrature nel periodo dell'assolutismo', *Annali della Scuola Superiore per Archivisti e Bibliotecari dell'Università di Roma*, 1, 1962
— 'La Guerra del Sale trecento anni dopo: cronaca di un convegno: fatti ed interpretazioni', in Lombardi, ed., *La Guerra del Sale (1680–1699): rivolte e frontiere del Piemonte barocco*, 3 vols. (Milan, 1986)
Lombardini, S., 'Appunti per un'ecologia politica dell'area monregalese in età moderna', in Lombardini, *et al.*, *Valli Monregalesi: arte, società, devozioni* (Mondovì, 1985)
— 'La costruzione dell'ordine: governatori e governati a Mondovì (1682–1687), in G. Lombardi, ed., *La Guerra del Sale (1680–1699)* (Milan, 1986)
Loriga, S., 'Un secreto per far morire la persona del re: magia e protezione nel Piemonte del '700', *Quaderni Storici*, 53, 1983; published as 'A secret to kill the king: magic and protection in Piedmont in the eighteenth century', in E. Muir and G. Ruggiero, eds., *History from Crime. Selections from Quaderni Storici* (Baltimore, 1994)
— 'L'Identità militare come aspirazione sociale: nobili di provincia e nobili di corte nel Piemonte del secondo metà del Settecento', *Quaderni Storici*, 74, 1990
— *Soldati: l'istituzione militare nel Piemonte del Settecento* (Venice, 1992)
Lovie, J., ed., *Histoire des Diocèses de France, vol. 11: Les Diocèses de Chambery, Tarentaise et Maurienne* (Paris, 1979)
Lovie, J., 'De l'institution d'un prince', *MDSSHA*, 84, 1971
Lucat, S., *L'Invasion française de 1691 dans la Vallée d'Aoste* (Aosta, 1893)
Mack Smith, D., *A History of Sicily: modern Sicily after 1713* (London, 1968)
Magrini, E., 'La popolazione di Torino nel 1705', *CGP*, VIII
Manno, A., *Il patriziato subalpino* (Florence, 1906) (A–B). (Complete text in 25 typed vols. in Biblioteca Reale, Turin)

'La marina sabauda (1388–1848)', *BSBS*, 62, 1964
'L'Esercito piemontese: lo stato attuale degli studi relativi', *BSBS*, 65, 1967
Marchisio, S., 'Ideologia e problemi dell'economia familiare nelle lettere della nobiltà piemontese (XVII–XVIII secoli)', *BSBS*, 83, 1985
Marini, L., 'La Valle d'Aosta fra Savoia e Piemonte 1601–1730', *Relazioni e communicazioni presentate al XXXI Congresso Storico Subalpino di Aosta, 1956*, 2 vols. (Turin, 1959)
Marroco, G., 'La storiografia piemontese di Carlo Denina', *BSBS*, 76, 1978
Massabo Ricci, I., and A. Merlotti, 'In attesa del duca: reggenza e principi del sangue nella Torino di Maria Giovanna Battista', in G. Romano, ed., *Torino 1675–1699: strategie e conflitti del Barocco* (Turin, 1995)
Massabo Ricci, I., and C. Rosso, 'La corte quale rappresentazione del potere sovrano', in G. Romano, ed., *Figure del Barocco in Piemonte* (Turin, 1988)
Mattone, A., 'La cessione del Regno di Sardegna dal Trattato di Utrecht alla presa di possesso sabauda (1713–20), *RSI*, 102, 1990
Menabrea, L., *Les Alpes historiques: Montmélian et les Alpes* (Turin, 1841)
Merlin, P. et al., *Il Piemonte sabaudo: stato e territori in età moderna*, vol. VIII/1 of G. Galasso, ed., *Storia d'Italia* (Turin, 1994)
Morandi, C., 'Torino e Napoli durante la guerra della Grande Alleanza nel carteggio dipomatico di GB Operti (1690–97)', *Archivio Storico per le provincie napoletane*, 1935
  'Il matrimonio di Maria Adelaida di Savoia', *Rassegna Storica del Risorgimento*, 23, 1936
  'Lo stato di Milano e la politica di Vittorio Amedeo II', *Annuario del Reale Istituto Storico Italiano*, 4, 1938
Mosca, E., 'La provincia di Alba e la comunità di Bra durante la guerra di successione spagnola (1703–1706), *BSBS*, 55, 1957
Narducci, C., Il Consiglio di Finanze del Regno di Sardegna: profili istituzionali con particolare riguardo alla prima metà del XVIII secolo', *BSBS*, 94, 1996.
Nicolas, J., 'La noblesse et l'état en Savoie au 18e siècle', *Cahiers d'Histoire*, 1977
  La Savoie au 18e siècle: Noblesse et bourgeoisie, 2 vols. (Paris, 1978)
  'Pouvoir et contestation en Savoie au XVIIe siècle: aux sources d'une culture populaire', in G. Mombello, L. Sozzi and L. Terreaux, eds., *Culture et pouvoir dans les états de Savoie du XVIIe siècle à la Revolution. Actes du Colloque d'Annecy–Chambéry–Turin (1982). Cahiers de Civilisation Alpine Quaderni di Civiltà Alpina*, 4 (Chambéry, 1985)
Oresko, R., 'The diplomatic background to the Glorioso Rimpatrio: the rupture between Vittorio Amedeo II and Louis XIV (1686–1690)', in A. de Lange, ed., *Dall'Europa alle Valli Valdesi* (Turin, 1990)
  'The House of Savoy and the Glorious Revolution', in J. Israel, ed., *The Anglo-Dutch Moment: essays on the Glorious Revolution and its world impact* (Cambridge, 1991)
  'The House of Savoy in search for a royal crown in the seventeenth century', in R. Oresko, G. C. Gibbs and H. M. Scott, eds., *Royal and Republican Sovereignty in Early Modern Europe: essays in memory of Ragnhild Hatton*

(Cambridge, 1997)
Owen, J. H., *The War at Sea under Queen Anne 1702–1708* (Cambridge, 1938)
Patrucco, C., 'Ivrea da Carlo Emanuele I a Carlo Emanuelle III', in D. Baudi di Vesme , et al., *Studi Eporediesi* (Pinerolo, 1900)
   'Il 1706 a Pinerolo in relazione colla guerra e colla battaglia di Torino', *BSBS*, 10, 1905
Pene-Vidari, G. S., 'La gabella del sale e le antiche franchigie monregalesi: un caso di esercizio del diritto di resistenza?', in G. Lombardi, ed., *La Guerra del Sale (1680–1699)* (Milan, 1986)
Perrero, D., 'Un carceriere vercellese del tempo antico: a proposito dell'acquisto per parte della Casa di Savoia del feudo di Desana 1683–1701', *Curiosità e ricerche di storia subalpina*, 3 (Turin, 1879)
Petrilli, P. 'Alle Origini dell' Intendenza in Piemonte. Il Caso della provincia di Pinerolo 1658–1717, tesi di laurea, University of Turin, 1989–90
Peyron, G., *Marchesato di Cavour: feudo contestato A.D. 1649–A.D. 1742*, no date or place (British Library, London, ref. YA.1991.b.7498)
Pignet, G., 'Eugenio Gaspare De Tillier uomo d'arme e di legge (1630–1699)', in *La Valle di Aosta: relazioni e comunicazioni presentate al XXXI Congresso Storico Subalpino di Aosta, 1956*, 2 vols. (Turin, 1959)
Pollak, M. *Turin 1564–1680: urban design, military culture and the creation of the absolutist capital* (Chicago, 1991)
Poni, C., 'All'origine del sistema di fabbrica: tecnologia e organizzazione produttiva dei mulini da seta nell'Italia settentrionale (secc. XVII–XVIII), *RSI*, 88, 1976
   'Misura contro misura: come il filo da seta divenne sottile e rotondo', *Quaderni Storici*, 47, 1981
Praj, G., 'La moneta piemontese ai tempi di Vittorio Amedeo I e di Carlo Emanuele II (1630–1675)', *BSBS*, 40, 1938
Prato, G., 'Censimenti e popolazione in Piemonte nei secoli XVI, XVII e XVIII', *Rivista Italiana di Sociologia*, 10, 1906
   La vita economica in Piemonte a mezzo il secolo XVIII (Turin, 1908)
   'Il costo della guerra di successione spagnuola e le spese pubbliche in Piemonte dal 1700 al 1713', *CGP*, X
   Problemi monetari e bancari nei secoli XVII e XVIII, 2 vols. (Turin, 1916)
Promis, D., *Le monete dei Reali di Savoia* (Turin, 1841)
Pugliese, S., *Le prime strette dell'Austria in Italia* (Milan, 1932)
Quazza, G., 'Guerra civile in Piemonte 1637–1642', *BSBS*, 57–8, 1959–60
   Le riforme in Piemonte nella prima metà del Settecento, 2 vols. (Modena, 1957)
   Il problema italiano e l'equilibrio europeo 1720–1738 (Turin, 1965)
Ramella, F. anmd Torre, A., 'Confraternite e conflitti sociali nelle campagne piemontesi di ancien regime', *Quaderni Storici*, 45, 1980
Ricuperati, G., 'Lo stato sabaudo e la storia da Emanuele Filiberto a Vittorio Amedeo II. Bilancio di studi e prospecttive di ricerca', *Atti del convegno 16–17 nov. 1979, numero speciale di Studi Piemontesi*, 1980
   'Gli strumenti dell'assolutismo sabaudo: Segreterie di Stato e Consiglio delle

Finanze nel XVIII secolo', *RSI*, 103, 1991; reprinted in Ricuperati, *Le avventure di uno stato 'ben amministrato': rappresentazioni e realtà nello spazio sabaudo tra Ancien Régime e Rivoluzione* (Turin, 1994)

Ricuperati, G., 'Il settecento', in Merlin, ed. *Il Piemonte sabaudo* (Turin, 1994)

Rochas d'Aiglun, E. A., *Les Vallées Vaudoises: étude de topographie et d'histoire militaire* (Paris, 1880)

Romagnani, G. P., 'Il "rimpatrio" nella storiografia italiana fra Sette e Ottocento', in A. de Lange, ed., *Dall'Europa alle valli valdesi* (Turin, 1990)

Romano, G., 'Resistenze locali alla dominazione torinese', in G. Romano, ed., *Figure del Barocco in Piemonte: la corte, la città, i cantieri, le provincie* (Turin, 1988)

Rondolino, F., 'Vita Torinese durante l'assedio (1703–1707)', *CGP*, VII

Rosso, C., *Una burocrazia di antico regime: I segretari di Stato dei Duchi di Savoia, I (1559–1637)* (Turin, 1992)

'Il Seicento', in Merlin, *Il Piemonte sabaudo* (Turin, 1994)

Ruata, A., *Luigi Malabaila di Canale: riflessi della cultura illuministica in un diplomatico piemontese* (Turin, 1968)

Salsotto, C., 'Fossano e la battaglia di Torino (1706). Contributo alla storia della guerra di successione di Spagna', *CGP*, VIII

Saluces, A., comte, de, *Histoire militaire du Piémont*, 5 vols. (Turin, 1818)

Saraceno, V., *Il corso delle monete negli stati del re di Sardegna dal 1300* (Turin, 1782)

Savio, C. F., *Saluzzo. Storia dal 1635 al 1730* (Saluzzo, 1928)

Sclopis, F., 'Delle relazioni politiche tra la dinastia di Savoia ed il governo britannico 1240–1815', *MAST*, 2nd ser. 14 (1854)

Segre, A., 'Negoziati diplomatici della Corte Sabauda colla Corte di Baviera dalle origini al 1704', *CGP*, VI

'Negoziati diplomatici della Corte di Prussia e colla Dieta di Ratisbona', *CGP*, VI

Sereno, P., 'Popolazione, territorio, risorse: sul contesto geografico delle Valli valdesi dopo la "Glorieuse Rentree"', in A. de Lange, ed., *Dall'Europa alle Valli Valdesi* (Turin, 1990)

Seyssel-Cressieu, Marc de, Comte, *La Maison de Seyssel: ses origines, sa généalogie, son histoire*, 2 vols. (Grenoble, 1900)

Silvestrini, M. T., *La Politica della Religione. Il Governo Ecclesiastico nello Stato Sabaudo del XVIII Secolo* (Florence, 1997)

Soffietti, I., 'La legislazione sabauda sui valdesi dal 1685 al 1730', in A. de Lange, ed., *Dall'Europa alle valli valdesi* (Turin, 1990)

Sperling, J., 'The international payments mechanism in the seventeenth and eighteenth centuries', *Economic History Review*, 2nd ser., 14, 1961–62

Stellardi, V. E., ed., *Il regno di Vittorio Amedeo II di Savoia in Sicilia dall'anno 1713 al 1719*, 3 vols. (Turin, 1862–66)

Storrs, C., 'Thomas Coxe and the Lindau Project 1689–90', in A. de Lange, ed., *Dall'Europa alle Valli Valdesi* (Turin, 1990)

'Machiavelli dethroned: Victor Amadeus II and the making of the Anglo-Savoyard alliance of 1690', *European History Quarterly*, 22, 3, 1992

'The Army of Lombardy and the resilience of Spanish power in Italy in the reign of Carlos II (1665–1700) (Part I)', *War in History*, 4/4, 1997

'The Army of Lombardy and the resilience of Spanish power in Italy in the reign of Carlos II (1665–1700) (Part II)', *War in History*, 5/1, 1998

'Savoyard diplomacy in the eighteenth century', in D. Frigo, ed., *Politics and Diplomacy in Early Modern Italy* (Cambridge, 1999)

Stumpo, E., *Finanza e stato moderna nel Piemonte del Seicento* (Rome, 1979)

'La distribuzione sociale degli acquirenti dei titoli del debbito pubblico in Piemonte nella seconda metà del Seicento', in *La fiscalité et ses implications sociales en Italie et en France aux XVIIe et XVIIIe siècles*, Ecole Francaise de Rome, 46, 1980

'I Ceti dirigenti in Italia nell'età moderna: due modelli diversi: nobiltà piemontese e patriziato toscano', in A. Tagliaferri, ed., *I ceti dirigenti in Italia in età moderna e contemporanea* (Udine, 1984)

'Guerra ed economia: spese e guadagni militari nel Piemonte del Seicento', *Studi Storici*, 27, 1986

'L'Organizzazione degli stati: accentramento e burocrazia', in N. Tranfaglia and M. Firpo, eds., *La storia dal medioevo all'età contemporanea, vol. 3, L'Età Móderna. I Quadri Generali* (Turin, 1987)

'Tra mito, leggenda e realtà storica: la tradizione militare sabauda da Emanuele Filiberto a Carlo Alberto', *RSI*, 103, 1991

Sturani, M. L., 'Inerzie e flessibilità: organizzazione ed evoluzione della rete viaria sabauda nei territori "di qua dai monti" (1563–1798), I: I presupposti strutturali (sec. XVI–XVIII)' *BSBS*, 88, 1990; II: 'Le trasformazioni del XVIII secolo', *BSBS*, 89, 1991

Symcox, G., *Victor Amadeus II: absolutism in the Savoyard state 1675–1730* (London, 1938)

'Britain and Victor Amadeus II: or, the use and abuse of allies', in S. Baxter, ed., *Britain's Rise to Greatness 1660–1763* (Berkeley, 1983)

'The development of absolutism in the Savoyard state', *Studies in History and Politics*, 1985

'Two forms of popular resistance in the Savoyard state of the 1680s: the rebels of Mondovì and the Vaudois', in Lombardi, *La Guerra del Sale (1680–2699)* (Milan, 1986)

'The Waldensians in the absolutist state of Victor Amadeus II', in A. de Lange, ed., *Dall'Europa alle Valle Valdesi* (Turin, 1990)

'L'Età di Vittorio Amedeo II', in P. Merlin *et al.*, *Il Piemonte sabaudo* (Turin, 1994)

'From commune to capital: the transformation of Turin, sixteenth to eighteenth centuries', in R. Oresko, G. C. Gibbs and H. M. Scott, eds., *Royal and Republican Sovereignty in Early Modern Europe: essays in memory of Ragnhild Hatton* (Cambridge, 1997)

Tabacco, G., *Lo stato sabaudo nel Sacro Romano Impero* (Turin, 1939)

Tabasso, E., Profilo biografico di Carlo Francesco Ferrero, Marchese d'Ormea Iesi di laurea, University of Turin, 1956–57

Tallone, A., 'Diritti e pretese sul marchesato del Finale al principio del secolo XVIII', *BSBS*, 1, 1896
'La vendita del Finale nel 1713 e la diplomazia piemontese', *BSBS*, 1–2, 1896–7
Tartaglino, R., *Storia di Cocconato* (Novara, 1966)
Torcellan Ginolino, F., 'Il pensiero politico di Paolo Mattia Doria ed un interessante profilo storico di Vittorio Amedeo II', *BSBS*, LIX, 1961
Torre, A., ed., *Stato e società nell'Ancien Régime* (Turin, 1983)
  'Elites locali e potere centrale tra Sei e Settecento: problemi di metodo e ipotesi di lavoro sui feudi imperiali delle Langhe', *Bollettino della Società per gli Studi Storici, Artistici e Archeologici della Provincia di Cuneo*, 89, 1983
  'Il consumo dei devozioni: rituali e potere nelle campagne piemontesi nella prima metà del Settecento', *Quaderni Storici*, 58, 1985; abridged version available in English in J. Obelkevich *et al.*, eds., *Disciplines of Faith* (London, 1987)
  'Tra comunità e stato: i rituali della giustizia in Piemonte tra 600 e 700', in G. Delille and F. Rizzi, eds., *Problèmes de l'histoire de la famille* (Rome, 1986)
  'Rivolte contadine e conflitti locali nel Piemonte tra Seicento e Settecento', in G. Lombardi, ed., *La Guerra del Sale (1680–1699)* (Milan, 1986)
  'Faide, fazioni e partiti, ovvero la redefinizione della politica nei feudi imperiali delle Langhe tra Sei e Settecento', *Quaderni Storici*, 63, 1986; trans. as 'Feuding, factions and parties: the redefinition of politics in the imperial fiefs of Langhe in the seventeenth and eighteenth centuries', in E. Muir and G. Ruggiero, eds., *History from Crime: selections from Quaderni Storici* (Baltimore, 1994)
  'Politics cloaked in worship: state, church and local power in Piedmont 1550–1770', *Past and Present*, 134, 1992
  Il Consumo di devozioni: religione e comunità nelle campagne dell'Ancien Regime (Venice, 1995)
Torta, M., *La Riunione al Demanio dei beni demaniali e feudali alienati sotto, Vittorio Amedeo II 1719–21*, tesi di laurea, University of Turin, 1958
Tron, D., 'Il reinsediamento in val Germanasca dopo la Rentrée', in A. de Lange, ed., *Dall'Europa alle Valli Valdesi* (Turin, 1990)
Valenti, P., 'Relazioni diplomatiche di Vittorio Amedeo II, Duca di Savoia, coi Cantoni Svizzeri e colla Repubblica del Vallese durante il secondo periodo della guerra in Italia per la successione di Spagna (1703–07)', *CGP*, VI
Venturi, F., 'Il Piemonte ai primi decenni del Settecento nelle relazioni dei diplomatici inglesi', *BSBS*, 54, 1956
  Saggi sull'Europa illuminista, 1: Alberto Radicati di Passerano (Turin, 1954)
  Settecento riformatore, vol. I: Da Muratori a Beccaria (1730–1765) (Turin, 1968)
Viora, M., 'Il senato di Pinerolo', *BSBS*, 29, 1927
  Le costituzioni piemontesi 1723–1729–1770 (Milan, 1928)
  'Nota sulla questione dell'osservanza delle feste della Chiesa cattolica da parte dei Valdesi dopo il ristabilimento del 1690', *BSHV*, 1928
  Storia delle leggi sui Valdesi di Vittorio Amedeo II (Bologna, 1930)

Vitelleschi, marchesa A., *The Romance of Savoy: Victor Amadeus II and his Stuart bride*, 2 vols. (London, 1905)

Wilkinson, S., *The Defence of Piedmont 1742–1748: a prelude to the study of Napoleon* (Oxford, 1927)

Winkler, L., *Der Anteil der bayerischen Armee an den Feldzügen in Piemont 1691 bis 1696*, 2 vols. (Munich, 1886–7)

Woolf, S. J. 'English public opinion and the Duchy of Savoy', *English Miscellany*, 12 (Rome, 1961)

'Sviluppo economico e struttura sociale in Piemonte da Emanuele Filiberto a Carlo Emanuele III', *Nuova Rivista Storica*, 46, 1962

Studi sulla nobiltà piemontese nell'epoca dell'assolutismo (Turin, 1963).

'The aristocracy in transition: a continental comparison', *Economic History Review*, 2nd. ser., 23, 1970

Relevant studies of other states

Anderson, P., *Lineages of the Absolute State* (London, 1974)

Beik, W., *Absolutism and Society in Seventeenth-Century France: state power and provincial aristocracy in Languedoc* (Cambridge, 1983)

Black, J., *European Warfare 1688–1815* (London, 1988)

Bonney, R., ed., *Economic Systems and State Finance: the origins of the Modern State in Europe Thirteenth to Eighteenth Centuries* (Oxford, 1995)

Brewer, J., *The Sinews of Power. War, Money and the English state 1688–1783* (London, 1989)

Bromley, J. S., ed., *New Cambridge Modern History, vol. VI: The Rise of Great Britain and Russia 1688–1725* (Cambridge, 1970)

Chittolini, G., A. Molho and P. Schiera, eds., *Origini dello stato: processi di formazione statale in Italia fra medioevo ed età moderna*, Annali dell'Istituto Storico Italo-Germanico di Trento, 39 (Bologna, 1994). A number of these contributions have been translated into English in J. Kirshner, ed., *The Origins of the State in Italy 1300–1600)* (Chicago, 1996)

Cornette, J., *Le roi de Guerre: essai sur la souveraineté dans la France du Grand Siècle* (Paris, 1993)

Dessert, D., *Argent, pouvoir et société au Grand Siècle* (Paris, 1984)

Evans, R. J. W., *The Making of the Habsburg Monarchy 1550–1700* (Oxford, 1977)

Fasano Guarini, E., *Lo stato mediceo di Cosimo I* (Florence, 1973)

'Etat moderne' et anciens états Italiens: éléments d'histoire comparée, *Revue d'Histoire Moderne et Contemporaine*, 45, 1, 1998

Fogel, M., *Les cérémonies de l'information dans la France du XVIe au milieu du XVIIIe siècle* (Paris, 1989)

Gestrich, A., *Absolutismus und Öffentlichkeit: politische Kommunikation in Deutschland zu Begin des 18. Jahrhunderts* (Göttingen, 1994)

Greengrass, M., ed., *Conquest and Coalescence: the Shaping of the State in Early Modern Europe* (London, 1991)

Hoffman, P. T. and Norberg, K., eds., *Fiscal Crisis, Liberty and Representative*

Government 1450–1789 (Stanford, 1994)

Ingrao, C., *In Quest and Crisis: Emperor Joseph I and the Habsburg Monarchy* (Lafayette, 1979)

Lopez, R. J., *Ceremonia y poder a finales del Antiguo Regimen: Galicia 1700–1833* (Santiago, 1995)

Lynn, J., *Giant of the Grand Siècle: the French army 1610–1715* (Cambridge, 1997)
The Wars of Louis XIV 1667–1714 (London, 1999)

Parker, D., *Class and State in Ancien Régime France: the road to modernity?* (London, 1996)

Parker, G., *The Military Revolution: military innovation and the rise of the West 1500–1800*, 2nd edn. (Cambridge, 1996)

Prodi, P., *Sacramento del potere: il giuramento politico nella storia costituzionale dell'Occidente* (Bologna, 1992)

Raeff, M., *The Well-Ordered Police State 1600–1800* (New Haven, 1983)

Raggio, O., *Faide e parentele: lo stato genovese visto dalla Fontanabuona* (Turin, 1990)

Redlich, O., *Weltmacht des Barock* (4th edn, Vienna, 1961)

Roosen, W., 'Early modern diplomatic ceremonial: a systems approach', *Journal of Modern History*, 52, 1980

Rosenberg, H., *Bureaucracy, Aristocracy and Autocracy: the Prussian Experience 1660–1815* (Boston, 1966)

Sahlins, P., *Boundaries: the Making of France and Spain in the Pyrenees* (Stanford, 1988)

Shennan, J. H., *The Origins of the Modern European State 1450–1725* (London, 1974)

Smith, J. M., *The Culture of Merit: nobility, royal service and the making of absolute monarchy in France 1600–1789* (Ann Arbor, 1996)

Symcox, G., *The Crisis of French Sea Power 1688–1697: from the Guerre d'Escadre to the Guerre de Course* (The Hague, 1974)

Tallett, F., *War and Society in Early Modern Europe 1495–1715* (London, 1992)

Tilly, C., ed., *The Formation of National States in Western Europe* (Princeton, 1975)

Trevelyan, G. M., *England under Queen Anne*, 3 vols. (London, 1930–34)

Vicens Vives, J., 'The administrative structure of the state in the sixteenth and seventeenth centuries', in H. J. Cohn, ed., *Government in Reformation Europe 1520–60* (London, 1971)

von Aretin, K. O., 'L'Ordinamento feudale in Italia nel XVI e XVII secolo e le sue ripercussioni sulla politica europea. Un contributo alla storia del tardo feudalismo in Europa', *Annali dell' Istituto Storico Italo-Germanico di Trento*, IV, 1978

Wilson, P., *War, State and Society in Württemberg, 1677–1793* (Cambridge, 1994)

INDEX

Absolutism: concept and historiography 11; war and 73; importance of cooperation and collaboration in 72–3; alternative models of integration 277, 285; and social change 221–2
Accademia Reale, Turin 135, 236, 254
ad hoc missions, importance of in wartime 182
Aglie, San Martino di, conte 232
Aiguebelle, baron d' 243
Aix, Seyssel, marquis d', Victor Amadeus (1679–1754) and family 144, 189, 239, 245, 250, 258
Alba, province of 39, 77, 181, 183, 184, 254, 271
Alessandria, town and province, newly acquired territory 30, 38, 193
Alley, Joly, d', *vibailli* of Duchy of Aosta 291
Alpine frontier 20, 123, 124, 144, 148
Anderson, Matthew 171
Andorno, marchese d' (d. 1719) 206, 245, 307
Anne, Queen, of England/Britain 152
Anne-Marie d'Orleans, Duchess of Savoy, Queen of Sicily and Sardinia, consort of Victor Amadeus II 151, 191
Annunziata, Savoyard Chivalric Order 193–94, 229, 250, 255
Aosta, Duchy and Valley 19, 55, 64, 65, 77, 79, 90, 102, 168, 174, 181; *pays d'états* 277; Conseil des Commis 278, 284–5, 293; Coutumier 278, 289; bishop of 279; ducal patronage 279–80; importance and role of in wars 281, 290; war devastation 247, 281, 283; ducal anxiety regarding 285; jealousy of privileges 285; attack on privileges 288; Cour des Connoissances 289; Estates of general 77, 277–78; (1694) 284, 286, 289; (1706) 292; (1712) 292; (1718) 292 nobility of 226, 228

archives, Savoyard 177
aristocratic constitutionalism, voiced by Chambre des Comptes, Chambery 251
army, Savoyard as reinforcement of ducal power 20–21, 41, 93, 271–2; as example of expanding state 61–2, 72; growth of 23; field army and garrisons 28; composition of ducal forces 31; recruiting 31; recruitment of criminals 35; pay 34–5; militia 36; use of foreign troops 43–59; reluctance to serve and desertion 40; dependence upon troops of allies 54; dependence upon allies for artillery and munitions 57–8; problems of dependence 60–1; organisational development and growing standardisation 61; development of uniforms 62; weaponry 62; continued lack of uniformity 34, 67; fraud 23, 34, 63–4; commissariat 65–6; non-military role of army 71; reform of militia after 1713 71
Arnaud, Henri, pastor 53, 295
artillery train 82
Asti, town and province 252, 253
Audiberti, official 139
Avigliana, community of (Piedmont) 29, 30

Bagnasco, Carlo Gerolamo del Carretto, marchese di (c. 1650–1712) 54, 231, 254
Balbiana di Colcavagno, Caterina (1670–1719), noblewomen 250–1
banditry 269, 273, 275
Barberis, Walter 17, 22–3, 40, 72, 224
Barbero, Alessandro 224
Barcelonette valley 4, 52, 94, 123, 144, 149, 182, 282, 309
Bard, fortress 27, 46, 65
Barge (Piedmont) 174, 302
Basilio, military contractor 66, 67

338

INDEX 339

battaglione, of Piedmont 36
Bava, noble family 235, 257
Bavaria, Max Emanuel, elector of, cousin of Victor Amadeus II 8, 32, 156, 160, 201
Beik, William 12, 265, 221
Belfanti, C.M. 265
Bellegarde, chevalier de 126
Bellegarde, marquis de, chancellor 287
Beltramo, Biagio 279, 289
Bély, Lucien 132
Benzo di Cavour, conte Giuseppe Antonio, secretary for war 50, 173, 174, 190, 191, 269–70, 299
Benzo di Santena, conte Carlo Ottavio, governor of Mondovi, Montmelian and Cherasco 274
Bern 45, 147, 164, 168
Bernardi, Giuseppe Tommaso, affair (1704) 212–13
Berta, Giovanni Antonio, conte di Mongardino, banker and councillor of Turin council, 249
Berwick, Duke of 132
Biandrate Aldobrandino di San Giorgio, marchese Guido Francesco and family 230, 254
Biella, province and town 45, 183, 214, 249
Birago di Vische, conte and family 232, 234–5, 242
Black, Jeremy 12, 21, 221
Blaeu brothers of Amsterdam and *Atlas de Savoye* 147
Blonay, Louis de, noble 243
Bolingbroke, viscount, Henry St John 135, 162
Bonney, Richard 76
Borel, Catherine 309
borrowing, ducal forced loans 95, 97, 98; salary and pension arrears 97; abroad 99; foreign subsidies and 108
Bra, commuinty of (Piedmont) 41, 94, 253, 257, 258
Brandenburg, elector of see king of Prussia
Brandizzo, Nicolis di, conte 129
Brewer, John 9, 13, 172
Briançon (France) 27, 169
Briançon (Brianzone), Carron de 52, 130, 134
Bricherasio, community of (Piedmont) 86, 302
Brussels 128
Bugey 169
Bulferetti, Luigi 222, 223
bureaucracy and its limits in the Savoyard state 142–3, 171, 186
Buschetti, conte di 288, 229
Buttigliera, community of (Piedmont) 68, 243

Cacherano di Mombello, conte 229; Cacherano d'Osasco, conte 256
Caissotti, Carlo Luigi 231
Camera dei Conti, Turin 78–9, 93, 201, 203–5, 228
Canale, Malabaila di, conte and family 227
capitation tax 90, 248
Caraffa, count, Imperial general 161
Caraglio, Isnardi di, marchese di and family 194, 206, 227, 255, 259, 260
career officials 175–6
Carignano, appanage, prince and house of 78,138, 140, 149–50, 196, 228
Carmagnola, community of (Piedmont) 269
Caroccio, Carlo, diplomat 126, 127, 133
Carron, conte Felice Dionisio, governor of Trino and Susa 182, 187–9
Carutti, Domenico see Risorgimento, historiography
Casa Savoia *see* House of Savoy
Casale (Monferrato), fortress, siege and surrender of (1695) 1, 30, 41, 49, 58, 61, 174, 250; senate of 248, 260, 266; militia 71
Caselette, conte di, Antonio, president of Turin Senate 212
Castellamare (Sicily), siege of 212
Catalonia, war in 7, 216
Catinat, marshal, French commander 37, 55, 65, 207, 270, 272
cavalcata tax 90, 247, 256
Cavallo, Sandra 17, 224, 230
Cerutti, Simona 17
Ceva, province and marquisate 42, 267–8, 270, 272, 274
Chabod, Federico 171
Chabod, marquis of Bourg-Saint-Maurice (Savoy) and family 239
Chambre des Comptes, Chambéry 78–9, 102, 201, 203–5, 266, 228, 230, 251, 261, 266
Chamlay, marquis de French diplomat 270
Charles Emanuel I, Duke of Savoy (1580–1630) 5, 24, 78, 79, 116, 178, 229, 269, 278, 288
Charles Emanuel II, Duke of Savoy (1630–1675) 22, 34, 76, 87, 133, 179, 194, 215, 222, 230, 240, 241, 278, 280,
Charles Emanuel III, king of Sardinia (1730–73) 92, 119, 125, 163, 198, 277
Châtillon, baron de, François-Jerome de Challant 279, 281, 285
Chaumont, marquis de, Louis Deschamps 175, 256
Chittolini, Giorgio 265
Chivasso 56
church clergy, taxation of, 91–2; clash with and Concordats (1727, 1741) 18, 91–2;

church *(cont.)*
  dévots in Turin 299; Inquisition 177, 300, 305
Cigliano, community of 21
Cinzano, della Chiesa, marchese di 128
clientage 142, 187, 269, 276
coinage, manipulation of 100
Colomba, banker 113
Compans di Brichanteau, Giovanni Giuseppe, senator 184
comparto dei grani (grain tax) 77, 89, 120
conquest, right of 20
Constitutions of 1723 21, 68, 194; of 1770 (170)
contadore generale 175–6, 191
contractors, use of 66–7, 173
contributions, military, levied by enemy in Savoyard state 100, 282, 284; and by allies in France 133
corruption, of officials 39
Cortanze, Roero di, Ercole, marchese and family 129, 146, 189, 259
Costa di Polonghera, conte 234; Costa della Trinita, conte 38, 247
Costeis, Antonio, banker 86
Coudrée, Allinges, marquises of 228, 239
Council for Artillery, Building and Fortifications 176
Council of Finances 79, 112, 120, 172, 175, 177
Council of State 189–90
court, Savoyard 191, 206, 246
Cumiana, community (Piedmont) 86
Cumiana, Canalis di, abbé Francesco 132
Cuneo, town and province (Piedmont) and siege 27, 52, 83, 92, 93, 185, 187, 250, 269, 273; militia of 273
Cyprus, kingdom of, claimed by Victor Amadeus 153

Danckelman, Eberhard von, Prussian minister 163
Daun, marshal, imperial commander 29, 66, 135
Dauphiné, invasion of (1692) 2, 6, 58, 61, 94, 100, 174, 270, 272, 282, 284
David, ducal patrimoniale generale 288–89
debts, owed by emperor 82; Savoyard 97
De Gubernatis 128, 132, 134, 189, 302
De la Tour (della Torre), Sallier, Filibert, count and president, marquis (1699) de Cordon 127, 134, 138, 140, 166, 167, 143, 202, 208, 256
Del Borgo, Solaro di Moretta, secretary of state for foreign affairs (1717–32) 134, 141, 145, 146, 161–2, 160, 166, 167., 258
Del Carretto di Monforte and Novello, Carlo Francesco 270

Delescheraine, president 212
Della Rocca, conte 38
Demonte 27, 63
desertion 41
Despine, G.-B., Savoyard secretary at The Hague after 1713 130
De Tillier, E.-G 279, 288
De Tillier, J.-B 249, 278
Des Hayes (Desais) 273, 254
Dijkveld, Everard van Weede, heer van, confident of William III 146, 162
diplomacy, Savoyard importance of 122; failures of 122–23; expansion after 1690 126–8; diplomatic ranks 129; unofficial and secret diplomacy 131–2, 143; posts and ciphers 132–3; growth of foreign diplomatic presence in Turin 134; diplomatic gifts 136; problems associated with expansion 138; organisation of Savoyard diplomacy pre 1717 138; correspondence 139; reform of organisation of in 1717 145; functions and objectives 146; as source of models for state organisation:147; general characteristics of 156; reputation of, and double-dealing 124, 161; dissimulation as sign of weakness 161; exploitation of weakness 161–2; methods 163; essentially 'reactive' 164–5; relazioni 165; impact on diplomats 165; 'new diplomatic history' 125. *See also* maxims of state, royal treatment
directors (direttori) of provinces 179
Dogliani, Solaro di Moretta, marchese di 255, 259
Doria di Ciriè, G.-B, governor of Aosta 289
Doria del Maro, Carlo Alessandro, abbate of Vezzolano (d. 1726) 253
Dronero, marchese di 137, 180
Druent, marchese *see* Provana

edicts, ducal, as propaganda 213–14
Einaudi, Luigi 75, 76, 213
Elias, Norbert 191
Emanuel Filibert (1556–80) 76, 77, 173, 175, 178, 215, 229, 269, 277, 279
étapes 33, 65, 173, 174, 180, 188, 284, 286
Eugene, Prince of Savoy of Soissons branch (d. 1736) 3, 27, 66, 56, 149, 160, 163, 196
Evans, Robert 9, 12
Exilles, alpine fortress, siege and conquest of (1708) 4

factions, Savoyard court 205–6, 300
Falletti di Barolo, marchesi di and family 90, 94, 98, 242, 244, 247, 260
farming of taxes 78; source of credit and loans 87; shift away from 88

INDEX

Fenestrelles   alpine fortress, siege and conquest of (1708)   4
Ferrero della Marmora, marchese, Tommaso Felice   279, 281
Ferrero della Marmora, Alberto   223
fiefs, revocation and sale of alienated (1719–22)   5, 120
Flanders, war in   7, 24, 33, 146
Finale (Liguria)   123, 272
finances, Savoyard   as sphere of state formation   75; system on eve of cycle of wars   77; growing expenditure   80; loss of territories and revenues in wartime   83; fiscal crisis (1696)   92, 93, 118; long-term growth of revenues   81; relative contributions to ducal revenues   87; growing fiscal uniformity   90, 101, 102; resistance   92–3; foreign subsidies   103; borrowing and debt   97, 120; war finance and social change   96, 248–9; contraband and state formation   80, 116; exemptions, fiscal, grant of in wartime   83–4, 275; communal debt   79, 119, 257
financiers, importance of and attack on by Victor Amadeus   88
Fontana, Giangiacomo, intendente generale and contador generale, conte di Monastero di Vasco (1722) and marchese di Cravanzana   66, 67, 96, 188, 277,
fortifications and garrisons   27; cost of   82, 83
Fossano, community of (Piedmont)   39, 40, 183, 187, 235, 257, 273
free companies   36, 53, 276
Frigo, Daniela   17

Gabaleone di Salmour, counts and family   229, 244
gabelles (taxes)   77, 78, 83, 88, 273
Gaja, R.   223
Gallino, intendant and director of Alba province   183
Galway, earl of, envoy of William III and commander of Huguenot troops   136, 138, 152, 208, 220, 301, 302
Gamba, barone Marcello, banker   82, 88, 92, 109
Gazette, Turin   220
Geneva, city of   99, 110, 148, 164–65
Genoa, Republic of   4, 24, 42, 67, 83, 99, 130, 131, 269
German troops, use of by Victor Amadeus   46
Gestrich, Andreas   12
Gioanetti, Turin banker   111
Govone, community of   84
Govone, Solaro di, conte   *see* Solaro
Great Powers, emergence of   122
Grimani, abbé Vincenzo   144
Gropello, Giovanni Battista (1650–1722), intendant, conte di Borgone (1699), generale delle finanze (1697–1717)   87, 97, 117, 132, 175, 180, 181, 184, 188, 204, 205, 212, 288, 289, 292, 304

Habermas, Jurgen   12
Hague: 127, 141; Hague congress   127, 154, 295
Hanover, duke and elector of   8
harvests, poor and impact on revenues   43, 84–5, 116
Hildesheim, bishop of, as supplier of German troops   47–8
Hill, Richard, English envoy   192
Hoffmann, P.   76
Holy Roman Empire   1, 10; imperial troops   55; imperial fiefs, purchase of by Victor Amadeus II   80. *See also* Reichsitalien
horses, purchase of   82
hospitals, military   65, 66
Huguenots   6, 52; troops (religionaries)   43; Victor Amadeus' distrust of as fifth column in valleys   298; expulsion of from Piedmont (1698)   306
Hungary, war in   60

indemnity, war, Victor Amadeus' desire of from LXIV for war damage   84, 274
infeudation   93–4, 118, 257
inflation, price, in Piedmont   84–5
Innocent XII, Pope   305
intendants, provincial, origins and development   178
Intendenza Generale (commissariat)   66, 88
invalids, corps of   63
Irish troops   31, 44, 51–2; French plan to colonise valleys of Piedmont using   302
Italy, not a concern of Victor Amadeus   148–9; war in, importance of   6–7
Ivrea   27, 184, 280, 282

Jacobites, Victor Amadeus II and   151–3
James II   61; *see* Jacobites

Kettering, Sharon   12

Lagnasco, conte di   212, 244
Lama, Bernardo Andrea, historian and university teacher   310
Lamberti, conte, intendant   182
Landriani, conte, Savoyard diplomat   126
Lanfranchi, secretary for war   132, 175
Langhe   4, 271
Lanteri   126, 127
Leone, Guglielmo, president of Senate of Turin   289
letters of change (for subsidy)   109
Leutrum, baron   46–7

342　INDEX

Levi, Giovanni　17, 187, 224
Lombardini, Sandro　17
Lombardy, Army of　55, 141
Loriga, Sabina　224
Louis XIV, king of France (1643–1715)　1–4, 6–7, 11, 158, 197, 301
Lullin and Nicholas, bankers　82, 99, 109

macina tax　88, 214
Madama Reale (Marie-Jeanne-Baptiste de Savoie-Nemours), Victor Amadeus' mother　11, 79, 93, 97, 173, 192, 206–7, 228, 229, 240, 267, 279
Maffei, conte Annibale　66, 130, 142, 143, 152, 162, 199
Malta, island and Knights　195
manifestos, ducal　213–14
Manno, A.　223
Mansfeld, Count, imperial diplomat　130
Mantua, Duchy of and Gonzaga dukes　4, 60, 128
Marelli, cavaliere　212
Marelli, conte, general of the finances　79, 191, 286, 299
Marie Adelaide, princess of Savoy and Duchess of Burgundy (d. 1712)　2, 196–8
Marie Louise, princess of Savoy and Queen of Spain (d. 1713)　3, 143, 196, 197
Marlborough, John Churchill, duke of　162, 163
Marolles, marquis de, Joseph de Mesmes　281, 284
Marsaglia, battle of (1693)　1, 25, 33, 63, 68, 83, 93, 94, 160, 243, 245, 255, 269, 272, 301
Martiniana, conte　126
Masserano, prince(s)/principality　242; abbé　132
maxims of state, as guide to conduct of policy　156
Melazzo, Gandolfi di, cavaliere　130, 146
Mellarède, Pierre, conte di Bettonet (1717), secretary of state for internal affairs (1717–)　45, 102, 141, 151, 160, 164, 166, 182, 189, 190, 219, 310
Micca, Pietro (d. 1706)　23, 31, 63, 64
Milanese (Lombardy)　2, 3, 6, 156, 159, 165; sought by Victor Amadeus　116, 123, 148, 159, 163, 165
Military Revolution debate　21
militia　36–41; reform of post- 1713　70
Modena, duke and duchy　60, 314
modernisation, of state　125, 145
Monaco, principality of, Victor Amadeus' designs on　169
Mondovì　19, 21, 77, 78, 102, 92, 93, 183, 184; Salt War (1681–2)　267; reduction of (1699)　267, 273; continuing anxiety about after 1699　274–75; integration after 1720　276
Monferrato, newly acquired territory　38, 39, 89, 101,128, 145, 148, 164–5
Monforte　271
Montaldo　273
monti (loans)　98–9
Montjoye, Pierre Anselme, lord of, exemplar of social mobility　248–9
Montmélian, fortress and siege of　27, 65, 102, 147, 282, 283
Morozzo, cavaliere　179
Mosso, community of　84
Münster, bishop of, source of German troops　47

Naples　128, 148, 151
national identity　218–20
navy, Savoyard　59, 71–2; English, Dutch and Spanish　59–60
Neuchâtel, rival claims to　149–50
Nice, County of and town　27, 29, 59, 60, 66, 83, 92, 201
Nicolas, J.　223, 226, 230, 241
Nine Years War (1688–97)　1, 2, 7
nobility, Savoyard　historiography　222; numbers and distribution　226–7; ennoblement　227; internal divisions　228–9; wealth　230–1; use of primogeniture and entail　232–3; nobles and the church　233–4; and court　234–5; noblewomen　237–8, 247; marriage patterns　238–9, 242; relations with the state　239; extinction　245; military role　242; financial pressures and opportunities　246–7; state's reliance on　254; as agents of state　256; as mediators between duke and subjects　257–8
Norberg, K.　76
Normandie, Savoyard agent at The Hague　127
Novello　273

oaths　194–95
Oberkan, Swiss soldier　53
Olivero, conte Silvestro, banker　88, 92, 94, 96, 109, 199
Oneglia　32, 59, 72, 90, 102
Operti, Costanzo　128, 150, 155
Operti, G.B.　128, 130
opinion, public　144–5, 213
Orbassano, battle of (1693)　*see* Marsaglia
Order of Saints Maurice and Lazarus　59, 72, 194
Ormea, marchese d', Carlo Vincenzo Francesco Ferrero (1680–1744), magistrate, intendant, general of the finances (1717–)　120, 124, 184, 186, 190

… INDEX 343

Ormea, community of (Piedmont)   276

Palatine, Elector, sends German troops to Piedmont   51
Palermo   133, 199
Pallavicino family   187, 189, 198, 229; Pallavicino, marchesi delle Frabose   281; Pallavicino, marchesi di Perlo   209; Pallavicino di Saint-Remy, baron   259
Palma di Borgofranco, conte (1722), Giovanni Francesco, intendant, controller general of the finances (1717–33)   185, 249
Pancalieri, community of (Piedmont)   79, 228, 257
Parella, San Martino di, marchese di   22, 142, 187, 189, 194, 206, 209, 268, 269, 223, 241, 242, 250
Parma, duke and duchy   195
Peracchino, avvocato   132
perequazione   6, 92, 101, 119, 173, 185, 306, 225, 231, 260, 261, 273, 306
Perrone di San Martino, noble family   227, 232
Peyrani, president   212
Philip V, king of Spain (1700–46)   3, 155, 178
Pianezza, marchese di   38, 41, 188, 209, 223, 241
Pianezza, community of   78, 84, 178
Piedmont, prince of (1699–1715)   123, 198–200
Piedmont, principality   91; provinces of, reorganisation (1697)   181
Pinerolo, fortress, siege (and preparations for) and cession by Louis XIV   1, 2, 7, 30, 37, 55, 58, 60, 85, 94, 118, 123, 148, 266, 273, 293, 306, 307; town and province   179, 182, 217; Conseil Superieur of   201–2; militia of   273
Piobesi, community of (Piedmont)   38
Pocapaglia, fief and noble family   243
Poley, Edmund, envoy of William III   136, 297
portraits, ducal, gifts, importance of   136
Portugal   127, 129, 153, 195, 267
Pragelato (Pragelas)   4, 20, 101, 185, 293, 305, 308
Pralormo   202
Prato, Giuseppe   75
Priè di Turinetti, marchese di   129, 131, 143, 144, 145, 161, 164, 228, 260
prisoners of war   33; nobles   245, 247; cartels for exchange of   34, 245
prefects (*prefetti*)   178
privateers, of Victor Amadeus   59, 72; of France   133
privilege   51, 67, 83, 316
propaganda, French   159, 165, 167; ducal   23–17

prophecy, political   208
Provana di Druent, marchese di   193, 209, 230 241; Provana di Frosasco, conte   29; Provana di Pratolongo, conte Orazio   129, 158, 190, 191, 205, 207, 208
Prussia, king of   8, 55, 59, 115, 129, 149, 155, 250; Prussian troops in Piedmont   49, 57, 60, 129
Pusterla, Marco Antonio   181

Quadruple Alliance   5
Quart, Carlo Filippo Perrone di San Martino, baron   281
quartiere d'inverno tax   89, 101
Quazza, Guido   17, 22, 222

Radicati di Passerano, conte and family   223, 231, 243
Raeff, Marc   18
Ratisbon (Regensburg)   126, 127, 133
reason of state   207–8, 299
recruiting, expenditure on   82, 83
Reding, Swiss commander, and 'military colony' scheme   43, 82, 205
referendaries (*referendari*)   178
regiments Aosta   32, 82; Asti   41; Cavalier   53; Chablais   31, 52, 273, 283; Cortanze   41; Desportes   53; Genevois (Chaumont) dragoons   31, 243, 245; Guards   34, 62; Marine   32; Miremont (Huguenot)   52, 54; Montauban (Huguenot)   52, 54; Montbrun (Huguenot)   52; Monferrato   182, 274; Nizza   32; Piedmont   41; Piemonte Reale   35; Saluzzo   24; Savoy   34, 62, 269; Schulemburg   46; White Cross   34, 271, 273
Reichsitalien, and Savoyard state, in Holy Roman Empire   2, 10, 49, 55, 61, 126, 128, 135. *See also* Holy Roman Empire
religionaries   *see* Huguenots
requisitioning, of animals, wagons by ducal officials for war   21, 66, 183–4, 209, 284, 286
Rezzano, Giuseppe Ignazio, intendant   181, 182
Rhebinder, baron Otto, exemplar of influx of German soldiers into elite   51, 249–50
Rhine, war on   7
Ricuperati, Giuseppe   18, 222
Risorgimento, historiography   16, 22–3, 92–3, 148, 153, 200
Rijswijk, peace of (1697)   2, 7, 123, 316
Rivera, di, conte   39
Roberts, Michael   21
Robilant, Nicolis di, conte auditeur de guerre, intendant   181, 229
Roccavignale, community (Monferrato)   38

344　　　　　　　　　　INDEX

Roero, noble family　di Guarene 246, 260–1; di Cortanze
Romani, M. 265
Rome 126, 127, 131
Rosso, Claudio 224
Rowen, Herbert 9

Saint-Thomas (San Tommaso), Carron de, marquis de, Carlo Giuseppe Vittorio (d. 1699) 68, 139, 143, 187, 189, 239, 240, 243, 257, 288, 299
Saint-Thomas (San Tommaso), Carron de, marquis de, Giuseppe Gaetano Giacinto Vincenzo (d. 1749) 139, 140, 143, 187, 189
sale of office　*see* venality
Sales, de, marquis de and family 32, 43, 192, 228, 245, 253, 254
Salmatoris, conte 204
Saluzzo, bishop of 214; militia of 273
Saluzzo di Paesana, noble family 181, 247, 261
San Benedetto (Lombardy), 'detention' of Savoyard forces (1703) 26, 63, 65, 214
San Martino, 'republic' of (1704) 254, 307, 308
Sardinia, island kingdom 5, 59, 72, 170, 177, 195, 199, 201, 266
Savigliano 213
Savoy, Duchy of 42, 185, 219, 39, 71; conquest by French 83, 102; plan to put under Swiss protection 164, 265–6; nobility of 192, 226–7
Savoy, House of　Saxon origins 133; as concern of Savoyard diplomacy 150–1
Savoyard state　strategic position and importance 6-7, 27; definition and identity 18–19; role in allied wartime strategy 60; still very 'personal' 147; typical composite state 19, 265
Saxe-Gotha, troops of, negotiations for 47, 57, 60
Scaglia di Verrua, noble family 234, 242, 246
Scalenghe, conte di 247
Schulemburg 39, 46
Secretariat for War 63, 173–5
Secretariat for Foreign Affairs 122, 142–3. *See also* Savoyard diplomacy
Shomberg, duke of (d. 1693), commander of religionaries 54, 137
Shroud, Holy 97, 100, 215–16
Sicily 4–5, 57, 144, 185, 201, 263, 264, 266; war for (1718–20) 5, 27, 57, 292
sieges, importance of 27
Skocpol, Theda 14
small states 76, 122
società dei grani 98
Soissons, Prince Thomas, comte de 150, 196

Sola, Giorgio, military contractor 67
Soleri, Turin diarist 35, 42, 198
Solaro di Govone, conte and family 127, 130, 147, 152　231; Solaro della Margherita 231, 241, 257; Solaro della Moretta, marchese di Chiusa 244
Sommariva Perno, community (Piedmont) 183
sovereignty: 10, 33, 101–2, 145, 153, 170, 195, 279, 285, 293
Spain　treaty of 1690 58, 129; troops of, *see* Army of Lombardy; fleet 59; subsidies paid by 103–4, 108–9, 114, 116
Spanish Succession 6
Staffarda, battle of (1690) 1, 33, 37, 63, 94, 132, 207, 245, 255
stamped paper tax 90, 288–9, 304
state formation,　processes and definition 8–11, 15, 313–18, 171–2; explanation and historiography of 11, 171; close connection between domestic and foreign spheres 170, 172, 177
Stumpo, Enrico 18, 76
subsidies, foreign in wartime　contribution and importance of 103; problems associated with 107 117–18; delays and arrears 113; trading of 115; influence on strategy 107
succession, Savoyard 196
Superga, monastery, monument to War of Spanish Succession 218, 275
Susa, marchese di 40
Susa, province and town 29, 134, 185, 187, 207, 212
sussidio militare 77, 78, 89
Swiss Confederation 123, 164–5, 265–66
Symcox, Geoffrey 17, 22, 222

tabellion/-ato, tax 101, 287–8, 289
Tallett, Frank 21
Tana d'Entraque, marchese and family 35, 230, 231, 253
Tarino Imperiale, conte 33, 48, 130, 134, 137, 138, 143, 179
tasso (Piedmontese land tax) 77, 78, 87; alienation of in wartime 90, 94–5, 118, 257
Te Deum, celebrations of Savoyard and allied succeses as ducal propaganda 216–17
Tessé, comte de, French soldier and diplomat 143
Tilly, Charles 14
Torre, Angelo 17
Toulon, naval base, abortive expedition against (1707) 4, 6, 59, 60, 99, 107, 133, 134
transports, military 64, 65, 83
Trino, province and town 77, 181

INDEX

Trivié, Wicardel de, marquis de   130, 134, 136, 166, 168,
Troops   Bavarian, serving in Piedmont in Nine Years War, 32, 49, 58; German 47–8, 551; Irish   31, 44, 51–2, 302; Prussian   49, 57, 60, 129; Saxe-Gotha   47, 57, 60; Swiss   44
Turin   1, 27; archbishop of   91, 189, 234; Academy   236, 241, 254; Arsenal   57, 58 siege of   22, 27, 29, 34, 56; battle of   56; ceremonial life   136; celebration of relief of after 1706 as source of new Savoyard national identity   217–19; Ospedale di Carità   185, 86; Senate of   178, 201, 278, 285, 228; University of   18, 186; Vicariato of   185, 252; treaty of (1696, 1701, 1703)   139; Jewish ghetto   90; financing of defences   98; mercantile community   98, 99; source of ducal loans   98; urban militia   30, 37, 39, 42; panic in in wartime   255; Company of San Paolo   304
Turinetti di Pertengo   238
Tuscany, grand duke/Duchy, as rivals of Victor Amadeus   130, 154, 195

Uditorato di Guerra   63
Ufficio (Generale) del Soldo (Army Pay Office)   63, 120, 175, 180, 191
United Provinces   diplomatic contacts with 126; 167
Utrecht, peace (congress) of   124, 132, 144, 148, 160, 163, 165, 167n

Vacca, president   207
Val Chisone   293
Val Luscina   296, 300, 304, 307, 309
Val Pellice   293
Val Perosa   266, 293, 309
Val San Martino   296, 298
Val San Martino di San Germano   230
Val Sesia, acquisition of   202
Valais   126
Valenza   30
Valfrè, Father   215, 218, 299
Valperga, noble family   di Rivara   246; di Masino   241, 243
Van der Meer, Albert, Dutch commissary (1690–96) and envoy (1703–13) in Turin   138, 307
Vaudois   19, 31–2, 140, 144; expulsion from Piedmont   294–95; Glorieuse Rentrée (1689)   1, 53, 179, 268, 281, 295; rebuilding of communities and reinsertion into Savoyard state from 1690   302; appeal to Maritime Powers   93, 144, 302; edict of 1694   91, 140, 203–4, 302; edict as focus for opposition to war   299; problems in enforcing edict 304; troops   32, 296, 307

venality   95–6, 118, 181, 205
Venice, Republic of   131, 134, 144, 148, 153, 154
Venturi, Franco   224
Vercelli, cavaliere   304
Vercelli, town and province (Piedmont)   27, 29, 30, 63, 182, 214, 273
Vernone, Balbis di, cavaliere, soldier and diplomat   212
Vernone, Balbis di, conte Carlo Emanuele, diplomat   131, 140, 159
Verrua, town and province (Piedmont)   27, 33, 56
Vicoforte (Piedmont)   275
Victor Amadeus II, duke of Savoy (1675–1730), king of Sicily (1713–20), king of Sardinia (1720–30)   contemporary and historical reputation   5, 15, 17, 158; illness (1692–93) and succession   196; key role in government   29, 68, 79, 135, 143–4, 146, 177, 190; limited objectives   102; preoccupation with dynasty   149; travels around state   190, 270; illness (1692–93) 191, 196–7; views   168; anxiety and procrastination   156, 158; use of 'non-nationals'   144, 248–9; plots to kill   4, 44, 200
Victor Amadeus III, king of Sardinia (1773–96)   18
Vienna   3, 127
Vigevano, treaty of (1696)   2, 139
Villefranche (Nice)   212

War of the League of Augsburg, *see* Nine Years War
War of the Spanish Succession (1701–14)   3
war   crucial importance of finance   74; devastation caused by   83–4, 215; conduct of influenced by non-military issues   85; importance of for ruler   68; need to avoid battle (and defeat)   142
warfare   influence of supply on strategy 64–5
Weber, Max   8, 171
William III   6–7, 32–3, 49, 104, 136, 139, 145, 147, 149, 150, 151–2, 154, 158, 165, 168, 190, 301, 305
Wolfenbüttel, duke of, source of German troops   47–8
Woolf, S. J.   223, 225, 226
Württemberg, Duke of, source of German troops   51

Zoja, G. A., intendant of Pinerolo province   182

CAMBRIDGE STUDIES IN ITALIAN HISTORY AND CULTURE

Family power and public life in Brescia, 1580–1650
The foundation of power in the Venetian state
JOANNE M. FERRARO

Church and politics in Renaissance Italy
The life and career of Cardinal Francesco Soderini, 1453–1524
K. J. P. LOWE

Crime, disorder, and the Risorgimento
The politics of policing in Bologna
STEVEN C. HUGHES

Liturgy, sanctity and history in Tridentine Italy
Pietro Maria Campi and the preservation of the particular
SIMON DITCHFIELD

Lay confraternities and civic religion in Renaissance Bologna
NICHOLAS TERPSTRA

Society and the professions in Italy, 1860–1914
Edited by MARIA MALATESTA

Herculean Ferrara
Ercole d'Este (1471–1505) and the invention of a ducal capital
THOMAS TUOHY

Numbers and nationhood
Writing statistics in nineteenth-century Italy
SILVANA PATRIARCA

The Italian garden
Art, design and culture
Edited by JOHN DIXON HUNT

Reviving the Renaissance
The use and abuse of the past in nineteenth-century Italian art and decoration
Edited by ROSANNA PAVONI

Railways and the formation of the Italian state in the nineteenth century
ALBERT SCHRAM

English merchants in seventeenth-century Italy
GIGLIOLA PAGANO DE DIVITIIS

Aristocrats in bourgeois Italy
The Piedmontese nobility, 1861–1930
ANTHONY L. CARDOZA

Italian culture in northern Europe
in the eighteenth century
Edited by SHEARER WEST

War, diplomacy and the rise of Savoy, 1690–1720
CHRISTOPHER STORRS

For EU product safety concerns, contact us at Calle de José Abascal, 56–1°,
28003 Madrid, Spain or eugpsr@cambridge.org.

www.ingramcontent.com/pod-product-compliance
Lightning Source LLC
LaVergne TN
LVHW091528060526
838200LV00036B/531